The Drug Wars in America, 1940–1973

The Drug Wars in America, 1940–1973, argues that the U.S. government has clung to its militant drug war, despite its obvious failures, because effective controls of illicit traffic and consumption were never the critical factors motivating its adoption in the first place. Instead, Kathleen J. Frydl shows that the shift from regulating illicit drug use and sales to criminalizing them both developed from, and was marked by, other dilemmas of governance in an age of vastly expanding state power. Most believe the "drug war" was inaugurated by President Richard Nixon's declaration of a war on drugs in 1971, but in fact his announcement heralded changes that had taken place in the two decades prior. Frydl examines this critical interval of time between regulation and prohibition, demonstrating that the war on drugs advanced certain state agendas, such as policing inner cities or exercising power abroad. Although this refashioned approach mechanically solved some vexing problems of state power, it endowed the country with a cumbersome and costly "war" that drains resources and degrades important aspects of the American legal and political tradition.

Kathleen J. Frydl is the author of *The G.I. Bill* (Cambridge, 2009), which won the 2010 Louis Brownlow Book Award from the National Academy of Public Administration. She received a fellowship from the Woodrow Wilson Center to support her research for this book.

The Drug Wars in America, 1940–1973

KATHLEEN J. FRYDL

CAMBRIDGE
UNIVERSITY PRESS

CAMBRIDGE UNIVERSITY PRESS
Cambridge, New York, Melbourne, Madrid, Cape Town,
Singapore, São Paulo, Delhi, Mexico City

Cambridge University Press
32 Avenue of the Americas, New York, NY 10013-2473, USA

www.cambridge.org
Information on this title: www.cambridge.org/9781107697003

First published 2013

Printed in the United States of America

A catalog record for this publication is available from the British Library.

Library of Congress Cataloging in Publication data
Frydl, Kathleen.
The drug wars in America, 1940–1973 / Kathleen J. Frydl.
p. cm.
Includes bibliographical references and index.
ISBN 978-1-107-01390-2 (hardback) – ISBN 978-1-107-69700-3 (pbk.)
1. Drug abuse – Government policy – United States.   2. Drug abuse – United
States.   3. Drug control – United States.   I. Title.
HV5825.F79   2012
363.450973'0904–dc23   2012025580

ISBN 978-1-107-01390-2 Hardback
ISBN 978-1-107-69700-3 Paperback

To Larry Janezich

Power obviously presents awkward problems for a community which abhors its existence, disavows its possession, but values its exercise.

John Kenneth Galbraith, *American Capitalism*[1]

[1] J. K. Galbraith, *American Capitalism: The Concept of Countervailing Power* (Cambridge: Riverside Press, 1952), 26.

Contents

Preface

There is no issue where government policy diverges from American popular opinion – let alone popular American practice – as drastically as it does in the handling of illicit drugs. This book was written to embolden the people's consensus and narrow the divide between the government and its citizens by presenting a history that casts doubt on the supporting tenets and presumed purposes of the so-called drug war.

It does so by offering an account of the federal government's original approach to illicit drugs, a scheme of taxes and tariffs, and tracing its demise. This story reveals that the shift from a regulatory regime toward a punitive and prohibitive one was not dictated by a surge in illicit drug use, crimes associated with drug use, or changes in drug potency or price, although it is most definitely the case that the availability of drugs rose dramatically in the years following World War II. Nor was this move in favor of prohibition brought about by changes to the constitutional powers accorded to the federal government, even though it is perfectly true that changes in judicial readings of the commerce clause during the New Deal and World War II made possible the sweeping legislation of the 1960s and 70s that provide the legislative basis for today's drug war.

Be that as it may, if one examines the reasons motivating the change in how the federal government handled illicit drugs by actually inspecting the historical record that bears witness to it, it becomes clear that some of the commonly cited reasons are consequences of that change, rather than causes, and others are events that coincided with and shaped the drug war but did not precipitate it. Instead, the government dropped one set of instruments and institutions to regulate drugs and substituted another because of the challenges posed by the unprecedented rise in power of the United States during the postwar era. Hence a larger ambition of this book is to chart and explain the federal government's abandonment of the tax code as the principal means to regulate citizens' behavior, and its adoption and reliance upon criminal punishment in its place. I argue that, more than anything else, the drug war extended or enabled certain state agendas, like policing inner cities embroiled in conflict, or wielding influence and power abroad, especially throughout the developing world. In its versatility and application, the drug war compensated for deficiencies in other institutions and instruments of government. Bereft of other tools, the state punished its way to power.

This history implicitly suggests – and I explicitly argue – that the drug "war" is not the only or best way to handle drugs. I want to note at the outset, however, that the paramount virtue of alternative schemes is merely that they are less bad. Although superior to a militant drug war, legalization and decriminalization are far from worthy goals in their own right. Perhaps it is because many Americans instinctively sense this that proposals to legalize or decriminalize possession of illicit drugs have stalled. After all, it is hard to muster troops to dismantle an entrenched system of power with just a rallying cry of sober pragmatism, and harder still to join the chorus of some of the most vocal drug reform proponents who seem only to be on a quest to secure better or safer drugs. Yet the many costs of the drug war exact their price regardless of our uninspired indifference; equally troubling, many precedents and practices of the drug war have found use in the government's current "war on terror," another sprawling government agenda that has not encountered the critical appraisal that either its expense or its incursions into customary freedoms would seem to demand. It is apparent, then, that Americans will have to either reverse course on the drug war and its progeny, or else sanction and support a government increasingly unaccountable to its people and the American political tradition.

Kathleen J. Frydl
Washington, DC, 2012

Introduction

In 2010, California voters considered – and rejected – a ballot proposition to legalize the cultivation and consumption of marijuana. Most voters wrestled with this decision while bearing in mind other illicit drugs, wondering whether legalizing marijuana would affect the moral and legal case for outlawing substances considered more potent and destructive. Could a pragmatic concession on one drug set an unwelcome precedent for the entire scheme of prohibition of illicit drugs?

Yet it is illicit drug prohibition itself that is the historical aberration, a labored and in many ways radical construction of some of the most formative decades in modern American history. Most assume that it is the result of President Richard Nixon's declaration of a "war on drugs"; in fact, his announcement only gave a name to changes that had taken place during the preceding two decades. Between World War II and 1973, the United States transitioned from a regulatory illicit drug regime to a prohibitive and punitive one. This book tells the story of that shift.

It does so differently than has been done before. Where others have focused on patterns of illicit drug consumption and trafficking and characterized the state-sponsored drug war as in some way a reaction to these, this book will treat the government's approach to handling illicit drugs as a subject worthy of its own story, one that is not adequately explained by dramatic increases in drug use or the sophisticated methods of drug smugglers. Instead I argue that in order to understand the construction of and ongoing commitment to the U.S. government's militant drug war, especially in light of its abject failure, we must examine the project's origins in decisions over how to manage state power in the context of global ascendancy abroad, and the difficult challenges to government posed by increasing affluence and accountability at home. It is a neglected but important fact that government officials adopted punishment and rejected illicit drug regulation as part of a calculus of power that initially had little to do with drugs, and that the government remains invested in the drug war despite its daily disappointments because the set of institutions and instruments that comprise it perform other tasks, and are valued for other reasons.

This emphasis on the state alters some well-established notions of how we currently understand the drug war. The first is chronology: in the main, students of the drug war focus their attention on illicit drug enforcement after Nixon's declaration of "war" in 1971, but, as we will see, the tactics deployed in that period have their roots in the postwar era. Even many scholars of the drug war assume that mandatory minimum prison sentences for drug possession and a focus on asset forfeiture (or seizing the money or material of drug smugglers for use by the state) came to the federal government in the 1980s; instead, both were important components of the government's strategy beginning in the 1950s. When we fail to provide an accurate chronology of the drug war, we also fail to appreciate the contemporaneous historical events that influenced its adoption and shaped its form and function. By restoring the drug war to its appropriate context, we add a new dimension to our understanding of it, and we also better understand the formation of and problems inherent in state power during a critical period of American history.

Second, when we concentrate on the state, we see continuities in and dialog between subjects normally presented as separate. For example, accounts of the drug war that do examine the pre-1971 period, what some call the "classical era," usually focus on one drug exclusively; histories of marijuana, for instance, are numerous, and several of them noteworthy.[1] Likewise, histories of licit addictive synthetics, first developed and distributed during the so-called classical era, also select one drug (or class of drug) for review, seldom drawing a connection between synthetics and the evolving priorities and nature of narcotics regulation.[2] Yet this

---

[1] See Richard J. Bonnie and Charles H. Whitehead, *The Marijuana Conviction: A History of Marijuana Prohibition in the United States* (New York: Lindesmith Center, 1999); for a more popular survey, see Larry "Ratso" Sloman, *Reefer Madness: A History of Marijuana* (New York: St. Martin's Griffin, 1979); on heroin, see Eric C. Schneider, *Smack: Heroin and the American City* (Philadelphia: University of Pennsylvania Press, 2008).

[2] Nicolas Rasmussen, *On Speed: The Many Lives of Amphetamines* (New York: New York University Press, 2008); Andrea Tone, *The Age of Anxiety: A History of America's Turbulent Affair with Tranquilizers* (New York: Basic Books, 2008); for an excellent history of different synthetics considered together, see David Herzberg, *Happy Pills in*

separation of older drugs from newer synthetics validates the different approaches constructed to regulate these drugs, and it also cheats history. Heroin and morphine were used for licit medical purposes for decades; moreover, when addictive synthetics like amphetamines and barbiturates were first manufactured in the United States, lawmakers weighed whether to add them to the regulatory machinery already in place for opiates and marijuana.

The reason they chose not to did not rest on any scientific or normative assessment of these different kinds of drugs; instead, the story was one of balancing and building state power, a story that is the focus of the pages that follow. In many ways, absent the specifics on drugs, this book describes how and why the federal government went from regulating citizens' behavior through taxation to doing so using the forces of criminal punishment. This story has historical interest to students of American political history, but it also has policy implications for today's debate. Are illicit drugs better conceptualized as a trade or a crime? If the former, then a regulatory regime makes more sense than criminal enforcement. Common sense dictates that it is easier to repeal drug laws than to overturn the law of supply and demand.

Not only is it impossible to punish a market out of existence, attempting to do so brings unintended consequences and costs. Some of these undesirable effects were in evidence as soon as the federal government began ratcheting up criminal punishment for possession and sale of illicit narcotics. While not unnoticed, the inability of punishment to deter drug traffic or consumption in any meaningful way failed to attract systematic or focused attention. This oversight underscored the power of the moral crusade waged against narcotics, as other scholars have noted, and it also advanced the many ways in which the more militant and resolute "war" against various illicit drugs served other purposes and solved

America: From Miltown to Prozac (Baltimore: Johns Hopkins University Press, 2008). One historian of science does relate narcotics to addictive synthetics; for a discussion of the social organization and "laboratory logics" of the scientific community dedicated to studying addiction, see Nancy D. Campbell, *Discovering Addiction: The Science and Politics of Addiction Research* (Ann Arbor: University of Michigan Press, 2007); for a recently issued call for historians to take more heed of addiction science and abandon polemical views of drugs in modern America, see David Courtwright, "Addiction and the Science of History," *Addiction* 107 (3): 486–92. I join Samuel Roberts (and, I presume, others) in noting that historical methodology can be rigorous in its own right, and hence a credible conversant with addiction scientists or any researcher. See Samuel Roberts, "Addiction, History, and Historians," http://pointsadhsblog.wordpress.com/2012/03/12/addiction-history-and-historians-samuel-roberts-response/ [accessed September 26, 2012].

other problems in the exercise of state power. Significantly, this alternative state agenda was more structural than partisan: despite occasional contours of party interest, the absence of durable party dimensions to the "drug war" political consensus is but one suggestive indication that deeper and more fundamental issues of governance were at stake in forging it. What is more, the dilemmas of power at the heart of the drug war have their own particular dynamic and historical trajectory, none of which can be fully accounted for or explained by attention to interests outside of the state.[3] At times, and paradoxically, the validity and importance of narrating the drug war through the lens of state power is best demonstrated by the role of unintended consequences – like those brought about by decisions of government officials made for reasons unrelated to drugs – in the evolution of drug prohibition and punishment. Yet, at the very same time, it is also the case that the government often acted with no uniform purpose, sometimes with no obvious purpose at all, and almost never with a motivation belonging only to itself. So, although the drug war can be considered from the perspective of the state – or more accurately, as a collection of decisions about how to manage state power – it is not a story that can be recited in one voice, let alone a voice that harbors only one motivation or acts with only one purpose in mind.

Nonetheless, a state-centered story of the drug war can be told, and it is one with a decidedly tragic cast to it. Ultimately, the drug war as waged by the U.S. government exposed more vulnerability than it shielded. Throughout the postwar era, more trade and greater ease of travel brought more drugs and, to a great and largely unappreciated extent, the smuggling of illicit drugs was the unwelcome but inevitable result of the country's expanded trade and global engagement. It was, in particular, the sinews of American economic power – trading channels and the movement of people and goods – upon which drug trafficking relied. In capitalizing on these resources, traffickers benefited from what I have elsewhere referred to as the advantages of the "pest" as opposed to the "predator": a cunning exploitation of the inevitable gaps in state power available to small-scale operators.[4] Thus, the very success of the American economy exposed new avenues of vulnerability. However small

---

[3] The state-centered approach here is analogous to Schneider, *Smack*, who recounts the history of heroin markets and the prosecution of them as an urban history, situating his "drug" narrative within the context of other transformations and dynamics of the city.

[4] Kathleen J. Frydl, "Kidnapping and U.S. State Development," *Studies in American Political Development* 20 (Spring 2006): 18–44.

or trivial these weaknesses, their flagrant persistence goaded lawmakers into imposing increasingly severe reprisals.

The United States undertook such measures and moved away from its initial drug regulations – literally a tariff and tax regime – incrementally, first by adding more punishment for violations, then transferring the oversight of the illicit drug portfolio from the Treasury Department to the Department of Justice, and finally by shifting the purposes and justifications for that portfolio from regulatory authority to criminalization. Scholars of the drug war as well as of American criminal punishment more generally have been divided in their assessment of the reasons for this change. Two of the most influential, David Garland and Michael Ignatieff, advance the modern industrial age and its attendant dislocations as the principal reason for the embrace of punishment and prisons more specifically – a tangible effort to restore order to a society unmoored or disconnected from previously binding conventions.[5] Legal scholar Jonathon Simon and sociologist James Whitman tailor this broader observation into distinct arguments: Whitman heralds the American preference for "harsh" punishment as a paradoxical result of the absence of aristocracy and a modern penchant for populist crusades, while Simon sketches the broad "episteme" or body of ideas shaping the modern understanding of punishment, including the critical discursive, political, and disciplinary moments that enabled a punitive paradigm to emerge as a structuring frame of governance.[6]

[5] David Garland, *The Culture of Control: Crime and Social Order in Contemporary Society* (Chicago: University of Chicago Press, 2002); Michael Ignatieff, *Just Measure of Pain: The Penitentiary in the Industrial Revolution* (New York: Columbia University Press, 1978).
[6] James Q. Whitman, *Harsh Justice: Criminal Punishment and the Widening Divide between America and Europe* (New York: Oxford University Press, 2003). Significantly, Whitman acknowledges the role that anti-statist political culture has played in the United States in the drive to rely more heavily on criminal codes, though he seems to take "weak" state claims at face value, agreeing with others that weak institutional capacity in the criminal justice system has made it susceptible to the influence of feverish moral campaigns: see also James A. Morone, *Hellfire Nation: The Politics of Sin in American History* (New Haven: Yale University Press, 2004); Samuel Walker, *Popular Justice: A History of American Criminal Justice* (New York: Oxford University Press, 1998); and William J. Stuntz, *The Collapse of American Criminal Justice* (Cambridge: Harvard University Press, 2011). Other scholars have taken issue with the notion of a weak American state: see William Novak, "The Myth of the 'Weak' American State," *American Historical Review* 113 (2008): 752–72; Brian Balogh, *A Government Out of Sight: The Mystery of National Authority in Nineteenth-Century America* (New York: Cambridge University Press, 2009); Stephen Skowronek, *Building a New American State: The Expansion of National Administrative Capacities, 1877–1920* (New York: Cambridge University Press, 1982). Those more apt to see an "uneven" state at work include: Gary Gerstle,

Where some see the collateral damage of modernity, others see a struggle for power as the central issue of the drug war, criminal punishment, and the impressive expansion of the carceral state, a formal term to describe mass incarceration and the "prison-industrial" complex. Academics who write in this particular vein prioritize categories traditionally subject to social control: class and race – and, far less so, gender.[7] David Courtwright and David Musto see drug war tactics shift according to changes in the class composition of drug users, with criminal sanctions directed toward only those drugs popular among the less powerful.[8] Rufus King, a lawyer active in the mid-century campaign to reform drug punishment who later became a historian of those efforts, takes a more classically materialist approach when he discerns the economic interests of pharmaceutical corporations at the heart of political decision making.[9] More influential, at least in terms of popular acceptance, has been the analysis of Naomi Murakawa and Vesla Weaver (and numerous others) who see the increased criminal punishment of the recent past as designed to check civil rights reform and, more broadly, as indicative of the persistence of institutionalized forms of white racism.[10]

"A State Both Weak and Strong," *American Historical Review* 115 (June 2010): 779–85; Kathleen J. Frydl, *The GI Bill* (New York: Cambridge University Press, 2009); and Theda Skocpol, *Protecting Soldiers and Mothers: The Political Origins of Social Policy in the U.S.* (Cambridge: Harvard University Press, 1995).

[7] See Nancy Campbell, *Using Women: Gender, Drug Policy, and Social Justice* (New York: Routledge, 2000); Stephen R. Kandall, *Substance and Shadow: Women and Addiction in the United States* (Cambridge: Harvard University Press, 1999); Gail A. Caputo, *Out in the Storm: Drug Addicted Women Living as Shoplifters and Sex Workers* (Boston: Northeastern University Press, 2008); Stephanie R. Bush-Baskette, *Misguided Justice: The War on Drugs and the Incarceration of Black Women* (Bloomington, IN: iUniverse, 2010). A rare first-hand account of opiate addiction written by a woman can be found in Helen MacGill Hughes, *The Fantastic Lodge* (New York: Fawcett, 1971).

[8] David Courtwright, *Forces of Habit: Drugs and the Making of the Modern World* (Cambridge: Harvard University Press, 2002); David F. Musto, *The American Disease: Origins of Narcotic Control* (New York: Oxford University Press, 1973).

[9] Rufus King, *The Drug Hang-Up: America's Fifty Year Folly* (New York: Norton, 1972).

[10] See especially Naomi Murakawa, "The Origins of the Carceral Crisis: Racial Order as 'Law and Order' in Postwar American Politics," in *Race and American Political Development*, Lowndes et al., eds. (New York: Routledge, 2008); Vesla M. Weaver, "Frontlash: Race and the Development of Punitive Crime Policy," *Studies in American Political Development* 21, no. 2 (Fall 2007): 230–65; Doris Marie Provine, *Unequal Under the Law: Race in the War on Drugs* (Chicago: University of Chicago Press, 2007). Only very recently have some scholars put forward explanations more grounded in political economy or institutional preferences: see Marie Gottschalk, *The Prison and the Gallows: The Politics of Mass Incarceration in America* (New York: Cambridge University Press, 2006); or the legal scholars interested in "overcriminalization" who note the importance of "external"

Michelle Alexander takes this analysis one step further, arguing that the racially selective enforcement of criminal punishment for possession of illicit drugs is the crucial difference separating the lives of young blacks from that of young whites in the United States. Despite equal rates of drug use *and* drug dealing between whites and blacks (and other minorities), the nation's prisons are disproportionately filled beyond capacity with African American inmates. As Alexander points out, criminal conviction and prison service in the modern-day United States stymies – if it does not altogether stop – social and economic mobility, and it can also disenfranchise a voter. Considered as a system and judged by its effects, Alexander proclaims a new Jim Crow system of legal discrimination at work in the U.S. criminal justice system, and the drug war, in its modern form, lies at its heart.[11]

Most recently, a conversation growing out of mainly law school circles has devoted attention to the "overcriminalization" of American law.[12] This subject bears an obvious connection to the cultural roots of punishment as well as to the expansion of the carceral state. Indeed, the availability of the criminal justice system to accommodate various political crusades, as well as the use of law enforcement for social control – arguments that play an important role in other literatures – strike legal observers as significant as well. William J. Stuntz, one of the guiding lights in the field, marries both into an insightful history of the evolution of American criminal law.[13] Douglas Husak cites illicit drug possession as the principal example of overcriminalization, a term he uses to refer to both too much criminal law and too much punishment.[14] Hence, more than just incidence of crime or enforcement tactics accounts for imprisonment: it is the law itself, including what it punishes as criminal, how it is written, and how it operates, that leads to such staggering rates of incarceration.[15] Ethan A. Nadelmann elaborates on this basic observation when he notes

factors: Douglas Husak, *Overcriminalization: The Limits of the Criminal Law* (New York: Oxford University Press, 2009); Daniel Richman, "Overcriminalization for Lack of Better Options," in *The Political Heart of Criminal Procedure* (New York: Cambridge University Press, 2011).

[11] Michelle Alexander, *The New Jim Crow: Mass Incarceration in the Age of Colorblindness* (New York: New Press, 2010).

[12] For a theory of criminalization, see Douglas Husak, *Overcriminalization: The Limits of the Criminal Law* (New York: Oxford University Press, 2008).

[13] William J. Stuntz, *The Collapse of American Criminal Justice* (Cambridge: Harvard University Press, 2011).

[14] Husak, *Overcriminalization*, passim.

[15] Stuntz, "The Pathological Politics of Criminal Law," *Michigan Law Review* 100 (2001).

that, in the recent past, federal statutes criminalized activities that "had not previously been regarded as criminal," and that these in turn played a crucial role in expanding the international activities and authority of U.S. law enforcement agencies, especially the Drug Enforcement Administration (DEA).[16] Significantly, as Daniel Richman argues – and as this account of the drug war will bear out – incentives outside the legal system can greatly affect the nature of criminal law, encouraging prosecutors to act as catch-all administrators who could "assume any number of new assignments," though, as Richman also notes, "without necessarily acting on them."[17] The discretion in the application of criminal law highlighted by Richman is a key factor in maintaining support for and the viability of aggressive criminalization. Without it, most of the country would be in prison: as Stuntz calculates, more than 70 percent of American adults have committed some sort of imprisonable offense in their lifetimes. Thus, support for "law and order" policies depends upon the selective enforcement of them, an observation validated both by logic and by the history recounted in the pages that follow.[18]

Individually and taken together, all of this scholarship sheds light on the shift from a regulatory framework to a punitive one in the handling of illicit drugs. Yet none explicitly makes reference to the history of or reasons for this shift. Unlike previous work on the drug war, this book takes the United States' first regulatory illicit drug regime – its initial tariff and tax apparatus – as an important expression of state power and, also unlike other work, it investigates the reasons for that regime's downfall. Scholars and sometimes contemporary observers dismissed the tax and tariff apparatus as a ruse, a fig leaf donned out of concern for the constitutional limits of federal power, the real purpose of which was to

---

[16] See Nadelmann, *Cops Across Borders: The Internationalization of US Criminal Law Enforcement* (University Park: Pennsylvania State University Press, 1993), quote from p. 1.

[17] Richman, "Overcriminalization for Lack of Better Options."

[18] For a sympathetic depiction of the rise and popularity of "law and order" rhetoric and its importance to the modern conservative movement, see Michael Flamm, *Law and Order: Street Crime, Civil Unrest, and the Crisis of Liberalism in the 1960s* (New York: Columbia University Press, 2007); and Stuntz, *The Collapse*, who holds low incarceration rates of the 1960s as responsible for the increase in violent crime in the 1970s. For a more critical appraisal of law and order rhetoric and the cultural appeal made "white ethnics" – as well as the contestations over employment that grounded that appeal – see Nancy MacLean, *Freedom Is Not Enough: The Opening of the American Workplace* (Cambridge: Harvard University Press, 2008); see also John Skretny and Thomas Sugrue, "White Ethnic Strategy," in *Rightward Bound*, Bruce Schulman and Julian Zelizer, eds. (Cambridge: Harvard University Press, 2008), 171–92.

disguise an enforcement operation.[19] Yet this depiction does not do justice to the fact that narcotics were relied upon as a medicine for decades;
thus, the licit purposes structuring the tax and tariff regime were concrete
and operational, not latent and abstract. Moreover, the abandonment
of this regulatory approach involved more than just the expansion of
federal constitutional powers beyond the power to tax or the advent of
newer, synthetic drugs; it bore an immediate connection to broader questions of governance and to other transformations in government power.
As the federal lawmakers and officials came to rely on income tax more
for revenue, they retreated from the indirect or excise tax portfolio – of
which narcotic regulation was a part – by leaps and bounds. In other
words, one important reason why the federal government abandoned the
tax regime for drugs is that officials of it favored taxes, and reliable tax
collection, more for revenue, and correspondingly were less invested in
the collection of taxes for the purposes of regulation.

Once severed from the tax structure, illicit drug enforcement was subsequently embraced as an instrument of state power in other venues, offering
a versatile set of tools for projects ranging from fashioning the terms of
international engagement to policing the inner city. These endeavors did
little to affect the drug market, but they remained useful in the eyes of their
proponents as a bridge between the task at hand and the political will and
institutional capacity available for it. Law enforcement in the United States,
for instance, previously had neglected inner city minority neighborhoods;
during the postwar era, they provided service in these areas for the first
time, but only with the benefit of the discretionary power afforded to them
under illicit drug enforcement, a policing agenda that, unlike other discretionary tools, remained impervious to civil rights reform. At the same time,
drug treatment clinics, even when sponsored by the state and pursued with
real conviction, withered on the vine. Although clinics regularly achieved
unprecedented success in managing the problems most associated with
illicit drug use, they offered none of the utility to the exercise of state power
as did punishment. The drug war performed with similar usefulness in the
nation's foreign policy portfolio. During the Cold War, Americans faced
the prospect of endorsing tremendous global aid packages; policymakers
mollified the country's long-standing reluctance for these by tying them to

---

[19] Most exemplary of this tendency in the scholarship to present taxing power as a conces-
sion to constitutional limits – and to downplay opiate's continuing use as a medicine – is
David F. Musto, *The American Disease: Origins of Narcotic Control* (New York: Oxford
University Press, 1999 edition).

drug interdiction efforts. Likewise, covert operations or a political interest too bald or embarrassing for open pursuit found cover in operations conducted under the aegis of drug suppression. After the U.S. defeat in South Vietnam, at a time when Cold War ideology suffered serious blows and American enthusiasm for global engagement flagged, the drug war revived and sustained elements of the foreign policy agenda.

At first, during the immediate post–World War II era and throughout the 1950s, government officials confined their interest in illicit drugs to specific agendas and venues. At home, the police investment in illicit drug enforcement was restricted to (overwhelmingly corrupt) urban vice squads and the work of a small band of (equally corrupt) Federal Bureau of Narcotics agents. Abroad, most mentions of illicit drug trafficking were made for the purpose of vilifying a political opponent or international rival of the United States. Alternatively, illicit narcotics trafficking was itself described as the work of an evil cabal, a depiction that spared expanding trade flows of routine inspections, earning the gratitude of business interests, and one that suggested that illicit drugs appeared as the result of a conspiracy of a morally dubious set of people, rather than the cold calculations made by a multitude of enterprises and interests.

Over time, official interest in punitive drug enforcement expanded, though its moralistic and sensationalized cast remained. By the time Nixon declared his "war on heroin" in 1971, most police officers could recognize illicit drugs – something that was not true just twenty years earlier – and they routinely made arrests for drug violations. In a sense, entire police departments had become vice squads with a primary interest in narcotics and, conversely, illicit drug enforcement emerged not just as something to police but as a *way* to police, especially in urban minority neighborhoods. During the same period, the U.S. foreign policy apparatus seized upon the illicit drug portfolio as an instrument to cajole allies, advance other international objectives, and justify certain political relationships. In shouldering so many difficult tasks, the drug war became a valued tool of statecraft, especially in regard to the developing world. Whereas the government's illicit drug agenda was once a discrete objective, it developed into less of a specific mission and more of a modality, a way to exercise state power. Of course, other complex and costly mobilizations of the state did not lack for applications beyond their original scope – uses of the Cold War, for instance, ranged far beyond military containment of the Soviet Union. Yet the drug war stands alone as a set of policy interventions, the value of which lay principally in their usefulness for other purposes of interest to the state, irrespective of (and frequently injurious to) the ostensible objectives of drug control. The modern drug war is, almost entirely and most importantly, a way for the state to accomplish something else. To use the apt terminology of sociologist Robert Merton, the drug war's "latent functions" eclipse and often undermine its stated objectives and goals.

These sorts of evolving and instrumental uses of "drug war" enforcement abetted its defining conceit: drugs were a crime, not a trade, and the culpable could be found and arrested. The persuasiveness of this logic was tied to, among other things, the willingness to believe that enforcement tactics provided a proportionate tally of addiction and use. Such a belief was only possible if one was willing to ignore major longstanding communities or sites of illicit drug traffic and consumption: the military, including veterans; the medical profession; and groups with unusual access to channels of distribution, like truck drivers. I tell the stories of these groups to integrate them into our drug war narrative and, more fundamentally, to make it clear that the punitive, prohibitive drug regime was itself composed of a set of choices, not a natural or purely reactive response to illicit drug use and traffic.

These choices, and the composite militant drug war that resulted from them, were undeniably shaped by several forces. Thus far the most important examinations of the drug war or the increase of "punishment" more generally present these forces either as self-interested political agendas or as a fundamental, if futile, response to the many displacements of modernity. Political and legal scholars who stress the importance of the immediate politics of power, especially the importance of race, find the latter analyses to be poorly specified: can modernity "cause" anything, even when broken down into discrete measurements of disorder? At the same time, sociologists and others who study the deep-seated and underlying currents of the shift toward punishment must certainly be correct in supposing that no single force or coalition, however passionate and powerful, can be credited with the long-standing and broad support for criminalization. Can decades of punishment be ascribed to racism or, as others would have it, to economic disadvantage alone? What is missing from both of these accounts, whether they focus on micro-analysis and proximate causes or macro-analysis and profound change, is the appropriate weighting of the middle tier of political economy, or the instruments and institutions of the state. Attention to these adds a crucial piece to the well-established stories of both the drug war and the modern embrace of punishment, making the state's struggle to regulate the pace of modern life concrete, while at the same time connecting the parochial agenda of white backlash and social control to more long-standing concerns of governance.

Moreover, with this focus, we can better understand how the drug war developed with relevance to and bearing on other activities and agendas of the state. Indeed, the most basic difference between this book and other scholarship on the drug war is its frame of reference: where others narrate the drug war from the vantage point of crime and punishment and look to clarify the cultural and political mechanics along those lines, I see a story of government power, and prioritize these dynamics and dilemmas as a way to define that story's scope and to derive argumentative force. Similarly, where others focus on causality in a narrow sense, either by examining the etiology of illicit drug use or by attempting to unravel drug trafficking patterns, I focus on the choices available to lawmakers – different options and possibilities in the exercise of state power – as they responded to various pressures to regulate (or, in the case of illicit use of pharmaceuticals, not to regulate) different drugs. Importantly, a focus on political economy answers more than just the question of "how"; with the drug war especially, it helps to answer "why." As a whole, the drug war has not succeeded in meaningfully affecting the factors that drive causality in other narratives of it: a militant approach has not substantially affected price or purity, or diminished the supply of illicit drugs; neither has it imperiled distribution by imprisoning traffickers. Yet it has churned away nonetheless, a "machine that would go of itself," to borrow a phrase from historian Michael Kammen. Rather than simply observe that the drug war is a hopeless failure, it is time to take seriously its everyday objectives, though these may have little to no bearing on illicit drugs, and read this routine and more instrumental agenda as more than just incidental achievements or expedient uses of the drug war.

Instead, these routine tasks deserve to be considered as causal factors in their own right. In the pages that follow, I argue that a militant drug war has served as a mechanism by which the federal government has reallocated functions, forged alliances, and channeled resources, and depicted, enhanced, and legitimized its sovereign power. The narrow political bandwidth available to the federal taxing project undid drug regulation, however unintentionally, as revenue generation to fund a superpower became a problem of the first magnitude, eclipsing all other taxing concerns. Officials of the federal government subsequently expanded punishment capabilities, both at home and abroad, to accommodate the "drug war" and to achieve much else besides. However else one understands the drug war, the evolution of its structure and basic purposes cannot be properly assessed without invoking the register of the state and deploying the language of political economy.

Naturally the construction of federal power in the twentieth century was Janus-faced, with one gaze directed outside of the country, and its adjoining and opposing gaze directed internally, to citizens and cities, and to individual states and local governments. Correspondingly, this book has both international and domestic components. Other scholars have examined the international patterns of illicit trafficking as well as the U.S. response to these; while this book benefits from that literature, my chief concern is how and when the U.S. international drug portfolio interacted with other foreign policy and domestic political agendas.[20] Likewise, much more can be said about the modern drug war as waged at the level of an individual state, and here we engage that story as well. In fact, I pay special attention to the District of Columbia, a preoccupation shared and occasioned by the U.S. Congress when it crafted some of the tools of the modern drug war. Still, students devoted to either international traffic or state-level punishment will find that these stories are engaged insofar as they illustrate federal power, and not on their own sufficient merits.

And both these objects of the gaze of federal power can be summoned to attest to that power's extraordinary breadth and expansion throughout the twentieth century. Taking just the degradations of civil liberties and common law heritage associated with the modern drug war – mandatory sentencing, no-knock searches, military operations on American soil, pre-textual searches, and possession as proof of a crime – enumerates a litany of practices jarring to the sensibilities of anyone familiar with the restraint on state power so revered in American political and legal traditions. And this is to say nothing of covert funding and operations abroad, or federal agents impinging upon the police powers constitutionally reserved for the states. Yet, as the story of the drug war that follows makes clear, power flowed in both directions: individual states and elements within the international community acted at least as much as they were acted upon. Hence, the story of the federal government's prosecution of the modern drug war is much richer than its more obvious failures would suggest. By seizing the cudgel of drug enforcement, agencies of the state embraced an unpredictable and to some extent a self-defeating instrument; nevertheless,

---

[20] See especially William O. Walker, *Drug Control in the Americas* (Albuquerque: University of New Mexico Press, 1981); William B. McAllister, *Drug Diplomacy in the Twentieth Century: An International History* (London: Routledge, 1999); Arnold Taylor, *American Diplomacy and the Narcotics Traffic, 1900–1939* (Durham: Duke University Press, 1969).

they did so in order to expand the margin and the discretion of operations perceived as being at risk in some way. This vulnerability implicit in the embrace of the drug war has been obscured by its many machinations – and so it remains, buried by the perception of a drug war that is necessary, reactive, and pre-ordained. To a surprising extent, then, the real fig leaf in this story has been the criminal punishment regime itself: a commanding expression of state power, to be sure, but one that has left deeper problems of governance unrecognized and unresolved.

The historical account offered in these pages suggests that the state's aggressive posture in the drug war is in fact a testament to the limits of its other resources, as well as to the fragile legitimacy of its institutions and activities. This perspective holds, I believe, both political and historical interest. Reading the drug war in relief, so to speak, both for what it is and what it is not, suggests that the room to reform its most egregious aspects entails greater acceptance of the taxing and regulatory powers of government. At the same time, it also suggests that historians of American politics ought to read coercive projects of the state, no matter how militant, as endeavors of considerable nuance, capable of collecting other agendas and compensating for other failures, and that these alternate and more subtle motivations extend beyond forging a political coalition to resolving basic dilemmas of governance. Behind the gun and the badge, and behind the edifice of conservative state-building more generally, there lies a story just as complex and contested as that which we commonly acknowledge as historical grounding for progressive causes.[21] Indeed, perhaps it is the failure to assimilate projects like the drug war into our comprehensive understanding of state power that accounts for the tendency to "naturalize" its radical nature and implicitly validate its proponents' claims of necessity. After all, sequestering something suggests that it can be understood separately and on its own terms. If so, then this book challenges such assumptions by unveiling the choices and struggles guiding the formation of drug prohibition and punishment, integrating this story into the narrative of modern U.S. state power, and providing a different way to discuss how the modern drug war came to be, and how it might come to an end.

---

[21] While assessments of James Q. Wilson's body of work have been monopolized by his "broken windows" theory on how disorder attracts crime, much of the rest of his scholarship – including, especially, *The Investigators* and *Bureacracy* – comprises the extent to which any scholar has attempted to assess conservative state-building across various domains as part of the modern government enterprise. See Wilson, *Bureaucracy: What Government Agencies Do and Why They Do It* (New York: Basic Books, 1989); *The Investigators: Managing FBI and Narcotics Agents* (New York: Basic Books, 1978).

PART I

1940–1960

I

Trade in War

For once, Harry Anslinger was satisfied. The bold and often irascible commissioner of the Bureau of Narcotics, known for his moralistic denunciations of drug use and enthusiastic promises of success in his campaign to eradicate the "demon of narcotics," must have grown weary of reports that contradicted his most assured public declarations. As confidently as Anslinger predicted certain victory, his own narcotics agents filed incident reports that chronicled a messy battle against illicit narcotic use; indeed, reading between the lines or judging by the heft of the correspondence alone, the campaign against illicit use of narcotics seemed not only uncertain, but much in doubt.

All that changed after the Japanese invasion of eastern China in 1937. Formerly dispirited narcotics agents turned triumphant as they fired off messages to their superiors, recording the sudden and exorbitant rise in the price of illicit narcotics and the "weak" or highly diluted content of drugs sold on the street. One district supervisor sent word in the fall of 1937 of the "high cost of bootleg narcotics," which he attributed to "strict enforcement of narcotic laws."[1] Other agents seemed likewise overcome by their own serendipity and success, though in fact this amounted to a gruesome catalog of behavior. The district supervisor in Seattle, Washington, observed that addicts who consumed highly adulterated drugs "subjected their bodies to unusual abuse." One barbiturate acid commonly "cut" into heroin sold on the black market

---

[1] Lawrence Kolb to Anslinger, October 28, 1937, RG 170, Record of the Drug Enforcement Administration, Subject Files of the Bureau of Narcotics and Dangerous Drugs, 1916–1970, *NARA*, Box 2.

deteriorated and ultimately destroyed the veins of its user, and those who consumed it in regular amounts resorted to "introduction through the head and particularly the forehead's small veins."[2] Narcotics agents in New York sent the Washington office a story of one woman who, "being unable to obtain narcotics, jumped from the fifth floor room in the Lexington apartments … landing 75 feet below on a pile of broken bricks in the alley." Because the Bureau kept records on all addicts known to them, it was not for poetic reasons that the narcotics agent added that the distraught woman "lived about four hours and died in the Mercy Hospital."[3] Other heroin users resorted to consuming gallons of paregoric sedative – usually dispensed in small bottles to quiet colicky babies – in order to get the two grains of opium present in each ounce.[4]

Similar stories were sent to Bureau headquarters from all over the country. Desperate narcotics users flooded the agency's doors, begging officials to send them to one of two recently opened hospitals sponsored by the Public Health Service to treat narcotic addiction.[5] A baffled district supervisor in Dallas admitted that "[t]his is the first time in my experience so large a number of addicts have applied for treatment." Those physically dependent upon narcotics told agents of the near impossibility of buying the necessary drugs, and, if obtained, the likelihood that these had been so diluted as to be worthless and so adulterated that even one "hit" put a user's life in jeopardy. "Whereas the streets of Dallas were formerly over-run with addicts," a supervisor wrote in a rare and certainly exaggerated admission, "it is not unusual at this time to cruise the streets for hours without sighting one known addict."[6] Months later, the same official followed with a report of a "panic" in the Dallas-Fort Worth area among those who used narcotics illicitly, and, like others, he credited the Bureau's own efforts in bringing this about. "We will, of course, continue

---

[2] Progress Report, District Supervisor [hereafter, DS], Seattle, Washington, January 1940, *NARA*, Box 2.

[3] Charles A. Burrows, Narcotics Agent [hereafter, NA] to Anslinger, New York, October 13, 1939, *NARA*, Box 2.

[4] "Paregoric Sold to Dope Users; Stores Raided," *Chicago Daily Tribune*, September 13, 1941, p.18.

[5] The first and more famous of these was located in Lexington, Kentucky; the second was in Ft. Worth, Texas. See Nancy D. Campbell, *Discovering Addiction: The Science and Politics of Substance Abuse Research* (Ann Arbor: University of Michigan Press, 2007).

[6] Joseph Bell, DS, to Anslinger, May 22, 1939, RG 170, Record of the Drug Enforcement Administration, Subject Files of the Bureau of Narcotics and Dangerous Drugs, 1916–1970, *NARA*, Box 2.

all possible enforcement efforts which will keep this condition more or less permanent," the supervisor pledged to Commissioner Anslinger.[7] All told, the tales of narcotics users who jumped to their death, shot up "bum stuff," or wandered the country in desperate search of drugs on the black market affirmed the commissioner of the Bureau of Narcotics in both his zealotry and his pursuits.

As Harry Anslinger surveyed the breathtaking disappearance of illicit narcotics from the United States, he, like his agents, viewed this turn of events as a credit to the Bureau of Narcotics, formed in 1930 and tasked with implementing a remarkable piece of Progressive-era legislation, the Harrison Anti-Narcotic Act of 1914. Though its name connotes an enforcement agenda, the legislation was, strictly speaking, a revenue measure that required anyone who handled opiates (including opium, morphine, and heroin) or cocaine to register with the Department of Internal Revenue, purchase a tax "stamp," and to record all transactions in which they dispensed narcotics.[8] Along with the tax liability that accompanied registration, legal sale of narcotics also depended upon filing a monthly narcotic report, which Internal Revenue shared with the Bureau of Narcotics, also housed within the Department of Treasury. The system of regulation explicitly recognized the legal manufacture and use of narcotics; at the time, opiates and cocoa-leaf derivatives were painkillers and anesthetics essential to the medical profession and used regularly. As one doctor who addressed a World War II gathering of his peers put it, opiates provided "the most blessed controller of pain and shock produced by God and discovered by man."[9] Singling out such addictive drugs for praise might sound strange to a modern ear, but that is only because it registers in a world that has grown accustomed to synthetic drugs of all kinds. In World War II, as in years before, such drugs were rare in the medical arsenal. To treat chronic pain or traumatic shock, physicians turned to narcotics.

[7] Bell to Anslinger, October 21, 1939, *NARA*, Box 2.
[8] The measure has been interpreted in light of the increased opium traffic coming from Asia to the United States through the recently acquired colonial possession of the Philippines; see David Courtwright, *Dark Paradise: Opiate Addiction in America Before 1940* (Cambridge: Harvard University Press, 1982). It has also been presented as principally, if not exclusively, a punitive enforcement measure: see David F. Musto, *The American Disease: Origins of Narcotic Control* (New York: Oxford University Press, 1999 edition).
[9] Address of Dr. William Charles White before the Harvard Club of Washington, October 31, 1942, found in RG 170, Records of the Drug Enforcement Administration, Subject Files of the Bureau of Narcotics and Dangerous Drugs, 1916–1970, *NARA*, Box 1.

The raw material used to create these drugs came from outside of the contiguous United States. This simple fact deserved more reflection at the time, and does so even more today. Because the United States does not grow poppies or cocoa plants to any appreciable extent, narcotics would always be, first and foremost, a trade. As such, the Department of Treasury seemed the natural location for the Bureau appointed to regulate it, though this assignment might also seem puzzling in hindsight. Yet the inherently commercial nature of narcotics production and sale, a natural fit within the Treasury, should in no way obscure the department's significant enforcement capabilities. Up until mid-century, the Treasury stood as the premier enforcement agency of the federal government. It is tempting to view this institutional fact as an accidental result of Prohibition, the short-lived constitutional amendment ratified in 1919 that outlawed the manufacture and sale of alcohol (also, technically speaking, a tax measure). Implementation of much of the brief and notorious reign of Prohibition fell to Andrew Mellon, Treasury secretary to Warren Harding, Calvin Coolidge, and Herbert Hoover – an unfortunate event, in the eyes of Prohibition's many ardent supporters, for this extravagantly wealthy and temperamentally prudent man held little enthusiasm for the so-called Noble Experiment.[10] In large part to counteract accusations from within the Republican Party that he had been too lenient in his enforcement of Prohibition, Mellon undertook a more concerted campaign against bootlegging under Hoover, and this effort has endowed popular culture and memory with lasting (and somewhat distorted) images of indefatigable Treasury agents confronting violent rings of organized crime profiting from the illegal distribution and sale of alcohol.

Untouchable or otherwise, these particular agents constituted only one part of Treasury's manifold enforcement duties. Traditional tasks demanded that the department keep "a vigilant superintendance over all accountabilities of public money," as its first secretary, Alexander Hamilton, instructed.[11] Collecting tax revenues, levying the tariff, or simply printing money certainly led to some serious-minded protection, but still other duties gave the department an altogether more militant cast. The Coast Guard, the nation's oldest maritime force, serves under the

[10] More on Mellon's service as Treasury secretary can be found in David Cannadine, *Mellon: An American Life* (New York: Vintage, 2008).

[11] See Alexander Hamilton, "The Examination, XI," originally in *New York Evening Post*, February 3, 1802, found in *The Papers of Alexander Hamilton*, vol. 25 (New York: Columbia University Press, 1977), p. 581.

Navy Department in war, but in times of peace it takes commands from Treasury. Among the most important of these are the numerous measures designed to prevent smuggling. In this light, the Coast Guard can be thought of as a floating Customs Service – another of the Treasury's enforcement components. Many people know that a president's personal protection comes from the Secret Service, also housed in Treasury, but few realize that this function was an offshoot of its original charge to suppress counterfeit currency and, as it evolved over time, conspiracies against the government of any kind. Finally, the government's efforts to collect taxes on alcohol, whether during the Whiskey Rebellion or in the present day, have long required an enforcement component, and, through a somewhat checkered lineage, the Bureau of Alcohol, Tobacco, and Firearms (ATF) can trace its evolution from colonial times to the modern Treasury Department.[12]

In historical context, then, readers of the *Washington Post* would not have been particularly surprised when, in 1941, the paper devoted an entire page to a pictorial review of Treasury's many enforcement functions.[13] Nor would its enforcement of the Harrison Act seem unusual: like other gate-keeping offices of the Treasury, the 1914 Act capitalized on the extraordinary legal authority available to the state at its borders. The Bureau of Narcotics performed a chemical assay of all known imported narcotics at the point of entry, and if it was to any degree unprocessed (and it often was), the government estimated "almost to a fraction of a grain," as one official claimed, how much finished product could be derived from the material.[14] Unexpected spikes anywhere in the distribution chain – manufacturers who asked for too much material or distributed too little; doctors who did the same – received the close attention of the Department of Treasury. In its review of narcotic circulation, the government held an economic (not necessarily criminal) threat: purveyors who were careless with a suspicious consistency did not go to jail, they went out of business. This point remains essential to the success of the government's narcotic scheme, and it bears emphasis here. The basic conceit of the Harrison Act was that if narcotics were a trade, then it would be taxed into the shape and scope that the government desired.

---

[12] ATF was transferred to the newly created Department of Homeland Security after September 11, 2001, and has since been reassigned again (somewhat incongruously to this author) to the Department of Justice.

[13] "The Treasury Helps Enforce the Nation's Laws," *Washington Post*, April 21, 1940, p. 85.

[14] Ewing, Oral History, Truman Presidential Archives, p. 58.

Since the goal of this tax and tariff endeavor was to govern behavior, the Harrison Act can be thought of as a classic sumptuary law – sometimes defined narrowly as regulation of luxury, but in fact much closer to a project, as Alan Hunt argues, of regulating "the social manifestations of consumption," including the moral or prescriptive component apparent in such attempts.[15]

Imperfections in this model were inevitable, and records of the Bureau of Narcotics attest to the government's struggle to remain one step ahead of schemes to divert narcotics. There was little the Bureau could do about occasional errors, and a resigned agency received monthly affidavits – required when any narcotic material was lost – testifying to incidents like the "full package of Hydrocain solution containing 162 grains of cocaine" that "was accidentally broken ... and the entire quantity destroyed," or the morphine that disappeared "when the New York and Worcester Dispatch truck fell into the river at Windsor Locks, Connecticut," or the seemingly endless stream of reports of burglaries from a doctor's office.[16] As in Europe, physicians in the United States were an important source of narcotics used for both licit and illicit purposes, and Bureau officials were quick to suspect practitioners who were burglarized with alarming regularity.[17] To avert suspicion, doctors often put forward a culprit. Such was usually a visitor who had come to the office earlier in the day, and with some unusual frequency this person was often a traveling carnival or circus performer.[18] It is interesting that, whether or not a suspect was

[15] Alan Hunt, *Governance of the Consuming Passions: A History of Sumptuary Law* (New York: St. Martin's Press, 1996), quote from p. 7. Hunt himself draws a comparison between sumptuary laws and the modern drug war, though he sees that parallel only in terms of moral regulation. Later I argue that theories of social control or prescriptive governance do not adequately account for the shift toward criminalization and the declaration of the "drug war," though I do not discount the importance of such logics either.

[16] Attributions, in order: French Affidavit, RG 170, Bureau of Narcotics, Correspondence of the BN with Collectors of Internal Revenue, 1928–1940, Box 1; Perkins Affidavit, RG 170, Bureau of Narcotics, Correspondence of BN with Narcotics agents, 1930–1940, Box 1.

[17] Also as in Europe, a significant number of these doctors were drug users and drug addicts themselves; Cf. David Courtwright, *Dark Paradise*, who argues that opiate use had, by this time, already become defined as a habit of the working class and racial minorities. Without doubt the drug's profile had changed substantially from its middle class and largely female beginnings, but evidence suggests diverse use prior to World War II.

[18] It is plausible that some performers had a drug habit, which they supported by criminal acts while on the road; performers who were injured, for instance, might well have developed an addiction to morphine. It is just as likely that this persona represented a "don't even bother" target for local law enforcement, and thus doctors could invoke it without rousing much of a police response.

named, agents of the Bureau of Narcotics left the burglary as a matter for local law enforcement. Theirs was not a criminal justice pursuit, but a tax investigation; if a doctor failed to pass it, he would be stripped of his "tax stamp" and lose his ability to deal in narcotics and, if the state medical society followed suit, he would in all likelihood lose his medical license as well. In two cases that quickly followed the initial implementation of the Harrison Act, the Supreme Court established a somewhat ambiguous formula to scrutinize medical professionals: if a doctor conspired with a pharmacist to furnish large amounts of drugs at a profit for himself, then a "prescription" could be treated as tantamount to a "sale" and he could be criminally charged with violating the Harrison Revenue measure.[19] Initially such charges were a misdemeanor; under the Bureau's leadership in the 1930s, many states made such violations a felony.

These minor incidents were all errors within the U.S. narcotics regime, not failures of it. Drugs were obviously lost or stolen in transit, and sometimes, as addicts themselves confessed, they were prescribed by physicians for uses not sanctioned by the government.[20] But these events were infrequent and trivial when compared to the much larger failures of the system itself: the importation of drugs without the knowledge of the U.S. government. In order to stymie the flow of unauthorized narcotic shipments, the Bureau of Narcotics and its supporters pressed a program of more stringent regulation of the market and its main suppliers. Unfortunately for them, the only institution or body with the requisite authority to consider an effective schedule, or trade regime, in narcotics traffic was the League of Nations – an international organization that the United States had declined to join, although Woodrow Wilson, the president at the time of its formation, was in some respects its ideological benefactor. Having rejected the treaty to ratify membership, the United States had only very limited influence over the activities of the League, and of course League members, still smarting from the insults of American critics, seemed quite content to deliberate and to decide without any serious American participation. But underestimating or ignoring the international body proved to be a miscalculation. While the League's interwar diplomatic stage in Geneva would be most remembered for the dramatic withdrawals of the Japanese, German, and Italian delegations after their respective nations

---

[19] *United States v. Doremus*, 249 US 86 (1919); *Webb v. United States*, 249 US 96 (1919); *Jin Fuey Moy v. United States*, 254 US 189 (1920).

[20] See oral histories, passim, in Courtwright et al., *Addicts Who Survived: An Oral History of Narcotic Use in America, 1923–1965* (Knoxville: University of Tennessee Press, 1989) [hereafter, *Addict Oral Histories*].

flouted the charter by acts of military aggression, this fateful ending has eclipsed the early, more heady days of the League, and overshadowed a number of its successful accomplishments.[21] As an operating international body, the League provided an important precedent for its successor institution, the United Nations. For instance, its struggle to reduce the global arms trade proved, for a time, successful.[22] And, during the 1930s, League members decided to attempt to govern the trade in narcotics.

Rather than accede to the treaty of membership, the United States preferred to send various informal representatives to oversee and attempt to influence the League's discussions. One of the most successful of these was Oscar Ewing, a young lawyer who would rise to some prominence years later in the Truman administration as leader of the Federal Security Agency. Interestingly, at the time when Ewing appeared before the League of Nations in the spring of 1931, the illegal importation of narcotics into the United States was tied, most often, to the businesses he represented: pharmaceutical manufacturers, in particular Ewing's client, Merck (of Dammestadt, but also incorporated in the United States), and other similarly large concerns. In many ways, Ewing's representation of Merck and Company, Inc., led him to the League's door. European drug producers supplied the licit market for narcotics, and, during this time, they supplied the lion's share of the illicit market as well.[23] Profits from illegal sales enabled these drug manufacturers to charge remarkably low prices for legal narcotics, underselling and thus undermining the competition, including the U.S. interests Ewing represented.[24] To the distress of the Americans, the European governments were indifferent in the face of illicit drug trafficking. Some, like France, developed a reputation that ranged beyond apathy into actual complicity, perfecting last-minute switches at the border and, if discovered, a practiced diplomatic silence in the face of repeated requests to account for how such large shipments of opium went astray.

---

[21] For a review of recent scholarship that has brought attention to some of these more successful ventures, see Susan Pedersen, "Back to the League of Nations: Review Essay," *American Historical Review* 112, no. 4 (October 2007): 1091–1117.

[22] David R. Stone, "The League of Nations' Drive to Control the Global Arms Trade," *Journal of Contemporary History* 35, no. 2 (April 2000): 213–30.

[23] Alan A. Block, "European Drug Traffic and Traffickers between the Wars: The Policy of Suppression and its Consequences," *Journal of Social History* 23, no. 2 (Winter 1989): 315–37.

[24] Not that the U.S. Merck and Company, Inc., was immune from the temptation to supply the illegal market; Merck occasionally purchased opium on the high seas, sealing a portion of its cartons for legal importation, and leaving the rest for other purposes.

To confront this embarrassing situation, the League initially determined that it should ration poppies and cocoa leaves for its member nations, though the narcotic quotas proposed by the League of Nations in 1930 had important loopholes as well as penalties.[25] In setting quotas, drug-producing nations like Turkey felt unduly penalized for illicit trading. Other objections emerged from Japan, with its fairly new manufacturing plants that were now stuck with quotas based on previous exports, a severe cap on their growth. Finally, and most significantly, there existed a gaping "colonial" loophole to the League's model. Quotas simply did not apply to territorial possessions, and this exemption is all the more extraordinary because it omitted the principal producers of the raw material for narcotics from review. Of these grave shortcomings, the United States was only concerned with Japan's grievance, for it was theirs as well. American business interests, represented by Ewing, struck a common cause with the Japanese and lobbied for the adoption of the U.S. model, the Harrison Act: rather than rationing the raw material for drugs using a quota based on previous trade, the Japanese proposed (and the Americans supported) a system whereby licit drug manufacturers would be allowed to import according to a much more generous quota, one arrived at with the help of recipient governments, and that those governments would then track, and be accountable for, narcotics traffic within their own country.

The adoption of the Japanese program had immediate and unintended effects. As historian Alan Block argues, the scheme imposed by the League of Nations meant that, by "disciplin[ing] legitimate drug firms, pharmaceutical traders and dealers, into servicing only this shrinking [licit] market," League mandates drove the illicit market underground. This was a shift of tremendous significance: where the illicit use and sale of narcotics was once closely tied to its licit use and sale, now, on the eve of World War II, ethnic gangs and, especially, connections to and penetration in the opiate market of China took center stage in the production, handling, and sale of illicit narcotics. Before the creation of League narcotic schedules, much of the illicit narcotics market received its supply through *diversion*, or the rerouting of material that was once a part of or destined for the process of legal manufacture and sale of drugs. After international controls were put in place, the illicit narcotics market would rely more on

---

[25] More detail of the intricacies of the politics and problems behind this proposal can be found in William B. McAllister, *Drug Diplomacy in the Twentieth Century: An International History* (London: Routledge, 1999).

subversion of the governing controls, or the knowing production, manufacture, or distribution of drugs in violation of international conventions and domestic laws.

One might assume that subversion resulted in a narcotic that was far less safe to consume – but, in reality, it led to a more ambivalent outcome. On the one hand, subverted narcotics generally meant a highly adulterated product: middlemen and dealers along the chain of production enhanced their profit by taking a "pure" drug and cutting (or mixing) it with other substances before resale. A less potent narcotic meant attenuated addiction and manipulated consumption, including – however unintentionally – incremental withdrawal. This is precisely the situation American opiate users found themselves in on the eve of their country's entry into World War II. As war embroiled Europe and the Pacific, it became obvious that an extraordinarily "weak" product wended its way through the illicit U.S. market, not least so because criminal suspects detained overnight or longer ceased to exhibit the physical symptoms of withdrawal. Police or custodial workers who had grown resigned to unsavory morning messes in jail cells happily noticed the change, and so too did the Bureau of Narcotics.

At the same time, subversion opened up new and dangerous prospects, both for user and trafficker. In a narcotics market supplied by subversion, a less addictive drug did not necessarily mean a "safer" one, since dealers selected lethal additives like arsenic as often as they used innocuous ones like sugar. In times of diminishing supply as well as in times of abundance, an unregulated drug represents an unknown risk for its user. Just as important, the shift from diversion to subversion meant that illicit narcotics use would be serviced by illicit narcotics networks, and this carried a potential for danger all the way up and down the supply chain, from poppy farmer to narcotics user. A criminal network has different elements, and many of these do not feel constrained to observe the law, much less market safe products. The compulsions driving illegal trafficking include the elasticity of the product, reciprocal fears of exposure or reluctance to lose business, and, of course, the threat of or willingness to use violence. Before, diverted narcotics had a plausible safe haven, or legal shelter, at any given point in its interception: a user could claim a legitimate prescription, a doctor could claim a legitimate supply, a drug manufacturer could claim legitimate shipments, and so on. But an entirely illegal and underground chain of supply exposed any single point within it to criminal retribution, and, ultimately, to state reprisals as well.

The fraught potentials of subversion represented, to the Bureau of Narcotics, new opportunities and incentives for interdiction. After all, a diverted narcotics market meant that illicit transactions were cloaked by and embedded in legal ones – and, more subtly, diversion shielded narcotics use as a whole from comprehensive denunciation. A physician who kept a heroin addict supplied was quite different from a street-level dealer with a list of prior criminal offenses; likewise Merck Pharmaceuticals selling under the table presented a different picture than a racketeer who merged his narcotics business with "white slavery" or illegal gambling. For the Bureau, diversion rankled not simply because of the difficulty of spotting properly credentialed actors engaged in foul play. More distressing was that doctors and drug companies' participation in licit and illicit narcotics use intertwined the two, and hence spared the black market from becoming a distinct entity for them to police, and to portray. And the Bureau was very invested in both: as energetically as it chased illegal drug deals, the agency invested still greater resources and evinced more commitment in constructing the image of narcotics in the American public mind. A shrinking supply through diversion, then, provided the Bureau with an opportunity to disentangle illicit narcotics use from legal consumption and depict it as sourced principally through subversion; a racket run by criminals for the benefit of addicts.

In this way, international narcotic conventions adopted by the League advanced the Bureau's agenda of marginalizing illicit narcotics use. To be sure, the Bureau's tendency to do so had long been apparent. Immediately prior to World War II, the United States had all but jettisoned the rehabilitative component to the Harrison Act – namely, the recognized authority of doctors to prescribe narcotics for addiction alone, and, in some cities, the creation of clinics designed for addicts to obtain therapeutic prescriptions and counseling.[26] By the mid-1920s, these approaches had been shunted aside, either through the courts or, just as important, by public opinion. The Jones-Miller Act of 1922, passed as the Narcotic Drugs Import and Export Act, enjoined the secretary of Treasury to restrict imports to only those narcotics needed for medicinal and scientific purposes, and to govern exports according to the same logic. This more stringent standard for trade signaled, among other things, a growing public disdain for these powerful drugs.

[26] Courtwright, *Dark Paradise*, and Susan L. Speaker, "'The Struggle of Mankind against Its Deadliest Foe': Themes of Counter-Subversion in Anti-Narcotic Campaigns, 1920–1940," *Journal of Social History* 34, no. 3 (Spring 2001): 591–610.

Several years later, the Bureau interpreted the Jones-Miller Act as strengthening their hand as the arbiter between licit and illicit narcotic use. From its earliest days, the agency launched a project of paramount importance: crafting the image of the "addict" in the American public mind.[27] While its construction of the addict would undergo several important revisions over time, some of the Bureau's key foundational components endured. First among these was that the Bureau believed, almost at an unspoken and implicit level, that illicit narcotic users were all addicts, each and every one. Recreational use of addictive substances would have struck agents and their allies as a contradiction in terms – though, according to modern pharmacology, even the most physically addictive substances do not lead to addiction in all of its users. Second, the Bureau of Narcotics publicly attacked and privately disavowed any notion that an addict could lead a functional life; that is, that those physically dependent upon narcotics could live, work, and socialize in the world without obvious markers of addiction or derangement. Here again the Bureau erred, as clinicians and medical professionals – an occupational group that suffers from disproportionate numbers of addicts within its own ranks – understand that the so-called functioning addict or functioning alcoholic is the most common profile in substance abuse.

Had the Bureau reconsidered its guiding assumptions regarding addiction, it might have been more hospitable to clinical care for addiction, including "ambulatory" or out-patient care, a system in which an office or clinic dispenses therapy and medical support to an addict in periodic installments without admission to a hospital or overnight stay in a medical facility. Instead, the Bureau viewed such approaches as anathema. Time and again proposals for ambulatory care would surface, and each time the Bureau responded with vituperative attacks. Long before a "war" on drugs was declared, a narcotics official volunteered its logic when reacting to yet another proposal for the adoption of the "British plan," or ambulatory care for addiction: such would be "opposed to our existing law and best medical judgment," though this was not altogether the case, and, he continued, the proposal "would constitute recognition that drug

---

[27] This was a project that some medical professionals and scientists supported with their research, while others – including those grouped around the Public Health Service Hospital in Lexington – used their research to denounce Anslinger's depiction of the addict. On collaboration with the Bureau's image of the addict, see Caroline Jeane Acker, *Creating the American Junkie: Addiction Research in the Classic Era of Narcotic Control* (Baltimore: Johns Hopkins University Press, 2002); on researchers who challenged Anslinger, see Campbell, *Discovering Addiction*.

addiction is to be tolerated, and consequently increased, representing an abject surrender to an evil which is unacceptable and repugnant to the moral principles of our people."[28]

From the first, Bureau agents believed that ambulatory care would increase addiction, and, in their minds, this assertion was not hypothetical. Officials argued that the initial experiments in clinical care undertaken in the early days of the Harrison Narcotic Act led to more narcotic use and hence addiction – a "fact" demonstrated by either the increased enrollment in such care or an increase in narcotic arrests in the same city as a clinic. While not statistically robust, these conclusions remained persuasive to the Bureau and to many Americans. In light of similar evidence marshaled against clinical proposals today, it seems important to note the principal fallacy in this critique of the medical model is the assumption that clinical admission and narcotic arrests represented a fair tally of use and trade, rather than artifacts of different treatment and enforcement approaches. The more strongly one feels that narcotic enforcement significantly affects narcotic consumption, including its price or purity, the more likely it is that one will concur with the Bureau of Narcotics and other similar arguments, and oppose ambulatory care. For those less convinced of the effect of enforcement methods, including those disposed to find them utterly futile, the medical model remains untested and unfairly maligned.

Just as important, opponents of a medical model often suggest clinical treatment of addicts condones narcotic consumption and promotes a permissive attitude that, if adopted, would tempt many more into narcotics experimentation and use. In their eyes, such a move could only be construed as defeat (or, as described previously, "surrender"). In this way, a state of war already reigned in the minds of those who had a fundamentalist view – as used here, a religiously tinged absolutism – regarding the narcotics trade. For them, the Bureau and its supporters were not simply fending off subversion of international drug conventions and illicit use; they also waged war against those who suggested alternate approaches and, with only a little exaggeration, one can say waged battle against sin itself. For narcotics officials, two dogmatic impulses merged into one: the depraved man of Catholic or Calvinist tradition, inevitably guided to sin, meets a more Enlightenment notion that man can himself devise

[28] George H. Gaffney, Deputy Commissioner, to J. A. Eashelman, September 17, 1964, Records of the Drug Enforcement Administration, Subject Files of the Bureau of Narcotics and Dangerous Drugs, 1916–1970, *NARA*, Box 38.

stratagems to avoid sin – not the perfectability of man quite, but of models. So strongly did Anslinger and the Bureau guard against "permissive" attitudes that they convinced the Hollywood production code authorities to eliminate images of narcotics from films and, more surprising, railed against anti-narcotic educational films, novels describing illicit drug use, or, for that matter, any open, public discussion of narcotics. For Anslinger especially, it seemed the mere image of an opium pipe would overcome enfeebled man's ability to resist; at the very same time, he regarded the Bureau's interventions as capable of totally smothering the last gram of narcotic from illicit use, sensing no contradiction between this grim view of man and confident belief in government.[29]

In these many ways, the Bureau openly professed its belief that it guarded morals as well as borders. From this conviction flowed little doubt, and it shaped the Bureau's views on addiction and, too, on addicts themselves. Despite evidence of the continuing diversity of narcotics use, Anslinger believed throughout his tenure in office that African Americans comprised the overwhelming majority of narcotic addicts. In the mid-1950s, one Hollywood producer hoping to secure an exception from Anslinger to the ban on narcotic images in film vowed to make an earnest, educational film, but Anslinger turned him away nevertheless, gesturing to the budding civil rights movement and its tactics: since "85 percent of the addicts are confined to a certain group," Anslinger wrote, more out of attempted propriety than desire to be oblique, "it would be impossible to give a factual portrayal of the addict situation without seriously offending this group and encountering the resulting boycott."[30] Though the Bureau maintained a registry of addicts, it is unclear how Anslinger arrived at this percentage; addict rolls had, by this time, been discredited in the eyes of the (normally credulous) agents who consulted them.[31] It seems more likely that Anslinger generalized from arrest rates or, perhaps, simply guessed; it was in fact customary for Bureau officials to assign statistical certainty to areas of doubt as a way of suggesting enforcement competence and control.

[29] Anslinger held a similarly exuberant confidence in Prohibition, which, as a Treasury official, he was charged with implementing: see Larry "Ratso" Sloman, *Reefer Madness: A History of Marijuana* (New York: St. Martin's Griffin, 1979), p. 35, for discussion of the essay contest Anslinger entered in 1928 designed to generate suggestions for ensuring Prohibition's success.

[30] Anslinger to Harry M. Goetz, July 11, 1956, RG 170, Records of the Drug Enforcement Administration, Subject Files of the Bureau of Narcotics and Dangerous Drugs, 1916–1970, *NARA*, Box 32.

[31] For further discussion, see Chapter 3.

Whatever the case, the commissioner believed himself to be squaring off against a largely black population of addicts, one that he and his agents viewed as criminal – either by the fact of their addiction, or in pursuit of it.[32] This was yet another conflation that warranted closer inspection. A memorandum summarizing a phone call between a Bureau agent and a Canadian official disclosed that, during the conversation, the American agreed with the proposition that an addict should be called "anti-social personality" rather than "psychopath." Both men reasoned that "anti-social personality is the better of the two because it comes closer to depicting a law-breaker ... and does not contain the implied word 'nut,' which so many persons read into the meaning of psychopath."[33] However slight the empathy elicited by use of the term "psychopath," these officials felt it would be too much. Discursive cues as well as enforcement tactics revealed quite emphatically that when the Bureau agents had an addict in hand, they felt they had apprehended a criminal. So severe and strict was the Bureau's social construction of addicts that when critics of it rallied around a 1938 publication called *Drug Addicts Are Human Beings*, the Bureau had the temerity to attack the book.[34] Its prolific author, the elderly and eclectic Dr. Henry Smith Williams, must have been taken aback that this single contribution to a body of work which included *Etching Is the Ideal Hobby* and *The Private Lives of Birds* should suddenly make him the object of such contempt.

Yet the pre–World War II reality of narcotic use did not conform to the narrow depiction put forward by the Bureau. Despite Anslinger's attempt to portray addiction as a habit of the "underclass," and despite scholars' willingness to substantially agree with this supposition in order to portray the narcotics regime exclusively as a project of social control,[35] much illicit narcotic use persisted through diversion of licit supply. To be blunt, doctors and nurses turned patients into addicts and then supplied

[32] Over time, the geography and demographics of heroin use as well as the effects of various enforcement strategies conformed to Anslinger's view that the majority of heroin users were black. Specifically, African Americans had increased exposure to heroin in urban America during the 1950s, and therefore increased their use of the drug; see Eric C. Schneider, *Smack: Heroin and the American City* (Philadelphia: University of Pennsylvania Press, 2008), passim.

[33] Memorandum of Telephone Call with Dr. James Hamilton, May 23, 1949, RG 170, Records of the Drug Enforcement Administration, Subject Files of the Bureau of Narcotics and Dangerous Drugs, 1916–1970, *NARA*, Box 1.

[34] Henry Smith Williams, *Drug Addicts Are Human Beings* (Washington, DC: Shaw Publishing, 1938).

[35] See Courtwright, *Dark Paradise*.

them in their habit. Some engaged in diversion as a practical concession; as one narcotic addict remembered, doctors who ventured into "under the table business" would "rather do it that way than have their place broken into or torn up" by opiate users in search of their drug.[36] Yet other physicians did so without much compulsion. Addicts recalled that disproportionately in small towns and especially in the south, doctors were willing to "write" – meaning, willing to sell narcotic prescriptions. Some of these doctors were addicts themselves: "every time I went" to the public health hospital for recovery, one addict remembered, "there were always three or four southern doctors there as drug addicts."[37] Many if not most of those supplied through diversion did not fit the mold cast by Anslinger. "Brenda," the pseudonym given to one user who recounted her experience shortly after World War II, recalled that in trying to "make" a doctor for a prescription, "everyone in the hallway was waiting for a narcotic prescription," and these fellow patients "were all white people." What was more, the women were in their fifties, and the men "were the same." The experience was an eye-opener for her; despite the Bureau's contentions, these addicts were "very home-like, very family-type people," not criminals and not disorderly.[38] The different racial connotations of the market supplied through diversion versus subversion were occasionally noted, and reinforced, by press coverage of narcotics arrests after the war. One 1949 story that appeared in *Afro-American*, for example, that headlined the arrest of a black "D.C. Dope Queen," also made a point of mentioning the arrest of a "white druggist" dealing heroin without a prescription in the same article. More often, racial categories went unstated, but understood, and it is likely that the *Afro-American* was in this instance seeking to draw attention to the comparison between the enforcement efforts directed toward street peddlers supplied through subversion versus the dwindling efforts aimed at pharmacies and druggists who continued to divert opiates from licit channels.[39]

In fact, medical complicity in narcotics diversion drove Henry Smith Williams, himself a doctor, to offer the surprisingly controversial

---

[36] "Mel," *Addict Oral Histories*, p. 89.

[37] "Mike," *Addict Oral Histories*, p. 137. Historian David Courtwright recounts the apex of the southern epidemic, though, contrary to the narrative and evidence offered here, he claims that it ended with the Supreme Court decision outlawing narcotic prescriptions for addict maintenance alone and the abandonment of clinics in the early 1920s: see David T. Courtwright, "The Hidden Epidemic: Opiate Addiction and Cocaine Use in the South, 1860–1920," *Journal of Southern History* 49, no. 1 (February 1983): 57–72.

[38] "Brenda," *Addict Oral Histories*, p. 138.

[39] NNPA, "D.C. Dope Queen Convicted," *Afro-American*, October 29, 1949, p. 1.

contention that addicts were human beings in the first place: like others in his profession, he decried the use of a revenue measure, the Harrison Act, to inspect and oversee their work. At the time of his writing, 25,000 physicians had been reported, and some imprisoned, for supplying patients with narcotics on the premise of addiction alone. Williams's brother, also a physician, was among those criminally charged and convicted, an event that undoubtedly spurred him into action. In many cases, infractions resulted in the loss of medical license. Though the Supreme Court repeatedly ruled that the federal government could not regulate a profession – that privilege being reserved for the states – the Bureau ignored these rulings at their convenience, routinely paying addicts to "set up" doctors willing to prescribe narcotics on a regular basis without a physical exam. Hounded by agents who monitored narcotics' dispensation, physicians and nurses resented the interference.

Indeed, throughout the 1930s, the Bureau and physicians across the country faced off in a protracted struggle to determine the scope and tenor of the medical profession's reliance upon narcotic drugs. And, despite the vocal indignation of physicians, there can be little doubt that the medical community varied greatly in its degree of responsibility and knowledge when prescribing these drugs. Before World War II, heroin was often prescribed as a "cure" for alcoholism, and, less frequently, a cough suppressant. Doctors with a confident sense that new drugs were necessarily less harmful than older ones also doled out heroin to treat opium addiction – the former being, unfortunately, a more powerful drug than the latter. And it was dismaying for Americans to discover how unscrupulous physicians set about promoting addiction. "There will always be a dope menace," Judge Harry McDevitt warned in 1926, "so long as there are doctors with prescription blanks, bank accounts, and no consciences."[40] One physician in Los Angeles added narcotic content to prescriptions without the patients' knowledge; upon his arrest in 1931, the state medical board must have been relieved to learn that he was also guilty of practicing medicine without a license.[41] This would have been small comfort, though, to a medical profession accustomed to assaults, justified and not, on its professionalism. In 1935, the *Washington Times* reported the comments of a federal judge who deplored "[b]ridge-playing nurses who quiet their patient with a

[40] "Scores Prescriptions for Drug Addicts," *New York Times,* July 10, 1926, p. 28.
[41] "Physician Seized on Drug Plant," *Los Angeles Times,* October 4, 1931, p. A2.

hypodermic needle rather than break up their card game," thus turning "neglected patients [into] drug addicts."[42]

Many cases of diversion involved more ambiguous circumstances; not a "bad" doctor coaxing an unsuspecting patient, but, rather, a genuinely injured person who developed an addiction out of a good-faith prescription intended to treat pain. These scenarios very often involved morphine, a drug used by doctors at this time to treat pain as well as various heart and pulmonary conditions, including asthma. A criminal case in Atlanta involved one doctor who watched patients testify to lying to him in order to obtain morphine, and who further noted that the doctor gradually decreased the amount of narcotic in prescriptions – yet the state proceeded with criminal charges nonetheless. "I told Dr. Freeman I had asthma," a former patient declared on the stand, "[b]ut I was an addict and was not suffering from asthma."[43] State medical boards were unsparing in their review all the same. When courts failed to convict, boards stripped physicians of their licenses in any event, fearful that the entire profession would fall into disrepute and lose the power to prescribe narcotics altogether.

If Anslinger or other Bureau of Narcotics officials sympathized with the plight of physicians who came under excessive scrutiny, they were careful not to show it. Narcotic agents did not even esteem the medical profession highly enough to rely on their advice for treating addiction – though, strangely enough, Bureau agents referred to their preferred approach as "the cure," and, stranger still, Anslinger himself tended to use public health discourse to describe narcotic addiction, often referring to it as a "communicable disease," the carriers of which needed to be "quarantined" to "take the cure."[44] Yet the cure "prescribed" by narcotic officials was nothing more than an extended stay in jail – or, for the well-off, a sanatorium – usually lasting about a week, but sometimes as long as month. Taking "the cure," a person who had grown physically

---

[42] *Washington Times*, July 13, 1935, as found in RG 170, Record of the Drug Enforcement Administration, Subject Files of the Bureau of Narcotics and Dangerous Drugs, 1916–1970, *NARA*, Box 28.

[43] Lamar Q. Ball, "Doctors and Drug Addicts Unfold Tragic Stories of Morphine's Grip," *Atlanta Constitution*, March 12, 1936, p. 1.

[44] For more on the deployment of public health discourse, see Virginia Berridge, *Marketing Health: Smoking and The Discourse of Public Health in Britain* (Oxford: Oxford University Press, 2007); for a review that includes a discursive and perceptual shift in the recent past, see Peter Conrad, *The Medicalization of Society: On the Transformation of Human Conditions into Treatable Disorders* (Baltimore: Johns Hopkins University Press, 2007). For more on contagion and addiction, see Chapter 3.

dependent on narcotics would stop "cold turkey" and suffer through
agonizing withdrawal until normal chemical and biological function
returned. Police watched over addicts who were there to "kick it out,"
as they often called it, and witnessing the wretchedness of the entire process must have evoked officers' compassion and, because so many addicts
returned over and over again, taxed it at the very same time. One reporter
filed a story in 1938 which described "the cure" as "literally hell on earth
for a week," and, in vivid detail, he encouraged his reader to imagine
enduring "chills, fever, sweating, terrific nausea, and pains that try to
throb your head off your backbone and seem to claw your nerves fiber
by fiber till every vertebra and joint and muscle in you is writhing and
screaming for the mercy that it will never get."[45] Officers delivered blan-
kets and meals as their charges suffered, and once appetite returned and
chills and fevers stopped, "the cure" had taken effect, and police released
their custody. Such was the nature of the Bureau's desired intervention
for addicts, delivered with the trappings of medical jargon, but offering
only a brief and brutal sequester – one that, in fact, could result in death.
Withdrawal from opiates could be so severe as to cause heart trauma
and, ultimately, a stroke.

No surprise then, that while Bureau officials invoked the discourse of
medicine regularly, they applied none of its protocols or rigor. One important example of this came in 1937, when Congress passed the Marihuana
Tax Act, using the Harrison Act as a template.[46] Adapting the Harrison
Act to regulate marijuana strained its legal premise, however, because,
unlike opiates, marijuana – the flowering portion of a hemp plant – was
indigenous and widespread. Since it was not an international trade, the
Treasury first attempted to solicit commentary from the pharmaceutical
industry that would classify the drug as addictive and deeply harmful,
in the hopes that the danger inherent in the drug would overcome legal
scruples regarding the constitutionality of federal legislation designed
to regulate it. But Treasury and Anslinger found little help from drug

[45] Guy Murchie, Jr., "The Truth About Dope," *Chicago Daily Tribune*, March 6,
1938, p. H3.
[46] The Spanish spelling of the law is directly indicative of the Central and South American
sources of the drug and, in the American mind, the majority of its users. For an excellent
history, see Richard J. Bonnie and Charles H. Whitehead, *The Marijuana Conviction: A
History of Marijuana Prohibition in the United States* (New York: Lindesmith Center,
1999); for a more popular survey, see Sloman, *Reefer Madness*. Musto, *The American
Disease*, reads much into the fact that marijuana was not simply added to the Harrison
Narcotic Act – though, since it was not imported as a medicine, it is unclear how or why
it would be.

manufacturers and pharmacists, one of whom called the contention that marijuana was habit-forming "absolute rot."[47]

Ignoring the views expressed in these expert assessments, the Bureau continued its drive to include marijuana in the class of "narcotics," confirming its spurious engagement with science, and marking the rise of a more stridently moralistic and hysterical rhetoric as well. It is almost as if Bureau officials and others hoped to compensate for the rather weak pharmacological properties of marijuana with the strength of their invective. Addressing one group, Anslinger declared that "those who are habitually accustomed to use of [marijuana] are said to develop a delirious rage after its administration during which they are temporarily, at least, irresponsible and liable to commit violent crimes" – an important claim, albeit a false one, because it allowed the commissioner to use fears of the "addict criminal" in order to pursue a more punitive approach to users.[48] In place of logic with scientific backing, Anslinger offered a historical one: "It is said that Mohammedan leaders, opposing the Crusaders, utilized the services of individuals addicted to hashish [a derivative of marijuana] for secret murders."[49] The reputation of marijuana as a drug of violent infidels occasionally appeared in the press – no doubt because narcotic officials promoted it as such – with one reporter going so far as to offer an etymology of "assassin" that traced the word's roots to the Arabic name for a hashish user (haschishin).[50]

Anslinger's promotion of what one historian has called the "marijuana-crime-insanity" edifice paved the way for the drug's addition to the Bureau's regulatory portfolio.[51] To be sure, it was an extremely awkward addendum, and Anslinger was himself wary of the extension. Not only did hemp grow wild in rural areas and even in vacant city lots, a number of legitimate industries relied on hemp cultivation.[52] To appease

---

[47] As quoted in Sloman, *Reefer Madness*, p. 39.

[48] Anslinger, remarks to General Federation of Women's Clubs, March 30, 1937, RG 170, Records of the Drug Enforcement Administration, Subject Files of the Bureau of Narcotics and Dangerous Drugs, 1916–1970, *NARA*, Box 3.

[49] Ibid.

[50] Murchie, "The Truth About Dope."

[51] See Sloman, *Reefer Madness*, p. 60; for spurious links to crime, see also Bonnie and Whitebread, *The Marijuana Conviction*, pp. 149–53.

[52] Drug war historians have sometimes offered conspiratorial ideas regarding Anslinger's anti-marijuana posture, including the theory that he was beholden to a DuPont family anxious to stamp out the native hemp industry. His wife was a niece of Andrew Mellon – a relation that probably accounts for Anslinger's quick rise in Treasury – but the DuPont connection is, as yet, unproven. As others have pointed out, and I have found in my own research, Anslinger initially resisted federal regulation, even as he demonized the drug

these vocal business interests, and to assuage legal concerns, the Marihuana Act taxed manufacturing uses moderately, not prohibitively, and levied the surcharge against production, manufacture, and transport only, exempting personal consumption and use. Crafting the bill's regulation so closely around the commerce clause of the Constitution might have spared the legislation from unfavorable judicial review, but it rendered the effort somewhat ironic: a crusade to rid the country of marijuana cigarettes resulted in a law to police every use of the plant except smoking it.

To bridge the gap, Anslinger called upon all states to adopt the draconian laws already in place in some, prohibiting the possession and personal use of the plant. Many did so, but to little effect. Numerous state laws banned the possession of narcotics and, during the early part of the twentieth century, marijuana as well; throughout the 1930s, Anslinger successfully pressured the rest to adopt the Uniform Narcotic Law. But local police rarely enforced these laws. In fact, during the 1930s, officers on routine patrol were not even trained to recognize opium use, a popular society drug regularly denounced by Commissioner Anslinger in invective laced with Asian stereotypes. Use of the drug gave off a distinctive odor, required elaborate accoutrements, and was most often used in a communal setting, all of which could be, one assumes, obvious and incriminating. Yet, as one user recalled, police officers who happened upon himself and several other users deep into a smoking session "didn't even know what [opium] was," and let the group off with a "nuisance charge."[53] Heroin, a more recent arrival to the drug scene, was even more obscure to police officers. One dealer intercepted by police feigned a medical condition, explaining (not without merit) that the drug was prescribed for his "asthmatic fits." "All right, put them away," the police officer shrugged, and released him with a warning not to engage in "numbers," an enormously popular underground lottery game.[54]

Many large police agencies resolved the dilemma of how to police narcotics by forming special units – squads that were themselves riddled with corruption and often complicit in illicit drug traffic. Clean or not, narcotic squads also suffered from lack of manpower until the 1960s. As one retired New York police detective explained, even though New York

and urged adoption of the Uniform Narcotic Act among the states prohibiting its possession. Interestingly, he presents a different picture – viz., that he supported marijuana legislation from the start – in Anslinger and Oursler, *The Murderers: The Story of Narcotic Gangs* (New York: Farrar, Straus and Cudahy, 1961), p. 38.

[53] "Al," *Addict Oral Histories*, p. 97.
[54] "Charlie," *Addict Oral Histories*, p. 183.

had a "police department of twenty-three thousand people," the narcotics unit only had "fifteen people in it" at the start of the 1950s, a skimpy allotment that underscored that there "was not a big priority for narcotics work at the time."[55]

Thus, faced with gaps of power inherent in the federal system, as well as the nonchalant approach to narcotic enforcement common among local police, Anslinger developed a series of partnerships to extend the reach of his authority and execute his agenda. In doing so, the commissioner was no great innovator; many "bureaucratic entrepreneurs" in the federal government resorted to the same strategy.[56] While not path-breaking, Anslinger was particularly effective in courting a set of government and civic organizations, lending his time, expertise, and good favor to his allies outside the Bureau. First among these was the powerful General Federation of Women's Clubs, founded in 1890, and home to a conglomerate of women's groups active on issues like temperance, widows' pensions, civic beautification and enlightenment, and suffrage – though, in the latter campaign, not initially in support of it. By the 1930s, the Federation and the "clubwomen" who participated in it had passed the height of their organizational power and political prowess, but they remained a formidable force, devoting themselves to a diverse range of community service activities, such as the creation of public parks and libraries, and embracing moral crusades like Prohibition in similar tones of civic commitment and political neutrality.[57] Not surprisingly, Anslinger sought close and continuing relations with the Federation, enlisting its support in the anti-marijuana campaign of the late thirties, and, in general, relying upon it to provide a speaking venue to like-minded advocates, and to deny the same to promoters of views that the Bureau disliked. Sometimes the anti-narcotic exuberance of clubwomen alienated potential

---

[55] "Ralph Salerno," *Addict Oral Histories*, p. 198.

[56] Phrase comes from Daniel P. Carpenter, *Forging Bureaucratic Autonomy: Reputations, Networks, and Policy Innovation in Executive Agencies, 1862–1928* (Princeton: Princeton University Press, 2001).

[57] As Catherine Rymph argues, the continued activities of these clubwomen formed an important component of the modern Republican Party: see Catherine E. Rymph, *Republican Women: Feminism and Conservatism from Suffrage Through the Rise of the New Right* (Durham: University of North Carolina Press, 2006); one Republican leader, Margaret Chase Smith, was an active GFWC member and the first woman to seek the nomination for president from a major political party. For a more extremist manifestation of post-suffrage, grassroots women's political involvement, see Lisa McGirr, *Suburban Warriors: The Origins of the New American Right* (Princeton: Princeton University Press, 2002), and Donald T. Critchlow, *Phyllis Schlafly and Grassroots Conservatism: A Women's Crusade* (Princeton: Princeton University Press, 2007).

partners, as when one leader of the Philadelphia Federation sent a letter, printed in the *Philadelphia Record*, charging the fair city with "one of the worst records" on marijuana infractions. "For fourteen years I have been a member of the Narcotic Squad," an irate detective responded, and declared himself "desirous of knowing how you reached the conclusions in the above quotations." With some condescension the officer added, "[u]ntil you know what you are talking about ... it is the suggestion of this writer that you keep quiet."[58]

Solicitous, if sometimes also cavalier, clubwomen regularly corresponded with Anslinger, inviting him to provide suggestions for the Federation and its future activities. The commissioner replied with detailed recommendations, usually expressing warm gratitude for the Federation's assistance, and relating his political objectives with an air of informality and confidence. When Anslinger addressed the Federation in 1937, he must have felt familiar to many of his listeners already. Not only did members support his crusade, including its latest incarnation against marijuana, they helped to effect Anslinger's project of censorship. In an ongoing effort to track speakers who deviated from the Bureau's "official line," Anslinger and his deputies attempted to act preemptively, alerting the local Federation and also the Parent-Teacher Association of any upcoming guest who espoused views "considered dangerous to moral welfare."[59] In the wake of such stark warnings, invitations were hastily withdrawn. Even one clubwoman felt the wrath of Anslinger: when Mrs. Marble Rewman of South Dakota took the podium of the Clark Garden Club in 1938 and announced that the dangers of marijuana "have been vastly exaggerated," offering the ambitious corrective that "50 cigarettes made from the stems and leaves of the plant would have to be smoked before feeling any harmful effects,"[60] Anslinger raced to send copies of the news story reporting the speech to Federation leadership and local

---

[58] William C. Leinhauser, sergeant of detectives, to Mrs. William Dick Sporborg, GFWC, April 13, 1939, found in RG 170, Records of the Drug Enforcement Administration, Subject Files of the Bureau of Narcotics and Dangerous Drugs, 1916–1970, *NARA*, Box 3.

[59] Often the admonition was accompanied by: "[views] are against the policy of the Federal Government," as was the case in this particular letter: Anslinger to Sporborg, September 11, 1939, *NARA*, Box 4. See also Christine A. Woyshner, *The National Parent-Teacher Association, Race, and Civic Engagement, 1897–1970* (Columbus: Ohio State University Press, 2009).

[60] Quoted in "Club Speaker Debunks Effects of Marihuana," *Daily Argus-Leader*, Sioux Falls, South Dakota, October 14, 1938, as found in RG 170, Records of the Drug Enforcement Administration, Subject Files of the Bureau of Narcotics and Dangerous

South Dakota members. One can only assume that reprimands followed
shortly thereafter.

Anslinger had a trickier relationship with his other key ally: the
International Association of Chiefs of Police (IACP). Comprised of
uniformed police executives and founded in 1902, the IACP was quite
national – despite its name – but, within that context, rather diverse in
that it brought together private detectives, an array of police chiefs and
their deputies, and the law enforcement leadership within the federal government.[61] After its founding, the IACP opposed proposals from within
the group intended to professionalize police through the adoption of new
technologies and analytical techniques, and this resistance spurred the
formation of other, smaller and more progressive groups, most notably
the National Police Conference (1921) led by renowned law enforcement
executive August Vollmer, Chief of Police in Berkeley, California. Though
not without rivals, the IACP was most definitely without peer: it was the
largest and best known law enforcement professional association in the
country. Its annual conferences represented important opportunities for
federal officials to forge alliances with local law enforcement; for this reason, Anslinger always insured a strong presence for the Bureau at these
events and often attended himself.

In this way as well as others, Anslinger followed the example set
by J. Edgar Hoover, leader of the newly christened "Federal" Bureau
of Investigation, and "bureaucratic entrepreneur" of truly remarkable
gifts.[62] It was Hoover who initially landed on the strategy of close relations with the IACP in order to mask the hostility his agents often encountered from local law enforcement, and this same desire to present a happy
front of cooperation induced Anslinger to follow his lead. Like the FBI

Drugs, 1916–1970, *NARA*, Box 3. I suppose the degree of "ambition" involved in her
assertion depends upon how one defines "harmful."

[61] For more on the IACP and its alliance with the FBI (discussed later), see Kathleen J. Frydl,
"Kidnapping and State Development in the United States," *Studies in American Political
Development* 20, no. 1 (2006): 18–24. Although police histories are not as numerous
as this author would like, excellent works on the subject include: Roger Lane, *Policing
the City: Boston, 1822–1885* (Cambridge: Harvard University Press, 1967); Eric H.
Monkkonen, *Police in Urban America, 1860–1920* (New York: Cambridge University
Press, 1981); Samuel Walker, *Popular Justice: A History of American Criminal Justice*
(New York: Oxford University Press, 1980).

[62] For more, see Frydl, "Kidnapping and State Development"; and, noting other conservative (or even reactionary) bureaucratic entrepreneurs, see Kathleen J. Frydl, *The GI Bill*
(New York: Cambridge University Press, 2009) for VA Administrator Frank T. Hines;
and, for more on Francis Cardinal Spellman, see Kathleen J. Frydl, "The Criminalization
of Distress: Foundlings in the Postwar United States" (forthcoming).

commissioner, Anslinger often praised the helping hand of local police, who, he remarked, never "fail to support us to the last degree."[63] While his own agents repeatedly derided the incompetence and corruption of local police – and local police leveled the same charges in return – Anslinger continued to commend the work and dedication of local law enforcement. In this tireless public relations effort, both Hoover and Anslinger hoped to cover well-known and recurring tensions between their agents and local police, and, even more important, to stave off plans to centralize all law enforcement under the auspices of a single agency of the federal government. "Most of us [in the IACP] are in agreement," Anslinger confided to his colleagues, "that there should not be, and need not be, any further centralization of police authority in this country; that we should make up in cooperation what we lack in consolidation."[64] While Progressives like Chief Vollmer and others argued for a national police force, Hoover and Anslinger sought instead to preserve their respective bureaucratic authority and portray a happy – though entirely superficial – front of efficient and cordial federalism. This scheme was one that individual police chiefs, similarly invested in preserving their bureaucratic domains, were happy to join.

Anslinger mimicked Hoover's bureaucratic tactics in other ways, too. Like the FBI commissioner, he harped on his agents' "modern training," contending that a small, elite, and undercover force produced gains that outstripped larger and more amateur outfits. On the eve of an important review of narcotics enforcement conducted by President Kennedy many years later, the Bureau reported maintaining only 435 positions – 297 of which were actual narcotics agents – and, though spanning the country with district headquarters in thirteen cities and branch offices in twenty-eight more, these offices and the few international posts were staffed by only a small number of agents. By the same time, the New York City police had, in comparison, grown to 115 officers in its Narcotic Squad, a figure that approached the Bureau's entire domestic force.[65] The Kennedy Commission produced the first official note of skepticism regarding the

---

[63] Quote from Anslinger to Superintendent Schoeffel, IACP Federal, State, and Municipal Cooperation Committee, April 28, 1949, RG 170, Records of the Drug Enforcement Administration, Subject Files of the Bureau of Narcotics and Dangerous Drugs, 1916–1970, *NARA*, Box 3.

[64] Ibid.

[65] Irwin I. Greenfield to Anslinger, Summary of Address by George P. Monaghan, Chief of Police, NYC, September 14, 1953, RG 170, Records of the Drug Enforcement Administration, Subject Files of the Bureau of Narcotics and Dangerous Drugs, 1916–1970, *NARA*, Box 3.

Bureau's manpower: while the Bureau insisted that "its present small force of mobile and highly trained narcotics agents is sufficient because these agents are supplemented in our cities of highest incidence by trained state and local narcotic officers," it was clear, at least to the commission, that drug trafficking overwhelmed this token federal force.[66]

Up until this review, publicly critical assessments of the Bureau's organization were few and far between, mostly because Anslinger also followed Hoover's lead in cultivating close ties to the press, especially the powerful Hearst newspaper chain. Friendly reporters were given special access to Anslinger and Bureau officials, a privilege made all the more desirable by Anslinger's otherwise energetic censorship of stories on narcotics trafficking or addiction. These glowing journalistic entrées into Bureau affairs could be easily detected by their tone, which bore a remarkable similarity to Anslinger's own voice and views: "Steadily and persistently the Federal Bureau of Narcotics wages an unending war against the insidious traffic [in narcotics]," read one typical example; though "the challenge is a large one, it has been met under the direction of Harry J. Anslinger."[67] While Hearst undoubtedly had many skilled and colorful writers in his organization, Anslinger sometimes crossed paths with a reporter who needed more guidance than others. In a revealing exchange, Anslinger congratulated one such journalist on his story in the *Milwaukee Sentinel*, declaring it "written exactly as it was discussed between us," and, patronizing him still further, the commissioner offered, "[y]ou are a good reporter. I suggest you show this [letter] to your editor."[68]

Because of his outsized personality and antics, Harry Anslinger has dominated histories of the Bureau of Narcotics.[69] Accordingly, students of the government's campaign against illicit drug use pay close attention to the commissioner, dwelling on his megalomania and blustering on the public stage; his international missionary sensibility, and his sycophantic relationship with certain politicians; and his insistence on personal

[66] Report of Kennedy Commision, *NARA*, Box 8, p. 39.

[67] "Narcotics Agents Unknown Heroes," *Houston Post*, April 18, 1961, *NARA*, Box 8.

[68] Anslinger to Tom White, Washington Bureau, Hearst Newspapers, September 11, 1956, *NARA*, Box 32.

[69] This personality is presented as more earnest in Douglas Valentine, *The Strength of the Wolf: The Secret History of America's War on Drugs* (London: Verso, 2004); but is typically more irascible in academic pieces, including Susan L. Speaker, "Demons of the 20th Century: The Rhetoric of Drug Reform," in *Altering American Consciousness: The History of Alcohol and Drug Use in the United States, 1800–2000*, Tracy and Acker, eds. (Amherst: University of Massachusetts Press, 2000): 203–24, as well as most histories of marijuana regulation.

control of bureaucratic power. In this way too, Anslinger resembles J. Edgar Hoover, who has endured a similar historical fate for very similar reasons. Both men used parallel tactics to build their organization – including, significantly, setting sharp limits regarding their function and their funding – and both had an impressive set of foibles and flaws, including a penchant for excessive secrecy. Hoover was known to investigate and keep a confidential file on members of Congress as a way of blackmailing them into support of his agency; likewise, Anslinger kept at least one member – Senator Joseph McCarthy of Wisconsin – supplied in his narcotic habit for the same reason.[70] Moreover, both men led their offices down complicated intrigues that have left historians with suggestive clues, bequeathing an almost obsessive desire to discover misdeeds and cover-ups.[71] Strangely, but perhaps understandably, the two men maintained a cordial but strained relationship with each other, with Anslinger positioned as a deferential and less powerful bureaucrat who endured Hoover's condescension, and Hoover's periodic resistance to adding illicit drug enforcement to his portfolio suggests that his knowledge of Bureau corruption was one source of that condescension.[72]

The intrigues were real, though they may not be fully recoverable, and so too were the idiosyncrasies and gaping flaws of these two men. Yet these have deflected attention away from the day-to-day, more prosaic realities of their bureaucratic styles, including the discourse and metaphors they invoked, the ways in which they promoted their agencies publicly, and the ways they managed them privately. In the end, these more mundane aspects of their careers mattered much more to the fate of their offices and their ideals. After all, the evolution and increasing legitimacy of a punitive approach toward illicit drug use did not arise from any particular intrigue orchestrated by Harry Anslinger, nor did the commissioner's most perceptive critics come from any number of the political enemies he earned through his aggressive and bombastic style.

On the contrary, one consistent source of skepticism regarding the Bureau was uniformed, local police. Irritation over the presence and supposed superior expertise of narcotics agents led to casual denunciation on a regular basis. Some police executives occasionally turned this frustration

---

[70] See John Caldwell McWilliams, "The Protectors: Harry J. Anslinger and the Federal Bureau of Narcotics, 1930–1962" (PhD diss., Pennsylvania State University, 1986).

[71] See Valentine, *The Strength of the Wolf*, who sees the Bureau's work as inadvertently stumbling into CIA plots, and hence curtailed for that reason.

[72] See James Q. Wilson, *The Investigators: Managing FBI and Narcotic Agents* (New York: Basic Books, 1978).

into more penetrating attacks. When retired chief and police reformer August Vollmer published *The Police in Modern Society* in 1938, his voice became the most prominent among these. Vollmer rejected Anslinger's punishment ethos, denouncing "stringent laws, spectacular police drives, vigorous prosecution of addicts and peddlers" as "useless and extraordinarily expensive." Chief Vollmer countered the crusading tone of the Bureau by adding his own moral rebuke, charging that the Bureau has behaved "unjustifiably and unbelievably cruel" toward "drug victims."[73] While he might have been unusual among police for his outspoken compassion for addicts, Vollmer certainly spoke for many in law enforcement when he claimed that "drug addiction is not a police problem ... and can never be solved by policemen."[74]

A fellow East Bay police official in Oakland, California, followed Vollmer's critique two years later with comments that the United States should support ambulatory clinics and forgo the awkward and unjust scheme of arresting addicts for failing to have an appropriate prescription for narcotic use. Lieutenant Barbeau probably could not have predicted the swift response that would come to him or any other uniformed officer who offered these views while still in active service.[75] In delivering his reply, Anslinger showed deft skill. The commissioner was too shrewd to confront Barbeau directly; after all, hostile remarks from a distant Washington bureaucrat would only add to the popularity of Barbeau among his fellow Oakland officers. Instead, Anslinger wrote an urgent appeal to a friendly judge in the area. "Any police officer who advocates clinics is ignorant of basic problems of narcotic control," Anslinger argued, and, referring to the near disappearance of narcotics from the country, he added that such an officer had also "not kept abreast with current progress in his city."[76]

But the Bureau did not rest with that exchange, though it likely meant that the lieutenant would hear an earful from a local judge. The agency's San Francisco district supervisor, Harry Smith, fired off a lengthy letter to the California attorney general, Earl Warren, future state governor and

[73] August Vollmer, *The Police in Modern Society* (Berkeley: University of California Press, 1938), excerpts found in RG 170, Records of the Drug Enforcement Administration, Subject Files of the Bureau of Narcotics and Dangerous Drugs, 1916–1970, *NARA*, Box 4.

[74] Ibid.

[75] But such an overreaction would not surprise many in law enforcement today: see Marc Lacey, "Police Officers Find that Dissent on Drug Laws May Come with a Price," *New York Times*, December 2, 2011.

[76] Anslinger to Judge Michelsen, May 21, 1940, *NARA*, Box 4.

U.S. Supreme Court Chief Justice. In it, Smith enumerated the points in support of the Bureau's approach, including the fact that the "narcotic addiction at the present time is the best it has ever been," and, like his boss in Washington, raised that possibility that revisiting a clinical approach risked this success.[77] Warren took a characteristically more moderate and reasonable view: "I know you have given a lot of thought to the subject," he wrote Barbeau, and, while he "never thought that [clinics would be an appropriate response]," Warren allowed that "whenever we are in the field of speculation, reasonable persons will differ."[78] Deliberate and cordial, the letter must have nevertheless made an impression on the lieutenant, who in all likelihood did not relish coming to the attention of his state's premier law enforcement official in this way.

These exchanges illustrate the preferred method of response by the Bureau to criticism or the promotion of views contrary to its sense of mission: quick censure, carried out indirectly, usually by officials who had no announced or obvious connection to the Bureau. Perhaps no one knew this better or saw through the ruse of Bureau reprisals more clearly than sociologist A. R. Lindesmith of Indiana University, a scholar of addiction who clashed with Anslinger regularly. From his very first publication in 1938, Lindesmith disputed the view that all users of narcotics were necessarily addicts, arguing instead that addiction was a learned process, informed in large part by the social context surrounding the appearance of withdrawal symptoms.[79] The Chicago-trained professor followed in 1940 with the provocative piece, "Dope Fiend Mythology," a still more emphatic challenge to the rhetoric and ideological tenets of the Bureau's enforcement posture.[80] As Lindesmith scoffed at the so-called addict criminal in print, Bureau officials mobilized. "One of the men" on the publishing journal's board "is on our side," Anslinger wrote to his superior in the Department of Treasury, and doubtless this "very close friend" would ensure that no future publication from Lindesmith would find a home there.[81]

[77] Harry D. Smith to Earl Warren, Attorney General, December 19, 1940, *NARA*, Box 4.
[78] Warren to Barbeau, copy in *NARA*, Box 4.
[79] See A. R. Lindesmith, "A Sociological Theory of Drug Addiction," *American Journal of Sociology* 43, no. 4 (1938): 593–613. These observations are echoed in the post–World War II research taking place at Lexington under Abraham Wikler; see Campbell, *Discovering Addiction*, 75–82.
[80] See Lindesmith, "Dope Fiend Mythology," *Journal of Criminal Law and Criminology* 31, no. 2 (1940): 199–208.
[81] Anslinger to Assistant Secretary Gaston, September 17, 1940, RG 170, Records of the Drug Enforcement Administration, Subject Files of the Bureau of Narcotics and Dangerous Drugs, 1916–1970, *NARA*, Box 4.

In fact this particular journal went out of its way to offer a response to Lindesmith, managed by the Bureau, but published under the name of an ostensibly independent author (who was also a prominent judge).[82] Not surprisingly, Lindesmith encountered difficulty when attempting to publish his work throughout his professional career.

But publishing his research was just one of the challenges Lindesmith faced. Indiana University officials regularly fielded anonymous calls claiming that Lindesmith was funded by drug racketeers or, even, that he was a drug addict himself.[83] A harassed Lindesmith could be forgiven for his guardedness: he believed the Bureau tapped his phone (and they may have), and that narcotics agents would "plant" illicit narcotics in his home or on his person if given the chance (and they might have). Remarkably, in the face of impressive pressure, Indiana University did nothing to remove Lindesmith, a fact made all the more surprising when considering that the controversial Alfred E. Kinsey, notorious student of American sexual behavior, labored away on the same campus. Through decades of a narrow political culture given to febrile moral crusades, Indiana University somehow managed more latitude and tolerance than the self-styled sophistication of its university peers on either the west or east coast, a fact that doubtless made Lindesmith and colleagues grateful to the campus leadership of Herman B. Wells, university president from 1938 to 1962.

Perhaps the close scrutiny that Kinsey attracted diminished the novelty and consequence of Lindesmith's dissent in the minds of university administrators. Not so Harry Anslinger: the Bureau commissioner latched onto Lindesmith as something of a nemesis, a revealing overreaction that suggests Anslinger's awareness that his own narcotics regime, comprehensive and convincing though it was, could be made vulnerable by its very dogmatism. The slightest chink in the armor, so to speak, could expose the fragile grounds upon which Anslinger's air of certainty rested.

Nothing manifested this latent apprehension more than the occasional legislative proposals for clinical care. In 1940, Washington State Senator Paul Thomas introduced a "clinic bill," or proposal for ambulatory care. The local Bureau district supervisor reassured Anslinger right away: "The

---

[82] See Twain Michelsen [San Francisco Circuit Judge], "Lindesmith's Mythology," *Journal of Criminal Law and Criminology* 31, no. 4 (1940): 373–400.

[83] John F. Galliher, David P. Keys, and Michael Elsner, "*Lindesmith v. Anslinger*: An Early Government Victory in the Failed War on Drugs," *Journal of Criminal Law and Criminology* 88, no. 2 (Winter 1998): 661–82.

fact that a Republican Governor was elected can certainly be considered in our favor," he wrote, "as it will have a very strong tendency to put both legislative houses in the hands of the conservative groups."[84] Such political calculations hardly assuaged Anslinger. He detailed Elizabeth Bass to Washington, and so went Mrs. George Bass, as she was more formally known, the only senior female official in the Bureau and a woman closely connected to the society of clubwomen.

Bass vowed to work "quietly" through women's groups and sent frequent updates to Anslinger. She shrewdly surmised that her best hope of defeating the bill was to keep it in committee too long, calculating that such a strategy would prevent Thomas's bill from a wide hearing and public debate, and perhaps finally a vote.[85] And who would dare to oppose humane treatment, if the proposal came to a more public review? The governor frankly confided to Bass that "he did not want to see that bill on his desk," signaling his reluctance to veto any bill that made it that far.[86] Bass was determined that this should never happen. Like her boss in Washington, DC, she disdained supporters of a medical model, deriding one of her clubwoman colleagues for her inability "to get rid of the belief that has settled itself in her system, that the addict is primarily a person to be pitied, coddled, treated medically, and saved from the stigma of court action."[87] Determined to put a stop to any gestures resembling this contemptible indulgence, Bass mobilized her friends and, finally, testified before Thomas's committee herself. "US Official Scores State Narcotic Bill," read the headline the morning after her testimony, and the story went on to describe Bass's effective, though unusual, deployment of the Progressive-era belief in state experimentation: clinical care in Washington would lead to "a state flooded with all the drug addicts in the country," Bass told a horrified group of legislators.[88] If Washington became the first state to reintroduce state clinics, then its citizens could expect to play host to desperate addicts from across the United States. With no great reluctance, the committee sat on Thomas's bill.

---

[84] A. M. Bangs to Anslinger, December 4, 1940, RG 170, Records of the Drug Enforcement Administration, Subject Files of the Bureau of Narcotics and Dangerous Drugs, 1916–1970, *NARA*, Box 4.

[85] Bass to Anslinger, January 29, 1941, *NARA*, Box 4.

[86] Bass to Anslinger, February 7, 1941, *NARA*, Box 4.

[87] Ibid.

[88] *Seattle Post Intelligencer*, January 30, 1941, as found in *NARA*, Box 4.

WORLD WAR II

Other political business soon overwhelmed the country, and the small cracks in the Bureau's narcotics regime seemed all the more imperceptible once the country was at war. While the rest of Washington mobilized in a confused and tense atmosphere, Anslinger exuded confidence. He had taken risks by moving aggressively in the late 1930s, but events now swung dramatically in his favor. Never in recent memory had narcotics been harder to obtain in the domestic United States. One heroin user remembered that, during the war, there were simply "no drugs on the East Coast," and as a result various scouting parties of addicts, or "wolf packs," would form networks to scour the city for drugs, or travel to small towns to visit doctors for prescriptions – who would often oblige, according to another user, "just to get you out of town."[89] The scarcity delighted the Bureau. If one politician or another academic had strayed from Anslinger's hard line, the commissioner could summon his agents, his faithful, and his statistics.

But Anslinger's confidence was grievously misplaced. The near total cessation of commercial trade – not the skill of narcotics agents, or the wisdom of their approach – produced this remarkable, albeit temporary, drought in illicit narcotics. It was trade that propelled narcotics traffic and consumption – the ease and volume of it, the regional diversity of it, its facilitation by domestic transport and business networks, and the international demand for it. All these dwarfed other considerations, including enforcement efforts, and Anslinger's inability or reluctance to acknowledge this basic fact led him to insist that he had landed on an effective narcotics regime long after objective or anecdotal evidence cast it well in doubt. Rather than revise, Anslinger fine-tuned his approach, whether in degree of punishment, moral opprobrium, or the persuasiveness of its presentation and censure of his critics. In this single-minded focus, the commissioner pinned the logic of his program to the early wartime plunge in illicit narcotics, not realizing that, in so doing, he staked his leadership on an exception that would be quickly overtaken by the rule: the flow of goods and people dictated the incidence, price, and purity of illicit drug use. Unfortunately for the commissioner, what seemed like a mighty blow from law enforcement was in fact a lucky stroke, a silver lining to the otherwise dismal picture of worldwide trade and transactions during global turmoil.

---

[89] "Arthur," *Addict Oral Histories*, p. 107; "Jack," *Addict Oral Histories*, p. 112.

War would ultimately disabuse the country of the idea that illicit narcotics had been banished. To be sure, hostilities vastly reduced commercial channels of trade, but they simultaneously expanded the presence and reach of the U.S. military. Indeed, as a component to U.S. illicit drug traffic and consumption, the military has not received the attention it deserves – though one particular episode of this legacy, the Vietnam War, has received so much scrutiny that the purported widespread drug use of U.S. soldiers has become a defining feature of that war in American popular culture.[90] In truth, the Vietnam War was a sensationalized installment in a larger story of U.S. military trafficking and use.

Military participation in illicit drug traffic had obvious, if overlooked, sources. Given that global reach and domestic flows of goods and people determine the scale and success of illicit narcotics trade and use, the U.S. military stood in a ready position to capitalize on both. And, as World War II military planners knew well, there was every indication that illicit drug use would surface as a problem; it had done so in every war since the discovery of opiates. During the Civil War, the first "modern" war in many ways, doctors used a free hand with morphine, so much so that one historian estimates that it was "doubtful ... that any soldier [in the Union Army] during the war escaped being dosed with some form of opium."[91] Opportunities for addiction abounded, and the post–Civil War unregulated circulation of heroin and cocaine only compounded the problem. The Great War produced yet another wave of soldiers who had grown dependent upon morphine, and both their addiction and the war injury that occasioned it kept European and American doctors busy tending to them for many years after the cessation of conflict.

No great surprise, then, that World War II military officers administratively classified "narcotics" next to veneral disease, another unwelcome yet recurring wartime problem that, like illicit drug use, the military preferred to manage quietly. The Bureau of Narcotics was inclined to do so as well, perhaps most particularly because an injured soldier did not fit well within their typology of addiction. Sensing the military's reluctance to pursue illicit drug use with any pronounced vigor, the Bureau sent district supervisors to local military bases, where they found officers to be "very cooperative," and, according to a military summary of the meeting,

---

[90] As we shall see, heroin use among soldiers increased after 1968. The consumption behavior which preceded that tipping point could be compared to World War II and Korean War use (described later and in Chapter 2).

[91] Byron Stinson, "The Army Disease," *American History Illustrated* 6, no. 8 (1971): 10–17.

the Bureau shared that "the number of cases in which the military establishment is involved is small and from widely separated regions."[92]

These assurances inadvertently revealed that the military remained aware of and apprehensive about the possibility that organizational resources could be used by military personnel to traffic in drugs. As the Bureau knew, this was no idle fear. High demand for drugs within the service attracted some entrepreneurial or reckless soldiers to broker deals, with their uniforms and their normal activities serving as a credible cover. Military luggage, though small, was almost never searched at the point of entry – nor were military ships, unless a captain had some reason to suspect contraband was aboard. In the 1930s, the Navy investigated its own base in the Panama Canal for marijuana traffic, concluding that its discoveries should remain confidential unless "mariajuana [sic] smoking by soldiers in the Panama Canal Department becomes a topic in the press."[93] Apparently it did not, nor did the instances of drug traffickers donning a military uniform to facilitate smuggling surface in public. In one such case, a drug smuggler went to Tijuana during World War II "wearing an army uniform, and [was reported] to have run 300 cans of opium across the line."[94]

Though it deserved closer scrutiny, military smuggling received no serious enforcement attention at the time. This remained so even as the Bureau continued to compile stories in the postwar era that featured snippets and signs of military involvement in drug trafficking.[95] What did attract notice, however, was the widespread anxiety that the nation would run out of painkillers and anesthetics – morphine and cocaine – at the very moment such medicine was urgently needed for the war wounded and replenishing stockpiles would be next to impossible. Government officials and medical doctors became so troubled by this possibility that Congress passed the Opium Poppy Control Act of 1942, authorizing licensed domestic production of poppies should the secretary of Treasury deem it necessary. He never did, but the army and navy voiced their concern nonetheless and urged the federal government to stockpile opium

---

[92] Memorandum for the Assistant Chief of Staff, G-1, by Brigadier General, Chief of the Moral Branch, RG 24, Bureau of Naval Personnel, U.S. Navy, General Correspondence, 1941–1945, *NARA*, Box 1756.

[93] Patrick J. Hurley, Secretary of War, to Secretary of the Navy, ibid.

[94] J. P. Sheehan, Customs Agent in Charge, Customs Bureau, to Supervising Customs Agent, August 13, 1946, RG 170, Records of the Drug Enforcement Administration, Office of Enforcement Policy Classified Subject Files, 1932–1967, *NARA*, Box 1.

[95] Discussed further in Chapters 2 and 6.

and its derivatives, a position they maintained into the early days of the Cold War.[96]

And stockpile the Bureau did. The military found that it had a plentiful supply at its disposal, placing morphine shots in all of the first aid kits supplied to medics. This portable set contained the notorious "quarter grain of morphine sulphate," which, as one postwar summary indicated, "soon found its way into profitable narcotics traffic."[97] In his controversial novel of 1949, Nelson Algren related a wartime vignette in *The Man With the Golden Arm* that would have a familiar echo to many soldiers and medics who served abroad: "I can't get him off," one private confided to Frankie Machine, Algren's protagonist, while in a military sick ward, a comment which referred to the "monkey" on his back, a slang expression for addiction. "The private was pointing to where, on the ward sterilizer, a GI syrette, out of some medic's first aid kit, lay with the GI quarter-grain ration of morphine beside it"; Frankie, a longtime morphine user, grew exhausted by his colleague's misery. "You can use my tie," he offered.[98]

Algren's fictional encounter did not take much dramatic license, but, because soldiers' non-medical use of morphine remained a quiet (and disquieting) subject for many years after the war, soldiers themselves were left as lone witnesses to illicit morphine use. And recreational use of opiates was by no means a sequestered or individual activity: one World War II soldier recalled that, after being pierced in the lung by a bayonet wielded by a Japanese prisoner of war, he was boosted with morphine in the hospital and, shortly after that, he sought it on his own, making contacts among his fellow soldiers.[99] Another remembered, "I didn't bother with drugs until I went into the service," with the medical kits in lifeboats serving as a replenishing source of morphine for himself and his companions in the navy.[100]

These episodic encounters only underscored the fear of U.S. military war planners, who anticipated the "only too probable" scenario, in the

---

[96] Newly arrived synthetics, including those produced by Germany during the war, had not yet been fully tested; see Chapter 3.

[97] J. Brian Lindsay, Recordex LTD, April 13, 1956, RG 170, Records of the Drug Enforcement Administration, Subject Files of the Bureau of Narcotics and Dangerous Drugs, 1916–1970, *NARA*, Box 32.

[98] Quotes from Algren, *The Man With the Golden Arm* (Garden City, NY: Doubleday, 1949), p. 16. The "golden arm" of Frankie Machine is a reference to his skills as a card dealer, as well as the deft trick Frankie uses to hang himself at the end of the novel – and not, as is sometimes interpreted, to his dope habit.

[99] "Stick," *Addict Oral Histories*, p. 56.

[100] "Mick," *Addict Oral Histories*, p. 69.

words of one journalist, that soldiers who grow accustomed to morphine "will take up the drug in peacetime." This expectation was heightened by the global military diaspora: "this war spread [soldiers] all over the globe," the reporter warned his readers, "taking them into some of the world's worst dope regions."[101] Indeed, according to one scholar, World War II military officers in Iran laid heavy pressure on their host country to reduce opium production out of a fear that U.S. soldiers would begin to use the drug in large numbers.[102] Significantly, abundant medical supplies for GIs revived the domestic market in diversion,[103] forcing the Bureau to return to investigating crimes like a hijacked medical delivery truck, a burglary of a warehouse storing narcotics (described in one press account as an "attack"), and such well-worn prewar tactics as the unauthorized printing of a physician's prescription pad.[104]

As distasteful as Anslinger and his agents found it to contend with diversion – subjecting a long-suffering cancer patient to interrogation as often as discovering foul play – the Bureau vastly preferred these duties to tackling the war's biggest drug problem: soldiers smoking marijuana.[105] Despite Anslinger's hysterical pronouncements regarding the drug, he was reticent to accept responsibility for the marijuana enforcement portfolio, a reluctance that stemmed from several factors. The first was practical: marijuana grew fairly easily and abundantly, a potential enforcement nightmare. Second, the Bureau had long ago ceded surveillance and policing priority over Latin America (and the Far East) to its bureaucratic colleague, and many ways its nemesis, the Customs Bureau. Created only four years prior to the Bureau of Narcotics, Customs officials jealously

---

[101] Philip Harkins, "Dope Racket Gets a Shot in Arm," *Washington Post*, July 14, 1946, p. B1.

[102] Bradley Hansen, "Learning to Tax: The Political Economy of the Opium Trade in Iran, 1921–1941," *Journal of Economic History* 61, no. 1 (March 2001): 15. As we shall see (Chapter 2), this pressure continued into the postwar.

[103] Wartime legal decisions reconsidering and refining the "physician" formula of the Harrison Act attest, indirectly, to the vast increase in diversion. See *United States v. Hipsch*, 34 F. Supp. 270 (W.D.Mo. 1940); *Nigro v. United States*, 117 F (2d) 624 (C.C.A. 8th, 1941); *United States v. Lindefeld*, 142 F. (2d) 829 (C.C.A. 2d, 1944); *United States v. Abdellah*, 149 F. (2d) 219 (C.C.A. 2d; 1945).

[104] Some of these crimes, a number of them quite audacious, are summarized in Harkins, "Dope Racket Gets a Shot in Arm."

[105] Some cultural historians have examined wartime marijuana smoking by ethnic minorities, noting the dominant view that such behavior was seen as yet another marker of ethnic difference. This is a perceptual and socially constructed "truth," but not an accurate assessment of wartime drug use. See, for example, Luis Alvarez, *The Power of the Zoot: Youth Culture and Resistance during World War II* (Berkeley: University of California Press, 2008).

guarded their prerogative to take the lead in smuggling investigations involving border traffic. "We feel as a matter of theory," Customs commissioner Kelly informed the Senate, "that if we have charge of the borders, then we have charge of everything that crosses the borders."[106] Marijuana, widely believed to be smuggled in from Mexico, struck Anslinger as a Customs Bureau responsibility, one that he was only too happy to pass off.

Dragging its feet and blaming others, narcotics officials nevertheless became entangled in marijuana politics and policy during the war. Their first foray came at the hand of the military itself, which, with some questionable legality, turned over the names of self-professed drug addicts discovered during draft board interrogations.[107] Like many of the later drug confessions by young men who desired to escape service, admissions of "marihuana addiction" must be taken with some healthy skepticism, including an appreciation for those men who cleverly turned the panicked rhetoric surrounding marijuana back on the government, claiming "addiction" and openly doubting their ability to serve in war. So, while the Bureau reported being involved in an impressive 3,000 investigations of "trading in marijuana around Army camps" by 1944, some of these cases no doubt involved "soldiers being deliberately caught with the contraband to obtain medical discharges."[108]

Still, even with this qualification, there can be little doubt that marijuana traffic and consumption surged during the war. Soldiers on furlough or a shorter leave from base sought out the drug, leaving narcotics agents in awkward enforcement positions. An arrest would not only be futile – as agents would be forced to turn over soldiers to military police – it would also constitute an admission of sorts, an unwelcome disclosure that the "addict" of the Narcotic Bureau's imagining was much too narrow to capture the diversity of drug use in the United States. Instead of revising their claims, Bureau agents chased the supply. In 1943, agents initiated a wave of arrests of cab drivers in Washington, DC, who, the

---

[106] Kelly to Daniel Committee, discussed at length in Chapter 3, in *Hearings Before the Subcommittee on Improvements in the Federal Criminal Code of the Committee on the Judiciary*, U.S. Senate, 84th Congress, June 2, 3, and 8, 1955 (Washington, DC: U.S. GPO, 1955), p. 135, found in Records of the Drug Enforcement Administration, Subject Files of the Bureau of Narcotics and Dangerous Drugs, 1916–1970, *NARA*, Box 9.

[107] Reports of the Military to District 2 (New York), RG 170, Records of the Drug Enforcement Administration, Subject Files of the Bureau of Narcotics and Dangerous Drugs, 1916–1970, *NARA*, Box 13.

[108] Unnamed author, "Marijuana Camp Sales Fought," *New York Times*, February 5, 1944, p. 19.

Bureau claimed, peddled "marihuana cigarettes to soldiers at nearby Army posts."[109] Coverage of the story related that "Federal agents refused to comment on rumors of soldier-use of marihuana," but the otherwise circumspect reporting inadvertently challenged Bureau norms nonetheless, disclosing the rumor that the heavy use of marijuana by soldiers in DC was fueled by the "exorbitant price of whisky" in the area, a tacit acknowledgment that much of marijuana use was simply soldiers looking for a good time, not addicts desperately trolling for their next fix.

In this way, some wartime recreational drug use comported with changing patterns of sexual behavior during the same period. New and accelerated migration patterns released young people from the supervision inherent in their former and more familiar contexts, and, at the same time, the stress, excitement, and opportunities of war fostered an atmosphere of social experimentation. As a result, interaction among and intercourse between young people increased.[110] Yet silence prevailed, and the secretive behaviors that went unremarked upon at the time are now unaccounted for in popular memory. Occasionally, however, some very salacious story demanded public recognition of youthful transgressions, furnishing a window to view the loosening of social mores of wartime.

No drama proved more titillating, if also unlikely, than the wartime adventures of Ursula Parrott, author of fourteen romance novels and a figure of some minor notoriety as a three-time divorcee and a regular in society scenes from Hollywood to New York. The forty-year-old Parrott, who *Time* magazine referred to as "aging," visited a soldier, presumably a paramour, while he was being held in stockade by military authorities, nominally for an unauthorized flight to New York, but in reality under investigation for running a "reefer flat" in Manhattan where "marijuana was smoked by soldiers and sailors."[111] This soldier was no ordinary grunt; he was a world-class guitarist with Benny Goodman's band before the war, and this may explain the military's relatively deferential treatment of him while in custody. Parrott was allowed to visit her "friend" at the army base in Miami Beach under apparently lax supervision. She

---

109   Unnamed author, "Cabby Taken: Suspected of Selling Dope," *Washington Post*, July 26, 1943, p. B1.

110   For more on the (temporary) sexual liberation introduced by the war, see Jane Mersky Leder, *Thanks for the Memories: Love, Sex and World War II* (Westport, CT: Praeger, 2006); on the simultaneous wartime policing of female sexuality and exaltation of male sexuality, see Marilyn Hegarty, *Victory Girls, Khaki-Wackies, and Patriotutes: The Regulation of Female Sexuality During World War II* (New York: NYU Press, 2007).

111   "US At War: The New Ursula Parrott Story," *Time*, January 11, 1943.

once took him to the back seat of her car for two hours; a guard was later asked about it and admitted that he checked on them, found them "making love," and apparently left the couple alone. Perhaps emboldened by such slackness, Parrott subsequently told her lover to hide in the back of her car (while being observed by guards), drove toward the exit and, upon being ordered to "halt," the novelist gamely stepped on the gas and crashed the gate.

This reckless escape filled the pages of newspapers and magazines, affording eager editors a pretext to print stories about sex and drugs. The subsequent trial of Parrott, who was arraigned on three counts, including a charge of impairing the loyalty and discipline of the fighting forces, allowed still more opportunities for prurient disclosures – including the "backseat" sex witnessed by the army guard. To be sure, Parrott also made for good copy in her own right, describing her decision to aid a military deserter as "a sudden impulse."[112] The novelist's apparently rash decision to break a man out of military prison added a whimsical air to her crime, appealing to the same romantic notions that fueled the sales of her books. But the charges the author faced were quite serious: the "impairing loyalty" charge in particular came as the result of a new law passed by Congress three years prior in anticipation and fear of fifth column activity, enemy propaganda, and sabotage. Yet Ursula Parrott, love-struck romance novelist, was the first person in the United States to be charged with violating it. Its application to her case remains curious; apparently federal prosecutors felt that something in Parrott's escapade, including perhaps the widespread circulation of it, undermined the morale and faithful service of the entire military.

In the same spirit of her now famous pluck, Parrott appeared in court and entered a plea of "innocent" to all charges, including aiding a deserter, a crime which, by her own admission, Parrott had clearly committed. In this plot of several twists, the court (and the all-male jury) delivered the last and most memorable, acquitting Parrott on all counts, and taking only twelve minutes to decide to do so. Close instructions from the judge to the jury probably spared Parrott from conviction of her most grievous crime, but what of absconding with an active soldier in the service? Here Parrott played her ace card: she did not flee military authority, she testified, but rather acted urgently to deliver a key witness to the Bureau of Narcotics for an investigation into marijuana dealing to World War II

---

[112] Widely quoted; see, for example, "Indicted on Three Federal Charges," *St. Petersburg Times*, January 9, 1943.

soldiers. Defense petitions filed before the court presented Parrott as a wily amateur narcotics agent – not an overwrought lover – and insisted that her interest in the man lay only in his ability to testify against the suppliers of his "reefer flat." "When she discovered the sale of narcotics to soldiers and sailors," one summary read, "Parrott ... gave the information to the prosecutor and to the Federal Bureau of Narcotics."[113] Like her fictional heroines, Parrott sought refuge and achieved redemption not by discarding cultural scripts, but by embracing them and carrying them to their most extreme conclusion. Playing upon gendered presumptions of her own innocence and the moral rectitude of drug enforcement, Ursula Parrott walked out of court a free woman.

The Bureau accepted Parrott's testimony, worked to produce charges against her lover, and continued in its grind, unwilling to cast a large net when it came to soldiers using marijuana. As before, narcotic agents generated certain stereotypes regarding the military men who used the drug; most notably, the Bureau seemed to feel that the majority of users were African American, musicians, or both. Much anecdotal evidence certainly supported the agents' views, but much did not, suggesting once again that the Bureau collapsed drug use into categories too confining to embrace adequately the degree and diversity of drug consumption.

Bureau officials maintained these assumptions regarding soldiers' use of marijuana well into the postwar era, a time when the military investigated drug use among soldiers with much greater conviction. In assisting military authorities and in advising newly occupied countries undergoing reconstruction in the postwar, the Bureau demonstrated some patterns of behavior worth noting. First, the Bureau "exported" its notion of the addict criminal, planting or supporting press accounts that linked violence to drug consumption. "Stop this Crime Drug," read one exemplary headline to a story that went on to attribute "an increasing number of unexplained murders throughout [Germany]" to marijuana use.[114] The fact that occupied countries typically ran on enormous exchanges within the "informal economy," or black market, gave Bureau officials grist for the mill; there were plenty of drugs in circulation.[115] Yet, rather than viewing narcotic and drug traffic as one of few profitable endeavors for

---

[113] "Defense Move Made by Ursula Parrott," *New York Times*, February 23, 1943, p. 24.

[114] "Stop This Crime Drug," *Daily Mail*, December 31, 1949, found in RG 170, Records of the Drug Enforcement Administration, Subject Files of the Bureau of Narcotics and Dangerous Drugs, 1916–1970, NARA, Box 16.

[115] See, for example, the fictional rendering of postwar Austria in Graham Greene's *The Third Man*, made into a film noir classic in 1949.

a struggling and starving people, it became, in the hands of American interlocutors, one of the specters haunting the moral reconstitution of wayward countries.

Second, Bureau officials sought to export enforcement features and tactics characteristic of their own approach, and, in so doing, they transferred the particularities of American politics to other settings. Bureau officials were quick to praise increased military penalties for soldiers using marijuana in Germany and even quicker to link such punitive measures to what they claimed was a decrease in consumption.[116] And, though it was an inevitable result of the shared project of German reconstruction, an independent native government came in for serious criticism from narcotic officials who felt that the "sketchy plan" for it also gave "priority and predominance to public health aspects of narcotics control, particularly drug addiction."[117] For the Bureau, attempts to install the reviled clinical model were too much to bear, prompting one agent to denounce his fellow Americans in the State Department as interested in "the democratization of Germany from top to bottom" – that is, allowing them to take their own approach to narcotic and drug control – without realizing that "[i]t will take at least 50 years to make even a democratic dent in the Teutonic skull."[118]

These differences in philosophy amounted to real departures in policy. Anslinger admitted as much when he congratulated one German narcotics official on his "lucid and convincing" memorandum arguing against clinics, adding "it represents our policy," but, "to what extent it runs contrary to the policy recently announced by the Secretary of State ... I do not know."[119] Of course Anslinger did know, as he consistently advocated more aggressive criminalization, tighter state controls, and greater deference on the part of German officials than other Americans espoused or desired. In this confrontation with American diplomats, Anslinger and his agents were quite right to detect friction, but they failed to properly account for its source. The Bureau explained the difference between its approach and that of the U.S. diplomatic corps in normative terms, including diverging views on the ethnic character or moral proclivities of reconstructed countries, a tendency that was emblematic of their approach

---

[116] Dyar to Anslinger, November 2, 1949, found in RG 170, Records of the Drug Enforcement Administration, Subject Files of the Bureau of Narcotics and Dangerous Drugs, 1916–1970, NARA, Box 16.

[117] Dyar to Anslinger, March 24, 1950, ibid.

[118] Dyar to Anslinger, November 2, 1949, ibid.

[119] Anslinger to Breidenbach, October 3, 1945, ibid., Box 17.

and understanding of drug use, one that was informed by, if not reliant upon, moral assessments and ethnic stereotypes. Instead, tension came first and foremost from the fact that other U.S. officials sought to restore trade, including close and favorable ties to America, and domestic stability, including functional independence for and the physical reconstruction of war-torn countries. These ambitions clashed with drug control in objective terms as well as the subjective sensibility of Bureau officials. New roads and bridges carried trade, and trade carried drugs.

Drugs were not the furtive passion of morally dubious people or countries; they were the secret and highly profitable package stowed away in the cargo ship and the larger project of global exchange of which it was a part. Chasing the darker side of capitalism, Bureau officials instead understood and rendered their mission as a battle with the dark forces of man. But traps laid to ensnare the demons of desire merely toyed with the larger forces of business. As American power grew to unprecedented heights following World War II, Bureau agents who launched phantom crusades at home and abroad left the real source of illicit drug traffic and use – trade and wealth – virtually untouched, and certainly unperturbed.

2

Presumptions and Pretense

The U.S. Response to the International Trade in Narcotics, 1945–1960

The ethnic stereotypes and dim prospects for post–World War II democratic reconstruction of Germany voiced by Bureau of Narcotics officials, while notable, were trivial compared to the Bureau's assessment of East Asia. Throughout the postwar years, Narcotics commissioner Harry Anslinger and his men projected their "good guys, bad guys" view of narcotics trade through the Asian prism, illuminating the essential character of nations for Americans to better apprehend, or so they believed. Anslinger seized on opportunities to nominate illicit narcotics trade as one more repugnant dimension to America's already hated enemies – first the Japanese empire, then Communist China. His purported knowledge of adversaries engaged in disreputable acts made his enforcement portfolio relevant to some of the most urgent issues of the day. By successfully insinuating himself into Asian politics, Anslinger presided over an awkward and occasionally hostile marriage between his Republican, religious missionary worldviews and an emerging democratic internationalism premised on trade and multilateral agreements and institutions.[1] However imperfect, the resulting hybrid of expanding global presence combined with a crusading impulse shaped much of the United States' experience of the world in the postwar era.

---

[1] For more on the former, the missionary model, and its role in the creation of a middle-class conception of Asia, especially China, see Christina Klein, *Cold War Orientalism: Asia in the Middlebrow Imagination, 1945–1961* (Berkeley: University of California Press, 2003); for more on the latter, the internationalism of Franklin Roosevelt and his followers, see Elisabeth Borgwardt, *A New Deal for the World: America's Vision for Human Rights* (Cambridge: Belknap Press of Harvard University Press, 2005).

In this way, Anslinger was both an architect and an emblem of American global engagement throughout the 1950s. Not surprisingly, his global vision resembled his domestic views, including his tendency to view illicit narcotics traffic not as an activity to detect and interdict, but as a proclivity, even a moral failing, to impute to unsavory types and denounce in strident terms. As before, this led to miscalculations, none more serious than Anslinger's incorrect though impassioned belief in the volume of and interest in narcotic smuggling by Communist China. When Bureau agents discovered ethnic (Han) Chinese suspected of illicit trafficking in Europe, they used this identity to sketch an unbroken chain back to the mainland; unfortunately for the agents who made these racial calculations, these entrepreneurs were part of a global Nationalist or Kuomintang (KMT) diaspora fleeing Communist China. In this and many other ways, it is impossible to understand Anslinger's historic blunders without acknowledging the racialized and highly reductivist views he and most Americans held regarding East Asia.

The penalty paid for Anslinger's East Asian forays was a heavy toll indeed. As the Bureau commissioner used his own moral certainty as a compass to navigate postwar international narcotics trade, this dynamic industry moved in new directions and flourished well outside his view. The commissioner was convinced – incorrectly – that Communist China doled out heroin or morphine to U.S. servicemen fighting in Korea, an error that obscured the chronic problem of military drug use until the U.S. war in Vietnam would reintroduce it to far greater media and public attention. Similarly, since Anslinger believed Italian gangsters dealt heroin, he hounded Charles ("Lucky") Luciano, living in exile in Italy, all the while missing the "French Connection" through Marseilles that supplied the bulk of the heroin reaching the United States. As before, throughout the tumultuous postwar years, the commissioner continued to prioritize international conventions that emphatically encouraged narcotic criminalization in other countries, convinced that laws and agreements could successfully govern a bustling world of travel and trade.[2]

Such a view was an article of faith, though Anslinger presented it as an unremarkable fact. In all his global pursuits, Anslinger demonized drug use and traffic, suggesting a dogmatic approach, and while on the international stage, he fingered certain countries as illicit traffickers, a reputation that, once established, would be difficult to cast off. This moralistic

---

[2] As McAllister notes, Anslinger opposed some international conventions, including the 1961 Single Convention (discussed further in Chapter 6), which failed to conform to his priorities. See McAllister, *Drug Diplomacy in the Twentieth Century: An International History* (New York: Routledge, 2000).

approach to international narcotics could be disingenuous in both direc- tions: sinners were sometimes not so bad, and saints were often anything but. In touchy and sometimes testy relations with Cold War ally France, Anslinger preferred to minimize the enormous flow of illicit narcotics coming from its shores. Thus the dogmatism of Anslinger was somehow also situational and relative – a precarious posture, albeit a recurring one in U.S. foreign policy. What was depicted to the American people as a compelling moral binary – good versus evil – was notable to crit- ical observers principally for its convenience. This impulse to sanctify political agendas and cloak them in moral trappings seems all the more likely, and altogether more potent, in the context of the developing world, where racial stereotypes and cultural ignorance render absolutist claims more plausible to the American mind.

In delineating this pattern, then, the United States' approaches to the narcotics trade from 1945 to 1960 illustrate a particular form of inter- national engagement that returns and resonates in other moments hospi- table to "us" versus "them" characterizations of the United States and the world. Indeed, the pattern is a familiar one to Americans in the modern day. Less well known are the shadings of this story, including the ways in which such deliberately simplified narratives advance certain institutional interests and political alliances. Specifically, Anslinger's depiction of the illicit narcotics trade as in the hands of an evil cabal reinforced the stat- ure and approach of his agency at the expense of his rival, the Customs Bureau, and it also greatly pleased business interests that depended upon the free movement of goods and people across borders, which aggressive Customs inspections would hinder. Rather than contend with the disem- bodied forces of trade and power, the Bureau of Narcotics declared its enemies to be fully embodied, sometimes even personified, thereby eas- ing the United States' global passage by focusing anxiety on specific and sinister targets while deflecting attention from other forces at work. As Commissioner Anslinger took to the world stage throughout the 1950s, he ranked effective illicit drug regulation behind certainty of purpose and the happy alignment of his own political preferences.

FROM JAPAN TO CHINA TO KOREA: MACARTHUR AND NARCOTICS IN ASIA

Few historical figures have evoked such diverging and deeply felt responses as General Douglas MacArthur of the U.S. Army. Many considered him a hero, who, as in the estimation of former President Herbert Hoover, represented the "reincarnation of St. Paul into a great General of the

Army who came out of the east."[3] The saintly succession cited by Hoover
to honor MacArthur, while startling, was no accident: Paul, among the
earliest of Christian missionaries, was alone among his peers in understanding his calling as one that extended beyond Jews to Gentiles. Paul
preached to the totally uninitiated, the "uncivilized" who had not subscribed to monotheism, much less to the emergent religious tenets derived
from the legacy of Jesus Christ. So it was with the legion of MacArthur's
admirers, who supported the general in his belief that his assignment to
East Asia – first to the Philippines, then as commander of the army in
the Pacific during World War II, finally as "Supreme Commander" of the
Allied Powers (SCAP) during occupation of the islands of Japan – held
religious portent, presaging the conversion of Asia to Christianity and,
perhaps, to western ways more generally.[4]

But, for as many who celebrated MacArthur in the same indulgent
terms favored by the general himself, there were at least as many who
denounced him. His legendary megalomania, his unenlightened simplifications, and his bombastic tirades all invited and came in for much
derision. When the author Truman Capote first heard MacArthur's most
famous address, the very one that prompted Herbert Hoover to exalt
MacArthur as a modern-day saint, he assumed that the melodramatic
and bloviated verse meant that he was listening to a parody of the speech
rather than an actual recording. It was an easy mistake to make: what
was to some hallowed was to others histrionic. Even many of the soldiers who served under MacArthur in the Pacific emerged with a great
deal of skepticism regarding his generalship, let alone his pretensions
toward monumental greatness. Following World War II, as the general
coyly contemplated running for president, returning soldiers formed
"Veterans-Against-MacArthur" clubs in almost every major city.[5] His
pompous demeanor and legions of devoted followers meant that each
time MacArthur ventured close to running for political office after the
war, some rejoiced, while others recoiled.

---

[3] Widely quoted response of Herbert Hoover to Douglas MacArthur's Farewell Address to
a Joint Meeting of Congress, delivered April 19, 1951, http://www.americanrhetoric.com/
speeches/douglasmacarthurfarewelladdress.htm [accessed January 25, 2010].

[4] A dialectic between the western ways and the eastern world had long been underway, of course, and had lately produced "syncretic" new forms such as the "muscular
Confucianism" that informed China's self-strengthening movement or the political and
institutional restructuring of the Meiji Restoration in Japan.

[5] See William Manchester, *American Caesar: Douglas MacArthur, 1880–1964* (London:
Arrow Books, 1979), p. 482.

Yet, even for MacArthur's greatest detractors, there remains one aspect of his career difficult to dismiss: the occupation of Japan after that country's leadership signed the instrument of "unconditional" surrender on September 2, 1945. MacArthur took charge of the sprawling and complex operation, with no task too big or small so as to be beyond the benefit of his personal attention. When unimpressed by Japanese politicians' efforts to formally renounce their ways, MacArthur drafted a new constitution for the country on a yellow legal pad, cobbling together principles and practices gleaned from his own study and idiosyncratic intellect. It was an extremely defensible effort – however jarring its improvised production – and the document remains in force to this day. This intervention as well as his early edicts showed a new side to MacArthur. As general, he was known for his conservative politics, chauvinist remarks, and manipulation of the press. As Supreme Commander, MacArthur put forward a constitution that granted women the right to vote, supported labor's right to organize, and allowed substantial freedom of the press and rights to assembly, provided these did not directly conflict with SCAP directives.[6]

Although MacArthur's leadership did not usher in a progressive utopia, it did allow for substantial give and take between U.S. forces and organized Japanese interests; it did successfully settle the terms of agrarian land reform, diminishing the power of large landowners and bolstering that of small tenants; and it did create a context for political stability that attended decades of economic prosperity. With only traces of vindictiveness,[7] and despite pronounced racialized ideas regarding the "Asian mind," MacArthur consistently showed a respect and degree of liberality during the occupation that greatly exceeded any expectations formed on the basis of his previous career – or, for that matter, those generated on the basis of American occupation elsewhere or the bitter intensity of its war with Japan.[8] As thousands of functionaries of the former Nazi Germany awaited either trial or political rehabilitation, MacArthur

---

[6] Japanese newspapers were required to carry SCAP messages in full; they also refrained from publishing criticism of the occupiers, though that criticism was common enough. Significantly, Communists' right to a general strike and free assembly were greatly curtailed after their 1946 show of strength.

[7] Manchester, *American Caesar*, and others view the execution of Masaharu Homma and Tomoyuki Yamashita as vindictive, and Yamashita as particularly so. These executions have been widely interpreted as MacArthur's revenge for his military defeats and for the notorious Bataan "death march."

[8] The barbarism and deeply felt animosity of the war is conveyed in horrifying detail in John W. Dower, *War Without Mercy: Race and Power in the Pacific War* (New York: Pantheon Books, 1986).

only selectively punished, agreeing to retain the Emperor as symbolic fig-
urehead, and crafted penalties that barred imperial professionals from
public life but did little else to persecute them.[9]

There is, however, one glaring exception to this picture of the surprisingly benevolent Douglas MacArthur, and it is a suggestive one: illicit drug
trafficking. From the first, the general was keen to depict imperial Japan
as the dealer of illicit narcotics to all of Asia, regardless of the fact that
making this case forced a reconsideration of history that MacArthur was
otherwise content to relegate to a politically convenient silence. In this
project to indict Imperial Japan with reckless narcotics trafficking, Bureau
of Narcotics Director Harry Anslinger – who addressed correspondence
to MacArthur with "My Dear General" – presented himself as a devoted
ally.[10] But why should these men spend so much time on drugs, especially
when more fundamental questions regarding Japanese military aggression
in China remained extraordinarily contentious, unacknowledged by many,
and of much greater consequence to all? The answer was clear: when it
came to drugs, establishing the guilt of one party, Imperial Japan, had
much more to do with exonerating another party, the purported victim of
Imperial trafficking, Chiang Kai-shek's Nationalist China.

Both MacArthur and Anslinger belonged to an important though
informal group dubbed the "China Lobby," a name first circulated during
the 1940s, a time when the term "lobby" held a pejorative connotation
for most Americans, and hence a designation that was initially meant to
call the group's activities into question. The unofficial circle of prominent
citizens who comprised the "Lobby" took as their main objective securing the unqualified support of the United States for Generalissimo Chiang
Kai-shek in his two wars: one against the external enemy of Imperial
Japan, the other against his internal enemy of Mao Tse-tung and the
Chinese Communists. By 1937, the time of Japanese invasion of mainland
China, it was difficult indeed to find any serious backing in the United
States for either Japan or the tattered band of forces led by Mao.[11] The
real project of the group, then, was not marginalizing Chiang's enemies

---

[9] Recently MacArthur's War Crime Tribunal has been the subject of controversy as to
whether it was lenient, equivalent, or in fact harsher than its corresponding body, the
Nuremberg trials in Germany. See John W. Dower, *Embracing Defeat: Japan in the Wake
of World War II* (New York: New Press, 1999).

[10] See, for example, July 23, 1946 correspondence and others like it found in RG 170,
Records of the Drug Enforcement Administration, Subject Files of the Bureau of Narcotics
and Dangerous Drugs, 1916–1970, *NARA*, Box 20.

[11] I note as an exception Edgar Snow's influential work, *Red Star Over China* (London:
V. Gollanz, 1937).

but to marginalize the very legitimate reservations American reporters, diplomats, and politicians held regarding the Generalissimo's leadership over a fractured, corrupt, and woefully impoverished China.[12]

For the China Lobby, Chiang's failures were the results of wavering American support for him. What others took as an indictment of the KMT regime, defenders of Chiang saw as a disturbing lack of conviction on the part of U.S. foreign policy. Restoring faith in Republican China and in Chiang thus became their major preoccupation, one that was well-suited to the skills and mind-set of many members of the Lobby, whose personal histories were rooted in Christian evangelical missionary practice and ideology.[13] Chiang ministered to these sensibilities with a deft skill, and his wife, Soong May-ling, advanced his cause by virtue of her own devout Christianity and her success in extracting a promise from Chiang to convert to Methodism as a condition of their betrothal. Madame Chiang Kai-shek's most ardent American supporter and the stalwart defender of Chiang and KMT rule in China, publisher Henry Luce, responded particularly well to direct appeals and vague invocations of the Christian mission in Asia. Luce, the son of missionaries to China, steered both *Time* and *Life* magazines to print sympathetic depictions of Chiang's rule.[14] Such stories were of considerable importance: as U.S. diplomats struggled to define a coherent and intelligent China policy, Luce, MacArthur, and Anslinger put forward what they viewed as a compelling and worthy cause. Amidst confusion, their escalating and strident calls to support Chiang at all costs resonated more powerfully for lack of an equally clear response.

This was a pity for those with more moderate inclinations, for Chiang Kai-shek emerged from World War II in real trouble. Battered Communist regiments who felt the brunt of Chiang's attacks in the 1930s capitalized on Japanese invasion of the mainland by retreating to rural areas

---

[12] Publisher Henry Luce notwithstanding, journalists generally had a skeptical view of the KMT and Chiang: see Stephen R. MacKinnon and Oris Friesen, *China Reporting: An Oral History of American Journalism in the 1930s and 1940s* (Berkeley: University of California Press, 1987) and the discussion of the reporting of Theodore (Teddy) White in Alan Brinkley, *The Publisher: Henry Luce and His American Century* (New York: Knopf, 2010), pp. 294–300.

[13] See Christina Klein, *Cold War Orientalism*; Ross Koen, *The China Lobby in American Politics* (New York: Macmillan, 1960); Joyce Mao, *Asia First: China and American Conservatives, 1937–1965* (PhD diss., University of California–Berkeley, 2007).

[14] For a nuanced portrait of Luce, including the ways in which his own publications occasionally deviated from his desires and a more muted depiction of his missionary impulse, see Brinkley, *The Publisher*; for more on his views and influence on U.S. policy in Asia, see Robert E. Herzstein, *Henry R. Luce, Time, and the American Crusade in Asia* (New York: Cambridge University Press, 2006).

and building peasant support for their cause in the hinterland. Chiang, obsessed with completely obliterating Mao and his followers, nevertheless had to contend with Japanese invasion, not to mention the pleas of American military advisors, so that he put aside his campaign against Communists to focus more resources and resolve on Imperial Japan. Chief among those who routinely implored Chiang was American military attaché to China, Brigadier General Joseph Stilwell. Frequently rebuffed by Chiang, Stilwell evolved into one of the most astute and vocal critics of the KMT regime.[15] He was in a distinct minority, and soon found himself the target of "China Lobby" attacks.

Yet even Chiang's most stalwart defenders recognized that China's reputation for both opium production and opium consumption hindered this project of legitimizing Chiang's rule. While the international trade in opium had been greatly reduced on the heels of Japanese invasion, domestic production and consumption continued under Chiang; in fact, the Generalissimo's tacit acceptance of opium trading on behalf of allied warlords and generals helped to consolidate his ruling regime – and to pay for it. In order to respond to the challenge opium posed to the China Lobby's efforts, Anslinger and his allies adopted a simple framework through which to view a complicated situation: it was all Japan's fault. KMT officials estimated "that in the provinces occupied by Japan," *Time* magazine reported, "30 million Chinese became opium, heroin, morphine or hashish addicts." What is more, according to *Time* reports, these tragic numbers came as the result of intentional Imperial policy: "Where the enemy advanced," the magazine reported, "he deliberately undid the patient, progressive work of Generalissimo Chiang Kai-shek's Opium Commission."[16] Anslinger and MacArthur both charged Imperial Japan with cultivating opium production throughout the 1930s, going so far as to bring these charges to the attention of the Permanent Central Opium Board of the newly created United Nations. Officials there remained skeptical; they had Japanese reports and their own estimates of what Japan produced during the war years, and these figures could not account for the entire drug trade in China. Anslinger worked the numbers, urging his staff to recalculate, until finally an agent reported finishing the tally

---

[15] See the excellent survey by Barbara W. Tuchman, *Stilwell and the American Experience in China, 1911–1945* (New York: Grove Press, 1970).

[16] Article in *Time*, January 7, 1946, found in RG 170, Records of the Drug Enforcement Administration, Subject Files of the Bureau of Narcotics and Dangerous Drugs, 1916–1970, *NARA*, Box 20.

sheet, adding that "this will account for all the stocks, since none of them came 'out of the blue sky' as stated by [officials in Geneva]."[17]

Though difficult to detect from just examining the books, officials and citizens of Imperial Japan did in fact conduct a considerable illicit drug trade in China throughout the war. This was not an official policy of the government, let alone a nefarious plan to use opium as a tool of conquest by addling the subjects of their occupation. It was a money-making proposition, and the result of what historian Adam McKeown refers to as Imperial Japan's own "racist ideas about the Chinese and their congenital need for opium and corruption."[18] Opium trafficking was condoned by the government and, in the sense that the Japanese government directed all military operations to "live off the land" – and insofar as this policy accounted for so much of the horrific events of the Sino-Japanese war[19] – then one can indeed say that unofficially, Imperial Japan trafficked in drugs in China. They were not alone, however. In his series devoted to Republican-era Shanghai, historian Frederic Wakeman demonstrates that residents in wartime China inhabited a "gray, equivocal zone," sometimes trading with the Japanese enemy, and sometimes trading with Chinese nationalists.[20] As Wakeman further notes, during the war, drug trade "soared, both nationally and in Shanghai.[21] Thus, when Chiang Kai-shek reported to the United Nations that Imperial Japan trafficked in "1,793,379 kilograms of opium" during the war, establishing "4958 opium shops and dens" and cultivating "200,000 acres of opium fields" to supply them, he was not really lying as much he was scapegoating.[22] Chinese dealers, middlemen, and growers had a hand in those figures, and their business thrived long after the Japanese left.

Continued opium production and use posed a real problem for the China Lobby after Japan's defeat. To deflect accusations away from Chiang,

[17] Ibid., Speer to Anslinger, October 20, 1948, Box 21.
[18] Adam McKeown, correspondence with the author, August 16, 2010. I am grateful to Adam more generally for his insights and knowledge regarding drug trafficking in East Asia.
[19] See Daqing Yang, "Convergence or Divergence? Recent Historical Writings on the Rape of Nanjing," *American Historical Review* 104, no. 3 (June 1999): 842–65. Timothy Brook makes this case explicitly with opium in "Opium and Collaboration in Central China, 1938–1940," in *Opium Regimes: China, Britain, and Japan, 1839–1952*, Brook and Wakabayashi, eds. (Berkeley: University of California Press, 2000), p. 340.
[20] See Frederic Wakeman, Jr., *The Shanghai Badlands: Wartime Terrorism and Urban Crime, 1937–1941* (New York: Cambridge University Press, 1996), p. 1.
[21] Ibid., p.111.
[22] Adelaide Kerr, "Man-made Morphine Substitutes Pose New Narcotics Problem," *Washington Post*, December 21, 1947, p. B8.

Anslinger and his agents deployed different tactics. One was just a simple whitewash. Longtime narcotics agent Ralph Oyler, one of Anslinger's most trusted lieutenants, went to China in the winter of 1945–46 and filed reports with Anslinger and military authorities that can be characterized as either disingenuous or astoundingly naïve (most likely the latter). Oyler accepted KMT assurances on faith as he toured the streets of Shanghai, relating every detail and, in so doing, inadvertently making it clear that KMT officials responded to his many questions by just showing him a good time. "Night club," read one summary, "Floor show very enjoyable. All nations were well represented."[23] "Visited the Japanese concession," or the former extrality of Japan, Oyler reported shortly thereafter. The KMT, he assured his readers, had "cleaned up [the area] completely," adding that "in place of the smoking opium signs are cures for addicts."[24] Having no facility with the language and relying on a translator, Oyler seems particularly gullible here; even taken at face value, it seems that he might have inquired after exactly what these "cures" entailed if he believed the story to be genuine. He preferred otherwise, triumphantly declaring to SCAP upon his return that the "Chinese government in Shanghai has eradicated virtually all vestiges of the serious narcotic situation created during the many years of Japanese occupation."[25]

While it was true that the American people in general knew very little about China, a total whitewash was nonetheless difficult to sell. After all, plenty of U.S. military soldiers remained stationed in the area, and they naturally caught glimpses of a very different situation. Anslinger grew distressed by the gap between what he would prefer to believe about opium in China and what he continued to hear: "we recently received another report," he wrote to one of his agents stationed in SCAP, "from a source considered reliable that the situation in Shanghai as of Feburary 1 [1946, the time of Oyler's trip] was about as follows: Plenty of narcotics were available in the city, and opium dens were flourishing."[26] Unable to "cure" or control China, Anslinger turned to his next best option: create an authoritative case that Japan must be held responsible. Indeed, Oyler openly discussed his mission to Asia as one to "prove beyond doubt that the Imperial Japanese Government has deliberately

---

[23] Oyler, "China Theater Mission," undated but contextually in winter of 1945–46, RG 170, Records of the Drug Enforcement Administration, Subject Files of the Bureau of Narcotics and Dangerous Drugs, 1916–1970, *NARA*, Box 20.

[24] Ibid.

[25] Oyler to Cresswell, Chief of Counter Intelligence, February 8, 1946, ibid.

[26] Anslinger to Speer, March 1, 1946, ibid.

and flagrantly violated its responsibility in this field," and, what is more, that the Imperial government, already officially pardoned or punished for its wartime activities, should nevertheless be "open to prosecution as an international peddler in illicit narcotics."[27] MacArthur even bandied about the phrase "war crime" – a new term used in the Allied trials of Nazis in Nuremberg to describe the longstanding principle of punishment of those who defy international conventions of war in some egregious and systematic fashion – in considering the Japanese record of drug dealing in China.[28] Though easy to proclaim, it was a difficult case to prove. Narcotics agents struggled, lacking clear evidence and swimming against the currents of reform and recovery in Japan. One agent showed signs of strain when he wrote to Anslinger (using capital letters for emphasis): "I want to stay here and see THIS THING THRU and above ALL PROVE TO THE WORLD THAT WHAT YOU HAVE BEEN PREACHING ABOUT THE JAPS WAS WELL FOUNDED AND THE RECORDS THEY SUBMITTED WERE FALSE ON THE FACE."[29]

Preaching was an apt word to describe Anslinger's efforts, and, when finished with his sermon, he meted out Japan's penance. MacArthur dutifully urged restrictive narcotics legislation on Japan, ordering the government to establish an "effective system for control, possession and the sale of drugs and to pass a law providing severe penalties for misuse."[30] As politicians mulled over the possibilities, Anslinger worked behind the scenes to shape the legislation. "I hope ... that the measure will be made a criminal statute instead of a revenue statute," he freely admitted in correspondence to one of his agents stationed in SCAP.[31] In this instance, as

---

[27] Oyler to General E. R. Thorpe, Chief of Counter Intelligence, January 9, 1946, RG 170, Records of the Drug Enforcement Administration, Subject Files of the Bureau of Narcotics and Dangerous Drugs, 1916–1970, *NARA*, Box 20.

[28] For more on these accusations, see William O. Walker III, *Opium and Foreign Policy: The Anglo American Search for Order in Asia* (Chapel Hill: University of North Carolina Press, 1991), pp. 164–8.

[29] Joseph Bransky to Anslinger, May 1, 1946, RG 170, Records of the Drug Enforcement Administration, Subject Files of the Bureau of Narcotics and Dangerous Drugs, 1916–1970, *NARA*, Box 20.

[30] "MacArthur Orders Control of Narcotics," *Fort Worth Star Telegram*, January 26, 1946, found in ibid. As with other elements of the occupation, scholars suggest that these policies had more indigenous sources. See Michael Auslin, *Negotiating with Imperialism: The Unequal Treaties and Japanese Diplomacy* (Cambridge: Harvard University Press, 2004); Richard Chang, *The Justice of the Western Consular Courts in Nineteenth-Century Japan* (Westport, CT: Greenwood Press, 1984).

[31] Anslinger to Speer, March 6, 1946, RG 170, Records of the Drug Enforcement Administration, Subject Files of the Bureau of Narcotics and Dangerous Drugs, 1916–1970, *NARA*, Box 20.

in others, Anslinger advocated more punitive legislation than that which existed in the United States, a discrepancy he attributed to the "constitutional restrictions" which kept the federal government "from approaching control by way of a criminal statute."[32] As Anslinger knew as he wrote those lines, there were many licit purposes to narcotic regulation, and Bureau officials were quick to cite them when proposals to transfer the Bureau to the Justice Department began to surface in the postwar era.

The result of MacArthur's efforts was the Narcotics Control Law of July 1948, passed the same year as the SCAP-engineered overhaul of the police in Japan, which decentralized the structure of law enforcement and rid it of the components notorious for policing the politics of Japanese citizens.[33] These two pieces of legislation evinced conflicting impulses regarding the best path for the SCAP's political reconstruction of Japan: whereas the police reform divested power from law enforcement and divided it structurally, the plan for narcotic control criminalized even small amounts of narcotics – an inventory of drugs that, repeating the idiosyncrasy of America, included marijuana – and invested the power of enforcement in one national office.[34] Significantly, both moves tracked well with U.S. police structure and U.S. drug policy, and hence U.S. preferences for Japan. In America, law enforcement operated on a decentralized basis, while drug enforcement (up to this point) was primarily a federal operation. The unique and in many ways odd negotiation of power in the United States seemed to American planners in Japan to be less a series of compromises and choices and more like the natural characteristics of democracy. Occupation authorities ushered in American policies and institutional patterns in Japan with no notion of anachronism or realization that, in so doing, they endowed a particularized power structure endemic to the United States with a universal relevance. And, unlike in Germany's occupation, where three other powers oversaw policy in their respective zones, American preferences went unchallenged in Japan but for the practical and political hurdles that imposing these preferences encountered.[35]

---

[32] Ibid. Department first surfaced (see Chapters 3 and 4).

[33] For more on the purges of Tokkō members, see especially David Bayley, *Forces of Order: Policing Modern Japan* (Berkeley: University of California Press, 1991).

[34] As Adam McKeown has pointed out to me, this was already a global idiosyncrasy: see James Mills, *Cannabis Britannica: Empire, Trade, and Prohibition* (New York: Oxford University Press, 2003).

[35] See H. R. Friman, "The Impact of the Occupation on Crime," in *Democracy in Occupied Japan: The US Occupation and Japanese Politics and Society*, Caprio and Sugita, eds. (London: Routledge, 2007), pp. 89–119, for a more detailed discussion of this comparison between occupied Germany and Japan (pp. 108–11).

Such hurdles turned out to be considerable indeed, so much so that the tension between U.S. proposals and dynamics on the ground in Japan produced new and unintended consequences.[36] As the political scientist H. Richard Friman argues, occupation policy as shaped by SCAP unintentionally paved the way for widespread trade in synthetic stimulants, especially methamphetamine.[37] This laboratory-engineered stimulant was new to the world in manufactured doses as recently as 1938, when Germany first introduced it; Imperial Japan followed, producing it in great quantities to endow military forces with a "fighting spirit" and workers with impressive energy. By the time Allied forces occupied Japan, methamphetamine stockpiles were considerable, as was the capacity to produce more of the drug as demand warranted. In the American obsession to tally and punish only narcotics, amphetamine storage and use escaped SCAP notice. At the same time, the police reforms introduced by SCAP resulted in the deployment of inexperienced (albeit uncorrupted) law enforcement officials who struggled to understand their new mission and organizational place. Large-scale syndicates, some comprised of Japanese and other Korean residents who were once legal subjects of the empire, moved into the gap created by regulatory omissions and inept policing, peddling stimulants and profiting from what Friman points out was Japan's "first domestic drug abuse epidemic."[38] Friman further argues that once U.S. officials became aware of the scale and seriousness of amphetamine traffic, they chose to ignore it, tacitly endorsing the power of ethnic-Japanese crime syndicates who, in turn, played a role in intimidating participants in the labor organizing undertaken by the Communist Party in Japan.[39] This Faustian bargain struck with racketeers for the benefit of appeasing the United States' increasing Cold War anxieties enhanced the power of the *yakuza*, the country's network of crime syndicates.[40]

Not surprisingly, as SCAP influence waned and the occupation drew to a close, Japan reverted to its own political inclinations, including a

---

[36] For more on the limits and ironies of the U.S. occupation policies in Japan, see Yoneyuki Sugita, *Pitfall or Panacea: The Irony of US Power in Occupied Japan* (New York: Routledge, 2003).

[37] Friman, "The Impact of the Occupation on Crime." Discussion that follows is also based on this work.

[38] Ibid., 95.

[39] Ibid., 106.

[40] As Friman and others point out, this includes the ethnically Korean members of Yakuza, the so-called enemy within of Japan that bears a rough comparison to Italian-American mafia syndicates of the postwar era in the United States, not least because of the popular conflation of a particular ethnicity to criminal activity.

more centralized police structure, and modified initial SCAP reforms. It also revised its drug policy to include penalties against those engaged in illicit dealing or use of synthetic stimulants. Like West Germany, Japan altered and amended the U.S. vision for drug policy and enforcement as its sovereign power was restored. Be that as it may, the U.S. occupation certainly set Japan down a path of criminalization, a path Germany successfully resisted at the outset, and a direction that has resulted in Japan sponsoring among the most punitive set of drug laws in the world today. By insisting upon criminalization, U.S. officials in SCAP sought to punish Japan for its past and expurgate the drug trafficking legacy that was embedded in its larger history of colonial occupation.

In this endeavor, U.S. officials weighed not just the occupation of Japan, but the fate of East Asia more generally, and, within that story, the fate of China most particularly. Political struggles elsewhere in Asia were never far from SCAP officials' minds, a fact that MacArthur disclosed in typically immodest terms when, in refusing invitations to return to the United States for a visit, he explained that, "[i]f I returned for only a few weeks, word would spread through the Pacific that the United States is abandoning the Orient."[41] Like the Greek Atlas, MacArthur bore the weight of East Asia on his shoulders, or so it seemed to him. As he and his subordinates pressed for changes in Tokyo, MacArthur hoped his agenda would ring out from Manila to Peking. The general's boundless ego was only the most trivial sense in which Japanese reconstruction was tied to the future of East Asia: former Japanese conquests now either returned to previous colonial occupiers, like France in Vietnam, or won independence, like Indonesia from the Dutch.[42] The Korean Peninsula was freed of decades of Japanese rule, only to be occupied by the Soviets in the north and the Americans in the south, a divided and uneasy resolution to its national destiny.

And then there was China. After evicting the Japanese from the mainland, many expected the Nationalist KMT under Chiang Kai-shek to make short work of the Communists. Instead, Nationalist power

---

[41] As quoted in Manchester, *American Caesar*, p. 442.
[42] There is, surprisingly, little in the English-language historiography that considers SCAP occupation and reconstruction with reference to the rest of Asia. I note as exceptions the following: Michael Schaller, *The American Occupation of Japan: The Origins of the Cold War in Asia* (New York: Oxford University Press, 1985), which considers reconstruction in the context of evolving U.S. policy during the Cold War; and Yoneyuki Sugita, *Pitfall or Panacea: The Irony of US Power in Occupied Japan, 1945–1952* (New York: Routledge, 2003), which discusses the ways in which U.S. decision making in Occupied Japan entailed a greater commitment to Japan specifically and to Asia more generally.

dissipated while a reenergized Communist Party added legions to its core of committed members. Some American diplomats began to distance themsevles from Chiang, most notably former World War II general and future secretary of state, George Marshall, who, at the request of President Truman, conducted a mission to China to try to negotiate a settlement between Nationalists and Communists. Beginning in 1945, the stoic Marshall mediated disputatious sessions between both parties in the hopes of forming a coalition government; when the effort collapsed in 1947, even the normally reserved general expressed his frustration at the deep mistrust of the Communists and the indifference of Chiang and the Nationalists. Convinced that the United States would never fail to back them, KMT officials saw no incentives to make any concessions to the Communists, incorrectly assuming that, if full-scale civil war returned, they could defeat Mao and his followers. Such was not the case: after years of fighting, Mao Tse-Tung formally declared the founding of the People's Republic of China (PRC) in October 1949.

The vast territory of China and its millennia of provincial rule fueled hope in some Chiang supporters – including in Chiang himself – that the PRC could not successfully consolidate power over the mainland. Likely Chiang's own appreciation of the problems encountered in governance of China instilled confidence that the evicted KMT forces, which regrouped in Formosa, could capitalize on any failures of the Communists to secure sovereignty or popular legitimacy. Such fundamental tests of governance would have struck Chiang as inevitable: since his own assumption of power in 1927, he was forced to accept alliances with warlords whose backing he needed. As leader of China he was, moreover, reluctant but willing to accede to a KMT monopoly over opium production and consumption, preferring eradication in some areas, but "addicted" to the tax revenues accrued from opium throughout the famous opium belt of Yenan and the southwest provinces.[43] As historian Edward Slack recounts, opium ranked third in non-borrowed income in Republican China, behind tariffs and the salt tax.[44] While Chiang undoubtedly committed real resources to the cultural campaign against opium-smoking, he also relied on generals and public officials who profited from the trade in his bargain to retain power. When he led American observers to public

[43] The most impressive English-language formulation of the KMT's relation with opium that I have seen is Edward R. Slack, Jr., *Opium, State, and Society: China's Narco-Economy and the Guamindong, 1924–1937* (Honolulu: University of Hawaii Press, 2001).
[44] "Borrowed income" being loans from the United States; ibid., 148.

burnings of large stores of opium, he failed, at the very same time, to disclose his dependence upon revenue that the opium trade produced.

Harry Anslinger, committed to believing that the symbolic opium burning of Chiang Kai-shek demonstrated his authentic agenda, now cast a deeply skeptical eye upon the People's Republic, convinced that remnants of opium production in the mainland represented Communist China's true intent. Although it is the case, as scholar Zhou Yongming writes, that Communist China embarked on a massive effort to purge opium production and consumption, this undertaking escaped the notice of Harry Anslinger and the Bureau of Narcotics.[45] This was hardly surprising, given that the anti-opium drive took place during a time of isolation for China, and, even more, PRC leaders did not desire much public notice of the program. As one official expressed it, the government avoided attention so as to prevent "American imperialists" from using even the mere mention of opium by the People's Republic as the foundation for "vicious rumors against us."[46]

Such concerns seemed to confirm the general paranoia of Chinese Communists detected by Marshall during his mission to China – but, as in other instances, such paranoia had legitimate sources. From the very beginning of the PRC, Anslinger was determined to trace every opium shipment back to the mainland and tarnish its international reputation, one that was already fragile and tenuous in the international community. The commissioner also showed a real determination to ignore the evidence that opium production had largely relocated from its former home in the southwest of China across the border, to a region that stretched from Burma to Laos and Thailand dubbed "the Golden Triangle."[47] What was more, former KMT military officials, driven out of China to the lush area of the Triangle, were responsible for the lion's share of opium cultivation. For many of these men, this was business as usual: supporting a militia through opium cultivation in the absence of a strong central government, whether in Republican China or in the mountainous and dense forests of the Triangle. Yet, as William Walker terms it, Anslinger

[45] See Zhou Yongming, "Nationalism, Identity, and State Building: The Anti-drug Crusade in the People's Republic, 1949–1952," in *Opium Regimes: China, Britain, and Japan, 1839–1952*, Timothy Brook and Bob Tadashi Wakabayashi, eds. (Berkeley: University of California Press, 2000): 380–403.

[46] As quoted in ibid., p. 390.

[47] As Adam McKeown notes, this pattern deserves to be considered in the context of the broader history of Chinese labor farms in Southeast Asia. See McKeown, "From Opium Farmer to Astronaut: A Global History of Diasporic Chinese Business," *Diaspora* 9, no. 3 (2009): 317–60.

deployed a "strategy of defensive avoidance" when it came to Nationalist opium production, an inability to acknowledge reality that stemmed from the certainty of his earlier positions and a subsequent unwillingness to acknowledge error or add subtlety to his views.[48]

In this way, during the early Cold War years, accusations of international narcotic trafficking became one very important way for U.S. policymakers to phrase moral opprobrium. The authority of illicit drug trafficking charges derived not from evidence but from previously assigned disapproval, and its gravity and trenchancy remained vague unless rendered in a context of preexisting censure. In the eyes of the commissioner and his supporters, drug trafficking did not amount to discovering certain trade patterns, but rather to unmasking a sinister identity. Within this moralistic frame, the Bureau used its new platform in East Asia, occupied Japan, as a base for its case against China. Anslinger's key narcotics agent in Japan sent word of a successful "bust" of "huge drug smuggling between Communist China and Japan," a highly unlikely node in the Asian trafficking network, given the estrangement of the newly formed Chinese government from Japan.[49] A year later Anslinger pleaded with this same agent, his man on the scene, to prepare "for me a memorandum showing the extent of heroin traffic in Japan during 1951 and how much of this can be traced to Communist China," with, he added, "striking examples." Anslinger all but pressured the agent, citing his need for a "good memorandum" so "that I will be fortified during the meeting of the United Nations Narcotics Commission" in New York, a venue in which Anslinger sought to revive the prewar international caps on narcotic production and trade, and, equally important, solidify his charges against Communist China's trafficking.[50] In typical fashion, Anslinger aimed to do so by relying on invective, accusing the People's Republic of "chemical warfare in the form of opium and heroin poisoning."[51]

---

[48] William O. Walker III, *Opium and Foreign Policy: The Anglo-American Search for Order in Asia* (Chapel Hill: University of North Carolina Press, 1991): 187.

[49] Report from Wayland Speer to Commissioner, February 17, 1951, Record Group 170, Records of the Drug Enforcement Administration, Office of Enforcement Policy Classified Subject Files, 1932–1967, *NARA*, Box 12.

[50] More on the UN Committee on Narcotic Drugs later. See Anslinger to Wayland Speer, February 6, 1952, Report from Wayland Speer to Commissioner, Record Group 170, Records of the Drug Enforcement Administration, Office of Enforcement Policy Classified Subject Files, 1932–1967, *NARA*, Box 12.

[51] Undated statement but contextually a draft for UN Narcotics Commissioner, which Acheson comments on (later), Record Group 170, Records of the Drug Enforcement Administration, Office of Enforcement Policy Classified Subjects, 1932–1967, *NARA*, Box 12.

When then-Secretary of State Dean Acheson reviewed the draft of Anslinger's presentation to the UN Commission on Narcotic Drugs (CND), he alerted the commissioner to several of his reservations and requested revisions. Acheson's instructions proved revealing: after examining the proposed statement, the State Department suggested that Anslinger place a "stress on evidence CHI[nese] Commies flooding the world with narcotics," apparently feeling that such evidence was either not sufficiently emphasized or not sufficiently present. "Avoid speculation CHI commies trying to undermine morale," Acheson further advised, "unless convincing evidence available which can be made public."[52] Here again the thrust of Acheson's comments was apparent: eschew rhetoric and conjecture in favor of evidence. Doubtless Acheson's role as secretary of state, and more subtly, his role as an architect of Cold War containment and the Democratic Party's Cold War foreign policy, made him sensitive to certain political realities – namely, that multinational engagement rested on multilateral relations. These in turn depended upon action that could be endorsed from differing perspectives and interests, hence his preference for information over accusations. If Anslinger had evidence, then so be it. But if he did not, then Acheson insisted that he keep his bombastic rhetoric and Manichean worldview to himself. In a divided and tense world, Anslinger's views were unnecessarily polarizing. For those not disposed to see "CHI Commies" as nefarious, there was little ground for constructive conversation put forward in Anslinger's diatribe.

Significantly, Acheson's admonishments came precisely at a moment when the United States sought to hold a multinational coalition together, a delicate balancing act that compelled the secretary of state to make his rather blunt observations. Just as Anslinger prepared remarks to deliver to the United Nations Committee on Narcotic Drugs, thousands of troops fought under a United Nations flag in South Korea. While the deployment force was overwhelmingly comprised of American troops (about 90 percent), it was not entirely so and, what was more, the mission derived political legitimacy from its United Nations auspices. Maintaining international support thus preoccupied Acheson and other U.S. diplomats. Initially, such support was not in great jeopardy – it was, after all, North Korean troops that had crossed the 38th parallel, the arbitrary designation separating the Korean peninsula between Soviet and American post–World War II zones of occupation and reconstruction. Invasion gave impetus and justification to the efforts to rally a multinational response in

[52] Acheson to Anslinger, May 2, 1952 cable, ibid.

support of South Korea and its army, and the Soviet absence from the UN Security Council – the result of a boycott undertaken to protest the exclusion of the People's Republic of China from the United Nations – made it an attractive venue for these efforts. Early military success under the command of General Douglas MacArthur also eased the work of managing UN coalition relations. From his command post in Tokyo (which he left only once during the war), MacArthur ordered a risky landing in Inchon, surprising North Korean forces and pushing them back on their heels. He then drove the North Koreans all the way back to the Yalu River, the geographical boundary between the Korean Peninsula and the People's Republic of China, and, at the outermost point, the Soviet Union as well.

MacArthur's mandate from the UN had been simply to repel the invasion and restore the 38th parallel, but, with no one willing to argue against success, he exceeded his orders and pushed through to the north. American diplomats and President Truman himself worried that MacArthur would trigger a larger war with the PRC – a credible concern, and one that was soon justified by MacArthur's decision to bomb the bridge over Yalu River, though, as if to appease his anxious political overseers, he bombed only the Korean side. Was this the moment when the general contemplated a bold political re-orchestration of East Asia by moving to topple the nascent PRC? If so – and it seems likely – then MacArthur had bitten off a lot more than he could chew. Chinese troops entered the war in late 1950, as they had covertly but rather predictably been organized and poised to do for some time. With Chinese support, North Koreans drove the UN forces back down the peninsula, capturing thousands of prisoners in their swift and chaotic attacks against overwhelmed and vastly outnumbered Americans.[53] In a deeply contentious move, Truman removed MacArthur from command in 1951; his replacement, Matt Ridgeway, unleashed a torrent of conventional bombs against the North, and for the remaining two years of this unpopular war, the Americans fought bitterly just to restore the original UN mandate and status quo ante, the 38th parallel.

It is an important but largely unremembered fact that narcotic drugs played a significant role in the Korean War. Reports trickled in from sources that alarming numbers of U.S. service personnel were discovered to have

---

[53] Prisoners of war became a potent component of the Korean War experience; later, we discuss drugs and prisoners, but more familiar to many is the effort of North Korea and China to politically reeducate their charge. This tactic was famously rendered as a kind of "mind control" experiment in the film *The Manchurian Candidate* (1959).

a heroin habit, including this fairly early assessment (September 1951) from Anslinger's most trusted narcotics agent in Japan: "A [soldier] … recently returned from occupation duty in Japan and action in Korea with the 24th Infantry [revealed] that during the time the 24th Infantry Regiment was stationed at Kobe, Japan, soldiers were approached with extremely cheap drugs for their use." The numbers, according to the informant, were not trivial: "up to 30% of the personnel of the 24th Infantry Regiment were believed to be drug addicts."[54] Soon reports extended to soldiers on active duty in Korea, and the same agent wrote to Anslinger several months later that narcotics are smuggled into Japan and Korea "by Chinese Communists to obtain funds for Communist activities" and, he added, "to lower the fighting strength of colored soldiers in Japan and Korea by narcotic smoking."[55] From the outset, Anslinger rushed to spread these "reports," amounting to accusations based on second-hand information, to his network of reporters and friends. "Red Chinese Dope Drive to Entrap GIs Charged," read one typical headline; or, later, a *Saturday Evening Post* story ran under the succinct banner, "Red China Exports Opium to Make Dope Addicts of Our Boys in Asia."[56] These accusations, premised on the authority of Anslinger, seemed credible to American readers, not least because of earlier stories claiming that, when PRC troops joined the fight, they were often "high" as they screamed and swarmed the better-equipped Americans to overrun their positions. The *Washington Daily News*, for example, informed readers in December 1950 that "Drugged Chinese Killed by Hundreds," and *St. Paul's Dispatch* related essentially the same story to its readers in March 1951 under a more sarcastic headline: "Dope-Happy: Chinese Puff Opium Pipes As UN Gunners Halt Leisure."[57]

[54] Speer to Anslinger, September 4, 1951, Record Group 170, Records of Drug Enforcement Administration, Office of Enforcement Policy Classified Subject Files, 1932–1967, *NARA*, Box 12.

[55] Speer to Anslinger, April 16, 1952, ibid.

[56] "Red Chinese Dope Drive to Entrap GIs Charged," *Los Angeles Times*, April 27, 1952, p. 18; "Red China Exports Opium to Make Dope Addicts of Our Boys in Asia," *Saturday Evening Post*, January 9, 1955, found in RG 170, Records of the Drug Enforcement Administration, Office of Enforcement Policy Classified Subject Files, 1932–1967, *NARA*, Box 12.

[57] "Drugged Chinese Killed by Hundreds," *Daily News*, December 4, 1950, found in RG 170, Records of the Drug Enforcement Administration, Subject Files of the Bureau of Narcotics and Dangerous Drugs, 1916–1970, *NARA*, Box 20; "Dope-Happy: Chinese Puff Opium Pipes As UN Gunners Halt Leisure," *St. Paul's Dispatch*, March 5, 1951, found in ibid.

Anslinger turned to his new sally port in East Asia, Japan, to validate his accusations against the PRC. Published reports in Japanese newspapers were cited as authoritative in American accounts, as when the Associated Press cited a story from the *Nippon Times* in August of 1953.[58] Yet these very reports presented details that raised questions about the veracity of Anslinger's charges against the PRC. As one army official deduced, if the narcotics circulated in Korea were the result of a plot, "we'd have a better grade of the stuff," as opposed to the diluted drugs available on the Korean Peninsula.[59] Another report featured a statistic that of those arrested in Japan for narcotics, a sizeable majority were "Chinese and Korean traffickers" – a point the reporter and others took as an indictment of PRC and North Korea, but, in fact, should have been read within the context of the East Asian diaspora of various nationalities.[60]

With suggestive but hardly robust data, Anslinger proceeded to recycle and recast his Asian narrative, replacing "Imperial Japan" with the People's Republic. Just as he prepared his most pointed remarks on the subject for the UN Committee on Narcotic Drugs, Dean Acheson checked him. The commissioner responded by airing his most devastating indictments outside of the committee chamber – formally submitting himself to Acheson's instructions, but defying them in spirit. When the commission reconvened the next day, the Soviet Union responded on behalf of the PRC, pronouncing the United States a debauched country that would naturally field an equally depraved fighting force – and, more pragmatically, pointing out that a naval blockade prevented shipments of any kind from mainland to Japan. Just how were these drugs reaching U.S. soldiers, a droll official from the Soviet Union wondered.

Records from the Bureau of Narcotics reveal that Anslinger must have known how, and known it long before reports of heroin and morphine use in Korea and Japan became common knowledge. In the early twentieth century, Korean subjects of the Japanese empire positioned themselves as key nodes in the Asian narcotic network, not just on the Peninsula but throughout Manchuria, the mainland, and ultimately Japan as well.[61] It

---

[58] Associated Press report picked up by *Chicago Daily Tribune*, August 8, 1953, p. 4.

[59] This official, who preferred to be anonymous, may have been Ridgeway or someone on his staff: see "No Dope Ring for GIs in Korea, 8th Army Says," *Los Angeles Times*, January 19, 1953, p. 8.

[60] See "Red Chinese Dope Drive to Entrap GIs Charged." On the Chinese diaspora, see Adam McKeown, *Chinese Migrant Networks and Cultural Change: Peru, Chicago, and Hawaii, 1900–1936* (Chicago: University of Chicago Press, 2001).

[61] See Timothy Brook, "Opium and Collaboration in Central China, 1938–1940."

was an attractive and profitable business to Koreans, who were deprived of rights tantamount to the Japanese, but still enjoyed special extraterritorial privileges as recognized Japanese subjects. These narco-entrepreneurs facilitated the interaction between empire and newly conquered lands, negotiating with local farmers and merchants and providing a valuable stream of revenue to the Japanese military. Because of their history with trafficking, a narcotics agent in postwar occupied Japan reported that South Korean President Syngman Rhee's proposal to repatriate all ethnic Koreans in Japan in 1948 met with the decided approval of Japan's law enforcement agencies, "as losing 600,000 registered Koreans plus some 250,000 unregistered Koreans, would lift a big load off our shoulders," he confessed. He added that the Koreans, along with "some 30,000 Chinese nationals, are the biggest black racketeers in Japan."[62]

Before a Korean War was ever in the offing – indeed, before there was even a People's Republic of China – Anslinger heard reports of ethnic Koreans and Chinese dealing in narcotics in Asia. In fact, two years earlier, in 1946, he had asked one of his staff in Japan to report on narcotics in Korea and relate "what measures were taken to correct the evils found there."[63] The agent proceeded to gather intelligence, reporting that "it is common for Koreans to have a small piece of opium in their homes which they eat for different ailments," and, in addition, "there were many indications that opium was grown secretly in remote areas of Korea."[64]

Anslinger knew even more than this. When the U.S. military began to wind down its occupation and reconstruction deployment in South Korea in 1948 – an attenuation of forces that encouraged North Korean leader Kim Il-sung to contemplate invasion in the first place – the commissioner's own agents informed him that when they discovered opium in South Korea, they opted to send it to Japan, rather than "leave it in the custody of the New Korean Government, as Koreans on the whole are so crooked," and their narcotic control system "is a farce."[65] After the chaos of artificial partition of the country in 1945 set off a wave of internal migration, the North Korean invasion in 1950 prompted yet another, and, as one soldier wrote to Commissioner Anslinger, "the illicit traffic [in narcotics] appears to be carried on by the many displaced persons and

[62] William F. Tollenger to Garland Williams, November 16, 1948, Records of the Drug Enforcement Administration, Subject Files of the Bureau of Narcotics and Dangerous Drugs, 1916–1970, *NARA*, Box 21.
[63] Anslinger to Theodore Walker, Narcotics Agent, September 10, 1946, ibid.
[64] Theodore J. Walker to Anslinger, September 18, 1946, ibid.
[65] Tollenger to Anslinger, July 26, 1948, ibid.

refugees from North Korea and the war zones. They brought with them things of value that could be readily changed into money," the soldier explained to Anslinger, assuming that the commissioner misunderstood rather than misrepresented the narcotic situation in Korea. He added, "Pusan and Taegu are the centers of this traffic with very little enforcement on the part of the Korean Government or local police departments," a trend that squared with previous reports from his own agents.[66]

It was Korean networks and other East Asian diasporas born from political turmoil or economic hardship that formed the backbone of narcotic trafficking in the Pacific. Be that as it may, American audiences, even soldiers, were inclined to take Anslinger at his word. One army investigator reported that "the heroin being peddled in Korea is coming from Red China," though, he added, "we found fields of opium poppies growing right there in Korea." On the heels of this startling admission, he explained, "It's supposed to be the problem of the Korean National Police, but" as Anslinger knew full well, "although they have the laws to enforce, they seem to turn their backs on the dope peddling," concluding, "it's a big business to them, no more and no less."[67]

There was no shrugging off the pattern of military use, however, regardless of who was accused of supporting the traffic. Records from Eighth U.S. Army, which, along with X Marine Corps, comprised the majority of the American fighting force in Korea, attest to problems military planners encountered in trying to curb heroin use among their soldiers. Eighth U.S. Army issued pamphlets like "Don't Be a Sucker," or "It's Not Worth It" to be circulated within its command.[68] Soldiers who read the material learned things like "Drugs are plentiful in Korea. Their purchase price here is small"; or that "Heroin appears as a white crystalline powder or as a fine talcum-like powder," all seemingly innocuous messages that would have alarmed Commissioner Anslinger with their neutral and educational tone. What was more, this material was transmitted in a mandatory company or unit discussion of heroin, during which the commanding officer was to stress "a narcotic addict faces a life of horror; Narcotic addiction leads to crime; and narcotic addicts corrupt

---

[66] D. F. Carpenter to Anslinger, April 28, 1951, ibid. For more on internal migration, see Bruce Cummings, *Two Koreas* (New York: Foreign Policy Association, 1984).

[67] CID Army officer quoted in "Narcotics Called Big Problem of Army in Korea," *Los Angeles Times*, January 18, 1953, p. A19.

[68] Found in RG 338, Records of the U.S. Army Operational, Tactical, and Support Organizations, Eighth U.S. Army, 1945–1956, Adjutant General Section, General Correspondence, Box 544.

others."[69] Interestingly, the draft order to conduct these informational sessions originally began with the declaration that "illegal narcotic use continues to be a serious problem within Eighth Army units," but this wording was altered by command to read, "the illegal use of narcotics is a continuing problem within Eighth Army units."[70] Even as military officers grappled with narcotic use among soldiers, they took care to minimize its scope and manage perceptions.

Word of heroin use by American soldiers in Korea reached Harry Anslinger as well. "Since January 1951," Anslinger's narcotics agent in Japan wrote to the commissioner, "a considerable number of military personnel in Korea have been arrested on narcotic charges."[71] While Anslinger attempted to portray this as a problem of principally African American soldiers or soldiers captured by the enemy and subjected to political reeducation programming and drugs, the military consistently found that "most of the offenders are service men stationed in rear areas in or near the large cities."[72] An increase in drug infractions also became noticeable once the movement of armies up and down the peninsula came to a halt and the two factions settled into their uneasy stalemate: whereas the military prosecuted 462 cases in Japan-Korea in 1952, they prosecuted 937 cases in 1953 (almost double). As the military knew very well, prosecutions represented an unknown share of actual drug use.

Military narcotic use raised the prospect of service personnel engaged in trafficking – though, in the Korean War, this prospect seems to have gone totally unmentioned. But the dire straights of soldiers returning home with a heroin or morphine addiction received considerably more attention. One story detailed the saga of a California veteran who, as he reported to the court, "experimented with morphine" while in the service in Korea and, after an honorable discharge, was caught with possessing heroin in violation of the Harrison Narcotic Act after he came home. "Numerous friends of his and his family," the reporter covering the trial

[69] RG 338, Rcords of the U.S. Army Operational, Tactical, and Support Organizations, Eighth U.S Army, 1946–1956, Adjutant General Section, General Correspondence, Box 544.

[70] Disposition form, January 27, 1953, RG 338, Records of the U.S. Army Operational, Tactical, and Support Organizations, Eighth U.S. Army, 1946–1956, Adjutant General Section, General Correspondence, Box 544.

[71] Wayland Speer to Anslinger, June 14, 1951, RG 170, Records of the Drug Enforcement Administration, Subject Files of the Bureau of Narcotics and Dangerous Drugs, 1916–1970, *NARA*, Box 21.

[72] Reported in "Narcotics' Use By Korea Yanks Worries 'Brass': 12 to 15 Service Men Tried Each Month," *Chicago Daily Tribune*, February 9, 1953, p. B12.

observed, "submitted letters to the court in support of statements that he was a faithful and honest worker before he went into the service," a sad and worrisome chronology that essentially held the war responsible for his addiction.[73] Less empathetic reports emerged from Illinois, where prison wardens noticed a sharp increase in incarceration of Korean War veterans and, within this group, addiction rates that ran about one in five, as opposed to one in ten for World War II veterans.[74] One report that related this news struck a tone of alarm rather than concern, most likely because the majority of veterans in the sample were African Americans, and thus the image of the "addict-criminal" was easily conjured in the case of these veterans.

In the face of growing public and military unease regarding heroin and morphine use by Korean War soldiers, Anslinger – despite evidence to the contrary – hewed tightly to the ideological course he had set for himself. In 1954, the commissioner appeared before the U.S. Senate Foreign Relations Committee to level the same charges against the People's Republic; if anything, Anslinger responded to doubts and contrary information by becoming more intransigent. Significantly, the commissioner's adamant and ideological views were part and parcel of a larger politicization of the Korean War and, broadly speaking, American foreign policy itself. The Korean War is often understood as a proxy war – a smaller, side conflict that substituted for a larger contest between two world powers – and as such the term is usually used to describe how the Korean Peninsula became the site of struggle between the United States, on the one hand, and China and the Soviet Union on the other. But there is a more figurative sense in which the Korean War could be considered a proxy war: divided views among Americans on the war related to preconceived notions regarding the "fall" of China to communism and, more generally, the role of the United States and the world. How one viewed the war said quite a bit about how one viewed the world, and in this sense, the Korean War served as a stage to enact and to sharpen political divisions within the United States itself. Those who fervently supported Chiang Kai-shek till the bitter end (and beyond), like Douglas MacArthur, very likely agreed with the general when he gave a speech to the American Legion in October 1951, criticizing what he viewed as a policy of "timidity" in Korea, a reluctance to use nuclear weapons or deploy the KMT

[73] "Ex-GI Sentenced for Narcotics Use," *Los Angeles Times*, March 11, 1954, p. 33.
[74] John H. Thompson, "Number of Vet Dope Users in Prison Grows," *Chicago Daily Tribune*, April 1, 1956, p. 24.

army in Formosa in the conflict, and a willingness to negotiate a settlement. Coming only six months after he was fired by Truman for insubordination and inflammatory tactics and rhetoric, MacArthur cautioned against a return to "isolationism," but condemned, at the very same time, what he viewed as excessive ministrations to Europe at the expense of East Asia.

This particular emphasis on "Asia First" was typical among those with a missionary sense of the role of the United States and the world;[75] it was a key component of the McCarthyism with which it coincided; and it was an effective tactic in "internationalizing" the broad sweep of the previously isolationist (and now largely Republican) Midwest. Whereas a kind of religious conviction once persuaded many to oppose U.S. global intervention in principle, this same set of attachments now argued on behalf of foreign campaigns – though only certain kinds, with certain "good versus evil" tropes embedded in their justification. It is not incidental or unimportant, then, that the same Legion convention that MacArthur addressed, and that gave him a standing ovation, also endorsed among its resolutions the program of Harry Anslinger and the Bureau.[76] For those who construed the Cold War as a religious crusade, the Bureau of Narcotics offered a lens through which to convey and to hone their views. In this way, illicit narcotics traffic played a disproportionately significant role in the U.S. foreign policy portfolio in the 1950s, establishing a shorthand for the missionary approach to world affairs.

Democratic internationalists, containment realists, and pragmatic politicians and policymakers struggled for a voice as this religious internationalism crested. As much as anything else, they fell victim to their own rhetorical excesses, their own distorted depictions, and their own policy gambits that rested on a fragile political mandate. Though Dean Acheson later justified the starkly worded 1950 National Security Council Memorandum 68 as an effort to make the U.S. Cold War international mission "clearer than truth" to the American people, there was little that separated it from propaganda. And such was a dynamic that would play out again and again: drawn out negotiations, compromise, and uneasy settlements did not seem to correspond to the stirring sentiments politicians had appealed to in order to win support for international engagement, and it was difficult to tame ideological passion with diplomatic prose after the fact.

---

[75] As a feature of Republican Party politics, this move dates back to Henry Cabot Lodge's denunciation of the Versailles Treaty for its "betrayal of Shantung."

[76] See "MacArthur Assails Defense Timidity," *New York Times*, October 18, 1951, p. 1.

Internationalists discovered this in the world of narcotics as well. American foreign officers occasionally developed sources and information that ran contrary to Anslinger's moralistic depictions, as when the consul general in Hong Kong wired the Department of State that one knowledgeable source "has no evidence whatever to show that opium and narcotics are being smuggled into Hong Kong or Macau directly from mainland," and, further, that "we have doubts that Communist China is trafficking in opium to anything like the extent indicated" by Anslinger.[77] No one was more blunt then Ansligner's rival from within the Treasury, Customs Chief Ralph Kelly, who took pains to correct the narcotics commissioner at length:

From my own observation and my many discussions with the enforcement officers in the Far East and from this dispatch, I see nothing to support your statement that "narcotics reaching Bangkok, Hong Kong, Japan, and other areas in the Far East and the United States are largely of Communist origin." ... The information I received from informed people in that part of the world is that approximately 500 tons of opium annually originates in the Burma-Laos-Yunnan area and flows to the outside world through the ports of Bangkok and Rangoon ... I found no indication to support the theory that Red China is flooding the world with opium. I did obtain very definite statements from the British and Hong Kong authorities as to their *resentment* as to statements made that a large volume of narcotics flows from Red China into Hong Kong and into the outside world. The effectiveness of customs enforcement operation in Hong Kong depends upon full cooperation with the British. Such statements relative to Red China being the source hurts our relations and hurts our effectiveness in the Far East.[78]

Colleagues who assumed that correcting Anslinger in private would amount to checking him in public failed to realize that Anslinger possessed better information all the while, he just preferred to ignore it. As a result, throughout the 1950s, the Bureau of Narcotics continued to make increasingly far-fetched assertions regarding the People's Republic. Like any conspiracy theorist, Ansligner interpreted facts that ran contrary to his expectations as evidence of a still deeper conspiracy. The United Kingdom, he wrote in disgust in 1958, "is trying to blame everything on Thailand. They do not want to offend communist China," he surmised, but his own narcotics agent, "who has been in the area, made a personal

---

[77] Everett F. Drumright, Consul General, AMCONGEN, Hong Kong, to the Department of State, May 7, 1956, RG 170, Records of the Drug Enforcement Administration, Office of Enforcement Policy Classified Subject Files, 1932–1967, *NARA*, Box 11.

[78] Ralph Kelly, Commissioner of Customs, to Anslinger, June 17, 1958, Record Group 170, Records of the Drug Enforcement Administration, Office of Enforcement Policy Classified Subject Files, 1932–1967, *NARA*, Box 10. Emphasis mine.

investigation and was convinced that most of the stuff came from China."
Remarkably, Anslinger brushed off reports of the now flourishing Golden
Triangle: "You will find the British authorities [crediting] the enormous
Singapore traffic point to the Yunnan-Burma-Thai area. For political reasons, they do not wish to single out China as such."[79] Hence, in an ironic
turn, Anslinger accused other officials of failing to understand international trafficking patterns as the result of political blind spots.

Yet political blind spots produced a blinkered vision for the Bureau
throughout the 1950s. Narcotics agents first of all missed the scale and
persistence of drug use by U.S. military personnel stationed abroad.
Customs officials certainly noted it, attributing the drop in heroin seized
from Thailand as a result of "the US pulling troops out of Korea, one
of the principal markets for drugs."[80] Second, they failed to survey the
production coming from the Thailand–Laos–Burma border, stubbornly
clinging to their theory of "ChiComm" production. The next time U.S.
military soldiers were deployed to Asia in great numbers, both of these
unacknowledged facts would converge into a drug epidemic that stunned
U.S. officials, overwhelmed the meager military resources devoted to
addiction, and left much of the American public completely at a loss to
understand.

This was not for want of explanations, but rather the inability of the
seamless and utterly certain theories promoted by Anslinger and the
Bureau to anticipate and account for patterns of drug use and trafficking in
the 1960s. If anything, Anslinger erred by linking too many dots together,
delineating an ambitious explanation of "evil" that was then susceptible
to any number of deviations. Still, it remained persuasive to those who
preferred political expedience above all else. In 1954, Rodney Gilbert, old
China-hand and editorial writer for the *New York Herald Tribune*, published his article "Dope From Red China," distilling Anslinger's most crucial East Asian interventions and, appropriately enough, weaving these
into a tale that explained behavior right down to the street-level drug
consumption of California juveniles. Noting with suspicion the "greater
and greater quantities of heroin" that "became available in the vicinity of
all [UN] military installations" in Korea, Gilbert addressed the skepticism

[79] Anslinger to Flues, May 8, 1958, Record Group 170, Records of the Drug Enforcement
Administration, Office of Enforcement Policy Classified Subject Files, 1932–1967,
NARA, Box 10.

[80] James Polk, Treasury Representative, to Customs Commissioner, October 28, 1957,
Record Group 170, Records of the Drug Enforcement Administration, Office of
Enforcement Policy Classified Subject Files, 1932–1967, *NARA*, Box 5.

over Anslinger's China accusations by stating categorically that there "is no longer the slightest doubt that the production and export of narcotics is the official business of what the Mao gang in Peiping [sic] have the effrontery to call the ... People's Republic of China." Moreover, Mao had long been keen on opium traffic, "for the support of a bureaucracy, educational institutions, an army and a propaganda machine" while in the hills of Yenan, and, though all this was "known to Chiang-Kai-shek's entourage," it was "never mentioned aloud in Stilwell's following," a dubious group linked to "anti-Chiang groups in the American Embassy." In this way, accusations of narcotics trafficking, though levied against a foreign government, were used to indict the politics of rivals within the United States. Taking stock of the rise in juvenile narcotic convictions, Gilbert noted that "the number of cases involving minors in California, where pure cheap heroin from China was already appearing in 1952, went up from 846 to 902."[81] By these leaps of logic, the abandonment of Chiang Kai-shek resulted in, among other things, teenage heroin addiction in California.

Gilbert published the piece in the *American Legion Magazine*, mouthpiece of the country's largest veteran organization, and one that was affiliated with much of conservative populism, including the "China Lobby." Yet its large readership meant that the article likely found its way into the hands of a Korean veteran who knew better than to suppose that narcotic use stemmed solely from a Communist cabal in Beijing. Indeed, it may have been striking to such a veteran that the article did not explicitly mention soldiers' drug use at all, though, in an awkward evasion, Gilbert conceded that "after every war there is an upsurge of narcotics addiction, for reasons too complex to explain here."[82] Whether too complex or just too discomfiting, the belief in certain evil purchased at the expense of awareness doubtless provided small comfort to those Korean War veterans whose struggles went unacknowledged and untreated.

LUCKY LUCIANO TO THE FRENCH CONNECTION

Anslinger's accusations against the People's Republic of China were but one way in which the Bureau of Narcotics commissioner commanded the international stage in the 1950s. His other more concerted campaign

[81] All quotes from Rodney Gilbert, "Dope From Red China," *American Legion Magazine*, September 1954, pp. 16–17, 50–53.
[82] Ibid., p. 52.

to depict the Sicilian Mafia, and gangster Charles Lucania, as the center of an international conspiracy to traffic in illegal drugs attracted more notice, garnered more credibility, and ultimately endured well beyond his denunciations of the PRC.

To be sure, key elements of Anslinger's drive against the mafia resembled his efforts against China. As before, Anslinger misrepresented or overstated his evidence. And, as before, Anslinger did not seek to make a case as such, but rather tossed out confident assurances and tendentious links, relying on derogatory ethnic suspicions and the inclination to discern a pattern and a motive in the midst of disorder and chaos to provide the tensile strength to his arguments and accusations. In this, Anslinger and his many supporters embraced a particular dynamic in history, one that medieval scholar R. I. Moore describes in his study of the Catholic Church's war against heresy as a "persecuting society," a drive against various groups initiated by first "welding scattered fragments of reality into coherent abstractions."[83] As Moore notes, such projects consolidate power of the ruling class – and, as we shall see, help to define and defend a particular form and station of bureaucratic power in the modern state. Nonetheless, the psychological impetus underwriting these campaigns deserves as much attention as their actual agenda. As is true elsewhere and at other times, Americans in the 1950s sought to project a kind of order onto a volatile world by subscribing to Anslinger's conspiratorial depictions. Evil and disorder existed because the mafia willed it into being, exploited it, and sought to create more. Seeking a kind of solace in the sinister, this imagining of an omnipotent criminal syndicate allowed Americans to take refuge in the notion that not only could the chaos and disruption of the modern world be explained, it could, if the right measures were taken, be controlled.

Anslinger benefited from the propensity to confer order onto disorder by subscribing to "evil" in whatever form; indeed, he presented the American public with its boldest incarnation and vowed to put a stop to it. For the commissioner, no person better fit this role of *bête noir* than Charles Lucania, dubbed "Lucky Luciano" (note the change in the spelling of the last name; narcotics agents went back and forth between his birth name, Lucania, and adopted name, Luciano. If not a quotation, I

---

[83] R. I. Moore, "The War Against Heresy in Medieval Europe," *Historical Research* 81, no. 212 (May 2008): 208, but see also R. I. Moore, *The Formation of a Persecuting Society: Authority and Deviance in Western Europe, 950–1250* (Oxford: Oxford University Press, 2006). My thanks to Bob Moore for bringing this historical parallel to my attention.

will henceforth use the second, more widely known spelling). A scrappy immigrant from the East Side, Luciano slowly worked his way into the inner circle of the infamous "Mott Street" crew of Little Italy during the era of Prohibition. Many misconceptions and half-truths surround his career: most observers date Luciano's reign as a criminal entrepreneur and then boss from 1919 to 1936, the year he was convicted as leader of a prostitution ring and sent to prison.[84]

Not so, argued Bureau of Narcotics agents, pronouncing Luciano heroin dealer to the world upon his release from prison and extradition to Italy in 1945 until his death in 1962. As a Bureau report on his career summarized, "the name of Lucky Luciano appears ... in all, or almost all, the investigations regarding traffic of narcotics, both in Italy and the United States," a fact that Bureau officials construed as "indicative of his importance."[85] Naturally it was Bureau agents who placed his name in these various records, a self-fulfilling and self-referential form of "evidence" that speaks to the many unexamined assumptions the Bureau employed when it came to Luciano.

Even the genesis of his nickname was in dispute. Various authors and observers date Luciano's vaguely sardonic moniker to the time when Lucky was "taken for a ride" by fellow mobsters – a casual term used to describe a mob-on-mob killing – yet "Lucky" Luciano survived, though he was slashed in the face and left on the street to an uncertain fate.[86] The Bureau of Narcotics preferred the Federal Bureau of Investigation (FBI) version: while working a job in a hat factory as a teenager, the budding criminal "tossed his earnings into a crap game and won $244. This unexpected sweepstake made such a deep impression on his young mind that he decided that he'd get all of his money the easy way. Why should he work hard for a living? Thereafter he was known as 'Lucky'."[87] The tale of a wayward youth with early criminal tendencies better suited

---

[84] Sid Feder and Joachim Joesten, The Luciano Story (New York: Da Capo Press, 1954), p. 6.

[85] Memorandum Report, April 6, 1962, In re: Salvatore Lucania et al., Record Group 170, Records of the Drug Enforcement Administration, Office of Enforcement Policy Classified Subject Files, 1932–1967, NARA, Box 2.

[86] See, for instance, Ellen Poulsen, The Case Against Lucky Luciano: New York's Most Sensational Vice Trial (Little Neck, NY: Clinton Cook Publishing, 2007), p. 93; or Feder and Joesten, The Luciano Story, p. 4.

[87] Copy of FBI report on Luciano, number 692920, found in Record Group 170, Records of the Drug Enforcement Administration, Office of Enforcement Policy Classified Subject Files, 1932–1967, NARA, Box 4. For all we know, the Bureau of Narcotics was the source of this story; it is cited as such for other doubtful components of the FBI file.

the didacticism of both Bureaus – not to mention their self-correcting hindsight, which, in this report and others, cast Luciano as precocious in his criminal career, though during the time these recollections describe, Luciano's escapades went largely unnoticed and unnoted by authorities. Like any savvy crime boss, Luciano kept his name out of the papers. After all, half the trick was in not letting the police or the prosecutors know the actual structure of a criminal syndicate, and Luciano was quick to berate enforcers who dropped his name with careless frequency.

And there is every indication that, for a long time, the Bureau had no idea who he was, even as Lucky cobbled together a franchise of vice, fronts, and legitimate business that stretched across the country during the Depression. Certainly his empire included narcotics, both in diverted (licit production) and subverted (illicit production) supply. Luciano also arranged the killing of two reigning mafia bosses, or "Dons," in New York City and then called a meeting of all powerful crime bosses, creating a kind of "corporate board" structure whereby certain gangs were assigned certain criminal ventures and turfs so as to reduce competitive tension and usher in an era of peace that would generate new prosperity.[88] Amazingly, Luciano's scheme worked; more than anyone else, Lucky "organized" crime in the United States. But it did not come without cost: Lucky's prominence in the underworld and notoriety throughout the city made him the target of law enforcement officials.

And it was not long before law enforcement made its move. "We were all set to nail him," lamented famed New York Narcotic Bureau chief Garland Williams to a New York columnist in 1947, but New York district attorney and future two-time Republican presidential nominee, Thomas Dewey, "got there first" when he charged Lucky with running a prostitution ring in 1936.[89] Williams offered no explanation as to why the Bureau could not also add to the indictment, even if it meant a separate set of charges, as Dewey would have welcomed the extra pressure for Luciano and his co-conspirators to change their plea of "not guilty." Years later, such evidence as the Bureau claimed to possess also would have presumably swayed the parole board or the New York governor against Luciano's appeal for release – a successful effort signed by none other than Dewey himself, who had been elected governor of New York

[88] The move echoes the plan and the logic behind Franklin Roosevelt's National Recovery Administration.
[89] Robert C. Ruark column, *World Telegram*, February 25, 1947, found in Record Group 170, Records of the Drug Enforcement Administration, Office of Enforcement Policy Classified Subject Files, 1932–1967, *NARA*, Box 1.

in the intervening years. Yet the Bureau offered none, most likely because it had none to offer. Luciano had spent his adult life learning how to cover his tracks and create layers to his criminal organization, so much so that Dewey won his battle in the courtroom only by inducing prostitutes to lie about direct meetings with Luciano, obviously in the hope that witness testimony would persuade the jury of the material but largely circumstantial case against Lucky.

It was a gamble, but one that the ambitious and young prosecutor was willing to take. He and his fellow attorneys made a name for themselves throughout the 1930s by charting a bold course in a new and some-what ambiguous legal terrain: racketeering. Technically (though rather loosely) defined as engaging in an illegal business, the term emerged dur-ing Prohibition, the same time when the phrase "organized crime" was coined. While organized crime could refer to any number of things, includ-ing bootlegging, its operation encompassed schemes for a "shakedown" or "protection racket," the kind of bread and butter extortion that vari-ous gangs employed by promising a business owner "protection" for a fee and, by using violence or the threat of violence, compelling the owner to pay, thus dispensing "protection" from themselves as much as anything else.[90] When it appeared, the term organized crime – a syndicate that made money from illicit endeavors, including racketeering – had multiple references. It could refer to the *mafia*, a Sicilian-born mode of sorting gangs by different crime families headed by a "Don," but it could also mean Jewish gangs (sometimes allied with the mafia), the well-established Irish organizations, new African American enterprises, Midwestern out-fits with no widely heralded ethnic affiliation like the Barker-Karpis gang, or the often overlooked Greek syndicates. The term racketeering was even more fluid: while it could refer to illegal shakedowns of licit businesses, it could also describe extortion committed against illegal enterprises – for instance, compelling "protection" money from prostitution madams, the charge Dewey pressed against Lucky Luciano – and, most confusing, it could also be used to refer to *legal* strong-arm tactics, the kind that craft and trade unions traditionally employed to retain their market share in any given business or city. As historian Andrew Wender Cohen argues, the invention of "racketeering" as a term in the 1920s had very much to do with undermining precisely this kind of organized labor sovereignty in local employment markets, the sort employed by the Teamsters Union, for

[90] Those who follow modern-day Italy are familiar with the term "pizzo," the "beak," or "pizzu," that southern Italian organized crime sticks into the metaphorical grain.

instance, which did not allow any trucks into Manhattan unless driven by a local union driver.[91]

Though it was possible to distinguish between and among the various uses of organized crime and racketeering, Republicans like Dewey encouraged the conflation and confusion of these terms. As organized labor gained new strength and legitimacy, it moved solidly in favor of the Democratic Party. Dewey and others hoped to portray this political shift in menacing tones, casting doubt on the integrity of unions and providing a conservative critique of ascendant Democratic power. Scholar William Howard Moore notes that "[i]ndustrial and labor racketeering, largely ignored by the federal government, provided the basis for prosecutor Thomas E. Dewey's meteoric rise to political prominence in the 1930s."[92] In carving this niche, the young prosecutor proved to be a resilient foe. His pursuit of Lucy Luciano was a painstaking effort: Dewey collared Luciano in Hot Springs, Arkansas, notorious haven for gangsters "on the lam," pressured witnesses into friendly testimony for a trial that lasted the better part of a year (an extremely unusual length of time for the era), and delivered a five-hour summation in his closing.[93] Clearly, Dewey had put it all on the line in order to put Luciano away.

And the guilty verdict and sentence of 30–50 years should have been the close of the Luciano saga. Instead it was only an interlude, and in 1946 Thomas Dewey and Luciano crossed paths again, though only in bureaucratic channels. The Parole Board of New York recommended commuting Lucky's sentence in exchange for services rendered to the U.S. Navy during the war effort – namely, Luciano's assistance in enlisting the support of mafia associates for the World War II allied invasion of Italy, and perhaps, as Luciano was later to suggest, a retrospective realization

---

[91] Andrew Wender Cohen, *The Racketeer's Progress: Chicago and the Struggle for the Modern American Economy* (New York: Cambridge University Press, 2004), chapter 7. As Cohen describes, the legitimacy (including the lawfulness) of trade organizing came at the cost of many of these self-governance mechanisms. The particular practice of the Teamsters Union cited earlier went all the way to the Supreme Court (*US v. Local 87, International Brotherhood of Teamsters*) in 1942 and, when the court ruled in favor of the Teamsters, disgust over the ruling inspired the drive behind the U.S. Congress "Hobbs Anti-Racketeering Bill" of 1943. While it is dubious to take an unsophisticated approach to these charges from anti-labor Republicans, it is equally so to take a quixotic view of unions. Corruption within organized labor was significant and, in some instances, prevalent; see, for example, Seymour Hersh's pieces on Sidney Korshak, *New York Times*, June 27–30, 1976.

[92] William Howard Moore, *The Kefauver Committee and the Politics of Crime, 1950–1952* (Columbia: University of Missouri Press, 1974), p. 17.

[93] Poulsen, *The Case Against Lucky Luciano*, p. 152.

that Lucky received a sentence that was grossly disproportionate to the crime for which he was convicted. With his sentence commuted, Lucky raised eyebrows once again, as a veritable VIP list of gangsters went to see Luciano off at Ellis Island before his extradition to Italy. And then, after his ship sailed, there was a silence of one year, when little was seen or heard of Lucky Luciano.

In January 1947, gossip columnist Walter Winchell reported spotting Lucky, who was under strict orders never to leave Italy, cavorting in Cuba, the preferred playground of gangsters because of the warm weather, close proximity to the United States, and accommodating government run by Fulgencio Batista. Thus began the Bureau of Narcotics effort to pressure the Batista regime into expelling Luciano and, more broadly, to present Luciano as kingpin heroin trafficker while raising suspicions regarding Governor Dewey's commutation of Luciano's sentence.[94] Much of the evidence for this latter charge lies in records produced by the Bureau or is attributable to leads promoted by them.[95] Still, it is hard to explain Governor Dewey's decision to release a convict he had pursued so doggedly as a prosecutor, and the nominal reason offered – that Luciano had assisted in the war effort, particularly the invasion of Sicily – seems a flimsy pretext.[96] Luciano or any other gangster's ability to influence a massive operation like the Allied invasion would certainly be marginal; invaders usually dictate the terms of coexistence, and it seems likely that the U.S. military would have been disposed to cooperate with Sicilian mafiosi in all events (and vice versa). Perhaps sensing these logical lapses, by the early 1950s Anslinger and his agents spoke publicly about their suspicion that Dewey accepted bribes in exchange for Luciano's commutation, charges they had dared only to whisper years earlier. Yet the very

[94] John C. McWilliams and Alan A. Block see a large but somewhat opaque conspiracy at work in Anslinger's attempt to discredit Dewey; see McWilliams and Block, "All the Commissioner's Men: The Federal Bureau of Narcotics and the Dewey-Luciano Affair, 1947–1954," *Intelligence and National Security* 5, no. 1 (1990): 171–92.

[95] Denial of Haffenden that he recommended release to Dewey, see Williams to Anslinger, February 27, 1946, RG 170, Records of the Drug Enforcement Administration, Office of Enforcement Policy Classified Subject Files, 1932–1967, *NARA*, Box 1; Breitel, former law partner of Dewey, accepts $500,000 in bribes, see RG 170, Summary of Luciano File, ibid., Box 2, p. 60; explanation of Frederick Moran, Parole Board Director, decision to recommend release in exchange for additional four-year term, see Siragusa to Commissioner, 3–23–53, ibid., Box 2.

[96] In terms of Luciano's service in war, what seems more likely is that he had his associates spread the word on the docks of New York City that longshoremen, controlled by mafia "protection," were to keep an eye out for German sabotage and take more responsibility for keeping the docks safe.

timing of their indiscretion raises suspicion: on the eve of the Republican National Convention, Governor Dewey had pledged all of New York State's delegates to the moderate candidate, Dwight Eisenhower. Conservatives upset by this move endorsed sensational news stories, like the one that named Luciano "one of the most depraved, inhuman monsters in history," who was now free "because Dewey turned him out of jail."[97] Undeterred, Dewey went on to throw his political weight behind Eisenhower, and Eisenhower proceeded to win the presidency, but the intrigue surrounding Luciano's pardon remains unresolved to this day.

Sordid or simply inexplicable, the terms of Luciano's release have diverted attention away from his escapades in Cuba and subsequent return to Italy. These warrant a closer look. In the postwar era, Cuba was notorious for its displays of debauchery. Mafia families and organized crime invested in resorts and vice "rackets" there, most especially casino gambling, and often availed themselves of the same, hosting famous entertainers, wealthy Americans, and their colleagues and associates in an atmosphere of venality and excess. Some brothels specializing in American tourism kept an attending physician on hand, ready to inspect for and treat venereal disease. Kickbacks were commonplace, and in this sense the Batista government was the biggest "racket" of all, demanding 30 percent of the money in any contract provided by the state. Yet the American government considered it a friendly regime, not least because Batista's presidency was the result of events set in motion years earlier by the U.S. ambassador to Cuba.[98] More important, over the years Batista had offered a radically pro-corporate setting, allowing American business enterprises (including crime syndicates) that invested in Cuba to repatriate profits, with a payoff to Batista being the only price exacted as the cost of doing business. Reluctant to cast aspersions on such a pro-business and anti-Communist ally, Anslinger and his agents insisted that Luciano was merely stopping over in Havana on his way to Mexico.[99]

[97] This story, which features the FBI version of the dice game that lead to the nickname "Lucky," also goes out of its way to discount the "taken for a ride" account: "At one point he made advances to a young Italian girl. The father, a New York City detective, took Lucky out for a ride and nearly stabbed him to death. Lucky has a permanent droop of his right eye as a result." See "Dewey Store: From Foe to Pal of Racketeers," *Chicago Daily Tribune*, May 30, 1952, p. 6.

[98] See, for example, Philip Dur and Christopher Gilcrease, "US Diplomacy and the Downfall of a Cuban Dictator: Machado in 1933," *Journal of Latin American Studies* 34, no. 2 (2002): 252–82.

[99] This was apparent from the consideration (and possibly the manufacturing) of such evidence as was presented in the anonymous letter to the Narcotics Bureau, March 24,

Events soon confirmed that Havana was in fact Luciano's destination, and his stay attracted some notice when other organized crime bosses, including Meyer Lansky and Frank Costello, joined Luciano. As the group gathered in Havana, Frank Sinatra gave his debut performance in Cuba in a show that all assembled crime bosses attended. This pretext for a meeting landed Sinatra in some trouble with the Bureau, leading some agents to tacitly endorse (and perhaps initially circulate) rumors that Sinatra was himself a narcotics addict. When the singer's savvy agent, George Evans, came in for a long talk with Bureau agent Charles Siragusa, he denied any narcotics use by Sinatra. According to Siragusa, Evans was then "asked for an explanation of Sinatra's recent meeting with Charles Lucky Luciano in Havana, Cuba" which, he noted, "had received publicity in the Hearst newspapers."[100] Unwilling to pursue such a high-profile client, the Bureau ultimately refused to pressure Sinatra for details that he likely did not have.

But the Bureau did not drop the issue. For many months, Bureau of Narcotics agents sought the real story behind Luciano's stay in Cuba, surmising that fixing heroin routes and allocating dividends dominated the proceedings, but they were unable to get hold of the particulars. Yet one of the most intriguing things that happened during Lucky's stay in Cuba was the success of the strategy the Bureau devised to get him out. At first, Anslinger remonstrated officials in the Batista regime, but this was of little use. As the commissioner wrote in a letter to the Cuban Ambassador to the United States, "Cuba has acquired an international reputation as one of the major illicit narcotic consumers and distributors in the western hemisphere."[101] Normally content to look the other way, the U.S. government could not sit by idly while its most notorious crime boss violated the terms of his extradition, especially when these violations attracted notice from the press.

When diplomatic exchanges did not produce results, Anslinger played his ace card. "You may inform your Ambassador at Havanna,"

1947, RG 170, Records of the Drug Enforcement Administration, Office of Enforcement Policy Classified Subject Files, 1932–1967, *NARA*, Box 1, as well as the Bureau's own speculations; see Anslinger to Bulkley, September 4, 1946, ibid., Box 1.

[100] Interview with George Evans, Theatrical Publicity Agent in re: his client Frank Sinatra, conducted by Charles Siragusa, April 12, 1948, Record Group 170, Records of the Drug Enforcement Administration, Office of Enforcement Policy Classified Subject Files, 1932–1967, *NARA*, Box 1.

[101] Summary of the file, March 7, 1947, RG 170, Records of the Drug Enforcement Administration, Office of Enforcement Policy Classified Subject Files, 1932–1967, *NARA*, Box 2.

the assistant secretary of Treasury wrote to the U.S. secretary of state in early March 1947, "that the Bureau of Narcotics intends to withhold exportation of narcotic drugs to Cuba as long as Salvatore Lucania is on Cuban soil. The Bureau feels that the risk of having drugs diverted is too great."[102] Here Anslinger deployed an economic threat, using the instrument most essential to the U.S. narcotic regime, licit trade. The legal commerce in narcotics allowed the commissioner to turn the carrot of trade into a stick for regulatory enforcement. Anslinger did not cajole with invective or condemn; he did not threaten criminal action or invasion. Shrewd and uncharacteristically staid, Anslinger's plan paid off in no time at all. On March 29, Lucky boarded a ship destined for Italy. Batista could tolerate many things, but he could not accept the loss of legal drugs for his country.

Efficient and fairly painless, Anslinger's attention to Lucky Luciano in Cuba nevertheless left him incensed. The commissioner began to insist that Luciano's name be placed atop the organization of international trade in heroin. To be sure, this was a role that Anslinger had been casting around to fill for some time. Just as he began to pressure the Cuban government, Anslinger granted an interview to the *Chicago Herald American* during which he divulged his thinking: of all World War II military personnel, the commissioner asserted that " 'fewer than you can count on the fingers of two hands' became addicted to narcotics while in the service," ignoring once again the reality of military drug use, but adding, "thousands have been discharged in the pain of their wounds and become susceptible to dope ... and it is this 'market' that the Mafia is trying to command."[103] Soon the word "kingpin" rolled off narcotics agents' tongues when they spoke of Luciano, as they hectored the Italian government about what they perceived as lenient treatment of Lucky, and goaded excitable congressional members to threaten Italy's share of U.S. foreign aid through the Marshall Plan unless officials did more to stop him.[104]

Fallible and predicated on slim evidence, the commissioner's view of Lucky's underworld standing was soon promoted in ways that assured nearly every adult American would learn of it. Throughout the 1950s, Anslinger's position as U.S. narcotics commissioner, the unsurpassed and

---

[102] Assistant Secretary of the Treasury to Secretary of State, February 21, 1947, ibid., Box 1.

[103] "Luciano's Chief US Aid Killed Building Dope Ring," *Chicago Herald American*, February 26, 1947, found in ibid., Box 1.

[104] "Luciano Called 'Kingpin' of US Narcotic Traffic," *Christian Science Monitor*, June 27, 1951, p. 11.

putatively objective authority in international illicit drug trafficking, sustained the circulation of his political views well beyond what credence these could command otherwise. Of course, his politics had long echoed beyond the halls of the Bureau, mostly because of his solicitation of the conservative populist press, a reliable venue to voice his views regularly. But in 1950, he was given an entirely new arena to offer his declarations and denunciations – the Senate Special Committee on Crime chaired by Democratic Senator Estes Kefauver of Tennessee. The bespeckled senator with a long face and Christian evangelical background projected an earnest indignation, an appealing image for the newly convened committee. Yet Kefauver was more sophisticated than his innocent country charm would suggest; he had fought doggedly for the committee's establishment and appointment as chair, overriding the will and wishes of more senior colleagues and his own party's leadership. His unlikely success came in large part because Kefauver sensed that the growing public concern over crime presented a vital yet somewhat apolitical issue, giving him an opportunity to raise his profile, and placing his opponents in the uncomfortable position of explaining just why they did not want a crime committee.

As public anxiety over crime propelled Kefauver's mission, this alarm took on new dimensions in postwar America. Kefauver capitalized on the fear that gangsters exploited an enfeebled U.S. federal government by citing explicitly "the manner in which the facilities of interstate commerce are made a vehicle of organized crime" as cause for his committee's concern. In so doing, he also clearly demarcated a purview for the federal government to intervene.[105] The ways in which the patchwork and disparate system of local law enforcement provided a safe haven for career criminals had troubled observers since at least the era of bootlegging, but the postwar era gave it a new spin.[106] "The Syndicate," two popular crime investigators explained in 1954, "no longer rules only from New York to Los Angeles, from Minnesota to Florida. The mob that operated from rock-bound coast to sun-kissed shore, now skips oceans and Federal boundaries with the same unhampered ease that it once crossed state lines."[107] Not just the ease of movement within the United States but the viability of travel overseas furnished new channels for licit trade, and

---

[105] Moore, *The Kefauver Committee and the Politics of Crime*, 49.
[106] See Kathleen J. Frydl, "Kidnapping and US State Development," *Studies in American Political Development* 20 (Spring 2006): 18–44.
[107] Feder and Joesten, *The Luciano Story*, p. 8.

also for smuggled goods. In a world where America's presence touched new shores with new power, some unwelcome contraband was stowed away in the United States' global passage.

Rather than confront the inevitability or daunting scale of the criminal consequences of the United States' powerful global position, Kefauver chose to emphasize a story he thought would comfort his American audience; he chose to map a conspiracy. In this and other compelling ways, Kefauver's crime committee resembled the politics and tone of another, more infamous committee under way, the Senate Subcommittee on Permanent Investigations of the Committee on Government Operations chaired by Republican Senator Joseph McCarthy from Wisconsin, another notable "voice" of the postwar era.[108] Though McCarthy and Kefauver came from different parties, their congressional investigations deserve to be grouped and understood together. Both men were relatively young and ambitious newcomers to the Senate who seized upon different issues – investigations of crime and communism – which they felt enjoyed a robust, bipartisan political mandate that the party leadership and political establishment was slow to apprehend. And, in both cases, Democratic congressional leaders and President Truman's advisors made the same calculation: sensing that crime or communism could be wielded as a tool to criticize them, they made a preemptive move to establish investigations of these issues, hoping to quiet the opposition. Kefauver and McCarthy stood as the beneficiaries of this decision, but the move hardly mollified critics; if anything, they were emboldened by the Democrats' recognition of these issues as "threats" worthy of review. In the hands of Kefauver and McCarthy, both crime and communism were defined and dealt with as insidious conspiracies engulfing an innocent American people.

Hence, more than any other single event, Kefauver's Crime Committee endorsed and promoted Anslinger's view of the narcotic trade.[109] While the odious and fraudulent nature of McCarthy's agenda was apparent to some from the very start, a wrenching but fairly brief period ended with his career discredited and his very name synonymous with demagoguery and political witch hunts. In contrast, the accusations, assumptions, and worldview of Kefauver and his committee have largely endured, illustrating the special purchase that conspiracy theories have when it comes to crime. Taking their cue from Anslinger and his agents, the Kefauver crime

---

[108] McCarthy assumed the subcommittee's chair in 1953.
[109] See especially the perceptive treatment by Moore, *The Kefauver Committee and the Politics of Crime.*

hearings presented an ethnic conspiracy, assuming and in many ways creating the image of a powerful and Sicilian-dominated crime syndicate. As William Moore argues, in testimony before the Kefauver committee, "the Federal Bureau of Narcotics revived the ethnic theme."[110] "For whatever reason," he observes, "Anslinger in 1950 was the only major federal official who stood squarely in favor of the proposition that organized crime was controlled by the Mafia" – that is, a Sicilian organization of confederated crime families.[111] Certainly there was crime, and also something that could be called organized crime, but to posit one overarching structure governing it misrepresented not just the nature of it but also its extent. Anyone familiar with the multiplicity of drug markets in just one city would find it difficult to believe in a single mechanism of control, let alone one group controlling multiple cities, national distribution, and international traffic. Yet, though Anslinger was the only "organized pressure on the Committee" to posit Luciano and the mafia as the dominant drug traffickers, senators "moved easily in that direction."[112]

The committee's inclination to accept uncritically Anslinger's assertions regarding Luciano and the Sicilian mafia had real significance. Sessions of the Kefauver crime committee were the first congressional committee hearings to be televised live across the country, and they quickly became a sensation. In fact, it is not too much to say that the hearings promoted the fledgling television industry, enticing consumers to purchase television sets by advertising their unique and remarkable appeal. Few households owned televisions when the first committee meeting was aired in 1951 from New Orleans; most interested viewers went to bars or even television stores to watch a program of interest, like a live boxing match, a popular choice for communal television viewing. Here was something different entirely: hours and hours of testimony that might at any moment produce titillating revelations in scandalous detail. This prospect sent customers flocking to stores to purchase their own television sets so that they could watch the unfolding drama firsthand. Gangsters previously confined to city newspapers' copy or racy cocktail conversation now appeared before the committee for hours, sometimes days, and Americans thrilled to observe, compare notes, and to judge these men who had once been so remote and so removed. Housewives kept the television on all day, working chores around compelling parts of

---

[110] Ibid., p. 21.
[111] Ibid., p. 114.
[112] Ibid., p. 132.

a hearing or, as was the subject of much cartoon humor, neglecting chores entirely. When Frank Costello, notorious gambling Don and legendary "diplomat" of the mafia, appeared before the committee, he declined to permit any broadcast images of his face. Ingenious camera operators instead focused on Costello's nervous hands; the Don's twiddling thumbs convicted him in the court of public opinion in a way that the senators' questions could not, a verdict that would have been impossible to reach in the era of radio.[113]

In addition to bolstering the appeal of television, the Kefauver hearings breathed life into Anslinger's efforts to revive the criminal career of Lucky Luciano, assuring Anslinger and his agents an audience that exceeded expectations. Yet, despite the fanfare, the committee did little that was constructive. No legislation resulted from its work. Not even the witness testimonies yielded much of anything useful; as William Moore observes, the committee did "not so much investigate the problem as it dramatized the perspectives" of senators and their favored witnesses. This was especially true when it came to drugs: though the committee heard testimony that challenged some of the worst distortions of the Bureau of Narcotics on marijuana, Kefauver and his colleagues endorsed the view that marijuana was a "gateway drug" leading ineluctably to heroin addiction and thus worthy of the utmost sanction. Worst of all, "the search for extensive conspiratorial power," as Moore contends, "obscured the need for a realistic examination" of different approaches to dealing with crime, including the legalization of various vice trades, most notably gambling, the issue to which Kefauver devoted the most time.[114]

The committee's many failings mostly escaped notice, but some critics were quick to question Kefauver's work when it came to Lucky Luciano. In their contemporaneous book, *Luciano Story* (1954), authors Sid Feder and Joachim Joesten detailed their skepticism regarding Luciano's purported narcotics role in a chapter entitled "Put Up or Shut Up," daring Anslinger and the Kefauver Committee to produce evidence for their assertions or retract them. "Many of the myths have sprung up as a result

---

[113] See Thomas Doherty, "Frank Costello's Hands: Film, Television, and the Kefauver Crime Hearings," *Film History* 10, no. 3, *The Cold War and the Movies* (1998), pp. 359–74.

[114] Moore, *The Kefauver Committee and the Politics of Crime*, p.113. The Kefauver hearings unwittingly promoted legalized gambling through its hearing held in Las Vegas. All gambling was legal there, and the expectation of salacious exposures was dashed as investors calmly laid out their business model. Not surprisingly, gambling entrepreneurs from all over the country closed up shop and headed for Vegas, where they could do business without the cost of police payoffs.

of statements by the United States Bureau of Narcotics or its agents," Feder and Joesten remarked, "but unfortunately [they] have failed, as of this writing, to come up with any solid evidence against him."[115] It is noteworthy the authors wrote an otherwise critical account of Luciano's life, hence their doubts regarding Luciano's drug dealing did not stem from an unwillingness to believe the worst about Lucky. And Luciano was himself adamant in his denials, insisting that he be given the privilege of appearing before the Kefauver committee to "vindicate" himself.[116]

The government refused, frustrating Luciano, who resorted to interviews in the American press in order to defend himself. "Listen," he told Earl Wilson of the *New York Post Home News*, "it's not necessary for me to fool around with dope, cause I'm not that hard up for money."[117] In fact, Luciano would have welcomed the opportunity to play a key role in the international narcotics trade. He most likely did broker the processing of raw opium into morphine (or morphine into heroin) in factories located throughout Italy, but his extradition undermined his ability to remain a real force. The Bureau of Narcotics received intelligence that confirmed Luciano's declining position, sometimes even unwittingly disclosing their knowledge of such by referring to traffickers as "former" associates of Luciano.[118] Already by 1949, a year before the first Kefauver hearing convened, the Bureau's New York district supervisor wrote to Anslinger of a lost shipment of heroin from Italy that, according to one informant, "subjected [Luciano] to considerable criticism by the leaders of the same mob in New York who believe that he may have been ineffective and that he may have lost his influence."[119]

Living in Italy placed Luciano at a real disadvantage, rendering him unable to negotiate or enforce deals convincingly. What's more, narcotics production and shipment began to relocate in response to market or enforcement pressures, as the Bureau also knew. By 1950, one source

[115] Feder and Joesten, *The Luciano Story*, p. 9.

[116] M. L. Harney to Mr. White, June 20,1950, RG 170, Records of the Drug Enforcement Administration, Office of Enforcement Policy Classified Subject Files, 1932–1967, *NARA*, Box 1.

[117] Earl Wilson, *New York Post Home News*, August 8, 1948, found in RG 170, Records of the Drug Enforcement Administration, Office of Enforcement Classified Subject Files, 1932–1967, *NARA*, Box 1.

[118] See, for example, Joe Pasci, "who was formerly a lieutenant of Charles 'Lucky' Luciano," Claude Follmer, Kansas City, Missouri, November 7, 1949, RG 170, Records of the Drug Enforcement Administration, Office of Enforcement Classified Subject Files, 1932–1967, *NARA*, Box 1.

[119] Williams to Anslinger, August 1, 1949, ibid., Box 1.

revealed that "there is a growing dearth of narcotics in Italy. Most of the narcotics," the informant told a narcotics agent, "originate in Switzerland, Genoa, and Torino, Italy, and they are not easily obtainable in Naples or Milan."[120] Just as Anslinger kept the Kefauver committee members rapt with stories of Sicilian domination, his own agency received indications that trafficking had moved to points north.

This new conduit would ultimately become known as "the French connection," familiar to many because of the eponymous film made in 1971, but known perhaps only in a casual sense. The tremendous flow of narcotics that came through southern French exchange points has not received an attention commensurate with its scale or duration; the film and the book on which it is based, Robin Moore's *The French Connection*, tells the story of one record-setting heroin seizure made in 1962. Joe Cesari, the most established chemist for the Marseilles heroin factory system, left legitimate work in 1954 and was first arrested in 1962. He served a short sentence, was arrested again in 1972, and rather than face trial and the prospect of twenty years behind bars, he hung himself in his jail cell. The chronology of his illicit professional life and his suicide coincides with the heyday of the so-called French Connection, a term that refers more generally to the relocation of manufacture of opium from Paris to Marseilles during the postwar years and the subsequent boom in the production and transit of heroin. The busy port city of Marseilles, long notorious for smuggling and corruption rackets run by ethnic Corsican gangs, presented several key advantages over competitors: France's war in Algeria (1954–62) added to bustling port traffic, and local city officials had even less interest than in Paris in monitoring narcotic flows. What was more, Corsican culture, with its many Italian influences, helped to forge close ties between Corsican crime families and the transatlantic Italian mob.

Added to easy trading access and ethnic networks for distribution of their product, Marseilles heroin production flourished in the face of almost farcical enforcement on the part of French authorities. Until 1970, the Marseilles Narcotic Squad consisted of only seven men whose faces, as one American official complained, were "as well known to the crooks as Brigitte Bardot's."[121] Indeed, heroin traffic in southern France benefited

---

[120] Greenfeld to Anslinger, October 24, 1950, RG 170, Records of the Drug Enforcement Administration, Office of Enforcement and Classified Subject Files, 1932–1967, *NARA*, Box 1.

[121] As quoted in Catherine Lamour and Michel Lamberti, *The International Connection: Opium from Growers to Pushers* (New York: Pantheon Books, 1974), p. 31.

from not just police apathy but also official complicity and powerful political support. Licit drugs manufactured by pharmaceutical firms owned by
wealthy French families often found their way to the illicit market; these
same families offered French president Charles de Gaulle unqualified
support, hence their illicit dealings escaped official scrutiny. Even more
remarkable, the key figure in narcotic traffic through Marseilles, Marcel
Francisci, was also an elected official serving the Gaullist conservative
party. Because of the political protection and local support enjoyed and
often purchased by smugglers, trafficking through Marseilles was mini-
mized or even publicly doubted by French officials. This posture soon
evolved into a kind of political theater, an elaborate act of delay, disgust,
and denial affected by French police when asked about narcotic smuggling; an arrest or two; and then a return to previous denials.

And, though the vast majority of heroin that reached the United
States came through southern French refining mills and transit points,
the Americans seemed content to play their assigned role in the performance, that of the earnest and occasionally irate narcotic official pleading for more robust enforcement from the French. Without question,
French officials put up more resistance to enforcement than any of the
sworn "narco-enemies" of Harry Anslinger, and these dilatory tactics
had much more consequence for the U.S. drug market. Yet, because the
tensions between French and American officials took place in the context of alliance – at least nominally so – under the guise of cooperation,
and without any obvious markers of ethnic difference, the French government was spared the repudiation that Anslinger was quick to deliver
in other circumstances. In the face of a heroin traffic of epic proportions
revealed to the American public by the famous "French Connection" seizure of January 1962, the Bureau of Narcotics gave a somewhat subdued
report to the American Embassy in Paris in March of that same year,
charging that the "full potential of [French and American] cooperation
has never been achieved due to the failure of the French Government
to ... provide the necessary manpower, equipment and operating funds"
to stymie flows, never hinting at a failure of political will or official
corruption.[122]

Yet as early as 1953, the Bureau was willing to go on record with a
German reporter that "France had during the past few months caught

---

[122] Cusack to Minister, American Embassy, Paris, France, March 8, 1962, RG 170, Records
of the Drug Enforcement Administration, Office of Enforcement Policy Classified
Subject Files, 1932–1967, *NARA*, Box 7.

up with the number one illicit narcotic drugs producing country, Italy."[123] Anslinger had guessed wrong when, in 1951, he located the Bureau of Narcotics overseas Europe office in Rome. That same year one of his most prized agents, Charles Siragusa, was obliged to start making regular trips to Marseilles.[124] Not surprisingly, agents thrown into the French milieu with little preparation used cultural analogues and familiar reference points to help them navigate the new terrain. "Although Marseilles is geographically and politically a part of France," Siragusa wrote to Anslinger, "[Corsicans] don't consider themselves to be French at all." Facing off against a disloyal ethnic "enemy within" generated some sympathy for French police on the part of narcotic officials, who construed trafficking at home in similar terms. Siragusa confided that "operationally," the commander of the French Narcotic unit, Director Hacq, "will always be hogtied in relation to the Marseille narcotics problem despite his best intentions."[125] Another narcotics agent scouting pharmacies dealing in illicit heroin in Marseilles reported that one suspicious outfit was a "small seedy looking establishment in a run-down neighborhood, very much like an East-Harlem drug-store."[126] Using these and other such assumptions as guiding lights, narcotics officials routinely portrayed overworked and outmanned French officials struggling to combat a disreputable ethnic conspiracy, a picture that resembled narcotics' officials' view of their own work at home.

Despite their pronounced sympathy for French police officials, Bureau officials soon found themselves caught in the internecine bureaucratic warfare of their ally. Informants who knew of official corruption began to seek out American agents to confide in, as one Inspector Duc did in 1955, hoping, as Bureau agents surmised, to advance his own professional prospects by discrediting his superiors. As narcotic trafficking became increasingly alarming, some Bureau agents grew tired of the delay and double talk. "I am at a loss to explain why they spend so much time ... in order to minimize or discredit the informant," one Narcotic official confessed to Washington, adding that the Sureté did not want to "start a police

[123] Translation of article in *Der Spiegel* as found in Summary of the file, 2–24–53, RG 170, Records of the Drug Enforcement Administration, Office of Enforcement Policy Classified Subject files, 1932–1967, *NARA*, Box 2.

[124] Record Group 170, Records of the Drug Enforcement Administration, Office of Enforcement Policy Classified Subject Files, 1932–1967, *NARA*, Box 2.

[125] Siragusa to Anslinger, November 2, 1960, Records of the Drug Enforcement Administration, Office of Enforcement Policy Classified Subject Files, 1932–1967, *NARA*, Box 7.

[126] Mertin Pera, November 13, 1961, ibid., Box 4.

investigation until such time as they have more ammunition."[127] Others condoned French inaction, offering excuses and validating the explanations offered by French officials. "There is no question but that [Director] Hacq and those who accompany him are professional officers," Bureau supervisor Wayland Speer wrote in 1960, "and their disturbance over the fact that they were in the dark on the real situation pertaining to France's being the source of the heroin reaching the United States was genuine. There is every reason to believe," he added, that "we will see a complete shake-up in narcotic enforcement in France by the first of the year."[128] And what supported this abiding faith in Director Hacq? He "had been completely stunned when he saw the more than 100 kilograms" that Bureau officials had seized in France; Hacq noted that "he had been told that the heroin was coming from Italy and that the Sureté was doing its job relatively well." Speer went on to counsel Washington headquarters that more constructive results would come from "our being able to develop cooperation rather than thinking we can outfox them."[129]

Less gullible agents had had enough. "If ... the efforts on the part of the Bureau to deal directly with M. Hacq fail," the District Supervisor in Rome wrote to Speer, then "I would suggest the shocking heroin situation in France be brought before the UN Narcotic Commission," citing a maneuver Anslinger had been willing to perform on far less evidence in other instances.[130] While the commissioner refrained from publicly humiliating French enforcement efforts, he stepped up his attempts to privately pressure government officials. The response was uniformly the same: France would be quite happy to devote more resources to heroin traffic, but the war in Algeria and the civil unrest it incited across France occupied all of its attention. "Since 1954," Narcotic Supervisor Cusack wrote to the American Ambassador in France, "the Algerian problem with its admitted drain on police manpower has been the excuse for not assigning more men to narcotic enforcement."[131] Cusack had reached the limit of his patience: "We have waited ... But how long can we accept the excuse of the Algerian problem and lack of manpower for not bringing

---

[127] Andrew C. Tartaglino, Memorandum Report, December 21, 1959, RG 170, Records of the Drug Enforcement Administration, Office of Enforcement Policy Classified Subject Files, 1932–1967, *NARA*, Box 4.
[128] Speer to Anslinger, October 19, 1960, RG 170, ibid., Box 7.
[129] Speer to Anslinger, October 10, 1960, RG 170, ibid.
[130] Cusack to Speer, November 22, 1960, RG 170, ibid.
[131] Cusack, March 8, 1962, RG 170, Records of the Drug Enforcement Administration, Office of Enforcement Policy Classified Subject Files, 1932–1967, *NARA*, Box 7.

this situation under control from a country as advanced and loosely allied with us as France?"[132] In 1961, the Marseilles Police Judiciare reassigned the only two police officers detailed to narcotics to assist in "the increased demands of the worsening political situation." Irritated Americans responded that, "out of 30,000 men, the Prefecture can spare at least two to work full time on narcotic investigations."[133]

American agents were right to suspect tactical delays and performative (rather than substantive) investigations. Martin Pera, a narcotics agent sent to work in Marseille after the Bureau opened an office there in 1961, noticed that older police officers in particular "treat the simplest narcotic investigations as extremely complex matters shrouded with great mystery which can only be understood after years of experience."[134] He countered by attempting to persuade French police officers of the scale of narcotic traffic through Marseilles, presenting sale and importation figures of chemicals used to refine morphine into heroin. But reason and circumstantial evidence were met with more bureaucratic intrigues, trying the patience of U.S. narcotics agents who lacked the ability to cajole or manipulate their French colleagues. U.S. agents could not operate on foreign soil except to collaborate with the indigenous police force; as guests of the police and allies of the French, there was no credible threat narcotics agents could muster. Doubtless the French were cognizant of the limited range of American power, and they took it for granted that nominal cooperation alone would suffice in preventing U.S. officials from publicly accusing the French government of complicity in narcotic traffic. Unless and until narcotic enforcement became a domestic priority, France would be a haven for illicit manufacture and trade, immune to U.S. entreaties and anger.

As Bureau officials alternated between sympathy and contempt for the French bureaucracy, their own institutional rivalry reminded them that overlapping organizational mandates could result in counterproductive clashes. Throughout much of the 1950s, Customs officials continued to question the Bureau of Narcotics' international scope, and Customs commissioner Kelly was emboldened further as he and others discerned the missed cues and wayward enforcement of Harry Anslinger's Bureau in Asia. Questioning the organizational competence of the Bureau, Customs officials sought more enforcement capability, particularly in Europe.

---

[132] Ibid.
[133] Pera to Anslinger, October 24, 1961, RG 170, ibid., Box 4.
[134] Martin Pera to Anslinger, October 20, 1961, ibid.

Since both offices shared a home in the Department of Treasury, they each maintained close contact with the assistant secretary of Treasury for enforcement. It was often he who served as arbiter in their disputes. Occasionally, Congress became involved as well, usually at the behest of Customs officials who were eager to activate political alliances in service to their cause. Senator Price Daniel, Democrat of Texas and chair of the Senate Judiciary's Subcommittee on Narcotics, visited Italy in 1955 to investigate the division of labor between Customs and Narcotics. While there he met with Charles Siragusa, who praised the Bureau's European efforts, which he held as "largely responsible for the passage of better narcotic enforcement laws in France and Italy and the establishment of specialized enforcement squads."[135] In this boast, Siragusa revealed much. Both he and his Washington superiors felt that adoption of certain kinds of legislation, undoubtedly punitive, and certain kinds of enforcement methods, undoubtedly the Bureau's own, represented "progress" of a genuine sort. Matching U.S. approaches or embracing their logic signaled to Bureau officials more than goodwill; it meant a genuine advance against illicit narcotic trafficking. Certainly trafficking could take place much the same as before even after adoption of U.S. techniques; in France, named as exemplary by Siragusa, illicit trafficking flourished. For the United States, then, submission to her will was the tacit but real measure of another country's seriousness of purpose in combating illegal drugs.

It was a presumption that the senator likely shared, but it remained to be seen whether the Bureau was the best instrument of U.S. policy. As Siragusa recounted for Anslinger, "Senator Daniel asked me to compare our accomplishments [to] those of the Bureau of Customs before the last war." It was a clever move by the senator. The Bureau had no European office prior to World War II; in a sense, he asked Siragusa to name what real difference the Bureau had made since expanding its operation overseas. Siragusa parried the thrust of the inquiry; "I mentioned that I had little knowledge of the pre-war accomplishments of Customs since I only came to our Bureau in 1939," he demurred, but quickly added that, "I thought our investigators were younger, more capable, energetic and resourceful than Customs Agents. I think that our undercover techniques of underworld penetration have never been duplicated by Customs." Here he seized upon the compositional difference between the two

---

[135] Charles Siragusa to Anslinger, August 15, 1955, Subject: Senators Daniel and Butler, Record Group 170, Records of the Drug Enforcement Administration, Office of Enforcement Policy Classified Subject Files, 1932–1967, *NARA*, Box 13.

organizations: Customs inspected, while the Bureau investigated. Daniel pressed Siragusa further, insisting that "he wanted my personal opinion whether or not it conflicted with Bureau policy." Siragusa responded by denouncing Customs more vigorously. "I said that it was virtually impossible to stop the flow of illicit narcotics into the United States by relying solely on random searches at our frontiers," he summarized for headquarters, and, for good measure, he added "that I thought narcotic smuggling enforcement at American borders should be taken away from Customs and given to us."[136]

Siragusa followed up this aggressive posture with a memorandum intended for submission to the Daniel Committee's formal deliberations over Customs and Narcotic duties. Here again he relied on organizational outputs, and not trafficking outcomes, to highlight the Bureau's contributions. In 1951, "Mr. Siragusa started a one room office in the American Embassy in Rome, bringing with him one briefcase of papers consisting of investigative targets for future undercover exploitation. The office is now composed of 5 rooms, with file cabinets, photo gallery, etc.," Siragusa detailed for Senator Daniel, hoping to project a mystique of a modern law enforcement of unquestionable competence.[137] Treasury officials were unwilling to forward Siragusa's memorandum to the Senate, claiming that doing so would necessarily make the document public, and "should it come to the attention of our European collaborators," they might take offense at the various characterizations of their own enforcement efforts, and, the assistant secretary of enforcement added in a mild rebuke, "there might even be an implied criticism of Customs" in the memorandum.[138]

By decade's end, Customs had won allies through persistence, and perhaps by virtue of Anslinger's bumbling as well. Assistant Secretary for Enforcement Ambrose appeared to favor expanded responsibilities for Customs when he approached European Narcotic Supervisor Cusack with a meeting "to get our ideas on the possibility of Customs re-entering narcotic enforcement in Europe." Cusack responded to the proposition in no uncertain terms by asserting that it was "impossible

[136] Ibid.

[137] Siragusa forwards draft of statement to Daniel committee to Anslinger, August 31, 1955. Record Group 170, Records of the Drug Enforcement Administration, Office of Enforcement Policy Classified Subject Files, 1932–1967, *NARA*, Box 13.

[138] M. L. Harney, Assistant to the Secretary for Enforcement to Anslinger, September 15, 1955, Record Group 170, Records of the Drug Enforcement Administration, Office of Enforcement Policy Classified Subject Files, 1932–1967, *NARA*, Box 13.

to separate the smuggling phase of the traffic from the source phase as Customs proposed," and that doing so "would only result in a duplication of effort." According to Cusack's summary, Ambrose took note of such warnings but remained convinced "that Customs can and should do more in narcotics."[139]

The Bureau's mishandled or biased enforcement efforts paved the way for a greater role for Customs, but so too did the steady pace and robust channels of illicit narcotic trafficking throughout the 1950s. Enforcement officials became particularly aware of drug smuggling that took place under the cover of diplomats and members of the U.S. military. Neither were the routine targets of Customs searches; in the case of diplomats, immunity exempted them from searches altogether. Opportunistic attachés and legation members capitalized on their frequent travels to act as couriers. The American Embassy in Lima recorded its suspicions that Peruvian diplomats participated in narcotic trafficking in 1952; in 1955, Air Force officers let other government agencies know of their contention that diplomats from Panama and Venezuela carried illegal drugs from Hong Kong to points beyond.[140] The most notorious instance of diplomatic smuggling came in 1960, when the Guatemalan envoy to Belgium was arrested by Bureau officials in New York carrying 110 pounds of heroin, a record-setting seizure exceeded only by the "French Connection" bust that followed shortly thereafter. Tellingly, the official was arrested in the company of a Frenchman from Marseilles, a sign that the busy port city had discovered the lucrative possibilities of diplomatic immunity – a claim that, once asserted in this case, was quickly turned aside by agents who noted that the diplomat was not presented in the United States for accreditation, and hence subject to local jurisdiction and arrest.[141]

The cooptation of diplomatic privileges for narcotic smuggling was an enticing prospect, but a rare one. Diplomats were unlikely to risk their privileged position on anything like a regular basis, but other world travelers – members of the U.S. military – had less to lose. Regrettably, the scale and frequency of U.S. military participation in narcotic trafficking can only be the subject of speculation. Files that might substantiate anecdotes with evidence have been withdrawn from Bureau of Narcotics records; particularly noteworthy is the withdrawal of the U.S. Air Force

---

[139] Cusack to Anslinger, December 29, 1959, RG 170, ibid., Box 5.

[140] AmEmbassy, Lima, to Department of State, January 14, 1952, RG 170, ibid., Box 11; C. A. Emerick to Customs official in charge in Hong Kong and Tokyo, August 23, 1955, RG 170, ibid., Box 5.

[141] "Arrest Envoy in Dope Ring," *Chicago Daily Tribune*, October 4, 1960, p. 1.

records in the Bureau's enforcement records throughout the 1950s.[142] Yet snippets and suggestive pieces of information indicate a routine participation in smuggling by some members of the military. As early as 1951, Anslinger wrote to Siragusa that a case that slipped through the fingers of enforcement officials in Athens would have likely implicated a "number of American civilians and Army personnel."[143] When Bureau officials looked to break the supply of French heroin in 1956, their "plant" in the operation posed as an American sailor.[144] It seems unlikely that agents would choose an identity that would jar the sensibilities of their suppliers, so their selection indicates that military participation in narcotic trafficking was perceived as commonplace. In 1957, the Bureau received information from the American legation in Tokyo that "US military personnel reportedly are being solicited by members of this group to act as carriers" for narcotics.[145] Significantly, the majority of allusions to military presence in narcotic smuggling throughout the 1950s involved the air force; not surprising, since travel and transport comprised basic duties of the service's personnel. Agents sometimes uncovered former air force pilots in the course of investigation;[146] just as often, they heard of U.S. Air Force personnel implicated in smuggling operations, particularly in Italy.[147]

In point of fact, the expansion of American air carriers in the 1950s, including the routinization of international flights, presented an entirely new arena for smuggling narcotics, military or otherwise. "Dope smugglers are learning new tricks," one witness told a congressional hearing, "[t]hey are using airplanes as well as jeeps to cover thousands of miles and to jump legal obstacles between the opium poppy ... and the dope addict."[148] Interestingly, the Bureau seems to have been at once aware of

---

[142] See withdrawal notices in RG 170, Records of the Drug Enforcment Agency, Office of Enforcement Policy Classified Subject Files, 1932–1967, *NARA*, Box 5.

[143] Anslinger to Siragusa, February 7, 1951, RG 170, Records of the Drug Enforcement Administration, Office of Enforcement Policy Classified Subject Files, 1932–1967, *NARA*, Box 11.

[144] "US-French Dope Ring Is Broken," *Washington Post and Times*, August 18, 1956, p. 3.

[145] Walter O'Brien, Treasury Agent, to Lester Johnson, Treasury Attache, Tokyo Legation, May 17, 1957, RG 170, Records of the Drug Enforcement Administration, Office of Enforcement Policy Classified Subject Files, 1932–1967, *NARA*, Box 5.

[146] Manfredi, CID Investigation, March 17, 1948, RG 170, ibid., Box 1; Drumright to Department of State, June 26, 1958, RG 170, ibid., Box 7.

[147] James C. Schofeld, Lt. Colonel, USAF to Anslinger, September 1, 1955, RG 170, ibid., Box 2.

[148] Congressman Sidney Yates, *Hearings Before a Subcommittee of the Committee on Ways and Means, House of Representatives, 82nd Congress, HR 3490 and HR 348, April, 7, 14, and 17, 1951* (Washington, DC: U.S. Government Printing Office, 1951), p. 45.

the possibility of airline smuggling and interested in minimizing awareness of it.[149] Harry Anslinger maintained close relations with Samuel F. Pryor, vice president of Pan American Airways, the largest American carrier. One of Pryor's employees, Dixon Arnett, was even enrolled for training at the Federal Bureau of Narcotics. Upon his return, Dixon Arnett conducted an informal survey of smuggling aboard aircraft, and returned the following verdict: "I have become convinced that [large-scale smuggling] is impossible to do unless employees of the airline are actually a part of the 'organization' of such an operation, and usually they are in some number."[150] Because of this, Arnett advised that the airline adopt full-time airline security, something air carriers remained extremely reluctant to do, for fear that security checks would emphasize the possible dangers of air travel to passengers. Instead, Pryor and Anslinger advocated a voluntary approach, encouraging captains to search their planes and watch for "associations between flight crew and ground personnel."[151]

Evidently the collaboration between Pryor and Anslinger went even deeper. When Narcotics Agent Siragusa paid a visit to Pryor in his hotel room during the summer of 1960, he listened as Pryor complained that his own inspector, Dixon Arnett, suspected one of his pilots of narcotic smuggling. Pan American "would like to discharge [the pilot]," Siragusa recounted in a memorandum for Anslinger, "but union regulations and other conditions preclude it." But this was not the reason Siragusa was summoned to the executive's hotel quarters. Pryor had heard that a Bureau investigation was already under way, and he "asked permission to accompany me to our Bureau office to learn just what we had in our files." More surprising, Siragusa attempted to reassure Pryor by remarking that "this must be a recent case otherwise you would have unquestionably already reported the pending case to him." Such familiarity bespoke a relationship that extended well beyond friendly cooperation, and the impulse behind this close collaboration soon became clear: "if and when arrests are made there is to be no publicity," Siragusa promised the Pan Am vice president, and "if publicity is unavoidable then only reference should be made to [pilot] but not the name of the airline."[152]

[149] At a 1954 conference discussing crime on airlines, Narcotic Agent Charles Siragusa was the U.S. representative. See "Deman Power to Put Irons on Air Travelers," *Chicago Daily Tribune*, October 10, 1954, p. 28.

[150] Dixon Arnett, March 20, 1961, RG 170, ibid., Box 4.

[151] "Suggested points for conference with Barney Brieskin," August 4, 1959, RG 170, ibid., Box 5.

[152] Siragusa to Anslinger, August 25, 1960, RG 170, ibid., Box 5. Emphasis not mine. Pan American was implicated in one heroin seizure in Hong Kong in 1960, for which

The relationship between the Bureau and Pan Am illustrates the carefully prescribed limits of Bureau investigations. Tourism, including expansion of international travel by airlines, offered a major conduit for smuggling narcotics. The enforcement strategy best tailored to that fact was regular security inspections, something that would slow down air traffic, inconvenience and perhaps intimidate travelers, and present the airlines with an additional expense. The natural federal government agency to oversee such an operation would have been the U.S. Customs office, charged with border security and interdiction of contraband. Instead, the Bureau and its business allies sought to convince the American public that such inspections would be fruitless, lacking, in Bureau agent Siragusa's words, "our undercover techniques of underworld penetration." In promoting investigation over inspection, the Bureau also endorsed its view that a band of criminals and not world trade flows and traffic was at the heart of drug smuggling. If narcotics came from all different directions, through all different guises, and by the hand of all manner of people, then inspections, including the method and frequency of travel, would be the wisest strategy. That was the least desirable scenario for the Bureau, as it would mean watching their bureaucratic rival, the Customs agency, ascend in importance and it would displace their own; just as significant, it was undesirable to business executives interested in facilitating international exchange as well.[153]

Belief in an "evil" cabal protected and legitimated the Bureau's bureaucratic power and station, then, in ways that acknowledging the consequences of international trade and traffic did not. The Bureau made a similar investment in international trade protocols for opium production and trade, guided by a similar logic. When the newly formed United Nations revived the League's efforts under its Committee on Narcotic Drugs (CND), Anslinger wasted little time. As historian William Walker observes, "[a]t the CND's first meeting in November 1946, Anslinger called for the reestablishment of international and national

---

it had to pay a fine. See Donald Fish, *Airline Detective* (St. James Place: Collins, 1962), p. 151.

[153] More can be said about the Bureau's relations with Pan American Airways. Apparently the airline had embarked on a campaign to build hotels near travel destinations; this project involved one Mr. Breeskin, who also kept close tabs on the Bureau (see, for example, article on Breeskin in *Washington Daily News*, June 22, 1960, as found in RG 170, Records of the Drug Enforcement Administration, Office of Enforcement Policy Classified Subject Files, 1932–1967, *NARA*, Box 5). This set of relationships also involved Joseph Holt, Republican Congressman from the San Fernando Valley.

controls."[154] His ultimate goal of consolidating the many separate international narcotics agreements into one convention would take, as Anslinger admitted in 1955, "many years," but the advantages of doing so went unquestioned, at least by the commissioner.[155]

From the first, Commissioner Anslinger attempted to enforce a basic symmetry between the U.S. Narcotic regime and international controls. In 1949, he reminded a colleague that under a recent U.S. law the "Secretary of Treasury is empowered to make a finding, with respect to any drug, that it has addiction-forming ... liability ... and when such a finding is proclaimed by the President, the drug is automatically covered under the Federal Narcotic Laws." So too with international controls: this "authority is given under a new Protocol to the World Health Organization [analogous, in some ways to the US Food and Drug Administration] and to the Commission on Narcotic Drugs of the United Nations."[156] His efforts to transform the U.S. approach into a universal model soon met with opposition, however. Annual CND meetings featured regular clashes between the United States and Soviet bloc countries. In 1953, the Soviet representative voted against all U.S. initiatives, carrying on what U.S. representatives deemed to be a "Russian policy which has been to abolish this Commission, probably because of the many discussions which take place in relation to Communist China"; or, as the commissioner allowed in his summary to Secretary of State John Foster Dulles, "[p]ossibly there is some other reason of which we are not aware."[157]

Soon other countries bristled at Anslinger's inflexibility and determination to impose U.S. norms on other countries. France proved even more obstructionist than the Soviet Union, no doubt part of the larger strategy of delay and avoidance undertaken by the French government in relation to narcotics traffic. French representative to the commission Charles Vaille "dominated debates," the U.S. representative reported in 1956, "deliberately throwing up a roadblock in the path of the Single

---

[154] William O. Walker III, *Opium and Foreign Policy: The Anglo American Search for Order in Asia* (Chapel Hill: University of North Carolina Press, 1991), p. 165.

[155] Memorandum of conversation, Anslinger visit to State Department to discuss 1955 Session of United Nations Commission on Narcotic Drugs, May 31, 1955, RG 170, Records of the Drug Enforcement Administration, office of Enforcement Policy Classified Subject Files, 1932–1967, *NARA*, Box 11.

[156] Anslinger's notation on March 9, 1949 memorandum, MH Seevers Project, RG 170, Records of the Drug Enforcement Administration, Subject Files of the Bureau of Narcotics and Dangerous Drugs, 1916–1970, *NARA*, Box 1.

[157] Anslinger to Secretary of State, May 7, 1953, RG 170, ibid., Box 10.

Convention."[158] When the normally dependable United Kingdom representative confronted the United States with his conviction that "the sources of smuggling in Southeast Asia are the Nationalists, specifically the remnant of Chiang Kai-shek's army in and around Thailand," the Americans brushed these assertions aside. As planning for the 1957 conference began, tensions arose within the U.S. government itself. Anslinger announced his intention to place Thailand's legal opium consumption on the agenda, and the U.S. Embassy was quick to respond. "It is felt here," the ambassador wrote the Department of State, "that it would be extremely unfortunate if the subject of opium smoking in Thailand were to be placed on the agenda of the April 1957 session of the Commission on Narcotic Drugs. The subject is an internal one," he contended, "and bears little relation to the more important question of how to prevent Thailand's being used as a pipeline for the exportation of opium."[159] Not so, objected Anslinger, who felt that "legalized opium smoking in Thailand is closely interlocked with the smuggling of opium," an assertion that the commissioner considered self-evident, and hence offered no supporting evidence for it.[160]

As the decade went on, more international defiance of Anslinger's goals and ideals became apparent. This dissatisfaction as well as Anslinger's intransigency all came together and collided in the Bureau's confrontation with revolutionary Cuba. There the Bureau and its depiction of the rebel insurgency, successful in its drive to overthrow the Batista regime and install Fidel Castro as the new leader of Cuba, recapitulated many of the Cold War dynamics and dilemmas of the decade. And the stand-off was long in the making: as had been the case when Lucky Luciano took shelter in Havana, the Batista regime had continued to offer a safe haven for criminal enterprises throughout the 1950s. When narcotics agents pressed Cuban officials, as they did in 1958, the police turned Bureau requests aside. In a refrain that should have struck a familiar chord with agents of the Bureau preoccupied with France and its Algerian "excuses," the commander "regretted he did not have more time to devote to narcotic enforcement," but Castro's insurgency required "investigations into

[158] Frederick T. Merrill, Confidential Report of Acting US Representative to the 11th Session of the UN Commission on Narcotic Drugs, RG 170, Records of the Drug Enforcement Administration, Office of the Enforcement Policy Classified Subject Files, 1932–1967, *NARA*, Box 10.

[159] AmEmbassy, Bangkok, to Department of State, August 30, 1956, ibid., Box 10.

[160] Anslinger to Calderwood, October 1, 1956, RG 170, ibid., Box 10.

revolutionary activities [that] took priority."[161] Bureau agents reluctantly concluded that the Batista regime's accommodating attitude toward criminals – namely "the facility with which [narcotic traffickers] can use Havana as a meeting place to affect the transfer of vast quantities of French heroin" – made Cuba "the most serious threat to the suppression of illicit heroin traffic at the present time."[162]

A little over a month after a narcotics agent shared this view with Anslinger, Castro celebrated his famous New Year revolution in Havana, completing his drive to expel the Batista regime. Thenceforth Cuban American relations entered into a strange interregnum, an often over-looked period of exploratory gestures that preceded the well-known animosity that came to define relations between the two countries. Not surprisingly, the Bureau raced to influence perceptions of the new regime. Days after the New Year's succession, Narcotics Agent Cusack accused Carlos Prio Socarras, former president of Cuba, of financing "the recent revolution" through cocaine traffic (a drug not much mentioned by the Bureau during this time).[163] Prio had in fact broken with Castro as the revolution gained momentum. Undeterred, the Bureau plowed on in its "case" against Cuba by presenting its records on one of Castro's most famous supporters, Australian actor Errol Flynn. Though Hollywood considered Flynn the ideal "swashbuckling hero," the Bureau had known since 1947 that Flynn "used narcotics when he had no medical need for them," citing, according to the Bureau, "painful hemorrhoids" as the reason for his morphine and heroin consumption.[164] Elsewhere Flynn's opiate habit has been attributed to his painful back injuries, but the Bureau seemed intent on giving Flynn no quarter. His typically flamboyant support of Fidel Castro – at one point referring to Castro as a "drinking partner" – instead seemed to Bureau agents to be behavior indicative of a narcotic addict, and therefore his "boasts of assisting in the Cuban revolution can and should be greatly discounted."[165] This dismissive attitude was something Flynn resented: "What makes anyone think I am less concerned for the verities of the world than anyone else?" he demanded to

---

[161] Cusack reporting on conversation with Colonel Piedra to Anslinger, November 3, 1958, RG 170, ibid., Box 7.

[162] Cusack to Anslinger, November 24, 1958, RG 170, ibid., Box 7.

[163] Cusack to Anslinger, January 12, 1959, RG 170, ibid., Box 7.

[164] January 16, 1959 unsigned memorandum, "The Illicit Narcotic Traffic in Cuba," RG 170, ibid., Box 7.

[165] Ibid.

know in his autobiography otherwise devoted to picaresque adventures. "Was it all a prank that I went to Loyalist Spain, that I sided with Castro, that I've plumbed the sea depths, and traveled the world?"[166]

Linking a prominent addict to the Castro government all but sealed the case against Cuba in Anslinger's mind, conflating, as he did, narcotic addiction with trafficking and vice versa. But, like other socialist or communist regimes, the new Cuban government actually showed a great interest in bringing gangsters to justice and expelling narcotics from Cuba. In March of his inaugural year of governing, Castro offered to extradite some of the "known drug smugglers" to the United States, vowing "Cuba will never again become the center of the narcotic traffic." In return Castro expected the United States to extradite "Cuban gangsters" – including, one can be sure, his political enemies – back to Cuba. "I don't see how the United States can ask us to deport American gangsters," he reasoned, "without saying anything about deporting the Cuban gangsters and war criminals in refuge [in the US]."[167] In this proposal, Castro hoped to get his hands on wealthy Cuban businessmen, only some of whom were criminals, and repatriate their profits and wealth back to the homeland. The United States wasted little time considering this request, emboldening Anslinger to present sharper and more public denunciations of the regime. In April, the commissioner claimed that a list "of 50 dope peddlers" living in Cuba that he sent to the new regime "mysteriously disappeared."[168]

Bureau records show that Castro's police chief Castroverde did in fact pursue the list furnished by Anslinger; when he telephoned for more information and details, a Bureau agent informed him that "under instructions from the Commissioner, we are not furnishing any further information since we consider it to be a waste of time."[169] The abrupt dismissal by the Americans, which was justified under the pretext of an uncooperative regime in Cuba, was met by officials there with persistent requests for more information and expressions of a shared interest in ridding Cuba of narcotic trafficking.

As the Bureau embarked on the predictable course of depicting Castro's government as involved in narcotic trafficking, the various tensions and

[166] Errol Flynn, *My Wicked, Wicked Ways: The Autobiography of Errol Flynn* (New York: Cooper Square Press, 2003), p. 22.
[167] "Gangster Exchange Suggested by Cuba," *Washington Daily News*, March 19, 1959, as found in RG 170, ibid., Box 7.
[168] "Dope Peddler List Got Lost in Cuba," *Washington Daily News*, April 1? (Friday), 1959, as found in ibid.
[169] Wayland Speer to Castroverde, June 2, 1959, ibid., Box 7.

tirades of the decade mounted into real resistance.[170] At an Inter-American Narcotic session held in Brazil in 1961, only months after the failed U.S.-backed "Bay of Pigs" attempt to overthrow Castro, U.S. representatives met with more than simply skepticism. A lengthy prepared statement was read by a Brazilian psychiatrist who insisted that "marihuana does not induce acts of violence"; this testimony, according to one U.S. delegate, "sparked a four-hour acrimonious debate." True to form, the United States and Canada insisted that the drug led to "aggressive criminal behavior."[171] Dissent from the U.S. ideological "line" was followed by still more signs of trouble. Cuban delegates worked the room passing around an anti-United States pamphlet, infuriating the Americans with this demonstration of Spanish-speaking solidarity (and perhaps upsetting the Brazilian hosts as well). Then, when Narcotics Agent Charles Siragusa raised his hand to be recognized, "the electrical current went off in the conference room," denying Siragusa the privilege of being heard and of being translated. The Cuban delegation undoubtedly effected this sudden loss of power, electric and otherwise. As the U.S. report of the meeting noted with regret, "Mr. Siragusa was then compelled to make his statement in a raised voice," and, once he was finished, "immediately the electric current returned."[172]

Throughout the 1950s, the Bureau made a number of moves that had undermined its authority and voice. Its strident and shrill denunciations, its policy contradictions and intelligence errors, and the provincial politics it projected onto a cosmopolitan world attracted serious critical attention. As the decade came to a close, Anslinger and his agents remained preoccupied with American exile Lucky Luciano in Italy, tracking him closely. They were rewarded for this effort with evidence of his dissolute and dissipated lifestyle, but little else. Luciano bet heavily at the tracks, consorted with aging gangsters like himself, and entertained a steady parade of U.S. military personnel and tourists who lined up at his favorite restaurant for a picture and an autograph. His finances dwindling, Luciano

---

[170] See Eduardo Sáenz Rovner, *The Cuban Connection: Drug Trafficking, Smuggling, and Gambling in Cuba from the 1920s to the Revolution*, trans. Russ Davidson (Chapel Hill: University of North Carolina Press, 2008), chap. 12.

[171] Gordon, Embassy Rio De Janeiro, to Secretary of State, December 12, 1961, RG 170, NARA, Box 5.

[172] Classified Report of the United States Delegation to the Second Meeting of the Inter-American Consultative Group on Narcotic Control, Rio de Janeiro, Brazil, November 27 to December 7, 1961, Submitted to the Secretary of State by Charles Siragusa, Chairman of the Delegation, RG 170, ibid., Box 5.

contemplated an invitation to collaborate on a movie script based on his life. He also continued to give interviews to prominent journalists when he felt it would serve his interests to do so.

One such reporter came to his villa in 1961, just a year before Luciano would die of a heart attack at an airport, awaiting the arrival of the screenwriter who promised to memorialize Lucky's life on film. Many months before that fateful day, Luciano gave a long interview to Ian Fleming, novelist and travel reporter for *The Sunday Times*. During this particular visit Lucky was feeling more expansive than usual; in addition to his usual carping about the Bureau, Luciano offered his views on the entire enforcement approach of the U.S. government. "These American narcotics people are always trying to frame me," Lucky told Fleming, and added that this was "the fault of the American government. They are not handling this narcotics problem right," he evaluated, presumably with some authority. "Washington is spending billions of dollars every year [sic] trying to stamp out the traffic, but that is not the way to stop it," Lucky insisted. "They ought to set up clinics all over the country where you can register as a drug-taker, like you do in England," a reference by Luciano to the UK's system of ambulatory care. "Ya see, Mr. Fleming," the author recorded Luciano as saying, "it's just the way you spend the money – on setting up clinics or on law enforcement that cannot work and only makes the problem worse."[173]

Coincidentally, Ian Fleming's best-known work, the novels chronicling the adventures of the fictional British secret service agent James Bond, captured well the mystique that the Bureau of Narcotics attempted to project for itself. Cleverness and guile would best their enemies, or so narcotics agents hoped. The conceit of the world of Agent 007 was the same as that of the Bureau: diabolical enemies could be countered by a force of valorous and elite men, never mind that both the Bureau and James Bond contended with disembodied forces more than devilish desires, and that they themselves acted on behalf of powerful nations that had their share of moral ambivalence. These fantasies cheated two sides of the story, presenting large and complex dynamics as the result of a nefarious few, and depicting a select cadre as the desirable response, perhaps mostly because a preference for the "excellent few" placated powerful business interests.

---

[173] Ian Fleming, "Luciano Has Solution to Drug Traffic," *Washington Post*, April 2, 1961, as found in RG 170, Records of the Drug Enforcement Administration, Subject Files of the Bureau of Narcotics and Dangerous Drugs, 1916–1970, *NARA*, Box 8.

It was a pleasant fiction, but one that, as Luciano lucidly pointed out in his broken and street-smart English, was counterproductive. Yet Ian Fleming's version of this indulgent fantasy made it all the way to the White House, amusing the newly elected John F. Kennedy so much that he listed Fleming as one of his favorite authors. Whatever psychic release *From Russia With Love* provided the young president, he did not let its romance extend to his view of the Bureau of Narcotics. When the new president took the reins of government, the international portfolio of the Bureau failed to impress him. Even less impressive was the Bureau's handling of domestic drug circulation and consumption throughout the postwar era. Indeed, however eventful the commissioner's management of global affairs, it was secondary when compared to the dramatic changes in the United States regarding illicit drug traffic and use during the 1950s.

3

"A Society Which Requires Some Sort of Sedation"

Domestic Drug Consumption, Circulation, and Perception

No decade of the recent American past is more distorted by popular culture than the 1950s. Commonly depicted as a time of complacent tranquility and rigid conformity, American life was instead unsettled and often contentious. Much of the turmoil was linked to the rise of a youth culture of unprecedented scope and importance – one that catered to the "teenager," a term invented in the 1950s to capture a stage of late adolescence between the dependency of childhood and the responsibility of adult life. The dynamics of the emerging youth culture often reinforced messages of conformity, but just as often they did not, and the emotions and expressiveness unleashed by rock 'n' roll music or adolescent pop movies could not always be monitored or checked by authority.[1] During the same time, the modern black freedom movement engaged in struggles that echoed elements of the power dialectic of youth culture. Mobilizing well-accepted notions of American life, civil rights leaders argued on behalf of enfranchisement or consumption opportunities for African Americans, even ones as seemingly banal as enjoying a drink at a soda fountain.[2]

---

[1] See Beth Bailey, *Sex in the Heartland* (Cambridge: Harvard University Press, 1999).

[2] Mary L. Dudziak, *Cold War Civil Right: Race and the Image of American Democracy* (Princeton: Princeton University Press, 2000); Thomas Borstelmann, *The Cold War and the Color Line: American Race Relations in the Global Arena* (Cambridge: Harvard University Press, 2001); Lizabeth Cohen, *A Consumer's Republic: The Politics of Mass Consumption in Postwar America* (New York: Knopf, 2003).

The quote in the title of this chapter is from a summary of Bureau of Narcotics Interview with Dr. Longo, found in Boston District to Administration, December 5, 1955, RG 88 Records of the Food and Drug Administration, Division of General Services, General Subject Files, 1938–1974, *NARA*, Box 2160.

Thus, while the dominant cultural script of American values survived the decade intact, its narration and particular applications changed – at times, radically so.

Not to be overlooked in a more careful assessment of the 1950s are the many tensions and transformations that were present within white middle-class America. While disaffected outsiders challenged dominant social norms, these norms also imposed hardships and entailed power negotiations among even those who subscribed to them. The familiar appearance of 1950s harmony projected in celebrated images of female domesticity masked, and to some extent helped mollify, concerns about the large numbers of married women entering the workforce. Similarly deceptive is the story of the "organization man," or male breadwinner, commonly supposed to have led a charmed life in the decade, but who in fact was tasked with new emotional responsibilities at home and professional obligations at work.[3] Historian Alan Petigny refers to these subtle contests during the 1950s as a "subversive consensus": an outward projection of conformity, but one that relied upon a reworked hierarchy of roles or understanding.[4]

The popular simplifications that shroud the 1950s also obscure our understanding of the American state. Generally the decade is considered a period of political and institutional stagnation, featuring an unambitious leader, Dwight Eisenhower, who presided over a largely dormant federal government, a misconception fueled by the tendency of academic scholars to see only progressive gestures as "activity." A more balanced view would herald the formation of the military industrial complex, a political fate that Eisenhower would later bemoan in his farewell address to the nation in the final days of his presidency.[5] Beyond just defense production, a nation of preeminent industrial power now became a nation of commercial activity as well, adding legions of white-collar and service-sector jobs to the employment rolls. To enhance commerce, the government invested billions in infrastructure and encouraged widespread use

[3] The "man in the gray flannel suit" would not have such power as a stereotype if either the eponymous book or movie, both complex and poignant stories, was consulted: see Sloan Wilson, *The Man in the Gray Flannel Suit* (New York: De Capo Press, 2002).

[4] See Alan Petigny, *The Permissive Society: America, 1941–1965* (New York: Cambridge University Press, 2009).

[5] Two fairly recent historical treatments present the political and institutional creation of the "military-industrial complex" carefully: see Michael J. Hogan, *A Cross of Iron: Harry S. Truman and the Origins of the National Security State* (New York: Cambridge University Press, 1998); Aaron L. Friedberg, *In the Shadow of the Garrison State: America's Anti-Statism and Its Grand Cold War Strategy* (Princeton: Princeton University Press, 2000).

of the automobile. As a result, Americans in the 1950s traveled more: goods and people moved about the country with greater efficiency and in far greater numbers.

Illegal drug consumption was a component to all of these stories. Drug use among teenagers typified their transgressive behavior and, in the hands of Bureau of Narcotics Commissioner Harry Anslinger and others, it became an instrument of censure and a tool to enact more punitive measures. The aspirational politics and carefully calibrated messages of African American civil rights leaders had to contend with another discursive construct of the decade, that of black criminality, an image its proponents anchored in the District of Columbia, which they depicted as rampant with drug use and overrun by violent crime. The District, in turn, became the proving ground for the U.S. Congress in its drive to reshape the criminal justice system, a significant though largely neglected aspect of state-building in the 1950s.[6] Illegal drug use also became a part of the fabric of commercial trade and internal movement, accelerating as these commercial ties grew. Importantly, the illegal trade in drugs featured new arrivals: synthetic drugs, especially barbiturates and amphetamines. These two classes of drugs were used illicitly and licitly predominately by white middle-class Americans, many of whom consumed copious amounts of them out of complete innocence, ignorance, or outright dependence.

This vibrant trade in illegal drugs strained the tenets of the country's regulatory enforcement regime. Anslinger responded by pushing for more punishment and criminalization; he also attempted to raise the profile of his "small but efficient" office. Though lacking apparent justification, the separation of narcotics and marijuana from newer synthetic drugs spared Anslinger the duty of policing the busy traffic in amphetamines and barbiturates. Instead, this portfolio fell to the Food and Drug Administration (FDA), an understaffed agency ill equipped to perform enforcement functions. The arbitrary line drawn between newer pharmaceuticals, synthetics, and older ones, narcotics, prompted some observers to question the

---

[6] One scholar who has emphasized the importance of DC in the drug war, but for a later time (the 1980s) and under the influence of the executive, not legislative, branch, is Clarence Lusane, *Pipe Dream Blues: Racism and the War on Drugs* (Boston: South End Press, 1991); David F. Musto also offers up a Progressive-era example of the District's importance: see Musto, *The American Disease: Origins of Narcotic Control* (New York: Oxford University Press, 1999 edition), p. 22. Finally, the dynamic detailed above bears a resemblance to the one described by Kate Masur in her examination of African American enfranchisement in the District and the subsequent efforts to undermine it. See Kate Masur, *An Example for All the Land: Emancipation and the Struggle for Equality in Washington, D.C.* (Chapel Hill: University of North Carolina Press, 2010).

country's entire approach to illegal drugs. As the decade went on, some very prominent voices joined in the denunciation of the punishment ethos pervading narcotics regulation; by the time John F. Kennedy assumed office, Anslinger faced a chorus of criticism.

As the commissioner clung to his prosecutorial approach and conspiracy theories, he defied a decade of expanding illegal drug use, a reality that punctures the myth of tranquility of the 1950s, to be sure, but one that amounts to more than simply exposing a seamier side to a nostalgic era. Interestingly, though other prominent cultural scripts of the decade have been all but discarded, when it comes to illicit drugs, the moralistic denunciation and punishment regime of Anslinger has largely endured. The reasons for its surprising longevity rest in the decade of the 1950s as well, including its utility in sustaining certain political relationships and institutional configurations. As Anslinger confronted massive drug use and faced off against perceptive critics, he furnished lawmakers an answer that, though it did little to affect drug use, "solved" other political puzzles, including acclimating a host of interests and people to a powerful U.S. state.

DISTRICT OF COLUMBIA: A "MODEL" CITY

By many measures, Washington, DC, is an unusual city. Article I of the U.S. Constitution grants Congress authority over the affairs of the city of Washington, a preemption of self-governance explicitly spelled out in a document otherwise dedicated to preserving local autonomy. This striking exception was born from a common fear that any other model would expose the nation's capital to a particular region's influence, or, as had been the case in Revolution-era Philadelphia, local attacks. Where Congress governed, Congress ruled, and in this calculation a budding nation hoped to neuter the District of Columbia of political power and, more fundamentally, a political identity.

This severe political compact subjugated District residents for decades, and its legacy is alive and well today: DC residents pay a federal income tax but possess no voting representation in Congress. This is but one of the manifold effects of federal control. Washington, DC, had no elected city government until the Home Rule Act of 1973; before that time, Washington's affairs were decided by committees of Congress and administered by a three-person Board of Commissioners, appointed by the president of the United States. Since District residents could not vote in presidential elections until 1964, the peculiar structure of governance in the District meant that, for most of its history, residents had the right to petition the government, a fundamental right from which all civil liberties emanate, only as subjects and not as citizens. Congress routinely reinforced this lowly status by taking up District business in "private bills," a bureaucratic designation that referred to trivial affairs, most often invoked to provide individual redress – to restore a particular veteran's pension, for instance – in the days before executive agencies possessed the plenary authority to dispose of such claims definitively.[7] In this way, Congress drew a procedural equivalence between governing a half million Americans and resolving a particular citizen's bureaucratic grievance.

Still more can be said about the distinctive political landscape of Washington, DC. Ever since the "Organic Act" of 1871 consolidated various territories of Washington into a "District," Washington has legally been a kind of city-state, albeit without the self-governance normally associated with other such entities. The fact that the city became a "District" – a state without political entitlements – combined with congressional oversight created an unusual jurisdictional footing for DC. In other states, serious crimes, including felonies, are defined and punished by state authorities: state legislatures create and amend the criminal code, "district" attorneys bring charges, and state judges preside over criminal cases in state courts. In Washington, all felonies and serious criminal infractions are presented before federal courts; they are prosecuted by the Department of Justice, in the person of the U.S. attorney assigned to the District; and, most significantly, in the era before home rule, the U.S. Congress passed the penal laws for the District. Criminal justice powers that would in other places be reserved for the state government are, in the District, a prerogative of the federal government.

This jurisdictional oddity grew in importance as the city changed over time. Prior to World War II, roughly one-third of the District's residents were classified as African American. In the postwar era, that percentage climbed dramatically, reaching its peak at 70 percent in 1970, and slowly declining since that time. For much of the twentieth century, then, DC had a large number of African American residents, and the fact that it was a

---

[7] For changes in administrative authority, see Joanna Grisinger, "Reform in the 'Fourth Branch': The Federal Administrative Procedure Act of 1946," Paper presented at the annual meeting of the American Political Science Association, Philadelphia Marriott Hotel, Philadelphia, PA. Online 2009–05–26 from http://www.allacademic.com/meta/p63452_index.html.

popular destination for black migrants from southern coastal states in the postwar years made it among the first majority black cities outside of the former Confederacy. As anthropologist Elliot Liebow pointed out in his well-known study of "streetcorner" men, *Tally's Corner*, the District "was the only major city in the country with more Negroes than whites living in it" by 1963.[8]

The relative security of federal government employment enticed waves of African American migrants in search of better work in a more stable setting. Though most often relegated to custodial and other menial jobs in the federal government, black employees in these positions had reasons to covet these jobs: unlike employment throughout the south, there was no race-based wage differential for work performed in the same position. In the federal government, a janitor's pay was a janitor's pay, regardless of the race of the person filling the position. What is more, World War II spurred a significant promotion of blacks into better classes of federal employment, especially clerical work. The prospect of work outside of domestic care for substantial numbers of African American women made DC unique among American cities – though, to be sure, many black women in the city worked as caretakers in private homes, and many other African Americans, both men and women, labored in menial jobs in and out of the federal government.

Yet even modest employment gains alarmed powerful segregationists in Congress. More troubling to congressional southerners, these strides were coupled with an increasingly vocal and powerful black freedom movement. In the postwar years, civil rights leaders fought to preserve wartime gains by extending the life of the Fair Employment Practices Commission (FEPC), arguing that its oversight helped to counter racial discrimination in hiring. Another major postwar civil rights goal was achieved when President Truman signed the Executive Order to desegregate the military in 1948, a move that leaders of the civil rights movement hoped would usher in desegregation in other areas of public life. At an uneven pace and frequently facing hostility, activists did effect an incremental desegregation of restaurants, movie theaters, and other businesses throughout the north in a scattershot fashion. In 1951, three years prior to the 1954 *Brown v. Board of Education* Supreme Court decision ordering the integration of public schools, Washington, DC, desegregated

---

[8] Elliot Liebow, *Tally's Corner: A Study of Negro Streetcorner Men* (Lanham, MD: Rowman & Littlefield Publishers, 2003), p. 10, n. 10.

restaurants and places of public recreation.[9] In that same year, a plan by the DC Board of Commissioners to extend these gains to Washington's firefighters met with the immediate opposition of Congressman James Davis of Georgia, chair of the House Subcommittee on District Police and Firemen and a relentless defender of segregation.[10] If the commissioners failed to reverse the order, Davis threatened to take action, up to and including cutting off the commissioners' salaries. In the end, the commissioners tempered their position, retaining an integration order in name but hiring and promoting very few black firefighters – a token gesture that the police force had pioneered years earlier.

This kind of imposition of segregationist priorities and a Dixie viewpoint onto the District was not an unusual occurrence; it was a regular and intended outcome of congressional oversight. Southern congressmen were routinely appointed to head the subcommittees charged with overseeing District affairs, a pattern that reflected upon the unmatched seniority southerners accrued through noncompetitive elections in the voter-suppressed south, and, too, the willingness of these southern congressmen to undertake a committee assignment that held little immediate reward for their own constituents – except, of course, those who took satisfaction in seeing a segregationist agenda dictate life in the nation's capital.

But overseeing DC's business was more than just incidentally gratifying for these legislators. Southern committee chairmen countered the civil rights agenda of the Truman administration and the increasing stridency of the black freedom movement by positing another agenda, and another image, using Washington, DC, as their stage: that of the propensity of black males toward crime, and the need for a strong punishment regime to check them. In this, sensationalized media accounts of crime or the periodic "discovery" of slums in DC gave credibility to congressional pronouncements that Washington was unsafe. "We've reached the point where it is risky for women and girls to be on the streets after dusk," Congressman Davis concluded in 1950, a time when DC's crime rate was one of the lowest of any major city in the country.[11] A *Washington Post* story of that same year declared that while the capital should be "America

---

[9] For more on civil rights activism throughout the north, see Thomas Sugrue, *Sweet Land of Liberty: The Forgotten Struggle for Civil Rights in the North* (New York: Random House, 2009).

[10] "Racial Order to Firemen Perils [sic] City," *Washington Post*, October 7, 1951, p. M1.

[11] As quoted in "Terror in Washington," *Washington Post*, June 18, 1950, p. B1.

in its Sunday best," it was besieged by crime instead, an appraisal the newspaper offered under the headline "Terror in Washington."[12]

The task of extending this rhetoric into policy fell to one of Congress's most powerful members, also from the southern delegation: Hale Boggs of Louisiana, a close but not unquestioning ally of Commissioner Anslinger. As a member of the House Ways and Means Committee, Boggs chaired the Subcommittee on Narcotics – an institutional assignment premised on the fact that narcotics were still regulated through a revenue measure, the Harrison Act, and hence would be monitored by a delegation from the taxing and appropriations committee. His colleague, James Davis of Georgia, chaired the subcommittee assigned to oversee the District's law enforcement issues. In a symbiotic fashion, the southern delegation put forward criminal justice reforms for the District that then eased the adoption of the same tactics in narcotic enforcement. At the same time, increased punishment at the federal level for narcotic infractions had an immediate and disproportionate impact on the criminal justice system of the District because of its anomalous jurisdictional structure. As the narcotic regime underwent significant revision in the 1950s, embracing in legislation the punishment ethos that had guided narcotic commissioner Anslinger's direction of the Bureau, DC played host to those changes – and foretold their consequences.

The prominence accorded to the District by Congress derived from obvious sources – white segregationists engaged in a project of social control over disempowered blacks – but it had less obvious impulses as well. In response to the enormous increase in illicit drug use in postwar America, Anslinger strove to depict illegal narcotic use as distinctly an urban phenomenon engaged in by African Americans or other similarly marginalized groups. In narrowing the identity and geography of addiction, he hoped to link it more explicitly with criminality. Like other legislators, Congressman Boggs readily helped to forge that link.

But it was one thing to do so rhetorically, and another to do it in fact. Three pillars of criminal justice reform, often simply presumed to emanate naturally from a punishment ethos, are instead better understood as measures undertaken to cajole a somewhat unwilling criminal justice system into processing and imprisoning greater and greater numbers of drug offenders. All three were either pioneered or put into widespread use in the early 1950s: asset forfeiture, presumption of guilt, and mandatory

[12] Ibid.

minimum sentencing.[13] The ability of law enforcement to confiscate assets seized in drug arrests – and realize some of the value of those assets – induced reluctant police to make drug arrests; the legal presumption of guilt of those possessing narcotics (rather than the state's burden to prove guilt) took away a judge's or jury's room for plausible doubt while weighing conviction; and the mandate to commit a convicted offender to a certain amount of time in prison sent an offender to serve a sentence, even if this option made little sense to judge or jury.

Each of these reforms was an affront to the common law tradition and the conservative temperament that sustained its values long after the common law's demise: innocent until proven guilty, restrained state power, and particularized judgment over universal codes.[14] Yet it was social conservatives who ushered in these radical changes. Significantly, these transformations were not sweeping but only selectively realized and pursuant to one another: arrests depended upon enforcement strategies, and applicable charges depended upon the particular drug and the amount seized. Thus, the criminal statutory reforms of the 1950s followed closely the discursive construct of the Bureau of Narcotics: punishment and, indeed, a powerful penal state, were devised so as to apply almost exclusively to marginalized illicit narcotic users in the city.

By far the most important reform engineered in the early 1950s was the enactment of mandatory minimum sentencing. Not surprisingly, the idea was first put forward by a southerner, the District Subcommittee Chairman Davis, who felt that attaching mandatory minimums to a series of offenses would help to deter the crime wave that he and others believed engulfed the District. Yet, despite the hysteria, some congressional members signaled trepidation regarding the idea. Congressman A. L. Miller, Republican of Nebraska, allowed that although "the District Commissioners are not even able to change the name of a street without coming to Congress," and while the District subcommittee had busied themselves with legislation concerning "the barbers, the undertakers, and the chiropractors, and all of the other things that you might have to

[13] "No Knock" searches became associated with the drug war at a later stage (1970); as noted in an unsigned piece in the *Journal of Criminology and Police Science*, these searches were explicitly authorized in the District of Columbia Court Reform and Criminal Procedure Act of 1970, a move that preceded the tactic's extension to the federal government in the Controlled Substances Act of 1970; see Chapter 5 and "'No Knock' Search and Seizure and the District of Columbia Crime Act: A Constitutional Analysis," *Journal of Criminal Law, Criminology, and Police Science* 62, no. 3 (September 1971): 350–62.

[14] See Roscoe Pound, *The Spirit of the Common Law* (Boston: Marshall Jones Company, 1921).

handle in a city council at home," the House should nevertheless carefully "listen to those who are opposed to [mandatory minimum sentenc-
ing]."[15] Indeed, it was an unprecedented move, as Pennsylvania Democrat
Herman Eberharter, the most outspoken critic of the bill, pointed out.
"We are proposing something to the residents of the District of Columbia
that is not required in any State of the Union," he reminded his colleagues,
adding, "We are attempting, in effect, to use the District of Columbia as a
guinea pig on which to try out a radical departure of new principles."[16]

As Eberharter elaborated upon his objection to the bill, he noted that
"[d]uring all the history of English jurisprudence it has been customary
generally to place in the hands of the court, the judge presiding over the
jury in cases of this kind, discretion," for they are the ones who "listen ...
to all the testimony" and are thus in the best position to "pass sentence
in accordance with those considerations."[17] As custom and as principle,
common law and Anglo jurisprudence abhorred the imposition of a code,
applied with no deliberation or discretion. Such universality was sanctioned by Roman or Napoleonic legal systems and abetted a powerful
central state. The ability to decide each case according to the offender
and *not* the offense separated Anglo law from other legal systems, much
to the pride and satisfaction of its defenders, and limited the ability of
the state's politicians to determine criminal justice outcomes. As advocates pointed out, judging the offender meant weighing previous offenses,
leading to a harsher sentence, and the absence of any generally led to
leniency. Both seemed warranted and just, proponents argued, and both
relied upon judicial discretion.

Democratic Congressman and future senator Harold Smith of Virginia
responded to these solemn objections by invoking the crime that the
southern delegation insisted terrorized Washington, contending that "no
one can feel safe in his house at night." Besides, "judges do not make the
law," he tossed off, "the judges are to carry out the law that you [the leg-
islature] make."[18] In this formulation, the traditional discretion belonging
to judges was recast as a usurpation of power that obstructed the will of

---

[15] Remarks of Miller of Nebraska, *Congressional Record – House*, 82nd Congress, June 5,
1951, p. 6167.
[16] Remarks of Eberharter of Pennsylvania, *Congressional Record – House*, 82nd Congress,
June 5, 1951, p. 6168.
[17] Remarks of Eberharter, *Congressional Record – House*, June 5, 1951, 82nd Congress,
p. 6170.
[18] Remarks of Smith, *Congressional Record – House*, June 5, 1951, 82nd Congress,
p. 6170.

the legislature. Judges had always consulted the sentencing parameters set out in the criminal code, and these parameters had always been determined by the state legislature or, for federal crimes, the Congress. While a judge might parole an offender or suspend a sentence, this too was within his normal power. Indeed, American judges in the early 1950s acted in the same way that judges had acted since the country's founding. But, in order to make this bold incursion of legislative power into the judicial branch more palatable, Smith insisted that it was the judges who acted peremptorily.

The House version of the District crime bill passed handily, despite the reservations aired in the debate. The Senate chose to put the bill to one side and conduct a thorough investigation of crime in the District. As they worked, another House committee put forward the idea of mandatory minimum sentencing once again – this time, it was Hale Boggs's Narcotic Subcommittee, and the legislation was designed to provide a mandatory minimum sentence for all repeat federal narcotic offenders. Early testimony before the subcommittee from Bureau of Narcotic officials revealed their support for mandatory minimum sentencing, as did the various statements proclaiming the effectiveness of mandatory minimums and harsh sentencing issued by Commissioner Anslinger in the press. These proclamations often took the efficacy of an enforcement approach for granted. Before a friendly Boggs committee, Bureau officials went on at length, extolling the work of their own agents by citing seven-day-a-week job performance and a tireless work ethic. But, in the face of an obvious increase in traffic in illicit drugs, legislators probed other parts of the criminal justice system, searching for a weak link. Just as Congressman Smith had done, they conveniently located it in the judiciary, a branch silenced by professional norms and barred from most political discussions. "The need for [mandatory sentencing] grows out of the fact that the Federal judges are not doing their duty," Congressman Harrison announced during the hearings, an emphatic declaration of the suspicions his other colleagues harbored but generally preferred to state more obliquely.[19]

Harrison was not alone in his bluntness, however. One witness called before the Boggs Committee went so far as to suggest a "collusion

[19] Congressman Harrison, "Control of Narcotics, Marihuana, and Barbiturates," hearings before a Subcommittee of the Committee on Ways and Means, U.S. House of Representatives, Eighty-second Congress, on H. R. 3490 ... and H. R. 348 ... April 7, 14, and 17, 1951, p.69; Hereafter, "Control."

between judicial officers and drug peddlers or addicts," a subversion of justice she felt would be broken only by passing mandatory minimum sentencing.[20] In a prepared statement, Bureau official M. L. Harney justified his agency's interest in mandatory minimum sentencing by linking it to the prevalence of traffic: the dope peddler "calculates risks exactly ... He knows the quality and amount of the narcotic law enforcement in the community; he knows whether narcotic cases move promptly on the criminal calendar or are stagnated for months; he knows the quality of prosecution; above all, he knows what is the likely payoff in the way of a sentence."[21]

Congressman Harrison took this theory to its logical conclusion. "Where are the areas in which [dealers] concentrate?" he asked Deputy Commissioner Cunningham. "The southern district of New York – Manhattan," Cunningham replied. "Can you give me the names of the judges in the Federal courts in the southern district of New York," Harrison requested, quite logically.[22] If the problem was one of a pattern of lenient sentencing, it would make sense to locate the specific judges responsible for it. Chairman Boggs interjected, "What about the District of Columbia?" "Well, they have been uniformly weak," Cunningham complained.[23] As Congressman Harrison chased names and hard numbers, Boggs cautioned against this approach. "You would probably find that these sentences differ from one judge and another and from year to year," he speculated, "and the question is whether or not you want to criticize the judiciary or the law. The law makes it a discretionary matter now."[24] This deft evasion thwarted a systematic review of sentencing – one that would have certainly found variation, as Hale Boggs predicted, and one that also would have contradicted the Bureau's most assured claims. Fond of citing Baltimore as a city of tough sentencing, and its beltway neighbor, DC, as a place of tremendous leniency, narcotic officials claimed that heroin had virtually disappeared from Baltimore as a result. Not only was this startling assertion easily rebutted on the Baltimore end, the Bureau's contention also erred factually in DC, where, as was discovered months later, judges handed down harsher sentencing than other cities in the region and maintained a sentencing average well above the national norm.

[20] Elizabeth A. Smart, National Woman's Christian Temperance Union, "Control," p. 119.
[21] M. L. Harney, "Control," p. 71.
[22] Exchange in "Control," p. 75.
[23] Ibid.
[24] Ibid., p. 76.

Thus, in the first sustained congressional discussion of mandatory sentencing legislation, actual sentencing practices figured little in the debate. Anecdotal evidence was summoned by the Bureau and by supportive legislators to denounce the practice of leniency, but, in response to any focused question regarding particular judges or specific patterns, these same officials declined to pursue the matter, presenting their reluctance as an effort to spare the judiciary of such an embarrassing review. To the extent that numbers or facts were put forward at all, they were to do with recidivist or repeat offender rates.[25] The Bureau of Prisons had found, for example, that in 1950, most inmates serving time for a narcotic offense had served time for the same offense before. Of 1,481 inmates, 63.6 percent had a previous narcotic conviction.[26] It is interesting how, then and now, recidivist rates are read as a failure of select components of the criminal justice system, rather than as a failure of the punishment and incarceration approach itself.[27] That is, legislators who reviewed the Bureau of Prisons' findings held lenient sentencing responsible for recidivism, presumably operating on the assumption that had an earlier conviction resulted in a longer sentence, the offender would be either unavailable to commit a future offense (or "incapacitated") or duly chastened by a punishment of such "hard time." A third possibility, that the incentives to peddle drugs outweighed the risks, no matter how formidable, did not occur to legislators – likely because they could not imagine a field of action constrained by addiction, poverty, or previous felony conviction, all of which rendered drug dealing more appealing for lack of realistic alternatives.

While actual sentencing practices did not figure greatly into the discussion of mandatory minimums, both the discourse of public health in

---

[25] A sentencing chart offered by the Administrative Office of United States Courts was tacked on to the end of one hearing session; it passed without comment. See "Control," p. 109. The chart not only showed stern sentencing from District judges; it indicated an average of 21.9 months – almost two years – as a sentence, a very long way from the "two or three" month sentences that proponents of the Boggs Bill complained about.

[26] Study reported in Statement of Julian Simpson, Attorney, Criminal Division, Department of Justice, "Control," p. 77.

[27] Sociologist David Garland, a leading analyst of the criminal justice system, distinguishes between policymakers' sense of "implementation failure," or a perception of a particular node of the institutional criminal justice framework in need of reinforcement or revision, and "theory-failure," which he sees as the discrediting of the institutional criminal justice framework as evidenced by a focus on private partnerships, prevention and community self-policing, and the almost complete abandonment of the rehabilitation ideal. See Garland, *The Culture of Control: Crime and Social Order in Contemporary Society* (Chicago: University of Chicago Press, 2001), p. 20.

general and the metaphor of contagion in particular played a much larger role. To be sure, communicable disease had an established and haunting place in the American imagination: since the yellow fever epidemics of colonial times, cities in particular struggled against vicious germs bred by unsanitary conditions and spread by close quarters. Periodic epidemics enhanced the regulatory powers of local government, as historian William Novak has noted, and in fact many of the earliest city incorporation charters were forged out of a common fear of exposure to disease.[28] Yet even these recurring and demoralizing encounters with epidemics did not compare to the devastation wrought by the influenza pandemic of 1918. As measured against the losses of World War I, the flu that spread the final year of that conflict unleashed staggering devastation, killing upwards of 40 million people worldwide – including close to 700,000 Americans, far more than the losses sustained by combat forces during the war.[29] Leaving no American family untouched or unaffected, the trauma of the flu pandemic cut a deep impression on the national imagination. Not surprisingly, the metaphor of contagion, including its pathology, potency, and coping mechanisms, entered commonplace discourse, even when the comparison was imperfect. Venereal disease, for instance, was often discussed in terms of a contagion in need of quarantine, even though sexually transmitted disease could not really be likened to a contagion that alighted indiscriminately and afflicted randomly.[30]

Capitalizing on the fears aroused by epidemics – as well as the government powers authorized in response to them – narcotics officials and

---

[28] William J. Novak, *The People's Welfare: Law and Regulation in 19th Century America* (Chapel Hill: University of North Carolina Press, 1996). For the ways in which ethnicity shaped and exacerbated fears of contagion, see Nayan Shah, *Contagious Divides: Epidemics and Race in San Francisco's Chinatown* (Berkeley: University of California Press, 2001); Alan Kraut, *Silent Travelers: Germs, Genes, and the Immigrant Menace* (Baltimore: Johns Hopkins University Press, 1995); Roberts Samuel Kelton, Jr., *Infectious Fear: Politics, Disease, and the Health Effects of Segregation* (Chapel Hill: University of North Carolina Press, 2009).

[29] For a popular account, see Gina Kolata, *Flu: The Story of the Great Influenza Pandemic* (New York: Touchstone, 2001).

[30] Still unsurpassed in its account of the history of the reaction to venereal disease is Allan M. Brandt, *No Magic Bullet: A Social History of Venereal Disease in the United States* (New York: Oxford University Press, 1987). Fears about the spread of venereal disease played a prominent role in predictions regarding the aftermath of a nuclear bomb, an anxiety predicated on conjectural loosening of sexual mores in the wake of widespread devastation: see Dee Garrison, "Our Skirts Gave Them Courage: The Civil Defense Protest Movement in New York City, 1955–1961," in *Not June Cleaver: Women and Gender in Postwar America, 1945–1960*, Joanne Meyerowitz, ed. (Philadelphia: Temple University Press, 1994): 201–28.

their supporters regularly applied the metaphor to describe drug use, especially when referring to mandatory minimum sentencing as a kind of "quarantine."[31] Before the Boggs Committee, Congressman Sidney Yates cited the story of one teenager addicted to heroin, vowing to "mak[e] sure that the men and women who furnished" the youngster with drugs would be "properly quarantined from the rest of society."[32] Commissioner Anslinger went one step further and sought to reify the comparison of narcotic use to contagion in explicit terms: "Cities should adopt an ordinance," he wrote in 1951, "which would class drug addiction as a communicable disease and require compulsory treatment."[33] Treatment, as Anslinger and his colleagues would have it, was "taking the cure" (forced withdrawal) in jails or, if mandatory sentencing passed the Congress, in prisons. "We have laws requiring quarantine for smallpox victims, lepers, and for venereal disease," the commissioner pointed out, adding that "[i]t is far more important to isolate the drug addict."[34] Significantly, "treatment," as used by the commissioner, was not an attempt to heal the sick but rather, as was true of other "quarantines," an attempt to preserve the health of the unaffected and assuage public anxiety.

This inventive use of the metaphor of epidemic coincided and had much in common with the emerging discourse used to describe the Cold War rivalry – and, like its counterpart, "contagious" understandings of communism were used to authorize new kinds of government power in order to "contain" the threat.[35] In both national security and crime discourse, policymakers faced with radical departures from previous practice – indeed, from revered political tradition – chose to cast U.S. state power as reactive and reluctant, a restrained and necessary response to an encroaching threat. Sociologist David Garland suggests that this narrative

---

[31] As Margaret Humphreys argues, quarantines are often more effective at quieting a panic than suppressing the spread of a disease: Humphreys, "No Safe Place: Disease and Panic in American History," *American Literary History* 14, no. 4 (2002): 845–57.

[32] Yates, "Control," p. 43.

[33] Anslinger, "The Federal Narcotic Laws," *Food, Drug, Cosmetic Law Journal* 6, no. 10 (October 1951): 748.

[34] Hearings Before a Subcommittee of the Committee on Appropriations, U.S. House of Representatives, Treasury Department Appropriation Bill for 1953, January 17, 1952, found in Record Group 170, Records of the Drug Enforcement Administration, Office of Enforcement Policy Classified Subject Files, 1932–1967, *NARA*, Box 12.

[35] Epidemics and contagion metaphors were not restricted to conservative viewpoints: political scientist James A. Morone notes Democratic presidential nominee Franklin Roosevelt used the image of "epidemic" to describe poverty and the legitimacy of a government response to prevent its spread. See Morone, *Hellfire Nation: The Politics of Sin in American History* (New Haven: Yale University Press, 2003), p. 19.

power is the very appeal of "crime control strategies," which, after all, "are not adopted because they are known to solve problems." Rather, they gain adherents "because they characterize problems and identify solutions in ways that fit with the dominant culture and the power structure upon which it rests."[36] In the case of the American experience, it would be more accurate to suggest that successful policy frameworks not only help to overcome scruples regarding the appropriate scope of government power, they often also discount or delimit some more aggressive plan for state action also under consideration.

This was true in the case of the Truman administration's adoption of containment, meant to present a militant front to the Soviet Union, to be sure, but also designed to quiet the voices calling for a "preemptive" nuclear strike on the Soviet Union, or the still greater chorus calling for Universal Military Training (UMT), the large standing army of peacetime so abhorrent to the American political tradition. The nuclear deterrence underpinning containment policy released the U.S. military from the need to place large numbers of "boots on the ground" in Europe, thus avoiding UMT and the subsequent "garrison state" that its critics feared.[37] Yet nuclear deterrence and containment did in fact spur a kind of militarization of American life by the posture it assumed, the commitments it entailed, and the influence it endowed to the military-industrial complex organized to execute its agenda. None of these, however, necessitated a legislative authorization of a powerful central state from the outset. As a narrative frame, "containment" seemed to strike a middle ground, and the ensuing and obvious fallacies of its anti-statist claims could not be predicted at the time of its adoption.

The same is true of mandatory minimum sentencing and the "contagion" rhetoric that helped to legitimize it. Even though the implementation of mandatory sentencing ultimately added thousands upon thousands to the prisons and the "penal state," during the policy's initial hearing, anti-statist strains were not difficult to discern. Congress had earlier voted to reduce the funding for customs officials who, as one congressman pointed

---

[36] Garland, *The Culture of Control*, p. 26. Penal theorists, or those who seek to explain the preference for criminal approaches, have noted the comparative legal advantages of U.S. criminal law and state power; among them, Daniel Richman also adds the important point that a preference for a "weak" central state can generate demand for criminal approaches: see Daniel Richman, "The Demand Side of Overcriminalization – A Celebration of Bill Stuntz," Paper Number 10–234, Public Law and Legal Theory Working Paper Group."

[37] Truman was himself a vocal supporter of UMT. See Hogan, *A Cross of Iron*.

out on the floor, "are there for ... preventing these drugs from coming into the country."[38] Yet, Congress collectively declined to enhance the capacity of Customs, concerned that doing so would obstruct the flow of goods and people in and out of the country. Moreover, at the very same time that the Bureau's officials appeared before Congress to insist on mandatory minimums, they eschewed plans to more closely regulate the illicit trade in barbiturates, claiming, as we shall see, that doing so would require a "tremendous bureaucracy."[39] Additional funds to the Bureau were carefully described as augmentations to Anslinger's "small bureau of 189 agents."[40] Congressman Canfield praised the commissioner's modest claim on government resources, reminding his colleagues on the floor of the House that "there was a period of more than 20 years in which the Bureau of Narcotics sought no increase in its appropriation."[41] "Here is a bureau which has played fair with the Congress and the taxpayer," Canfield concluded; "[t]here was no inclination to maintain an organization for organization's sake. The size of the force was closely adapted to the problem at hand."[42] If the Bureau sought an increase in funds or change in the sentencing laws, then Congress should measure such a request against the fact that it "has the highest number of persons serving time in penitentiaries per officer employed of any federal agency."[43] Summing up this logic, Hale Boggs argued that his mandatory sentencing legislation "will be giving support to Commissioner Anslinger and his small but efficient staff."[44] In this way, a selective and harshly punitive approach spared the American people, and American businesses, from a more "bureaucratic" approach – although, in the end, this preference would lead to its own bureaucratic empire in the penal state. Never empowering a more robust system of surveillance and oversight of the country's trade, and having never wished to, Anslinger and his allies in Congress assigned blame for the influx of illicit drugs into the country to the criminal justice system and what they claimed to be leniency within it.

---

[38] Remarks of Fogarty, *Congressional Record – House*, 82nd Congress, July 16, 1951, p. 8210.
[39] Exchange in "Control," p. 229.
[40] Remarks of Canfield, *Congressional Record – House*, 82nd Congress, June 30, 1951, p. 7545.
[41] Remarks of Canfield, *Congressional Record – House*, 82nd Congress, March 20, 1951, p. 2688.
[42] Ibid.
[43] Ibid.
[44] Remarks of Boggs, *Congressional Record – House*, 82nd Congress, July 16, 1951, p. 8204.

Even in these early discussions, the fact that the efficiency of the Bureau was judged in terms of incarceration rates raised the possibility that the Bureau might be arresting addicts for possession or petty dealing – and, if true, that the Boggs bill would only exacerbate this token effort at law enforcement. When a congressman mentioned this concern during the Boggs hearings, the deputy narcotic commissioner clarified that "[i]t is not an offense to be an addict under federal law."[45] Yet only moments later he added, "it is an offense for an addict or anyone to buy out of an unstamped package."[46] If this seeming contradiction gave legislators any pause, the deputy commissioner quickly dismissed concerns by adding that he and fellow narcotic officials felt that, "with reference to these addicts that roam the streets, they are a problem in that narcotics addiction seems to be contagious."[47]

Yet the prospect of imprisoning those guilty of merely addiction or petty dealing remained, despite the Bureau's deflections. A longstanding legal anomaly instituted under the 1922 Jones-Miller Act declared possession itself to be "prima facie evidence," as Cunningham reminded the legislators in his testimony, and it was up to the carrier of it to "satisfy the jury as to how he obtained the drugs." In other words, anyone found with narcotics was guilty until proven innocent. Knowing this, a small number of congressmen did in fact announce objections to the Boggs bill on the House floor. Congressman Simpson denounced "a mandatory prison sentence for an individual who uses narcotics but in no way distributes them."[48] Boggs responded by pointing out the "prima facie" rule of the Jones-Miller Act, "which has been the law for many, many years," and held to discern "no distinction between possession and peddling."[49] Besides, he added, "the judge can send [an addict] to the Federal institution in Lexington, Kentucky," referring to the U.S. Public Health Service (PHS) hospital designated to treat addiction. Congressman Fogarty dismissed this facile response from Boggs, wondering out loud "how that judge is going to send someone to Lexington when they already have a waiting list of 300 to 400 down there."[50]

---

45 Cunningham, "Control," p. 63.
46 Ibid., p. 64.
47 Ibid.
48 Remarks of Simpson, *Congressional Record – House*, 82nd Congress, July 16, 1951, p. 8205.
49 Remarks of Boggs, *Congressional Record – House*, 82nd Congress, p. 8206.
50 Remarks of Fogarty, *Congressional Record – House*, 82nd Congress, p. 8210.

In all, the most sustained objection to the Boggs bill came forward in a speech by Congressman Celler. His tack differed from other critics: he did not raise the potential cost, nor did he dwell on the incursion into judicial discretion. Instead, he described a spectrum of drug use that extended well beyond the "city" and the marginalized groups Anslinger had insisted represented the principal users of illicit narcotics. "Unfortunate victims of narcotics" defied categorization, Celler observed, adding that "not a few of them are veterans." "Another type of case" common in illicit narcotic use, Celler correctly went on, was "doctors and nurses." "What Congress is doing in this bill is prejudging all of these cases," and Celler meant the term rather precisely.[51] With mandatory sentencing, Congress was not eliminating discretion, but rather relocating it, replacing the discretion normally available to the judge or the jury with legislative discretion in setting the terms of sentencing, and individual police officer discretion in deciding whether and what to charge in an encounter with a suspect. Congressman Simpson, another critic of the Boggs bill, stated as much when he flatly declared that the proposed legislation would "substitute for the discretion of the judge arbitrary and discretionary actions on the part of the arresting officer."[52]

Opponents mounted cogent arguments, but, in the main, the House steered the bill toward an easy victory. Congressman Donovan rallied supporters by reminding them of the District Crime Bill, taken up only weeks prior to the Boggs discussion. "In case there should be any doubt as to the actual position of those who oppose the bill," he chided critics, "I ask the House to jog its memory and remember the position that was taken by some when the District of Columbia bill was before this body not long ago, dealing with the question of mandatory sentences."[53] The opponents were the same in both instances, for the most part, and this seemed reason enough to dismiss their voices. Besides, Commissioner Anslinger promised lawmakers that mandatory minimum sentencing "would just about dry up the traffic" in illicit narcotics.[54] Who could resist such an

---

[51] Remarks of Celler, *Congressional Record – House*, 82nd Congress, p. 8210.

[52] Remarks of Simpson, *Congressional Record – House*, 82nd Congress, p. 8205. The Congressman's prophecy extends to the tremendous discretionary powers now afforded to prosecutors, who can wield mandatory sentencing laws to effectively threaten defendants into a "guilty" plea, vastly reducing the number of cases that go to trial. See Richard A. Oppel, Jr., "Sentencing Shift Gives New Leverage to Prosecutors," *New York Times*, September 25, 2011.

[53] Remarks of Donovan, *Congressional Record – House*, 82nd Congress, p. 8209.

[54] Anslinger testimony before Boggs Committee, quoted in *Congressional Record – House*, 82nd Congress, July 16, 1951, p. 8198.

easy assurance? Not the House of Representatives, which had likewise been informed by the commissioner that illicit narcotics was "limited to the major cities," with "little of it in small cities and rural areas," totally discounting the still-vibrant practice of narcotics diversion.[55] Yet, in the minds of lawmakers, the unprecedented departure from legal custom initiated under the Boggs bill would be focused and effective, or so Congress thought. "We have 180 agents," Anslinger proudly noted in an interview. "It's like using blotting paper on the ocean," he observed in a startling metaphor. "But we catch them," he promised his readers, against insurmountable odds: "the smugglers, the syndicates, the pushers, the wholesalers, and the users. We can catch them. But we can't keep them in."[56] With victory in the House and the Senate for the Boggs bill, Congress had attempted to "keep them in" – with "them" understood more closely in terms of residential area and race than criminal offense. As congressional members filed out of the Capitol, they could easily fix their gaze down North Capitol Street and the city's impoverished second precinct, catching a glimpse of "them" and the world lawmakers intended to reshape.

If the District was to serve as template and exemplar of criminal justice reform, it was in a sense altogether different from what proponents had hoped. The impressive powers delegated to Congress to govern the District's business might have enticed lawmakers into thinking that they controlled the District's fate, but the same forces that influenced the drug trade elsewhere also dominated DC's experience. More than anything else, Washington's drug history in the 1950s exposed the failures endemic to the criminal justice or punitive approach. Yet these failures did not deter supporters, mostly because police enforcement of narcotic laws was not used to control narcotic traffic, but rather to negotiate the terms of policing in predominantly black neighborhoods.

And the District certainly had many of these, though they varied greatly. Reporters investigating crime in the city harped on the second precinct, the arbitrary police map designation that covered what is today downtown and parts of the Shaw neighborhood. The impoverished second was known as "wickedest precinct" to DC residents, thanks to a series of articles that ran under that headline in the *Washington Post* in 1954, and few from outside it ever ventured into the most degraded parts of its territory behind Union Station and up toward Florida Avenue on

---

[55] Interview with Commissioner Anslinger in *US News and World Report*, June 29, 1951, inserted in the *Congressional Record – House*, 82nd Congress, June 26, 1951, p. 7149.
[56] Ibid.

either side of North Capitol Street. As Elliot Liebow put it, the second encompassed "the heart of a Negro slum area," a fact made poignant to observers, Liebow included, when noting the national monuments that were within walking distance, and some, like the U.S. Capitol, that were within sight.[57]

But Shaw also included one of the nation's most illustrious historically black colleges, Howard University, which, throughout the postwar years, boomed with GI Bill enrollments and exuded an atmosphere charged with excitement and defiant pride. And, if Howard students wanted to experience more of the city, they needed only to take the short walk to U Street, one of the nation's premier African American neighborhoods, which hosted black-owned business, jazz hot spots, and theaters.

Ghettos and slums abutted the fabric and institutions of established African American life in Washington, and perhaps the desolate out-skirts discouraged outsiders from exploring these areas too closely. DC's Metropolitan Police Department did not seem overly concerned with life in the second either: they routinely "pocketed," meaning they did not offi-cially report, black on black crime in the worst parts of the area. Though police sometimes chose to record the crime in an unofficial tally – per-haps to be used later when interrogating a suspect for a different crime – the decision to not report a crime officially was tantamount to a decision not to police it. In the eyes of the police, the crime simply did not happen. The police considered this practice of "pocketing" crimes to be natu-ral, as it or similar methods had been practiced for as long as anyone could remember, and the DC commissioner charged with overseeing the police, John Russell Young, officially condoned it, maintaining that his apathy regarding black on black crime in impoverished neighborhoods was shared by the public and most of the press.[58]

When the *Washington Post* exposed the practice of pocketing crime to its readers in 1947, it did so using the standard euphemisms employed to discuss race in the District. The *Post* revealed that, already in 1947, "more than 300" robbery complaints had been placed "in secret files in the Detective Bureau and an additional 300 others recorded in police pre-cinct record books and marked 'hold'."[59] Alluding to a "peculiar psycho-logical attitude toward complainants" in its official report to the Senate, the *Washington Post* treaded carefully in discussing the story, never once

[57] Liebow, *Tally's Corner*, p. 8.
[58] "Police Investigation," *Washington Post*, July 15, 1947, p. 8.
[59] "Police Conceal Crime Reports," *Washington Post*, July 15, 1947, p. 1.

mentioning race or racism.[60] Police Superintendent Robert J. Barrett refused to disavow the practice of pocketing before the Senate hearing held in response to the newspaper's expose, instead admitting that "confidential" files had been used since 1941, and prior to that, "other methods were used."[61] That this statement could be made without any elaboration suggests that his audience understood him quite well. What Barrett meant was that, before 1941, the police employed other methods to deny police services to black residents.

This worked to the advantage of police in two ways: first, by pocketing suppressed knowledge of the extent of crime in the District, keeping crime statistics artificially low. Impressive crime records earned the police a sterling reputation in the eyes of those ignorant of the situation, and it robbed many "home rule" advocates of an important argument. If city services were being managed so superlatively under the current system, what practical reason was there to shift control from Congress to the citizens of DC? Second, and more important, low crime numbers spared police outside scrutiny and review, and this autonomy remained critical to the success of the numerous shakedown rackets conducted by the police. Any observant person who spent time in Shaw knew that the police demanded payoffs from illicit drug dealers and gambling outfits, but even this off-hand knowledge did not do justice to the extent of police corruption under Superintendent Barrett. Only after his departure did citizens learn that, according to one Senate committee, Barrett had run the police force as "ruthlessly as a private army, to serve his friends and harass his enemies."[62] During the time he led the District's police force, Barrett profited from the fact that the use of telephone wiretaps went unregulated, enabling him to order phone taps on those who interested him for political reasons or for possible blackmail. In managing his private empire, he demanded absolute submission from his deputies, at one point initiating a transfer of a police captain who "glared contemptuously" at him.[63] At a time when police corruption was common and commonplace, Barrett maintained an exceptional standing. Not only did police take payments, they provided protection, using their uniforms and marked squad cars as legitimate cover for illegal operations of all kinds.

[60] "Text of *The Post's* Report on Its Police Department Inquiry," *Washington Post*, July 15, 1947, p. B1.
[61] "Police Conceal Crime Reports."
[62] "Neely's Committee Deduces Ex-Chief and Aides Got Graft," *Washington Post*, June 29, 1952, p. M1.
[63] "Richitt Misbehavior Listed in Report," *Washington Post*, March 5, 1950, p. M13.

Yet police autonomy remained largely untouched after the *Post's* expose of pocketing. In 1948, the Metropolitan Police Department (MPD) changed its crime reporting system, including adding a requirement that all aggravated assaults be reported and filed and that crimes such as purse-snatching and pick-pocketing be tabulated as assaults. These changes led to the first of many "bumps" in the crime rate – prompting cries of DC's descent into chaos from southern congressmen – and it was the most significant consequence of the *Post's* series. To be sure, the story may well have raised some skepticism regarding Chief Barrett's leadership and Commissioner Young's oversight, since neither seemed particularly exercised that the Metropolitan Police Department discarded roughly half of all the crime reported to it. Yet such skepticism was by no means widespread. At the time, crime reports of an official sort were relatively new to all of law enforcement. Police considered collection of these data as a mark of professionalization, a voluntary but widely adopted standard initially advanced by the International Association of Chiefs of Police (IACP) throughout the 1920s and given to the Federal Bureau of Investigation in 1930 in order to compile its Uniform Crime Reports.[64] If Washington, DC, had not yet perfected its method of collecting and organizing official data, it was by no means alone.

Police and much of the public were not overly concerned with the practice of pocketing, recognizing without acknowledgment that law enforcement operated under a vague and evolving mandate when it came to policing the city's worst ghettos. In this too, DC was not alone. In the south, post–Reconstruction era efforts at formal policing drew from the region's longstanding practice of using law enforcement as an instrument of social control over black residents. So pronounced were these efforts, in fact, that it is common for historians of policing in the United States to trace the roots of policing in the south to antebellum slave patrols – that is, the vigilante groups formed to capture escaped slaves. In the north, urban police departments gradually embraced a bureaucratic model, often adopting professional practices pioneered out west or in smaller towns, so that by the early twentieth century many urban police forces wore a uniform, staffed their precincts on a twenty-four-hour basis, and hired and promoted at least ostensibly on the basis of performance and

---

[64] Political historians recognize this dynamic as an example of the "associationalism" touted by commerce secretary and President Herbert Hoover: private professional organizations partner with the federal government to produce information-gathering of interest and benefit to all parties.

examinations. In DC, a mid-Atlantic locale with cultural ties to both north and south, the police had not moved decisively toward the more bureaucratic northern model or the more militant southern example. Neglect of slums by police was thus a critical component of this larger dilemma of institutional posture, and it was one that remained unresolved until the police professionalization movement of the 1960s.[65]

In this ambivalent setting, police presence in poor minority neighborhoods was not uncommon, but their purpose in being there could not be assumed. In DC especially, they could be there to collect money or ferry drugs; they could be there on behalf of a business proprietor interested in scaring away loiterers; they could be there to arrest a suspect who normally preyed upon marginalized victims, but who had recently ventured on to victims with more status. Any number of things could bring a police squad car to the slums of the city's second precinct; practically none involved keeping the neighborhood safe. There was simply no interest or imperative to do so on the part of the police, and this remained the case even after the *Washington Post* exposed the practice of pocketing.

In 1952, two coincident but separately tracked events would change the way the police approached policing in the city's poorest neighborhoods. The first came in response to the celebrated Kefauver crime hearings, when U.S. Attorney General Howard McGrath ordered U.S. attorneys across the country to impanel federal grand juries to investigate local rackets. Charles Irelan, U.S. attorney in charge of the District of Columbia, formed a grand jury in February 1952 and placed his assistant, Thomas Wadden, in charge of the narcotics component of the investigations. Wadden approached the Bureau of Narcotics for help in his investigation, expecting immediate and substantial assistance, since the Bureau shared enforcement duties for the District with the Metropolitan Police Department. He received one young and relatively inexperienced narcotics agent instead. Determined to make the best of it, Wadden set about "the destruction," as he put it, "of Washington's vicious, hydra-headed, multi-million dollar narcotic monster."[66]

Only months before, Senator Alexander Wiley called for a congressional investigation into District crime. Wiley, a Kefauver Commission member, clearly saw an opportunity to expose major illicit operations in DC, as well as suspected police connivance and complicity in those

---

[65] See Chapter 5.
[66] Thomas A. Wadden, Jr., with Thomas Drake Durrance, "We Put the Heat on Washington Dope Peddlers," *Saturday Evening Post*, October 1953, p. 20.

operations. Not surprisingly, Police Superintendent Barrett was cool to the idea, and for several weeks, the Senate did nothing. Then, upon receipt of the House's District Crime Bill calling for mandatory minimum sentencing, the Senate convened a committee to investigate crime in the District so that members could consider the House proposal in a more informed light. By the time the Senate decided to proceed in this fashion, Irelan had already seated his grand jury. Though there was no "conscious rivalry," as Irelan assured reporters when he learned of the Senate investigation, the U.S. Attorney must have harbored some doubts on that score.[67]

Such doubts proved justified before long: it was the Senate Committee, not Irelan's grand jury, that produced the first groundbreaking results. Senate investigators quickly narrowed their focus to Barrett's police lieutenant, H. H. Carper, head of the narcotic squad. On the eve of Carper's testimony, the committee's counsel held his cards close to his chest by explaining that Carper's appearance represented a natural progression in the committee's work: "as head of the narcotics squad ... he is the logical man" to call in for an interview, he told reporters. On March 17, 1952, the day of Carper's appearance before the committee finally arrived, notwithstanding the distracting reports of the lieutenant's ill health and recent hospitalization. Two local television stations carried the program live, and radio station WMAL agreed to rebroadcast the interview in the primetime evening hours. As with the Kefauver hearings, an air of anticipation buzzed around the committee room. Senators confronted Carper with his own financial records and asked him to explain the more than $4,000 in deposits to one of his checking accounts; Carper claimed that he could not recollect making them. Senator Neely remarked that he found such a lapse in memory to be highly suspicious, and then blurted, "Lieutenant, I am going to probably break the injunction of secrecy, but I think I should tell you that in executive session this committee will hear evidence of payment after payment of cash that was made to you by dope peddlers for protection."[68]

This astonishing accusation shocked some viewers, but not others. For many black DC residents, the remarkable thing about the Carper testimony was not police corruption but the willingness to discuss it publicly. One African American lawyer interviewed along with a dozen fellow DC

---

[67] Quote from "Senators Decide to Proceed Now with Inquiry Into Narcotics Racket," *Washington Post*, March 13, 1952, p. B1.

[68] As quoted in "Irelan Says He'll Launch Immediate Investigation," *Washington Post*, March 18, 1952, p. 1.

residents admitted that the "hearings brought to light what a large segment of the population has known all along," undoubtedly a reference to the fact that police corruption was common knowledge among the city's black population.[69] On the other hand, those without such knowledge were shocked, some openly professing their disbelief.[70] Yet even those deeply skeptical of Neely's charges had plenty to be disturbed about: the red-faced Carper admitted to personally disposing of seized narcotics, often opting to "flush them down the toilet" of police headquarters. Senate investigators ticked off a list of suspected narcotic peddlers, using their colorful nicknames like "Peter the Rabbit," or "Daddy Twine," and demanded that Carper estimate their relative importance in the DC dope traffic. The lieutenant shunned the exercise, and without any official record of seizures – most of which, according to Carper, went down the drain – the committee could not directly challenge Carper's dismissals of these men as mere peddlers.[71]

Senator Neely's shocking charges against Carper were vindicated the very next day, when the imprisoned dope peddler James "Jim Yellow" Roberts appeared before the senators. The calm demeanor and saturnine face of Roberts presented Senate investigators and the general public with a picture of a thoughtful, if not remorseful, man, as he quietly told the story of his history of dealing in illicit drugs and his interactions with DC's narcotic squad during that time. From 1947 to 1949, Lieutenant Carper received $18,000 to $20,000 in payoffs, Roberts revealed, always tendered in small bills, and always paid on the first of the month, often by wrapping cash in a newspaper and dropping it in a squad car. He stunned his listeners when he related that one time, Carper picked up a package of drugs from National Airport and delivered it directly to Roberts's home. But Carper did not simply betray his duty as sworn officer – he betrayed others as well, showing Roberts pictures of police informants and keeping him apprised of police investigations. For these services, Roberts was charged extra, and his thriving business in heroin dealing bankrolled a similarly flourishing industry of police shakedowns. Yet Carper could not control the Federal Bureau of Narcotics, which, as Carper warned

---

[69] Aubrey Robinson quoted in "Additional Comment on Narcotics Inquiry," *Washington Post*, March 24, 1952, p. B2.

[70] Howard Hardy, "Additional Comment on Narcotics Inquiry," *Washington Post*, March 24, 1952, p. B2.

[71] This was a refrain that Carper had long invoked to explain his low arrest rate; see, for example, "Jail Terms Curb DC Drug Sales, Police Assert," *Washington Star*, June 15, 1951, Found in Martin Luther King Library [hereafter MLK Library], Washingtoniana Room.

Roberts, was inching his way closer to him. Finally, in 1949, Roberts walked into Bureau headquarters and surrendered.

Interestingly, a month before he testified before the Senate, Roberts had been called before Irelan's special grand jury. He said nothing, fearing police reprisals. Those quick to doubt the word of a convicted dope dealer must have paused when they learned of the special protection given to Roberts and other witnesses who testified against the police; "Bucklejaws" Johnson had two detectives assigned to keep "constant guard" on him after he followed Roberts as a witness.[72] In total, four witnesses took an oath before the Senate in order to share the sordid details of police corruption. Barrett suspended Carper from active duty and awaited charges – which, after all, could very well have included him. Over a relatively short period of time in mid-March of 1952, the Senate Committee successfully collected a set of jaw-dropping testimonials.

It was to be the Committee's major contribution to illuminating the world of illicit narcotic dealing in DC. From then on, the special grand jury took the lead in making headlines. Reporters planted outside the grand jury hearing room attempted to surmise the proceedings based on identifying faces in the parade of witnesses that marched in and out. A month before the Carper scandal broke, Irelan and his chief assistant Thomas Wadden called in agents from the Federal Bureau of Narcotics. By the end of February, rumors circulated that indictments would be handed down by the grand jury for the biggest dealers in DC. Not to be outdone by the Senate, Irelan pressed forward with his strategy of charging drug dealers in successive rounds, hoping to move closer to major players with each one. As the grand jury issued its indictments, the first signs of strain between it and the Bureau of Narcotics appeared when officials from the agency downplayed the work of the grand jury publicly. These indictments were not "big-time peddlers but street-corner peddlers," Thomas Andrew, Washington chief of the Bureau, informed the press; they were a "thorn in the side of law enforcement."[73]

One day after the Carper testimony in the Senate, Irelan issued a new round of indictments for fourteen suspects; most notable among these was Randolph "Catfish" Turner, reputed leader of the DC's largest organized illicit heroin ring.[74] Over the course of several months, Irelan developed

[72] "Guards Assigned Witnesses in Dope: Death Threats Reported," *Washington Daily News*, March 21, 1952, Found in Martin Luther King Library, Washingtoniana Room.

[73] "23 Arraigned Here in Dope Crackdown," *Washington Post*, January 6, 1952, p. M1.

[74] "Catfish" was one of several DC versions of Bumpy Johnson of New York City, a dealer vilified by authorities but quietly celebrated, if not admired, among African Americans

a case against nine of these defendants, arguing it in court as 1952 came to a close. U.S. Attorney Irelan presented Turner as the real "prize," the suspect whose imprisonment would justify his work. It was a heated trial, with defense lawyers launching accusations of inexperience, targeting Wadden, Irelan's young assistant, in particular. Fuming at the defense counsel's suggestion that he ought to wear rompers, Irelan thundered in his closing argument that the defense counselors were "clowns," prompting them to rise for an objection. "No lawyers are on trial here," the judge interrupted, and instructed the jury to ignore the name-calling.[75]

Shortly after adjournment, the jury returned to file guilty verdicts for six of the other suspects as well as for Randolph Turner, convicted on all counts. The result was heralded by the *Washington Post* as a "smashing climax to the year-long anti-dope crusade waged by United States Attorney Charles M. Irelan."[76] This victory was all the more sweet because Turner had proven to be a worthy adversary, or a "cagey target," as the *Post* put it. The newspaper then launched a series of articles describing Turner's case, including the traps Wadden laid to capture him, a dramatic tale of betrayal that featured a *femme fatale* from within Turner's organization. These articles repeatedly made mention of some material aspect of Turner's lifestyle – whether it was his maroon and cream Cadillac ($4,000) or his $20,000 home in northwest with "downstairs drapes costing $700," and "a television set in the parlor and another in the bedroom."[77] When Wadden later recounted the story of the special grand jury for *The Saturday Evening Post*, he also harped on Turner's consumption habits: "Almost overnight [Turner] developed a penchant for high-priced hats, sixty-dollar slacks, and expensive shirts with 'Cat' monogrammed on the pockets," Wadden scoffed. "He bought a cashmere polo coat for $500," and, adding a new twist to the oft-cited Cadillac purchase, he noted that Turner "picked up an expensive car and a big, black-faced boxer dog."[78] The consistent mention of and the prominence accorded to such details suggest that, in the eyes of mainly white readers, these trappings of an upper-middle-class lifestyle somehow indicted Turner as much as his drug

who relished in his independence and lifestyle. For more on Johnson, see Eric C. Schneider, *Smack: Heroin and the American City* (Philadelphia: University of Pennsylvania Press, 2008), p. 104.

75 "Jury Weighs Fate of Nine in Dope Plot Trial in DC," *Washington Post*, December 12, 1952, p. 1.
76 "Turner and 6 Convicted of All Counts, Jury Frees 2," *Washington Post*, December 13, 1952, p. 1.
77 "Narcotics Peddler's Saga," *Washington Post*, January 5, 1953, p. 1.
78 Wadden, Jr., with Durrance, "We Put the Heat on Washington Dope Peddlers," p. 21.

dealing. Not only was he a despised dope king who made regular payoffs to the police, Turner was a black man who had the effrontery to live stylishly off of his ill-gotten gains.

When it came time for sentencing in the case, the government invoked the newly passed Boggs Act. Turner had no prior convictions, but three of his fellow co-conspirators did; as repeat offenders, they were now subject to mandatory minimum sentences. With this impressive courtroom victory, Irelan and Wadden might have rested on their laurels. Instead, they aired doubts regarding the ultimate benefits of their labor. "The narcotics racket is unique," Wadden told the *Washington Post*, "as soon as one big pusher gets locked up, another one takes his place."[79] Two weeks later, an interview with a self-identified peddler confirmed Wadden's fatalistic view. "Who was peddling junk on the night Catfish was convicted?" a *Post* reporter asked. "Nobody peddling that night," he answered; "There was a panic on the street that night." How long did the panic last? "Almost 24 hours," the peddler shrugged. Wadden was interviewed for the same piece, and while he reiterated his resignation to the flow of illicit narcotics, he also took the time to shatter another conceit of the Bureau of Narcotics. "As it turns out," the young prosecutor confessed, "this group [the Turner ring] consisted primarily of Negroes here ... [but] the narcotic traffic ... knows no racial or geographic boundaries. We have found addiction and peddling among various racial groups and in many parts of Washington."[80]

That Wadden should so boldly contradict the claims of the federal Bureau of Narcotics underscored the tension between the special grand jury and the agency. In point of fact, the Bureau had been the real target of the investigations of the U.S. Attorneys' office all the while – an accusation that Commissioner Anslinger was quick to make, though he did so in personal terms, construing Irelan's embarrassment of the Bureau as a political challenge to his leadership. Such an interpretation suggested a calculated effort, but it seems that, more than anything, the U.S. Attorneys' office stumbled into its suspicions regarding the quality of the work performed by the Bureau. As late as March 1952, at the same time the Senate heard its testimony regarding police corruption, Wadden was willing to go on public record praising the Bureau.[81] But as he called in

[79] "Dope Flow Unabated Here, Wadden Says," *Washington Post*, December 14, 1952, p. M22.
[80] "Beginning of the End," *Washington Post*, January 9, 1953, p. 1.
[81] "Grand Jurors Again to Call Jim Yellow," *Washington Post*, March 20, 1952, p. 1.

witness after witness before the special grand jury, edging his way closer to "Catfish" Turner, he uncovered slip-shod work. Then in May, Wadden and his boss, Charles Irelan, discovered an illicit drug supply connection that came directly from the Treasury Department – in fact, from the Bureau of Narcotics' storage room. As Wadden later told the story to *The Saturday Evening Post*, his boss initially "decided to give the Federal bureau a chance to clean up what appeared to be a mess within its own shop."[82] The agency responded by picking up one of its janitors, Eddie Gregg, and secretly questioning him.

If this interrogation of their suspect by the Bureau aroused any resentment from the U.S. Attorneys' office, they did not harbor it long. Instead, they watched in disbelief as the Bureau chose to release Gregg and deny that any narcotics escaped its storage room, confident in their vault door and lock, and maintaining the validity of repeated declarations that narcotics were weighed and stored "down to the last grain."[83] "So far as the Bureau was concerned at that time," Wadden wrote, "there was no case. Eddie Gregg was all mine."[84] The enterprising lawyer decided to take a field trip with his witness and visit the Bureau's storage room. There, a willing Eddie Gregg demonstrated how he successfully picked the storage room vault with an ordinary string. "The demonstration proves nothing!" shouted Deputy Commissioner Cunningham. The Bureau had "actively hindered" the U.S. Attorneys' office in its investigation, Wadden concluded.[85] The U.S. Attorneys' office forged ahead, but, "while we were preparing our indictments" on the Gregg case, Wadden and his colleagues could not help but notice that "Commissioner Anslinger made public statements which tended to disparage our claims."[86] Upon closer examination and testimony from Bureau agents, Irelan and Wadden learned "that no one in the bureau was capable of telling exactly how much narcotic was in stock at any given moment."[87] Without an accurate ledger, the office was forced to drop the indictments, despite sworn testimony and Gregg's crafty display.

This embarrassing episode irritated the commissioner. It also aroused real suspicion within the U.S. Attorneys' office regarding the quality of the

---

[82] Wadden, Jr., with Durrance, "We Put the Heat on Washington Dope Peddlers," p. 131.
[83] Anslinger quoted in "Addicts Still Buy Dope Here," *Washington Post*, March 27, 1952, p. 3.
[84] Wadden, Jr., with Durrance, "We Put the Heat on Washington Dope Peddlers," p. 134.
[85] Ibid.
[86] Ibid.
[87] Ibid.

work performed by the Bureau. As Irelan and Wadden aired some of these doubts before the special grand jury, they did so in secret; Commissioner Anslinger, however, decided to fight the U.S. Attorneys' office in the public eye. First the commissioner tried to steal the thunder of the special grand jury by initiating his own raid on illicit narcotics in DC. After much fanfare, Wadden wrote in the *Saturday Evening Post*, "the commissioner's commandos were back at base, their nets squirming with a catch of small fry – punks, addicts and errand boys." Wadden's critique of the exercise suggested that the Bureau did not manage to penetrate from the world of addicts and street-corner dealers through to the bigger sources of supply and distribution. Yet, as Wadden recalled, while the "haul was hardly an impressive one," you would not know it from the newspaper headlines the next day, which suggested that "the city had been scoured clean in one magnificent thrust."[88] There could be no mistaking the gist of Wadden's comments: he believed that the Bureau misrepresented itself to the public, claiming an enforcement competence that exaggerated the reach and the relevance of its arrests, and that a gullible press corps chasing sensation headlines was none the wiser, accepting the Bureau's claims at face value.

After months of work, the special grand jury declared in its final report that the Bureau of Narcotics was "lax in its enforcement of the narcotic laws of the District of Columbia."[89] The report detailed the grand jury's criticism of the Bureau's handling of narcotic material, denouncing the Bureau's errors and subsequent attempt to cover up the storeroom thefts. Just as intriguing was the material that went unrecorded in the final version of the special report: one Bureau agent learned from a newspaper reporter covering the special grand jury that its members "had received information that when the US Attorney's Office called for assistance from [the] Bureau, the local men were generally out on special assignment driving the Commissioner or Mrs. Anslinger around on personal business."[90]

The discovery that enforcement officers were enlisted as private errand boys never made it into the final report. But the material that remained attracted plenty of notice, however. The *Post* ran a front page story on the

[88] Ibid.
[89] Federal Grant Jury Report, found in RG 170, Records of the Drug Enforcement Administration, Office of Enforcement Policy Classified Subject Files, 1932–1967, *NARA*, Box 12.
[90] Memorandum signed LWM, January 9, 1953, RG 170, Records of the Drug Enforcement Administration, Office of Enforcement Policy Classified Subjects, 1932–1967, *NARA*, Box 12.

report, which it claimed "slapped at the Federal Bureau of Narcotics for what it called 'antiquated and inadequate' methods of investigation," and, not surprisingly, "record keeping."[91] The war of words escalated months later, when Wadden left his job as assistant U.S. attorney. In an interview given the day before his departure, Wadden again charged the Bureau with slackness and, more serious, he once again alluded to the duplicity of the Bureau's work. Despite the repeated comparisons between sentencing in Baltimore and Washington, he noted, the "sentences here [in DC] are much tougher."[92] This claim called the premise of mandatory minimum sentencing into question: if traffic flourished even where tough sentencing reigned, then it seemed the effect of sentencing on narcotic flows could not be assumed to be directly correlated, despite Bureau assertions to the contrary. In May 1953, Judge Bolitha J. Laws put her agreement with Wadden on the public record: for the past seven years, she noted, sentences for narcotic offenders in the District were above the national average and had been "far stiffer than those meted out" in Baltimore (national average, 37.8 months; DC, 58.3 months).

As Wadden's criticism of the Bureau became public, Anslinger interpreted it as a personal, politically motivated attack on him. "It has come to my attention that members of the office of the US Attorney, Washington DC, are engaged in a smear campaign against the Bureau ... and against you personally," one former employee wrote to Anslinger.[93] "The US Attorney's office in Washington has been conducting an 'antinarcotic' campaign in the newspapers with what appears to be an obvious intent to embarrass Commissioner Harry Anslinger at a critical period," another former employee wrote to Senator Wiley when the special grand jury released its report in January. As Anslinger had almost certainly instructed, the employee continued that "it would be a tragedy if a lame-duck administration succeeded in breaking apart the tough, efficient, and economical Bureau built by Commissioner Anslinger over the past twenty five years in the face of considerable opposition from an administration politically unsympathetic to a Republican Commissioner."[94] The

---

[91] "Jurors Call for Clean-Up of Narcotics Traffic Here," *Washington Post*, January 17, 1953, p. 1.

[92] "Wadden Says Federal Drug Squad Is Lax," *Washington Post*, June 27, 1953, p. 15.

[93] Price Spivey to Anslinger, May 1, 1953, RG 170, Records of the Drug Enforcement Administration, Office of Enforcement Policy Classified Subject Files, 1932–1967, *NARA*, Box 12.

[94] George H. White to Julius Cahn, Administrative Assistant, Senator Alexander Wiley, January 12, 1953, RG 170, Records of the Drug Enforcement Administration, Office of Enforcement Policy Classified Subject Files, 1932–1967, *NARA*, Box 12.

key words used to describe the Bureau evoked the particular institutional features the commissioner hoped to keep most prominent in lawmakers' minds – small, highly skilled, and effective – but the grand jury report and the U.S. Attorneys' office offered a different view: sloppy, out of touch, and deceitful. By depicting the report as a personal and political attack, Anslinger avoided a more systematic institutional review and maintained his hold on power.

Thus the saga of DC's narcotic experience in the early 1950s was a confused and dispiriting affair. Wadden decided to end his account of the special grand jury in the pages of the *Saturday Evening Post* on an upbeat note with the sentencing of Catfish Turner. Readers wrote in with other ideas. "Washingtonians have no voice whatsoever in the conduct of the affairs of their own community," Kenneth P. Armstrong protested in a letter to the editor. "They have no vote. They are governed by the Congress of the United States, which normally is too busy to give much attention to the affairs of the nation's capital, and by three commissioners appointed by the President of the United States."[95] Another reader wrote in to share his view that "the narcotics traffic can only be stopped when the profit has been taken from this vicious, illicit business," and, to accomplish that, "[c]linics or dispensaries should be established in every metropolitan area."[96]

Despite these readers' focus on structural features and enforcement strategies, problems that arose under a punitive approach were generally depicted as problems or failings of a particular person – Lieutenant Carper, for instance, or Police Superintendent Barrett. Likewise, "solutions" were sought in the promise and potential of new people, like Barrett's replacement, Police Superintendent Murray, who reassured DC residents that the firing of Barrett ushered in a new era for DC police; or Carper's replacement, Captain John Barry Layton, "a choir singing cop with a marksman's eye" – and future DC Chief of Police – thought to be incorruptible.[97] When the *Post* reported that Layton "would arrest his grandmother if he caught her jaywalking," the newspaper also took care to record the rise in narcotics arrests as a measure of progress: "In 1950, there were 178 arrests on narcotics charges; 443 in 1951, and 875

---

[95] Kenneth P. Armstrong, Letters to the Editor, *Saturday Evening Post*, November 1953, p. 4.
[96] J. Edward Slavin, Letters to the Editor, *Saturday Evening Post*, November 1953, p. 4.
[97] *Washington Post*, March 25, 1952, found in MLK Library, Washingtoniana Room.

in the first nine months of 1952."[98] The 1951 and 1952 figures were unusually high; as the sense of urgency passed, arrest figures for narcotics dropped to their pre-investigation levels and remained there for the rest of the 1950s.

Layton's squad was consolidated under one vice section of the Metropolitan Police Department, headed by Inspector Clarence Lutz, who signaled he meant business when he dismissed all twelve members of the gambling squad to make room, as he put it, "for new ideas, methods, and faces."[99] Despite even drastic changes in personnel, several problems remained. First, the police continued their practice of under-reporting crime. A former DC police officer acknowledged that "the low rates of crime in the middle 1950s were partly the result of under-reporting by police." Not surprisingly then, "some of the increases in the late 1950s and middle 1960s were the result of improved reporting," which was itself the result of changes in institutional incentives within police management such that the MPD responded to higher rates of crime in a precinct by deploying more resources to it.[100]

As the MPD attempted to clean house in the mid-1950s and beyond, crime was reported as going up in the District, though crime rates fluctuated according to shifts in enforcement strategies and reporting as much as to actual increases in the incidence of crime. As police began to enter into the city's ghettos for enforcement purposes and deploy significant resources to them, crime rates went up on paper. To respond to this "increase" in crime, law enforcement executed more arrests, with illicit narcotic possession ranking behind public drunkenness and loitering arrests as the tools used most often by police. In 1953, District commissioners declared that the mere presence of someone in a "dope den" – not defined, and left at the discretion of the police to designate – without good cause – again, a point left for the police to decide – to be illegal and hence grounds for arrest. The federal "presumption of guilt" in narcotic law now extended, at the city level, simply to being at the wrong place at the wrong time.

---

[98] "DC Crime Curbs Await Congress," *Washington Post*, January 4, 1953, p. B1.

[99] "Lutz Relieves All Members of Gambling Squad," *Washington Star*, December 3, 1951, found in MLK Library, Washingtoniana Room.

[100] Jerry V. Wilson, "The War on Crime in the District of Columbia, 1955–1975," National Institute for Law Enforcement and Criminal Justice Law Enforcement Assistance Administration, U.S. Department of Justice, February 1978, found in MLK Library, Washingtoniana Room [hereafter: Wilson, "War on Crime"].

Naturally, the addicts routinely supplied through the capital's pharmacies escaped such legal vulnerability, despite the fact that occasional investigations continued to find drugstores (and diversion more generally) to be major suppliers of illicit narcotics.[101] Dilaudid, a synthetic opiate, was prescribed for medical purposes, and it was relied upon to supply addicts throughout the decade via pharmacies, joining the more carefully tracked dispensation of naturally derived heroin and morphine. Yet arrest and incarceration rates did not reflect this broader and more diverse use: already by 1955, two thirds of the drug offenders at the Public Health Hospital in Lexington were African Americans in prison for heroin use; as scholar Nancy Campbell notes, "only seven years prior, two thirds had been white."[102] It defies evidence and common sense to suggest that some dramatic transformation in the demography of heroin use had taken place in such a short time; what had changed, rather, was enforcement.

Drug laws, including sentencing changes, targeted toward inner city and minority neighborhoods, were followed by subsequent policy elaborations designed to enhance enforcement in those particular neighborhoods. As urban law enforcement assumed large-scale enforcement duties in poor black neighborhoods for the first time, episodic waves of drug arrests by a narcotics squad became one of the ways in which police announced and understood their presence in those neighborhoods. This was true of inner city neighborhoods, but nowhere else, even though, as assistant to U.S. Attorney Thomas Wadden made a point of observing, illicit drug use extended to all neighborhoods and all ethnic groups.

This expanded police mission to inner city neighborhoods and the illicit drug portfolio exacerbated two problems: police corruption and police brutality. Both existed well before the narcotic reforms of the early 1950s, but these reforms undoubtedly exposed greater and greater numbers of citizens to police corruption and the illegitimate use of force. Corruption in particular is endemic to a punitive approach to narcotics: assigning police officers to enforce narcotic laws means that they are asked routinely to confiscate large amounts of cash or

---

[101] "A close check of Washington drugstores has led police to uncover enough violations by doctors and pharmacists to indicate a number of dope addicts are being supplied with narcotics through legitimate channels, it was learned yesterday," read one newspaper article in 1957. See *Washington Star*, June 23, 1957, found in MLK Library, Washingtoniana Room.

[102] Campbell, *Discovering Addiction*, p. 148.

assets readily convertible into cash that are unaccounted for in regular inventories.[103]

For decades, many police officers understood that taking some personal profit from "vice," be it gambling, illicit drugs, or prostitution, was a legitimate method of augmenting their salary – and, of course, some truly "dirty" cops gravitated toward narcotic enforcement for precisely this reason. Anslinger had an ingenuous, though highly unusual, method for seizing assets for another purpose: in 1950, Congress amended the Depression-era "Vehicle Forfeiture Law" to provide, as Anslinger explained, "for the seizure and forfeiture of vessels, vehicles and aircraft used to transport, carry or convey contraband narcotic drugs or to conceal or possess any such drug whether actually in the vessel." As he observed in 1951, already "an appreciable number of vehicles are seized under this act by the Bureau of Narcotics and forfeited to the United States. After forfeiture, some of these vehicles, as authorized by law, are used in enforcement work in the investigation, detection and arrest of other violators."[104] Thus the whole logic of asset forfeiture was to claim the valuable resources of illicit drug dealers on behalf of the organization – the particular police department or enforcement agency – rather than episodically and erratically (and illegally) claim them for use by the individual police officer. In this way, asset forfeiture at the federal level in the 1950s or at the local level as adopted throughout the 1980s[105] motivated police agencies not just to police illicit drugs, but to do so with less corruption from within their own ranks. After all, confiscating narcotics was always attractive – it was always possible to realize the value of those assets for cash – the question was how to see to it that some of that value would be realized by the police agency in general and not the officers handling the assets only and in particular.

---

[103] It is important to note that corruption can take place under a regulatory approach, and may go well beyond routine diversion of drugs: the Bureau of Narcotics was formed in 1930 in the wake of an IRS scandal where one agent of the Treasury helped a heroin dealer hide his earnings in order to exempt him from federal income taxes. It is an obvious but equally important point that such collaborative schemes are more difficult to execute than police corruption, and much less damaging to the public good.

[104] Anslinger, "The Federal Narcotic Laws," *Food, Drug, Cosmetic Law Journal* 6, no. 10 (October 1951): 746.

[105] See Blumenson and Eva Nilsen, "Policing for Profit: The Drug War's Hidden Economic Agenda," *University of Chicago Law Review* 65, no. 1 (Winter 1998): 50–6, for a discussion of "equitable sharing," or the sharing of the value of drug assets with state and local law enforcement by federal agents, even when only federal agents are involved in the arrest; see also Conclusion.

Yet, in encouraging more narcotics enforcement, law enforcement only increased the opportunities for corruption. Although confined to narcotic squads, local police enforcement of the illicit drug portfolio saw corruption from the very start. Since narcotic units were generally lumped with or under vice squads, the culture of payoffs common to vice filtered through and animated police narcotic enforcement. As one dealer remembered, while working in a "house that dealt in sex, alcohol and drugs" before World War II, police visits to the establishment were conducted only to "come by and pick up their pay-off."[106] As houses of "ill-repute" became harder to sustain after the war, illicit drug dealers moved to their now-familiar pattern of street-dealing, with one dealer testifying that his stake in East Harlem required the payment of "two thousand dollars a month" to the New York Police Department, a figure that ensured that he "couldn't get busted" while dealing within his territory.[107] As police agencies invested more in narcotic squads and planned to enforce the law more forcefully and routinely, the payoffs that accompanied narcotics enforcement grew accordingly.

Police enforcement of illicit narcotics laws also produced a clash between officers and the inner city neighborhoods in which they ventured to provide services for the first time. On the one hand, the police understood themselves to be evolving toward a more professional and accountable model of policing. By 1955, Police Superintendent Murray could claim with some credibility that DC police had been "professionalized." Under Murray, the MPD became a 24-hour police force, a latecomer to this hallmark of a professional squad. He used police trial boards regularly, disciplining and occasionally firing officers who had violated police procedures. He continued to argue for police institutional autonomy, construing the freedom from the control of politicians as a major precondition of a professional force, a credible standard that had much history to support it. On the heels of Barrett's dismissal, Murray testified to the House that the police should be allowed to "clean its own house."[108] "By 1955," one history recounts, "everyone believed that Chief Murray had largely eliminated corruption from the department."[109]

The problem with the discourse of professionalization was that, although popular and persuasive, it gave an incomplete picture of police

---

[106] "Teddy," *Addict Oral Histories*, p. 49.
[107] "Arthur," *Addict Oral Histories*, p. 156.
[108] "Police Setup Can Clean Its Own House," *Washington Post*, March 25, 1952, p. B1.
[109] Wilson, "War on Crime," p. 31.

actions. In the worst parts of the "wickedest" precinct, police operated closer to a model of Barrett's personal army than Murray's professional officers. Institutionally there was no question that Murray enforced discriminatory policies – the NAACP filed suit against him in 1957, and significantly, they added that the segregated police environment "condoned police brutality."[110] In the second district, police used their power of arrest expansively, routinely clearing "loiterers" and vagrants from places of business, even though small groups typically gathered on particular street corners in search of employment.

This militant and capricious approach set the context in which police brutality would be understood within Shaw: just yet another transgression by an arrogant police force. The beatings in and of themselves were bad enough, but community reaction to them depended upon the entire framework within which the police operated and were perceived. At the very moment that Murray claimed to steward a "northern" and more professional force, the second precinct felt the brunt of the "southern" slave patrol. The geographic boundaries of racial residential segregation facilitated this duality, as did the tremendous discrepancies in illicit narcotic enforcement. In this way, the escalation of punishment in the narcotics enforcement agenda of the early 1950s coincided with and shaped police behavior in inner city neighborhoods. With good reason, the police applauded themselves as progressive for venturing to offer services in these areas for the first time, while, with equally good reason, residents in those neighborhoods felt alienated from police, and even oppressed by them.

SYNTHETIC "SEDATION"

At the same time as a statutory and policing framework was constructed to deal with narcotics in the inner city, the country reckoned with an entirely new drug menace involving recently developed synthetic drugs: amphetamines (stimulants) and barbiturates (sedatives). Like the narcotics, doctors relied on these drugs to treat a variety of ailments, and, also like narcotics, some doctors dispensed them with a cavalier disregard for their apparent addictive properties and psychotropic effects. And, just as they had done with narcotics years before, drug companies flooded the market with amphetamines and barbiturates knowing full well that a good portion of their product would be "diverted" to illicit consumption.

[110] Ibid., p. 32.

If morphine and heroin sales before World War II provided any precedent to explain this behavior, then drug manufacturers overproduced in the hopes that profits from illicit sales would allow them to charge less for their licit product, driving out competition. The sad market imperatives guiding the production and sale of addictive drugs reemerged, dictating a story fundamentally similar to that of narcotics.

But this was true only in terms of the dynamics of production and demand. While the market impulses guiding the use of narcotics and addictive synthetics correspond closely, the government response to illicit diversion for these drugs differed markedly. A number of reasons explain the disparity. The development and sale of addictive synthetic drugs in the United States was separated from the regulatory regime in place for narcotics by about thirty years, and much had happened in the interval. Most notably, the Food and Drug Administration (FDA) had promulgated a new distinction between over-the-counter and prescription drugs, including non-narcotic prescription drugs. The ensuing confusion and battles between the FDA and retail pharmacies shaped the regulatory pattern within which amphetamines and barbiturates would be placed and ultimately policed.

But this is an incomplete explanation, at best. Many congressional members themselves did not understand why amphetamines and barbiturates should be handed to the FDA, rather than classified under the Harrison Narcotic Act and given to the Bureau of Narcotics for enforcement. This confusion of legislators is also lost in the other, more scholarly accounts of why the government treated these drugs so differently, an explanation that typically rests on the difference in the economic class and social background of their respective users, including especially their illicit users.[111] While no one can definitively map out the contours of a market purposefully hidden from view, there can be little question that the popular perception of a narcotic addict (black, inner city) differed from that of an amphetamine or barbiturate addict (white, middle class), not least because the U.S. medical profession stood in defiance of the World Health Organization for more than thirty years and refused to class the latter as addicts, but rather as unfortunate victims of a "habit-forming" substance.[112] The medical denial of withdrawal symptoms and physical

[111] David T. Courtwright, *Forces of Habit: Drugs and the Making of the Modern World* (Cambridge: Harvard University Press, 2001).

[112] For a summary of the World Health Organization's position, see New York Academy of Medicine, "Report on Barbiturates," *Public Health Reports* 71, no. 11 (November 1956): 1146.

tolerance evident in any number of heavy amphetamine and barbiturate users supported the tendency to treat them differently from narcotic users, as did the knowledge that many synthetic users, illicit and otherwise, were whites of significant social and economic status. These two tendencies reinforced each other, so much so that it was not surprising to readers of the *Los Angeles Times* to come across the term "sleeping-tablet victims" for barbiturate users who overdosed.[113] No one ever discussed "heroin victims."

Yet this account raises questions as well. First, it perpetuates omissions in and simplifications of the diversity of users of these drugs.[114] Second, it assumes that a consequence – different generalizations about users of these drugs that emerged as the result of different enforcement tactics – was itself a cause. Congressional wrangling over how to regulate these drugs preceded their social stereotyping and enforcement outcomes. While this legislative debate featured race and class dimensions, its determining factors lay elsewhere – namely, in a story of the state. Congress classed amphetamines and barbiturates differently from narcotics because lawmakers were profoundly reluctant to further burden the taxing powers of the federal government at a moment when, for the first time, a majority of Americans paid a federal income tax absent a total war.

Beset by complaints and challenges to the legitimacy of this new and awesome taxing power, Department of Treasury officials pleaded with congressional stewards that the task of policing amphetamines and barbiturates be placed elsewhere. Ultimately, congressional leaders agreed, though only with great reluctance, for they recognized that they were in fact creating a new office in the FDA, the Bureau of Dangerous Drugs, to replicate the work that was already being done in the Treasury's Bureau of Narcotics. This bureaucratic redundancy would be implicitly acknowledged in 1968, when the two Bureaus were removed from their respective "homes" and joined together in the Department of Justice to create the newly christened Bureau of Narcotics and Dangerous Drugs, later renamed the Drug Enforcement Administration. Once united, these different offices trailed different sets of institutional baggage. Whereas the Bureau of Narcotics brought with it a punitive approach forged in the District of Columbia and later exported elsewhere, the FDA held a

---

[113] Estes Kefauver, "Let's Stop Sleeping Pill," *Los Angeles Times*, March 20, 1949, p. C4.

[114] One very important point about these drugs that was true at the time and remains true today is that the millions of people who have a drug dependency actually mix their use of narcotics, synthetics, and alcohol, a point I discuss further in the Conclusion.

regulatory posture that more closely resembled earlier years of Harrison Narcotic Act enforcement. Like its later-day institutional partner, the FDA fashioned the logic and defining features of this approach in the 1950s.

Amphetamines and barbiturates had different pharmacological properties and medical applications. The initial application of amphetamines was to ease pulmonary suffering, especially that brought on by allergies or asthma. Nicolas Rasmussen, author of a comprehensive history of amphetamines, details the aggressive moves made by drug companies in the 1930s as they eagerly secured patents for this chemical synthesized in the laboratory: not only did companies claim medical use for amphetamines to help breathing, they noted its use in treating depression, literally stimulating users into productive activity, and touted its success as a weight-loss drug as well.[115] The more treatment applications drug companies claimed, the more secure their patent. Barbiturates, another product of laboratory experimentation derived from barbituric acid, sedated users, even to the point of anesthetizing them for surgery, one of the drug's first medical uses. Most Americans became familiar with the drug as a sleeping pill or as a treatment for anxiety, including neurotic behavior. It is simple but fundamentally correct to note that these two drugs act in an opposite fashion on the body – and hence, by the mid-1950s, drug companies sold compounds of amphetamine/barbiturates to offset the side effects of the principal drug prescribed. Weight-loss patients who complained of frenetic activity were sedated with barbiturates, for example, and, conversely, insomniacs who felt lethargic received a chemical boost from amphetamines.

The chemical combination of these synthetics reinforced the joining of these two drugs in the public mind, though this was done only belatedly and for reasons other than their pharmacological compatibility. Policymakers and others grouped amphetamines and barbiturates together because they posed similar problems. By the middle of the decade and about ten years into their widespread use by the American public, these new synthetics acquired a kind of public health stigma, as anecdotal and sometimes authoritative evidence of their pernicious effects could no longer be ignored. Initially, public alarm focused only on barbiturates and, as a result, early hearings on addictive synthetics were devoted exclusively to discussing them. By 1955, Congress added amphetamines to its consideration of how to regulate addictive synthetics. Lawmakers by

---

[115] See Nicolas Rasmussen, *On Speed: The Many Lives of Amphetamines* (New York: New York University Press, 2008), esp. chapters 1–2.

and large still struggled with the correct pronunciation of "barbiturates," sometimes confused it with marijuana, and in the main neglected to bring up amphetamines at all, even while considering the drug's fate, a sign that they were perhaps overwhelmed by the obscure technical jargon and "hipster" slang for drugs in equal turns.[116] In his 1955 hearings on "Traffic In and Control of Narcotics, Barbiturates, and Amphetamines," Subcommittee Chairman Hale Boggs forgot to mention amphetamines in his opening remarks describing the purpose of the hearing.

The ignorance that confounded congressional deliberation was in evidence throughout the country as it struggled to come to terms with the implications of addictive synthetics. To make matters more complicated, the country's encounter with these drugs took place without a clear assignment of government regulatory authority. By mid-century, revolutions in medicine, including the advent of synthetic drugs, combined with the growing prestige of doctors made for an impressive medical establishment – but, as historian Nancy Tomes recounts, both drugs and doctors had to compete with a flourishing world of "alternative healers" in what was still a "largely unregulated marketplace."[117] A sick person might go see a doctor, but this was an expensive option; just as likely, she might visit the pharmacy to see what patented medicine promised to treat her symptoms or heal her sickness. This second approach belonged to a long and lively American tradition of self-medication, a widely practiced and occasionally hazardous way of obtaining healthcare. Harmless "snake oil" tonics shared the medicine shelf with more potent formulations, including dangerous or addictive derivations. According to one scholar, these patented medicines "accounted for half of all drug sales" on the eve of the Great Depression.[118] Then, in 1937, disaster struck: the Massengill Company delivered to market a new sulfa drug treatment for sore throats containing an untested solvent, diethylene glycol, known to many today as the chemical name for antifreeze. The toxic solution killed more than a hundred people, including children – and it did so with excruciating pain, described in harrowing detail to readers of newspapers and magazines across the country.

---

[116] See *Subcommittee of the Committee on Ways and Means, House of Representatives, 84th Congress, October, November, December 1955 and January, 1956* (Washington, DC: U.S. Government Printing Office, 1956): 1 [hereafter: Boggs 1955, 1956].

[117] Nancy Tomes, "Merchants of Health: Medicine and Consumer Culture in the United States, 1900–1940," *Journal of American History* 88, no. 2 (September 2001): 524.

[118] See Peter Temin, "The Origin of Compulsory Drug Prescriptions," *Journal of Law and Economics* 22, no. 1 (April 1979): 91.

As the American public reeled from these horrid disclosures, they also learned that under existing statutes, the only crime that the company could be charged with was mislabeling their product; no statutory authority existed to prosecute Massengill for the deaths it had so carelessly caused. Leaders of the Food and Drug Administration who had previously sought an opportunity to clarify and expand their agency's function now seized on this public health disaster. Produced in the wake of the Massengill tragedy, the 1938 Federal Food, Drug, and Cosmetic Act provided for FDA approval before drugs were sold. Yet two related but distinct components of the act seemed to be at odds with each other and, the FDA and others determined, would probably need an authoritative court decision to reconcile them. One section of the act mandated that all drugs be labeled with adequate directions for safe use. Given the countless numbers of people who self-medicated themselves, lawmakers reasoned, they ought to be given directions on how to do so. In regulations issued to guide implementation of the act, the FDA announced an exemption from the labeling requirement for prescription drugs. A separate section of the act allowed drug companies to place a "Warning" label on a drug that was to be sold only by prescription – up until this point, a restriction placed only on narcotic drugs. Economic historian Peter Temin makes clear the dramatic difference the act instituted in pharmacy practice: before the act, he notes, "consumers could get any non-narcotic drug they desired without going to see a doctor."[119] Without any explicit recognition of doing so, the FDA had effectively created a distinction between over-the-counter drugs, which must be labeled for safe use, and prescription drugs, which could not be considered safe unless used under the care of a physician. This second group was much broader than just the narcotics, yet precisely how it should be defined remained unclear.

A legal showdown was not only inevitable but imminent: the nation's powerful and highly organized community of pharmacists felt that the FDA's new position endangered their standard practice of selling any non-narcotic drug to customers without interference. In essence, as Peter Temin again notes, "the FDA had appointed doctors as the consumer's agents in selecting drugs."[120] As expected, the pharmacists searched for an opportunity to take their grievance to court. So too did the FDA, which recognized that bringing the right kind of case before the courts could work in their favor if the verdict sustained their regulatory authority. As

119 Ibid., 98.
120 Ibid.

a result, the FDA cited only egregious cases for violations of the 1938 Act, cases that had, as FDA memoranda often put it, plenty of "background" or "atmosphere." These vague terms referred to details of a case of the sort that would galvanize any judge or jury into siding with the FDA. When regulators cited Sullivan's Pharmacy in Columbus, Georgia, for selling sulfa drugs without the appropriate "Warning" label and without a prescription, they knew the pharmacy in question was surreptitiously repackaging drugs and acting in bad faith. The case and its appeal went all the way to the Supreme Court, finally decided on the 1948 docket in *U.S. v. Sullivan*. When the majority sided with the FDA, officials at the agency must have breathed a collective sigh of relief.

Yet opinions accompanying the ruling raised new concerns, because the Supreme Court did not even weigh in on the question of whether the FDA had the authority to designate certain drugs for sale by prescription only. Instead it discussed whether the government's interstate regulatory powers stretched down to the final (local) sale of the drug, with a majority deciding that it did. Around the time of the *Sullivan* decision, many Americans began to consume barbiturates, which, like sulfa drugs, the FDA determined should be sold by prescription only. Significantly, the demand for barbiturates derived from both medically sanctioned and non-sanctioned purposes. In the midst of unsettled regulatory questions and exploding barbiturate sales, stories began to surface about the drug's potential for addiction and abuse. Already in 1945, the *Saturday Evening Post* reminded readers that "Sleeping Pills Aren't Candy," in the title of one its feature articles.[121] New York City held Board of Health hearings in 1947 to discuss the possibility of curbing barbiturate use, with one doctor offering his view that "a barbiturate addict is just as much a danger to society as the narcotic addict."[122] This comparison would become something of a refrain for the next several years, one that was frequently drawn to convey both the potency of barbiturates and the need for some sort of government regulation.

When manufacturers and pharmacists opposed any attempt to regulate the barbiturate trade, as they did in New York City in 1947, proponents of regulation escalated their rhetoric.[123] By the time New York reconvened hearings on barbiturates in 1951, the *New York Times* framed its

---

[121] March 9, 1945.

[122] "Barbiturate Curb Backed by Doctors," *New York Times*, April 3, 1947, p. 26.

[123] Commissioner Trichter of the New York Board of Health tried "for many years," to have "barbiturate control vested in the Federal Bureau of Narcotics." See "Grave Peril Seen in Sleeping Pills," *New York Times*, December 16, 1951, p. 1.

coverage of the proceedings with the declaration that barbiturates "are more of a menace to society than heroin or morphine."[124] New York Health Commissioner John Mahoney decried barbiturates "as causing a steady increase in human wreckage in this city," a reference both to accidental overdoses and to alarming traffic accidents involving a driver under the influence of sleeping pills. One doctor after another recorded the view that "addiction to sleeping pills is far more dangerous to the patient and to society than is heroin addiction," not least because, as one witness described, users may "be far more aggressive, acting out angers and sex behavior."[125]

The fact that pills were so easy to get, either with a prescription legally or on the black market illicitly, only exacerbated the danger. Though the FDA cited pharmacists for sale of barbiturates without a prescription, there was nothing they could do to prevent "under the counter" sales, as *Time* magazine put it in 1950, which usually took place between a pharmacist and someone they had known for a long time – or else, direct mail sales, unlimited refills on a legitimate prescription, or simply an illicit sale on a street corner. Barbiturate drugs were everywhere. A tragic parade of famous entertainers or local notables died from barbiturate overdose; by 1949, these included actors Carole Landis, Ralph Holmes, and socialites Ellen Wilson McAdoo, granddaughter of President Woodrow Wilson, and Evelyn McLean Reynolds, heiress and teenage bride to Senator Reynolds of North Carolina. That same year, Metropolitan Life Insurance Company reported that barbiturates were the leading cause of accidental poisoning, estimating that upwards of 350 people died per year. Other estimates were steeper, and no one could know for certain. Hospitals did not routinely investigate suicides as suspicious, and it was usually difficult to separate an accidental overdose from a suicide.

Blame, and thus responsibility, seemed to the drug industry and pharmacists to lie exclusively with those who abused barbiturates. One professional journal published an article in 1950 that showed some disdain for what it called "the laity," defined here as anyone who was not a medical professional, and in a resigned fashion the author acknowledged this group as "perpetually alert for means of self-medication."[126] Alarmed public officials did not find much solace in the clerical aloofness of the

[124] Ibid., p. 1.
[125] Ibid.
[126] Unnamed author, "Barbiturate Control," *Food Drug Cosmetic Law Journal*, September 1950: 598.

drug industry and began to search for ways to protect the public from serious harm. The first proposal was a logical one: treat barbiturates like the other known addictive drugs. Though the plan to add barbiturates to the purview of the Harrison Narcotic Act had several backers, the first formal bill proposing to do so was sponsored by Edith Nourse Rogers, Republican of Massachusetts, and hence she became the figure most associated with the idea. It is not obvious why this longtime congresswoman representing the textile area of northeastern Massachusetts remained so committed to barbiturate regulation; it was, perhaps, her devoted attention to veterans' medical issues.[127] Whatever her motivation, she proved a resilient advocate: after consecutive defeats, Rogers altered her bill to mollify critics and re-introduced it.

During the proposal's first serious hearing, considered as HR 348 in the 82nd Congress, Rogers remarked that she "had a bill in for some years."[128] Called up on short notice to testify before the Boggs Subcommittee, she recited her office's estimates on deaths relating to barbiturates: in 1945, 965 deaths, and in 1948, 1,058. The congresswoman's solution was to place barbiturates under the taxing and regulatory powers of the Harrison Act, a move which, she acknowledged, the Treasury Department had opposed. According to her, this was "not that they were against the idea or provisions of the bill," but rather, "they were against it because they did not have the money to enforce it." To rectify that, Rogers had added $1 million for enforcement to her latest version of the bill.[129]

Unfortunately for the congresswoman, her bill came up for consideration at the very moment – indeed, during the very same hearing – as Boggs's proposal for increased penalties in narcotics. Not surprisingly, the committee paid the most attention to their chair's legislative agenda, and the conversation regarding Rogers's bill was desultory and uninformed. Such lack of focus assisted the bill's opponents, including congressional allies of Anslinger's Bureau of Narcotics, in their effort to create confusion surrounding what exactly the bill would accomplish. Congressman Donovan of New York seemed to read directly from a script provided by the Bureau when he echoed almost verbatim Bureau officials' remarks that barbiturates were "strictly a domestic problem of the United States.

[127] Her first remarks on the floor of the House discussing barbiturates mention "nervous veterans" who are taking the drug in excess amounts. See Remarks of Rogers, *Congressional Record – House*, November 26, 1945, Appendix, p. A5091.

[128] Rogers, "Control," p. 3.

[129] Ibid., p. 7.

This whole narcotics traffic, morphine and its derivatives, and marijuana, is the subject of international treaties between the government of the United States and [other nations]. If you try to tack on any bill something that covers barbiturates," he warned, "you will be interfering with the treaties we have with other nations." This thesis was floated in Bureau testimony before the committee as well, and with a gravity that suggested that somehow levying a tax on barbiturates and enforcing it would wreck the entire intricate machinery of international conventions.

Because there was no mandate that signatories to a convention regulate anything other than the substance(s) listed in the convention, the point was a moot one, but a successful diversion. Yet even legislators unfamiliar with the particulars of international conventions recognized something askew and prodded the Bureau to discuss marijuana, a domestic plant, in relation to the Bureau's reluctance to take on barbiturate regulation. In response, Anslinger testified that there is "little interstate traffic" in barbiturates, so federal power was not implicated.[130] This astounding assertion was taken at face value, it seems, by all but Congressman Simpson, who pressed Anslinger further. In his typical straightforward fashion, the congressman wondered, "[w]hy would it be harder to control the production of barbiturates than it is to control the production of marijuana?" Anslinger responded by pointing out that "[w]e do not manufacture marijuana," and insisted that agricultural cultivation was easier to monitor. In fact, Anslinger boldly declared, when it came to marijuana, the Bureau had "practically eradicated illicit production."[131]

With his typical bravado, and his characteristic indifference to the truth, Anslinger turned aside suggestions that his Bureau regulate barbiturates. Boggs's subcommittee moved on to discuss barbiturates with the Food and Drug Administration, quite obviously aware that the agency had placed the drug in the recently invented category of prescription-only non-narcotic drugs. When FDA Commissioner Paul Dunbar appeared before the subcommittee, he noted first of all that his agency had no authority to deal with bootlegging, hence all illicit traffic would be well beyond their capabilities to control. Dunbar then confessed that he had remarked "on some occasions … that I think the narcotic type of control was the answer," but in the face of Anslinger's strident opposition, he no longer advocated such a move – at least not openly. His biggest concern seemed to be the scope of any regulatory regime. Barbiturate

[130] Anslinger, "Control," p. 204.
[131] Exchange in "Control," p. 210.

traffic reached into every city and town in America, and there was simply no federal office equipped to monitor it. Congressman Hale Boggs objected: "You are not saying to us, are you, that it is a problem, it is a very definite problem, it is a serious health problem, and that it is such a big problem that the Congress of the United States cannot do anything about it?" Dunbar backtracked: "I am thinking something in this way, Mr. Chairman, that while a bill like the Rogers bill would give absolute control, it would require the setting up of a tremendous bureaucracy, and there is probably some approach that does not go that far."[132] The general counsel of the FDA recast his superior's objections as having originated in the Bureau of Narcotics. "As I understand it," he reminded legislators, "the trouble with [the Rogers bill] is that it would involve so much record-keeping and so much policing that the Narcotics Bureau says it is impractical."[133] The subcommittee concluded its intermittent examination of barbiturates by viewing in seclusion disturbing films of barbiturate use provided by the Public Health Service hospital in Lexington.[134] When the hearings adjourned, narcotic penalties had been increased, and nothing whatsoever had been done on the issue of regulating barbiturates.

Subcommittee Chairman Hale Boggs had remained somewhat reticent on the subject of barbiturates throughout the hearings. The thorny questions raised by the congresswoman's bill distracted focus from his goal of increasing narcotics sentencing, so Boggs hurried through barbiturate discussions in a way that might lead one to suppose that he was unsympathetic to Rogers's plan. But such was not the case. Instead, Boggs resolved to convene a separate set of hearings devoted exclusively to barbiturate regulation in March 1952, almost a full year after his subcommittee had studied Rogers's proposal.[135] On the first day of that second round of hearings, officials from the FDA sat before the subcommittee members. From their testimony and in a second-hand fashion, Boggs and his colleagues learned one of the most important – though totally neglected – pieces of information that would guide the federal government's prosecution of the modern drug war. William Goodrich, Assistant

<hr>

[132] Ibid., p. 229.
[133] Goodrich, "Control," p. 233.
[134] At this time, Lexington was the leader in research on addiction; researchers assigned to the hospital tested many drugs, barbiturates among them, on behalf of drug companies before the advent of randomized clinical trial requirements (1962). See Campbell, *The Discovery of Addiction*.
[135] Committee on Ways and Means, Hearings, Subcommittee on Narcotics, U.S. House of Representatives, 82nd Congress, March 3, 5, 13, 1952 (Washington, DC: U.S. Government Printing Office, 1952) [hereafter: "Barbiturate Hearing"].

General Counsel for the FDA, understood the legislators' reluctance to place barbiturates in his agency's portfolio, but, he told the subcommittee, "the Bureau of Internal Revenue [later the Internal Revenue Service, or IRS] was against any new tax measures that were primarily regulatory in nature," adding, evidently, that the Department of Treasury felt that it was "such a big job" just collecting revenue. Apparently the legal counsel for the Bureau of Internal Revenue had drawn a sharp distinction between income tax or other direct (payroll) taxes paid to the government for the purpose of funding government operations, and an indirect or excise tax, like the Harrison Narcotic Act, levied on consumption or a particular occupation, and something that was generally not a significant source of money for the government.[136]

Boggs paused to consider the matter more closely. Why should the Bureau of Internal Revenue's preferences dictate policy? Excise and indirect taxes had been a major source of government regulatory power since the country's founding. FDA officials then went on to disclose that the American Medical Association opposed any sort of increased barbiturate regulation whatsoever, part and parcel of their deeper conviction that any government role in medicine represented a dangerous step toward socialized healthcare. The committee's efforts seemed stymied at every turn. Just then Congressman Simpson, perhaps the most engaged legislator on these issues after Boggs, posed a critical question: "Hale," he addressed the chair in an informal fashion, "I am behind the eight ball here. Am I correct that the reason we do not add this [barbiturates] to the current narcotics law is because Mr. Anslinger's people say it could not be enforced?"[137]

This interjection brought a new direction to the proceedings, as congressmen renewed their sense of confusion over why the Bureau of Narcotics should be spared the duty of policing barbiturates and, if they were to be spared, just who would do it in their place. George Larrick, deputy commissioner of the FDA, only added to the mounting frustration when he admitted that, if given the barbiturate portfolio, "we will have to learn techniques that we do not know now."[138] Boggs seized upon this admission: If Congress gave barbiturates to the FDA, then "it seems that we are creating a new bureau to do this job. We could have done the same thing with marijuana," he correctly noted, citing the 1937

[136] For more discussion of sumptuary law, see Chapter 1.
[137] Simspon, "Barbiturate Hearing," p. 10.
[138] Larrick, "Barbiturate Hearing," p. 14.

addition of marijuana to the Harrison Act.[139] Why did marijuana warrant Department of Treasury attention and barbiturates not? "I think we ought to get Mr. Anslinger back up here," the chairman concluded at the end of the day's discussion.

When the next hearing convened two days later, Boggs grouped all of the government officials around one large table and began the proceeding by having a letter from E. H. Foley, acting secretary of the Treasury, read out loud by one of his subordinates, Alfred L. Tennyson, chief counsel of the Bureau of Narcotics. "It is the position of the Treasury Department," Tennyson recited from the copy, "that the Bureau of Internal Revenue, as the tax-collecting agency of the Federal Government, should not have imposed upon it any duties which are not intimately related to the collection of revenues."[140] Boggs addressed the legislative counsel of the Bureau of Internal Revenue in his opening question: "What intimate relation, Mr. Kirby, is there of the collection of revenue with the enforcement of the marijuana statute, for instance?"[141]

It was a point the legislators just could not get their minds around, and for good reason. Perhaps there was a medical reason to class barbiturates separately – but congressmen knew this was not the case, since, as Boggs reminded them, the films they viewed as a committee "showed that [barbiturates] constituted a problem as far as addiction was concerned just as bad as any other narcotic."[142] Perhaps then, there was an institutional reason to class barbiturates separately – and here Boggs showed particular disdain for Anslinger's distinctions between the "importation" of narcotics and production of synthetics, since the addition of domestically produced marijuana to the Harrison Act totally undermined any validity to this point. "[I]f we pass legislation and turn [barbiturates] over to the Federal Security Agency [and the FDA]," the chairman observed to his colleagues at the table, "we are creating another agency for enforcement which is operating substantially in the same field that Mr. Anslinger is operating in," an evidently nonsensical approach.[143]

That the Bureau opposed the addition of barbiturates to its enforcement agenda was an unequivocal and unsurprising fact. Representatives from the agency gathered around Boggs's table continued to cling to Anslinger's importation theory, going so far as to deny the domestic

---

[139] Boggs, "Barbiturate Hearing," p. 14.
[140] Letter published in "Barbiturate Hearing," p. 18.
[141] Boggs, "Barbiturate Hearing," p. 18.
[142] Ibid., p. 19.
[143] Ibid.

production of marijuana, but Boggs, drawing on his experience in his
home state of Louisiana, would have none of it. "Now and then I see a
field" back home, he chided, "that some agent of the Bureau of Narcotics
had gone to and burned it up," the scorched remains of the Bureau's
busy enforcement work.[144] Like before, narcotics representatives dwelled
on the difficulty of regulating the robust market of barbiturates. Boggs
greeted these testimonials with contempt: "It seems to me that what you
people in the Bureau are saying, to be frank with you, is that there is
a problem here and it is a tough one, and you would rather not have
it."[145] "Apparently," the congressman observed, "the reason you do not
want it is because you are afraid you may not do such a good job on
barbiturates."[146] To break the tension building around the table, Boggs
then suggested that all drug enforcement be moved to the Department of
Justice – where it would in fact end up more than ten years later – but
now the room greeted this suggestion as absurd, with the hearing report
recording no response except the notation: "[Laughter]."[147]

Boggs was not alone in his growing impatience with Treasury.
Representative Jenkins elaborated on Boggs's assertion that the department ought to accept taxing and regulatory responsibility for barbiturates
by pointing out the limits of law enforcement. "[T]his confounded stuff,"
a frustrated Jenkins responded to Treasury disclaimers, "this marijuana,
these narcotics and these barbiturates, the average policeman or the FBI
man I say cannot handle. He could not," Jenkins conjectured in an intriguing choice of imagery, "go to some home where some poor old lady takes
this stuff and turns up dead."[148] With the tables turning against them,
Treasury officials requested that the entire hearing go "off the record,"
presumably to allow for a more candid discussion. The exact exchange
that then took place is lost to history, but when the hearing reconvened
again on record, Boggs and his colleagues had suddenly changed their
minds and decided that Treasury would not be burdened with barbiturate
enforcement after all. Just what did Treasury officials say, and why did
they need to say it off record?

While the specifics of the discussion cannot be recovered, any reasonable reconstruction of the confidential exchange between Treasury
administrators and congressional members would focus on the many

[144] Ibid., p. 22.
[145] Ibid., p. 23.
[146] Ibid.
[147] "Hearing on Barbiturates," p. 23.
[148] Jenkins, "Hearing on Bariturates," p. 27.

problems that dogged the Bureau of Internal Revenue at precisely the time Boggs held his roundtable meeting. Congressional investigation of the Bureau exposed instances of corruption, and the unwelcome attention the Bureau received as a result marks a crucial though neglected chapter in American history and state development. Without recovering that history, we cannot understand or appreciate the significance of a pivotal moment in the federal government's enforcement approach to illicit drugs, a moment when some of these substances were delegated to the Bureau of Narcotics, yielding a punitive approach, and others went to the Food and Drug Administration, to be handled under a regulatory regime. Had barbiturates and amphetamines been assigned to the Bureau of Narcotics, it is unlikely that the punishment ethos Commissioner Anslinger encouraged would have been sustained for these newer drugs. A shared home between narcotics and addictive synthetics would have made it difficult, if not impossible, for Anslinger to construct the perception of the "addict" in such narrow terms, to portray traffic in illicit drugs as in the hands of an evil cabal, and to deny that the illicit users of these drugs extended well beyond the numbers of those addicted to them. All had been fictional but foundational conceits the commissioner relied upon to invest more criminal punishment into U.S. narcotic regulation – hence, the institutional separation of narcotics from newer synthetics was a decision of utmost significance.

This division between narcotics and addictive synthetics occurred in order to protect a politically valuable instrument, the federal income tax, and to help to repair the reputation of the Bureau of Internal Revenue charged with collecting it. The decision, insofar as one could call it that, had nothing whatever to do with some laborious examination of different drug properties, or still less the manifest class or racial biases routinely fielded as part of official drug discourse. Rather, lawmakers ultimately agreed to place barbiturates outside the Treasury because there were so many serious problems inside it. Drug regulation, up till now a taxing operation, was the incidental victim of efforts to shore up the political legitimacy of a powerful central state and its most significant revenue generator, the federal income tax.

This legitimacy was gravely imperiled by the time Hale Boggs convened his March 1952 hearings on barbiturates – though, to be sure, problems with Treasury's Bureau of Internal Revenue were a long time in the making. Some of these were masked by the reign of Bureau Commissioner Guy Helvering, who, much like Anslinger or Anslinger's bureaucratic role model J. Edgar Hoover, enjoyed a long tenure in office

(1933–43), dispensing favors and, as a result, cultivating political protection that shielded the Bureau from close inspection. By the time of Helvering's leadership, such inspection was well warranted. Founded in 1862 to collect the first income tax levied to pay for war, the Bureau of Internal Revenue ranked second only to the U.S. Post Office when it came to dispensing patronage – both in the form of jobs and in the form of tax favors. The collectors office was, in particular, "continuously providing patronage to the party in power," according to public administration scholar Clara Penniman.[149] In her study of the Bureau, Penniman provided an indication of the tax collector's public profile by quoting one Chicago lawyer who observed, "[the collector is] a man who would be regularly seen at prize fights."[150] As Penniman deduced, the tax collector, a shrewd local operator, knew "his way around politically" and "would listen sympathetically to requests for delays in tax payments or other tax problems."[151]

The political nuances of tax collection were of less public concern when few Americans paid a federal income tax, as was the case prior to World War II. After the Civil War, the United States rescinded the tax and, when it was constitutionally sanctioned by the Sixteenth Amendment in 1913, only those who earned a great deal were subjected to it.[152] On the eve of World War II, most Americans did not pay the tax; they did not even file forms proving their exemption. All that changed, swiftly and dramatically, with the war. In 1942, all deputy collectors were covered by the Civil Service merit system for the first time, an obvious attempt to induce faith in the fairness of tax collections; in 1943, the government mandated extension of the income tax to everyone with an income of $600 or more, and this tax was to be collected by "withholding at the source," meaning, it would be taken out of an employee's paycheck directly.[153] This astounding expansion of taxing power probably struck most Americans as necessary for the war and in line with precedents set in other conflicts.[154] Remarkably, Secretary of the Treasury Fred Vinson

---

[149] Clara Penniman, "Reorganization and the Internal Revenue Service," *Public Administration Review* 21, no. 3 (Summer 1961): 124.

[150] Ibid.

[151] Ibid.

[152] Interestingly, government reliance upon wealthy peoples' income as a source of federal revenue led many of these well-off citizens to support the repeal of alcohol Prohibition, and hence the return of the excise tax on alcohol as a viable alternative, or so they hoped, to federal income tax.

[153] Penniman, "Reorganization and the Internal Revenue Service," 122.

[154] Which is not to say that paying federal income taxes came "naturally" to Americans: see Carolyn C. Jones, "Creating a Tax Paying Culture, 1940–1952," in *Funding the*

determined that, immediately following the war, "the personal income tax should be the chief source of tax revenue on as broad a base (number of tax payers) as possible."[155]

Here was a striking departure from the past: before World War II, the income tax had been levied *en masse* only in times of war. In peace, the federal income tax had been reserved as a tool to generate revenue from only the very rich. But, as one reporter who wrote a celebratory article of Vinson's peacetime taxing philosophy stated matter-of-factly, "if large revenue must be raised it cannot be had entirely, or even in major part, from the wealthy – there are not enough wealthy people."[156] Debts incurred during war would now have to be paid for many years into the peace. As the Bureau continued to levy the federal income tax, the brisk pace of business strained the fragile agency. As Penniman notes, the weakness of the office, "tolerable perhaps with a prewar 1940 tax return load of 19.2 million," was "a serious strain when the tax return load had grown to 83.8 million in 1945 and continued to grow."[157]

Given the size of the war debt, there was consensus for perpetuating the federal income tax in the postwar, but it was by no means a universal view. It was most definitely the view of Treasury officials and its Bureau of Internal Revenue, however. Committed to the income tax, the "Treasury Frown[ed] on Other Taxes," as one subtitle of a *Wall Street Journal* article from 1947 read.[158] In a direct challenge to the income tax and the powerful central government it funded, some key Republicans launched a series of challenges to Treasury's preference for and increasing dependence upon the income tax. These politicians proposed an alternative, an "excise" tax, a tax on goods (like a whiskey tax, the country's first excise tax)[159] or services (like a value-added tax, or VAT, which extracts money from each stage of the production process and is commonly used throughout Europe). Some proposals, like a service tax, would be new to the United States, but others already had a home in the federal tax portfolio. Government taxed narcotics and marijuana through the instrument of the Harrison Act and its amendments; these were excise taxes, and like many taxes of this kind, they were not designed to generate revenue

Modern American State, 1941–1945 (New York: Cambridge University Press, 1996), pp. 107–47.

[155] "The Man at the Head of the Treasury," *New York Times*, October 14, 1945, p. 16.

[156] Ibid.

[157] Penniman, "Reorganization and the Internal Revenue Service," 122.

[158] W. C. Bryant, "Key Republicans Toss Political Dynamite Into Laps of Leaders: Ask Excise Tax Raise," *Wall Street Journal*, October 21, 1947, p. 5.

[159] The liquor tax was levied by the government of the United States in 1791, inciting the "Whiskey Rebellion" during President Washington's presidency.

but rather to regulate behavior. An alcohol excise tax could be lucrative, however, as could a tobacco tax, and both produced very respectable amounts for the federal government throughout the postwar era. World War II brought a whole regime of new excise taxes, and these were more in the vein of the narcotics tax – that is, they were designed to regulate behavior and limit consumption on frivolous items like mink coats or toiletries. These multiple taxes understandably annoyed consumers once the war ended, and working-class political voices such as the Congress of Industrial Organizations (CIO) called for their end. The same levies irritated businessmen even more, since they considered heavy excises as effective only in suppressing consumption and diminishing demand.

But some Republicans chose to view the situation from the opposite viewpoint, preferring to keep excise taxes in the hopes of weakening the formidable instrument of the federal income tax.[160] As the *Wall Street Journal* reviewed the various proposals put forward by Republicans in 1947, the article reminded readers that all were meant to "pave the way for a big income tax cut."[161] Critics of the proposed shift to reliance on excise taxes were numerous, not least because these excises were unwieldy, hard to calculate, and hard to enforce. As this battle unfolded, Treasury officials made it plain that they considered excise taxes to be "nuisance taxes": difficult to collect and almost never worth the effort of doing so.[162] Despite criticism from some Republicans, consensus on retaining the federal income tax remained strong. Rebuffed from overhauling the tax regime directly, political opponents of the perpetuation of the mass federal income tax turned to their attention to the Treasury Department itself, particularly the Bureau of Revenue.

This move was hastened and perhaps inspired by the first of the so-called Hoover Commissions, blue-ribbon panels chaired by former President Herbert Hoover charged with "reorganizing" the chaos in federal government that followed in the wake of the New Deal and World War II. It was no secret that the conservative Hoover and many of his allies on the commission crafted their proposals to not only make the

---

[160] There is every reason to suppose that here conservatives hoped to revive the tradition of anti-tax politics discussed by David Beito, *Taxpayers in Revolt: Tax Resistance During the Great Depression* (Chapel Hill: University of North Carolina Press, 1989). The foremost historian of taxation, W. Elliot Brownlee, has, in my opinion, overestimated the degree of bipartisan consensus on fiscal policy during the postwar: see Brownlee, *Federal Taxation in America* (New York: Cambridge University Press, 2004), p. 121.

[161] Bryant, "Key Republicans Toss Political Dynamite."

[162] Ibid.

federal government more efficient but also less powerful, narrowing its scope and reducing its operations. In his initial committee release of 1949, Hoover recommended that the Bureau of Narcotics be transferred to the Department of Justice; he was the first and for a long time the only one to suggest the move. The recommendation fell flat, but critics of the Treasury Department recognized a new tack: rather than argue for the merits of one form of taxation over another, they would assess the Bureau of Internal Revenue as a bureaucracy, and a failing one at that. By the beginning of 1950, most congressional Republicans abandoned their "excise tax" agenda, joining Truman in his call for cuts in the excises that irritated consumers and business leaders alike.[163] They began to focus on the Bureau of Internal Revenue instead.

A little more than a year later, Senator Estes Kefauver unearthed some suspicious practices by some tax collectors in his investigations of organized crime. The senator from Tennessee, always attuned to his popular appeal, denounced from his hearing room a tax system that struck him as "tough on the honest citizen and easy on the gangster."[164] This arresting comparison came on the heels of the revelation that some tax collectors on the west coast had formed a "dummy" company made available to racketeers as an investment in exchange for overlooking tax obligations. To follow up on various Kefauver allegations, the House formed a congressional investigation out of the Ways and Means Committee chaired by California Democrat Cecil King. Through this venue, over the course of the next twelve months, "scandal of as yet unknown proportions" in the Bureau, as one reporter surmised in the fall of 1951, was revealed to the American public "piecemeal." As a result, indignation mounted steadily since, as the reporter also noted, "taxes are high and most people are paying them."[165] Various collectors left office either immediately before or after their testimony before the King committee; all told, 166 Bureau of Internal Revenue officials were either expelled or had resigned by March 1952.[166]

Some of these departures came amidst colorful stories and scandalous testimony. Denis Delaney, tax collector for Boston, was ousted long after

---

[163] "Truman Urges 'Improved' Tax System for U.S.," text of message to Congress found in *Chicago Daily Tribune*, January 24, 1950, p. 8.

[164] In William Moore, "Probers Rip US Laxity on Gangster Tax," *Chicago Daily Tribune*, March 28, 1951, p. 1.

[165] George Draper, "Revenue Scandal Is Reaching High," *Washington Post*, September 2, 1951, p. B1.

[166] "US Tax Bureau Soon to Take on New Form," *New York Times*, March 30, 1952, p. E12.

he enjoyed the use of his new Cadillac and two new Chevrolets, all three of which happened to come from a local car dealer in tax trouble.[167] Carefree car rides were the least of Delaney's transgressions. According to testimony, the tax collector performed regular "shakedowns" of taxpayers under investigation. The record of one potential sign of trouble, Delaney's motion to file bankruptcy years earlier, somehow disappeared from the federal court entirely. Another episode involving a tax collector under the patronage of the aging Democratic Senator Kenneth McKellar of Tennessee, Lipe Henslee, revealed the hand of the Bureau of Narcotics in the tax scandals, as well as some of the partisan dynamics in play. The Bureau's participation fit a larger pattern: all of the congressional investigations of the early 1950s, including the anti-communist crusades of Senator Joseph McCarthy, were used by Republicans to clear as much room as possible within various executive agencies, led for twenty years by Democratic presidents and staffed under their power of appointment. The Bureau of Narcotics, a Republican island in the sea of a Democratic Treasury, was only too happy to lend a hand to the efforts to expel Democrats from federal jobs. Lipe Henslee was, Commissioner Anslinger confided to reporters, a drug addict bound to enter into a hospital for treatment. "I have never considered going to [the public hospital in] Lexington, Kentucky," an irate Henslee told the press, "and why Mr. Anslinger felt called upon to make a statement at all I cannot understand."[168] When the Bureau director personally delivered some damaging files on Henslee to an outraged Senator McKellar, the senator tossed them aside and declared the director "unfit to hold public office." In fact, the senator went on in full theatrics, the Bureau's director was "the most despicable man" McKellar ever met; the senator then brandished his cane and threatened to "beat the tar" out of him. His target was in no humor to suffer such insults: "If you were forty years younger," the incensed director retorted, "I'd knock your teeth down your throat."[169]

Clearly the investigations into the Bureau took a toll on the Democratic administration. Internal Revenue officials responded to congressional attack by emphasizing their expanded workload. In the short span of ten years' time, between 1940 and 1950, the Bureau processed ten times as many tax returns. Sympathetic politicians like Congressman Burnside

[167] "Reveal Fired Revenue Aide Had a Record," *Chicago Daily Tribune,* October 23, 1951, p. 1.
[168] "He Didn't Offer Tax Records to Probe: Truman," *Chicago Daily Tribune,* November 16, 1951, p. B13.
[169] "National Affairs: Spoilsman's Threat," *Time Magazine,* November 19, 1951.

concluded that "[f]air-minded men," such as himself, "recognize the great difficulties which the Bureau has had to meet in adjusting its organizational structure to absorb the burden created by the increased tax collections necessary to finance the last war and support the defense effort."[170] Penniman notes just how beleaguered the Bureau felt in the postwar years, when "a sense of impossible task in controlling the work load apparently permeated the organization."[171] Treasury officials tended to view streamlining their operations as a natural and desired outcome of their postwar crisis. For them, streamlining meant jettisoning any business that did not raise meaningful revenue.

Significantly, congressional reports reached the same conclusion, even when steered by the most vociferous of Bureau critics, Congressman Cecil King of California. "It is clear," his Ways and Means Subcommittee concluded, "that any proposal to use the Bureau [of Internal Revenue] as a law enforcement agency must be carefully weighed by both the Congress ... and by the Executive branch." Echoing the sentiments of Treasury officials, the report warned that "the diversion of Bureau enforcement personnel to non-revenue-producing work will have a serious effect on the federal revenues."[172] To underscore the point, the report cited Treasury testimony that chasing alcohol tax violations in particular could "have no result other than to hurt, impede, and confuse the Bureau's principal mission of administrating the internal revenue laws."[173] Enforcement work cost money, and it raised precious little in return.

Streamlining Internal Revenue's functions became an acceptable way for Democrats to answer Republican charges of corruption and, along those lines, President Truman submitted a reorganization plan for the Bureau in January 1952 – a proposal that was under discussion at the very moment Boggs convened his barbiturate review. The reorganization plan increased the number of collectors who fell under civil service, thus eliminating the suspicion of corruption that haunted politically appointed collectors. It also decentralized the Bureau's business and placed the alcohol and tobacco tax in regional offices with no operating responsibility under

[170] Remarks of Burnside, *Congressional Record – House,* January 30, 1952, 82nd Congress, p. 649.
[171] Penniman, "Reorganization and the Internal Revenue Service," p. 129.
[172] *Subcommittee on Administration of Internal Revenue Laws, Report to the Committee on Ways and Means Committee, U.S. House of Representatives* (Washington, DC: U.S. Government Printing Office, 1952): 20.
[173] Ibid., 23.

the District director. As Penniman notes, "the alcohol and tobacco tax … retain[ed] a separateness reminiscent of the old tax-by-tax structure," meaning the excise tax model; Treasury Secretary John Snyder acknowledged as much when discussing the Bureau's reorganization, noting the "semi-segregated status of the alcohol and tobacco tax operations."[174] The only reason Treasury and the president kept it this way, or kept these taxes at all, was owing to the substantial amount of money they raised – and, too, it is important to note that these excises were levied against manufacturers and distilleries directly, not against consumers at the point of purchase, simplifying their collection. Truman's tax reorganization, which eventually went into effect despite conservative opposition,[175] also created a Bureau-wide investigation office, led, interestingly enough, by an important Bureau of Narcotics official, Garland Williams – who was forced to return to Narcotics when embarrassing discrepancies in his income tax returns became known.[176] As a capstone to these reforms, in 1953 the Bureau was rechristened the Internal Revenue Service, a change intended to advertise its new professional footing and citizen-oriented disposition.

While Internal Revenue scandals forced legislators contemplating barbiturate regulation to confront certain political realities, deeper impulses influenced their ultimate decision to move away from excise taxes. The first and most obvious of these was the ascendancy of Keynesian economics.[177] This theory, based on the principles set forth by British economist John Maynard Keynes, stipulated in part that government should spend to counteract economic downturns; for the most part, throughout the 1950s, only Democrats and young economists subscribed to this particular view. On the other hand, a correlate Keynesian supposition, that government ought to tax to suppress inflation, enjoyed widespread acceptance, even to the point of being considered conventional wisdom among both policymakers and the public. One assumption embedded in

---

[174] Penniman, "Reorganization and the Internal Revenue Service," 127. John Snyder, "The Reorganization of the Bureau of Internal Revenue," *Public Administration Review* 12, no. 4 (Autumn 1952): 225.

[175] This opposition came from both southern Democrats and some Republicans. It was framed as concern that the plan did not go far enough, but there is every reason to suspect that concerns ranged well beyond that, including a concern that Republicans were about to lose an important seat of patronage on the eve of a national election in which they expected to win back the White House.

[176] "Tax Aide Resigns, Own Returns Eyed," *New York Times*, November 27, 1953, p. 36.

[177] For more on the shift toward Keynesianism, see Alan Brinkley, *The End of Reform: New Deal Liberalism in Recession and War* (New York: Knopf, 1994).

this view of taxation deserves special attention here: namely, that taxing power was more than simply a tool to raise revenue, it was an instrument to shape the economy. As postwar Keynesian economists teased out the consequences of this assumption, they realized that excise taxes could not be deployed for countercyclical purposes – people buy alcohol or cigarettes regardless of the economic outlook – and, what is more, the businessmen who detested excises were most likely correct in supposing that these taxes discouraged consumption. Believing, as they did, that consumption fueled overall economic growth, Keynesian economists led the call for the repeal of excises.[178] As their numbers grew, the support for excises dwindled, paving the way for cuts throughout the 1950s and, finally, a dramatic withdrawal of the federal government from the excise tax business in 1965.[179]

Yet in one particular place excise taxes remained an appealing option: individual states. This fact was the second and very much overlooked reason why the federal policymakers elected to rely more on direct taxation; state governors and legislatures were eager to get their hands on excises as a source of revenue for themselves. As the federal government assumed more powers in World War II and beyond, it is sometimes suggested or inferred that the individual states enjoyed less. The opposite is the more correct assumption: individual states were necessary partners in the expanding federal apparatus. On some issues, like civil rights protections, state sovereignty suffered, but in all else, especially institutional capacity and revenue generation, states grew, and they grew dramatically and in tandem with federal power.[180] In need of more financial support, states turned to excises. Already by 1947, governors attending their annual conference in Salt Lake City supported Horace Hildreth, governor of Maine, in his citation of "tax studies ... [that] indicate that it would be desirable for the federal government to withdraw from the so-called nuisance tax field, in favor of the several states."[181] As the influential economist Roy Blough noted only months later, "mutually helpful federal-state fiscal relations would not be promoted by expanding

---

[178] See, for example, O. H. Brownlee, "The C.E.D. on Tax Reform," *Journal of Political Economy* 56, no. 2 (April 1948): 166–72.

[179] Discussed further in Chapter 4.

[180] See Kathleen J. Frydl, *The GI Bill* (New York: Cambridge University Press, 2009), chapter 4.

[181] As quoted in Roy Blough, "The Issue of Diversification in Federal Tax Policy," *NYU Tax Law Review* 3, no. 1 (1947–1948): 21. See also Mabel Newcomer, "Taxation and the Consumer," *Annals of the American Academy of Political and Social Science* 266 (November 1949): 58.

the federal use of excise and sales taxes."[182] States embraced the excises cast off by the federal government throughout the postwar era; by 1969, states relied on consumer taxes (sales and excise taxes), for roughly 60 percent of their revenue generation.[183]

There can be little question, then, that during the "off the record" discussion of the Boggs Subcommittee, Treasury officials expressed a profound desire to get out of the excise tax and enforcement business. They had enough on their hands just levying the federal income tax. At this point, no move was made to transfer the Bureau of Narcotics out of Treasury, but agency officials must have been persuasive in pleading that no new drugs be added to its responsibilities, especially since this would involve devising a new tax on the rather robust trade in barbiturates. Faced with the challenge of bankrolling federal power, the Treasury abandoned its traditional roles in regulation and enforcement. Significantly, new constitutional interpretations of the powers rooted in the interstate commerce clause abetted the willingness to invest the regulatory powers of the federal government in something other than the power to tax.[184] As Anslinger wrote months before Boggs's barbiturate hearing, his colleagues at the Bureau of Internal Revenue did not want "new tax measures that are primarily regulatory in nature unless there were clear constitutional reasons why the taxing power must be exercised and the commerce power is inadequate."[185]

This shift in legal rationales is important, but so too is the institutional context in which it took place. One part of the reason that the federal government moved from regulating behavior by using the forces of the market to regulating behavior through the forces of punishment is that the Treasury Department was being asked to do new things, and stretched beyond institutional capacity, its leadership made choices. They chose to follow the money and focus on those instruments most essential to raising revenue.

This left an enormous vacuum in the regulation of the illicit synthetic drug market, and it was not immediately obvious that criminal punishment would fill it. Throughout the 1950s, it was the Food and Drug

---

[182] Blough, "The Issue of Diversification in Federal Tax Policy," p. 21.

[183] For further discussion, see Chapter 5; see also L. L. Ecker Racz, "Tax Simplification in this Federal System," *Law and Contemporary Problems* 769 (1969): 770–71.

[184] Cass Sunstein, "Constitutionalism After the New Deal," *Harvard Law Review* 101 (1987–88): 421–96.

[185] Anslinger, "Barbiturate Legislation," *Food, Drug, Cosmetic Law Journal*, March 1951: 212.

Administration that cobbled together makeshift efforts in the place of a
formal directive and in the place of the Bureau of Narcotics. Years later,
George Larrick of the FDA would describe his agency's entry into barbiturate and amphetamine enforcement as "by the back door," an incidental addition to its core mission of protecting consumer safety, and
perhaps something of a justification for the agency's negligible results
in enforcement.[186] To be sure, the task was a substantial one: already
by 1948, barbiturate production reached 335 tons, or "about 24 therapeutic doses per man, woman, and child in the country," as one industry insider marveled.[187] By the same token, the FDA concentrated what
little enforcement resources it had on barbiturates and amphetamines,
with one examination of their efforts concluding that from the 1940s and
1960s, "the agency devoted more regulatory work" to these synthetics
than "to all other drugs combined."[188]

At the same time as enforcement responsibility shifted to the FDA,
amphetamine use, both licit and illicit, emerged as a major issue in its
own right. The scale of licit use and widespread illicit use of the stimulant
may have been new to most of the public, but misuse of amphetamines –
most typically, stripping the medicinal paper out of a Benzedrine inhaler
for an amphetamine hit – had been frequently practiced since the end
of World War II, and known to the FDA since at least that time. Agency
inspectors had in fact contemplated a court case on the issue, fearful that
the popularity of a Benzedrine hit would spread among young people;
they dropped the case for want of "background," since the particulars
involved an army camp in Virginia that did not offer up any stereotypes
or stories that might galvanize a judge or jury.[189]

Stripping Benzedrine inhalers and sucking on the strip of amphet-
amine-soaked paper soon became a popular drug fix among a variety of
groups: author Jack Kerouac and poet Allan Ginsberg joined their circle
of friends in taking Benzedrine hits, just one of the illicit drug practices
that formed a part of Beat life and the larger urban hipster culture of
which it was a part. Stateside military camps provided an ideal breeding

[186] George Larrick at the White House Conference on Drugs, 1962, as quoted in "Narcotic
and Drug Abuse: Report of Advisory Commission Prescribes for Old Problems, New
Dangers," *Science* 143, no. 3607 (February 1964): 664.
[187] I. Phillips Frohman, *American Journal of Nursing* 54, no. 4 (April 1954): 433.
[188] John P. Swann, "Drug Abuse Control Under FDA, 1938–1968," *Public Health Reports*
112, no. 1 (1997): 83.
[189] Winton B. Rankin, Inspector, to Chief, Baltimore Station, March 10, 1945, RG 88
Records of the Food and Drug Administration, Division of General Services, General
Subject Files, 1938–1974, *NARA*, Box 794.

ground for the somewhat arcane practice; if one soldier knew what to do and how to do it, then ready access to the over-the-counter inhaler meant that it would soon spread. The same was true for prisons, where inmates were supplied, as one FDA investigation uncovered, by "several of the guards" who "were buying unusual numbers of the Benzedrine inhalers." Their unauthorized dealing had much in common with prison guards who do similar things today: the FDA learned "that the Benzedrine Inhalers were being purchased for 60 cents a piece and sold to the convicts for $5.00."[190] The profit margin on drugs meant that guards who were willing to flout prison rules were well-compensated.

These venues for illicit use all paled in comparison to the larger, licit use of amphetamine drugs. When doctors noticed weight loss among amphetamine users during World War II, it was a welcome side effect for a drug most often prescribed as a mood enhancer and treatment for depression. This "off-label" benefit soon emerged as a major use in its own right. In 1947, the American Medical Association approved amphetamine use for weight loss.[191] Not surprisingly, steep increases in the production and sale of amphetamines followed quickly on the heels of this decision. One reporter writing in the midst of the amphetamine boom extrapolated the following from U.S. Tariff Statistics: "In 1949, drug manufacturers produced 15,500 pounds of amphetamine, which was converted into a billion and a half pills; in 1951 they produced twice that much, and the latest available figures show that they are now turning out 52,000 pounds annually for a total of 5,200,000,000 pills, or, to put it another way, 33 pills for every man, woman and child in this country."[192]

As amphetamine use surged, its users were grouped under a common stereotype, that of the overwrought housewife. "Has someone you know recently become a dish-throwing witch?" one *Chicago Daily Tribune* asked its readers in 1958. If so, then the reason, the reporter speculated, might be found in the medicine cabinet and the extreme irritability that often accompanied amphetamine use for weight loss.[193] Other stories

[190] 8/13/48 Chief Inspector, Seattle, to Chief, Seattle Station, RG 88 Records of the Food and Drug Administration, Division of General Services, General Subject Files, 1938–1974, *NARA*, Box 1065.

[191] See Nathan William Moon, "The Amphetamine Years: A Study of the Medical Applications and Extramedical Consumption of Psychostimulant Drugs in the Postwar United States," PhD diss., Georgia Institute of Technology, December 2009: 225.

[192] "Dope: 50 Cents a Shot," A. E. Hotchner, *This Week Magazine*, supplement to Sunday Newspapers, RG 88 Records of the Food and Drug Administration, Division of General Services, General Subject Files, 1938–1974, *NARA*, Box 1994.

[193] "Is She Irritable? Better Check," *Chicago Daily Tribune*, October 12, 1958, p. E6.

depicted a much more sanguine view of these new wonder drugs. "You are," one writer addressed his readers, "entering the heyday of pills for your moods. They are, in fact, a triumph of chemical science and medical research," he reassured his audience; "[y]ou are the lucky consumer."[194] Occasional stories of dependence punctuated the otherwise glowing coverage of these diet drugs throughout the 1950s, and the reports of nervousness or insomnia seemed to be regrettable but rare side effects to a drug that helped women conform to stylized and ever more popular images of the ideal female form.[195]

Within a relatively short period of time, the mounting pace of synthetic drug consumption altered the landscape of medicine in ways that have come to seem natural today. But when they first appeared, the authority of just who should dispense these drugs, and how, had not yet been definitively settled. In the fall of 1951, Congress decided to clarify the FDA's regulatory posture on prescription drugs by providing, for the first time, a statutory definition of "prescription drug" in the so-called Durham-Humphrey amendments to the 1938 Food, Drug, and Cosmetic Act. The legislation reinforced the FDA's interpretation of the 1938 Act and, in addition, set out the specific criteria by which prescriptions could be refilled by order of a doctor – and not by prerogative of the pharmacist, as had often been the case in years past.

Yet the bill also responded to the concerns of retail pharmacists by sharply limiting the FDA's right to inspect the prescription files of any given pharmacy. "I am sure," FDA Commissioner Charles Crawford lamented, "that any court interpreting the language of inspection legislation would deny the Food and Drug Administration prescription-inspection in light of the debate of the House floor when the bill was passed."[196] One of the bill's co-sponsors, Hubert Humphrey, who came from a family of pharmacists, acknowledged the need for additional regulation on the floor of the Senate, noting that "further legislative consideration must be given to adequate barbiturate controls."[197] None was forthcoming. In the

---

[194] "Mood Pills-Safe New Drugs that Give You Peace of Mind," *Washington Post and Times Herald*, May 6, 1956, p. AW4.

[195] The demand for these drugs as weight loss tools has strengthened the inclination to view twentieth-century drug users as consumers with agency, and not simply as unwitting patients duped into addiction. See Moon, "The Amphetamine Years," 259, n. 59; David Herzberg, *Happy Pills in America: From Miltown to Prozac* (Baltimore: Johns Hopkins University Press, 2009).

[196] "Drug Unit Fears Loss of Authority," *New York Times*, August 6, 1953, p. 28.

[197] Remarks of Humphrey, *Congressional Record*, October 15, 1951, 82nd Congress, p. 13128.

end, the Durham-Humphrey amendments clarified the premise by which the FDA could monitor licit traffic in barbiturates, but, at the same time, it did little to enhance the mechanisms by which the agency could do so.

In wrestling with this mandate, the FDA drew on its past. Given the agency's experience monitoring the consumption of everyday products, it cannot be surprising to learn that, in its new and expanded role in synthetic drug regulation, the FDA directed its attention to pharmacies rather than drug companies.[198] This point bears some emphasis. The narcotic regulatory regime began at the point of production, whereupon every licit manufacturer was expected to account for the importation of raw or refined opium down to the last grain or, if imported in finished form, for every dose. Licensed manufacturers had to purchase a tax stamp and affix it to each and every shipment; lost or stolen shipments raised suspicion, and distribution of any unstamped narcotic was a violation of the Harrison Act. In the case of the synthetic drugs, however, no attempt was made to regulate production, or even to monitor it. What is more, the institutional culture of the Food and Drug Administration relied much more on voluntary and cooperative efforts than enforced regulatory practices. Thus, when the FDA approached drug manufacturing giant Eli Lilly in 1945 to suggest a reporting procedure for synthetic drug production, company officials dismissed the idea with the remark that they "entertain[ed] some rather serious reservations concerning the propriety of their firm assisting in actions which are to be directed against their customers."[199] Clearly, production tallies could be used to track diversion, including the substantial amount of diversion beginning in the production plant itself, and hence companies preferred to produce – and produce and produce, and not to disclose their output totals to anyone for inspection.

When the FDA got wind of diversion by drug manufacturers, they proceeded cautiously. One inspector wrote to Washington that, "[w]ithout detailing the results, it may be reported that the Halperin firm is still permitting unauthorized persons [from within the production plant] to acquire dangerous drugs." How did they do this? "The firm is invoicing sales for "delivery to Dr. ***", when, in fact, the invoicing as such is a subterfuge because delivery is made directly to unauthorized

---

[198] See Swann, "Drug Abuse Control Under FDA, 1938–1968."

[199] Memo of Interview, October 22, 1945. Mr. Ward Rice, Director of Chemical Control, EL, RG 88 Records of the Food and Drug Administration, Division of General Services, General Subject Files, 1938–1974, *NARA*, Box 794.

persons."[200] In 1951, and in the face of staggering synthetic drug production, the FDA headquarters sent a message to its New Orleans branch office investigating Southwestern Drug Corporation that, naturally, they "realized that this practice of selling drugs to employees and friends may quite probably be found in other wholesale drug houses"; "however," the commissioner preferred to think "that the top management of many of these concerns would welcome an opportunity to put an end to the practice, if that can be done tactfully." The qualification underscored the agency's reluctance to police manufacturers directly; in fact, FDA officials advised New Orleans inspectors that, in this instance, they "call upon a responsible officer of this corporation" and essentially warn him that an arrest of a druggist in the area may lead to information that implicated the firm, obviously in the hope that such a message would rouse the company into controlling its distribution more carefully.[201]

While the FDA avoided confrontation with drug companies, the agency pursued a more vigorous approach to retail pharmacies. Indeed, it is not too much to say that throughout the 1950s, the FDA endeavored to reshape the professional norms of pharmacy retailers, a contentious engagement similar to the professional struggle between doctors and the Bureau of Narcotics thirty years before. Yet this latter-day dispute had distinct features as well: not only did the FDA refuse to systematically monitor synthetics from the point of production, it also refused to interfere with the professional judgment of doctors who prescribed addictive synthetics or the pharmacists who sold them. Instead, the agency occupied itself almost exclusively with the proper mechanics of the sale of addictive synthetics. The rules for dispensing non-narcotic prescription drugs were new to pharmacists, and the Durham-Humphrey amendments clarifying those rules were newer still. Not surprisingly, pharmacists cited the resentment of customers as one reason why they did not always comply with regulations to the letter. One pharmacist wrote to the agency that "the public does not show a friendly attitude when we tell them that they cannot buy what they want until they have a prescription from a physician."[202]

[200] Boston District to Administration, June 24, 1949, RG 88 Records of the Food and Drug Administration, Division of General Services, General Subject Files, 1938–1974, *NARA*, Box 1184.

[201] Administration to New Orleans District, November 20, 1951, RG 88 Records of the Food and Drug Administration, Division of General Services, General Subject Files, 1938–1974, *NARA*, Box 1449.

[202] William F. Harrison, Harrison's Old Reliable Drug Store, to FDA, October 26, 1945, RG 88 Records of the Food and Drug Administration, Division of General Services, General Subject Files, 1938–1974, *NARA*, Box 794.

In response, the FDA supported an effort to post signs in drugstores that pleaded with customers accustomed to simply getting any drug they wished not to ask pharmacists to deviate from the new procedures. And, too, the FDA was quick to remind those who complained that the agency was not presenting "restrictions upon the sale of drugs, but rather [attempting to] fence off a field in which they may be legitimately distributed."[203]

One bone of contention between pharmacists and the FDA was the question of refills – before the 1938 Act and subsequent amendments, considered to be the prerogative of the pharmacist and a question settled according to his professional judgment. After the 1938 Act, the FDA ruled that it was to be the doctors, not the pharmacists, who decided how much of any given prescription drug ought to be dispensed. The agency pulled no punches when justifying this new regulation. In a speech before a retail pharmacy industry group, one FDA official indulged in plenty of "background" and "atmosphere" when regaling his audience of the case of *US v. Harry Skepner*, trading as Skepner's Rx Pharmacy in Hollywood, California. The official invited his audience to form a mental picture: "It's late afternoon of Dec. 12, 1946; Place – a middle income neighborhood in North Kansas City. There's a police car out front – and the morgue wagon is there. It's a coroner's case." Then he narrowed in on his subject. "The neighbors all knew there was something wrong with Mrs. Frank Phelps," he said, as if reading from a radio script, "but they didn't know the whole story, except that she acted very queerly at times and that her husband had left her and she lived alone." When she disappeared without warning, neighbors called in the police. As officers broke down the door to her home, "they found everything in a mess. The body was on the living room floor; it had been rather badly disfigured by rats, she had been dead about three days." What caused this appalling tragedy? Barbiturate shipments sent to her on unlimited refills by the defendants in the case, and the FDA official reciting this horror story noted that the height of blood stains on the walls suggested that Mrs. Phelps had managed only to crawl in her final hours.[204]

---

[203] A. G. Murray, Acting Chief, Interstate Division, FDA, to E. W. Constable, State Chemist, North Carolina, April 22, 1948, RG 88 Records of the Food and Drug Administration, Division of General Services, General Subject Files, 1938–1974, *NARA*, Box 1065.

[204] "Over the Counter or Prescription Only?" speech by Wallace F. Janssenn to Federal Wholesale Druggists Association, Atlantic City, October 6, 1948, RG 88 Records of the Food and Drug Administration, Division of General Services, General Subject Files, 1938–1974, *NARA*, Box 1065.

Obviously it was difficult for pharmacists to defend a practice that led to a tortured death followed by a mauling by rats. And it was difficult to argue with numbers as well; *Lilly Digest* reported that "prescription refilling runs over 40% of total prescription volume" and, just as noteworthy, "barbiturates are the most prescribed of all drugs."[205] A couple of years later, amphetamines would rank second on that list. Where exhortations failed, the FDA resolved to regulate pharmacists more forcefully. This determination launched a strange chapter in the agency's history, one where inspectors trained in consumer safety assumed "undercover" identities and attempted to make "buys" from pharmacists using unauthorized or flawed prescriptions or refills.

At first, the inspectors seemed to think that a kind of "skid row" look best fit the task at hand – so, as one inspector described for the Washington office, he "dressed in old clothes, refrained from shaving for three days, and visited drug stores" in sketchy areas of town.[206] It was surprising to the agency that this gumshoe detective approach did not yield results. But, as they soon learned, to the extent that pharmacists sold addictive synthetics illicitly, they tended to do so only to people already familiar to them. "It's common knowledge that some druggists sell dangerous drugs to their friends and people that they know," inspectors wrote in to headquarters. When they gained access to one pharmacy's files, FDA officials "were amazed to find that some customers were buying more dangerous drugs than the average neighborhood store sells," and, just as noteworthy, "a routine check revealed that the purchasers were school teachers, oil men, contractors, and well-to-do people."[207]

Without an obvious "cover" or disguise and with even less chance of being familiar to a pharmacist, FDA inspections got off to a slow and inauspicious start. One FDA branch office reported to headquarters in 1955 that "although it is becoming more difficult for our inspectors to make over-the-counter purchases of amphetamines in our territory, the druggists are simply becoming more wary of strangers who might be enforcement officers, and are still selling large quantities of amphetamines ... to customers whom they know well." The inspectors

[205] Ibid.
[206] Leonard M. Levin and William Vir Walker, St. Louis station, to Chief, March 15, 1948, RG 88 Records of the Food and Drug Administration, Division of General Services, General Subject Files, 1938–1974, NARA, Box 1066.
[207] Administration Information Letter No. 129, April 8, 1949, RG 88 Records of the Food and Drug Administration, Division of General Services, General Subject Files, 1938–1974, NARA, Box 1185.

surmised as much because "whether or not a prosecution action includes charges based on the sale of amphetamines to our inspectors, the close-out investigation almost invariably shows a considerable shortage of amphetamine drugs."[208]

As a tool to transform the professional culture of retail pharmacy, undercover work, though pursued throughout the 1950s, brought uneven results and was clearly inadequate. The agency tended to agree with those who supported a voluntary and educational approach rather than undercover investigation and possible criminal charges. When the FDA interviewed the secretary of the New York Board of Pharmacy, he admitted to knowing of "hot spots" (sources of dangerous drugs) and declared himself "100% for wiping them out." But, as the FDA official reporting the conversation went on to observe, "his [inspection] force is limited too, and is giving what he believes to be greater public protection by a general coverage of pharmacies" through educational campaigns "rather than concentrated effort in 'hot spots'; if he did concentrate on these 'spots',” the FDA official quoted him as stating, "he would force the traffic further underground with the same number of transactions at higher prices." For these reasons, "he believes in relying on a cooperative and educational program first and 'scare' or pressure tactics second."[209]

These observations, and the FDA's endorsement of them, bring up another important distinction between government regulation of addictive synthetics and the regulation of narcotics (and marijuana). It is a simple yet somehow also a subtle one: whereas Anslinger steered his Bureau toward focusing its energy on eliminating the illicit market, the FDA chose to focus on disciplining licit sales. Naturally the two agendas overlapped to some extent; the FDA used the threat of criminal punishment against pharmacists who flouted prescription rules, and the Bureau continued to check up on licit narcotic prescriptions. The fact that the Bureau did so throughout the postwar era is a point that often goes unremarked upon, not least because Commissioner Anslinger himself chose to minimize if not disparage the licit use of narcotic drugs. Yet records from the Bureau provide evidence of the routine inspections of narcotic prescriptions, as

[208] E. C. Boudreaux, New Orleans, to Administration, November 18, 1955, RG 88 Records of the Food and Drug Administration, Division of General Services, General Subject Files, 1938–1974, *NARA*, Box 2160.

[209] Inspector Hirschberg to New York District, February 7, 1949, RG 88 Records of the Food and Drug Administration, Division of General Services, General Subject Files, 1938–1974, *NARA*, Box 1183.

well as the ways these errands tested the patience of the agents sent on them. Agents inspected the records of Dr. Larson in Omaha, Nebraska, for example, and found him to be dispensing narcotics to three patients, all of whom resided in a nursing home.[210] No follow-up seemed necessary to them. Another report related the results of an inspection in what seemed to be a mild rebuke: "Examination of the narcotic prescriptions and other information ... discloses that practically all the Dilaudid tablets purchased are used to fill prescriptions ... for Captain S. E. Anderson, a Second World War Veteran. Captain Anderson has undergone several operations for amputation of the limbs," the agent continued, "and the narcotics are prescribed to allay pain; Captain Anderson is 40 years old, married, and was a former Post Office employee in Mt. Vernon, Washington. The local athletic field bears his name."[211] Clearly agents took no satisfaction in prying into the affairs of patients. One Bureau official in Portland, Oregon, sent to check on a "Mrs. Knox" found her to be a "pitiful case" in that "no one has ever diagnosed her affliction." Her symptoms included extreme pressure on the brain, which her doctor treated with narcotics, though, he admitted, even with these painkillers "Mrs. Knox loses all control of her extremities and is unable to walk or even to move her arms." The agent ended his report on a plaintive note: "What are you going to do other than give her narcotics?"[212]

Though the Bureau continued its efforts to ensure compliance in the licit narcotics market, it concentrated its efforts on eradicating the illicit one supplied through subversion (even though there was evidence that much of the illicit market was supplied through diversion). When the agency underwent outside review in the early 1960s, analysts found that "80 percent of the Bureau's time is spent in actual investigation and control of the illicit traffic," while "the remaining 20 percent is devoted to regulating the legitimate manufacture and transfer of narcotics."[213] FDA

[210] "Apparent Excess Purchases of Demerol," M. R. Frederickson, NA, Omaha, Nebraska, September 29, 1952, Records of the Drug Enforcement Administration, Subject Files of the Bureau of Narcotics and Dangerous Drugs, 1916–1970, NARA, Box 31.

[211] Walter G. Graben, NA, Seattle, Washington, October 22, 1952, Records of the Drug Enforcement Administration, Subject Files of the Bureau of Narcotics and Dangerous Drugs, 1916–1970, NARA, Box 31.

[212] Jack M. Merrill, NA, Portland, Oregon, November 19, 1952, Records of the Drug Enforcement Administration, Subject Files of the Bureau of Narcotics and Dangerous Drugs, 1916–1970, NARA, Box 31.

[213] Herbert Miller, Jr. to Nicholas deB. Katzenbach, Feburary 27, 1964, Dean Markham File, *John F. Kennedy Library*, Box 13.

officials chose to allocate their time in the opposite fashion, and it is a difference of emphasis that entailed different tactics, to be sure, but also a different operational premise. In the case of the Bureau, "the norm" or regular target of its efforts was the illegal sale, whereas in the case of the FDA, it was the legal sale of addictive synthetics. The differing institutional choices structured the market dynamics of their respective drugs. Because of the Bureau's actions, the risk of dealing in narcotics was higher and, to extend the logic of the New York Board of Pharmacy secretary, the same number of transactions went underground, with higher prices to compensate for risk. In contrast, there was really no subversion to speak of in addictive synthetics – every dose produced was done legally, even if diversion of the drugs occurred the moment they left the manufacturing plant. By differences of degree, the FDA positioned itself to regulate a trade, focusing on enforcing the standards of a licit transaction, whereas the Bureau moved in the direction of policing a crime, embracing a punishment ethos and an enforcement mentality.

So far was the FDA from a punishment mind-set, in fact, that its officials, including its commissioner, occasionally expressed sympathy for pharmacists forced to adapt to new rules. As leader of the FDA in 1949, Paul Dunbar confided to a friend that "[f]rankly, I don't see why pharmacy should carry the whole burden of maintaining the integrity of the so-called physician–pharmacist–patient relationship." For Dunbar, others deserved attention as well. "Whatever may be the reason," the commissioner observed, "physicians do not always carry out their obligation to the patient and the pharmacist by remembering to mark prescriptions 'non-refillable' when their nature is such that continuous use would be dangerous."[214]

Though Dunbar and many of his colleagues empathized with pharmacists, the scale of illicit trade in addictive synthetics soon drove them to explore more enforcement tactics – a move that ran counter to their institutional preferences as well as their standard repertoire of activity. Tentatively and reluctantly, the FDA steered itself into policing the illicit trade. As far back as 1948, Dunbar sent an important directive to all branches that began by noting that "our present methods of [undercover 'buys'] are not revealing material indiscriminate sales of dangerous drugs." Yet the FDA knew that such sales took place, not least because

[214] P. B. Dunbar to Dean L. F. Tice, College of Pharmacy and Science, Philadelphia, February 2, 1949, RG 88 Records of the Food and Drug Administration, Division of General Services, General Subject Files, 1938–1974, *NARA*, Box 1184.

"continuing newspaper reports of deaths due to over-dosages of barbiturates, complaints from State pharmaceutical associations, and a continued high production of barbiturates by pharmaceutical manufacturers lead us to believe ... that dangerous drugs are still reaching the public through other than prescription channels." The commissioner then faced the facts, admitting that "[t]he practice of visiting drugstores and attempting to purchase over-the-counter dangerous drugs without any advance knowledge that the drugstore may be engaged in the sale of such drugs has proved to be rather nonproductive."[215]

The commissioner invited his branch offices to continue undercover work and to explore alternate methods of grappling with the illicit market. In the main, the correspondence from his branch office inspectors confirmed the commissioner's suspicions. "It is our opinion that in localities where action has been taken against druggists for the indiscriminate sale or refilling of prescriptions," one inspector remarked in a carefully worded message, "the pharmacists have become more cautious, if not actually reformed."[216] New Orleans, an unusually active and alert branch, agreed: "Our recent efforts reveal that due to our previous activities in the larger cities such as Dallas, Houston, and perhaps New Orleans, sales of barbiturates, Benzedrine, etc. are being made only to known individuals and peddlers who in turn distribute in smaller quantities to juveniles and others who are contacted in dark alleys and other secluded locations. It seems that now under-cover methods of sale are used which approach the status of a bootleg racket. Therefore our present technique of dealing with the problem is rapidly becoming ineffective."[217] The more FDA inspectors chased the illicit market, the more they drove it underground, making it harder to track and harder still to thwart.

Yet consumption and sales (legal or otherwise) of addictive synthetics only escalated throughout the early 1950s. "In 10 years, manufacture of barbiturates – principal ingredient of most sleeping pills – has risen more than 300 per cent, in the United States," a 1953 *Boston Traveler* newspaper article read. Significantly, this report took cognizance of the

---

[215] P. B. Dunbar to Chiefs of Stations, August 25, 1948, RG 88 Records of the Food and Drug Administration, Division of General Services, General Subject Files, 1938–1974, *NARA*, Box 1065.

[216] Kenneth Lennington, Chief Inspector, Minneapolis District, to Administration, February 28, 1951, RG 88 Records of the Food and Drug Administration, Division of General Services, General Subject Files, 1938–1974, *NARA*, Box 1577.

[217] E. C. Bourdeaux, New Orleans District, to Administration, February 28, 1951, RG 88 Records of the Food and Drug Administration, Division of General Services, General Subject Files, 1938–1974, *NARA*, Box 1577.

illicit market as well: "The goofballs plus alcohol – 'A bolt and a ball' is the underworld slang for the combination – provide the artificial courage and deadening of morals and common sense behind many a robber's gun," and, just as noteworthy, the reporter reminded his readers that "those addicts aren't from among the city's dregs; their ranks are filled from the business world, from the professions and from among all social and economic levels."[218] Another news report was even more forthright about the illegal trade in addictive synthetics, warning readers that "[g]angsters have started to move into the lucrative barbiturate drug trade as demands for this sedative grow."[219] Unfortunately for the FDA, news of the illicit trade in diverted synthetics surfaced just as the regulatory burden fell more on their own agency, if only by default or, as the commissioner put it later, "through the back door."

The agency reconciled its traditional mores and its belief in the futility of undercover buys with the mounting urgency that something be done about the illicit traffic in synthetics by focusing its enforcement work on one particular venue of that traffic: American trucking. Its ambitious investigation of truckers in the 1950s – as illicit dealers, buyers, and users of addictive synthetics – is a startling chapter in the agency's history, and it is also an instructive episode in the federal government's prosecution of the modern "drug war." If nothing else, the illicit traffic in synthetics that centered on the nation's highways and truck stops attests to the fact that drugs were a trade, and anything that enhanced or eased the flow of goods would bring more drugs, and more demand for them.

The first and most famous of the FDA's trucking investigations took place between 1953 and 1955, just at the time when the trucking industry experienced phenomenal growth.[220] "The outlook now for the truck-trailer industry," one industry executive declared in 1954, "is perhaps the brightest it has ever been."[221] His optimism seemed justified, as the nation's

---

[218] "Goofballs Habit Tops All in Dope," *Boston Traveler*, March 16, 1953, RG 88 Records of the Food and Drug Administration, Division of General Services, General Subject Files, 1938–1974, *NARA*, Box 1728.

[219] "Sleeping Pill in Drug Probe," *Boston Herald*, Friday, January 23, 1953, RG 88 Records of the Food and Drug Administration, Division of General Services, General Subject Files, 1938–1974, *NARA*, Box 1728.

[220] The politics and political economy of trucking in the 1950s and later deserve much more attention; for an excellent treatment of these during an earlier time and trucking's formative years, see Shane Hamilton, *Trucking Country: The Road to America's Wal-Mart Economy* (Princeton: Princeton University Press, 2008).

[221] F. E. Burnham, "The Trucking and Truck-Trailer Industry," *Analysts Journal* 10, no. 2 (May 1954): 118.

expanded highway network afforded a new competitiveness to long-distance freight delivery, traditionally a network dominated by the trucking industry's arch rival, railroads. Material moved by trucks grew in tons from 14 billion in 1936 to 92 billion by 1950, with a projected growth to 248 billion in 1960.[222] The federal gasoline tax levied to help pay for Eisenhower's ambitious construction of the interstate highway system – the only man-made structure visible from space other than the Great Wall of China – added to the cost of leisure driving, certainly, but diesel trucks avoided this surcharge. Capitalizing on new opportunities, freight-carrying highway trailers were built during the 1950s at an unprecedented pace, and companies hired hundreds of young men to drive them.

As long-distance trucking matured into a vital industry, a trucking culture was born in its wake. "It's a lonesome job," trucker Charley Bell confided to the *Saturday Evening Post* reporter who accompanied him on his cross-country trip. Truckers who stopped along the highway spoke in their own kind of dialect, where police anywhere were known as "Big Bad Joe," and a trailer could "fishtail" or skid as a driver "squeezed-down" or stepped on the brakes.[223] On the road, truckers signaled "trouble ahead" to passing colleagues by forming a two-fingered salute, and this could refer to anything from an upcoming Interstate Commerce Commission checkpoint, a tedious stop that would no doubt include an inspection of the driver's logbook of his hours and his route, a quicker and more routine weight and mileage check at the state line, or an accident ahead. A quick flash of headlights was a more ambiguous and benign signal; depending upon the situation, it could mean "hello" or "do you need help with your mechanical problem?" or "you have room to pass me." Truckers bridged the isolation of their jobs by communicating with other truckers in these ways and, as a group, they tended to be young men, not on the college track, and from the southern or western plains states. Truckers also developed their sense of vocational identity by engaging with their hard-nosed union, the International Brotherhood of Teamsters, though this led to a shared resentment of the union's corruption at least as often as gratitude for its service. Whichever the case, truckers in the 1950s carved out their own cultural landscape – one that had physical parallels as well, as they dominated the highways during the midday and virtually owned them at night.

[222] Ibid.
[223] John Reese, "I Crossed America in a Moving Van," *Saturday Evening Post*, January 1, 1955.

Some elements of trucking culture were more raucous. Penny ante poker was a common and subdued enough pastime, and truckers who worked on relay, shuttling between trailers and work, could often be found passing the time between jobs at a truck stop with cards in hand.[224] But, as the 1940 film noir classic *They Drive By Night* let on with its suggestive allusions and seductive plot, many truckers indulged in a racy side of life as well. Truck stops held different sorts of sexual opportunities for drivers who stopped, ranging from flirtation from the waitress hired for her good looks to outright prostitution. As the trucking industry boomed, it gradually became apparent to observers that young women from the local area would visit a truck stop in search of an escape from everyday moral constraints. In a cross-country trip taken with a trucker in 1955, a *Saturday Evening Post* reporter briefly remarked on this when he disapprovingly observed, "night also brings out the teenage girls who hang around truck-stop cafes in the small towns of the Midwest." "It's not a pretty picture," he concluded, "but the local law enforcement officers seem to be blind to it."[225]

Undoubtedly one reason for the reporter's dismay at this social exchange was the presence of drugs – specifically amphetamines, or "bennies" as they were dubbed in trucker slang. By the 1950s, amphetamines had a well-established place in trucking culture, and not just the seamy side of it. Close monitoring by the Interstate Commerce Commission (ICC) mandated that truckers work only a certain number of hours consecutively, and they were to record these faithfully in their logbook. Unscrupulous employers all but demanded that truckers routinely violate these working codes, and unscrupulous Teamster representatives often tacitly signed off on this abuse of work standards in exchange for a "cut" or payment under the table. Because of punishing work hours, even a straight-laced trucker who had no interest in sordid escapades would be tempted to buy amphetamines at a truck stop; some companies sold "bennies" to their drivers directly. A combination of work demands and a transgressive subculture produced a vibrant drug trade in the trucking industry – one that would last well into the 1980s, when Ronald Reagan signed an executive order mandating drug testing and, with the gradual implementation of that order, the great "purge," as industry insiders called it, began.

[224] Richard Thruelsen, "Men at Work: Road Driver," *Saturday Evening Post*, June 14, 1941, p. 18.
[225] Reese, "I Crossed America in a Moving Van," p. 57.

Trucking drug culture was hidden from view and embedded in a specific work context, so it is not surprising that government officials were slow to comprehend the magnitude of the problem. The first inkling came with accidents, including those that were horrific and otherwise inexplicable were it not for drugs. Unlike long hours, accidents were something that trucking employers cared a great deal about. In 1953, a Pennsylvania trucking company, Eastern Truck Lines, approached the FDA with stories of amphetamine abuse. To an unusual degree, truckers were involved in serious accidents that they could not explain to the satisfaction of the company. Very often they complained of an approaching car on the wrong side of the road, a drug-induced hallucination that sent more than one rig out of control. Sometimes amphetamines convinced a trucker to push beyond his endurance – and well beyond the law – with the tragic result of falling asleep at the wheel. The *Saturday Evening Post* reported one such story in 1954, detailing for readers how Larry Allen Rowley succumbed to his exhaustion and sent his rig off road in Alabama, on to a "non-stop trip to eternity." Police discovered a bottle of amphetamines in the truck, as they had in many similar accidents.

As was common with heavy amphetamine use, hallucinations drove truckers to offer fabulous tales to explain their accidents, or even sometimes to speak to officers while still suffering from a delusion. One trucker who drove off the road was found asleep in his cabin and, when questioned by the police, he told them that "Benny and I were driving along very nicely and I got very sleepy. Benny was doing so well at the wheel, I decided to crawl up in the bunk and let Benny drive."[226]

The FDA had already begun some investigative work by the time industry insiders approached. In St. Louis in early 1953, investigators attempted "buys" of amphetamines at "filling stations and truck stops" in order to trace the pills back to their source.[227] It was a difficult if not impossible task. The pink heart-shaped pills could come from anywhere, and the FDA needed more direct clues in order to uncover the sources of supply. Soon investigators took the logical next step. "Dressed as a truck driver and at 9:50 a.m. on 12/8/54, I entered the WC Sharp Drug Store

---

[226] Arthur L. Davis, "Death in Small Doses," *Saturday Evening Post*, January 21, 1955, pp. 25, 89.

[227] St. Louis District to Division of Microbiology, January 3, 1953, RG 88 Records of the Food and Drug Administration, Division of General Services, General Subject Files, 1938–1974, *NARA*, Box 1994.

FIGURE 3.1. Horrific truck accidents like the one pictured above (undated) spurred lawmakers and the Federal Drug Administration to assume a more aggressive posture in policing the illicit trade in amphetamines.

[in Knoxville, Tennessee]," one FDA investigator reported to Washington headquarters. He offered a verbatim script of what took place next:

Inspector: Some of the boys want me to get some more those heart-shaped stay awake pills – Dexedrine pills.

Moon: Dexedrine?

Inspector: Yes.

Moon: Who do you work for?

Inspector: Mason and Dixon Lines.

Moon: How many do you want? Do you sell them out to the other fellows?

Inspector: Yes. I haven't got a lot of money for them now ...

Moon: ... We have an in at the wholesale place and we can get it for cash so that no record is made of it. After Christmas it will be easier, I know, but if you buy it in the 1000's it will be a little cheaper.[228]

---

[228] Memo to accompany investigation in Knoxville, December 8, 1954, RG 88 Records of the Food and Drug Administration, Division of General Services, General Subject Files, 1938–1974, *NARA*, Box 1994.

A drug store ready to deal in units of 1000s must have been an eye-opener for the FDA, but, unfortunately for the agency, such was the scale of illicit amphetamine traffic they faced.

At first the FDA believed the opinion of older truck drivers that the problem of amphetamines was restricted to freelance, younger truckers who had yet to find an established job with one of the bigger companies. They soon learned that this was not the case. "We know in our truck investigations on the illicit sales of amphetamines that there were a great many more users than actually covered," an Atlanta inspector acknowledged. "We can cite here the 16 truck stops and 3 drug stores involving one or more dispensers who sold to an unknown number of users," but "since the publicity on our investigation," the investigators began receiving even more "complaints on continual illicit sales of this drug by truck stops and cafes."[229] Even more telling, in a FDA survey of 180 truckers, "not one ... claimed ignorance of the use of bennies" and "thirty or so admitted using" amphetamines themselves.[230] To stem the tide of amphetamine use among truckers, the FDA fielded their most audacious investigation yet. Two FDA investigators were sent to trucking school at an undisclosed location in the south and, after graduation, they cruised the nation's highways in search of major amphetamine suppliers and willing stooges. In the beginning, they made rookie mistakes, including crisscrossing the country with empty trailers. "Anybody in a service station could see by looking at the springs that the trucks were empty," one FDA official later remembered, so the inspectors went the extra distance in correcting their error. After loading their trailers with "junk," they "also found out that the greatest thing was to sprinkle a little sugar on the tailgate"; that way, "if anybody asked what you were hauling, you could always tell them sugar, because," in the south especially, such a load was almost always understood to be an illegal delivery to a moonshiner. After that, "buys were then very easy to make."[231]

After months of traveling, the FDA issued forty-three warrants for arrest in the fall of 1955. All of the arrests were made against those who

---

[229] Atlanta District to Administration, November 21, 1955, RG 88 Records of the Food and Drug Administration, Division of General Services, General Subject Files, 1938–1974, *NARA*, Box 2160.

[230] Davis, "Death in Small Doses," 89.

[231] Interview with Clifford Shane found in John P. Swann, "The FDA and the Practice of Pharmacy: Prescription Drug Regulation Before 1968," *Pharmacy in History* 36 (1994): 55–70. We need to know much more than is currently known about the illicit production of alcohol, or "moonshine," during the 1950s, a thriving underground industry that bore a direct relationship to the heavy excise tax levied against alcohol during this time.

distributed amphetamines without a prescription – that is, who made an illegal sale. Truckers themselves were spared indictment; there was no law against illegal possession, contrary to narcotics. In fact, the FDA understood that many truckers were "surprised to learn [amphetamines] are dangerous, so commonly are they taken for prolonged periods."[232] Less innocent aspects of the investigation also received attention. FDA Commissioner Larrick informed Congress that the agency had uncovered an "extensive problem in the Springfield, Missouri area involving delinquent girls engaging in sex orgies with itinerant truck drivers and local individuals. This investigation developed evidence that amphetamines and barbiturates ('sleeping pills') played a part in the picture."[233] Years later, the FDA continued to note a link between sexually transgressive behavior and addictive synthetics, as it directed investigators to take particular interest "in North Carolina truck stops where prostitution and the sale of 'bennies' go hand-in-hand."[234]

The success of the 1955 arrests really only served to bring attention to a problem that had grown well beyond the scope of enforcement. In 1957, the *Chicago Daily Tribune* still ranked amphetamine use among long-distance truckers as "one of the greatest highway hazards."[235] Clever investigations could foil a supply channel, but these efforts were costly, and most amphetamine suppliers did exactly what pharmacists did when selling illicitly: they sold only to those whom they knew. Since no tabs were kept on production, it was impossible to track supply or even make reliable estimates on the amount of drugs diverted to illicit sales. In one common ruse, truckers making a delivery of amphetamine drugs would mark some of the boxes as "damaged" upon delivery – lost to inventory at that point – and the shipment's recipient, complicit in the scam, would then sell the boxes back to the trucker "under the table." Who could ever hope to penetrate this insiders' game?

Certainly not the FDA, uncomfortable with investigating the illicit drug market, and burdened with a number of other, competing demands.

[232] Baltimore District to Administration, November 21, 1955, RG 88 Records of the Food and Drug Administration, Division of General Services, General Subject Files, 1938–1974, *NARA*, Box 2160.

[233] Larrick, Deputy Commissioner, FDA, to Donald M. Counihan, Legislative Liaison, October 19, 1953, RG 88 Records of the Food and Drug Administration, Division of General Services, General Subject Files, 1938–1974, *NARA*, Box 1994.

[234] John J. McAuliffe to Baltimore District, November 29, 1957, RG 88 Records of the Food and Drug Administration, Division of General Services, General Subject Files, 1938–1974, *NARA*, Box 2360.

[235] "The Facts About Thrill Pills," *Chicago Daily Tribune*, March 10, 1957, p. D19.

While beginning illicit sale enforcement in 1949, investigators in St. Louis confessed themselves to be "greatly confused. With the effort which we thus far spent," they explained, "we have developed approximately 15 cases during the first half of this fiscal year. Frankly, there appears to be no end as to the number of cases that could be developed if the time is spent on [illicit drug market]."[236] Years later, as the first trucker investigation wrapped up in 1955, the New York branch of the FDA drew limits on the scope of its enforcement work during a congressional hearing: "Our investigations were undertaken only on follow-up of specific complaints. We had neither the manpower nor sufficient funds to make exploratory investigations or to try independently to develop leads." Still more explicit, the branch told Washington officials that "our experience in this area points to the general conclusion that the illegal sales of dangerous drugs, particularly the barbiturates and amphetamines, constitute a very serious, unsolved, social problem ... In fact, we were barely able to handle the gross complaints received." According to its own assessment, the branch office had managed only to scratch the surface. "Without a comprehensive survey of exploration into established channels of drug distribution and thence into underworld bootleg traffic," the office report disclosed, "we do not know the extent of the work that remains to be done."[237]

The FDA was overwhelmed, and the feeling that the problem of addiction to and illicit dealing in synthetic drugs was spiraling out of control was palpable throughout the country as well. "Side by side with narcotics addiction," the *Christian Science Monitor* noted to its readers in December 1955, "there has been growing for many years now the addiction to barbiturates and amphetamines – sleeping pills and stimulant drugs."[238] During that same month, the FDA's Boston branch paid a visit to a leading psychiatrist to learn more about what was fueling licit and illicit demand for these drugs. His answers followed the consensus views developing among psychiatrists, a set of notions that combined a kind of observational sociology and medical diagnosis. The FDA's expert source

---

[236] Chief, St. Louis, to Administration, December 16, 1949, RG 88 Records of the Food and Drug Administration, Division of General Services, General Subject Files, 1938–1974, NARA, Box 1305.

[237] Statement of C. A. Herrmann, Chief, New York District, FDA, November 8, 1955 before the Subcommittee on Narcotics, Committee on Ways and Means, U.S. House of Representatives, found in RG 88 Records of the Food and Drug Administration, Division of General Services, General Subject Files, 1938–1974, NARA, Box 2160.

[238] "Worse Than Narcotics: Sleep Pill Traffic Assailed," *Christian Science Monitor*, December 31, 1955, p. 2.

felt that "barbiturates pose[d] a greater problem than do narcotics," not least because "[t]heir use has increased greatly." What drove this seemingly unstoppable demand? Experts agreed that "people are more tense and that they are very concerned about the future (the present cold war and the possibility of atomic warfare, etc.)." This anxiety was juxtaposed with "the increased leisure time enjoyed by people today." Citing one of the principal profiles of barbiturate use, the doctor noted that this extra time "affords the housewife more time to worry about her problems, while at the same time she does not become physically tired and consequently may suffer from insomnia." In general, the doctor concluded, "the lack of physical exertion plus the increased mental tension produces a society which requires some sort of sedation."

FDA investigators pressed the doctor; just how bad was the problem? "Regarding barbiturate addicts," the doctor claimed "that they are the worst kind, being much worse than narcotic addicts. He pointed out that a barbiturate addict reaches the lowest level in our society – usually he is not even able to care for himself – whereas a narcotic addict may remain self-sufficient for years" – a position the Bureau of Narcotics most certainly would have challenged, but one that fell well within the norm of a so-called functioning addict. The FDA officials pressed on, curious as to how so much addiction could go unnoticed and untreated. The doctor felt that in "those cases where the addict or injured is a prominent member of the community," there was embarrassment or, even "a covering-up of such cases in the past, particularly in small communities." "Because of their widespread popularity with the medical profession," the doctor warned the FDA, "barbiturates have been introduced to practically every household."[239]

A world of privilege punctuated by moments of deep foreboding, this affluent America occasionally forced to contemplate nuclear annihilation, created, according to these doctors, a nearly insatiable appetite for sedatives. By mid-decade, the increasing notoriety of addictive synthetics prompted government officials and lawmakers to review the entire federal drug regime. The result – the Senate Daniel Subcommittee hearings and its companion in the House, the Boggs Subcommittee – revised and reaffirmed the drug regulatory mechanisms that would take the country well into the 1960s.

---

[239] Boston District to Administration, December 5, 1955, RG 88 Records of the Food and Drug Administration, Division of General Services, General Subject Files, 1938–1974, *NARA*, Box 2160.

DANIEL COMMITTEE

When the U.S. House of Representatives and Senate sent their respective drug committees on a traveling circuit throughout the country to collect testimony, neither group could have suspected that their public engagement would focus so heavily on young people. Certainly there was evidence that teenagers were connected to the older narcotic culture and to the newer traffic in synthetics as well. In 1955, New Orleans FDA investigators noted that the illegal distribution of amphetamines was "closely connected with that of barbiturates," and that "[t]his connection appears to have become more common during the past two years, particularly insofar as abuses by juveniles and by the outright criminal class are concerned."[240]

And, to be sure, the "youth" angle had always been a popular one in the press, an easy "hook" for a sensational drug story. In 1951, the *Alameda Times-Star* offered a typical example, informing readers that "Federal authorities moved ... to stop teen-agers in Colorado, New Mexico, and Texas from using sleeping pills and wine spiked with gasoline to produce 'thrill jags'." As the reporter also noted, "[p]eddlers of the sleeping pills – known as 'goof balls,' 'red birds,' 'yellow jackets' or 'blue heavens' – even circulated among school children."[241] The prospect of peddlers dealing drugs to young people, particularly to young girls, had long been used as a cudgel to authorize new kinds of federal regulatory authority; only twenty years prior, Commissioner Anslinger decried opium-dealing "Chinamen" in San Francisco who seduced innocent white girls with "incense-laden" depravity.

But now the commissioner saw his own tactics turn against him – namely, that similar stories about young people in the 1950s would undermine his claim to have narcotics traffic under control. One reporter sympathetic to Anslinger – and, most likely, writing under his specific instructions – took note of the rising alarm regarding teenagers and illicit drugs. The story he wrote quoted a grand jury report in Detroit that found "conditions of the most shocking nature were revealed in the testimony adduced before them; that young people ranging in age between

---

[240] E. C. Boudreaux, New Orleans, to Administration, November 18, 1955, RG 88 Records of the Food and Drug Administration, Division of General Services, General Subject Files, 1938–1974, *NARA*, Box 2160.

[241] "Teen-Age 'Thrill Jags' Investigated in Mid-West," *Alameda Times-Star*, May 18, 1951, RG 88 Records of the Food and Drug Administration, Division of General Services, General Subject Files, 1938–1974, *NARA*, Box 1450.

fourteen and twenty-one have become confirmed and inveterate users of heroin, morphine and cocaine; that these young people, enslaved through their addiction to narcotics, resorted not only to thievery in the homes of their parents and relatives but become shoplifters and common thieves, and that many of the young girls became prostitutes." Yet the reporter concluded that "[t]here is no 'national epidemic'. The teen-age problem is mainly confined to a few metropolitan centers" – a geographic focus that matched Commissioner Anslinger's own agenda.[242]

Yet several voices began to question the scope of the youth illicit drug problem, and the tension over the extent and precise dimensions of this problem had much more to it than simply a desire to calibrate the appropriate degree of alarm. It had real stakes when it came to enforcement assignments and legislative ambitions. If there was a youth "epidemic," then it was a battering ram for more extensive government powers and perhaps increased punishment as well. If not, then the current system would be presumed to be working well. If teenagers used barbiturates and amphetamines illicitly, then such drugs would most likely be regulated under a more stringent regime. If not, then the system of relying exclusively on the judgment of a prescribing physician and the rules governing the sale of prescription drugs would continue. There were also smaller arguments that related to teenage drug use that called aspects of Commissioner Anslinger's drug posture into question. Should young people be educated about the dangers of narcotics? The famous actor and highly decorated war hero Audie Murphy thought so, testifying before the Senate that "with young folks being impulsive, as they are, if you hide something from them, they immediately become interested in it."[243] Such a view questioned the wisdom of Anslinger's approach of treating illicit drug use as an unspeakable taboo, a wicked power, the mere mention of which only added to its allure.

In these numerous ways, the sensationalism of teenage drug use and its potential for attracting new voices to the debate presented challenges to Commissioner Anslinger's monopoly on official drug discourse and policy. In 1955, the Senate ran a high-profile set of hearings devoted to juvenile delinquency, a volatile topic that periodically erupted in

[242] Albert Deutsch, "What We Can Do About the Drug Menace," Public Affairs Committee, Inc., found in RG 88 Records of the Food and Drug Administration, Division of General Services, General Subject Files, 1938–1974, NARA, Box 1994.

[243] *Hearings Before Subcommittee on Improvements in the Federal Criminal Code, Committee on the Judiciary, U.S. Senate, 84th Congress, July 12–15, 1955* (Washington, DC: U.S. Government Printing Office, 1956): 907.

controversy throughout the decade. Called before the special Senate Subcommittee on Delinquency, Anslinger testified that, although drug use among teens appeared to be declining, it was nevertheless too distressing "for complacency."[244] Since escalating teenage illicit drug use would seem to condemn his own handiwork, the commissioner became, in a strange way, a sober voice of reason amidst the delinquency hysteria, desirous of minimizing the evidence and skeptical of anecdotes recited in order to elicit an aggressive response. And Anslinger was by no means alone: when Price Daniel, Democrat from Texas, formed his special subcommittee in the Senate to study illicit drug use, and Hale Boggs followed suit with a companion committee in the House, some of the experts called before both subcommittees substantiated Anslinger's claims. Before the Boggs Subcommittee, for instance, Dr. Kenneth Chapman of the National Institute of Mental Health agreed that the problem of teenage addiction was "not as great as it was" in the early 1950s.[245] Yet politicians picked up on it nonetheless, and Senator Payne of Maine was not alone in his belief that "[t]he increased use of narcotics by teenagers has been of greatest concern since it is closely related to the increase in juvenile delinquency."[246]

The obsession with teenage drug use helps to explain the major outcome of the 1955 Daniel Subcommittee and its corollary investigation in the House: approval of increased penalties for narcotic offenders, including a mandatory ten-year minimum and a maximum of the death penalty for selling illicit narcotics to a minor, should a jury conclude, as the congressional committees had, that the crime was tantamount to "murder on the installment plan."[247] Even still the invocation of the death penalty was a remarkable turn of events, perhaps most so because of a kind of technical nonchalance on the part of lawmakers. Though the difficulty of differentiating between possession of illicit narcotics and selling them came up for some discussion, it did not receive anything like the careful examination that the severe penalties the committee contemplated would seem to require. Congressional members also did not take a great interest in the difference between selling to an addict and moving supply;

---

[244] Rebecca Carroll, "The Narcotic Control Act Triggers the Great Nondebate: Treatment Loses to Punishment," *Federal Drug Control*, 102.

[245] Chapman, "Traffic In and Control of Narcotics, Barbiturates, and Amphetamines," in Boggs 1955, 1956, p. 37.

[246] Remarks of Payne, *Congressional Record – Senate*, 84th Congress, p. 9032.

[247] See, for example, Remarks of Daniel, *Congressional Record – Senate*, 84th Congress, p. 9014.

"[a]nyone who sells drugs is a trafficker, in our opinion," Anslinger told the Boggs Subcommittee, a disturbing indication of the Bureau's blanket approach to enforcement.[248] Also noteworthy in the Daniel legislation was the fact that its penalties for narcotics traffic were so severe that it enticed Bureau agents to place as many cases as possible before federal courts – as opposed to state courts – and this, in turn, led to a less centralized system of illicit narcotics dealing, with many powerful members of organized crime deciding to construct a buffer between themselves and narcotics operations previously under their direct supervision.

While the "narcotics conspiracy" charges now available to prosecutors at the federal level had the greatest impact, it was the death penalty provision that attracted the most attention. Daniel's success in passing a death penalty for sale to a minor was in many ways the culmination of Commissioner Anslinger's agenda, effectively a moral and largely symbolic demonstration, part of what David Garland calls "expressive justice," but one that was cloaked, importantly enough, as a pragmatic deterrent, an odd but effective alliance of purposes that the commissioner was a master in crafting.

Yet in some respects, the work of both the Daniel and Boggs subcommittees represented a serious defeat for him. Many of the commissioner's seemingly unassailable positions became vulnerable under close scrutiny. First to fall was the certainty Anslinger routinely adopted when claiming to affect – even to control – heroin supply. There was no doubt in any serious observer's mind that the illicit narcotics reaching the country had grown substantially; despite all of the "deterrents" already in place and the work of Anslinger's "small but efficient force," "[i]llicit drug use has trebled in the United States since World War II," Senator Daniel claimed when introducing his bill.[249] Second, when the committees interviewed self-professed addicts or spoke with medical doctors down at Lexington, cocaine regularly came up in the litany of substances enumerated. Anslinger had tried his hardest to ignore this drug and, in fact, to ignore the Central American countries from whence it came, preferring instead to delegate both the cocaine and the region that it came from to the enforcement portfolio of his archrival, U.S. Customs Commissioner Ralph Kelly. But there was no ignoring Kelly's portfolio in the work of the committee – especially since Price Daniel represented Texas, and saw

---

[248] Anslinger, "Traffic In and Control of Narcotics, Barbiturates, and Amphetamines," in Boggs 1955, 1956, p. 132.
[249] Remarks of Daniel, *Congressional Record – Senate*, 84th Congress, p. 9013.

his subcommittee as a springboard to a run for governor of that state. As a result, Mexico especially took a new and prominent role in the trafficking discussion, heretofore considered only as a producer of marijuana. To underscore the importance of border relations, Daniel conducted two on-site committee hearings at San Antonio and Houston along with the other committee visits to Philadelphia, New York, Austin, Fort Worth, Dallas, Los Angeles, San Francisco, Chicago, and Detroit.

Texas border hearings introduced another important (though little noted) development in both subcommittees: lawmakers had difficulty comprehending the staggering scale of global exchange. When Price Daniel learned of Mexican "shooting galleries," or the daily crossings undertaken by Americans to shoot heroin on the Mexican side of the border, he confessed later to Customs commissioner Kelly that the hearings "along the Mexican border actually brought out facts that were surprising to all of us."[250] He insisted to Kelly that Customs officials keep a list of all those who made the crossing, an idea made plausible to him by the assured fashion in which the Narcotics Bureau bandied about its "addict rolls," but one that was preposterous to anyone familiar with the border. "As you know," the commissioner gently reminded Daniel, "there is a tremendous flow of traffic at the large centers like San Ysidro ... over 50 million people a year cross in the stretch of border in between El Paso and San Ysidro."[251]

In San Francisco the Boggs subcommittee had another rude awakening when Senator Baker questioned Chester MacPhee, the collector of Customs stationed there. "Mr. MacPhee, the attorney general of the State of New York recommended to this committee that 5,000 members of the armed forces on a voluntary basis in effect be loaned to Customs in New York to make a complete check of all vessels, all methods of entry, that perhaps you could stop the smuggling of narcotics," the senator informed MacPhee. "If you had 5,000 or 3,000 men, do you think you could absolutely or practically stop narcotic smuggling in San Francisco?" the senator wondered. "I think that is an excellent question," MacPhee replied, "and the answer is absolutely 'no'."[252]

[250] *Hearing Before the Subcommittee on Improvements in the Federal Criminal Code, Committee on the Judiciary, U.S. Senate, 84th Congress, S.3760, May 4, 1956* (Washington, DC: U.S. Government Printing Office, 1956): 21.
[251] *Hearing Before the Subcommittee on Improvements in the Federal Criminal Code, Committee on the Judiciary, U.S Senate, 84th Congress, S.3760, May 4, 1956* (Washington, DC: U.S. Government Printing Office, 1956): 24.
[252] Exchange in "Traffic In and Control of Narcotics, Barbiturates, and Amphetamines," in Boggs 1955, 1956, p. 854.

FIGURE 3.2. This photo from the El Paso Texas Border Crossing taken in 1964 shows a U.S. Customs agent performing a cursory check of a car traveling across the U.S. border.

The conceit of control so often proffered by Anslinger and his allies, whether it be control of the heroin supply, or control of the number of addicts, broke down at the borders, a literal observation that held even more metaphorical truth. Customs officials knew that the first fact of the illicit drug trade was the larger global exchange of which it was a part. Any plan that failed to acknowledge that broader context was more of a symbolic gesture, a performance of enforcement rather than the provision of it. Lawmakers and countless others failed to make this distinction, seeing illicit drugs as trafficked in isolation, a contained activity or crime only waiting to be caught. Congressman Herbert Zelenko of New York actually seized on the idea that 5,000 members of the armed forces be seconded to Customs and formally proposed it before the Boggs Committee. For those who failed to see global trading networks at work, the performances of "security" could become more extravagant, and more and more militant.

Price Daniel seemed to struggle between which of these two frameworks to adopt: were illegal drugs brought into the country by an evil cabal that could be identified and defeated, or were they a part of the larger flows of people and goods in and out of the country? His dilemma was captured by his initial ambivalence about the feud

FIGURE 3.3. Nightlife was a popular draw for American visitors who crossed the border, as this photo from Juarez, Mexico (1964), attests, with its English-language advertising.

between Customs and the Bureau of Narcotics. The tension between the two offices remained a sore point – in fact, institutional feuding led to the Daniel Subcommittee in the very first place. The original idea to initiate congressional examination of the illicit drug situation actually came from Daniel's colleague, Senator Fred Payne, Republican from Maine, who successfully steered a resolution urging a formal review through the chamber. The Senate lodged the matter with the Senate Finance Committee for disposition – the natural place, of course, given that the Harrison Act was a taxing measure. But one particular part of the resolution prevented it from coming up for consideration at all; as Senator Payne later reflected: "for a time it looked as if the whole idea of comprehensive study might be lost because of opposition to one of the more controversial provisions – the proposed transfer of the Bureau of Narcotics from the Treasury to the Justice Department as had been recommended by the first Hoover Commission."[253]

When Payne had included Hoover's widely ignored reorganization recommendation, no doubt the congressional allies of Commissioner Anslinger sprang into action to stall the review. Eventually this item was

[253] Remarks of Payne, *Congressional Record – Senate*, 84th Congress, p. 9032.

dropped and the entire review was transferred to the Senate Judiciary Committee, which formed the Daniel Subcommittee to execute its mandate. This turn of events was considered a political compromise at the time, but, with the benefit of hindsight, it deserves greater prominence. The Senate thenceforth considered drugs to be an issue belonging to the Judiciary Committee and thus a part of a criminal justice discussion, and not a taxing measure – not formally, at least.

Yet Price Daniel was himself not immediately persuaded of the virtue of the Bureau of Narcotics. The geographic division of labor between Customs and the Bureau, where Customs assumed responsibility for Central and South America and Asia and the Bureau did the same for Europe and the Middle East, struck him as odd. During formal questioning in subcommittee, Anslinger spoke of the division as if it was as natural as an act of God, but Daniel remained unconvinced.[254] Informally Daniel pushed the matter even further, visiting Europe and questioning Bureau officials in Rome about their genuine feelings on how best to set up an international enforcement network. Charles Siragusa reported to Anslinger that Daniel had repeatedly pressed him for his "personal opinion," regardless of whether "it conflicted with Bureau policy." Siragusa reported his reply to the senator directly to Anslinger: "I said it was virtually impossible to stop the flow of illicit narcotics into the United States by relying solely on random searches at our frontiers [sic]." For good measure, Siragusa added that he "thought narcotic smuggling enforcement at American borders should be taken away from Customs and given to us."[255]

No doubt Daniel came away impressed with the fiery loyalty of Bureau agents abroad, but perhaps what impressed him most was the consistent narrative confidence of the Bureau, their promise to "control" illicit drugs. Customs Commissioner Kelly offered no such promises, instead telling the Daniel Subcommittee that "the world is simply so heavily supplied with illicit narcotics that we can hardly have a reasonable hope of keeping them all out of this country."[256] As the hearings unfolded, Daniel came to reject this view that underscored the limits, if not the futility, of

---

[254] *Hearings Before Subcommittee on Improvements in the Federal Criminal Code, Committee on the Judiciary, U.S. Senate, 84th Congress, June 2, 3, 8, 1955* (Washington, DC: U.S. Government Printing Office, 1956): 94.

[255] Charles Siragusa to Anslinger, August 15, 1955, Subject: Senators Daniel and Butler, Record Group 170, Records of the Drug Enforcement Administration, Office of Enforcement Policy Classified Subject Files, 1932–1967, NARA, Box 13.

[256] Kelly before Daniel, *Hearings Before the Subcommittee on Improvements in the Federal Criminal Code of the Committee on the Judiciary, U.S. Senate, 84th Congress, June 2, 3, and 8, 1955* (Washington, DC: U.S. Government Printing Office, 1955): 141.

enforcement work and that conveyed such a sense of resignation. Instead Daniel seized upon the energetic voice of the Bureau, so much so that, when on the floor of the Senate defending his legislative package of new criminal penalties, the senator bristled at the suggestion that heroin traffic could not be stopped. "No I do not agree [with that view]," Daniel told his colleagues, "because during World War II the narcotics traffic in this country did a nosedive," a reference to the totally aberrational cessation of *all* trade flows that the Bureau routinely offered as validation of its particular enforcement approach. From that singular event, Daniel deduced that, "whenever we have the personnel to watch it and stop it at its source, the traffic can be stopped. If that cannot be done, we are just wasting our time trying to legislate."[257]

Daniel's remarks warranted a literal and ironic gloss; instead his colleagues joined him in earnest and all too casual agreement. Also in need of more thoughtful reflection were the numerous warnings both committees had received regarding the utility of mandatory minimums that, after all, had been in place for second offenders since the Boggs Act of 1951. Assistant Attorney General Warren Olney raised concerns about the Boggs Act, claiming that under its rigorous demands juries had been more unwilling to convict.[258] Dr. Chapman of the Lexington Hospital equivocated in response to a question from Subcommittee Chairman Hale Boggs about the deterrent effects of the mandatory minimums implemented years earlier, then finally admitted, "we have noticed about the same percentage of new faces at Lexington as we had before the increased penalties."[259] At the final hearing of the long-running Daniel Subcommittee, the Department of Justice shared its view that "vesting the courts with discretion," meaning putting a stop to mandatory minimums, would lead to fewer suspended sentences.[260] Raymond Del Tufo, U.S. Attorney from New Jersey, told the committee that he felt mandatory minimums undermined plea bargains.[261]

---

[257] Remarks of Daniel, *Congressional Record – Senate*, 84th Congress, p. 9032.

[258] *Hearings Before Subcommittee on Improvements in the Federal Criminal Code, Committee on the Judiciary, U.S. Senate, 84th Congress, June 2, 3, 8, 1955* (Washington, DC: U.S. Government Printing Office, 1956).

[259] Chapman, "Traffic In and Control of Narcotics, Barbiturates, and Amphetamines," in Boggs 1955, 1956, p. 38.

[260] *Hearing Before the Subcommittee on Improvements in the Federal Criminal Code, Committee on the Judiciary, U.S. Senate, 84th Congress, S. 3760, May 4, 1956* (Washington, DC: U.S. Government Printing Office, 1956): 8.

[261] Tufo, "Traffic In and Control of Narcotics, Barbiturates, and Amphetamines," in Boggs 1955, 1956, p. 505.

This impressive array of testimony was forcefully countered by Commissioner Anslinger, who appeared before the companion Boggs Subcommittee with a map, and with numbers, all purporting to chart the remarkable deterrent effects of the first Boggs Act.[262] In places where states had adopted mandatory minimums in their own codes, Anslinger claimed that drug dealing declined. It was not a perfect comparison, especially since all indications were that heroin traffic had surged since mandatory minimums were instituted. Consequently the commissioner turned to another measure of success. "Without that [Boggs] act," Anslinger surmised, "we would not have been able to hold the fort,"[263] a clever downgrading of expectations, the persuasiveness of which rested on a counterfactual: how much worse would things be without the Boggs Act? And, of course, the commissioner stood ready to nominate other components of a lax criminal justice system as culpable. "In those areas where probations are high the traffic has increased," Anslinger informed the committee.[264] More crucial, according to the commissioner, was the fact that the Boggs Act did not apply to first offenders, the majority of whom, the commissioner now claimed with certainty, accounted for the increase in trafficking.[265]

In sum, Anslinger stressed, it was up to the states to adopt mini-Boggs Acts in their Uniform Narcotic Code. "In the 16 States which have enacted the same penalties as the Boggs Act ... we have no problem," Anslinger assured Subcommittee Chairman Hale Boggs. "You couldn't have any better evidence than that, could you?" the chairman responded, almost marveling at his handiwork of years earlier. Anslinger dismissed those who harbored doubts about the justness or effectiveness of mandatory minimums; "We are in the door," Anslinger noted, meaning mandatory minimums have already been accepted in principle and should now be extended.

As before, the District of Columbia appeared prominently in legislators' discussions regarding mandatory minimums and narcotic punishment in general. Senator Daniel convened one of his subcommittee's hearings in DC during the summer of 1955, and the final testimony solicited by the Boggs Subcommittee was that of Metropolitan Police Department Chief Murray. Senator Payne traced his original interest in

[262] Anslinger testimony, "Traffic In and Control of Narcotics, Barbiturates, and Amphetamines," in Boggs 1955, 1956, pp. 87–120.
[263] Ibid., p. 88.
[264] Ibid., p. 120.
[265] Ibid., p. 127.

"more effective Federal narcotics legislation" to his "service as a member
of the Senate District of Columbia Committee."[266] His colleague, Senator
John Sparkman, Democrat of Alabama, informed colleagues in the chamber of his view that the District "alone needs at least a dozen new laws, or
amendments to old laws, to cope with the narcotics problem here."[267] In
extended mandatory minimums, Congress had a ready test case at hand.
When it came to the energetic pursuit of narcotic punishment, Congress
invoked illicit narcotics in the District as an imaginary template on which
to map their efforts. Even more ambitious, some southern congressmen
began to present the District, or their version of the District, as predicting
the fate of civil rights reform and integration. In September 1959, Senator
Olin Johnston, Democrat of South Carolina, took the floor to relate "cold
statistics of crime in Washington," a sad state produced by "the practice
of forcing integration" which necessarily would eventuate in "this kind of
antisocial attitude." Without spelling out the causal connection, Johnston
nevertheless expressed his disbelief at "people in high office who insist
that forced integration has nothing to do with the crime rate."[268] As the
next decade unfolded, additional assertions of black criminality, focused
on the District and illicit narcotic use, would be deployed regularly to
counter or to stall the black freedom movement.

No similar attention was paid to the thriving business of illicit traffic in amphetamines and barbiturates. Though the Daniel and Boggs
subcommittees heard testimony regarding addiction to synthetics and
the illegal markets for both, the institutional impasse reached in 1952
remained unresolved. This was deeply frustrating to some, including
Senator Frank Karsten of Missouri, who could not believe that "[t]his
is 1955," three years after the Boggs hearing in 1952, "and we still have
no policy."[269] In general, experts in the synthetic market adopted none of
the assured claims of Anslinger and his agents; they sounded more like
Customs officials who were suitably awed by the tremendous explosion
in trade flows. Whereas narcotics seemed to have a numerical certainty in
terms of addicts and amounts, barbiturates and amphetamines had none.
"I know there is a problem," M. L. Harey admitted before the Boggs

---

[266] Remarks of Payne, *Congressional Record – Senate*, 84th Congress, p. 9032.

[267] As quoted in Carroll, "The Narcotic Control Act Triggers the Great Nondebate,"
p. 106.

[268] Remarks of Johnston, *Congressional Record – Senate*, 86th Congress, p. 17488.

[269] Karsten, "Traffic In and Control of Narcotics, Barbiturates, and Amphetamines," in
Boggs 1955, 1956, p. 232.

Subcommittee, "but I do not pretend to know how big it is."[270] In search of any easy answer, Congress had none before it, and legislators left the existing regulatory mechanisms, such as they were, intact.

Doubtless lawmakers' refusal to authorize additional mechanisms to regulate synthetic drugs had a definite relation to the persuasive influence and growing political clout of U.S. drug manufacturers. Companies like Eli Lilly that once clamored for government protection from more competitive European rivals – and got it, in the form of the tariff and tax system of the Harrison Narcotic Act of 1914 – now saw greater advantage in less government interference as their market share grew, an evolution that mirrored the larger trade and business dynamics of which drugs were a part. The Bureau of Narcotics had long kept tabs on the preferences of American drug companies, and one can only assume that congressional members joined Bureau officials in their sensitivity to the concerns raised by this promising sector of business. And, as we shall see, drug companies continued to exert decisive control in the regulatory debate over addictive synthetics throughout the 1960s; their interventions remain the principal reason why possession of these drugs is not assumed to be illegal, as is the case with heroin.

The work of the Daniel Subcommittee resulted in the heaviest narcotic penalties up to that point, including mandatory minimums for first offenders (two years). Initially Daniel also wanted to sanction the use of wiretaps against drug dealers as part of his omnibus bill. He was forced to relinquish this particular provision in Senate chamber owing to the objections of Wayne Morse, Democrat from Oregon, best known to history for casting one of two votes against the Gulf of Tonkin Resolution in 1964, the proposition that endorsed use of force by the United States against North Vietnam. Almost a decade earlier, Morse demonstrated glimmers of that same moral courage as he played upon the rhetoric of drug reformers to make his point. If the Senate agreed to wiretapping, Morse argued, it would be tantamount to "injecting this procedural drug into the veins of our body politic in an endeavor to make our people even more insensitive to their liberties than millions of people already are."[271] In order to preserve an uncontroversial voice vote, Daniel dropped the section from his bill.

Other, more penetrating objections to the work of the Daniel Committee were heard as well, though they attracted far less notice and concern.

---

[270] Harvey, "Traffic In and Control of Narcotics, Barbiturates, and Amphetamines," in Boggs 1955, 1956, p. 1120.

[271] Remarks of Morse, *Congressional Record – Senate*, 84th Congress, p. 9038.

Senator Lehman of New York pointed out on the floor that Congress had "already tried the punitive and repressive approach. Experience has shown that that alone will not solve this tragic problem." It is surprising that this train of thought went almost ignored; that is, that Congress had already passed the Boggs Act, and "[n]ow," as Lehman pointed out, "almost 5 years later, we are told that the drug traffic is again on the increase." How is it that the Boggs Act escaped a reputation of failure; or, as Lehman, put it, "[h]ave we any assurance that the higher penalties will work any better than those in the present law?"[272] Rather than confront this question, lawmakers subscribed to an incremental logic. It was not that penalties failed, they reasoned, but the fact that punishment was not serious enough or imposed universally. Daniel exemplified this willingness to commit more to punishment when he told his congressional colleagues in the chamber that his subcommittee believed "that law enforcement officers should be equipped to meet [drug dealers] weapon for weapon," thus presenting his escalation of punishment as merely a reaction to the militancy of drug dealers.[273] This stormy rhetoric did not escape the notice of the *Decator Herald,* which ran a story that observed with approval that the "new narcotics legislation written by a Senate Judiciary Subcommittee ... really declares war on the drug traffic in this country."[274] In this way, the "war" metaphor gave a sense of mission and meaning to the ratcheting up of punishment, implying a concerted and uncompromising effort against illicit narcotic traffic.

This policy direction failed to account for the total absence of evidence that a punitive approach worked at all. Often the "get tough" tone of this rhetoric was construed as a kind of hard-nosed pragmatism, but there was nothing to demonstrate the practicality of punishment in the first place. In fact, the opposite was the case. Reviewing occupations of the patients in treatment at Lexington, both congressional subcommittees must have noticed that medical professionals (doctor, nurse, dentist, and "other health worker") followed service workers and "proprietary managerial, and white collar," as the most numerous among patients,

---

[272] Remarks of Lehman, *Congressional Record – Senate,* 84th Congress, p. 9033.

[273] Remarks of Daniel, *Congressional Record – Senate,* 84th Congress, p. 9016.

[274] As found in *Congressional Record – Senate,* 84th Congress, p. 9026. This is the first direct reference to a drug war that I have found in the postwar United States; references to a "war" on dope or other similar formulations were common enough during the 1930s, when the newly christened "Federal" Bureau of Investigation waged a "war on crime." See, for example, Edward Atwell, "America Declares War on Dope, the Mighty Maker of Criminals," *Washington Post,* March 24, 1935, p. F6.

followed by skilled and unskilled labor and then housewives. These were not the occupations of those who were in prison. By process of deduction, then, legislators could have reasoned that imprisonment bore a relation to different enforcement strategies and not to illicit drug use per se. Judge Jonah Goldstein testified before Boggs in New York City and made this point explicitly: "In the 24 years of my judicial service I have never had a rich narcotic user brought before me, nor have I heard of a rich narcotic user being brought into the criminal court before any other judge. Yet there is no doubt in my mind that there are rich users."[275] Some went even further, suggesting not only that Anslinger's figure of 60,000 addicts was absurdly low, but that the narcotic addict as depicted by the commissioner was an unrecognizable stereotype. Drug addicts were, as Dr. Berger of the New York Board of Medicine testified, "very much like the rest of us." "Drugs do not incite him to violence," he corrected the legislators, though "if addicted, lack of drugs might do so easily. An addict is not coaxed into sexual promiscuity; if anything, drugs stunt her natural sex drive."[276] Berger went so far as to suggest that the true problem of the addict was that he was self-medicating, a relic of an earlier time, who somehow remained ignorant of the development that doctors, not patients, dispensed drugs now.[277]

The subcommittees downplayed or ignored these voices. After passing his narcotics legislation, Price Daniel went on to become governor of Texas in 1956; Hale Boggs stayed in Washington and continued his rise in House leadership and numbered among the most powerful of congressmen. But in some real measure, the voice of Harry Anslinger grew slightly fainter in the rising din. Other views of illicit drugs, including the number of addicts and the nature of addiction itself, were presented to Congress during the Daniel hearings. Anslinger no longer exercised an exclusive monopoly over the public discussion of illicit drug use. Yet not even the commissioner, a jealous guardian of his official domain, could predict the extent to which an alternative view of drugs, only glimpsed at in the hearings, was about to gain ascendancy in the very highest halls of power.

---

[275] Goldstein, "Traffic In and Control of Narcotics, Barbiturates, and Amphetamines," in Boggs 1955, 1956, p. 529.

[276] Berger, "Traffic In and Control of Narcotics, Barbiturates, and Amphetamines," in Boggs 1955, 1956, p. 649.

[277] Berger, "Traffic In and Control of Narcotics, Barbiturates, and Amphetamines," *Hearings Before a Subcommittee of the Committee on Ways and Means, U.S. House of Representatives, 84th Congress, October, November, December 1955 and January 1956* (Washington, DC: U.S. Government Printing Office, 1956): 650.

PART II

1960–1973

4

Review and Reform

The Kennedy Commission

When witness Judge Jonah Goldstein appeared before the Boggs Subcommittee in 1956, he admonished the very legislators who had been instrumental in crafting a punishment regime for illicit narcotic use: "Common sense and experience," he told the congressmen, "dictate that habits cannot be controlled or cured by criminal law."[1] Doubtless Goldstein drew on knowledge he gained while serving on New York's Court of General Sessions, but, as the congressional members knew well, Goldstein's view was also one that was gaining traction in a variety of professional circles. A short time later, the American Medical Association (AMA) and the American Bar Association (ABA) would issue reports critical of the criminal punishment approach in dealing with illicit drug use. For the medical society in particular this was a striking departure, as the new stance on illicit drugs recanted previous claims, and the positions that the AMA now saw fit to renounce had once been essential in sparing professional medical authority from the review and contempt of U.S. Bureau of Narcotics Commissioner Harry Anslinger.

Such authority now flourished well beyond the reach of Anslinger's reproach, and the medical profession relied on its popular esteem in striking new ground. Doctors also seemed to be influenced by more mundane forms of social engagement as well: new ideas regarding "addiction" came from several corners in the late 1950s, and these contemporary

---

[1] Goldstein, "Traffic In and Control of Narcotics, Barbiturates, and Amphetamines," *Hearings Before a Subcommittee of the Committee on Ways and Means, U.S. House of Representatives, 84th Congress, October, November, December 1955 and January 1956* (Washington, DC: Government Printing Office, 1956), p. 528.

views reinforced the revised medical consensus on illicit drug use. While doctors and others recast public perceptions of the "addict," legal professionals took stock of the now-unwieldy set of criminal punishments in place for illicit narcotic use. At the same time that the medical community held out the possibilities for a new way of dealing with addiction, important legal circles were at work discrediting the old one.

Of course there had been muffled voices of dissent all along, including those grumblings that came from within law enforcement. Some of these more traditional critics of Anslinger's approach were emboldened by the new willingness to reconsider the validity of the punishment model, and none was more animated than Los Angeles Police Chief William Parker in taking on the Bureau of Narcotics and its leadership. As the storm of criticism gathered, a new president, John F. Kennedy, sensed a critical moment and, more acutely, a political opportunity. The Bureau of Narcotics had been a festering sore of histrionics, embarrassing the United States internationally with wild accusations, and out of touch with changing norms of drug use and treatment at home. To set the United States on a new path, the president formed a blue-ribbon commission to review drug policy; importantly, the commission's broad mandate included the new addictive synthetic drugs and the problems that persisted in the federal government's decade-long refusal to regulate their production and use.

Under the leadership of E. Barrett Prettyman, a U.S. Appeals Court judge and father to a close friend of Attorney General Robert Kennedy, the commission asked the "big" questions and endorsed much of the new professional consensus in answering them. Anslinger's critics had been heard. Yet, in the end, the commission still recommended institutional changes that would ultimately advance the punishment regime. The reasons for this once again came down to calculations made based on the range of political options available to lawmakers – and, just as was the case with the decision to shift power away from taxes and toward criminal punishment, these moves had as much to do with the world outside of drug policy as any determinations made from within it.

Punishment as a political logic endured, even at the hand of reformers who urged a new path. Yet, critically, the function and application of prohibition and punishment were altered: whereas its previous uses at home and abroad had been polemical and polarizing, drug policy in the hands of reformers would be operative and intended to consolidate the sovereign power and penetration of the state. In the past, illicit drug enforcement had been an agenda handled by only select agencies and for certain purposes. Starting with the Kennedy administration, drugs became less a mission and more a modality of a state power, a way for the state to achieve goals outside the ambit of typical drug policy concerns.

ADDICTION AS DISEASE

For decades, U.S. Bureau of Narcotics Commissioner Harry Anslinger had devoted himself to crafting the image of the narcotic addict in the American public mind. Anslinger's book *The Murderers*, published in 1961 and written with the assistance of Will Oursler, recounted the themes and characterizations of "narcotic gangs" that were familiar to his audience from the countless public statements Anslinger had issued throughout his tenure. Depraved addicts with a perverse sex life and a proclivity toward violent crime lay at the heart of narcotic gangs and, as the commissioner colorfully described it, such "substrata vermiforms" worked to spread the sinister "tentacles of addiction."[2] In tone and in substance, Anslinger's jeremiad struck the same chord as his previous pronouncements. Yet by 1961, the commissioner's customary sermon redounded in a new setting. Certainly by the time of this publication, Anslinger considered many of his readers in need of a reminder of what he viewed as the inalterable perniciousness of the addict.

For the five years prior, the American public began to learn of new ways to think about addiction. Revised and more expansive depictions of who was an addict and just what addiction actually meant endangered key assumptions supporting Commissioner Anslinger's punishment regime, and so, not surprisingly, the Bureau of Narcotics leader was unsparing in his response. If the commissioner had his druthers, most would accept the Bureau's assertions of addiction at face value and, even more, readily believe the Bureau's repeated claims to have all addicts accounted for on the so-called addict roll. Yet even within the Bureau the roll was suspect, and had been for a long time. In 1948, New York Bureau Chief Garland Williams selected eighty names at random from his "addict roll" and found only twenty-nine of them to be involved in drug use in any way. "I am forced to the conclusion that [the survey of addiction] is incorrect," Garland wrote to Washington headquarters, "and should in no way be relied upon as a guide to the number of addicts in New York City."[3]

[2] Harry Anslinger, *The Murderers: The Story of Narcotic Gangs* (New York: Farrar, Straus, and Cudahy, 1961), pp. 192 and 173.

[3] Williams to Anslinger, November 22, 1948, Addiction Survey, RG 170, Records of the Drug Enforcement Administration, Subject Files of the Bureau of Narcotics and Dangerous Drugs, 1916–1970, *NARA*, Box 1.

If Anslinger had heeded such warnings earlier, perhaps it would have spared him the even greater skepticism generated by his insistence to have all "60,000" addicts active throughout the 1950s on record; as it was, the commissioner sat unperturbed, but surely discredited, as Customs Bureau Chief Kelly testified before Congress that such a number did not even account for all those who crossed the Mexican American border in search of heroin.

Given that Anslinger was wrong about the number of addicts, perhaps he was wrong about the nature of addiction as well. This leap of logic was by no means obvious at the time, and it took several different converging forces to render it plausible or even possible to make. First among these was the changing discourse on alcoholism, a shift that registered on many surprising fronts throughout the postwar era. As historian Alan Petigny points out, the 1950s are too often remembered as a time of rigid cultural norms and powerful constraints. It is more accurate, he argues, to acknowledge the numerous ways in which the United States evolved into a more "permissive" society – and, as he argues, the ways in which Americans began to rethink alcoholism spoke to this newfound tolerance and liberality. Spurred by the vocal efforts of a few prominent voices, Americans once accustomed to regarding alcoholism as a moral failing instead increasingly endorsed a view that alcoholism was a disease – an allergy, even – that afflicted some who consumed alcohol, but not others. In 1944, only one in eighteen Americans thought of alcoholism as an illness; already by 1954, six out of ten considered it as such.[4]

The story of the acceptance of the so-called medical model of alcoholism touches upon powerful forces at work throughout the decade. It was not hard to detect the influence of the social sciences, both as profession and popular discourse, in the reworked ideas on alcoholism. As it turns out, this was no mere brush with a popular trend. It was a concerted and collective engagement to emerge from various parts of the academy; a "new science of alcoholism," as historian Jonathan Zimmerman terms it, centered around the multidisciplinary group at Yale's Center for Alcohol Studies.[5] Founded in 1942 and directed by biostatistician E. M. Jellinek since its start, the Center promoted what Jellinek called "the disease

---

[4] Alan Petigny, *The Permissive Society: America, 1941–1965* (New York: Cambridge University Press, 2009), p. 265.

[5] See Jonathan Zimmerman, "'One's Total World View Comes into Play': America's Culture War over Alcohol Education, 1945–1964," *History of Education Quarterly* 24, no. 4 (Winter 2002): 471–92.

concept of alcoholism," endowing the "disease" framework with the imprimatur of higher learning and hastening its acceptance.[6]

As important as this academic blessing was, jettisoning the old notion of alcoholics as sinners who lacked moral fortitude was most dependent upon the activism and outspokenness of recovering alcoholics themselves. This activism took many forms, but almost all could be traced to the formation of the first and still most famous of the various "recovery" movements, Alcoholics Anonymous (AA). One founding principle of AA is that all members remain anonymous – hence the name – and so its two most famous organizers are often referred to simply as Bill W. and Dr. Bob. Because of their organization's success and their future renown, their full names – Bill Wilson and Dr. Bob Smith – are widely known and not shielded. Bill W. and Dr. Bob first encountered each other in the 1930s as part of a loose support group in Akron, Ohio, organized under the auspices of a local church. Gleaning from his conversion experience, or the admission that he was powerless over alcohol and offering to submit to a "higher power" to aid him in his struggle to stay sober, Bill W. encouraged Dr. Bob toward a similar epiphany. Their shared experience and willingness to approach others generated the famous "Twelve Steps" of Alcoholics Anonymous; soon, Bill W. put the steps and powerful personal stories of gaining sobriety in the "big book" of 1939, *Alcoholics Anonymous: The Story of How 100 Men Have Recovered from Alcoholism.*

After publication of this foundational text, Bill Wilson actively solicited support from donors to purchase copies of the book and fund expansion of his budding movement. Through a connection to the famed Riverside Church of New York City, he found a willing benefactor in John D. Rockefeller, Jr., who considered the AA, or organized "moral suasion" to stay sober, the best recourse for temperance advocates following the repeal of Prohibition.[7] With the benefit of Rockefeller support, the AA attracted public notice and elite backing. Soon local affiliates

---

[6] See Penny Booth Page, "E. M. Jellinek and the Evolution of Alcohol Studies: A Critical Essay," *Addiction* 92 (December 1997): 1619–37. Patricia A. Morgan points out that the Yale Center, as well as the larger movement toward the disease model, had substantial financial support from the alcohol industry: Morgan, "Power, Politics, and Public Health: The Political Power of the Alcohol Beverage Industry," *Journal of Public Health Policy* 9, no. 2 (Summer 1988): 177–97.

[7] Leonard U. Blumberg with William L. Pittman, *Beware the First Drink! The Washington Temperance Movement and Alcoholics Anonymous* (Seattle, WA: Glen Abbey Books, 1991), p. 8.

organized meetings, banding strangers together with a shared commitment to the twelve steps. One of the most important early groups was
located in Washington, DC. This particular AA chapter confirmed Bill W.
and Dr. Bob in their suspicion that many among the "respectable" classes
struggled with alcoholism, and it also provided some early challenges.
Washingtonians and other like-minded AA members wanted to position the movement at the forefront of several policy debates, including,
importantly, efforts to "decriminalize" public drunkenness. AA leadership probably agreed with these efforts in principle, yet they could easily
see how this and similar endeavors could factionalize and splinter the
group. From this dilemma as well as other organizational challenges, Bill
W. fashioned the "twelve traditions" of AA, a set of rules intended to
depoliticize the group, guarantee membership to anyone who wishes to
stay sober, and limit the amount of governance coming from outside of
any given local chapter. So long as a chapter disengaged from anything
other than staying sober and welcomed anyone who wished to stay sober,
it was free to conduct itself as it pleased.

  These traditions enshrined the AA as dedicated to recovery and support
and very likely, guaranteed the group's enduring relevance and success.
Yet the traditions also opened up a gap between the growing activism of
the recovery movement and what the AA as an organization would itself
take on. This vacuum was soon filled by one of the first women who
went through the twelve steps to stay sober, Marty Mann, a well-known
society figure who turned her talent and connections to forming the
National Council on Alcoholism (NCA), later rechristened the National
Council on Drug Abuse and, even later, the National Council on Drug
Dependence, still in existence today. Formed by Mann in 1944, the NCA
took the "disease model" public, booking speaking engagements and providing support to Yale's Center on Alcohol Studies, including, at times,
furnishing the center subjects for research. The striking vision of a refined
society woman speaking openly about alcoholism attracted notice for
Mann's activities and, as Alan Petigny argues, "forced people to reconsider old stereotypes" of alcoholics as only men, and only those who were
"skid row" types, destitute and vagrant.[8] But Mann hoped to do much
more than debunk popular myths. She put the NCA and its numerous
local affiliates, including the Washington Council on Alcoholism, to work
as advocates. Throughout the 1950s, the NCA argued for revised school
instruction on alcohol, launching an impassioned battle waged with real

[8] Petigny, *The Permissive Society*, p. 27.

conviction on both sides. For decades students had been warned about "evil rum" and the deleterious effects of just one sip of alcohol. Yet the fact that school curricula subscribed to a teetotaler agenda long after the repeal of Prohibition created a cognitive dissonance for the students who were exposed to it, since many who learned about the sinfulness of alcohol went home to find their parents enjoying a drink. Mann and the NCA used this disconnect as an opportunity to advance an education agenda that instead emphasized the innocuousness of light to moderate drinking, and introduced students to the "disease model" of alcoholism, whereby some simply could not tolerate any amount of alcohol and were susceptible to a dangerous dependence. Historian Jonathan Zimmerman observes that this dispute between "slippery slope" fundamentalists who defended the older curriculum and the reformers who argued for change remains unresolved to this day.[9]

In addition to attempting to sway school boards, the National Council also attempted to repeal the common criminal punishment of public drunkenness, the primary tool of "disorder" policing – arrests for minor infractions in the hope of deterring more serious crime – for decades. Taking a cue from another prominent social movement, civil rights, the NCA focused first of all on generating legal cases to challenge the criminal statute. Some of this casework began to bear fruit by the late 1950s, as lawyers argued, with some success, that alcoholics who consumed drink were doing so not as an act of volition but out of physical compulsion. This line of argument culminated in the *Easter v. District of Columbia* ruling of 1966, in which the U.S. Court of Appeals decided that alcoholics lacked *mens rea*, or "guilty mind," a criminal standard inherited from the common law that held that in order for a person to be culpable for a crime, she had to have had the intent to commit it. *Easter* set a new precedent for decriminalization and, as we shall see, became a springboard for political efforts to rescind punishment of public drunkenness nationally, a movement that ultimately prompted renewed questions over the logic and justness of criminal punishment for illicit drug use.

Perhaps not surprisingly then, the activities and increasing acceptance of the recovery movement fueled, in turn, a series of attempts to chart a similar path in illicit drug use.[10] Also not surprising, the translation of

---

[9] Zimmerman, "'One's Total World View Comes into Play.'"

[10] Perhaps because drug research was confined to the insular world of the Public Health Hospital at Lexington, Kentucky, scientific discourse and backing played a far less prominent role. For more on this community of researchers and their evolving understanding of addiction, see Campbell, *Discovering Addiction*.

certain recovery tactics and ideas from alcohol to illicit drugs was imperfect, if not impossible, and these difficulties led to a number of false starts. The first known recovery group comprised of illicit drug addicts, the "Narco Group" formed at the Lexington Public Health Hospital, carefully replicated the practices of the AA.[11] Tweaking the twelve steps, the group enunciated principles that deviated somewhat from the AA model and, sounding a note of anguish, added a thirteenth step that simply said, "God help me." One member of this group, Danny Carlsen, went on to found a "Narcotics Anonymous" organization tied closely to the work of the Catholic Church, YMCA, and Salvation Army. His fledgling organization based in the urban northeast evolved into less a support group and more of a social services network designed to provide stable housing, food, and job connections to an addict who desired recovery.[12]

Time magazine revealed the existence of Carlsen's group to its readers in a 1951 article entitled "The White Stuff." This particular off-shoot of Narcotics Anonymous petered out over time, as did several other attempts centered in and around southern California that followed the support group and recovery model more closely. Jimmy K, an influential member of the first chapter from which the modern-day Narcotics Anonymous claims its heritage, criticized these various California groups as he floated in and out of them for not following the apolitical "traditions" that Bill Wilson of AA had spelled out. But clearly the NA faced more obstacles than internal bickering. When the head of the Los Angeles Sheriff's Department Narcotics Division asked one recovering addict, Jack P., to organize an AA for narcotic addicts, evening meetings of the group adjourned to the scrutiny of local police who camped outside, hectored attendees, and recorded license plates.[13] Jack P. pleaded with the narcotics captain and the officers were called off. Still, the fact that consuming narcotics without an appropriate tax stamp was a criminal offense with progressively more punishment attached to it obviously deterred members from attending meetings held in the public gaze, and it made the NA's work quite distinct from that of the AA. Users who coped with the stigma of illicit drug use carried the additional burden of its illegality. Yet, despite internal setbacks and external pressures, the resilient stewardship of Jimmy K. and other southern California

[11] See Narcotics Anonymous World Services, *Miracles Happen: The Birth of the Narcotics Anonymous in Words and in Pictures* (Chatsworth, CA: NAWS, 1998), p. 18.
[12] Ibid., pp. 18–19.
[13] Ibid., pp. 27–8.

members ultimately led to the modern, formal organization of Narcotics Anonymous in late 1959.

Compared to the membership ranks and the public reception of Alcoholics Anonymous, the NA was off to a slow start. Still, altered ideas of addiction in general had very real effects on how narcotic use in particular was portrayed and discussed in the late 1950s. By increments and in small ways, the code of silence imposed by Commissioner Anslinger on the media regarding illicit drug use was broken. Some of these lapses could be found in motion pictures, the venue in which Anslinger had the most leverage – playing off the already existing Hollywood codes governing cinematic production – and hence violations of his "narcotic" moratorium were all the more surprising. Certainly one of the most stunning of these came in Universal's 1958 *Touch of Evil*, directed and adapted by Orson Welles, who also starred in the film. The film noir classic was based on the novel *Badge of Evil* by Whit Masterson, but the book itself does not touch on narcotics; adding this dimension was among the changes Welles worked into his screenplay. The film follows the travails of a Mexican narcotics detective, played by Charlton Heston, who recently married an American woman. Heston's character, Detective Vargas, investigates a major cross-border drug ring and, in revenge for his success, members of that gang kidnap his wife from a deserted motel in Mexico.

In telling his revised story, Welles offered his audience the kind of imagery that Commissioner Anslinger had long railed against: narcotic use portrayed with sexually tinged titillation. As Vargas's wife awaits her husband alone in her motel room, she hears a voice from the neighboring room. "You know what the Mary Jane is?" a sinister-sounding whisper from behind a motel wall asks the stranded Mrs. Vargas. "You know what a 'main-liner' is?" Mrs. Vargas, presumably exposed to this drug jargon as the wife of a narcotics detective, is nevertheless puzzled by these questions. "I think so," she replies with some confusion. "But what's that got to do with me?" "It will make you feel real good," the voice replies. Vargas's wife recoils from the wall in horror, the picture of innocence in a billowy and chaste white cotton nightgown. Just then her captors enter, dressed in black leather and bopping to rambunctious rock 'n' roll music, providing the audience with certain cultural "cues" to suggest their menacing nature. Members of the gang surround her and, the audience is left to assume as it views the closing of the motel room door, administer her drugs against her will. The oppositional symbolism and illicit excitement engendered in the scene suggests a parallel between drug use and sexual defilement, precisely the kind of erotic transgressiveness that Commissioner Anslinger feared but, in truth, one that he routinely deployed as a trope in his own speeches and writing as he paired seduction with illicit drug use.

Even the mere mention of the drug jargon like "mainlining" or "Mary Jane" would have been unthinkable even just a few years prior, as would allusions to actual drug use or a portrayal of addicts themselves. These daring moves in *Touch of Evil* had been made possible years earlier, when irate motion picture executives wrote to Anslinger, expressing their upset over the fact that television had been "allowed" to depict narcotic use during that year. Anslinger wrote back that he felt "reasonably certain that TV will have to come around to the Code," at least on the "subject of juvenile delinquency," by which Anslinger meant the code's insistence that adult authority be portrayed respectfully and that the misbehavior of young people not be celebrated or redeemed by the outcome of a plot.[14] Yet months later, in October 1955, the action series *Highway Patrol* featured yet another image of a young woman seduced by narcotics. "Bolo," the young woman's supplier, "always had plenty of 'H' for me," the bed-ridden recovering addict – once again the picture of innocence in a diaphanous white nightgown – confessed to the series' lead, a State Patrol chief played by Broderick Crawford. "H" skirted the explicit mention of heroin, as the television's writers surely intended, but only just.

In fact, illicit drug rings had long been fodder for television (and radio) crime dramas, an indirect result of the fact that each particular network had its own censor and hence its own code of conduct.[15] This patchwork system yielded a more fluid system of oversight than was the case in films produced under the uniform code. ABC, for example, felt that children's shows should never show a stuttering child or the image of a snake, unless it was a "zoo" program, in which case snakes were allowed.[16] These idiosyncratic standards varied from network to network and were inherited from radio, a medium that was generally allowed to broadcast much racier plots than cinema. As a result, narcotic plots could appear on television, as they had on radio, but not in movies. The

---

[14] Anslinger to Martin Quigley, Jr., March 24, 1955, Records of the Drug Enforcement Administration, Subject Files of the Bureau of Narcotics and Dangerous Drugs, 1916–1970, *NARA*, Box 32.

[15] For a review of youth-targeted media that transgressed or skirted established standards, see Ronald D. Cohen, "The Delinquents: Censorship and Youth Culture in Recent U.S. History," *History of Education Quarterly* 37, no. 3 (Autumn 1997): 251–70.

[16] See John Crosby, "Thank Your Stars for TV Censors," *Washington Post and Times Herald*, May 27, 1956, p. J6.

interesting early 1950s series *Treasury Men in Action* enacted such plots regularly, alongside its standard fare of counterfeit operations and illegal alcohol production, or even the occasional income tax fraud case. Taken together, *Treasury Men* certainly confirms the more militant cast of the Treasury Department during this time, still the federal government's premier enforcement department. And of course, the first run of the famed Los Angeles Police Department crime series, *Dragnet*, also sometimes took on the subject of illicit drug smuggling.

Yet images of addicts or actual depictions of drug use were not to be found among these episodes. NBC, for example, insisted that "narcotic be treated as a vicious habit and that its effect not be shown in sensational detail."[17] Most construed this as a ban on showing addicts. Then, in 1955, television suddenly broke that taboo, and the cinema followed quickly on its heels with the release that same of year of *The Man with the Golden Arm*, based on the novel by Nelson Algren. The movie, starring Frank Sinatra as the heroin-addicted musician Frankie Machine, represented an altogether stunning departure from the code, placing an addict at the center of its story and featuring numerous and graphic allusions to drug use, drug slang, and drug paraphernalia. The radical nature of the project was not lost on the Motion Picture Association of America, which refused to certify the film and award it MPA's "seal of approval."

Despite its limited release, critics lavished praise on the film and, in the wake of the acclaim, the Motion Picture Association revised the code to allow for more images of addiction and drug use. This change paved the way for *Touch of Evil* and other early path-breaking films, including the 1957 drama *Monkey on My Back*, a story that begins in the Pacific theater of World War II, where the copious amounts of morphine were by now a familiar starting point to many stories of addiction. The Bureau of Narcotics remained steadfast in its disapproval of these and all such images of drug use. "Many young people who have become addicted," one Bureau official wrote several years later, "have done so, not because of ignorance of the consequences, but because they have learned too much about the effects of drugs and have developed a morbid curiosity and unwholesome interest regarding narcotics."[18]

[17] Ibid.
[18] Gaffney, Deputy Commissioner, to J. A. Eashelman, September 17, 1964, Records of the Drug Enforcement Administration, Subject Files of the Bureau of Narcotics and Dangerous Drugs, 1916–1970, NARA, Box 38.

Fictionalized representations of drug use and addiction upset Bureau officials, and they continued to do so for many years. But this irritation was slight when compared to that elicited by press coverage that deviated from Bureau orthodoxy. The slightest infraction raised suspicion, as was the case when society columnist John Crosby, writing for the *Washington Post and Times Herald* in 1956, recalled for his readers his train of thought while in the hospital. "And when did they invent this stuff, morphine, anyhow?" Crosby mused. "I don't know how many of you have ever looked at [television star] Red Skelton while hopped to the ears on morphine," the columnist ventured to wonder, but, he added, "brother, it's the greatest."[19] The Bureau recorded the columnist's name and the offending piece in its records, awaiting some manner of disposition should another infraction come to light. Sometimes the commissioner did not wait. Anslinger wrote immediately to KTLA-TV of Los Angeles after the station hosted a frank discussion of drug use among various local figures in 1956. An incensed Anslinger informed producers that one panelist, a Dr. Crane, "stated that [narcotics use] was engulfing the nation." To the contrary, Anslinger insisted, "it is not found in the New England states, Minnesota, the Dakotas," or, astonishingly enough, "the south," though the Commissioner hedged this assertion by adding, "except in New Orleans and Texas."[20]

As Anslinger struggled to maintain the integrity of his statements before the Daniel Subcommittee – that heroin use was confined, if not decreasing, and that the penalties instituted under the Boggs Act served as an effective deterrent – he left editors and producers with the impression that they had run afoul of the government just by reporting what was evident: illicit drug use was apparent and on the rise. Yet a rebuke from the commissioner did not necessarily suffice in silencing the press, at least not anymore. A new generation of aspiring journalists no longer had to contend with the cultural constraints of the early 1950s and the height of McCarthyism. By the middle of the decade, only vestiges of that climate of censure remained. Chet Huntley of the *New York Times* took advantage of new license when he filed a series on Los Angeles addicts in December 1955. Two years later, an article in the *San Fernando Valley Mirror News* detailed the work of the burgeoning Narcotics Anonymous in southern

---

[19] John Crosby, "Radio and Television" Column, *Washington Post and Times Herald,* January 30, 1956, found in Records of the Drug Enforcement Administration, Subject Files of the Bureau of Narcotics and Dangerous Drugs, 1916–1970, *NARA,* Box 32.

[20] Anslinger to Clinton Thienes, October 11, 1956, ibid.

California, including the organization's desire to see "realistic" narcotic instruction in schools, an agenda clearly patterned after the National Council on Alcoholism.[21]

In many ways the most remarkable challenge to Anslinger's publicly iterated dogmas of illicit drug use and addiction came in 1958 from CBS News, at the hands of famed journalist Walter Cronkite and television producer Al Wasserman. When Cronkite narrated a two-part story written and directed by Wasserman as part of their "Twentieth Century" series, CBS News must have worried about the show's reception. After all, in the series, "The Addicts," Cronkite and Wasserman discarded so much of accepted wisdom promoted by the Bureau of Narcotics. Perhaps television executives assuaged themselves with the thought that the episodes mentioned the Bureau by name only once, citing the commissioner's (suspiciously durable) figure of 60,000 addicts. "Some other estimates have been considerably higher," Cronkite remarked following his reference to the statistic, a glancing blow to Anslinger that fell deliberately short of direct defiance.

Still, much in the two programs amounted to just that. The first part of the series, "Portrait of a Young Addict," told the story of Fred through his own voice and those who knew him best. Cronkite introduced the piece by observing that addiction was "not the most important of our social problems," but, he noted, it was "among the most complex ... and misunderstood." Close-up camera shots of Fred's friends and colleagues followed, each declaring Fred's struggle with addiction to be implausible; he struck those who knew him as "as normal." Then another addict, Dave, admitted to knowing him since Fred was nineteen, when he started "using junk." As Fred's health and quality of life declined, his mother described a cycle of detention and release from Riverside Hospital, the island-sequestered treatment facility off of New York City dedicated to the recovery of juvenile addicts. Once, while confined at Riverside, Fred and a friend used the inner tube of a tire to support a swim across the East River, back to Manhattan's shore in search of their next hit. Finally, as the psychiatrist at the hospital recalled with relief, Fred took an interest in some shop classes, demonstrating real skill and a desire to stay sober.

"We look upon drug addiction as a symptom of an emotional disorder," the same bespectacled psychiatrist observed in an aloof academic fashion, "plus an accident – the accident being exposure to drugs." Here

[21] *Miracles Happen*, p. 38.

the audience listened to a credible authority articulating the "disease model" of addiction directly, a model that influenced the work of Fred's next step in his journey, a small gathering of the northeast branch of Narcotics Anonymous. The camera recorded a simulated meeting of the group, closely focused on various participants as they stepped forward to tell their story. Most, like Fred, were white; some were women; a few, like Dave, were middle-aged. As a visual and in their testimonials, the NA meeting ran counter to Anslinger's depiction of addiction as principally comprised of blacks or down and out criminals. Instead, a diverse and rather subdued group spoke with disarming candor, narrating their struggle to stay sober. Dave, the leader of the group, revealed to the group and to the television audience that after four months of sobriety, Fred had a relapse and was now detained in prison. A careful but introspective conversation followed, as Dave, visiting Fred in prison, pleaded with Fred not to try to go it alone, but rather to rely on his NA support group even as he served time. Some would say the story of Fred was a failure, but, as Dave observed with a compassionate sensibility, four months of sobriety was a triumph in its own right. "Prison is neither the answer, nor the end," he reflected to a closing shot of Fred being led away in handcuffs.

If this first part of "The Addicts" made bold though largely anecdotal claims, the second installment affirmed and elevated them to the level of explicit argument. Probably nothing broached heresy of the Bureau of Narcotics' various dogmas as clearly as this episode entitled, appropriately enough, "Addict: Criminal or Patient?" The program opened in a context that was at once familiar and jarring: an addict attempting to buy heroin, watched at a distance from police. Viewers of television crime dramas were probably accustomed to this scenario, yet CBS News broadcast actual footage. As a police squad car followed the addict out of camera frame, law enforcement officers who watched from a viewing post yelled at their colleagues, "Come on! Step on it!" fearful that this presumptive criminal would shake his pursuers. As Walter Cronkite concluded, this encounter epitomized the reigning view of the addict as well as the government's response. "But how accurate is this image [of the addict]?" Cronkite wondered, this supposed "dope fiend" who would mercilessly commit crime in support of his habit.

The episode next cut to an interview with the soft-spoken Carol, a recovering addict who had a melancholy and confiding demeanor. As she spoke about her addiction, her interviewer asked her whether she had "ever 'boosted'," a slang term for shoplifting, "or prostituted when you weren't using drugs?" "No," she replied with some resentment, as she shook her head. The question was of some importance, as Commissioner Anslinger often described addicts as born criminals whose lives just happened to veer into illicit drug use. Following Carol there was Jimmy, whose tale of addiction came the closest to conforming to the picture of an addict as painted by Anslinger. A shoplifter who stole prodigiously in order to support his habit, Jimmy disclosed the impressive frequency of his crimes in the interview. And yet, as Cronkite observed, property crimes were the extent of addict criminality. Charges of violence or sex crimes were simply inconsistent with the addict profile, he asserted, and a parade of addicts followed to confirm this view. Addiction turned a user into a lethargic and listless person; Carol returned on camera to describe the desire to get high as akin to "a baby in a crib" who needed "formula." The only time he exhibited any hyper activity, one unnamed addict offered, was when he was running "to a connection" or "from police." After discrediting the Bureau's claims on criminality, Cronkite made a still more forceful point: "Yet our attitude has been to treat addiction as if it were a moral one," and, regrettably, "treatment facilities are almost non-existent."

The episode then cut to footage shot in a prison ward, perhaps the most haunting scene of the entire series. The men in the sick beds were taking "the cure," as Anslinger would have it: they were going cold turkey and suffering through withdrawal. As they writhed in pain, no medical staff was present to supervise them, nor did they benefit from any counseling or recovery personnel. Cronkite emphasized that most, if not all, of these addicts would relapse. Two had committed suicide. Just who was served by structuring the response to the addict in this way? Certainly not the criminal justice system, New York Commissioner of Corrections Anna Kross appeared on screen to say. Her extended monologue ended the series, summing up its crucial interventions. "Drug addicts consume a great deal of the facilities of the courts and criminal justice system," she remarked, yet, "in spite of over forty years of increasingly punitive measures, we're confronted today with a costly problem and a growing one." Punishment as a deterrent had not worked. What the country needed, Kross suggested, was a "climate of opinion" that addiction is a "medical, social problem and a health problem" that would "permit us to view the addict as a sick and troubled human being."[22]

---

[22] Series available for viewing at the *Library of Congress*, Moving Images Division, LC Control No: fi 67000144 and 67000145.

At the vanguard of promoting just such a change were several important professional voices. First among these was the medical profession, which had every reason to concern itself with addiction. Not only did most healthcare providers object to criminalization on medical principles, an estimated 1 out of every 100 medical workers was an addict himself, a ratio that even Commissioner Anslinger endorsed as accurate, though only quietly in correspondence. The California State Board of Medical Examiners published confirmation of this high addict ratio in the Bulletin of the Los Angeles County Medical Association in April 1958.[23] So, when the chairman of the groundbreaking Committee on Alcoholism and Narcotics of New York State Medical Society, Dr. Herbert Berger, revealed the results of his work to *New York Times* readers in July 1956, it is not surprising that he began by asking "What manner of person is the addict?" A shy, reticent person, he answered, who is "employable and [can] carry on difficult and precise work as long as they receive narcotics regularly." Addicts are "found in all businesses and professions," Dr. Berger insisted, "[m]y own, unfortunately, has many of them."

The work of Berger's committee built upon the precedent set years ago by a New York City Committee on Public Health convened to study marijuana in 1948.[24] The LaGuardia Report issued on the committee's findings took exception to key assertions by Anslinger regarding the drug; namely, the committee did not feel that marijuana incited users to violent behavior, nor did it agree that it was a "gateway" drug leading ineluctably to other illicit drug use. Worst of all, at least from the commissioner's perspective, the committee observed no physical or mental damage from long-term marijuana use. The Bureau naturally denounced the results as unwarranted from the research and improper, yet the LaGuardia Report achieved its most immediate purpose nonetheless. For years following its release, defense lawyers waved the report in front of a judge while attempting to gain leniency for a client charged with a marijuana infraction in New York City courts. Anslinger viewed even this limited circulation and use of the committee's work as reprehensible. "I say the report was a government printed invitation to youth and adults – above all teenagers," he warned, "to go ahead and smoke all the reefers they felt like."[25]

[23] Anslinger confirmation in response to Earl L. Douglass, December 8, 1952, Records of the Drug Enforcement Administration, Subject Files of the Bureau of Narcotics and Dangerous Drugs, 1916–1970, *NARA*, Box 38; Study referenced in ibid., April 3, 1958.

[24] For more on this committee, see Eric C. Schneider, *Smack: Heroin and the American City* (Philadelphia: University of Pennsylvania Press, 2008), chap. 2.

[25] Anslinger, *Murderers*, p. 40.

When the New York Medical Society took up the gauntlet to argue for leniency years later, they did so in a more tolerant authorizing environment and political culture. After all, discussing addiction more openly and along the lines of a disease had made significant headway in the intervening years. Perhaps that is why Dr. Berger felt he could challenge Anslinger so pointedly: "We keep hearing about a cure," Berger wrote, "and this error ... leads us to the faulty conclusion that the addict is responsible for his relapse. One might as well be indicted for having a recurrence of cancer," Berger remarked, revealing his rather robust notion of the "disease model" of addiction. The chairman went on to flout Anslinger's orthodoxy where the narcotics commissioner would feel it most: politics. As the Daniel Subcommittee deliberated, Berger reminded his readers of the original logic of the Boggs Bill. "[W]e were promised that the stiffer sentences [the Boggs Bill] provided for would control the narcotic problem," and yet, "only five years later, we are urged by Congress that application of the death penalty will help to remedy the situation."[26] Was the ineffectiveness of punishment a sign of its leniency, as Congress supposed, or did it reflect upon the failure of punishment itself?

The ensuing denunciations of Berger by Federal Bureau of Narcotics officials could not stall the growing ranks of professional discontent with the punishment approach. More and more, the legal and medical professional communities found themselves locked in a relationship of common dissent, with healthcare workers railing against the conceit of addiction as a crime, and legal experts emphasizing the deleterious effects of such an approach on the criminal justice system. Rebecca Carroll recounts the story of the group that formally represented that common dissent, the ABA-AMA Joint Committee formed in 1955 to study addiction and the punishment of addicts.[27] By the time the six-member group began its work in earnest, Carroll notes, members of the Council on Mental Health of the American Medical Association had already made their views known in a set of recommendations put forward in 1956. The first among these observed that the "operations of clinics which dispensed drugs to addicts between 1919–1923 shows that data available on these

---

[26] All quotes of Berger from "To Dispel the Nightmare of Narcotics," *New York Times Magazine*, July 8, 1956, found in Records of the Drug Enforcement Administration, Subject Files of the Bureau of Narcotics and Dangerous Drugs, 1916–1970, NARA, Box 32.

[27] Rebecca Caroll, "The Narcotic Act Triggers the Great Nondebate: Treatment Loses to Punishment," in *Federal Drug Control: The Evolution of Policy and Practice*, in Erlen et al., eds. (New York: Haworth Press, 2004), pp. 101–45.

clinics are not sufficiently objective to be of any value."[28] In one fell
stroke, the AMA challenged the Bureau of Narcotics' frequent assertions
that these early clinics offered unequivocal evidence against the clinical
model specifically, and a treatment approach more generally.

The Bureau disagreed, and vehemently so. Characterizing the renewed
attention to clinics as a proposal for "feeding stations" for narcotics,
Bureau officials reminded medical groups that "public health authorities"
agree that "narcotic addiction is contagious," and hence, "these so-called
experts who would establish clinics are simply advocating the spread of
narcotic addiction."[29] At times the Bureau could not resist even more disparaging commentary, including conjuring the vision that, should a treatment approach go forward, it ought to be in "a government building,
the first floor of which should be a bar for alcoholics, the second floor a
narcotic dispensary for teen-agers and other addicts where they can be
furnished heroin, marihuana and cocaine, the third floor a department
store for kleptomaniacs, and the fourth floor a brothel for sex deviates."[30]
Such alarmist condemnations of the treatment approach revealed many
of the key suppositions of the Bureau's understanding of addiction. In the
eyes of Bureau officials, addiction was sinful, a depraved indulgence that
could only lead to more sin; it was "contagious"; and licit dispensation
of narcotics was tantamount to approval of them.

The AMA-ABA joint committee was not too impressed with the
Bureau's denunciations, and opted to embrace the Mental Health
Council's recommendations without question. And, even though
the council had couched its suggestions in a deliberately diplomatic
language – agreeing, for instance, that there were probably "not more
than 60,000 addicts in the United States at present" – the thrust of its
intervention could not be more antithetical to the Bureau's purposes.
"Opiates do not directly incite persons to commit violent crimes," the
council concluded, and, what was more, the current "treatment of

---

[28] Summary and Recommendations of Report on Narcotic Addiction by the Council on
Mental Health of the American Medical Association (1956), included in *Drug Addiction:
Crime or Disease? Interim and Final Reports of the Joint Committee of the American Bar
Association and the American Medical Association on Narcotic Drugs* (Bloomington:
Indiana University Press, 1961), p. 169.

[29] R. T. Mitchell, Assistant to the Commissioner, "Narcotic Law Enforcement," Speech to
the IACP and response to the San Francisco AMA's endorsement of a clinic system in
New Orleans, September 28, 1954, Records of the Drug Enforcement Administration,
Subject Files of the Bureau of Narcotics and Dangerous Drugs, 1916–1970, *NARA*,
Box 3.

[30] Ibid.

addiction is unsatisfactory." Hence the council recommended that states develop care and treatment facilities, including measures to support recovering addicts post-treatment, and that the AMA investigate ways to confine criminal punishment more closely to illicit sales for, in the council's estimation, "mandatory minimum sentences for addict violators [interferes] with the possible treatment and rehabilitation of addicts and therefore should be abolished."[31]

Accepting the council's conclusions without question resolved some of the most important medical aspects of the addiction review charged to the joint committee. Not surprisingly, legal voices took the lead, and none was more vocal than attorney Rufus King, a drug circle activist for decades who would ultimately use his experience to write a blistering attack on the Bureau of Narcotics in 1972 called *The Drug Hang Up: America's Fifty Year Folly*. Another notable member of the joint committee was Abe Fortas, a lawyer who would go on to become a Justice of the Supreme Court in 1965. Perhaps it was Fortas's acumen and political judgment that prevailed in the joint committee's decision to proceed "slowly" on the question of narcotics. Despite its caution, the joint committee aroused the suspicion of Anslinger, who responded to its formation by creating his own advisory committee – chaired by close ally Louisiana Representative Hale Boggs – and replete with notables who, according to Rufus King, "never actually convened" as a group.[32]

When the joint committee issued an *Interim Report* in 1958, its members probably believed its recommendations were tentative and designed for discussion. For example, the committee members observed that a treatment approach to addiction might be a good idea, so, they suggested, perhaps one ought to be established in the District of Columbia for experimental purposes. The chair sent a copy of the *Interim Report* to Anslinger for review and comment; the commissioner responded with a vicious attack and a total failure to engage the joint committee on any issue of substance, despite numerous invitations issued to do just that. King attempted to mollify Anslinger by pointing out that the joint committee had not recommended the establishment of clinics per se, merely that one ought to be started for research purposes and on an experimental basis. These good faith attempts to reach out to Anslinger were to no avail and, as might be expected, the commissioner's total dismissal of the

---

[31] All quotes from Council, ibid., 169–73.
[32] This is according to Rufus King as quoted in Carroll, "The Narcotic Act Triggers the Great Nondebate," p. 113.

joint committee's work propelled its members toward greater skepticism of the Bureau.

Undeterred by Anslinger's dismissal of their work, the joint committee saw its *Interim* recommendations ratified by both the ABA and AMA Houses of Delegates that same year.[33] The Bureau responded with a report from its own advisory committee, rejecting the joint committee's work in a sloppy effort that appeared simply to cobble together previous position papers in a haphazard and disjointed fashion. Three years after the *Interim* findings, the joint committee released its *Final Report* and chose to use funding from the Russell Sage Foundation to publish its results, along with the *Interim Report*, with the Indiana University Press under the title, *Drug Addiction: Crime or Disease?* The introduction to this collection of material was written by Anslinger's old *bête-noir*, Alfred R. Lindesmith, Indiana University professor, addiction researcher, and an enterprising critic who was doubtless instrumental in securing the publishing contract for the joint committee in the first place. The decision to collect the full work of the committee in one volume, Lindesmith explained in his introduction, was owing to "the comprehensive attack upon it [that] was published in 1959" by the Bureau. While the joint committee never imagined a need to circulate its *Interim Report* beyond professional circles, Anslinger's widely noted denunciations of it seemed to warrant a wider distribution of the report.

Though still cautious, the joint committee's *Final Report* clearly articulated the need for more research and alternative programs, including treatment programs. Clearly the professional authority of its authors weighed heavily in the report's reception, with even the *New York Times* offering that the careful and heavily qualified prose amounted to "one of the strongest attacks ever made" on Anslinger and the Bureau.[34] Accordingly, Narcotic officials reacted to the joint committee's efforts with tremendous suspicion and contempt. When the commissioner received the report, he had only very recently read Ian Fleming's interview with that famous gangster in exile, "Lucky" Luciano, in which the former narcotic dealer criticized the Bureau's enforcement and punishment approach. For Anslinger this coincidence represented an opportunity. The commissioner "blasted" the joint committee's work, one

[33] Carroll discusses Anslinger's attempts to publish a similar looking "interim report" of his own advisory committee, perhaps to dupe unwitting readers into thinking that the Bureau's views were in fact the findings of the AMA-ABA joint committee. See Carroll, "The Narcotic Act Triggers the Great Nondebate."

[34] "Report Questions Narcotic Policy," *New York Times*, April 30, 1961, p. 76.

reporter friendly to the Bureau wrote, by noting that the "the only person who has given it 'unqualified support' is Charles 'Lucky' Luciano, one-time New York vice king." AMA and ABA members must have been surprised, and many chagrined, to find themselves aligned with one of the most notorious criminals of his day. Still more upsetting was the fact that Anslinger ordered one of his agents out to Indiana University to "investigate" the publication of the joint committee's report. Though the commissioner dismissed these intimidation tactics as a "routine check," Dr. Lindesmith was certainly not the only one to invoke the specter of McCarthyism and wonder how this inquiry fell under the purview of a law enforcement agency.[35]

Indeed, the commissioner's willingness to overstep his agency's bounds earned him a fair share of critics – many of whom resented, in one way or another, the Bureau's incursion into their own affairs. Of this group, none was more important than uniformed local police. The sources of friction between Bureau agents and local law enforcement were numerous and varied. At its most base, the rivalry was contested over which agency would enjoy the spoils of narcotic work: money from the black market, or "informal economy," not reported as income or earnings and thus ideal for taking surreptitiously. At a more professional level, police often derided the Bureau's eagerness to use their local informers, usually drug addicts, but to do nothing with them other than arrest them. The willingness of the police to turn over an informer hinged upon the Bureau's presumptively superior ability to "connect the dots" and make meaningful arrests at higher levels of the supply chain. Yet time and again, the Bureau showed neither the ambition nor competence for doing so. "Small fry," in the words of U.S. Attorney Thomas Wadden, was enough to satisfy the Bureau, especially when such arrests could be presented to a gullible or tractable press corps as major breakthroughs. But local police knew better and, after a time, became reluctant to share resources with the Bureau. Finally, there was a more fundamental antagonism between some police, especially police reformers, and the Bureau; there were those, like Progressive-era Police Chief August Vollmer, who just did not believe that drug use should be in the law enforcement portfolio at all.[36]

[35] Charles D. Pierce, "Drug Addiction Stirs Federal Criticism," *Washington Evening Star*, April 19, 1961, found in Records of the Drug Enforcement Administration, Subject Files of the Bureau of Narcotics and Dangerous Drugs, 1916–1970, *NARA*, Box 8.
[36] The *New York Times* reports that not only is this particular law enforcement critique of the drug war alive and well, its proponents are often punished for their views: Marc Lacey, "Police Officers Find that Dissent on Drug Laws May Come with a Price," *New York*

Of these different tensions, the public would come to learn of the latter first, and pay it the least regard. Vollmer's criticism of the Bureau and the punishment approach had been on record for nearly twenty years, and to little effect. The last source of tension, the competing corruption of narcotics agents and police officers, became publicly known only in the late 1960s and, once known, it attracted the most notice. But it is the middle tension – the clash between professional cultures, and the sycophantic use of local police resources and information by the Bureau without reciprocation or an end result that would placate local law enforcement – that, at least numerically speaking, won the most police support. And, though this tension was obvious to anyone involved in a big city police department by the late 1950s, it would be one of the nation's best known and most controversial police chiefs, Los Angeles Chief William Parker, to first give it public voice.

Typical for Parker, that voice was an accusatory and irate one. The chief who assumed the head of his agency based on a reputation of "incorruptiblity" was in fact a devoted engineer of police autonomy – autonomy from corrupt officials and mobsters, as well as autonomy from reformers and city officials who desired more police accountability. The heavy-drinking Parker was also given to flashes of temper and sometimes rage. He divorced his first wife after beating her and was, throughout his career, prone to outbursts and intemperate remarks. These episodes unfolded alongside Parker's other pronounced features and public performances: his dogged approach to police work (famously lionized by the radio and then television series *Dragnet*), his impressive ministrations to his local American Legion Post and the Roman Catholic Archdiocese, and his refusal to return Los Angeles to "open" city status – that is, "open" for business with organized crime. Under his watchful eye, Parker insisted that police hold no truck with gangsters.[37] For many in LA, the chief was the revered engineer of a "professional" police force. For others who were familiar with his agency's remarkably powerful "Intelligence Division," his routine violations of civil liberties, including covert spying and the collection of information regarding those he deemed "radical," Chief Parker was a reactionary who regularly indulged in dictatorial methods for dubious purposes. In this strange admixture of autocratic tendencies

Times, December 2, 2011, http://www.nytimes.com/2011/12/03/us/officers-punished-for-supporting-eased-drug-laws.html?_r=1&hpw [accessed December 3, 2011].

[37] See John Buntin, *L.A. Noir: The Struggle for the Soul of America's Most Seductive City* (New York: Harmony Books, 2009).

combined with the celebration of a professional ethos, Parker resembled two national law enforcement figures quite well: FBI Director J. Edgar Hoover, and U.S. Bureau of Narcotics Commissioner Harry Anslinger.

Both would become detested rivals of Chief Parker, most likely because Parker harbored an ambition to become a national law enforcement figure himself.[38] In 1956, Senate aide Robert Kennedy reached out to Chief Parker during his investigations into organized crime after finding the FBI to be without useful information.[39] From that point on, Parker, an outspoken Republican, would always have a special relationship with the ambitious Kennedy family. As he consolidated his hold over LA's police and nourished political ties outside of his city, the chief ventured to offer proposals for a national clearinghouse of police information – something that the FBI and Hoover were correct to surmise as a threat to their status as the nation's chief coordinator of law enforcement.[40] Parker's relations with the Bureau, however, remained amicable, at least outwardly so.

All that changed in April 1960, a presidential election year, and a time when change seemed imminent. Chief Parker was in no position to commit a heresy against Bureau orthodoxy, as he had long subscribed to Anslinger's idea that addiction promoted crime, and vice versa. In fact, in most respects, Parker's rhetoric on illicit drug use matched Ansligner's platform of ideas closely. Just two years prior, Parker denounced local judges for "coddling" narcotic addicts by virtue of "lenient" sentencing.[41] Nevertheless, when Eisenhower's Interdepartmental Committee on Narcotics visited Los Angeles for a special hearing in the spring of 1960, Parker (and others) sensed an opportunity. Seizing the moment, the chief laid into the Bureau. A Mexican heroin syndicate was fully known to the narcotics officials, Parker claimed, and yet they failed to act. The *Los Angeles Times* reported the gist of Parker's comments as urging the Bureau to strike at the source and chase the supply coming from Mexico. "If the Los Angeles Police Department can learn the identity of that syndicate," the chief remarked to the committee, "the federal agencies have it, too." Parker then went on to suggest that the committee consider

---

[38] On Hoover's sense of Parker, see ibid., p. 192.

[39] This would come as no surprise to anyone familiar with the output, rather than outcome, measures toward which J. Edgar Hoover steered his agency: See Kathleen J. Frydl, "Kidnapping and U.S. State Development," *Studies in American Political Development* 20, no. 1 (April 2006): 18–44.

[40] See Buntin, *L.A. Noir*, p. 162.

[41] Walter Ames, "Parker Blames Dope Traffic for 50% of All LA Crime," *Los Angeles Times*, June 17, 1956, p. 2.

"closing the border," a rather loose (and perhaps inebriated) comment that caught his listeners off guard. "Are you recommending that the border be closed?" an incredulous committee member asked. "I didn't say that," Chief Parker replied, confusing his listeners even more, then adding, "but if that's the only way you can get anything done then maybe that's the solution."[42] Parker went on to encourage a White House conference on illicit drugs, with all of the power and prestige of the executive behind it, so as to impress upon Mexican officials the importance of suppressing drug traffic.

Not surprisingly, the chief's testimony made headlines. Interestingly, the Bureau's own report of Parker's appearance before the committee emphasized different aspects of his statement. Trusted Anslinger aide Charles Siragusa filed his summary of Parker's comments directly with the commissioner, noting at the outset that the chief "spoke at great length, extemporaneously ... His remarks were inflammatory, virtually vitriolic against our Bureau," he warned the commissioner, and he had no choice but to believe that Parker "delivered himself of a great cargo of long nurtured hate against our Bureau." What was the substance of Parker's remarks? To Siragusa it seemed to be Parker's assertions that the Bureau "washes its feet in the same bathtub his men do" and, moreover, that narcotics agents were "angry at him because we want him to give us informers and information; that he will not do it; that he never will." The chief went on to praise the LAPD's special narcotics unit, and he told the committee that "[t]he Federal Agency looks for quantity in cases rather than quality."[43]

Interestingly, the chief's more workaday objections, carefully recorded by Siragusa, failed to make news; his call for a White House conference, however, did. Commissioner Anslinger was already on record declaring those who supported such an idea "crackpots," although when the *Los Angeles Times* editorial board, one of the several prominent proponents of a conference, took exception to this, Anslinger backed off and insisted that he referred only to a "medico-legal group," meaning the Joint AMA-ABA committee. "We really don't care what he calls us," the paper's editorial writers admitted shortly thereafter, "if he will give the White House conference his influential support."[44] When Chief Parker

[42] Ibid.
[43] Siragusa to H.J. Anslinger, April 1, 1960, Records of the Drug Enforcement Administration, Subject Files of the Bureau of Narcotics and Dangerous Drugs, 1916–1970, *NARA*, Box 2.
[44] "A Hopeful Reconciliation," *Los Angeles Times*, March 23, 1960, p. B4.

joined the chorus of those calling for a White House review, the idea seemed to have the support of a diverse California coalition, including that of one of Parker's great enemies, Democratic governor Pat Brown. The subsequent acceptance of and deference to the conference idea marked, among other things, the rising importance of California in national life and, especially, in electoral politics. Accordingly, a new president, John F. Kennedy, defied Anslinger's wishes and called for a White House conference. For several years prior, lone critics of Anslinger had multiplied into respectable pockets of dissent, and there was now ample room to challenge the Bureau of Narcotics. As the editorial board of the *Washington Post and Times Herald* observed only months after Kennedy assumed office, "there is nothing sacrosanct about the 1956 [Daniel] act," and practical experience suggested that there was "very little reason for continuing that law in force of adhering longer to the policy [of deterrent punishment] it sets forth." "[R]examination," they concluded, was "long overdue."[45]

There was yet another force at work, inchoate but powerful, in calling for change, and that was the way in which Jack Kennedy embraced and embodied youth, and the corresponding forces that were unleashed by the energies he tapped into. A kind of youthful exuberance and, at times, insolence, was evident in the ways in which countless teenagers and young adults rejected the government's outmoded ideas regarding illicit drugs. Though this dismissal has been most often associated with the beatniks—a cadre of disaffected artists, many of whom took illicit drugs with reckless abandon—the most significant facet of the youth movement was the way in which far greater numbers of young people rejected the government line on marijuana. Through films like *Reefer Madness*, young viewers encountered the laughable claims that constituted the "official" view: namely, that marijuana induced violent behavior and was physically addictive.[46] A young person did not have to be a stalwart member of the "beat" generation to regard these as specious; marijuana was not yet common among college undergraduates, but it was not unheard of either. Jazz festivals like Newport attracted thousands of co-eds, at least as much for its atmosphere of rowdy party behavior as for its exceptional

---

[45] "Throw the Book at Them," *Washington Post and Times Herald*, April 25, 1961, p. A14.

[46] "Is the campy appeal of a film such as *Reefer Madness* ... the product of a half century's distance, or were midcentury audiences in on the joke?" historian Regina Kunzel wonders. The latter seems more likely, at least to some extent: see Kunzel, Review [untitled], *Journal of American History* 87, no. 4 (March 2001): 1549–50.

musical offerings.[47] At places and at times like these, marijuana circulated widely, second only to alcohol. Through social networks and personal observation or use, marijuana earned a far less nefarious reputation among young people. This savvy and slightly cynical *savoir-faire* fit well with Jack Kennedy's urbane sophistication and dry wit. When the candidate's flashy campaign played Frank Sinatra's special recording of the song "High Hopes" in 1960, countless young Americans listened to the jazzy theme, perhaps some with a wry smile, and sensed that Kennedy was a political figure in step with their generation.

KENNEDY COMMISSION

Jack Kennedy's appeal to young people was, at first, less sardonic than idealistic – and, in fact, boundlessly so. The programs he introduced and the tenor of his administration verged on the quixotic, with calls ranging from placing a "man on the moon" before the end of the decade to the recruitment of select volunteers to change the world either through the militant "Green Berets" or service in the Peace Corps. Apart from new initiatives, the romance of the administration extended to the confident and even cocksure fashion in which it addressed old and seemingly intractable problems – illicit drug use among them. "We are a proud and powerful Nation," the president's brother, Attorney General Robert Kennedy, reminded his audience of drug officials in 1962; "There is no affliction to which we have to surrender." In the same tone of muscular idealism, the attorney general continued,

We have conquered our environment by conquering ignorance. Sewage systems protected us from cholera and typhoid, vaccinations guard us against other diseases. Public and private institutions working with wide public awareness and financial support continue to wage an unremitting campaign against cancer, heart disease, and other afflictions ... Such efforts are not limited to natural afflictions. Increasingly, we are devoting the same kind of urgent effort to socially spawned problems, and our efforts are constantly improving in such areas as mental illness and juvenile delinquency. Yet our approach to the great social product of narcotics and drug abuse reflects none of the same dedication, confidence, or progress. Not only do we not have a comprehensive program; we do not have sufficient reliable information on which to even base such a program.

---

[47] For a discussion of the Newport Jazz Festival that addresses its role in mainstream and affluent white American culture, see Scott Saul, *Freedom Is, Freedom Ain't: Jazz and the Making of the Sixties* (Cambridge: Harvard University Press, 2003).

"To say this about a Nation which won two world wars and sends men into orbit sounds like lunacy or lethargy," Kennedy observed, almost castigating his audience.[48] In the administration's new tack, not many courtesies would be extended to the old way of doing things.

And not much deference was given to Commissioner Anslinger, now viewed as more of a crank than policy leader. In May 1962, Anslinger submitted his resignation to the president, as was his duty to do upon reaching the age of seventy, the mandatory retirement age of government officials unless given an exemption by the executive. Kennedy did not have much time to weigh the decision of whether to extend Anslinger's career in a disinterested fashion; only days after sending it, the commissioner publicly denounced China and Cuba as drug traffickers in Geneva. Both of the targets of his accusations were countries that Kennedy hoped to conciliate: China, because he received intelligence of a growing Sino-Soviet split, and Cuba, because he had badly fumbled his relations with the country by backing an ill-conceived coup against Fidel Castro. Yet here was an official in his administration offering inflammatory remarks, fraying already strained diplomatic ties. What was worse, the accusations rested on suspect evidence, including Anslinger's assertion that the United States had "been free of cocaine addicts for twenty years until the Cuban traffic began," a deceitful remark that obscured years of cocaine-related seizures by the Bureau that Anslinger chose to minimize or ignore.[49] Now he suddenly "discovered" cocaine, and it seems likely that the commissioner deliberately held knowledge of the drug's use in abeyance so that he could invoke it, at the time of his choosing, as a charge against a political enemy.

The president did not take well to this discretionary initiative and refused to allow Anslinger to continue in service. The commissioner clearly had expected him to do so, as he told a reporter in early July that he was "not anxious to retire."[50] Only days later the president's press secretary, Pierre Salinger, announced that Anslinger would leave government shortly. Some newspaper articles describing the departure stopped short of the fulsome praise the commissoner had grown accustomed to in years past, acknowledging instead that he was "one of the most controversial

[48] RFK remarks to the White House Conference on Drug Abuse, September 27, 1962, transcript found in Dean F. Markham File, *John F. Kennedy Library*, Box 4.

[49] "Narcotics Rise Laid to China and Cuba," *New York Times*, June 1, 1962, p. 2.

[50] "Narcotics Foe Anslinger Reluctantly Retires Soon," *Washington Post Times Herald*, July 2, 1962, p. A2.

men in government."[51] One story written with the benefit of an unnamed source claimed that "the administration was mindful that [Anslinger] has made many enemies who challenge his tough-minded approach to narcotics control," a description that could have been intended to refer to an array of medical professionals, legal experts, law enforcement officials, recovery groups, or various governments abroad equally and alike.[52]

A little more than a month after his comments in Geneva, Anslinger was out of office, though he remained as the U.S. representative to the UN drug convention treaty talks. Still, it was a remarkable turn of events. The personal empire of a powerful government official was now up for grabs, and not just that. Because Anslinger was the architect of a particular approach to illicit drug traffic and use, his removal raised the prospect that the country's entire illicit drug regime would be open to review and, perhaps, revision. Henry L. Giordano, Anslinger's deputy and replacement, signaled at least some willingness to consider change. The new commissioner cited his belief that "we should do everything we can to treat addicts whenever we find them, and not wait for them to commit a crime," a fate he felt awaited each and every addict eventually.[53] Still, he was at least open to approaches other than punishment, as well he would be, given that when his boss, Treasury Secretary James Dillon, administered the oath of office to Giordano, Dillon also took care to "hint" to reporters that "under its new chief" the Bureau "might be more receptive to suggestions that narcotics addiction be treated as a disease as well as a criminal offense."[54] And, although Giordano was one of dozens of Anslinger disciples in the Bureau, he had none of the press or congressional contacts that his mentor possessed, despite serving as the Bureau agent "on loan" to the Daniel Subcommittee of 1956.

Hence the Kennedy administration now had an opening to review illicit drugs. They also had an obligation: in the heat of the presidential campaign, Kennedy had promised the attorney general of the state of California that, if elected, he would hold a White House Conference on Narcotics "as soon as it was possible."[55] The attorney general had the

[51] This phrase comes from a UPI story printed in several places; see, for example, "US Narcotics Chief Due to Retire Soon," *Hartford Courant*, July 2, 1962, p. 13D.
[52] Quote from "Narcotics Foe Anslinger Reluctantly Retires Soon."
[53] "Narcotics Policy Divides Officials," *New York Times*, July 9, 1962, p. 21.
[54] "Dillon Swears in Giordano as Narcotics Bureau Head," *New York Times*, August 18, 1962, p. 11.
[55] Undated memorandum explaining conference, Dean F. Markham File, *John F. Kennedy Library*, Box 3.

good sense to extract this concession in writing, and the delegation from California, crucial to Kennedy's electoral success, regularly referred to the telegram. But the White House also took cognizance of other factors in determining that a White House conference should go forward. Once Anslinger stepped down from the Bureau in July 1962, preparations for a conference began in earnest. Only weeks later, former Kennedy lover and Hollywood starlet Marilyn Monroe was found dead in her Brentwood, California, home. Her death was caused by an overdose of sleeping pills, another in a litany of famous people to die this way, either accidentally or as suicide. Dean Markham, White House Special Projects Officer and point man for the conference, mentioned the tragedy specifically in a memorandum that set out the reasons for convening the conference.[56]

Monroe's shocking death gave a poignant aspect to Kennedy's resolve to include the abuse and illicit circulation of prescription drugs in his review, as did his own dependence on amphetamines, a prescription Kennedy relied upon to project an image of a healthy, energetic person rather than someone beset by numerous ailments, including crippling back pain, as indeed he was.[57] For all these personal ties to synthetic drug use and dependence, his administration was preoccupied with a broader, professional crisis as well. Not only had Congress deferred any obligation to regulate addictive synthetics for several years running, but questions regarding the entire system of drug safety and inspection were revived, in horrific ways, early on in the president's term. Thalidomide, a sedative used for cough and headaches introduced in the late 1950s, had been refused FDA licensing because of insufficient clinical trials, though only as a result of the determined efforts of one pharmacologist, Frances Kelsey, one of a handful of doctors hired to review drugs for consumer safety. Despite pressure from the drug industry, Kelsey stood her ground. Months later, evidence of the drug's link to birth defects surfaced around the world, horrifying readers who learned of babies born without arms or legs as a result of prescribing the drug to treat morning sickness.

Some doses of Thalidomide had in fact reached the American public as part of the clinical trials; all were quickly recalled. This disturbing close call affirmed the Kennedy administration's decision to include synthetic drugs as part of its review, or, as Dean Markham put it, to define the

---

[56] Ibid.
[57] See a discussion of Kennedy's amphetamine use specifically, see Nicolas Rasmussen, *On Speed: The Many Lives of Amphetamine* (New York: New York University Press, 2008), pp. 168–70.

conference as an effort to "re-examine the whole problem of narcotics use in the United States and evaluate it in the larger context of the abuse of drugs."[58] This agenda struck some as a dilatory tactic. Senator Keating, Republican from New York, thought the conference was a tool to delay deliberation on federal legislation.[59] Others took the opposite view, that the vision of the conference was too bold and unsettling. The most vocal of this number were officials from the Bureau of Narcotics, who, according to one assistant to the attorney general, "insist there is no need for a conference" and who exhibited "considerable reluctance ... even to offer ideas for a suggested format."[60] This did not deter Dean Markham, conference organizer, and friend and occasional sailing companion to Robert and Ethel Kennedy. Providing regular updates of setbacks and difficulties to Lee White, White House counselor and his supervisor, Markham must have relished the moment when he finally could send the conference "kit" to White in preparation for his attendance to the two-day event. "Dope on Dope Conference," the portfolio was labeled, and White probably had the good sense to carry Markham's jest discretely as he made his way to the State Department auditorium, the venue for the event, in late September 1962.

Included in this portfolio was the conference working paper, prepared by a group led by David Goddard, botanist and provost of the University of Pennsylvania. This ad hoc panel provided a summary of recent drug legislation, though not from a sympathetic vantage point. "The economic burden which [mandatory sentences] may eventually create for the American citizenry is enormous," the panel noted, and added that its members believed that "prolonged incarceration of [addicts] represents as much of an admission of incurability as does the continued dosage of drugs to maintain compulsive abuse."[61] Here the panel made a compelling point: in invoking the Bureau of Narcotics' criticism of the ambulatory clinic plan of drug maintenance – that is, that it represented an abject surrender – the panel proceeded to liken it to mandatory sentencing. After

[58] Undated memorandum explaining conference, Dean F. Markham File, *John F. Kennedy Library*, Box 3.

[59] Markham to White, September 22, 1962, Lee C. White File, General File, *John F. Kennedy Library*, Box 11.

[60] John Seigenthaler, Administrative Assistant to RFK, to Lee C. White, Assistant Special Counsel to the President, Undated, Dean F. Markham File, *John F. Kennedy Library*, Box 3.

[61] Progress Report of an Ad Hoc Panel on Drug Abuse, White House Conference, filed September 7, 1962, found in Records of the Drug Enforcement Administration, Subject Files of the Bureau of Narcotics and Dangerous Drugs, 1916–1970, *NARA*, Box 8.

all, neither approach was structured around the prospect of rehabilitation and recovery. In equating the two and dismissing the fatalistic pessimism of both, the panel hoped to strike a political middle ground. Yet many of the panel's findings that followed were provocative, including: alcohol, which met the "World Health Organization definition of addiction," was the "outstanding addictive drug in the United States and is available without control"; marijuana was not physically addictive and its "hazards ... have been exaggerated"; and amphetamine use was "considerable" yet "difficult to ascertain."[62]

Perhaps because the working paper prepared for the conference represented such a departure from the official government line, President Kennedy took care in his opening remarks to compliment the work of the Bureau of Narcotics. "In recent years we have seen a drastic and dramatic reduction in the volume of illegal narcotics and drugs brought into this country," the president maintained, and, while this putative reduction was the result of collaborative efforts, Kennedy claimed that he "must single out the Federal Bureau of Narcotics for special note. Under the forceful and purposeful leadership of Commissioner Anslinger," a man that Kennedy had forced into retirement only weeks prior, "the Bureau has reduced this misery-producing traffic."[63] As the president set the stage for the conference with deliberately uncontroversial comments, his brother, Attorney General Robert Kennedy, succeeded him with politic, though transparently disingenuous remarks. "We have somehow assumed that the narcotics problem is so intensely dangerous and vicious that the solution is principally punitive," and, consequently, "we have persisted in letting almost the entire burden fall on the Federal Bureau of Narcotics," the attorney general declared. It was time to distribute this burden more justly, Kennedy implied. But it would be difficult to know how to do so, he complained, in light of the lack of basic and applied knowledge in the field of addiction. "We spend too much time debating how to [strike at the root of addiction] without knowing whether we are using a hoe where a bulldozer is needed," Bobby Kennedy observed, and it is typical of his robust belief in the power of government action that he did not sketch the opposite imagery – that is, the possibility that the government might be using massive instruments to little or no avail.

This rhetorical tactic of easing the Bureau's burden or turning the agency's own arguments back on itself repeated throughout the conference.

[62] Ibid.
[63] Transcript of Conference, Dean F. Markham File, *John F. Kennedy Library*, Box 3.

Perhaps the most clever version of these sorts of remarks came from Richard Kuh, administrative assistant to the district attorney of the City of New York, who noted that he was "aware that addiction, although not a virus spread, was a 'highly' contagious matter," and so he and his fellow prosecutors in New York reasoned that "criminal courts, burdened with the laws' technicalities and delays, were not the ideal place in which to deal with it."[64] These satiric observations did not suit those who wished to confront Bureau dogma more explicitly, and nearly everyone present seemed intent on doing so when it came to mandatory minimum sentencing. Senator Dodd of Connecticut read the results of a confidential poll of federal district judges, revealing that 73 percent of them opposed the mandatory minimum sentencing provision and 86 percent opposed the prohibition against probation or parole. To render these impressive numbers less impersonally, the senator quoted one district judge who regretted that he was "compelled to impose a five-year sentence on a Marine veteran of the Korean War who was found with three or four marijuana cigarettes."[65] The otherwise circumspect attorney general offered his view that mandatory minimums did not provide the solution to illicit narcotics traffic; "the solution," Kennedy told the assembled officials, "does not rest in making sentencing equal, but in making our sentencing philosophies agree."[66] Judge William Smith spoke plainly when he said, "under the existing rules, the judge is a robot," an insulting position for a federal judge whose intellect and professional judgment received the endorsement of both the president and the Senate.[67]

Given the near universal disgust over mandatory minimums at the conference, a bystander would have been entitled to wonder how the legislation passed in 1952 and, even more, how the policy was reaffirmed and strengthened in 1956. One California lawmaker shed some light on this when he acknowledged that "the public," led by "unreliable sources for knowledge" that went unnamed, "seems to have accepted as true major premises such invalid appellations [as dope fiend], thus permitting, and even demanding, the adoption of unrealistic laws. Imprisonment has become," he observed with regret, "a source of great satisfaction for having 'done something' about a bad problem and to bad people."[68] Even if a lawmaker recognized the public clamor for punishment as faulty in

---

[64] Transcript of Conference, Dean F. Markham File, *John F. Kennedy Library,* Box 4.
[65] Ibid.
[66] Ibid.
[67] Ibid.
[68] California State Senator Edwin Regan, in ibid.

logic and doomed to failure, how could she escape the political pressure to "do something"? The conference discussion of amphetamines and barbiturates shared this same sense of resignation, as panelists confirmed the drugs' wide circulation and abuse, but dismissed prohibition as the appropriate response. "It is quite clear from history," one doctor told the audience, "that if one drug is suppressed, another will rise to take its place."[69] It must have been a relief to conference organizers that the president had already announced his intention to form a commission based on the proceedings, for, although the conference successfully challenged Bureau of Narcotics orthodoxy, it supplied no clear alternatives in its place; if anything, attendees seemed overwhelmed by the complexity of illicit drug use.

All except one contingent, that is. At the close of the conference, the Bureau of Narcotics representative, chief counsel Carl DeBaggio, approached the microphone. "I might say as I have sat here this afternoon I began to have the feeling that I might have been thrown to lions," he began. "I am pretty sure of it now. I would not say that the [law enforcement] panel was stacked, but I leave that to your judgment," and DeBaggio's not so veiled criticism garnered applause from Bureau attendees and their allies. What about protecting "society at large," he wondered; the Bureau has been "forced ... into the position of being the sole defender of the existing legislation which was adopted, incidentally, by a unanimous Congress only six years ago." If you want to treat addiction, DeBaggio tossed off, go right ahead; but "why wait until [a criminal offense has been committed] to show so much sympathy for him?" DeBaggio ignored the fact that criminal offense might indeed be possession of unstamped narcotics, instead emphasizing that addiction did not excuse a perpetrator from accounting for his crime, nor would doing so protect public safety.

The conference adjourned to the disappointing realization that the Bureau would cling to its traditional approach. With this in mind, attendees mulled over the composition of the proposed narcotics commission. Morris Ploscowe, leader of the joint AMA-ABA report, offered himself to the administration as a member only five days after the conference adjourned.[70] Days later, the attorney general received a more tactful letter from Alfred R. Lindesmith, addiction researcher at Indiana

[69] Ibid.
[70] Ploscowe to David R. Goddard, October 1, 1962, Dean F. Markham File, *John F. Kennedy Library*, Box 5.

University. The professor raised the regret expressed at the conference over the lack of reliable information on drug addiction. "It is unhappily necessary to observe in this connection," Lindesmith pointed out, "that the main source of many of these misconceptions over the past decades has been an agency of the Federal government itself, i.e., the Federal Bureau of Narcotics."[71] Perhaps Bobby Kennedy gave the notion of seating Lindesmith on the commission a brief thought; he asked for a review of the letter from Keith Killam, professor of pharmacology at Stanford. The contents were "appropriate, pointed, and slightly biased," the professor concluded, and he could not refrain from expressing his disdain over Lindesmith's support for ambulatory clinics; "he really can't be serious that the clinic structure," Killam wrote, "should be the starting point even for research in this area."[72] In the end, it seemed that anyone with an established profile on the subject of illicit drugs would be viewed as less desirable for the commission than a well-respected outsider whose views or opinions were as yet unknown. Just as important, since the commission was really an instrument to impose the attorney general's will on the nation's approach to illicit traffic, Robert Kennedy wanted people whom he knew and trusted.

And the attorney general had just the man for the job. While at law school at the University of Virginia, Kennedy befriended E. Barrett Prettyman Jr., and the two remained close as Prettyman developed his private law practice in DC and Kennedy entered government service. Prettyman's father, E. Barrett Prettyman, was a highly regarded district judge in Washington; in honor of his legacy, the main federal courthouse in downtown DC bears his name. It was Prettyman's father, known to almost all as Judge Prettyman, who struck Kennedy as the ideal chair of his narcotics commission – perhaps most because, although Prettyman had expertise and a track record on many subjects closely related to illicit drugs, he had never been professionally linked to any school of thought on addiction or any particular approach to illicit drug traffic and use. As a result, his views would be accepted as impartial and authoritative. Prettyman had recently retired from official duties as chief of the Federal District Court, and very soon after that the president selected him to lead the panel to review whether Gary Powers, the U-2 spy plane pilot shot down over Soviet air space, had handled himself appropriately during his

---

[71] Lindesmith to Robert Kennedy, October 9, 1962, ibid.
[72] Keith Killam to Peter S. Bing, Office of Special Assistant for Science and Technology, October 19, 1962, Dean F. Markham File, *John F. Kennedy Library*, Box 5.

capture and eighteen-month internment. It was a sensitive assignment, as many Americans projected the international embarrassment generated by the episode onto the figure of Powers himself, questioning his decisions and indignant that the pilot did not commit suicide before falling into Soviet hands. Judge Prettyman and his colleagues absolved Powers of any personal responsibility and concluded that the classified information revealed as a result of the crash was negligible. In an emotional and charged atmosphere, Prettyman allayed fears and dispelled ungrounded accusations. He was most definitely the man to lead the narcotics commission, the attorney general decided.

Judge Prettyman's professional career offered up many connections to the task the attorney general hoped he would accept, and it offered a glimpse of his temperament as well. A southerner cast in a "New South" mode, Prettyman longed for the economic development of his home state of Virginia, though he lived in Maryland most of his adult life. Still, his upbringing clearly shaped his views. An inveterate writer – frequent essayist, and occasional poet – Prettyman set down his thoughts at a young age on "the destiny of the Anglo-Saxon."[73] This was no simple homage to racial purity, however; though Prettyman accepted the dominant views of the superiority of the white race, his own tribute combined racist ideology with an expansive evaluation of the rise and fall of civilizations. As a young Prettyman saw it, the "God of Nations" took "the rugged strength of the Saxon, the love of liberty of the untamed highland Scot, the dogged perseverance of the Welch, the boldness of the Dane, the polish of the Norman French, and from the blending of these bloods, He brought forth upon the face of the earth a race of Kings, the Anglo-Saxon people."[74] America, in Prettyman's eyes, was the crowning achievement of this racial heritage – yet, in this young southerner's view, this inheritance was being squandered. It was not the result of racial or ethnic impurities, Prettyman argued, it was because of an "aristocracy of wealth" that concentrated power in the hands of a few, contrary to the ambition of the country's founding. "There is yet one generation," Prettyman concluded, of "pure-blooded Anglo-Saxon" who could redeem the "stagnant civilization" America had become, and that was the "rising generation of the New South."[75]

---

[73] Undated essay, but contextually placed before the Great Depression, Barrett Prettyman Papers, *Library of Congress*, Manuscript Division, Box 122.

[74] Ibid.

[75] Ibid.

Prettyman probably set down these effusive thoughts during the 1920s, as he advanced in his law career and began a family. Most of his other essays and published writing concerned themselves with far more pragmatic subjects, and, indeed, Prettyman's fair-minded approach to everyday problems earned him the respect of his colleagues and, ultimately, his reputation. As a mentor, he later advised young lawyers to come before the court as a "well-prepared country boy," an earnest demeanor that resembled Prettyman's own approach. With a folksy deference and no apparent guile, Prettyman met with considerable success as a tax lawyer and, long after he became a judge, he continued to advise lawyers who went up against Internal Revenue or some other federal agency. Yet it was not Prettyman's tax expertise that recommended him to Attorney General Robert Kennedy, but rather his long service on the Federal District Court of DC, much of it as chief judge. At his court, the judge was known as a procedural innovator. Prettyman insisted on instructing the jury before it began deliberation, sensibly enough, and not, as was then common, after it returned a sentence. He also set up a legal aid system for indigent defenders, using talent culled from local law schools, a forerunner to the provision of public defenders. Finally, and most pertinent to the attorney general, Prettyman had been vocal among the growing number of judges who questioned criminal culpability for the insane or those otherwise not in control of their actions. Judge Prettyman went so far as to send the common law dictum instructing judges on this principle – *Actum non facit reum nis sit mens rea* – to a Georgetown University Latin scholar for translation. The elaborate exegesis that came back to him ended in a succinct translation that squared well with Prettyman's own views: "The action does not render a man answerable for that action unless his mind (in some way) also participated in the act."[76]

This doctrine, often referred to simply as *mens rea*, would become instrumental in the decriminalization efforts for public drunkenness and, eventually, in cases that attempted to do the same for drug addiction.[77] Thus, Prettyman's experience and credentials made him an ideal candidate to lead Kennedy's drug commission: though he did not devote himself to issues of illicit drug traffic or addiction, he was conversant and well-experienced on issues ranging from procedural fairness, the rights of the accused, and the difficulties faced by the less privileged defendant.

[76] Exchange dates February 17, 1961, Barrett Prettyman Papers, *Library of Congress*, Manuscript Division, Box 7.
[77] Already by the time of the White House Conference and Commission, some drug defendants began to actually plead insanity in federal and state courts.

Prettyman also had enough Washington experience to play hard to get, whether he wanted to chair the commission or not. After the retired judge turned the position down some time in November 1962, Attorney General Robert Kennedy sent the assistant secretary of the Treasury, supervisor of the Bureau of Narcotics –and special projects assistant and White House conference organizer Dean Markham to Ocean City, Maryland, to plead with the judge while he vacationed with his wife.[78] This impressive effort gave the experienced judge a gauge as to just how interested and invested the White House and the attorney general were in the proposed commission. Not one to waste his time or his talent, Prettyman later confronted the president directly on this subject, in a quiet corner after the official appointment ceremony of the White House Commission and all of its "fluff-de-duff," as Prettyman put it. According to Prettyman, Jack Kennedy "sat down, turned to [him] and said, 'Now Judge, what do you think you can do with this Commission?'" Prettyman responded that it depended upon whether the president wanted a paper or a program, his way of summarizing the choice between a token effort or real reform. "I want a program," Kennedy replied.[79]

Other members of the small commission were selected by the White House, the Treasury, or by the attorney general through an informal process channeled through Dean Markham's office. Obviously the president wanted a balance of legal and medical experts, hence the invitations to serve on the commission were accepted by James P. Dixon, former director of the U.S. Public Health Service; Roger Egeberg, former medical director of the LA County Hospital who then held the same position for the Los Angeles Department of Charities; and Rafael Sanchez-Ubeda, physician and director of Out Patient and Emergency Department of St. Vincent's Hospital in New York. The latter had no national profile. Because his ethnic roots were Puerto Rican, Markham felt both happy and defensive about this connection to a community over-represented in drug arrests. We "would not have had a Puerto-Rican just to have a Puerto-Rican," he told his boss, Lee White.[80] On the legal side, the commission members included Austin MacCormick, former assistant director of the U.S. Bureau of Prisons and commissioner of corrections in New York City, and then, at the time of his appointment, professor of criminology. Two

[78] Longhand memorandum dated July 19, 1964, Barrett Prettyman Papers, *Library of Congress*, Manuscript Division, Box 123.
[79] Ibid.
[80] Confidential discussion of Commission members, January 1963, Lee C. White File, General File, *John F. Kennedy Library*, Box 11.

political types were also appointed, and, following the pattern of other selections, one was from New York and one was from California: James R. Dumpson, commissioner of Welfare, New York City, and Harry M. Kimball, second only to Prettyman in his influence on the commission – though, oddly, as a general manager of a hotel, seemingly the least well-qualified. Yet Kimball possessed several credentials of note: he was a former FBI agent, he was a Republican, and, most important, he served as chairman of the governor of California's Special Narcotic Commission (1960–1961). He also represented "business," Markham informed White, in a way that could be expected to "counterbalance other professions on the Commission."[81]

The commission set to work at the start of 1963. Members were surprised and probably disheartened to learn that the president expected specific recommendations for legislation almost immediately, a preference that cut short their time for fact-finding and deliberation. Prettyman decided to hold one meeting in late January and another in March, and then to prepare an interim report, scheduled for release in April, with recommendations intended to satisfy Kennedy's desire for action. The judge was originally skeptical that he could produce something meaningful in such a short time, but he was pleasantly surprised when feedback from the meetings indicated broad areas of agreement.

Consensus was enhanced by the commission's shared reaction to early testimony. The commission heard first from officials in the Bureau of Narcotics and the Bureau of Customs, with the latter agency sending two men, one of whom clearly viewed the interview as an opportunity to secure more manpower for Customs. "Ellis [of Customs] was very confident that the Customs Bureau could get 50% of heroin smuggled if they had everything they needed," the meeting transcript read, though his colleague differed with him, leading the transcriber to note parenthetically, "Ellis is an eager beaver."[82] Still, Ellis's confidence made a deep impression on the commission, guiding members to agree with the judge that heroin smuggling was a failure on the part of the executive branch to control the country's borders, and that such a failure could be meaningfully remedied with a more concerted effort. At the commission's second meeting, the judge flatly stated his belief that it is a "direct responsibility of the

[81] Ibid.
[82] Meeting Trancript, January 28–30, 1963, Dean F. Markham File, *John F. Kennedy Library*, Box 6, p. 23.

executive branch ... to stop [heroin] smuggling."[83] Austin MacCormick agreed, arguing, "we need to flood the major areas like California and New York with men."[84]

In addition, even at this early date, the commission began to broach the subject of transferring the Bureau of Narcotics from the Treasury Department to the Department of Justice – something that Prettyman and others felt that Attorney General Robert Kennedy would welcome. During the closed session of the second meeting in March, Kimball declared to his colleagues that he was in favor of such a transfer, and the commission began to collect legal opinions as to whether the government could regulate or control traffic in narcotic drugs under the commerce clause of the Constitution, rather than relying on the taxing power and regulatory regime currently in place. The group also considered what it could do on the subject of addictive synthetics, with MacCormick warning that the commission needed "more studying of dangerous drugs" because the "pharmaceutical people ... shovel lots of snow," by which he meant that the drug companies performed a lot of politically useful favors.[85] "The pattern we set in the matter of dangerous drugs may be the most important work that we accomplish," Egeberg suggested, and warned that certain drugs, "amphetamines and barbiturates in particular," were used "clinically for chronic illness, and therefore if they are placed in the same categories of control as the hard narcotics" – which, Egeberg failed to note, were also used clinically – "one would needlessly and officiously interfere with good treatment of patients."[86]

From the outset, then, regulation of addictive synthetics in the same fashion as narcotics was not seriously considered by the commission. Probably Prettyman did not think much of the idea himself, as he personally requested that the Pharmaceutical Manufacturers Association (PMA) "furnish the Commission with its view as to the type of regulation that should control the amphetamine-barbiturate problem" almost as soon as the commission began its work, essentially inviting the drug industry to write its own regulatory framework. When Dean Markham

[83] Transcript of Second Meeting, March 11–12, 1963, Dean F. Markham File, *John F. Kennedy Library*, Box 6, pp. 4–5.

[84] Ibid., p. 5.

[85] Transcript of First Meeting, Dean F. Markham File, *John F. Kennedy Library*, Box 6, p. 21.

[86] Roger O. Egeberg to E. Barrett Prettyman, February 18, 1963, Dean F. Markham File, *John F. Kennedy Library*, Box 6.

and his aide met with PMA representatives to deliver this request, the association took the opportunity to state that if the FDA were given the power to declare new drugs habit-forming, the "industry should be given an opportunity to be heard on any particular declaration," and, moreover, that "illegal possession as such should not be made a crime," as was the case with narcotics.[87] The industry's subsequent submissions to the commission underscored these points. Robert McNeil Jr., chairman of McNeil Laboratories, a subsidiary of Johnson and Johnson and manufacturer of the largest selling barbiturate prescription, went so far as to cast doubt on the "extent of the misuse and abuse of stimulant and depressant drugs," which, to the best of their knowledge, had never been "adequately documented."[88] The PMA's formal submission to the commission agreed that there was no "adequately documented" data demonstrating the "real extent of misuse," and, as for the numerous stories of overdoses, association officials observed that "the Chinese ... are known to commit suicide by consuming excessive quantities of ordinary table salt," an analogy intended to suggest that, taken in improper doses, most any substance could be harmful.[89]

By the time the commission received these testimonials, the problem of diverted synthetic drugs was too grave for such cavalier dismissals. Clearly the PMA would have to offer more: "In general," the association informed the commission, "the PMA favors legislation requiring the registration of all those engaged in the production and distribution of these drugs, and," they added, "requiring these persons to maintain adequate and accurate records."[90] It was not much of an offer, especially since the association gave no hint of what, if any, enforcement mechanism would inspect such records. Already by the commission's second meeting, members were aware that Senator Dodd, Democrat of Connecticut, had introduced legislation to Congress to regulate what he and others were now calling "dangerous drugs," a label that included amphetamines and barbiturates, newer tranquilizers like valium, and psychotropic drugs like LSD, a little known drug that had been the subject of several military

[87] Paul Laskin, Memorandum for the File, February 5, 1963, Dean F. Markham File, *John F. Kennedy Library*, Box 20.
[88] McNeil to Prettyman, March 8, 1963, Dean F. Markham File, *John F. Kennedy Library*, Box 6.
[89] "Statement to the President's Commission," Pharmaceutical Manufacturers Association, February 27, 1963, found in the Records of the Drug Enforcement Administration, Subject Files of the Bureau of Narcotics and Dangerous Drugs, 1916–1970, *NARA*, Box 8.
[90] Ibid.

trials and had also produced a recreational following in elite Hollywood circles. Content to simply endorse these efforts without articulating specifics, the commission resolved to do so in its interim report – but, to appease Egeberg and others, also to state flatly that such regulation should be distinct from the regime in place governing narcotics – a separation justified, the commission argued, by the continued medical use of dangerous drugs.

The commission also decided to make other recommendations in its interim report. Most attention was given to the commission's resolution in favor of a joint commission to address illicit drug smuggling from Mexico to the United States as well as its suggestion that more personnel and money be added to control the border between the two countries. The vocal California drug reform coalition welcomed these recommendations with enthusiasm. The topic was considered a sensitive one, with American diplomats reluctant to make accusations against the government of Mexico while, at the same time, California state officials routinely depicted Mexico as being at the root of all the state's drug problems. For the commission to have sided squarely with California seemed to be a real victory in the minds of the state's delegation; less appreciated was the extent to which these recommendations indicated that the commission viewed the international traffic in illicit drugs as something that could be confronted at the border and meaningfully contained.

Other recommendations included more money for federal research on all facets of the illicit drug problem and, mimicking the agenda of the National Council on Alcoholism and their efforts to reform instruction on alcohol, a resolution urging the Department of Health, Education and Welfare to prepare educational material on addiction to be made available to public schools, welfare agencies, professional groups, and any interested member of the public. Obviously members were not persuaded to agree with Harry Anslinger that the subject of illicit drugs should remain taboo. The commission also stated its preference to see a distinction between the criminal penalties for trafficking and possession, and that the latter not be subject to any mandatory sentencing requirements at all. This was clearly an attack on the Boggs and Daniel framework. Upon hearing of it, Price Daniel, recently retired from service as Texas governor, expressed his "shock and surprise."[91] Yet it was not this recommendation that generated the most speculation in Washington, but

---

[91] Quoted in Dean Markham to Price Daniel, May 15, 1963, Lee C. White File, General File, *John F. Kennedy Library*, Box 11.

rather the commission's resolution that a new and separate investigative task force be formed within the Department of Justice to pursue charges against large-scale traffickers in illicit drugs.

By all appearances this was a move that Attorney General Robert Kennedy had encouraged and anticipated. Throughout the 1950s, the young lawyer had earned his reputation by joining the efforts of aggressive investigations, first (and briefly) with Senator Joseph McCarthy's anti-communism hearings, and later and more prominently as chief counsel for Senator McLellan's Labor Rackets Committee. His work sparked his near obsession with organized crime, as well as an appreciation for just how well the image of the fearless prosecutor suited him politically. His growing interest in the subject also introduced him to the Los Angeles Police Chief William Parker, who shared his disgust over how little the FBI seemed to know about organized crime, and it led him to collaborate with New York Bureau of Narcotic agents who, despite whatever enforcement or ethical flaws would soon surface, could at least quite adequately outline a structure of New York crime families.[92] The commission's recommendation for a special unit, including its insistence that it be "highly mobile," suggested that its members were attuned to Kennedy's political agenda and that they were, moreover, calling plays from a familiar playbook, as they seemed to be recommending a "flying squad" of elite investigators, a technique made famous by J. Edgar Hoover during the country's "war on crime" in the 1930s.

Bureau of Narcotics officials interpreted the recommendation, correctly, as an initial move to dismantle or transfer their agency. As was typical for the Bureau, although they did not challenge the interim report directly, narcotics officials tapped allies who would. First among these were the powerful allies the agency had won through its refusal to add addictive synthetics to its purview: namely, the Pharmaceutical Manufacturers Association. A representative from the group wrote to commission director Dean Markham that forming a special unit in the Department of Justice "would be a forerunner to others calling for the ultimate dismemberment of the Bureau of Narcotics," a decision PMA characterized as wrong-headed and without justification.[93]

As the Bureau mobilized allies, it also produced for the commission a list of the high-echelon traffickers its agents apprehended, an obvious

[92] Buntin, *L.A. Noir*, pp. 221, 243.
[93] Austin Smith, PMA, to Dean Markham, August 29, 1963, Dean F. Markham File, *John F. Kennedy Library*, Box 20.

attempt to render the commission's interim recommendation moot. The agency's introduction to the document was an impressive effort to recast organizational failures: contrary to other dangerous drugs, the Bureau wrote to the commission, very little of the supply of narcotics was diverted from licit production. This was a silver lining in the dark cloud of subversion; to wit, the fact that the Bureau had driven production, distribution, and most consumption entirely underground. Bureau officials also saw fit to view other criticisms in a benevolent light. Rather than clogging the criminal justice system with nonviolent offenders convicted of trivial crimes, the Bureau depicted the 17.6 percent of inmates in federal prisons there as the result of drug charges as evidence of "the scope of productive investigations of the Bureau of Narcotics."[94]

The interim report had done its job. While the *Wall Street Journal* attacked the document as too timid, calling for a radical new approach, public reception was otherwise positive.[95] Just as important, the White House seemed satisfied with the project and the recommendations submitted. In fact, if anything, the lack of critical response to the commission's resolutions emboldened its members to go one step further in their final report. Project director Dean Markham seemed particularly intent to take on the Bureau of Narcotics more aggressively. As the commission continued its work, Markham requested that one law enforcement official compile a list of drug smugglers who had *not* been apprehended by the Bureau; as the official sensibly noted in his response to this request, it was impossible to sketch the dimensions of that which was unknown, and, in addition, impossible to assess the guilt of a person without adjudicating evidence.[96] Still, the request spoke to Markham's determination to undermine the Bureau's defense of its own work. As the commission's deliberations stretched into the summer of 1963, its staff did what they could to make preparations to strengthen the proposal to transfer the Bureau from Treasury to Justice. Dean Markham personally visited Richard Kimball in August, encouraging the influential Republican to tour Washington and drum up support for the proposed move.[97] Kimball declined, citing

[94] "Brief Summary of the Results of the Efforts by the Federal Bureau of Narcotics," May 1, 1963, Records of the Drug Enforcement Administration, Subject Files of the Bureau of Narcotics and Dangerous Drugs, 1916–1970, *NARA*, Box 8.

[95] "Narcotics Policy: Addiction to Failure," *Wall Street Journal*, April 17, 1963, p. 16.

[96] Howard Chappell to Dean F. Markham, September 17, 1963, Lee C. White File, General File, *John F. Kennedy Library*, Box 11.

[97] Dean Markham, Memorandum of Record, August 19, 1963, Dean F. Markham File, *John F. Kennedy Library*, Box 5.

business obligations, but recommended some contacts among former associates in the FBI. Markham labored on his own to construct arguments that justified the move; months later, he would tell one audience, the transfer of the Bureau was advantageous because it would allow "the Attorney General to more completely integrate [illicit drug trafficking prosecutions] with his campaign" against organized crime.[98]

Obviously the commission staff worried over the reception of the recommendation to transfer the Bureau. While the Hoover Commission had endorsed the same move ten years earlier, it did so as part of a largely unnoticed series of proposals. The White House Commission on Narcotics and Dangerous Drugs, on the other hand, provided a more visible platform. Its members seemed aware of the potential for controversy; Judge Prettyman, who had endorsed the move in meeting transcripts, nevertheless voted "no" in response to Markham's poll put to the commission's members as to whether the transfer should be recommended in the group's final report.[99] Perhaps the judge had second thoughts, but it is more likely that he decided to move gingerly on the transfer and provide any dissenting members (and himself) political cover in the event that the recommendation proved unpopular. Dean Markham also proceeded cautiously, soliciting opinions throughout the executive branch on the proposed move – even though, as he and others stated numerous times, the commission's work was considered confidential. In September, Markham assured his boss, Lee White, that the commission received testimony on all points of view and held all the requisite meetings with the agencies involved. Members knew, for example, that FBI Director J. Edgar Hoover opposed the move, as he had in the past. Perhaps the commission was too dismissive of Hoover's formal letter of objection, which noted, among other things, that "effective narcotics enforcement" might be "weakened if it is separated from regulatory control."[100]

In general, the commission and its supporters elected to interpret the various positions on the proposed transfer through the lens of institutional self-interest. Treasury opposed the move; certain elements in the Department of Justice supported it. The neat and predictable alignment of these preferences perhaps encouraged commission members to minimize

[98] Markham, Speech to Wisconsin State Board of Pharmacy, May 19, 1964, Dean F. Markham File, *John F. Kennedy Library*, Box 22.

[99] Questionnaire response, June 14, 1963, Dean F. Markham File, *John F. Kennedy Library*, Box 14.

[100] J. Edgar Hoover, Director, FBI to Attorney General, February 17, 1964, Dean F. Markham File, *John F. Kennedy Library*, Box 13.

the concerns raised, and to weigh opinions from within the White House most heavily, as a kind of referee in the dispute. When the steering office of the White House, the Bureau of the Budget, endorsed the transfer in October 1963, the commission felt it had received a green light.[101] While the group set aside objections to the plan as motivated solely by self-interested politics, it viewed its own actions as more disinterested, and thus enlightened. Members considered the proposed transfer of the Bureau as a rejection of an outdated and objectionable approach to illicit drugs, and not without reason. Anslinger's punishment ethos had so thoroughly dominated the Bureau's approach to illicit drugs that it would have been natural to conflate the two. Moreover, the commission's appraisal of the Bureau would have taken cognizance of the way in which Anslinger staffed the agency with acolytes. To get beyond a punishment mind-set, then, it would have struck members as necessary to go beyond the offices and agents of the Bureau, maybe even to undermine them.

Indeed, to a person, the commission rejected the stridency of the punishment model. After the final report was released, Judge Prettyman continued to insist that the stereotype of "the raging 'dope fiend,' frothing at the mouth, indiscriminately seeking victims for his violence, was largely a myth."[102] Addicts were "the victims, not the knowing creators of crime."[103] In the discursive war over the image of the "addict" waged between the Bureau and its critics, including those from the ranks of the legal and medical professions, the commission came out decisively in favor of the latter. An important joint National Research Council and American Medical Association committee convened at the same time as the commission ratified the growing medical consensus that addicts were "sick people, not criminals." This conclusion from such an esteemed group supported the commission's already well-formed consensus on the need to replace punishment with treatment.

At the very same time, Judge Prettyman and his colleagues remained critical of what they saw as a failure to interdict drugs at the border and beyond. A new commissioner of Customs, Philip Nichols Jr., wanted very much to capitalize on this perception. "World trade and travel has expanded almost four times in the last twenty years without any

[101] Comments on report, October 12, 1963, Lee C. White File, General File, *John F. Kennedy Library*, Box 11.
[102] Prettyman, "The Relationship Between Drugs and Crime," *Combating Crime and the Forensic Quarterly* 41 (August 1967): 446.
[103] Ibid.

corresponding increase in Customs enforcement personnel," he informed the commission as it approached the end of its work in September 1963.[104] Customs wanted to secure a recommendation for 500 more agents; Dean Markham could not resist noting that, "speaking unofficially," it appeared "that the Customs Bureau was using the Commission ... to increase their overall personnel requirements."[105] While Markham was skeptical, Judge Prettyman argued that more should be done at the borders. "It seems quite clear to me that the Federal Government should shoulder full responsibility for traffic," he wrote to his colleagues over the summer, and that the "authorities ought not dodge their responsibility in this area by saying that these are difficult problems."[106] Harry Kimball carried this view to the public when he addressed the California Peace Officers Association. "The Commission believes that our ports of entry and our borders are inadequately manned," he told a gathering of state officials known to be receptive to this opinion. "I do not mean to imply that with more agents [in Customs] we can eradicate smuggling," he offered, in an interesting qualification, but rather that "the Commission is convinced that we can significantly increase our interceptions of smuggled drugs and thereby have a marked deterrent effect on smuggling."[107]

As the commission prepared to scale back the punishment approach to illicit drug use, it simultaneously worked to endorse its justifying logic, deterrence, when it came to illicit drug traffic. Members of the group consistently represented this posture as an adoption of the "middle road" approach: tougher penalties for sale and distribution, more compassion when it came to addiction and use. In a polarized and politically sensitive environment, this appearance of compromise was attractive, and it reinforced the perception of impartiality. It was, however, a flawed conceit, both in practice and in theory. Had an experienced law enforcement official or criminal prosecutor been placed on the panel, the assumption that one could meaningfully isolate traffic from use would most certainly have received more critical attention. Confidential informants, usually small-time peddlers or users (or both), were essential in understanding

[104] Statement of Philip Nichols Jr. to the Commission, September 4, 1963, Dean F. Markham File, *John F. Kennedy Library*, Box 14.
[105] Markham to James Reed, July 30, 1963, Robert F. Kennedy Papers, Attorney General's Files, General Correspondence, *John F. Kennedy Library*, Box 35.
[106] Prettyman to Commission, June 24, 1963, Dean F. Markham File, *John F. Kennedy Library*, Box 5.
[107] Kimball to California Peace Officers Association, San Francisco, California, May 29, 1963, found in Dean Markham File, *John F. Kennedy Library*, Box 5.

and tracking larger illicit drug networks, and informants disclosed what they knew by and large because of the threat of criminal charges against them. Without punishment, the ability to extract information would be seriously damaged. What was more, the logic of deterrence rested upon a presumption of control over a defined range of action as well as a universally shared decision-making calculus. Addicts or traffickers sentenced to long prison terms would think twice about returning to their former habits – or so proponents of mandatory minimums argued, without consideration of the ways in which criminal records, personal histories, and addiction constrained the choices of convicts, nor any acknowledgment of the ways in which adding more risk via criminal punishment to a sale also added to its profit margin, thus enticing some to attempt to navigate those risks despite penalties. Similarly, increased seizures of drugs at the border would dissuade traffickers – or so the commission hoped – without any serious consideration of the possibility that drug runners would continue in the face of such risks, and that an occasional seizure only added to the profit of a successful shipment. Deterrence advocates assumed a limit to the amount of illicit drugs or number of willing couriers; even if they only caught a small portion of these, they projected the effect of this capture along what they assumed to be a finite range. In a sense, deterrence was an implicit admission that enforcement could make only a minor dent in traffic or use, but it was, in addition, a claim that this little bit actually worked to much larger effect. Yet it was just as plausbile that interdiction would simply provide incentives for traffickers to expand their supply or market, or add greater efficiency to these.

In sanctioning the logic of deterrence via punishment, the Kennedy Commission limited the scope of its reforms. As much as the commission intended to propel acceptance of treatment for addicts by presenting such reforms as a hard-headed compromise – or, as the preface to the final report stated, a rejection of the "extreme attitudes" of an exclusively punishment or permissive approach – its approval of punishment for trafficking bespoke its failure to conceptualize illicit drugs as a trade rather than a crime. "The full power of the federal government," the commission concluded, should be brought to bear on trafficking, thus making "the price for participation in this traffic … prohibitive. It should be made too dangerous to be attractive," the commission clarified, and then followed up that remark with the view that "the individual user should be rehabilitated."

Commission members readily accepted the view that a more concerted effort on trafficking would lead to such great effects because they perceived current efforts to be "fragmented," with institutional divisions necessarily amounting to "a lessened emphasis on the problem of drug abuse." To correct this, the commission made a series of recommendations to reorganize the government agencies involved. By far the most controversial was the resolution to transfer the functions of the Bureau of Narcotics "relating to the investigation of the illicit manufacture, sale, or other distribution, or possession of narcotic drugs" and marijuana to the Department of Justice; in a similar fashion, the commission recommended that the office in the Food and Drug Administration (FDA) devoted to investigating the illicit sale of addictive synthetics be transferred to Justice as well. Far less noticed was the commission's follow-up recommendation that the functions of the Bureau related "to the regulation of the legitimate importation, exportation, manufacture, sale, and other transfer of narcotic drugs" be transferred to the Department of Health, Education, and Welfare – and presumably therein to the FDA.

This particular point did not generate much attention because the Bureau itself was quite content to carry out its mission as if the licit sale of narcotics was not a part of it; after World War II and under the leadership of Harry Anslinger, it had decisively shifted the weight of its efforts and its rhetoric to targeting illicit sales. Yet, though a neglected piece of the commission's work, licit sales nevertheless raised the possibility that FBI Director J. Edgar Hoover was correct in his letter to the commission: that is, that the best way to discipline the illicit market was to regulate the licit one, and that detaching the one from the other hampered enforcement efforts. Some of the points necessary to appreciate the importance of this connection came directly from the Bureau's own enforcement history, episodes of which disclosed that the best check against illicit diversion was to place licit supply in some sort of jeopardy. When Commissioner Anslinger wanted gangster Lucky Luciano expelled from Cuba, he threatened the legal sale of drugs to that country. When doctors diverted narcotics illegally throughout the 1930s, the Bureau threatened them not with jail time but with the loss of their license and continued narcotic supply. Deterrence as a strategy to discipline markets seemed to influence those who had an investment in protecting their legal status – a little bit of enforcement could in fact work a larger effect on someone who held legitimate standing and an interest in keeping it – yet there was no way to maintain that investment once licit and illicit sales were separated. The best threat was not criminal punishment but the loss of business, and its best target was not the nodes of an illicit network but the transaction points of a legal sale. Driving a market underground drove the effectiveness of deterrence down with it.

The commission finished well short of this reckoning, and thus it paid little mind to the separation of licit from illicit sales, nor did it ascribe much significance to its abandonment of taxation as a tool for enforcement. But the commission did acknowledge that execution of its reorganization proposals would require the enactment of new legislation. In rejecting the Harrison Act, the Kennedy Commission presented its alternatives as fitting a more enlightened legal model. "This method of regulation by taxation," the commission's final report argued, "can only be understood in its historical setting. When the Harrison Act was drafted," the group explained, "Congress was concerned about its constitutionality." While this was undoubtedly true, it was also true that Congress was equally concerned that licit sales of narcotics continue without undue interference. Taxation was much more than an antiquated enforcement option for the federal government; it was the tool by which licit sales were defined. As the arbiter between what was a legal sale and what was not, taxation brought the project of licit regulation and illicit enforcement together. Later in the report, the commission acknowledged that an estimated 20 percent of the Bureau's work still involved regulation of licit sales, but seemed to dismiss these efforts all the same because they did not raise much revenue. "The amounts collected under the Harrison Act are relatively minor," commission members noted with disapproval, and added, "taxation is in fact only a guise for law enforcement regulation."

And so the commission mounted a direct assault on the country's illicit drug regulatory and enforcement regime. Often its decision to do so is presented as a desire to do all possible favors for Attorney General Robert Kennedy, but there is no reason to see the commission's recommendations as anything other than a good faith effort to dismantle the punishment approach former Commissioner Anslinger had constructed during the twenty years prior. As one newspaper noted, the Bureau of Narcotics had, after all, "become a symbol of a single theory of drug addiction."[108] Most of the commission's recommendations were directed toward encouraging departures from that theory, including the securing of research funds for addiction and generating more treatment options – and less punishment – for illicit drug users. The commission recommended that mandatory minimums be abandoned and that probation and other

---

[108] "Review and Outlook," February 7, 1964, found in E. Barrett Prettyman Papers, *Library of Congress*, Box 8.

incentives for rehabilitation be relied upon in its place. In addition, the commission lent its endorsement to the regulatory efforts of so-called dangerous drugs, clarifying that, although illicit traffic in these should be policed by the Department of Justice, the Department of Health, Education, and Welfare should establish an office to monitor the safety and efficacy of dangerous drugs, as well as the regulation of the production and sale of such drugs.

If President Kennedy wanted a new program and a fresh approach, then the commission certainly delivered. In early November, the group formally submitted its report to the president, and members were told to stand by for "quick notices of invites" to the White House.[109] And then they waited. Barrett Prettyman went to the White House for another event; while there, he spoke with Dean Markham and Lee White. Curious and slightly annoyed, the judge asked them, "What about the report?" Lee White, Markham's supervisor, responded, "That's no report. That's a bomb."[110] Prettyman might have been taken aback by the remark, but the two assured him that Kennedy would decide what to do with the commission's recommendations after he returned from some necessary campaign travel. The next day, John F. Kennedy left to mend political fences in Texas.

The president never returned. As his limousine caravan wended its way through Dallas on a bright November afternoon, gunman Lee Harvey Oswald stood perched inside a book depository awaiting his target. When shots rang out, bystanders and victims in the line of fire had difficulty comprehending what was going on. Within a matter of seconds, the president had been mortally wounded; he was moribund – technically alive but with no hope of recovery – by the time he arrived at the hospital minutes later. A priest administered Last Rites as witnesses stood by in complete shock. An hour and a half later, Vice President Lyndon Johnson, a native Texan who had joined Kennedy on his trip to Dallas, took the oath of office aboard *Air Force One*, with Kennedy's bloodied corpse stowed several rows behind him.

It is difficult to recover the grief of a stunned nation. Resentment lingered and took a different, more indirect form for many who nurtured a belief that, had the young and dynamic president lived, the nation's course would have been charted differently. Those who think so have been the

---

[109] Prettyman, longhand account written on July 19, 1964, Barrett Prettyman Papers, *Library of Congress*, Box 123; hereafter: "Longhand memo."
[110] Ibid.

most tenacious when assessing the government's deepening involvement in South Vietnam, arguing that, despite the fact that President Kennedy endorsed an aggressive policy while alive, he would have had the wisdom to put a stop to American participation in the escalating crisis in the days ahead. At the very same time, some of the earliest domestic achievements of the Lyndon Johnson administration have been presented and understood as the fulfillment of the Kennedy agenda, a perception that Johnson himself did much to advance. Whether it was the steep tax cut for business or the enactment of Medicare, Johnson signed legislation that had been many months in the making. On all of these important issues, whether foreign crises or domestic agendas, President Kennedy and his successor Lyndon Johnson benefited from the intellect and attention of numerous advisors. Each was a saga of multiple chapters, and each installment was shaped by many voices. The decisive effect of the sudden removal of one person, no matter how charismatic and powerful, is questionable.

But Kennedy's attempt to reform the country's illicit drug regime was an altogether different matter. The commission was the result of his own discretionary judgment and, perhaps, his desire to enhance the stature of his brother, Attorney General Robert Kennedy. In a counterintuitive fashion, the low profile and relative unimportance of drugs made policy departures more likely, not less. It was Kennedy who encouraged his commission to think in terms of sweeping reforms and new approaches, and it was Kennedy who elevated the discussion of illicit drug policy to such prominence. Now the sudden loss of the president threatened the substance and the relevance of the commission's work. Its members endured a frustrating waiting period while other issues took precedence over their work. A month after Kennedy's assassination, Dean Markham wrote to the commission to assure them that he had been trying to "get a definite release date from President Johnson's office for the report," which, he reminded them, "has been in the President's Office since November 1st," a somewhat uncharitable framing of the chronology in the sense that, on November 1st, the president was John Kennedy. Markham also took the opportunity to let members know that their recommendation to transfer the Bureau had excited considerable controversy and, more surprising, that reports now circulated that the attorney general had come to oppose the transfer.[111]

---

[111] Dean Markham to members of Commission, December 18, 1963, Dean F. Markham File, *John F. Kennedy Library*, Box 5.

The delay in releasing the report, its subsequent downgrading as the work of a "Citizen's Commission" upon release, and Attorney General Bobby Kennedy's reported change of heart regarding the transfer of the Bureau of Narcotics all served to give the impression that the commission's most important recommendations were either rejected or ignored. Instead, it is more accurate to say these delays and interruptions obscured the eventual adoption of much of the Kennedy Commission's ideas. Contrary to the popular notion that, during the 1960s, the government meted out progressively more punishment for drug offenses, with only an increasingly self-conscious and radical youth movement obstructing or criticizing the drive to impose stiffer penalties, the commission simultaneously sanctioned the logic of punishment and launched a drive to provide more and more realistic treatment options as well.

Indeed, after the commission, experiments and ideas of treatment and punishment coexisted and competed with each other. In fact, for a considerable time treatment options gained the upper hand, both in terms of legislation introduced and in terms of structuring ideas and perceptions of addiction. In three major areas, the federal government eventually adopted the commission's recommendations: the regulation of dangerous drugs; addict rehabilitation instead of prison; and the reorganization of federal agencies, including, years later, the relocation of the Bureau of Narcotics to the Department of Justice. If anything, some of the Kennedy Commission recommendations were too successful, insofar as they were incompatible with others. Notwithstanding the growing acceptance of sentencing leniency and the increasing availability of treatment options, the ultimate transfer of the Bureau from Treasury to Justice in 1968 supplanted the operating premise and instruments for rehabilitative and regulatory approaches, providing for only a political economy of punishment instead.

Despite eventual success, months after completing their work, commission members could be forgiven for feeling that their report went neglected. Lee White, Markham's supervisor, was unwilling to stir up controversy with the recommendation to transfer the Bureau; in December he decided to start referring to the group as a "Citizen's Commission," removing the White House from the political implications of the report's recommendations, or so he hoped.[112] When Press Secretary Pierre Salinger announced that the commission's report was a "citizen's report, and would be duly filed," Prettyman "hit the ceiling," as he characterized

[112] White on December 13, 1963, Dean F. Markham File, *John F. Kennedy Library*, Box 8.

it, and sent blistering comments to Markham and to the Department of Justice reminding him of the circumstances of his appointment.[113] As the report dwindled in a "state of limbo," Markham set about finding another job and chasing leaks about the commission's final report.[114] One Washington paper reported that, while the attorney general had once supported the transfer of the Bureau, he now endorsed the growing view within Justice that such a move would not be advantageous.[115] When Narcotics Commissioner Giordano began to speak openly of Kennedy's disapproval, a bewildered Markham wrote to the attorney general to "wonder[ ] if you have made such a statement."[116]

Those scholars who have analyzed the work of the commission tend to assume that the attorney general remained supportive of the transfer until his last days in office, and that Lyndon Johnson, wary of a potential political rivalry with a new Kennedy, deliberately withheld the transfer in order to stymie the attorney general's political aspirations. But the commission and its staff had received indications that the attorney general felt differently about the recommendation on its own merits, and it is possible these reservations existed even before his brother was killed – perhaps, for instance, Kennedy got wind of the rampant corruption dogging the Bureau's field work. What was more, Kennedy left the Department of Justice in the summer of 1964 in order to run as the Democratic nominee for senator from the State of New York, yet the transfer of the Bureau did not take place for another four years after that, a lapse of time that cannot be accounted for by the testy rivalry between Kennedy and Johnson.

Whatever his genuine feelings, in his final days as attorney general, Kennedy decided to do well by a patron who had done well by him. He asked Judge Prettyman if he would be willing to meet Lyndon Johnson to discuss the Narcotics Commission Report. The judge agreed and joined Kennedy for a visit to the White House. As the judge later remembered it, the attorney general struck him as "subdued" and "out of sorts," evidently still smarting from the loss of his brother and all of the power that accompanied his close relations with him, not to mention his overt

[113] Longhand memo, July 19, 1964.
[114] Phrase is from Markham to William B. Eldridge, May 19, 1964, Dean F. Markham File, *John F. Kennedy Library*, Box 20.
[115] "Justice, originally believed to be favorable, opposed transfer of narcotics to the Dept., reportedly with approval from the Attorney General." Found in attachment in Dean Markham to members of commission, December 18, 1963, Dean F. Markham File, *John F. Kennedy Library*, Box 5.
[116] Dean Markham to RFK, January 14, 1964, Dean F. Markham File, *John F. Kennedy Library*, Box 8.

and visceral resentment of his brother's successor. Johnson only added to Kennedy's rancor when he abruptly decided to take a walk outside, keeping his two guests waiting. Finally the president joined them. Prettyman immediately "bore down on the necessity for a presidential declaration" on illicit drugs, the commission's first recommendation, and one that they felt would endow the entire reform agenda with a sense of priority and cohesiveness. Johnson responded by indicating his "long-time interest in the narcotics problem," and he mentioned the work of his fellow Texan Price Daniel specifically. The President then said that he would name Lee White to direct a narcotics program and that he would support the Dodd Bill, currently making its way through the Senate, to control "dangerous drugs." Next he mentioned the transfer recommendation, assuring Prettyman "that he agreed with me, explaining that it made little sense to him to have big time racketeers prosecuted by 'dollar people,' i.e., the Treasury." The judge must have been heartened to hear of Johnson's approval, and perhaps this emboldened him to explicitly denounce the work of the Bureau as unsatisfactory, intercepting "165 pounds of heroin out of an estimated 3,000 pounds imported"; "the whole narcotics and drug abuse problem," the judge concluded, "arises from law enforcement failure on the part of the federal government," again choosing to believe that a more alert or better organized agency would interdict more drugs, and this would in turn affect the availability, price, and purity of all drugs in the black market.[117] Shortly after the meeting, Lyndon Johnson issued a presidential statement directing all concerned agencies to review their efforts on illicit drug traffic and use, to recommend improvements in these, announcing that Lee White would act as a special coordinating liaison in conducting this review. His remarks said nothing about a transfer of the Bureau.

A month later, the first congressional hearings conducted following Johnson's lukewarm endorsement of the Presidential Narcotics Commission report were held. These were devoted to the subject of the regulation of addictive synthetics or "dangerous drugs," and legislative proposals in this field had been quite far along even when the Kennedy Commission first convened. This was largely due to the efforts of one man, Senator Thomas Dodd, Democrat of Connecticut and chair of the Subcommittee to Investigate Juvenile Delinquency. Since 1963, Dodd had sponsored legislation to require recordkeeping from drug manufacturers and criminal charges for those found to be trafficking in dangerous drugs

[117] All quotes from longhand memorandum, July 19, 1964.

illicitly. "The house is on fire," he told his Senate colleagues in August 1964, referring to the tremendous flows of dangerous drugs outside of legal channels, and added that, since he began his investigation into illicit traffic, he learned that "the volume of extremely dangerous 'pep pills' and 'goof balls' sold illegally equal, and might actually exceed, the amounts sold legally in the nation's drugstores."[118]

The FDA commissioner underscored the need for additional legislation, as well as more authority for his agency's enforcement work. "In recent years," he informed the Senate, "our investigations have become more hazardous ... because hardened criminals are taking over the [illicit dangerous drugs] rackets."[119] The commissioner sought – and eventually received – the power for his investigators to carry firearms, serve and execute search and arrest warrants, and seize evidence. As one historian of the FDA observed, when Dodd's bill passed, FDA officials charged with its enforcement "were given powers that more closely resembled those of Federal Bureau of Narcotics agents than those of food and drug inspectors."[120] Indeed, John Finlator, the newly appointed director of the office formed to conduct this enforcement work, the Bureau of Drug Abuse Control (BDAC), told industry professionals at a conference convened to explain the new law to them in 1966 that his employees were no longer "inspectors" but "agents."[121]

Commissioner Larrick also secured vehicle asset forfeiture provisions for his new enforcement office, a power that the Bureau of Narcotics had possessed for more than ten years, but one that came as a surprise to the congressional committees hearing the Dodd bill, a different set of committees than those that had heard narcotics enforcement issues in the past. Oren Harris, an Arkansas Democrat who chaired the Interstate Foreign Commerce Committee, could not disguise his surprise to learn that the government confiscated vehicles of criminals, sometimes selling them, sometimes using them in investigations, and other times placing them at the disposal of government officials in Washington should the

---

[118] Dodd in "Control of Psychotoxic Drugs," *Hearing, Subcommittee on Health of the Committee on Labor and Public Welfare, U.S. Senate, S. 2628, August 3, 1964* (Washington, DC: U.S. Government Printing Office, 1964), quotes from p. 51 and p. 47.

[119] Larrick in ibid., p. 40.

[120] John P. Swann, "The FDA and the Practice of Pharmacy: Prescription Drug Regulation Before 1968," *Pharmacy in History* 36 (1994): 85.

[121] Finlator in "Proceedings," Food and Drug Administration Conference on Drug Abuse Control Amendments, March 11, 1966 (Washington, DC: U.S. Government Printing Office, 1966), 29.

FIGURE 4.1. This photo, taken at the scene of a 1965 arrest of a suspected illicit dealer of amphetamines, shows an FDA BDAC official brandishing a gun, a power the agency's "agents" acquired only months before.

General Service Administration find it an "economy" to do so. "That is revealing," he told Commissioner Larrick in testimony, perhaps alluding to the concrete benefits that helped to generate institutional interest in pursuing illicit drug enforcement.[122]

Despite this more organized and muscular approach to undercover investigations, the Dodd Bill, as eventually passed in the Drug Abuse Control Amendments of 1965, did not impose any limits on the manufacture or distribution of dangerous drugs. And, while the legislation did oblige manufacturers of dangerous drugs to register and keep records of transactions involving these drugs, the records were to be made available to FDA "agents" only upon request. This requirement fell short of the stringent accounting procedures in place for narcotics, which, since 1914, had necessitated that all transactions be filed with the Treasury

[122] Chair, "Drug Abuse Control Amendments of 1965," *Hearings, Committee on Interstate and Foreign Commerce, U.S. House of Representatives, H.R. 2, January and February 1965* (Washington, DC: U.S. Government Printing Office, 1965): 115.

Department and that the department would, in turn, perform a continuous review of these records and look for suspicious entries. Moreover, there was no attempt to determine an overall quota for legitimate manufacture of these drugs – a cap or a ceiling – as had been the case for narcotics since the 1922 Drug Import and Export Act. Such a production quota would have forced drug manufacturers to become their own enforcement agents, since each illicit sale would mean one less legal one, and manufacturers would have every reason to preserve as much legitimate profit as possible. A cap on production would have also meant that imports of dangerous drugs would have to be inventoried as soon as they entered an American port – as was the case with narcotics – and that these imports would count against the overall quota. Without a cap on the manufacture or importation of dangerous drugs, every conceivable enforcement mechanism could be substantially overcome or evaded simply by manufacturing or importing more drugs. CBS news reporter Mike McMullen made this point dramatically when he printed some letterhead for a fictional "McMullen Services" and used it to successfully purchase more than a million barbiturate and amphetamine tablets.

Significantly, Congress agreed to this loose system of regulation despite substantial evidence of the harm that resulted from traffic in dangerous drugs. Pictures of grisly vehicle accidents were duly deposited in the congressional record, as was the FDA estimate that approximately half of all dangerous drugs wound up on the "bootleg" market.[123] Various committees also learned that acute intoxication or poisoning from barbiturates accounted for roughly 25 percent of all patients admitted to a hospital for some form of poisoning. Some advocates called for the formation of a "Barbiturates Anonymous."[124] Even with the appalling cost and personal tragedies, Congress did not venture to consider more stringent forms of regulation, deferring to the pharmaceutical industry. In fact, while the bill placed the burden of proof for illegal possession on law enforcement officials, it also stipulated, in accordance with drug company wishes, that criminal penalties (as opposed to civil remedies) would be invoked for copyright infringement and copycat drugs. In Dodd's bill, the enforcement power was exercised to protect drug company profits rather than regulate their products.

Also surprising, Congress gave short shrift to an examination of the legal tenets supporting the Drug Control Amendments. In years past,

---

[123] Larrick, "Control of Psychotoxic Drugs," p. 42.
[124] Both found in "Drug Abuse Control Amendments," p. 73 and p. 81.

drug regulation and illicit drug enforcement had been defined through taxing authority; now Congress elected to rely on the powers endowed to them by the Constitution to regulate interstate commerce instead. Doing so meant endorsing a particular interpretation of the interstate commerce clause, one sanctioned by the Supreme Court in a series of late New Deal cases where it ruled that economic activity that was purely local in character could nevertheless fall under the interstate clause, and hence congressional powers of regulation, if the transaction or others like it could be reasonably supposed to affect interstate commerce in some significant way.[125] Formerly a strict guardian of what was and was not deigned to be "commerce," the courts followed the lead of the Supreme Court and allowed the legislative branch more discretion in making this determination.[126] In correspondence and official memoranda, it was not unusual to see public officials refer to this new and potentially revolutionary expansion of the scope of the commerce clause, yet its adoption and widespread acceptance lagged behind its legal purchase. "Well I must confess that I get a little bit confused," Congressman Oren Harris admitted as he gaveled the final set of hearings on the Dodd bill into recess; "the Constitution does not give the power of Congress to pass laws that would affect purely and solely intrastate operations," he proclaimed, at the very moment he and his committee approved a bill written to allow just that.[127]

Reading new federal regulatory powers into the commerce clause provoked criticism almost as soon as Congress showed a willingness to rely on this expansive interpretation to accomplish new goals. None was more controversial than the 1964 Civil Rights Act, premised on the commerce clause and designed to make discrimination based on race, gender, or religion by any business that serves the public a federal offense.

---

[125] Critical cases were: *NLRB v. Jones & Lauchlin Steel Corporation* (1937); *US v. Darby* (1941); and *Wickard v. Filburn* (1942). The timing of these have lead observers to catalog this expanded scope of the commerce clause as part of the New Deal; strangely, Cass Sunstein does not provide much discussion of the commerce clause in his influential article, "Constitutionalism After the New Deal," *Harvard Law Review* 101 (1987–88): 421–96, focusing instead on the New Deal "attack on the common law," which, he argues, was misguided in important respects. A closer analysis – with findings more consonant with the arguments made here – can be found in Stephen Gardbaum, "New Deal Constitutionalism and the Unshackling of the States," *University of Chicago Law Review* 64 (1997): 483–566.

[126] For a more critical appraisal of the expanded readings of the commerce clause that hinges on precisely this point, see Richard A. Epstein, "The Proper Scope of the Commerce Power," *Virginia Law Review* 73, no. 8 (1987): 1387–1455.

[127] Harris, "Drug Abuse Control," p. 42.

More than any other piece of civil rights reform legislation, the 1964 act galvanized opponents and engendered a populist backlash, especially across the south, as segregation's supporters rallied behind white business owners who refused to serve black patrons the same as whites.[128] Lester Maddox, owner of Pickrick cafeteria in Atlanta, Georgia, attracted notice and notoriety when he turned away African American customers with violent threats, becoming the public face of southern resistance and a hero to stalwart segregationists.[129] Often photographed brandishing an axe handle as a gesture to emphasize his adamant refusal to abide by the Civil Rights Act, Maddox followed his flamboyant public performances by filing a suit against the legislation, claiming that as a business owner, he should have the right to serve and to associate with whom he wished. The Pickrick case was joined with another local holdout, The Heart of Atlanta Motel, in the federal courts; together the claim went all the way to the Supreme Court for adjudication. The ruling in the case upheld the Civil Rights Act, but it launched Maddox to prominence nonetheless, endearing him especially to working-class whites in the south and paving the way for his successful 1966 run for governor of Georgia. Less visible amidst the theatrics, but no less important, was the fact that *Heart of Atlanta v. U.S.* upheld the legislative use of the commerce clause to command the integration of commercial public space.[130]

During the 1960s, the commerce clause took on different functionality in another respect as well: new readings sanctioned individual states to tax interstate commerce for the first time, a paradoxical finding that enabled states to levy a uniform sales (excise) tax. For most of American history, as the Tax Foundation explained to its members, the courts had interpreted the commerce clause to mean that "a state had no right to impose a tax on interstate commerce" – a rather straightforward reading of the Constitution, given that this power was explicitly reserved for the federal government. Beginning in 1959, the Supreme Court issued rulings that invited states to contemplate imposing a uniform tax on interstate

---

[128] Jason Sokol, *There Goes My Everything: White Southerners in the Age of Civil Rights* (New York: Vintage, 2007).

[129] For more on Maddox and southern resistance in Atlanta, see Kevin M. Kruse, *White Flight: Atlanta and the Making of Modern Conservatism* (Princeton: Princeton University Press, 2005).

[130] Vesla Weaver's observations regarding the ways in which the crime and punishment agenda and civil rights reform interacted can have no more concrete validation than the fact that both rested on the expanded powers of the commerce clause. See Weaver, "Frontlash: Race and the Development of Punitive Crime Policy," *Studies in American Political Development* 21 (Fall 2007): 230–65.

commerce.[131] This move underscores the importance of the arguments made by legal scholar Stephen Gardbaum, who argues that the New Deal court enhanced the regulatory authority of both the federal government and the individual states, and that to present federal gains as coming at the expense of the states is to miss the larger and more important story of the expansion of state authority at all levels of government.[132]

Precedents established to allow a uniform sales tax at the state level speak directly to this point: prior to these court rulings, the sales taxes among the various states, almost all created as a new avenue of state revenue during the Great Depression, featured a mind-boggling array of legislative dictums crafted to avoid running afoul of the commerce clause.[133] Starting in the early 1950s, sales taxes were proposed by southern governors who argued that revenue generated from them would go toward upgrading schools dedicated to serving blacks, thus equalizing them with those dedicated to whites and thwarting the federal government's attempts to integrate schools.[134] Even after the 1954 *Brown v. Board of Education* ruling that commanded school integration, these states remained interested in the sales tax as a source of revenue and, in the wake of new interpretations of the commerce clause, legislatures encountered fewer hurdles in imposing it.

Yet for many states, especially those in the south, greater attention to their revenue stream also exposed their relaxed approach toward tax collection. For decades many states were content, in the words of the Tax Foundation, to have certain tax liabilities "'negotiated' rather than 'computed,'" a practice that harkened back to a feudal noble requesting fealty from a vassal rather than the operations of a modern nation-state.[135] In the face of scrutiny, states professionalized their revenue practices, but consumer taxes continued to pose a conundrum. Even with the liberal readings of the commerce clause that allowed them to tax interstate goods, the states still struggled with how best to levy (and measure) a tax on consumption; for most, a single-rate sales tax for all commodities imposed at

---

[131] *Northwestern Cement v. Minn.*, 358 US 450 (1959).

[132] See Gardbaum, "New Deal Constitutionalism."

[133] Haig and Shoup discuss the diversity as well as the legal exemptions of the various state taxes in Haig and Shoup, *The Sales Tax in the American States* (New York: Columbia University Press, 1934).

[134] See Robert Sherrill, *Gothic Politics in the Deep South* (New York: Ballantine Books, 1968), p. 60.

[135] Tax Foundation, "Current Problems and Issues in State Taxation of Interstate Commerce" (New York: Tax Foundation, 1966): quotes from pp. 1 and 3.

the point of purchase became the most attractive mechanism.[136] All but four states endorsed the uniform point-of-purchase tax, paving the way for an expansion in individual state institutional capacity and growth. By 1969, consumption and sales taxes accounted for almost 60 percent of the revenue stream for individual states.

As the states entered the field of sales and excise taxes in a more robust fashion, the federal government beat a strategic retreat from the same. In June 1965, Lyndon Johnson signed the sweeping Excise Tax Reduction Act, repealing most remaining excise taxes either immediately or through a scheduled withdrawal. Earlier in the year Wilbur Mills, longtime chair of the House Ways and Means Committee, introduced the bill to abolish these federal taxes to his colleagues on the floor of the House as if it were an obvious move, despite the breadth and financial consequences of the bill: "frankly," he told congressional members, "I think we will find it difficult to explain why we waited so long to repeal the bulk of these taxes."[137] While he hailed rescinding excise taxes as a great saving to the American consumer and a boost to business, he also admitted that, "local and State governments will increase their sales taxes" because, as he noted, "the Federal Government has not left [them] many sources for additional revenue."[138] Mills, a southerner and one of the most powerful men in Congress, chose to reflect upon this shift in revenue streams by echoing his political forebears' resentment of federal power. Perhaps if state and local government collected more in excise taxes, he speculated, they might "assume more of the responsibilities which they have been passing on to the Federal Government."[139] Instead, it was the case that as the federal government increased its institutional capacity and revenue generation, individual states did the same, a concomitant growth in power between the two tiers of government. To ease this process and effect smooth relations, the federal government essentially gave the consumer taxes portfolio to the individual states. Though this bargain made for more harmonious intergovernment relations, it robbed the federal government of the tools to levy and implement a broad tax and regulatory regime on a specific set of goods, like drugs. In other words, the

---

[136] Some of these difficulties are discussed in "State Taxation of Interstate Commerce: Roadway Express, the Diminishing Privilege Tax Immunity, and the Movement toward Uniformity in Apportionment," *University of Chicago Law Review* 36, no. 1 (Autumn 1968): 186–219.

[137] Remarks of Mills in *Congressional Record*, 89th Congress, p. 304.

[138] Ibid., p. 306.

[139] Ibid.

federal government forfeited the tools to target a particular behavior and regulate it through taxation.

While the nation's tax machinery was revised and refined, other pieces of the Kennedy Commission's work made progress. As the president himself noted, the Drug Abuse Control Act, signed by Johnson in July 1965, was only the "first new legislation to come out of the recommendations ... of the President's Advisory Commission on Narcotic and Drug Abuse." The next was a two-step effort to direct federal narcotic offenders toward rehabilitation rather than prison: the Narcotic Addict Rehabilitation Act of 1966 and, two years later, the 1968 Alcoholic and Narcotic Addict Rehabilitation Amendments. The first piece of legislation, sponsored by New York Senators Robert F. Kennedy and Jacob Javitz, allowed judges to offer addicted defendants the option of civil commitment for treatment as an alternative to criminal prosecution; it also allowed eligible offenders (with no prior convictions) to volunteer for such treatment. During his introduction to the proposal, the newly elected Senator Kennedy acknowledged his debt to the President's Commission and, perhaps, discharged an obligation to Judge Prettyman for such long overdue recognition. It was revealing that, in unveiling his plan, Kennedy adopted a different tone regarding illicit drug use. Once brash and filled with confidence during his brother's administration, Kennedy now couched his proposals in a melancholy tone. Illicit drug use was a "most difficult" problem, he acknowledged; "Now, more than any other time in our history, the addict is a product of a society which has moved faster and further than it has allowed him to go," he remarked, a far cry from his assurances, years earlier, that this same energetic society would undoubtedly produce a "cure" for addiction. Instead, the world, with "its complexity and its increasingly material comfort," had left addicts behind.[140]

Echoes of this sad resignation were evident throughout the debate on the rehabilitation proposals, and even Lyndon Johnson's measured remarks on the legislation, offered during his Message on Crime in March 1965, promised that offenders would be afforded "a maximum opportunity for return to a normal life" in a somewhat muted fashion.[141] Federal officials demonstrated such a lack of enthusiasm for rehabilitation in part because they were goaded into action by individual states, most especially

---

[140] Testimony of Robert F. Kennedy, July 15, 1965, before the House Judiciary Committee, Dean F. Markham File, *John F. Kennedy Library*, Box 19.

[141] Lyndon Johnson, Special Message to the Congress on Law Enforcement and the Administration of Justice, March 8, 1965, Hein Online – 1965 – Book I Public Papers 263.

by New York and California, which began to support treatment programs several years earlier.[142] Some of these were voluntary, ambulatory clinics, the very apostasy denounced by the Bureau of Narcotics for decades. The fact that, starting in 1964, a small number of these clinics embraced methadone maintenance – a synthetic narcotic dispensed to an opiate addict to prevent her from lapsing into physical withdrawal – made these enterprises even more politically jarring.[143] New York City seemed almost defiant in its pursuit of such treatment programs: "We are ... determined," New York Mayor Robert F. Wagner announced at a 1965 Gracie Mansion Conference and in front of White House officials, "to pursue our demonstration program of utilizing a maintenance drug, in other words, a substitute for heroin, on an ambulatory basis."[144]

Lagging behind states determined to carve a new path in narcotic rehabilitation, the federal government crafted a more conservative plan. If an offender had no prior convictions, or if a judge deemed a narcotic offender to be suitable for treatment, an offender could go to treatment rather than to prison. Illicit drug use, if discovered, would automatically reinstate prosecution. As the new Attorney General Nicholas Katzenbach explained in testimony, the legislation was "the first step in disentangling medical and criminal elements in the knot of problems we call drug addiction."[145] Its proponents intended for the act to provide for more humane and progressive alternatives than had been the case under the regime of "the cure," or the forced withdrawal and imprisonment favored by Anslinger and his successors; the act also sponsored new research on addiction that would result, supporters hoped, in new treatment findings.

Treatment options were scarce and availability was extremely limited; for the rest of the decade, reformers who hoped to dismantle the punishment approach to illicit narcotic use tied their fortunes to the success of various state-level programs and fledgling city experiments. Still, even as they waited on progress, supporters scored a rare rhetorical and

[142] California had civil commitment for narcotic addicts since 1961, and New York since 1963.
[143] For succinct review of the development of methadone, see Herbert Kleber, "Methadone: The Drug, the Treatment, the Controversy," in *One Hundred Years of Heroin* (Westport, CT: Auburn House: 2002), pp. 149–58; for more on clinics, see Chapter 5.
[144] Remarks of Robert F. Wagner, February 4, 1965, Gracie Mansion Conference, found in Dean F. Markham File, *John F. Kennedy Library*, Box 22.
[145] Katzenbach in *Hearings before Special Subcommittee of the Committee on Judiciary, U.S Senate, 89th Congress, January–July 1966* (Washington, DC: U.S. Government Printing Office, 1966), p. 14.

important symbolic victory. The 1966 act embraced the logic that addiction, including narcotic addiction, was an illness in need of treatment and not a crime liable to punishment. Congress sustained this premise when it passed the Alcoholic and Narcotic Addict Rehabilitation Amendments in October 1968. Even just the joining of narcotics with alcohol in the title of the legislation signaled acceptance of arguments that Narcotics Anonymous had struggled to make only eight years earlier: addiction was a disease, and addicts were not derelicts or criminals but afflicted people who needed support and treatment. To that end, Congress passed the 1968 legislation to hasten progress in treatment centers nationwide by providing for federal funding, not just for treatment and rehabilitation, but for prevention and education as well. Without attracting much notice or, at the federal level, without engendering much controversy, the viability of a treatment approach over punishment gained adherents and much-needed support throughout the late 1960s.

The battle waged to reorganize the institutional setting for the federal government's illicit drug portfolio garnered much more attention. The Kennedy Commission's recommendation to fold the Bureau of Narcotics into the Department of Justice launched an intense bureaucratic struggle, episodes of which occasionally spilled into public view. For the most part, early discussions were confined to internal government exchanges, but as early as January 1964, when the Kennedy Commission report was finally made public, the *New York Times* informed readers that its recommendation to transfer the Bureau had been roundly denounced by Treasury insiders and, in addition, that the Justice Department "reacted coldly to the commission's proposal that it absorb the Narcotics Bureau."[146] Other vested parties followed suit, including the American Medical Association (AMA), which took the opportunity to remind President Johnson that the Bureau of Narcotics had developed a working relationship with physicians and was thus the profession's preferred partner, given the "significant and beneficial use of narcotic drugs in the practice of medicine."[147]

But for the most part, reaction to the proposed transfer was stormiest and the most heartfelt within the corridors of the federal agencies

---

[146] Homer Bigart, "US Study Urges Shift in Command in Narcotics War," *New York Times*, January 25, 1964, found in Records of the Drug Enforcement Administration, Subject Files of the Bureau of Narcotics and Dangerous Drugs, 1916–1970, *NARA*, Box 8.

[147] F.G.L. Blasingame, AMA, to Lyndon Johnson, March 11, 1964, Records of the Drug Enforcement Administration, Subject Files of the Bureau of Narcotics and Dangerous Drugs, 1916–1970, *NARA*, Box 8.

involved. Indignant narcotics agents filed rebuttals to the proposal to transfer the Bureau with Commissioner Giordano in Washington; these were then summarized and filed with the Bureau of the Budget. Narcotics District Supervisor Ross Ellis voiced a widely shared view when he singled out the 1956 Daniel Act as an effective deterrent to narcotic traffic, claiming that "fewer new addicts [have] come to the attention of all authorities ... and there has been a steady decrease in the availability of heroin," the result, he felt, of the stiff mandatory minimums instituted under the act.[148] "The progress is evident," he concluded, and neither he nor his colleagues could see how "we could have applied these provisions and enforced the law generally any better under the U.S. Department of Justice than has been done under the U.S. Treasury Department."[149] In what was a common refrain among narcotics agents, Ellis posed the question: why argue with success?

Spiraling rates of illicit drug use, while not registered in official Bureau tallies, nevertheless robbed this argument of much of its persuasive force. Dean Markham responded to the Bureau's single-minded devotion to mandatory minimums by simply noting that, despite harsh sentencing, "narcotic abuse continues to be a problem of serious dimensions in the United States."[150] Another difficult argument for the Bureau to parry was the fact that so-called dangerous drugs, like amphetamines or barbiturates, were often sold and used alongside narcotics, rendering the separate enforcement of the two drug portfolios an awkward bureaucratic concession that defied common sense. As early as 1952, then-Commissioner Anslinger recognized that many narcotic users turned to barbiturates when the opportunity presented itself;[151] years earlier, in fact, New York Bureau chief Garland Williams claimed that "90 percent of persons involved in violation of narcotic laws used barbiturates also."[152] Though such assertions stretched credibility – and demonstrated (once again) Bureau officials' tendency to provide statistical "facts" as a way of suggesting competence in the face of the unknown – there was little doubt that the traffic and consumption of "dangerous drugs" mingled with

---

[148] Ellis to Giordano, March 20, 1964, Records of the Drug Enforcement Administration, Subject Files of the Bureau of Narcotics and Dangerous Drugs, 1916–1970, *NARA*, Box 8.

[149] Ibid.

[150] Markham to Walsh, June 24, 1963, found in ibid., Box 8.

[151] H. J. Anslinger, "Barbiturate Legislation," Paper at the Seventh Annual Meeting of the Section on Food, Drug, and Cosmetic Law of the New York State Bar Association, January 23, 1952, reprinted in *Food, Drug, Cosmetic Law Journal* (March 1952): 224.

[152] "Barbiturate Curb Backed by Doctors," *New York Times*, April 3, 1947, p. 26.

illicit narcotic use.[153] Faced with this persistent pattern, Bureau agents could only reply, somewhat meekly, that joining all enforcement work under one agency "would greatly dilute the effectiveness of the agent insofar as it concerns narcotics [because] narcotic enforcement requires the full attention of the agent."[154]

In point of fact, the only viable argument that opponents of the proposed transfer could muster was one that the Bureau had itself done much to undermine: its neglected role in licit narcotic regulation. "It is regrettable that the Commission ignores the great work of the Bureau of Narcotics in perfecting [narcotic] registrant control," one agent wrote to Giordano; "nowhere in the [Kennedy Commission's] report is there a comment on the fact that annually under licenses issued by the Commissioner of Narcotics, the United States imports almost 100 tons of opium for medical needs," he observed.[155] Such activities had a natural home in the Treasury department which, as the agent noted, had regulated commerce, including contraband, since the country's founding; the "fact that in 1964 the Bureau of Narcotics devotes most of its efforts to suppressing illicit traffic should not be cause," he argued, "to divest it of its registrant function where it quietly maintains a remarkably efficient system to prevent diversion."[156] Quietly indeed: the Bureau had discounted the importance of licit regulation for many years, preferring instead to emphasize the police aspects of its illicit enforcement work. Four years later, when Congress finally found itself in the position of deliberating on the transfer of the Bureau from Treasury to the Department of Justice, Congressman Don Edwards, Democrat from California, posed a question on licit regulation directly. "The major part of drug enforcement relates to the enforcement against legitimate industries, wholesalers, druggists, doctors, retailers, and so forth," the congressman observed. "How will enforcement in this field be improved by transfer to the Department of Justice?" he asked the assistant secretary of Treasury.[157] No answer was forthcoming.

[153] Theodore M. Porter, *Trust in Numbers: The Pursuit of Objectivity in Science and Public Life* (Princeton: Princeton University Press, 1995).

[154] Wilbert Penberthy to Giordano, March 20, 1964, Records of the Drug Enforcement Administration, Subject Files of the Bureau of Narcotics and Dangerous Drugs, 1916–1970, *NARA*, Box 8.

[155] John T. Cusack to Giordano, March 25, 1965, Comments on the Final Report of the President's Advisory Commission on Narcotic and Drug Abuse, Records of the Drug Enforcement Administration, Subject Files of the Bureau of Narcotics and Dangerous Drugs, 1916–1970, *NARA*, Box 8.

[156] Ibid.

[157] Edwards in *Hearings Before a Subcommittee of the Committee on Government Operations, U.S. Senate, Reorganization Plan #1 of 1968: Drug Abuse and Narcotics,*

Despite the obvious superiority of Treasury when it came to licit regulation, elements from within the Department of Treasury had, over the previous two years, begun to question the legitimacy of keeping narcotic enforcement work within its purview. David C. Acheson, son of former Secretary of State Dean Acheson, served as assistant secretary of the Treasury for enforcement from 1965 until shortly before the agency transfer, and notes from his office occasionally evinced a real skepticism regarding the Bureau, an agency he supervised directly. The "problem" with federal legislation on narcotics, he wrote to a friend appointed to serve as the newly elected district attorney in Philadelphia, Arlen Specter, is that it "represents a panic point of time and almost exclusively the enforcement point of view." As a result, the current enforcement regime "has made the mandatory sentences rather unmanageable and," moreover, "has failed to differentiate sharply enough between addicts who commit the crime of possession and sellers who commit the crime of possession."[158] Such frank admissions, even while given off the record, spoke to the larger skepticism regarding narcotics work from within Treasury.

Yet it was mostly the fact that Treasury remained preoccupied with so much else that made its decision to forsake the Bureau relatively easy. Two things specifically helped to make the Bureau anachronistic, if not an outcast, from the rest of Treasury's work. First, like other executive agencies engaged in policy work, Treasury was asked to submit to PPBS: Planned Programming Budget System.[159] This technocratic review, pioneered at RAND and first applied to the Defense Department in the 1950s, attempted to match budget expenditures to program objectives and measure success in cost-effective terms. When applied to the work of the Bureau, the basic information needed to measure the effectiveness of its work was found wanting. As the consultant hired to do the work explained, without a reliable estimate of total worldwide opium production, the Bureau's interdiction efforts could not be assessed meaningfully,

---

90th Congress (Washington, DC: U.S. Government Printing Office, 1968) [hereafter, *Reorganization Hearing*]: 130.

[158] Acheson to Paul Michel, Assistant to Arlen Specter, District Attorney, Philadelphia, October 20, 1966, Record Group 56, Department of the Treasury, Office of Secretary, Special Assistant to Secretary for Enforcement, Narcotic Enforcement Subject Files, 1965–1968, Box 2.

[159] For more on PPBS, see Stephanie Young, "Power and the Purse: Defense Budgeting and American Politics, 1947–1972," PhD diss., University of California–Berkeley, 2009; and Jennifer S. Light, *From Warfare to Welfare: Defense Intellectuals and Urban Problems in Cold War America* (Baltimore: Johns Hopkins University Press, 2005).

despite the vaunted claims made on behalf of it.[160] David Acheson replied that neither he nor the Bureau had the capability of assembling such data,[161] and his subsequent defensiveness on the issue suggested that, in a federal government increasingly enthralled with sophisticated measurement, the Bureau and its antiquated addict rolls and poorly managed storage room were laughable vestiges of a bygone era.

Second, and most important, Treasury legal counsel had, in the mid-1960s, begun to discard the legal precepts supporting the Harrison Narcotic Act of 1914 – and so too, presumably, did then-Secretary of Treasury Henry Fowler. This fact surfaced in an exchange regarding Treasury's broader consideration of an increase in user charges, the fees associated with levying a tax that benefits a certain entity, like the gasoline tax levied to fund highway expansion and maintenance. As an excise tax, the narcotics regime of course came in for consideration for an increase in user fees, but legal authorities within Treasury concluded that "[t]he federal system for control of narcotics ... is designed to provide a different type of benefit which does not warrant trying to recover Government expenditure thereon by direct charges to those making use of the products involved." Rather, the system is "not intended to reflect the benefits derived by legitimate users but to prevent uncontrolled use," a formulation that discounted licit use and regulation entirely. Counsel was even more blunt when he concluded that the Harrison Act and its successor amendments "are an indirect method of giving the Treasury Department police power in this area and to provide a means of penalizing illegal activities."[162]

Of course the Bureau had heard this before, but never so explicitly from within the halls of the Treasury Department itself. The acting narcotics commissioner took special care to correct his colleague for the record. The Harrison Act, he observed, "was a revenue measure and was not intended merely to accomplish a moral end." The fact that Treasury

---

[160] Benjamin Caplan, Office of Planning, Treasury Department, to David Acheson, June 30, 1966, Record Group 56, Department of the Treasury, Office of Secretary, Special Assistant to Secretary for Enforcement, Narcotic Enforcement Subject Files, 1965–1968, Box 4.

[161] Acheson replies, July 1, 1966, Record Group 56, Department of the Treasury, Office of Secretary, Special Assistant to Secretary for Enforcement, Narcotic Enforcement Subject Files, 1965–1968, Box 4.

[162] Betts to Surrey, internal tax memorandum, User Charges Survey, Narcotics Taxes, September 20, 1965, Record Group 56, Department of the Treasury, Office of Secretary, Special Assistant to Secretary for Enforcement, Narcotic Enforcement Subject Files, 1965–1968, Box 4.

officials thought otherwise spelled the end of the Bureau's days in that department. Nevertheless, the commissioner made sure that his superiors in the department understood that the "declared object of the Act of 1914 was to provide revenue, and," hence, "there is a need to keep the taxing provision in its proper perspective. Any official pronouncement that it is solely for the purpose of controlling drug abuse will cast grave doubts upon its constitutionality," and, he might have added, the legitimacy of retaining narcotics work within Treasury.[163]

With the upper echelon of management persuaded that narcotics enforcement was not a natural fit with its core purposes or evolving institutional culture, Treasury officials acceded to the most controversial of all the Kennedy Commission recommendations – the transfer of the Bureau to the Department of Justice. Thus, what had once been the dispositional preference of Harry Anslinger – emphasizing illicit enforcement over licit regulation – was ultimately instantiated in a bureaucratic structure, and into the practice and understanding of policy as well. Anslinger had doggedly peddled the image of agents pursuing illicit narcotics enforcement; years later, this left little room for the Bureau to reclaim the fundamental importance of licit regulation.

And, in fact, the demand for more robust enforcement work to respond to spiraling rates of illicit drug use is what drove Lyndon Johnson to propose the transfer in early February 1968, a reorganization plan offered as part of his "message on crime," an attempt to construct a bulwark against escalating rates of violent crime, disorder, and drug use. The president had the power to reorganize any executive agencies as he saw fit, but he was required to present the plan to Congress, which could then veto it, should the plan arouse such determined opposition. The transfer of the Bureau of Narcotics to Justice, as well as the companion proposal to transfer the FDA's Bureau of Drug Abuse Control (BDAC) to the same, did in fact meet with skepticism in the House, with a resolution to defeat it failing by only ten votes. But then this particular vote was taken only days after Johnson announced that he would not seek reelection, and thus opposition to the move was more motivated by a desire to deny reorganization power to a lame duck president than it was to defeat the specific proposal at hand. In the main, like so much else in the drug debate, the agency reshuffling that created a new "Bureau of Narcotics and Dangerous Drugs" in the Justice

---

[163] Gaffney, Acting Commissioner of Narcotics, to Acheson, September 30, 1965, Record Group 56, Department of the Treasury, Office of Secretary, Special Assistant to Secretary for Enforcement, Narcotic Enforcement Subject Files, 1965–1968, Box 4.

Department was viewed by lawmakers with a kind of resigned skepticism. When, for example, Congressman Don Edwards of California asked John Finlator, the director of BDAC, whether he thought it was a good idea to give the attorney general (instead of the FDA) the power to exempt prescription drugs from regulatory controls, and Finlator answered in the affirmative, an unconvinced Edwards followed with, "Do you think that is proper?" "Yes," Finlator repeated. "You really do?" the seemingly disbelieving congressman responded.[164]

As Edwards and others shook their heads, the FDA witnesses were undeterred from their testimonials of emphatic support for the transfer. Their agency had recently gotten into a minor public relations scuffle with the Bureau of Narcotics for suggesting that marijuana penalties were too severe, a view that was gaining more and more support throughout the country, but one that rarely was voiced by any official in the federal government. The subsequent backlash only served to underscore the FDA's resolve; officials there clearly had had enough of gun-toting enforcement work. In a telling exchange, Finlator reminded Congress that if it was a "cop and robbers outfit" that they wanted, then the FDA was not the appropriate agency for the job. Just three years after his agency's authorizing legislation, the Drug Abuse Control Amendments of 1965, had passed, Finlator agreed that it was "better to place upon the shoulders of the Attorney General the total responsibility, the social responsibility, of the drug abuse problem," and, in a revealing elaboration, Finlator clarified that he wanted to "forc[e] upon [the attorney general's] shoulders the responsibility to determine why we are doing these things."[165] After chasing trucks and traffic, inspecting factories and pharmacies, searching college dorm rooms and houses of ill repute, the Food and Drug Administration was clearly eager to wash its hands of illicit drug enforcement work. BDAC, which Finlator later declared to be an outfit of "inscrutable origin that died almost before its honeymoon was over," was a short-lived FDA experiment that lasted only three years.[166]

Lawmakers raised various reservations, including the fact that the Department of Justice was not equipped to perform licit regulation and, more generally, if mounting rates of illicit drug use was really the result of social disaffection and dissent, as many contended, then at least one lawmaker wondered whether the Justice Department was the appropriate

---

[164] Exchange in *Reorganization Hearing*, p. 28.

[165] See Finlator, *Reorganization Hearing*, p. 16.

[166] Finlator, *The Drugged Nation: A "Narc's" Story* (New York: Simon & Schuster, 1973), p. 22.

agency to assign cases of "alienation."[167] Others were intent on scaling back expectations. Chair Blatnik advised his colleagues to not give the public "an impression ... that now we have a new super-duper bureau, by combining these two bureaus, and now we have the problem under control."[168] Several lawmakers were careful to pick up on this cue, with Congressman Rosenthal going so far as to wonder whether the whole proposal was "an overreaction to crime in the streets, an enforcement kind of attitude."[169]

In responding to these misgivings, government officials drew heavily on the rationale first offered by the Kennedy Commission, one that was crafted originally to suit Bobby Kennedy's initial approach and agenda to drug enforcement. The problem, Treasury officials argued, was that organized crime had thoroughly infiltrated traffic in illicit narcotics and dangerous drugs, hence the solution was to place enforcement within the halls of Justice. The reemergence of this argument several years after it had first been made was dubious, and not just because illicit drug traffic had expanded well beyond the mafia. Even if one accepted the logic on its face, as Congressman Rosenthal did, it cannot be, as he then observed, that "organized crime is the cause of the narcotics situation in the United States. It is just an adjunct to it," he argued; "It is a vehicle for it to be sold in the commercial markets."[170]

His point was as valid then as it is today. In some sense, organized crime was just a designation, and in this case a slightly inaccurate one, to describe the vendors supplying the market. Supposing that every last member of the mafia was caught, a new set of people would appear to perform the same function. "The jails are not big enough," Rosenthal observed.[171] In a subsequent session on the reorganization plan, Rosenthal expanded on these remarks to the attorney general directly, questioning the very logic of a prohibitive approach. "Is it possible," he asked Ramsey Clark, "that we can stamp out narcotics abuse and the taking of narcotics by a massive enforcement program? Do you think that is at all possible?"[172] After all, the transfer of the Bureau begged this larger question. In Treasury, narcotics work was essentially a regulatory project governing a trade; in Justice, it would be fundamentally an enforcement

---

[167] Ibid., pp. 36–7.
[168] Blatnik, ibid., p. 13.
[169] Rosenthal, ibid., p. 37.
[170] Ibid., p. 38.
[171] Ibid.
[172] Ibid., p. 77.

portfolio directed against a crime. "I would say that that is probably possible," Clark offered, a reply that was not equivocal, but not bristling with confidence either.

And on such a meager assurance, Reorganization Plan #1 of 1968 went into effect. The United States now held an institutional posture that indicated that drugs were a crime and not a trade; it was only a matter of time before the requisite political will and rhetorical powers were summoned to christen this change a "war on drugs."

5

Police and Clinics

Enforcement and Treatment in the City,
1960–1973

As the federal government restructured its illicit drug regime in a stag-
gered fashion throughout the 1960s, the cities that lawmakers invoked as
the intended beneficiaries of their efforts underwent spectacular change.
In large cities across America, the demographics of residential life were
altered as the result of Puerto Rican immigration and African American
migration – and, just as significant, white middle-class exodus to the suburbs. By the middle of the 1950s, as the housing market stabilized after
a tumultuous postwar era, a steady stream of roughly one million people
per year moved to suburban homes, leaving city life behind. These massive movements of people reshaped the modern landscape of American
life, including its political geography. Whereas the country had once been
divided along sectional lines – the south, the west, and the north – now
its most durable political boundaries were residential: urban, suburban,
and rural.

For the first time, the identity of "city" by that reckoning became
linked to a sizeable presence of racial minorities; Washington, DC,
registered the most dramatic of all the demographic shifts and was
declared majority African American by 1963 (54 percent). That same
year, African Americans made up more than a quarter of the population in New Orleans, Baltimore, Cleveland, Detroit, St. Louis, and
Philadelphia, with Chicago not far behind. During this same time, in
these cities and others, urban police departments expanded aggressive
drug enforcement from vice squads to general patrol officers, though
these were tactics applied primarily to poor, minority neighborhoods
most affected by the demographic changes underway. And, although
law enforcement embraced a professional ethos, aggressive use of force

in these neighborhoods was commonplace – and so too was corruption, especially in narcotics work. Strained relations with police resulted in tense community life defined by racial hostility. In Washington, DC, a young activist named Marion Barry forged his reputation in the community by denouncing police brutality and the autocratic control of the city by its appointed commissioners. In the District and elsewhere, throughout the latter half of the 1960s and especially in 1968, volatile police encounters occasionally escalated into riots. In the worst of these, entire neighborhoods burned.

The eruption of seemingly random violence and destruction shocked affluent Americans who had grown unfamiliar with the everyday realities of city life in its poorest neighborhoods. Equally jarring for some was a different approach launched to curb the violence associated with illicit drugs in the inner city: methadone clinics. Pioneered in New York City, clinics were nowhere more successful than in Washington, DC. Not only did DC embrace these controversial clinics, residents also fielded important legal challenges to the criminalization of public drunkenness and, later, drug addiction. As DC reformers worked to breathe life into the nascent treatment approach to illicit drug use, they confronted challenges both from within and outside of the community. But by the close of the decade, they had every reason to believe they had weathered the storm.

Yet such was not their fate. Encouraging signs that the federal government favored a treatment approach were embedded in, and beholden to, a larger consolidation of its illicit drug portfolio, a move greatly advanced by the transfer of the Bureau of Narcotics and the Bureau of Drug Abuse Control to the Department of Justice to form the Bureau of Narcotics and Dangerous Drugs (BNDD). As government officials assembled their new platform to confront illicit drug use, they faced growing criticism and alarm over escalating rates of illicit drug use among the young. Not surprisingly, officials mobilized resources within their new institutional setting to respond to political pressure, setting new precedents and shaping the institutional culture of the BNDD. In this way, the ability to turn episodic panic into lasting public policy was abetted by the drug agency reorganization of 1968. With a punishment preference securely in place institutionally, all that was needed was the political logic to justify its escalation and expansion. Richard Nixon, the newly elected Republican president and the first to call for a "war on drugs," would provide it, but not before seriously courting the treatment approach for one last time.

POLICE IN THE CITY

It is a natural tendency to assume that those things that surround us in the present day, especially those like religion or the law, that evoke tradition as a way to command obedience, operated in a similar though perhaps slightly less elaborate fashion in the past. When police don a uniform, respond to calls for service, patrol to prevent crimes, and work to solve them, it seems normal to speculate that they performed some crude version of these tasks since their formation. But even those most refined systems of power are not exempt from the laws of history: they are, in fact, dynamic institutions that change over time.

Nothing could be more true of the modern police mission. As late as the 1960s, reformers urged DC police officers to adopt and wear a recognizable uniform with some consistency; the idea that police could – and should – prevent crime was a novel theory with little evidence or rank-and-file enthusiasm to support it; and calls for police service could go unanswered or, even worse, jeered at by citizens accustomed to police more interested in shakedowns for personal profit than apprehending criminals. Dire calls for police assistance typically did not require a police report or an investigation; most involved a police officer exercising what one retired New York Police Department (NYPD) investigator remembered as "bare-knuckle law enforcement," or "getting down and dirty as criminals."[1]

In any big city in 1960, a police officer summoned to the scene of a disturbance would probably recognize his antagonists; in all likelihood, this was not their first encounter. And, though an officer was typically recruited for his brawn and willingness to fight, he might well have felt some trepidation if he was outnumbered or if his opponent had a weapon. When fights broke out, both sides – cop and criminal – put in their punches. If alarmed, a police officer would quickly go to a call box or, as was the case in New York, take his nightstick and bang it furiously on the sidewalk, a distinct and recognizable distress signal to his fellow cops on the beat who would come running, always ready to back one of their own. In New York City, as elsewhere, officers used a preponderance of force since, as one of them put it, "fairness was not our creed but winning on the street was."[2] In the end, arrests were made, and very possibly a few more punches were thrown before suspects were charged.

---

[1] Jim O'Neil with Mel Fazzino, *A Cop's Take: NYPD, the Violent Years* (Frontlee, NY: Barricade Books, 2004), p. 15.
[2] Ibid., p. 37.

This kind of justice through brute force has since been condemned for any number of reasons, not least because it sometimes attracted sadists to the force, men who inflicted physical harm beyond what was deemed necessary even under such crude standards. It is not a defense of these men – or of any of the disturbed criminals police routinely faced off against – to note that, its numerous flaws notwithstanding, this rough style of policing fit the resources police were given to handle the problems they regularly encountered. Police officers were alone on the beat, or, at best, paired with a colleague, hence every call for service could mean danger. Officers compensated for their lack of advance knowledge or efficient deployment by using overwhelming physical force, or perhaps by wielding a firearm or a nightstick. It was not uncommon for police to carry "dirty" weapons with them on the beat – or later, in their squad car – to plant on a citizen injured or killed by police so that officers could claim self-defense. These ploys probably struck a typical cop of the time not as sinister, but as a necessary form of protection. After all, a police officer's safety was on the line; sometimes he was the target of assaults himself. Performing a job that regularly asked him to oblige a neighborhood tough looking for a fight, a police officer could never be sure what was around the next corner.

With such stressful demands placed upon them, policemen were known to seek release in a number of ways. First and foremost was drink. Without question, law enforcement attracted and cultivated men who had a dependence upon alcohol.[3] Excessive drinking was so pervasive that, in an era before internal investigative units, the most feared man on the police force was the person who could send an officer "to the farm" for a mandatory drying-out period of thirty days. This banishment was invoked only in the worst instances of misconduct. Most policemen who struggled with alcohol were circumspect or well-liked enough to avoid "the farm." With frightening regularity, and with little to deter them, countless policemen both on and off duty engaged in heavy drinking. It was not unheard of for police leaving a shift to engage in riotous and drunken behavior, sometimes discharging firearms as they left the police station; in neighborhoods suspicious of police, this behavior took on a menacing cast.

---

[3] In a relative sense, this remains the case today, although police supervisors have shown an awareness of alcoholism and incidents of domestic violence among their ranks. Yet the heavy drinking of today's police force is just not comparable to historical standards, when heavy drinking was more pervasive and more openly tolerated.

Second, police officers who risked so much of themselves on the beat expected some compensation in return. Salaries were not adequate for their efforts, or so many police felt, and with good reason. It was unspoken covenant of urban policing that the department would tax the city treasury only lightly, instead relying on payoffs for the real costs of its operation. "Everyone knew about corruption on the job," a NYPD officer admitted, "and I'm not talking about a free cup of coffee or a meal on the arm. I'm talking about enormous amounts of money."[4] Supervisors from a precinct commander or higher had their own "bag man" to count and handle the money, and the "nut" or the total take from shakedowns and buyoffs was distributed up the chain of command, sometimes including the mayor, and back down to the police officers responsible for its collection. Gambling and prostitution supplied regular and handsome payoffs to police; in some cases, certain illicit narcotic traffickers did as well.

Not every police officer was a drunk or on the take, but the numbers of those who were remained significant enough to make these defining and endemic features of law enforcement culture. But the practices and accepted norms of police behavior underwent dramatic change starting in the 1950s – though, to be sure, the evolution of a more modern or "professional" form of policing was an uneven and at times faltering process. At the forefront of the change was William Parker of the LAPD, who proved to be a transitional figure by bridging the rough-and-ready style of policing with a more bureaucratic, and to some extent more accountable, mode of operation. Throughout his tenure as LA's chief of police, Parker remained unapologetic about police use of force and his own exercise of discretionary powers. Yet he was equally stern in his efforts to professionalize the force by adopting rigorous and test-based recruiting and promotions, improving the technology at the disposal of his officers, centralizing command and operations, and insisting on police autonomy and the right of police command to manage its own house without interference from politicians. Despite these impressive efforts, police autonomy had only an imperfect relationship to professionalism, and Parker ultimately reinforced the insularity of policing culture more than anything else. And vestiges of older norms were not hard to discern: nothing captured the chief's abiding attachment to the culture of rough justice more than the phrase he made famous: "the thin blue line" (a play on the "thin red line" of the British in the Crimean War), a metaphor for the small number of police officers who stood between the lawless and

[4] O'Neil, *A Cop's Take*, p. 55.

the well-ordered community, ready to repel the greater numbers that may, at any moment, join the forces of mayhem and destruction.[5]

Chief Parker had many professional admirers, and one in particular, O. W. Wilson, rose to prominence. Wilson viewed Parker's transformation of law enforcement in Los Angeles as the modern interpretation of the legacy of his mentor, progressive police reformer and chief August Vollmer. Trained by Vollmer at UC Berkeley, Wilson took up a post at the criminology school of the university and eventually became its dean. From his academic perch, Wilson issued warm praise for Parker, who, in his judgment, made the "most of his opportunity to modernize and professionalize the police service."[6] Throughout the decade, as academic circles devoted to evaluating the policing function grew in influence and number, reformers who grappled with "lawless police" or, more euphemistically, "the police problem" put forward Parker and the LAPD as the exemplar of professionalism and, they hoped, a harbinger of the future.

Such a future seemed fast and certain to arrive in sunny California, where new and expanding suburbs raked in tax dollars and enthusiastically expanded city services, including law enforcement. The pages of *The Police Chief*, the monthly journal of the largest police professional organization, the International Association of Chiefs of Police (IACP), featured triumphant updates from western and principally Californian police departments with sleek new headquarters, eager recruits capable of making the grade, and enviable salaries. In 1950, O. W. Wilson, who was himself a former a police chief in a suburb of California, published his classic text, *Police Administration*, a book that amounted to a handbook for this new kind of police force – so much so that Wilson left no detail to imagination, specifying the ideal design of police office space (open and separated by counters, so as to both symbolically suggest and visibly effect transparency). Disciples realized Wilson's vision in detail, noting for *The Police Chief* readers the exact measurements and design of headquarters, and reveling in their handsome allotment of new squad cars, a necessity in spacious California but a luxury and still somewhat discounted addition to older big-city departments in the east.

Above all else, Wilson encouraged police to move toward a more hierarchical organizational model, which, he argued, would eliminate confusion and allow for greater control of management over police operations.

---

[5] For more on Parker, see John Buntin, *L.A. Noir: The Struggle for the Soul of America's Most Seductive City* (New York: Harmony Books, 2009).

[6] Wilson in *Parker on Police*, Wilson, ed. (Springfield, IL: Charles C. Thomas, 1957), p. vii.

For a chief like Parker, centralized operations allowed him to bring the entire force under heel; Wilson, on the other hand, felt that such changes made the police force more accountable, both in terms of vetting out malfeasance and in performing and measuring the police mission. In truth, centralization and empowering management could enable both schemes, depending upon the predilection of the chief and the culture and context of any given police department. What the centralized management model inevitably did, regardless of who was at the helm, was to grant more autonomy to the police. City managers, mayors, and county supervisors who funded this organizational transformation wanted police performance, not police payoffs. Operating under such a broad mandate, politicians ceded – and police command actively sought – the power to manage law enforcement.

Despite the uniqueness of the law enforcement mission, such management enterprises resembled, in broad outline, corporate organizational development elsewhere. Reformers like Wilson and more idiosyncratic figures like Parker both agreed on the importance of a police union – though organizers could not call it one and were barred from striking – and they introduced grievance procedures for officers to use in the event of serious disagreements with management. Both also argued passionately for increased pay, as well as the importance of training recruits in an academy setting with other recruits, rather than simply deploying rookies to a veteran precinct and having them learn on the job. All of these various incentives and mechanisms gave these police managers the ability to shape and to discipline police culture, prerogatives that had once been left to the ethnic and political networks that had connected the top of city hall to the cop on the beat.

Importantly, the only significant check on the police as they amassed tools for self-governance was the courts, particularly the Supreme Court of Chief Justice Earl Warren. At the very same time as police professionalized and distanced themselves from their political overseers, a string of rulings from the state and federal courts set formal limits on the manner in which the police could interact with civilians. One area of judicial intervention was to limit the ability of police to collect intelligence via tapping telephones (or putting in a "wire").[7] It is indeed surprising to learn the extent to which such "wires" went unregulated and were indiscriminately used by police (and the FBI) for any number of reasons, including tapping the phone of a political rival. Starting in the individual states and

[7] Buntin, *L.A. Noir*, p. 208.

culminating in the Supreme Court ruling in *Katz v. US* (1967), courts determined that police had to obtain a warrant in order to tap telephones. The courts also clarified the standard for what was admissible evidence against a defendant in a criminal case – for the federal government, this came much earlier in *Boyd v. United States* (1886) and *Weeks v. United States* (1914), and for the states (and hence for most felonies in most jurisdictions) this came later in *Mapp v. Ohio* (1961). All of these precedents established the principle that evidence that was improperly obtained must be excluded from criminal proceedings. Finally, and most controversially, the Supreme Court responded to concerns over forced or false confessions by charging police with the responsibility of prompt arraignment and the duty to inform suspects of their rights upon arrest in its *Mallory v. United States* (1957), and *Miranda v. Arizona* decision in 1966; for similar reasons, the court also held that a suspect had the right to counsel during police interviews in *Escobedo v. Illinois* (1964).[8] The oversight once exercised by politicians and directed toward primarily police command had now moved to the courts and constrained the behavior of the entire department, right down to the cop on the beat. This relocation of oversight, as well the reconfiguration of its priorities and targets, produced a sweeping backlash from within the ranks of law enforcement.

Significantly, denouncing court decisions that impinged upon police discretion was one of the few things that united police leaders across the country. Baronial police chiefs accustomed to arbitrary rule resented judicial decisions just as much as those who held themselves out as paragons of professionalism. Court rulings were also a prominent and, in the minds of many police, artificial barrier to achieving full police effectiveness, supplying police leaders with an easy scapegoat. As one police chief admitted, "blaming crime increases on court restrictions furnished a convenient excuse for police commanders to escape their responsibility to reduce crime."[9] Yet there can be little doubt that court decisions altered the standards of behavior for each and every patrol officer on duty, a marked transformation wrought by a new taskmaster, and one that many police viewed with suspicion, if not hostility.

[8] I exclude here the "right to counsel" decision of *Gideon v. Wainwright*, 372 US 375 (1963), which provided a right to counsel during trial and hence did not substantially alter police practice.
[9] Jerry V. Wilson, "The War on Crime in the District of Columbia, 1955–1975," National Institute for Law Enforcement and Criminal Justice Law Enforcement Assistance Administration, U.S. Department of Justice, February 1978, Found in MLK Library, Washingtoniana Room, p. 3.

The protest against court decisions united a police profession that was otherwise disparate and, in some cases, in disarray. No outfit was more assailed than the Chicago Police Department (CPD), which, according to one law review article in 1955, was "by far the most demoralized, graft-ridden and inefficient among our larger cities."[10] When members of its force were discovered to be running a burglary ring in 1959, news stories that announced the police to be "crooks with badges" punctuated the sense of crisis. Lost in the outcry was the way in which the burglary ring was an extension of traditional police corruption: store owners who had been burglarized routinely invited police to "help themselves" to what was left, since insurance would cover the losses in any event. In Chicago, some cops decided simply to drop the pretense and helped themselves to whatever they wanted, whenever they wanted.[11] As the probe into the burglary ring extended into the new year, newspapers reported to readers that the city's police department was in fact "riddled with corruption," and that promotions were blatantly political, something that, as one U.S. attorney sneered, "you'd have to be stupid or blind" not to know.[12] To silence his critics, Chicago Mayor Richard Daley appointed a blue-ribbon commission to recommend changes in the police department. The group concluded that Chicago's police needed organizational changes decreed from the very top, and, as the result of their efforts, O.W. Wilson was brought in as the new police superintendent.

With his typical energy and thoroughness, Wilson set about restructuring the CPD into a modern, professional, and what he sometimes called a "scientific" organization. Only nine months after his appointment, Wilson assured the city council that he "no longer consider[ed] corruption a serious problem in the police department."[13] His confidence was based on his successful program to centralize the CPD, a move that eliminated many precinct posts and clarified the chain of command, and, as a result, strengthened management's ability to supervise the force. Yet by far Wilson's most aggressive initiative was his program to put more CPD officers in squad cars or motorbikes with two-way radios to patrol the city, taking them off the pedestrian beat and, just as important, enabling

---

[10] As quoted in *Parker on Police*, p. 129.

[11] See Kenneth Rexroth, "The Fuzz," tearsheets from *Playboy*, July 1967, found in NAACP, Part IV: Box A59.

[12] "Chicago Police Scandal Faces Probe by Jury," *Washington Post Times Herald*, January 18, 1960, p. A3.

[13] "Corrupt Cops No Longer Are Worry: Wilson," *Chicago Daily Tribune*, November 16, 1960, p. B15.

their radio command to contact them – and check on them – at any time. No single change did more to transform the practice and the culture of Chicago policing: instead of belonging to the streets, Chicago police officers were now extensions of central command. By 1963, 95 percent of Chicago's patrol worked on wheels.[14]

Wilson introduced other reforms as well. He joined other chiefs in the state to successfully push the Illinois legislature into passing state-wide minimum standards for police recruits and law enforcement training since, as the IACP observed in its professional journal, too many "men were being employed as police officers without any formal training whatsoever."[15] He invested heavily in the latest technology, including a high-speed computer, an important part of what Wilson called "an accelerated program to make our city's law enforcement procedures the best in the country."[16] Using such sophisticated tools, Chicago tracked the deployment of patrol vehicles, cutting response times and keeping a watchful eye on the force. When the new electronic computer center of the Chicago police was highlighted in *The Police Chief* in December 1961, the superintendent could take pride in the fact that his accomplishments in Chicago now stood comparable to the ideal police force he had envisioned only ten years before in *Police Administration*.

Nevertheless, and not surprisingly, elements of old Chicago police culture remained. Reports of corruption dogged the department, such as the ones that surfaced in 1963 in response to federal agents threatening to leak damaging information about the "dishonesty of certain policemen" in the city, or the 1965 allegations that police managed to run a prostitution racket, busting wealthy "johns" who were willing to pay in order to avoid arrest and exposure.[17] Wilson met these and similar charges by insisting that such incidents were now isolated and atypical, and often he and other police chiefs complained that the press sensationalized accusations of corruption but left honesty and good police work unreported. When Denver's police force was found to have forty-five officers active in a burglary ring in 1962, the IACP attempted to place the scandal

---

[14] Harley Davidson advertisement, *The Police Chief* 30, no. 4 (April 1963).

[15] "Illinois Chiefs Draft Standards Bill," *The Police Chief* 27, no. 5 (May 1960): 25.

[16] "Chicago High Speed Computer," *The Police Chief* 38, no. 9 (September 1961): 27.

[17] "Wilson Probes Corruption in Police Ranks," *Chicago Tribune*, July 20, 1963, p. 1; "Near North Sex Racket Reports Draw O.W.'s Fire," *Chicago Daily Defender*, October 28, 1965, p. 1. In the latter scandal, two prostitutes who came forward to report the scam were found dead days later.

in context by pointing out that "the other 742 Denver police officers" received "very little space" in press accounts.[18]

As the persistence of crooked cops occasionally stole headlines from the larger story of Chicago's modernization, a more fundamental concern went almost entirely neglected: did Wilson's changes, even if implemented to the fullest, actually make for more effective police? The *Christian Science Monitor* posed this question just weeks prior to the Chicago police force's brutal attack on Vietnam War protestors gathered in the city for the 1968 Democratic Party Convention. "Car patrols relentlessly cruise inner-city areas," the article noted, and both the force and its downtown headquarters had received "a drastic facelift" since reforms began in 1960; yet, the reporter wondered, were these many changes "proving effective in fighting crime?"[19] With violent crime on the increase, many Chicago citizens were dubious. Two years later, *Time* magazine presented the same dilemma in even starker terms. "The realization is growing," the author observed, "that even the best police work ... is little more than a symbolic response to crime."[20]

The ultimate purpose and effects of the police function was a question asked but rarely, yet it was one that could have been put before the entire burgeoning police professional movement of the decade, a drive begun in incipient form in the LAPD of the 1950s and one that was fully apparent in most big-city departments by the 1960s. Michael J. Murphy, police chief of New York City starting in 1961, raised training and recruiting requirements and kept the force on the same footing as other departments. His occasional letters to the IACP's *Police Chief* were welcomed by the organization's president at that time, DC Chief Robert Murray, who had installed similar training standards only a few years earlier.[21] Murray had also established formal criteria for promotion, though these included subjective factors vulnerable to manipulation. He was also unabashed about letting *Police Chief* readers in on changes in DC police practice that he felt attested to his modernization efforts, like his institution of more elaborate categories of racial categorization than just W (White) and C/B (Colored/Black), even though the newly

[18] "Rebuilding a Scandal Torn Police Force," *The Police Chief* 29, no. 4 (February 1962): 4.
[19] "Chicago Presses Modernization of Police Force," *Christian Science Monitor*, July 16, 1968, p. 3.
[20] "What the Police Can – and Cannot – Do About Crime," *Time*, July 13, 1970, found in MLK Library, Washingtoniana Room, Vertical Files, "Police."
[21] "Police Chief to Restore Academy," *Washington Post and Times Herald*, May 11, 1958, p. A1.

added groups of Mongolian, Brown Indian, and American Indian did not speak to major demographic shifts under way in the District; or his use of color photography to capture the image of detainees, something he felt added "tonal quality" and helped in identification efforts. "Recently we have found that color has greatly assisted us in squelching false charges of police brutality," Murray confided to *Police Chief* readers.[22] His contention that such was the case rested on the fact that color photos of detainees did not show any apparent bruising on the face. While Murray applauded his own modernization efforts, it was not difficult to detect a dimension of racial hostility in his endeavors.

Likewise, another source of pride for Murray was DC's canine force, the largest in the country. Though he promoted it with evident satisfaction and published stories in *The Police Chief* extolling the virtues of trained police dogs, other chiefs, including Parker in LA and Murphy in New York, wrote in politely to demur, claiming no use for a canine force in their department. Yet police command from the south endorsed Murray's belief in the value of the unit, a regional bias that was made manifest to many in the country as they stood aghast at televised images of fierce police dogs set upon young children participating in a civil rights march in Birmingham in 1963. In fact, it seemed the whole issue of a canine unit stood in as an indirect measure of the police department's posture toward the civil disobedience sponsored as part of the modern civil rights movement and, it is not too much to say, toward the local black community more generally. While it is safe to assume that no major police department embraced civil rights protests, some viewed them as only contemptible, while others viewed them as existential threats to the social order. The latter were more likely to have canine units, and more likely to openly profess indifference in the face of the black community's continuing objections to the use of aggressive dogs. When the issue of the District's canine unit came up for review in the mid-1960s, reformers encouraged the police force to abandon plans for expansion of the canine unit and instead gradually phase it out,[23] while southern congressional supporters of police chief Murray praised it and urged its retention.[24]

---

[22] "Use of Color Photography in DC," *The Police Chief* 29, no. 1 (January 1962): 12.

[23] President's Commission on Crime in the District of Columbia, *Report on the Metropolitan Police Department* (Washington, DC: U.S. Government Printing Office), p. 55.

[24] *Hearings Before the Special Subcommittee on the Metropolitan Police Department of the Committee on DC, House of Representatives, 90th Congress, February, March 1967* (Washington, DC: U.S. Government Printing Office, 1967), p. 130.

This was but one component of policing that was set in a new and volatile context of change in the nation's cities. At the same time as police reformers embarked on their drive to professionalize law enforcement, the civil rights movement embraced the tactics of direct, nonviolent confrontation. Students and other volunteers who rode on interstate buses in the south as part of the Congress on Racial Equality (CORE) project to desegregate transportation were firebombed on deserted roads. In one instance in Montgomery, Alabama, civil rights volunteers departed the bus under presumptive police protection only to be savagely attacked. CORE volunteer and future Congressman John L. Lewis was struck so forcefully that he had to be taken to the hospital for a fractured skull. Sit-ins and marches throughout the country attracted the hostility of local communities; the police, who were caught in a dangerous stand-off between the movement and its detractors, sometimes negotiated a peace, and other times were complicit and perhaps even participated in violence.

So, in a provocative coupling of events, at the very moment in 1960 when the IACP ventured that "the idea of a professional police force should not come as a shock to anyone," the proposition surely would have been a welcome surprise to civil rights participants who held a more jaundiced view.[25] Their cynicism was shared by the larger black urban community that had expanded and, by most measures, suffered during the same time. Mistrust of the police was a routine fact of life in the city's toughest black neighborhoods. Often an arrest made on one of these streets attracted spectators who hassled cops in an effort to ensure that the police remained circumspect, but also surely to subject officers to verbal abuse while they were too preoccupied to do anything about it. As tensions rose, they became impossible to ignore. One police commander attempted to appeal to blacks alienated from local police by comparing the plight of the black freedom movement with that of modern police: "policemen should be understanding and sensitive to the Negro and his status," he wrote in 1963, but, at the same time, "the Negro should certainly be able to see the police officer in much the same light as he sees himself."[26] Both suffered from stereotypes, and, he argued perceptively, both perpetuated them as well. In one passage, the commander argued that the police force's sensitivity to its reputation had been "dulled by the

[25] Quote from "Technical Competence is Not Enough: The Policeman as a Professional," *The Police Chief* 27, no. 9 (September 1960), p. 20.
[26] James J. Allman, "The Public Attitude Toward Police," *The Police Chief* 30, no. 1 (January 1963): 12.

many thumpings they have received that, at this stage of the game, one more knot on the head doesn't make a difference."[27] Such language would ring hollow to those bandaging real and not metaphorical wounds. It was nonetheless a heartfelt plea, and police from many corners shared a genuine belief in their own victimization and, at the same time, a determination to better their relations with inner city minority neighborhoods. San Francisco Police Chief Thomas Cahill took note of the transformation of American cities and informed his colleagues in 1964 that, "the social structure [in most cities] is completely changed, and in many we find restless, moving, ever-growing populations, resulting in new tensions, new conflicts, and new demands for service."[28] And so it was that when sending a squad car into the ghetto in the 1960s, the ascendant and self-aware movement of police professionalism passed into its crucible.

THE DISTRICT

Narcotics enforcement served as the most reliable way to perpetuate the practices of "rough justice," and to retain the discretion of police autonomy despite judicial scrutiny, and in the new era of police professionalism, the southern model of police as an instrument of social control over blacks became the way to chart – and to delimit – the domain that would be subjected to it. In restructuring the valences of police power and its geography, the District of Columbia once again proved essential.

Like other cities, life in the District had changed in the late 1950s and early 1960s. Lost in the much-heralded news of DC as a majority black city was the fact that much of that majority was comprised of migrants who were new to the city. Ulf Hannerz, a Swedish anthropologist who chronicled 1960s street life on "Winston Street," a fictitious name given to a block in Shaw, estimated that only about one third of the residents in his study were born in DC.[29] Yet newcomers assimilated quickly, by necessity, as kinship ties from mainly coastal southern states facilitated close community, and residential segregation and exclusion from white neighborhoods demanded it. To be sure, black neighborhoods expanded as the city's African American population grew. As George Pelacanos writes in *Hard Revolution*, a novel set in Washington that opens in 1959,

[27] Ibid.
[28] Quoted in IACP Conference Summary, *The Police Chief* 31, no. 7 (July 1964): 47.
[29] Ulf Hannerz, *Soulside: Inquiries Into Ghetto Culture and Community* (New York: Columbia University Press, 1969), p. 25.

this expansion was hastened by "blockbuster real estate agents" who, sensing a quick profit, "had begun moving colored families into white streets with the intention of scaring residents into selling their houses on the cheap."[30]

As scores of white residents relocated and many left for the suburbs, black neighborhoods that stretched farther and farther north of the U.S. Capitol building maintained a varied and in many ways vibrant community life. U Street still hosted an impressive array of sophisticated, established, and bourgeois city life – though one of DC's most infamous narcotics corners, T and 7th Street (Georgia Avenue), sat uncomfortably close to the flourishing center of Washington's black community. And of course, ghettos expanded too. The slums of the second or "wickedest" precinct encroached onto new terrain, albeit in ways that would not be fully obvious until riots burned out the retail that had clung to corners and cross-streets. But, as Hannerz pointed out, even a typical ghetto street could not be stereotyped or simplified. Any such block had its "mainstreamers," residents who had full-time or reliable seasonal employment; in the second district, for example, one in five workers were employed by the federal government, a rate that fell below the city average of two in five workers, but one that nevertheless represented a steady stream of income.[31] Even the "streetcorner men," who snuck into alleys to drink liquor while avoiding police detection, could not be counted as completely hostile, since they were familiar figures and most likely to inflict harm on each other.[32]

The real danger detected by the ghetto's residents, according to Hannerz, were the "gorillas," the disparaging yet frightening name given to young men attracted to a life of violent crime, and the police, who, along with certain retailers, were the only ambassadors of life outside the ghetto to make frequent appearances inside of it. And the police stood out: as many observers noted throughout the 1960s, while the majority of DC was black, a majority of its police force – four out of five officers – was white. This racial disparity only fueled a view of the police from within the ghetto that was, Hannerz argued, highly ambivalent and "tinged with more hostility than respect." Like others, he acknowledged

---

[30] George Pelecanos, *Hard Revolution* (New York: Little, Brown, 2004), p. 7.
[31] Statistic from *Washington Post*, June 28, 1968 found in MLK Library, Washingtoniana Room, Vertical Files, "Police."
[32] This practice of "alley" drinking belonged to the history of alley life in DC: see James Borchert, *Alley Life in Washington: Family, Community, Religion, and Folklife in the City, 1850–1970* (Chicago: University of Illinois Press, 1980).

that many residents on Winston Street recognized the need for police in their community, and, quite frequently, the police were condemned most strongly for their *lack* of presence in the ghetto. Yet, at the very same time, Hannerz noted that young teenagers and "streetcorner men [felt] they [were] being harassed quite unnecessarily in their everyday lives," a resentment derived mostly from enforcement of the controversial disorder statute of the DC city code – specifically, section 1121 and section 1107, the "move along" and noise provisions – stipulating that anyone making disruptive noise or who failed to "move along" after police commanded him to do so was subject to arrest.

Under these disorder charges, an incredible number of people were arrested for public drunkenness, a "crime" without any real victim, or for failing to behave as a policeman wished; one precinct in DC claimed an astonishing 4,352 disorderly arrests in 1966.[33] Because disorderly charges were such an expansive enforcement tool at the disposal of police, the statute operated, in the broadest sense, as a cudgel to establish police power in black neighborhoods. Not surprisingly, the charge and police reliance upon it became ensnared in controversy in the era of civil rights.[34] Washington, DC, Student Non-Violent Coordinating Committee (SNCC) chair Marion Barry denounced "move along" arrests as a capricious instrument in the hands of white and often openly racist police; such arrests, numbering some 21,000 annually, meant that police were "wasting their time," Barry insisted, "while people are being raped and murdered."[35] "Move along, boy," countless black men and teenagers heard white police say; any gesture that a policeman then construed as dilatory or defiant could be grounds for an arrest, and sometimes a brutal one. Adding to the ample amounts of law enforcement discretion, the District's Narcotics Vagrancy Act (1961) declared any person a "vagrant" who was found to be close at hand to illicit narcotics and authorized arrest on those grounds. As often as not, then, arrests for disorderly conduct or vagrancy depended upon what a police officer chose to investigate, how he perceived the situation unfolding around him, and whether or not he operated under an informal arrest quota in his precinct.

And it was the case that some police reported to precincts with unannounced arrest quotas – typically, the worst precincts, like the second or

---

[33] Nicholos Horback, "A Wide Ranging Charge," *Washington Daily News*, no date given, MLK Library, Washingtoniana Room, Vertical Files, "Police."

[34] Quotes from Hannerz, *Soulside*, pp. 162–3.

[35] Carl Bernstein, "DC Police Waste Time," *Washington Post*, July 1, 1967, p. B2.

adjacent precincts like the 13th – the new "wickedest" precinct.[36] Such aggressive (and illegal) tactics bespoke a militant enforcement approach, but crime in the District was, for the first half of the 1960s, not particularly bad. That changed quickly in the middle of the decade: in 1957, DC ranked twelfth among sixteen comparable cities in crime, yet by 1967, it was second.[37] As was typical, rhetoric about crime did not match the official statistics. Well before violent crime rates spiraled to new heights, some political leaders continued the practice of invoking the District as a kind of synecdoche or stand-in for black criminality in urban America and railed against it accordingly. On a national television broadcast in June 1963, southern Senator Allen J. Ellender referred to DC as a "cesspool" of crime.[38] Not long after, Barry Goldwater focused on black criminality as part of his efforts to forge a common social cause with white southern Democrats. When accepting the Republican party's nomination for president in the summer of 1964, Goldwater took special care to note that the "growing menace in our country tonight, to personal safety, to life, to limb and property, in homes, in churches, on the playgrounds, and places of business, particularly in our great cities, is the mounting concern, or should be, of every thoughtful citizen in the United States." A measured response from President Johnson pointed out that crime was a responsibility of local government, a demurral that, as historian Michael Flamm argues, contradicted decades of Democratic efforts to empower the federal government with tasks once reserved for state and local bodies. Yet even Johnson's attempts to dismiss the question of crime as a local preoccupation left an open door – the District of Columbia, a property of the federal government – and Goldwater was quick to walk through it. A month after his acceptance speech at the Republican convention, Goldwater criticized President Johnson for declaring many "wars," but no "war on crime," especially for the District, where the federal government's authority was uncontested. While the capital should be "the one city which should reflect most brightly the president's concern for

[36] "Inspector Stargel, former commander of precinct 2, was highly regarded for his civic participation as precinct captain but reports persisted at that time that the official exacted quota arrests from his men." Found in "Stargel Must GO – NAACP," *Afro*, November 13, 1965, MLK Library, Washingtoniana Room, Vertical Files, "Police."

[37] "The Bitter World of the Policeman," *Nation's Business*, October 1967, p. 85.

[38] Jerry V. Wilson, "The War on Crime in the District of Columbia, 1955–1975," National Institute for Law Enforcement and Criminal Justice Law Enforcement Assistance Administration, US Department of Justice, February 1978, Found in MLK Library, Washingtoniana Room; quote from p. 6 [hereafter: Wilson, "The War on Crime"].

law and order," instead, Goldwater lamented, it was a "city embattled, plagued by lawlessness."[39]

Despite his early dismissals, Johnson was in fact extremely mindful of crime in the District; according to Flamm, he was "fixated" on it.[40] After a triumphant election result in the fall, the president responded to his critics by appointing a special Commission on Crime in the District of Columbia in July 1965, one of several actions taken in the wake of Johnson's address on crime to the nation months before. The task force spent a good part of its time assessing the work of DC's Metropolitan Police Department (MPD), and concluded its analysis with a stark admonition: "No one in the District of Columbia should underestimate the gulf of experience and misunderstanding which separates police from poorer Negro citizens."[41] The commission was determined to usher in changes that would bridge the divide between these residents and the police, so in its interim report published in early 1967, the commission restricted itself to a focus on internal reforms of the MPD, deferring its discussion of crime and its causes, and some might say dismissing them. "In some cities," the group noted, "the professionalization of a police force has been accompanied by an apparent rise in the crime rate, as official reporting techniques are improved and increased public confidence in the police results in more crimes being reported by citizens."[42] This was perfectly true, though, at the same time, it was a point that read so technically as to seem indifferent.[43]

To form the base of its police recommendations, the commission recruited the IACP to recommend structural changes to the MPD, and the professional association was by now well accustomed to its role as experts consulted to speed the transition to a more professional police culture. The first thing the IACP noted – because it surprised them – was how large the police force in DC was, and how much it cost: by the mid-1960s, it was per capita the largest department in the country as well as the most expensive. Yet all this investment represented good money after bad because the department, according to the IACP, was poorly managed. As it had done elsewhere, the group urged the MPD to refine its

---

[39] See Michael W. Flamm, *Law and Order: Street Crime, Civil Unrest, and the Crisis of Liberalism* (New York: Columbia University Press, 2005), p. 42.

[40] Ibid., p. 132.

[41] President's Commission on Crime in the District of Columbia, *Report on the Metropolitan Police Department* (Washington, DC: U.S. Government Printing Office, 1966), p. 63.

[42] Ibid., p. 2.

[43] See Flamm, *Law and Order*.

chain of command and internal supervision by centralizing operations and to shift police from desk work, hiring clerical staff in their place, and transfer them to patrol. Less than half of the department's personnel were available for patrol at any one time, the IACP pointed out with obvious disapproval.

The other facet of MPD institutional life that jumped out at the IACP was the fact that DC's police force had one of the highest resignation rates in the country. The reasons for this police exodus became the subject of contentious debate, as well as a kind of Rorschach test of police and race relations in the city. For its part, the IACP and the commission focused on those internal failures that would foster discontent. The MPD's building was old, its equipment inadequate, its patrol cars antiquated; even uniforms varied in shade and were haphazardly worn.[44] Remarkably, officers had to purchase handcuffs at their own expense, a miserly indicator of an apathetic police command. And, as both the IACP and the commission were quick to point out, police in the District needed only to look over the city's boundaries to well-staffed, well-paid, and well-run suburban police departments that were, in all likelihood, closer to the police officer's home than the District. The decision to resign from the MPD was made easier by the attractive offers that were well within reach.

While the commission took all of the IACP findings to heart, it also made some remarks independent of that group. For a city that was now mostly black, the commission could not but help to find a mostly white police force to be anachronistic at best, and antagonistic at worst. "Frequent instances of arrests," the commission reported, "many unjustified, [have been issued] under the 'failure to move on' provision of the disorderly conduct statute," and these stoked resentment in the city's expanding black neighborhoods.[45] Moreover, despite complaints from police of false accusations, transgressions were found in the majority of complaints filed with the Trial Board by the Citizens Board.[46] Aggressive and unjustified use of force, whether it was arrest, physical brutality, or both, led black residents in impoverished areas to view the police "not as protectors but as part of an oppressive social order."[47] "There is a psychological setting of police brutality," as one DC activist observed, a charged atmosphere that meant even routine interactions could escalate

---

[44] Ibid., pp. 39–43.
[45] Ibid., p. 67.
[46] Ibid., p. 77.
[47] Ibid., p. 2.

into a police-community standoff.[48] The commission concluded that it was common sense and perhaps even necessary to preserve the peace to hire and promote more African Americans to the MPD.

Congressional response to the president's commission and its findings was quick and emphatic. Not content to rely on the IACP, Congress employed its own expert analyst, M. L. Harney, longtime assistant to Harry Anslinger in the Bureau of Narcotics and perhaps his most trusted lieutenant. Through the figure of Harney, the Bureau's racialized views and particular brand of moral panic was projected onto the District of Columbia, a welcome and illuminating lens for the southern Democrats in charge of District affairs in Congress, including Basil Whitmer, the North Carolina congressman placed in charge of the special subcommittee on the Metropolitan Police Department. In hearings held by Whitmer to review his report, Harney dismissed the president's commission as "a contribution from outsiders of varying 'expertise' in the police field."[49] Instead of institutional failings, Harney attributed the impressive personnel exodus from the MPD to *Mapp v. Ohio*, the Supreme Court ruling of 1961 that held that evidence procured as the result of improper searches could not be used in court. Harney did not explain just how this affected the District, which, as a federal entity, had been operating under the "exclusionary rule" for federal law enforcement established in the courts many years earlier. Moreover, Harney insisted that recruiting blacks to the force was not the answer, for such efforts amounted to little more than "speculat[ion] in numbers or play[ing] with color."[50] For Harney, morale in the MPD was low because "Washington streets are crawling with felons"; for this reason, the committee should "watch very closely any attempts made to weaken the 'move on' ... provisions." "Sometimes their application can be abrasive," Harney admitted, "but the alternative to non-enforcement may well be a curfew with soldiers and bayonets on every block."[51]

This depiction of the District as teetering on the precipice of chaos sustained southern congressmen in their view that nothing needed to change

[48] Marion Barry quoted in "Is Nation's Capital Heading for a 'Watts?'" *Hartford Courant*, September 18, 1966, p. 46A.

[49] *Investigation and Study of the Metropolitan Police Department, Report of the Committee on the District of Columbia, House of Representatives, 89th Congress, February 1967* (Washington, DC: U.S. Government Printing Office, 1967), pp. 7–8.

[50] Ibid., p. 19.

[51] Ibid., pp. 20, 24.

in the Metropolitan Police Department, except perhaps the formation of a "civilian guard" or "reserve police," a favorite suggestion of Basil Whitener that referred to the southern practice of arming white civilians in the event of a disturbance in black neighborhoods. All in all, the presiding members of the congressional committee found "no basis for nor does it see any probability of expectation that [police] reorganization can bring about any substantial improvement in the laws of DC."[52] Indeed, reforms were regarded as an effort to soften the department's approach to law enforcement, leaving criminals, in the words of M. L. Harney, "unwhipped of justice."[53] Some members of Congress objected, characterizing Harney's intervention as "one of defensiveness" that encouraged the unfortunate feelings of "isolation and fear" already haunting the MPD.[54] Congressman Adams pointed out that the reforms suggested by the president's commission were akin to efforts elsewhere, all part and parcel of a recognizable drive to "bring down the time and modernize these police departments in less than twenty five years"; "through use of the money and techniques," he added, that was "precisely what we are going to try to do in DC."[55] The congressman then went on to make a crucial observation: the courts in DC were overcrowded, and the judicial system was literally "at a point where it is burning out from the overload."[56] Whitener disregarded this notion; "I do not believe this is a real estate problem," he responded.[57] Instead, Congress endorsed the contention of DC police command, including its new chief, John Layton, that the department's structure and its methods were fine; it was the streets of DC that were the problem.

Layton, the department's "choir singing cop with a marksman's eye," brought in to clean up a corrupt narcotics unit in the early 1950s, had subsequently gone on to lead the department's internal investigation unit.[58] Widely viewed as beyond reproach, Layton was also a comfortable choice to replace Chief Murray in the sense that, while not corrupt

---

[52] McMillan, *Hearings Before Special Subcommittee on MPD of the Committee on DC, House of Representatives, 90th Congress, February, March 1967* (Washington, DC: U.S. Government Printing Office, 1967), p. 4.

[53] Ibid., p. 62.

[54] Gude, ibid., p. 47.

[55] Ibid., p. 62.

[56] Ibid., p. 104.

[57] Ibid.

[58] *Washington Post*, March 25, 1952, Found in MLK Library, Washingtoniana Room.

himself, neither had he had turned the department upside down vetting
out corruption. When Lyndon Johnson heard that the DC commissioners selected Layton to run the MPD just days after the president's phenomenal 1964 election triumph, he was irate, no doubt because he had
not been consulted.[59] Layton seemed content to run the department just
as his predecessor had done, and Johnson, who had some clear ambition to reform and exert more authority over the MPD, finally resorted
to circumventing the new chief. In 1967, Johnson appointed Walter
Washington, the last presidential appointment to the DC commission,
and the first one to be designated mayor-commissioner – and, later under
Home Rule, the city's first elected mayor. Upon appointment as mayor-
commissioner, Washington brought in Patrick Murphy, former chief of
police in Syracuse, New York, as Director of Public Safety. Widely viewed
as a progressive, Murphy launched an aggressive recruitment drive to
hire blacks to the MPD, and he also implemented the various recommendations of Johnson's Crime Commission. In 1968, he orchestrated a
leadership change, selecting a technocrat with progressive leanings, Jerry
V. Wilson, to replace Layton as MPD police chief. With or without the
help of Congress, Johnson showed determination in his efforts to professionalize DC's police force.

The resulting drive to recruit more blacks to the MPD – and, of course,
the fact that blacks comprised more and more of the employment pool for
the agency – converged to produce a number of tragic or embarrassing
episodes that initially only served to emphasize the racism that pervaded
the department. A good number of African Americans who joined the
MPD before the commission's report either quit the force or retired early
as a result of frustrations encountered on the job. One such retired officer,
Charles Dixon, was ordered to "move along" by two white officers who,
when dissatisfied with Dixon's response, arrested and beat him.[60] Such
incidents of harassment of former or off-duty police galvanized black
police officers within the MPD. As *Washington Post* columnist William
Raspberry reported in 1966, black officers once "shrugged off such
abuse," but "now that it is happening to the other officers, they want

[59] Flamm, *Law and Order*, p. 129. Jerry V. Wilson speculates that Johnson's irritation came
from damaging information leaked to the press about one of Johnson's assistants that,
the president believed, could only have come from the MPD. See Wilson, *War on Crime
in the District of Columbia* (Washington, DC: U.S. Government Printing Office, 1978).
[60] "Charges Police Brutality," *Washington Post*, September 24, 1965, found in MLK Library,
Washingtoniana Room, Vertical Files, "Police."

FIGURE 5.1. "Wear It With Pride" (1969). In the wake of riots and years of tension between officers and the community, the Metropolitan Police Department of Washington, DC, began a concerted drive to recruit African American officers to the force.

action."[61] African American cops working undercover felt particularly aggrieved: frequently mistaken for fleeing criminals or streetcorner men, they worked in grave danger. One was shot and killed by a uniformed officer in 1968; shortly thereafter, the MPD adopted the practice of rotating a universal cap that all undercover cops would wear on the streets so as to alert other police of their covert identity. But ill-targeted violence was by no means restricted to the MPD; retail proprietors accustomed to using a shotgun to respond to even trifling burglaries could accidentally threaten an off-duty cop arriving at the scene. In 1969, one shop owner shot and killed an off-duty cop who he assumed was the "henchman" of the man who stole a six-pack of beer from him.[62]

As forces throughout the city and from within police command moved to build a more progressive police force, these kinds of incidents raised the stakes of the transformation, underscoring its necessity but, by stoking resentment, impeding it at the very same time. Hostility for the police from especially African American components of the community spilled over into DC city politics. In 1967, when Lyndon Johnson designated Walter Washington mayor-commissioner and appointed a "city council" to advise him, members of the group immediately voiced criticisms of the police.

Yet, as was typical for DC, city officials only watched as the courts and the federal government interceded and preempted their fledgling efforts at self-governance. In 1968, the DC Circuit Court declared much of the vagrancy violations unconstitutionally vague, hence arrests under that charge dropped off precipitously – so much so that by 1972, they were "virtually non-existent," according to the police reports.[63] In the summer of 1968, the MPD also issued a clarification on its "police rules on arrests," under the guidance of the Department of Justice. This particular adumbration modified the criteria for disorder arrests, stating explicitly that the "mere refusal to move on at the order of a police officer is not sufficient to constitute a breach of the peace."[64] So there would be no confusion, the next year the MPD decided that disorder arrests should be

[61] William Rasberry, "Police Rift Widens Here Among White and Negro Officers," *Washington Post*, September 23, 1966, found in MLK Library, Washingtoniana Room, Vertical Files, "Police."

[62] "Off-Duty Policeman Is Shot by Mistake," *Washington Post*, June 6, 1969, MLK Library, Washingtoniana Room, Vertical Files, "Police."

[63] Wilson, "The War Against Crime," p. 75.

[64] "Excerpts from Police Rules on Arrests," *Washington Post*, July 13, 1968, MLK Library, Washingtoniana Room, Vertical Files, "Police."

subject to a pretrial hearing, essentially a bureaucratic review meant to discourage officers from relying on disorder arrests except in very specific instances.[65]

By the early 1970s, the once-standard tools of policing in the District, vagrancy and disorder statutes, were all but extinct. Police officers had traditionally used both to arrest for public drunkenness: Lyndon Johnson's DC Crime Commission observed that in 1965, the MPD arrests totaled more than three times the number of public drunkenness arrests per capita as any other city over 250,000 in population. This rigorous arrest policy was forsaken for several reasons, not least because of the U.S. Court of Appeals ruling in 1966, *Easter v. District of Columbia*, which held that a person could not be arrested for public drunkenness if he was an alcoholic, since inebriation was the result of a disease and not a voluntary act of a person in possession of his faculties. Combined with the controversy over vagrancy and disorder arrests, the MPD, within a span of about five years, went from an enforcement agency that made thousands upon thousands of arrests for drunkenness to one that made hardly any at all.

During the same time, arrests for illicit possession of narcotics surged. Before 1960, the Department of Corrections sentenced an average of fifty heroin addicts to jail per year. This number grew at a gradual pace, such that in 1966, the figure was roughly 150 annually. However, as drug war historian Clarence Lusane points out with astonishment, by 1969, "only three years later, the average had risen to 1400!" Likewise, by February 1969, heroin addicts comprised 15 percent of the city's jail population. By August, addicts were 45 percent of the same.[66] By the early 1970s, it was clear that the District's drug laws and the federal criminal code provided police much of the discretion and even more of the brute force that had once been afforded to them via the now-discarded disorder and vagrancy statutes.

For the MPD, the transition to a drug enforcement regime was a halting one. Narcotic arrests – that is, charges levied for illicit possession – had long been the exclusive province of the narcotics squad. Throughout most of the 1960s, the MPD's squad totaled twenty-one men, an unimpressive force that was further augmented in 1969 to thirty-one officers.[67]

[65] Wilson, "The War Against Crime," p. 79.
[66] Clarence Lusan with Dennis Desmond, *Pipe Dream Blues: Racism and the War on Drugs* (Boston: South End Press, 1991), p. 158.
[67] "City Fails to Launch New Attacks on Growing Drug Sales, Addiction," *Washington Post and Times Herald*, June 22, 1969, p. 1.

As a rule, patrol officers were expected to refer drug cases to the narcotic squad – something they rarely did, if only to spare themselves the nuisance. As a result, most drug arrests by patrol fell under "narcotic vagrancy" charges, at least until the statute was declared unconstitutionally vague in 1968.

With this ruling and from a variety of other sources, the MPD came under pressure to train more of its patrol officers to identify illicit drugs and make street arrests for violations of the Harrison Narcotic Act, always a felony, or the District's Uniform Narcotic Code, which could be a felony or misdemeanor depending upon the charge. When Maryland Senator Joseph Tydings opened hearings to survey the District's narcotics problems in 1970, he learned from the District's new police chief, Jerry V. Wilson, that both patrol units and the narcotics squad had increased the number of their drug arrests and, in addition, more and more officers had completed training with the Bureau of Narcotics and Dangerous Drugs (BNDD) so that they would be better equipped to enforce illicit drug laws.[68]

Significantly, one important reason why the local police picked up street-level narcotic enforcement was because the BNDD was so eager to give it away. The transfer of the Bureau from Treasury to the Department of Justice in 1968 resulted in, among other things, a change in leadership for the agency. Henry Giordano resigned shortly after the move, and in his place Johnson appointed John Ingersoll, a California police official who had most recently served in the IACP's leadership. Johnson evidently hoped that Ingersoll's background would placate local police chiefs who grew suspicious of the initiative or interference of federal agents. And true to expectations, Ingersoll did not upset the balance of authority between local police and federal narcotics agents, but he did rattle the BNDD itself. Upon taking office, the young administrator was aghast at the corruption that ran rampant in his new agency. To be sure, doubts about the Bureau's capabilities, especially its enforcement methods, were hardly new. In 1964, the *Washington Post* freely criticized the agency's reliance upon informers, noting that this strategy was "more effective in netting hapless small-time peddlers than cracking the big under world drug rings."[69] No one unfamiliar with the underground economy of drugs could know, however, that the arrests executed by the Bureau were at least

[68] Jerry V. Wilson in *Hearings Before the Committee on the District of Columbia, US Senate, 91st Session, on the Narcotics Crime Crisis in the Washington Area* (Washington, DC: Government Printing Office, 1971), p. 2676.

[69] "Narcotics Law Stresses Rehabilitation," *Washington Post*, January 20, 1964.

as much the result of agents' connivance with drug dealers as the agency's network of informers. Traffickers furnished the Bureau with payoffs and with information for trivial arrests so that agents could meet their arrest quota; in return, agents left the bulk of a dealer's business alone.

IRS agents in the Department of Treasury worked to uncover the extent of the Bureau's corruption, perhaps motivated to avenge the Treasury's loss of the agency, but more likely pursuing an agenda that the IRS had been keen on for some time. Edward Epstein, historian of drug policy in the Nixon administration, surely understates the case when he calls the reaction of Ingersoll and Attorney General Ramsey Clark one of "dismay" as they were apprised of the extent of corruption in the Bureau.[70] Shortly after Ingersoll's appointment, investigations by the IRS led him to conclude that especially in the Bureau's New York office, the agency's largest and most important field station, not a single Bureau agent could be trusted and, what was worse, the Bureau had "itself been a major source of supply and protection of heroin in the United States."[71] To a man, almost every field agent in New York was either transferred or fired. Attorney General Clark could only conclude that longtime agency leader Harry Anslinger had, at the very least, been woefully "derelict" in his supervision of the Bureau, and that the former narcotics commissioner had apparently determined that it was simply a matter "of self-preservation not to address" it.[72]

Ingersoll's solution to the crisis within his agency was to get it out of the business of street arrests. Informal arrest quotas – a set number of arrests that narcotics agents were asked to execute every month as a measure of their agency's performance – had, Ingersoll surmised, led the Bureau down a seedy path. According to Epstein, the new director "reluctantly came to the conclusion that the quota system would almost ineluctably tend to corrupt agents in the field."[73] Ingersoll detached his Bureau from street-level business and from arrests, steering the BNDD to focus instead on seizures of illicit drugs, both abroad and at home. DC Police Chief Jerry Wilson joined other big city police chiefs in signing a pact with the BNDD in 1970 that formalized the division of labor: the Bureau would concentrate on international trafficking and interstate violators and the MPD, or any other designated local police force, would address

[70] Edward Jay Epstein, *Agency of Fear: Opiates and Political Power in America* (New York: Putnam & Sons, 1977), p. 105.

[71] Ibid.

[72] Ramsey Clark quoted in Jill Jonnes, *Hep-Cats, Narcs, and Pipe Dreams: A History of America's Romance with Illegal Drugs* (Baltimore: Johns Hopkins University Press, 1999), p. 197.

[73] Epstein, *Agency of Fear*, p. 107.

local drug dealers. Police chiefs who eagerly signed the memorandum of understanding in order to minimize federal intrusion into their work could not know that what John Ingersoll was really doing was washing his hands of the dirty business of street enforcement.[74]

Another source of the pressure on the MPD to adopt a more robust drug enforcement approach was the simple but important fact that illicit drugs were more widely available on the streets of the District. The reopening of the East and Southeast Asian heroin supply chain, hastened by the U.S. war in Vietnam, supplemented the production coming from the Middle East and traveling through Marseilles, returning the United States to the vibrant opiate market that existed before World War II.[75] Significantly, heroin that arrived from Asian networks was consistently more pure than its Atlantic counterpart, so much so that its success in the American market exacerbated addiction and all of its attendant problems. As a result, at the same time as the MPD decided to make more arrests for illicit possession, addicts themselves were committing more crime, especially property crime, in order to maintain their habit. Thus, it was not surprising that Washington's Chief Wilson noted a proportionate rise in both drug and robbery arrests in the late 1960s: robberies accounted for 3 percent of all offenders in 1956, 13 percent in 1969, and 25 percent in 1973; likewise, narcotics violations constituted 3 percent of offenders in 1956, 6 percent in 1969, and 10 percent in 1973.[76] This latter trend was all the more interesting given Wilson's own estimate that heroin use "dropped off sharply" after 1969.[77] As he himself suggested, the arrest and subsequent conviction rates for drug violations reflected upon police enforcement tactics at least as much as it did upon incidence of illicit drug use.

The decision to police drugs at the street level carried many consequences for a local police department, some manifest in changes, and others apparent in what did not change. To be sure, policing drugs hastened certain recognizable departures. The routine of a narcotics squad officer, for instance, deviated from that of the normal patrol officer, as Bruce Jackson, a sociologist conducting an observational study on police and drug enforcement, chronicled in his article for the *Atlantic Monthly* in January 1967. A change in routine could bring a change in views.

---

[74] Wilson describes the compact in *Hearings Before the Committee on the District of Columbia, U.S. Senate, 91st Congress, on the Narcotics Crime Crisis in the Washington Area* (Washington, DC: U.S. Government Printing Office, 1971), p. 2849.

[75] See Chapter 6.

[76] Wilson, "The War on Crime," p. 54.

[77] Ibid.

For many officers, the experience of drug enforcement led them to question conventional wisdom or the doctrinaire statements regarding the danger posed by drug use. One police officer in Houston confessed to Jackson that the "talk and newspaper articles about violent addicts are nonsense"; in fact, most officers seemed to have some kind of empathetic relationship with addicts who were familiar to them, especially those who served as informers, even if occasional contempt was apparent as well.[78] What struck Jackson most was the shared world, and almost mutual dependence, that the local cop and the local junkie inhabited. "Little Pavlovian mechanisms set junkies and cops in the same motions," he observed, though the particular "*elan* varies with the jurisdiction." Cops assigned to narcotics began late in the morning because that is what their informers did, and they finished late at night for the same reason. Both were fixated on drug deals. Police officers even adopted the addicts' slang. For all these reasons, Jackson wrote, "the junkie and the cop find themselves bound to one another in one agonizing coil."[79]

That same year Kenneth Rexroth, Beatnik poet and essayist, provided an extended and very astute reflection on the state of policing in the pages of *Playboy* magazine. In it, he speculated that many policing decisions were actually made to further cultural objectives – that is, to impose an Irish Catholic, middle-class morality onto an increasingly permissive society. To support his point, he cited a police raid on a nude party in Berkeley, performed under a false pretext and for the purpose of simply harassing attendees. "In a sense," Rexroth argued, "the police are caught in the middle of a class war, a war between antagonistic moral, rather than economic classes" – a view that was no doubt informed by his life in San Francisco, a city that displayed cultural cleavages more dramatically than most.[80] Narcotics enforcement fit into this picture only awkwardly – a weakness echoed in academic attempts to explain the drug war in exclusively cultural terms – since drug enforcement did not put thousands of rich but "deviant" people in prison; rather, it put underprivileged drug violators in jail.

The exceptions to this rule, the arrest of relatively privileged drug offenders, inadvertently shed light on the way in which drug enforcement

---

[78] Bruce Jackson, "Exiles from the American Dream: The Junkie and the Cop," *Atlantic Monthly* 219 (January 1967) found in *Police in America*, Skolnick and Gray, eds. (New York: Little, Brown, 1975), p. 196.

[79] Bruce Jackson, "Exiles from the American Dream," p. 203.

[80] Kenneth Rexroth, "The Fuzz," tearsheets from *Playboy*, July 1967, found in NAACP, Part IV: Box A59.

sustained one element of older policing culture: police brutality. Called
before the Senate in 1969, one "Mr. X," the son of foreign service parents who was caught dealing marijuana, informed the Senate Committee
on the District of Columbia that there were "a couple of ... aspects of
my case that the committee should hear about. One is the nature of my
arrest," he told the assembled legislators. Mr. X let the committee know
that, more than anything, he felt "hustled" into selling the undercover
police officer marijuana, and, when he "finally did sell him some," a
detective sergeant came and "broke down [his] door. He did not have
a warrant for my arrest," and, "[d]uring the process of arresting me he
also beat me up."[81] Lucy Carmichael, a resident of Georgetown and self-
proclaimed socialite from Washington's "high society," came before the
same committee to tell her story of addiction and to let the committee
know that "drug use is as heavy among middle and upper middle class
students as among students in lower economic areas."[82] Arrested on a
narcotics vagrancy charge when her group house was raided, Carmichael
suffered through an agonizing withdrawal process as she waited in jail.
The committee and a local DC television audience listened as Carmichael
described the police indifference to her wretched pain, and how occasionally police attendants scorned her pleas for help because they held addicts
in such contempt.

If these offenders, who did not lack for resources, suffered through
cruel treatment at the hands of police, then one can only infer that brutality accompanied much of the drug enforcement that took place in neighborhoods and with people who had little to none, even if their stories
went unrecorded. One white illicit drug user recalled a "bust" of a heroin shooting gallery in Harlem, where a police officer let him off with a
warning: "Get out of here you son a bitch," the cop told him, and "don't
ever let me see you here again or I'll break your chops." "See," he told
his interviewer, "I got out because I was white," while the "black and
the Puerto-Rican addicts, [the police] knocked the piss out of them."[83]
Anecdotes such as these occasionally received more evidentiary support. An eight-week investigation by the *New York Times* conducted in
the early seventies, for example, concluded that drug raids were often

[81] "Crime in the National Capital," *Hearings before the Committee on the District of
Columbia, US Senate, 91st Congress* (Washington, DC: U.S. Government Printing Office,
1969), p. 208.

[82] Ibid., p. 135.

[83] "Mick," in Courtwright et al., *Addicts Who Survived: An Oral History of Narcotic Use
in America, 1923–1965* (Knoxville: University of Tennessee Press, 1989) [hereafter:
Addict Oral Histories], p. 258.

conducted "against innocent people," and, moreover, frequently involved "threats and abusive language."[84]

In fact, police brutality and excessive use of force in general became an explosive issue in cities across the country in the mid- to late 1960s. On the defensive, police command portrayed actual brutality as rare and the work of a few rogue officers, consistently responding with hostility to suggestions of civilian review boards. More than any other single component of police-community relations, stories and incidents of police brutality, and law enforcement's perceived or actual indifference to it, fanned the hostility many African Americans felt for police. Denounced as "pigs," police were written off wholesale and with contempt – so much so that elements of the civil rights community grew alarmed. In Oakland, California, the local NAACP initiated a call to "Adopt a Cop" in 1968, urging residents to "[b]egin to see [the policeman] as a human being charged with a social function in an organized society."[85]

Community pleas designed to humanize police in the eyes of inner city residents faced another obstacle, a second feature of traditional policing culture maintained in the era of drug enforcement: police corruption. Addiction researcher and longtime Bureau nemesis Alfred Lindesmith was among the first to suggest that corruption was endemic to drug enforcement: "When the door of the drug seller's room or apartment has been battered down and he has been taken away, the police state that the premises are frequently looted by unknown persons," he informed readers in 1965. "Actually," he disclosed in a confidential tone, "these 'unknown persons' are sometimes the police themselves."[86] Narcotics enforcement attracted "policemen who are not above the temptation of easy money," Lindesmith observed, and several within police professional circles agreed.[87] Yet, as one police chief lamented in the pages of the IACP magazine, while "[t]here have been several national reports concerning crime, civil disorders, and police-community relations ... the issue of police corruption has been summarily treated, if at all."[88]

All that changed when a gifted young social scientist named Al Reiss performed an observational study for the President's Commission on

[84] "US Cutting Narcotics Treatment Programs," *New York Times*, July 5, 1973, p. 25.

[85] NAACP, Part IV: Box A59.

[86] Alfred R. Lindesmith, *The Addict and the Law* (Bloomington: Indiana University Press, 1965), p. 58.

[87] Ibid., p. 59.

[88] Chief James C. Parsons, "A Candid Analysis of Police Corruption," *Police Chief* (March 1973), reprinted in *Police in America*, Skolnick and Gray, eds., p. 255.

Crime. Reiss sent his team of young researchers into the field to accompany law enforcement in order to observe and to record how police spent their time in various big cities (including DC). The social scientists were taken aback by the nonchalant corruption they observed first hand, especially in the city's poorest neighborhoods. In a report initially suppressed by the government, Reiss calculated that more than 20 percent of police stationed in the inner city were on the take – and his team felt that this finding understated the amount of corruption since, after all, the figure represented only the corruption that police were willing to let outsiders observe.[89] As one police official remarked in the pages of the IACP journal, the Reiss study "exploded the myth that there are occasional 'rotten apples.'"[90] He further noted that, according to the study, the ghetto hosted a disproportionate share of corruption because "[t]he black minority poses no security risk to the corrupted officer." After all, he asked his fellow police readers, "Who will listen to him?"[91] Moreover, this corruption fed a vicious cycle of violence because, "[o]nce compromised, the officer has problems with his conscience and projects his guilt feelings to the scapegoat, the minority member." The author concluded on a reflective note: "Frustration is a concomitant manifestation of a lack of self confidence which results from facing complex problems one does not understand."[92]

The Knapp Commission formed in the wake of NYPD Detective Frank Serpico's startling revelations of narcotics enforcement corruption struck a plainer but equally grim chord: "We found police corruption to be widespread," the Commission, named after chair Whitman Knapp, concluded.[93] While gambling featured the most "standardized" form of corruption, narcotics enforcement, while lacking "the organization of the gambling pads," commonly featured "individual payments – known as 'scores' [that] ... could be staggering in amount."[94] One narcotics payment totaled $80,000, and, the Commission added, "the size of this score was by no means unique."[95] It is not generally known that, upon

[89] "Misconduct Laid to 27% of Police in 3 Cities' Slums," *New York Times*, July 5, 1968, p. 1.

[90] Parsons, "A Candid Analysis," p. 255.

[91] Ibid. See also Lawrence Sherman, "Becoming Bent," in *Moral Issues in Police Work*, Elliston and Feldberg, eds. (New Jersey: Rowman and Allanheld, 1985), pp. 253–65.

[92] Parsons, "A Candid Analysis," p. 258.

[93] Knapp Commission, "Police Corruption in New York" (August 1972), reprinted in *Police in America*, Skolnick and Gray, eds., p. 235.

[94] Ibid.

[95] Ibid., p. 236.

the conclusion of the Knapp Commission's revealing work, Senator Claude Pepper, Democrat of Florida, had the idea of conducting a similar investigation of DC police. Certainly his concern was justified: by the summer of 1970, four police had been arrested on narcotic charges in eight months.

When Pepper made public his intention to investigate, Chief Wilson assigned eight new sergeants to the MPD's internal affairs division to assist in a "crackdown on illegal drug activity by policemen."[96] President Richard Nixon backed the chief, one of his favorites, by suggesting that an investigation was unnecessary and could only detract from police autonomy by undermining the prerogative of the police to put their own house in order.[97] After meeting with Chief Wilson and Mayor Washington, Senator Pepper backed down. Thereafter, as before, when DC police were caught using illicit narcotics or dealing in them, the sensational headlines that followed depicted these as lapses in police conduct rather than a problem endemic to narcotics enforcement.

The public's willingness to overlook or remain uninterested in police narcotic corruption bore an inverse relation to its concern about rising crime and the desire to see police undistracted from their pursuit of criminals. As violent crime in cities across America increased, politicians who had been disposed earlier to dwell on crime in public remarks now harped on it, none more successfully than Republican candidate and then President Richard Nixon. Periodic riots in various cities, beginning in 1965 in Watts and erupting in 1968 after the assassination of Martin Luther King on April 4, seemed to confirm to outsiders that the inner city had descended into lawlessness. Street crime and riots, both as a perception and in reality, dominated any assessment of quality of life in urban America. Yet residents of the city's poorest neighborhoods felt that riots in particular reflected upon a decade of culpable neglect. By 1968, for example, standards in the District had deteriorated dramatically. Only one out of three students graduated from public high school. What was more, riots elicited from police (and the military) just the sort of aggressive response that reaffirmed the bleak view residents held of these institutions in the first place. When one policeman from New York called in to suppress a riot watched as a colleague shot an unarmed woman who was looting a pair of shoes

---

[96] "Unit to Stem Police Drug Use Enlarged," WP, October 28, 1970, 1969, MLK Library, Washingtoniana Room, Vertical Files, "Police."

[97] Stephen Green, "Nixon Prefers Police Handle Own Inquiry," *Washington Post*, January 18, 1972, MLK Library, Washingtoniana Room, Vertical Files, "Police."

right in front of them, he recalled that "she probably didn't believe that a cop would shoot her over a lousy bunch of shoes," but in fact "a shot was fired and she was left bleeding in the street."[98]

Nevertheless, even those victimized by or aware of police violence could not fail to notice the surge in street crime and violent crime in the city. Some observers familiar with the criminal justice system considered court congestion to be one of the principal drivers in the escalation of crime. Significantly, in the District, the April 1968 riots greatly exacerbated this problem, since roughly 400 looters were charged with felonious robbery in an apparent effort by police to demonstrate to congressional overloads, particularly southerners, that police were not being "soft" on looters. But if riots and the subsequent police crackdown overwhelmed the system, it was only in the sense of a final straw; court congestion had plagued the District for several years prior. Reflecting upon his years as police chief, Jerry Wilson traced court congestion back to the particular court structure in the District and the Bail Reform Act of 1966. Two kinds of courts existed in DC: the municipal court, called the Court of General Sessions up until 1970, and the U.S. District Court, the federal court that heard felony cases argued by U.S. attorneys. What would elsewhere be a state court was, in the District, dependent upon federal labor for its operation. Hence it was not surprising that overburdened U.S. attorneys routinely reduced felony charges to misdemeanors just to get a case out of their dockets and into someone else's hands. Because of this, General Sessions was chronically behind in its docket, so much so that Senator Robert Byrd developed a plan for "visiting judges" to come to the District and help to clear the backlog. Just as his plan was gaining support, riots and the resulting arrests plunged the District further behind.

Court overload meant that, in the considerable interval between arrest and trial, a suspect would be at large if he could post bail. Doing so was made easier by congressional passage of the Bail Reform Act, a law designed to apply to federal courts, and thus one that had an unusually large influence in the District. The legislation sought to diminish the court's practice of setting high bail for suspects, something that was viewed at the time as imposing a financial bias in determining who could and could not obtain pretrial release. The Reform Act instructed federal judges to detain a suspect in jail only if they could be uncertain about her future appearance for trial. According to Chief Wilson and others, releasing suspects on their own recognizance brought down the number

[98] O'Neil, *A Cop's Take*, p. 47.

of guilty pleas: if a suspect knew that she could be released for as long as a year before trial, there was no incentive to plead guilty and start serving out the time of a sentence right away. This tendency was only abetted by the District of Columbia Criminal Justice Act, which provided counsel to suspects who could not afford one. With these new rights and privileges extended to criminal defendants, the deterrent effect of arrests was weakened considerably.

In failing to instruct judges to use public safety as one component of their calculation to release a suspect or to set a steep bail, suspected criminals were returned to the streets of Washington, often with even less of an incentive to live within the law. As city officials struggled to impose order on its criminal justice system, they were forced to reckon with a disturbing new pattern, that of probationers who committed another crime while on conditional release. Recidivism added significantly to the District's crime problem: out of roughly 4,000 people on probation in 1975, almost 1,000 were rearrested on new criminal charges.[99] The system was so overwhelmed, in fact, that it was even difficult to execute bench warrants for arrest when a suspect failed to appear for criminal trial. One DC Superior Court judge complained that more than half of the cases before him could not be tried because of the "apparent inability" of police to find and arrest the suspect charged with the crime.[100]

In spite of the forces that sapped the criminal justice system of its efficiency, few outside city government or law enforcement acknowledged the problem of repeat offenses committed by "major violators."[101] Instead, many equated illicit drugs with crime, and Washington with both of these. Not surprisingly, then, the District served as a template for national drug policy in a multitude of ways. One of the most subtle was the way in which Washington's lack of political power shaped the discourse on the harmfulness of drugs. When Maryland Senator Joseph Tydings convened his series of hearings to examine illicit drug use in the District, he began each with a preamble that described the cost of addiction to public safety, underscoring the reach of both illicit drugs and addict-fueled crime into the surrounding suburbs, including those located in Tydings's home state. While the senator understandably set the terms of his inquiry to justify

---

[99] Wilson, "The War on Crime," p. 45.
[100] Mary Ann Kuhn, "Halleck Hits Police Ability in Rearrests," *Washington Post*, December 1972, MLK Library, Washingtoniana Room, Vertical Files, "Police."
[101] For an examination of the police response to handling major offenders, see Mark H. Moore et al., *Dangerous Offenders: The Elusive Targets of Justice* (Cambridge: Harvard University Press, 1984).

his interest in the District, no politician from the city itself could effectively counter Tydings's ranking or prioritization of the dangers posed by illicit drug use. The only person who challenged it in any way was New York Senator Charles Goodell, who rebuked the governing conceit of the hearings by noting that addiction had "ramifications far beyond it spreading to the suburbs. This is sort of the selfish white people's view," and, even more pointedly, Goodell went on to remark that "the other selfish white view is that we want to make the streets safer in the metropolitan area from criminals who are trying to feed a habit. We had better start thinking about this in terms of the exploitation of the black people from ghetto areas."[102] Yet Goodell's intervention was a lone one. Instead, the sense of problem or crisis in illicit drug use was inflected through a city that was politically impotent, unable to exercise an authoritative voice and beholden to the attentiveness of neighboring states. In this way, the District's anomalous political status greatly advanced the tendency to construe addiction as a problem of urban black residents that exacted a cost from white suburban society.[103]

Other legacies of congressional experimentation with the District were more obvious and direct. Despite assurances from both Police Chief Jerry Wilson and Mayor-Commissioner Walter Washington that "no knock" authority – the ability of police to enter a premises without warning if they believed issuing one would result in the destruction of evidence – was unnecessary for the District, officials in the Nixon administration insisted on putting it in the District's anti-crime legislation of 1970; months later, the same authority appeared in Nixon's overhaul of the country's drug regime, the Controlled Substances Act of 1970. Opposition to no-knock authority, led by Democratic Senator Sam Ervin of North Carolina, was a distinct minority when it came to the District bill. As Senator Gaylord Nelson of Wisconsin explained, when no-knock authority came before the Senate in the District bill, "grave doubts were expressed by many over the wisdom and the justice of including" it in the legislation. Yet there was no need to act on such reservations, because no constituent would demand an explanation; as Nelson put it, "the District of Columbia crime

---

[102] "Crime in the National Capital," *Hearings before the Committee on the District of Columbia, US Senate, 91st Congress* (Washington, DC: U.S. Government Printing Office, 1969), p. 93.

[103] Arrest rates for narcotic violations in neighboring Maryland counties skyrocketed in 1970, suggesting both increased law enforcement attention to the problem and increased illicit drug use.

bill would not touch home."[104] When the same provision came before the Senate in the Controlled Substances Act, proponents were quick to cite the precedent set by the District bill. Congressman Springer dismissed opposition to no-knock by reminding his colleagues that they had already consented to it. "We had it in the District of Columbia crime bill," he reminded his colleagues; "We voted for it then."[105]

Finally, the evolution of law enforcement in the District – much of it hastened by federal courts, and much of it guided by police command and revised by various kinds of community activism – provided a model for policing elsewhere. Southerners had delayed the acceptance of a professional policing culture just long enough; when it was finally adopted in Washington, DC, it coexisted with a drug enforcement agenda that retained some of the practices and much of the discretion of traditional policing. Significantly, widespread adoption of narcotics enforcement also provided law enforcement with a ready explanation for inner city crime – both when the numbers of narcotics addiction and nature of the crimes correlated, and when they did not. As drug enforcement took on greater prominence, expectations for successful police resolution of violent crime in neighborhoods afflicted with the drug epidemic were lowered. This indifference was particularly costly to black neighborhoods: as Will Cooley argues, the emergence of a new, more insular African American gang culture that was successful in driving out white organized crime figures turned to extreme violence among and between their own factions in order to settle disputes and gain control of the drug trade.[106] And, as Eric Schneider argues, patterns of heroin dealing in these same neighborhoods led to widespread vacancies and the degradation of the fabric of residential life. Not surprising, then, that in such areas cause and effect intertwined in a mutually reinforced descent into urban blight.

To be sure, the transition to narcotics enforcement and its ultimate effects was a complex story that unfolded during a turbulent time. Nevertheless, it was clear that whereas Congress had established the principle of severe criminal penalties for illicit narcotics in the 1950s, it was only by the end of the 1960s that local law enforcement stood ready to arrest and enforce those statutes to an appreciable degree, and that, despite a surge in drug use across a spectrum of users, mainly African

---

[104] *Congressional Record – Senate*, October 7, 1970, p. 35538.
[105] *Congressional Record – House*, September 24, 1970, p. 33642.
[106] Will Cooley, "'Stones Run It': Taking Back Control of Organized Crime in Chicago, 1940–1975," *Journal of Urban History* 37, no. 6 (November 2011): 911–32.

Americans who lived in the inner city would be the target of that enforcement. Once established as an acceptable police tactic, drug enforcement did not alter the operations of criminal justice, it overwhelmed them.

TREATMENT IN THE CITY

Arrest and incarceration of drug users became such a pronounced feature of criminal justice in Washington, DC, that it actually served as the impetus to develop a comprehensive system of clinics to treat narcotic addiction. In 1968, a much-discussed study of DC jail admissions found that 46 percent of arrestees tested positive for drugs.[107] Most viewed this result as evidence of a concrete and causal link between drugs and crime, even though Police Chief Jerry Wilson was careful to note that this finding reflected upon, among other things, the MPD's decision to commit more resources to drug enforcement and execute arrests for drug violations. Nonetheless it became apparent to District corrections that, whatever the reason, more and more addicts entered their facilities. While there, they would need treatment and, once released, they would need to be monitored and, if possible, spared a relapse. Hence, paradoxically, the District's initial investment in community-based clinical care could be traced back to the decision to arrest drug users on a more concerted and consistent basis.

Certainly the city's move to invest in clinics did not come as the result of specific judicial rulings, despite the fact that the logic of some closely related decisions held obvious relevance for the rationale for criminalizing drug possession. At the start of the 1960s, reformers who sought a ruling that drug addiction was a disease that should be subject to treatment instead of punishment received encouragement when, in 1962, the Supreme Court struck down a California state law criminalizing addiction in its *Robinson v. California* decision.[108] This rare venture for the Supreme Court into the actual substance of state criminal law was also a decisive one. California could not put a person in prison for addiction any more than it could incarcerate for the "common cold"; to do so, the majority held, would constitute "cruel and unusual punishment" and was thus prohibited by the Eighth Amendment. Using either this constitutional

---

See Kozel and DuPont, *Criminal Charges and Drug Use Patterns of Arrestees in the District of Columbia* (Washington, DC: Department of Health, Education, and Welfare, NIDA, 1977).

Robinson v. California, 370 US 660 (1962).

tack – that incarcerating for addiction or any of the activities that addiction compelled constituted cruel and unusual punishment – or by asserting a common law argument, that drug addicts lacked *mens rea* ("guilty mind" or a culpable volition), legal reformers hoping to capitalize on the *Robinson* decision began to mount challenges to the criminal penalties for possession of illicit drugs.

Much of this legal project was argued through the DC Court of Appeals. Indeed, its first and most enduring success came from that circuit: the 1966 *Easter v. District of Columbia* decision, which held that an alcoholic could not be arrested for public drunkenness.[109] To do so, the court found, would be tantamount to identifying a symptom and proceeding to punish the disease. Significantly, the court relied on the *mens rea* plea of the defendant in its holding, a sign, perhaps, of judicial willingness to expand on the *Robinson* ruling still further. Yet, though the question was put before the courts in the DC circuit and elsewhere, the judiciary continued to reject both *mens rea* and cruel and unusual punishment defenses for narcotic addicts arrested for possession, though sometimes by only a slim margin. Still, the DC Court of Appeals decisions were particularly devastating to reformers since they were issued *en banc*, meaning the full panel of judges participated in the ruling, so the possibilities for orchestrating a different outcome by arguing a similar case were remote.

By the mid-1970s, federal and state courts had turned back an array of cases designed to decriminalize illicit drug possession for what reformers termed the "addict-possessor" or the "non-trafficking offender."[110] Judicial rationale proved revealing. Distinguishing the alcoholic from the addict did not rest upon differences of disease or behavior – for, as it turns out, bodily harm generated by alcohol dependence could be severe, and more crime was committed by those who wished to obtain alcohol than any other type of drug (something that is still true today). Instead, judges writing for the majority rejected reformers' efforts by pointing out that illicit drugs were prohibited – whereas alcohol, at that time,

---

[109] Ironically, as Irene Sullivan points out, it was "in fact in the area of alcoholism that *Robinson* was first given its broadest reading." See Sullivan, "Comments," *Fordham Law Review* 396 (1973–74): 371. For more on *Easter* and its aftermath, see Arronson, Dienes, and Mucheno, "Changing Public Drunkeness Laws: The Impact of Decriminalization," *Law and Society Review* 12, no. 3 (Spring 1978): 405–36.

[110] *Lloyd v. United States*, 343 F.2d 492 (1964); *Castle v. United States*, 347 F.2d 492 (1965); *Watson v. United States*, 439 F.2d 442 (1970); *United States v. Moore*, 486 F.2d 1139 (1973); *Gorham v. United States*, 339 A.2d 401 (1975).

was not – and that the entire prohibition regime rested upon the ability to punish the contraband right up until it reached its "final repository," as one Superior Court justice put it in a 1971 case that went all the way to the Supreme Court.[111] Without criminal sanctions for possession, the justice argued, the judiciary would undermine the legislature's efforts to assert "the pressure of criminal law ... against the entire heroin trade."[112] Here and elsewhere, judges found possession to be criminal for no other reason than to sustain illicit drug prohibition – or, put in more tautological form, illicit drug possession remained illegal because it was illegal.

With little help from the courts, reformers' hopes of advancing treatment options rather than prison rested entirely with the country's lawmakers. Happily for them, the prospects for changing the discourse of addiction from a degenerate failing to a crippling disease had been greatly strengthened by different sorts of activism in the late 1950s and early '60s, and these in turn bore fruit in Robert Kennedy's Narcotic Addiction Rehabilitation Act (NARA) of 1966. Though underfunded and, by most assessments, uncharitable in its determination of who was eligible for treatment, the Act set an important precedent insofar as it created a role for the federal government in civil commitment of at least some of those arrested for illicit possession, allowed voluntary commitment in other cases, and invested federal dollars in researching the science of addiction; NARA also transformed the Public Health Service's institution at Lexington, eliminating all elements of prison life within its walls, and placing a greater sense of priority and prestige on the drug research that had been well under way at Lexington for more than a decade.[113] So, at the same time as lawyers crafted their legal challenges to criminal possession, medical professionals reentered the world of narcotic addiction treatment for the first time since Harry Anslinger had policed them out of it more than thirty years before.

They did so haltingly, unsure of their legal status if their treatment plan included the prescribing of narcotics. As late as the mid-1960s, with a medical community still haunted by Bureau of Narcotics investigations, the overwhelming majority of treatment plans did not prescribe for addiction. Instead, most offered addict-to-addict counseling, usually in some form of group therapy and individual mentoring patterned after Alcoholics Anonymous. Only the federal hospital at Lexington had an

[111] *United States v. Williams*, 401 US 646 (1971).
[112] Ibid.
[113] See Campbell, *Discovering Addiction*, chap. 5.

explicit policy of managed withdrawal of narcotic (and other) addicts, gradually decreasing narcotic doses while administering sedatives or other medicine. Doctors who happened to learn the science of managed withdrawal during an internship at Lexington returned home to serve as informal and covert advisors to other physicians who could not bring themselves to turn a narcotic-addicted patient away, despite the threat to their medical license. Coached in nightly telephone conversations with Lexington alumni, doctors manipulated doses until a patient no longer suffered withdrawal from the drug – only to watch, almost invariably if not inevitably, as the psychological and emotional compulsions that drove drug use returned the patient as an addict to the doctor's care once more.

This frustrating cycle of purely physical withdrawal and relapse led some medical groups to question the government's punitive approach and their own profession's abdication of treatment and research. Determined to forge a new path, the Medical Society of the County of New York decided in 1962 that doctors who engaged in supervised clinical research could treat patients for addiction. Shortly thereafter, the Rockefeller Institute funded drug researcher Vincent Dole for a sabbatical year researching the science of addiction in preparation for crafting a new, more scientifically based treatment regime. While reading up on the scant published offerings in the field, Dole encountered a book by Dr. Marie Nyswander, published in 1956, entitled *The Drug Addict as Patient*. One of his first moves when he returned from his leave was to call Dr. Nyswander to suggest collaboration. In their partnership, a new approach to treatment was born.

Like most doctors familiar with addiction, Marie Nyswander was most concerned with heroin, though, as an intern at Lexington, she certainly encountered a fair share of barbiturate addicts as well.[114] While at the federal hospital, her iconoclastic personality bristled against its rigid practices, including its obvious racism as well as the staff's customary brusqueness in handling addicts. Determined not just to humanize her patients but to connect with them, Nyswander charted a lonely path for herself at Lexington, as colleagues derided her association with addicts and even some patients chastised her for her willingness to strike a rapport with black patients and staff. Nevertheless, difficult though it was, her service at Lexington made her a resource for other doctors once she returned to

---

[114] For more on Nyswander, see Nat Hentoff, *Doctor Among the Addicts* (New York: Rand McNally, 1968).

New York City. To preempt or curtail the stream of phone calls soliciting advice, Nyswander wrote her first book, a brave intervention in 1956, a time when few accepted narcotics addiction as a disease. As years went by and the view gained more currency, doctors like Nyswander continued to hear of the heartbreaking stories of addicts desperately seeking treatment, including the sad and recurring story of those who broke into a mailbox and then called a postal inspector, a routine designed to convict them of a federal felony just so they could be sent to federal prison, in the hope that they might be assigned to Lexington for treatment in lieu of prison.

When Vincent Dole called her in 1963, then, Nyswander was quite ready to embark on formulating a treatment program. To fend off any Bureau of Narcotic intrusion, the two doctors conducted their first clinical experiment in the corridor of a hospital in studious compliance of New York County medical practice guidelines. For their first trial, they selected two difficult subjects for narcotic treatment: an Italian American male, aged thirty-four, and a twenty-one-year-old Irish American male. Both had been using heroin for eight years, and both had committed property crimes in order to fund their habit. Because of their reluctance and their criminal past, the two posed challenges for any other contemporaneous treatment plan, all of which relied on voluntary subjects who had "burned out" and come to therapy on their own. If their program met with success with such tricky subjects, the doctors reasoned, it would bode well for its prospects.

At first Nyswander did what any doctor who had trained at Lexington would be likely to do: instead of weaning her patients off of heroin, she attempted to replace the craving for it entirely by substituting another drug. She chose morphine, also a logical choice in that it is a close cognate of heroin. Dole and Nyswander soon grew discouraged as their patients grew listless and despondent, completely addicted to a narcotic only slightly less harmful than heroin and, what was worse, in need of gradually increasing amounts to overcome their fast-developing tolerance for the drug. To manage morphine withdrawal, Dole began to administer a synthetic narcotic formulated by the Germans in World War II called methadone. While this had been common practice at Lexington, what was unusual in this case was the dose.[115] Because the two patients were on so much morphine, Dole prescribed double and triple the amounts of methadone than normal. Right before the doctors' eyes, the pair returned

---

[115] See Herbert Kleber, "Methadone: The Drug, the Treatment, the Controversy," in *One Hundred Years of Heroin* (Westport, CT: Auburn House, 2002), p. 150.

to functional life. One began to paint again, the other expressed a desire to go back to work (and eventually did). More surprising, doses of morphine seemed to no longer have any effect on the men. Not only did methadone satisfy the physical craving for a narcotic, it blocked out its effect or "high." Nyswander watched in disbelief as her two patients turned into "dynamos of activity." When she ran them through a battery of tests, she was still more astonished to discover that methadone seemed to have "no deleterious effects anywhere."[116] To doctors long accustomed to the discouraging cycle of heroin dependence, methadone seemed nothing short of a miracle drug.

If so, then Nyswander was careful to point out that the miracle was only in the sense of restoring an addict to functional life, not ridding her of addiction. Regular methadone doses, Nyswander and Dole argued, gave a patient a normal existence, one that could be used to explore and possibly address other components of her life driving addiction – or not, something Nyswander in particular was not very judgmental about. To her and to many of her colleagues, the proper criterion for evaluating methadone was that of reinstating a patient back to functional life, a goal that promised many ancillary benefits, such as subtracting the patient from the illicit heroin market and thus obviating the need for crime committed in order to purchase heroin. As one methadone user previously addicted to heroin remembered, her first trip to a methadone clinic in 1968 was a "godsend"; "nobody really wants to be an addict," she confessed, and the doctor who first told her about methadone gave her "new life."[117] Another methadone user recalled that once admitted to a program, he "stopped everything." "I was living again," he told his interviewer in what was a familiar refrain among methadone patients; "I got back to my old self."[118] In light of these experiences, doctors administering methadone chafed at others' insistence on ridding a patient of addiction or producing a completely self-reliant human being as a result of treatment. Nyswander brooked no criticism from those who espoused such admirable goals. In a world saturated with dangerous prescription drugs and alcohol, just who could be judged as completely self-reliant, she wondered, and why should a heroin addict be penalized for a dependence on methadone that was less pernicious than many licit substances? Nyswander was adamant: the perfect should not be the enemy of the

---

[116] Ibid., pp. 114–15.
[117] "May," *Addict Oral Histories*, p. 164.
[118] "Al," *Addict Oral Histories*, p. 148.

good, especially when many who embraced the standard of perfection could not be held to it themselves.

The discovery that methadone acted as a narcotic-blocker stimulated researchers to search for a different narcotic "antagonist," something that blocked the effect of narcotics, as methadone did, but was not addictive in and of itself.[119] While this quest, ultimately fruitless, was under way, Nyswander and Dole devised a treatment protocol using methadone that they soon expanded to other facilities. Within months, they treated more than a thousand patients, varying their neighborhood, ethnicity, and race to assess the scope of methadone's effectiveness. In explaining their novel approach to others, Dole nominated an insulin model, referring to the regular doses of insulin that a diabetic needs in order to remain functional.[120] Insulin did not cure diabetes, he noted, but it did make it possible for a diabetic to live a normal life.

This metaphor and the logic supporting it met with some immediate hostility from within the treatment community, especially from support-ers of programs that strove for a "drug-free" existence achieved through addict-to-addict counseling and group therapy. One speaker from a well-known example of just such a group gave a talk at Lexington in 1966 and, when responding to a question about the promise of methadone, he churlishly offered that "methadone maintenance is a great idea: we should give money to bank robbers, women to rapists, methadone to addicts."[121] To those unaffiliated or only loosely committed to the twelve-step approach, especially to doctors and psychiatrists, methadone was unfairly maligned by traditional treatment programs. To those greatly invested in those standard approaches, like Narcotics Anonymous, Synanon, or Daytop Village, methadone was a spurious solution, a false promise of recovery issued under the guise of medical treatment.

Thus, from the outset, methadone treatment was condemned not for its failures, but its success. Critics from within the therapeutic commu-nity were discomfited not by the drug's inconsistency or ineffectiveness, but by its nearly universal applicability and use – a seductive panacea, they suggested, that left the sources of addiction untreated and lulled a patient into a false sense of normalcy. While tensions festered, Dole and Nyswander pushed forward with another, equally radical idea: out-patient clinics. Long anathema to the Bureau of Narcotics, such clinics

---

[119] See Joan Lynn Arehart, "The Search for a Heroin 'Cure,'" *Science* 101 (April 15, 1972): 250–51.

[120] Kleber, "Methadone," p. 150.

[121] Ibid.

were nonetheless gaining new supporters in the mid- and late 1960s. The resurgence of the outpatient clinic idea derived from a number of different sources. One was simple common sense: as longtime addiction researcher Alfred Lindesmith pointed out, police and Bureau payoffs to drug informants who were addicts meant that they were, in effect, operating "what might be called a kind of 'clinic' system of their own," but without any of the public health or criminal justice benefits.[122] The other and more significant influence was the movement under way to "deinstitutionalize" mental illness – that is, to take patients once confined to specialized state hospitals for the mentally ill and assign them to community-based, outpatient care. President Kennedy had argued for this transition years before, making it one component of his "New Frontier" reform proposals; accordingly, in 1963, Congress passed the Community Mental Health Centers Construction Act. An extraordinary wave of deinstitutionalization took place in its wake, and, since much of the medical community considered addiction to be a form of mental illness, it followed that, in their judgment, addicts should be incorporated into the move toward community-based outpatient care. Robert Kennedy's Narcotic Addict Rehabilitation Act certainly advanced this notion, but, as Senator Goodell pointed out, while the act put treatment on a national footing, only a "minimum amount of money [was] made available for it."[123] In 1968, Congress strengthened its commitment to community treatment with a formal amendment to the 1963 Mental Health Centers Act, instructing community providers to devote resources to the prevention of alcoholism and the treatment of narcotic addiction.

Just as Congress issued this new mandate, the District began to execute arrests for drug violations at an unprecedented rate. Jails and prisons were soon filled beyond capacity, as Kenneth Hardy, director of DC's Department of Corrections, informed his congressional overseers in 1969. For that calendar year, he estimated that Washington "will have booked into the District of Columbia Jail more than 1500 narcotic-involved offenders. This is more than double the number we booked in 1968," he informed the new Senate chair of the Committee

---

[122] Alfred R. Lindesmith, *The Addict and the Law* (Bloomington: Indiana University Press, 1965), p. 51. For more on the current use of informants, including the dangers they are exposed to when they work as undercover agents, see Sarah Stillman, "The Throwaways," *New Yorker* (September 3, 2012): 38–47.

[123] "Crime in the National Capital," *Hearings before the Committee on the District of Columbia, US Senate, 91st Congress* (Washington, DC: U.S. Government Printing Office, 1969), p. 80.

on the District of Columbia, Joseph Tydings, "and more than seven times the number we booked in 1965."[124] "Unfortunately," he added for emphasis, "my jails and prison do not have elastic walls."[125] Joining Hardy before the Senate committee was Robert DuPont, a psychiatrist employed by the Department of Corrections. It was DuPont, a Harvard-educated researcher who came to DC initially to work for the National Institutes of Mental Health, who ultimately pioneered a new vision for narcotic treatment in the District. He did this on the heels of his sensational research project that found roughly 45 percent of inmates in DC jails tested positive for some type of illicit drug use – a study that made headlines across the country, and was cited over and over again as evidence of the link between drugs and crime. But, as Hardy told the Senate committee, neither he nor DuPont viewed jails or prisons as the best option for addict-offenders. "We now feel," the director informed the Congress, "that we can handle the narcotic offender in community-based programs."[126] Hardy's Department of Corrections simply could not accommodate any other option.[127] When asked about the possibility of methadone treatment in these community facilities, DuPont admitted that, since other rehabilitation programs depended upon motivation for abstinence, these traditional programs would just not work for the majority of inmates. In order to treat the bulk of addicts, methadone maintenance held the greatest promise.

Guided by this pragmatic endorsement of methadone, DuPont committed himself to creating a network of community-based narcotic treatment programs. In assessing the scope of the problem, DuPont dismissed Bureau of Narcotics addict rolls as totally outdated, insisting that the District faced a heroin epidemic that was "without known precedent in the United States," and that the city was mired in a crisis that extended well beyond prison walls.[128] Overwhelmed public health officials declared

---

[124] Ibid., p. 237.

[125] Ibid., p. 238.

[126] Ibid., p. 239.

[127] This dilemma bore a resemblance to California, where, in 1957, the State Board of Corrections drew attention to the lack of rehabilitation options for ex-convicts. To remedy this, the board created a Narcotic Treatment Control Project that tracked former prisoners known to have a narcotics addiction. See Dean F. Markham File, *John F. Kennedy Library*, Box 22.

[128] *Hearings Before the Committee on the District of Columbia, U.S. Senate, 91st Congress, on the Narcotics Crime Crisis in the Washington Area* (Washington, DC: U.S. Government Printing Office, 1971), p. 2723. Like other public health officials, DuPont followed the "Baden Formula," an estimate of total number of addicts based on Dr. Michael Baden's calculation that roughly 0.5 percent of addicts died of overdoses per

heroin dependence to be the most common serious disease afflicting teen-agers and young adults in DC. Expecting help from other components of city government, DuPont got only double-talk and delays. Finally, Dupont and Hardy approached Mayor-Commissioner Walter Washington directly, extracting from him a promise to create a single agency to deal with DC's heroin problem. From this agreement came DC's Narcotics Treatment Administration (NTA), an agency devoted exclusively to nar-cotic rehabilitation and addiction prevention. Bob DuPont, an obvious choice for its first director, intended to craft an approach that could be imitated elsewhere, a model for successful treatment with unassailable methods and incontrovertible results.[129]

It was an ambition that Senator Joseph Tydings shared, a reformist counterpoint to congressional conservatives' designs on the District as an entryway to their criminal punishment agenda. In hearing after hear-ing, Tydings monitored the fledgling NTA. The methadone component of treatment was operational by April 1970, and the senator was eager to learn of its progress.[130] Mayor Walter Washington appeared before the Senate committee to testify, gingerly acknowledging the many prior missteps by noting that the District was "moving toward treatment in a relatively short period of time."[131] That was all well and good, the sen-ator responded, but his ambition was to make the "drug treatment pro-gram in the District of Columbia ... into a national model," hence he had little patience for excuses. DuPont stepped forward to report on his progress: the NTA already had an estimated 20 percent of the District's 10,400 addicts under its care.[132] The director then confessed that he faced a choice between raising the quality of services provided or increasing the number of addicts enrolled in the program. Tydings was emphatic in his advice: the NTA should do a "100% job with 20% of the addicts."[133]

year. If one knew the total number of heroin overdoses, one could therefore extrapolate the total number of addicts.

[129] In order to gain the support of existing treatment programs, DuPont shrewdly wrote contracts to include them under the ambit of the NTA: see DuPont, "Treating Heroin Addicts in Washington," *Delaware Medical Journal*, February 1972, p. 36.

[130] *Hearings before the Committee on the District of Columbia, U.S. Senate, 91st Congress, on the Narcotics Crime Crisis in the Washington Area* (Washington, DC: U.S. Government Printing Office, 1971), p. 2658.

[131] Ibid., p. 2743.

[132] DuPont, like other medical researchers, arrived at his estimate for addicts by extrapolat-ing from overdoses and tetanus deaths.

[133] *Hearings before the Committee on the District of Columbia, U.S. Senate, 91st Congress, on the Narcotics Crime Crisis in the Washington Area* (Washington, DC: U.S. Government Printing Office, 1971), p. 2818.

The reason, Tydings explained, was simply a matter of public relations. "I think it is fair to say there are a lot of discredited people … who would like nothing better than to see this narcotics program fail," Tydings advised, referring to the therapeutic "drug free" proponents who assailed methadone maintenance. "These people are almost psychotic about abstinence," he remarked, and that was one important reason why he wanted DuPont's program to be "letter perfect" so as to withstand their criticism.[134]

As DuPont began to administer methadone maintenance on a large scale, defenders of traditional abstinence programs were by no means its only critics. In government support for methadone – and, in particular, in its ties to a federal government now led by Republican president Richard Nixon – many community activists were quick to suspect ulterior motives. William Rasberry, an influential *Washington Post* columnist and probably the most recognized African American voice in the city behind the mayor and Marion Barry, editorialized against methadone treatment in February 1969. In a piece entitled, "Methadone: Crutch Not a Cure," Rasberry presented to his readers the views of a veteran drug counselor who was skeptical of methadone, noting that under the new treatment curbing an addict's desire for heroin was now achieved "by the dubious means of addicting him to methadone."[135] Nation of Islam followers also denounced methadone maintenance, instructing their own rehabilitation counselors that "the only way to treat the drug addict is to tell him the truth of self, kind, religion and the devil."[136] Still greater misgivings were voiced by various branches of the local Black Panthers, with some members equating methadone maintenance to race genocide.[137] One doctor who started a methadone program in New Haven, Connecticut, described the views of the Panthers he met with as regarding methadone as "a sort of Band-Aid on the ghetto, an attempt to avoid the total revolution they believed would soon happen."[138] For the Panthers and others, methadone preempted the rage that they hoped to foment in order to precipitate a crisis that in their eyes represented the best hope of transforming the

---

[134] Ibid., p. 2823.
[135] William Rasberry, "Methadone: Crutch, Not a Cure," *Washington Post*, February 26, 1969, p. B1.
[136] Dr. Lonni Shabazz of Muhammad's Mosque No. 4, as quoted in Jack Smith, "A Comparison of the Black Muslim's Drug Rehabilitation Program with the Methadone Maintenance Program," MA thesis, Howard University, 1973, available at Moreland Spingarn Research Center, Howard University, Washington, DC.
[137] Kleber, "Methadone," p. 151.
[138] Ibid.

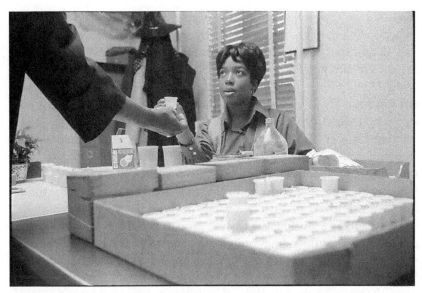

FIGURE 5.2. NTA counselor dispenses a methadone dose to a client in Washington, DC, 1971.

inner city. This feeling was analogous to the objections aired by support-ers of traditional treatment programs who felt that methadone placated its user, forever delaying a personal crisis that would ultimately lead to recovery. Whether the register was the individual or the inner city, it was clear that, for some, methadone worked only too well, staving off a bout of suffering that was necessary and long overdue.

Despite criticism from various quarters, methadone maintenance made converts on Capitol Hill – and congressional supporters were not alone in proposing that Bob DuPont's treatment plan should serve as a national model for treatment. Journalist Michael Massing traces the evolution of drug policy in the Nixon administration in his book, *The Fix*, revealing the unusual prominence accorded to DuPont's efforts in the District among White House staffers. Leading the administration's efforts to curb addic-tion nationwide was Jerome Jaffe, kindred spirit and colleague of DuPont. Like his DC counterpart, Jaffe did not have dogmatic views on the supe-riority of certain treatment approaches over others and, also like DuPont, he resolved the tension between methadone maintenance and abstinence advocates by giving money to them both. Yet it was clear that Jaffe felt methadone offered the most hope in delivering the results that the White House most wanted to see: a drop in crime. In appealing to Nixon's advi-sors on drug policy to invest more in methadone, Jaffe faced a daunting task. Not only were many of them deeply conservative and apt to see addiction as a moral failing, some were practicing Christian Scientists and thus skeptical of medical treatment of all kinds. Foremost among these natural skeptics was Egil ("Bud") Krogh, a young but influential presence in the White House who served as presidential advisor for the District of Columbia. His duties led him to adopt a vocal position on drug policy: "The District of Columbia became a laboratory in my mind," as he expressed it years later, "a place where we could put more funding into treatment and see what happened."[139] His intensive consultations with DuPont "gave ... some assurance," as he wrote to White House counsel John Ehrlichman, that efforts in the District could serve as a model to "go forward with a development of a nation-wide addict treatment policy."[140]

Soon DuPont's work in the District outpaced even the most optimistic projections. The most prized result was a reduction in crime, one that ran counter to national trends. Whereas the country's overall crime rate for 1970 increased by 11 percent, the crime rate for the District declined 5.2 percent during the same period.[141] While no one could make a direct and empirical claim about crime that did *not* happen, FBI figures disclosed that most of the drop in crime came after the Narcotics Treatment Administration was operational.[142] Nixon seized on the results to create a Special Action Office for Drug Abuse Prevention, placing Jaffe in charge. As a White House official detailed exclusively to drug policy, Jaffe served, in effect, as the nation's first "drug czar." It was notable that Jaffe's legacy was a singular one, as his successors were devoted more to enforcement than to treatment. A related and equally striking historical anomaly was the fact that Jaffe oversaw a budget in which funding for treatment outpaced the funding for drug enforcement by roughly a 2 to 1 ratio. By 1973, the United States had around 400 methadone programs serving more than 60,000 patients, and a new spoke in the research wheel of the National Institutes of Mental Health, the National Institute on Drug Abuse (NIDA), fostered this expansion, although it did so with some considerable ambivalence, resenting White House interference and still loyal to traditional treatment approaches.

Nevertheless, treatment – and methadone maintenance in particular – had made tremendous strides in a short period of time. The reasons for

[139] Michael Massing, *The Fix* (Berkeley: University of California Press, 2000), p. 102.
[140] Ibid., p. 103.
[141] For more, see Robert L. DuPont, "Treating Heroin Addicts in Washington," *Delaware Medical Journal*, February 1972, pp. 35–7.
[142] Massing, *The Fix*, p. 106.

this extended beyond just the favorable results. Nixon himself did not seem to have much use for Jaffe or other treatment experts until two congressmen revealed the extent of heroin use among U.S. soldiers stationed in South Vietnam;[143] once exposed, soldiers' drug habits forced the country to revise – however temporarily – lingering perceptions of heroin use as almost exclusively an inner city phenomenon. And, of course, the special obligation that the federal government bore for the care of soldiers and veterans hastened Nixon's acceptance of treatment.

But the president's pragmatic calculation was just that; he never fully embraced treatment or methadone maintenance specifically. While Nixon happily visited DC police headquarters for an unannounced morale booster, Michael Massing notes that the president never visited a treatment clinic (of any kind). Indeed, his support for a public health approach was a quiet one. Though Nixon funded an unprecedented expansion in treatment programs, he never openly endorsed a "disease" paradigm for addiction. When a high-level conference to discuss treatment convened at the White House, Nixon walked in late, recognized football great Gayle Sayers and exchanged pleasantries with him, and then left. "It made you wonder about the man's commitment," one of Nixon's advisors admitted.[144]

No one wondered long. By 1974, his last year in office, Nixon had cut $87 million from drug abuse treatment and prevention programs. Even more revealing was the fact that the enforcement side of Nixon's drug policy was not forced to endure similar budget cuts. Just the opposite: during the reelection year in 1972, the president created a new White House office – the Office of Drug Abuse Law Enforcement (ODALE) – and appointed its director, former Customs official Myles Ambrose. Ambrose vowed to use his powers to make a "dent" in the street trade in illicit drugs, a goal he announced in total sincerity, and one that was warmly received in the halls of the Nixon administration, despite the fact that no enforcement approach had ever had anything other than a temporary effect on street traffic.

What was more, Nixon's preferences, though important, were only part of the story. Public health clinics, especially methadone clinics, rested on the none too popular approach of harm reduction. The unease over methadone remained even as powerful circumstantial and correlative

---

[143] For more on this, see Chapter 6.
[144] Falco and Pekkamen, "The Abuse of Drug Abuse," *Washington Post*, September 8, 1974, p. B1.

evidence indicated that increased availability of drug treatment led to significant decreases in property crime. Nationwide data on crime for 1972, the first year of expanded treatment, showed the first drop registered in close to twenty years; crime rates for major cities fell by anywhere from 4 to 20 percent. This combination of awkward alliances and unspoken political aims paired with demonstrable results fit a pattern common to many public health initiatives – and, interestingly, it was one that stood in contradistinction to the politics of punitive drug enforcement. Enforcement promised easy and emphatic consensus paired with negligible if not deleterious outcomes. In contrast, an array of uncomfortable public officials quietly funded methadone treatment that produced real results, but only in a fashion that these same public officials were unwilling to trumpet or defend.

Unfortunately for treatment proponents, the enforcement equation had far greater political durability than its treatment counterpart. As early as 1972, when Nixon began his reelection campaign in earnest, his enthusiasm for methadone clinics had subsided, while his embrace of militant enforcement became more powerful and pronounced. This was in spite of several of Nixon's own advisors' support for methadone, support that suffered in the wake of the assignment of these same advisors to a White House working group called the "plumbers," a project dedicated to marginalizing Nixon's political rivals using dubious and frequently illegal tactics. Once caught breaking into Democratic Party headquarters in the Watergate hotel, "plumbers" who had been active in drug policy became even more distracted with the subsequent Watergate cover-up and criminal charges. Bud Krough, the president's point man on DC and a stalwart (if unlikely) Jaffe supporter, resigned as a result of the Watergate scandal and was later tried, convicted, and sentenced. No single personnel change within the White House had a more detrimental effect to the future of White House support for the burgeoning network of clinics.

Of more immediate and obvious concern to methadone supporters was the bad reputation that the drug began to acquire. "Some methadone patients sell all or part of their allotted dosage," the *New York Times* reported in 1972, "so as to purchase heroin, barbiturates," or, increasingly popular and plentiful, "cocaine."[145] As medical researchers began to discover to their dismay, while methadone did not provide a "high" to a person physically addicted to narcotics, it did provide one to someone

[145] "Methadone Found Rising As Killer," *New York Times*, March 14, 1972, p. 48.

who was not, and was thus subject to recreational abuse. Even more distressing, because coroners in big cities adopted the practice of testing the
deceased for toxicology, traces of methadone would sometimes appear
in dead bodies – and this was the case whether or not methadone was
actually a cause of death. A spike in coroners' figures set off a wave of
concern: in 1971, the District had seventeen methadone-related deaths,
yet by November 1972, the District tallied twenty-eight of the same (and
nineteen more deceased with both heroin and methadone in their systems).[146] Jaffe protested that, like any drug, methadone could be dangerous if misused.[147] He and DuPont also felt that persistent waitlists for
methadone treatment in various cities accounted for instances of diversion, and that these in turn led to misuse and overdose.[148] In controlled
settings, they insisted, methadone provided essential relief. Responding to
the growing concern, in 1972 the FDA tightened methadone dispensation
by prohibiting physicians from prescribing it privately, sanctioning its use
only in the context of clinics.[149]

Most damning was the fact that methadone maintenance never
escaped the stigma of addiction. "Are we merely substituting one habit
for another?" Senator Birch Bayh of Indiana wondered at the start of
hearings he conducted to evaluate the treatment in late 1972 and early
1973.[150] Officials from the Bureau of Narcotics and Dangerous Drugs
underscored the senator's reservations in testimony, claiming that,
although methadone treatment was widely available in California, "there
is still a devil of a lot of heroin available."[151] The intended inference was
that treatment could not be relied upon to stem the tide of illicit drugs,
while enforcement presumably could. Director Ingersoll was more explicit
in his testimony before the committee, claiming that Bureau agents could
obtain diverted methadone easily.[152] In the context of the gnawing fear
that methadone was a dangerously addictive drug, the revelation of

[146] "The Heroin Epidemic," *New York Times*, November 21, 1972, p. 28.
[147] See his remarks in William C. Selover, "US Warned on Use of Drugs to Fight Heroin," *Christian Science Monitor*, November 12, 1971, p. 1.
[148] James Markham, "Study Finds Black Market Developing in Methadone," *New York Times*, January 2, 1972, p. 1.
[149] See Kozel and DuPont, *Criminal Charges and Drug Use Patterns*, p. 18.
[150] "Methadone Use and Abuse," pp. 172–3, *Hearings before Subcommittee to Investigate Juvenile Delinquency, Committee on the Judiciary, US Senate, 92nd and 93rd Congress* (Washington, DC: U.S. Government Printing Office, 1973) [hereafter: "Bayh Hearings"], p. 4.
[151] Bayh Hearings, p. 82.
[152] Ibid., pp. 644–5.

diverted methadone along with occasional misuse or overdose damaged its public reputation. Rather than being defined by its overall success, methadone was tarnished by its failures.

Despite the bad press, treatment programs did not suffer from lack of demand. In DC, for example, NTA Director Bob DuPont recalled that, "[f]rom the day it opened its doors in February 1970, NTA has never had unused treatment capacity."[153] To guard against public disapproval, the director also carefully managed expectations. He outlined four objectives for the NTA: to treat "as many heroin addicts as possible"; restore the patient to functional life and gainful employment; stop illicit drug use; and stop criminal activity.[154] DuPont demonstrated progress on all fronts. Moreover, his decision to allow a diversity of approaches allowed him to compare the effectiveness of each. He found that, unlike methadone maintenance, which boasted a remarkable retention rate of 86 percent, only 15 percent of the patients enrolled in traditional abstinence programs were still with NTA six months later.[155] DuPont aggregated the assessment of his work by posing a simple question: "Will the community benefit from the expensive effort needed to treat thousands of heroin addicts?" His answer was an unequivocal "yes."

But by 1972, DuPont encountered difficulty sustaining financial support for the NTA, a difficulty that he felt could be attributed to "the thought that we are just substituting one addiction for another."[156] NTA's future seemed in greater doubt when Jerome Jaffe left the Nixon administration following his office's post-reelection expulsion from the White House and banishment to Rockville, Maryland. Not only did the NTA lose an influential voice with Jaffe's departure, Nixon chose Bob DuPont to replace him, and so the NTA lost its resourceful leader as well. After DuPont departed for the federal government, a series of crises befell the agency in quick succession. In 1974, the NTA abandoned take-home (usually weekend) doses of methadone so as to limit the problem of diversion to an illicit market and to discourage the mugging of patients leaving the clinic. This fairly innocuous change meant that patients had

---

[153] DuPont and Greene, "The Dynamics of Heroin Addiction Epidemic," *Science* 181 (August 1973): 719.
[154] Robert L. DuPont, "Treating Heroin Addicts in Washington," *Delaware Medical Journal*, February 1972, p. 36.
[155] Ibid.
[156] "Doctor Links Methadone Treatment to a Decline in Crime in the Capital," *New York Times*, March 13, 1972, p. 18.

to appear at the clinic daily, something that interfered with the self-sustaining vision set forth by Nyswander and Dole as key to methadone's success. The following year, budget cuts forced the agency to fire twenty drug counselors. The next year NTA's budget fell even further; one NTA official complained that the agency had "counselors with case loads over 50, which is unrealistic when you're talking about getting people off drugs."[157] When the budget for 1976 was finalized, NTA was forced to declare its services closed to new patients, or else risk violation of FDA codes regarding appropriate staff-to-patient ratios. Yet the city's clinics were so understaffed that the FDA threatened to sue the NTA even after this drastic move, forcing the agency to close three clinics until they could be properly staffed and the methadone being dispensed could be properly monitored. By the time the clinics reopened in 1977, the city decided to skirt the problem of appropriate safeguards for methadone by rededicating two out of the three clinics to drug-free abstinence programs.

These local decisions typified the national move away from methadone as well as the declining investment in treatment more generally. Once Nixon cast off Jaffe's office from the White House, NIDA assumed control over the federal government's treatment portfolio. Housed in the larger National Institute of Mental Health bureaucracy, the research and risk-averse culture of NIDA's institutional surroundings only strengthened its leaders' preference for distancing themselves from methadone maintenance clinics. As much as anything else, methadone languished because, as NIDA director Bertram Brown bluntly admitted in 1975, "defining the appropriate criteria for evaluating treatment is a major problem."[158] Fairly or not, methadone was often implicitly or explicitly evaluated according to the precepts of a medical model: individual diagnosis, treatment, and cure. But in fact, as a public health initiative, methadone's supporters would have argued for a different framework: the public good rather than individual care, a targeted intervention rather than a complete treatment plan, and harm reduction rather than a cure. Under the former and more exacting medical standards, occasional failures of methadone programs, like diversion, overdose, or prolonged dependence upon the drug, discredited its use. Those who invoked the demanding criteria of the medical model, whether in or out of the treatment community,

[157] "City Drug Unit Fears Budget Cuts," *Washington Post*, February 17, 1976, p. B2.
[158] Bertram S. Brown, "Drugs and Public Health: Issues and Answers," *Annals of the American Academy of Political and Social Science* 417 (January 1975): 117.

could be assured that adoption of their standards would mean that every success could be celebrated – whereas, in the public health approach, success could only mean less to be dismayed about. Perhaps this thought assuaged them as it became increasingly obvious that success – a drug-free life – could be so rarely achieved, and was most often a provisional, not permanent, victory.

Nixon and other conservative leaders eventually adopted the standards of the medical model as the appropriate evaluative criteria for treatment because it fit well with other absolutist views of drug abstinence that became more important to them over time. Methadone maintenance might have been a success, and it might have been a success precisely along the criteria nominated by its pioneers, but it lacked a broader political utility. In the end, Nixon shunted clinics aside as part of a larger calculation, one that would not allow him to countenance treatment for fear that it would appear to condone drug use of any kind. It was a sad irony indeed: clinics, born from a desire to confront the damage caused by one of the world's most addictive drugs, ultimately fell victim to a backlash against the widespread recreational use of one of the least harmful, marijuana.

YOUTH AND THE CULTURAL DRUG WAR

It is sometimes said that if a person can remember the 1960s, she did not really experience them. Common reference to broad and casual drug use by especially young people was one reason why many found the decade to be so divisive, and continue to do so today. For young and mainly affluent people, the addition of marijuana to alcohol and cigarettes as commonly used drugs in their birth cohort was a marker of generational identity and a sign of progress. To others, especially to older Americans, the youthful embrace of marijuana and the blithe acceptance of drug use more generally signaled a dangerous moral decline. It was a divide not easily bridged, nor one easily denied. One researcher appearing before Congress in 1970 to testify on marijuana use revealed that more than 50 percent of an entering class of medical students had used marijuana at one time. "And if it is this high in the medical students," he remarked, his voice trailing off. "Then the saints preserve us," one congressman jumped in to finish his thought.[159]

---

[159] *Subcommittee on Public Health and Welfare, Committee on Interstate and Foreign Commerce, U.S. House of Representatives, Hearings on Drug Abuse Control Amendments* (Washington, DC: Government Printing Office, 1970), p. 563.

Saints who interceded on behalf of those on a quest to alter their state of mind through drug use would have been busy indeed. Marijuana use skyrocketed, but so too did other forms of drug use, including licit and illicit consumption of prescription drugs. Lawmakers struggled to stay abreast of new drug discoveries and their subsequent misuse, all the while choosing to present themselves as preoccupied with exploding marijuana use, but, in reality, keen on refashioning the government's approach to all drugs and bring them under one framework. Their efforts culminated in the 1970 Controlled Substances Act, a statute that was in many ways the result of the decision to place drug enforcement entirely in the Department of Justice, and one that separated drug control from taxing power once and for all. While lawmakers viewed their labors as an effort to impose logic and coherence upon the sprawling and inconsistent world of drug laws, their success was a mechanical one, for, in severing drug regulation from taxes and the world of trade, they put forward crime, and rejected trade, as the appropriate framework within which to consider and regulate illicit drugs.

Many of the young people who remained at least the rhetorical target of lawmakers' censure were not shy about placing their drug use in a different and more celebratory perspective. Throughout the late 1960s, college and high school students across the country embraced cultural markers and behaviors that put them at odds with the mainstream, whether their dissent took the form of civil disobedience, long hair, or a heretical celebration of illicit drug use.[160] Historian Ken Cmiel argues that young baby boomers adopted a kind of deliberate incivility, meant to expose the dishonest and corrupt aspects governing the adult world's notion of civility, a hollow concept that encompassed things like the tacit approval for the bombing of North Vietnam, or polite endorsement of white racism.[161] This suggestion places an ennobling and rather uncritical cast on baby boom drug use, an activity that first and foremost deserves to be assessed as part of that

---

[160] Literature that addresses youth activism in the sixties, especially the late 1960s, includes: Terry M. Anderson, *The Movement and the Sixties: Protest in America from Greensboro to Wounded Knee* (New York: Oxford University Press, 1996); Stewart Burns, *Social Movements of the 1960s: Searching for Democracy* (Boston: Twayne Publishers, 1990); David Farber, *The Age of Great Dreams: America in the 1960s* (New York: Hill and Wang, 1994); Todd Gitlin, *The Sixties: Years of Hope, Days of Rage* (New York: Bantam Books, 1987); Gael Graham, "Flaunting the Freak Flag: *Karr v. Schmidt* and the Great Hair Debate in American High Schools, 1965–1975," *Journal of American History* 91, no. 2 (September 2004): 522–43; Edward K. Spann, *Democracy's Children: The Young Rebels of the 1960s and the Power of Ideals* (Wilmington: Scholarly Resources, 2003).

[161] Kenneth Cmiel, "The Politics of Incivility," in *The Sixties: From Memory to History*, David Farber, ed. (Chapel Hill: University of North Carolina Press, 1994), pp. 263–90.

generation's tremendous affluence and, too, the country's own preeminent
standing at the center of western wealth and trading networks.

Whatever the motivation, wealth was the necessary context to understanding young people's use of drugs – as well as that of their elders,
something that baby boomers made rich use of in justifying their own
recreational indulgence. "Every time I come home even just a little
stoned," one boomer complained, "my old man thinks I've been shooting up [heroin]. Then he sits down and dares to drink his alcohol while
telling me the evils of drugs, between puffs on his nicotine-loaded cigarettes." Similarly, when his mother upbraided him for his marijuana use,
she failed to mention her own habit of taking tranquilizers for sleep and
amphetamines "to get her going in the morning."[162] A still more pointed
reference to mainstream drug use and dependence could be found at one
drug dealing spot in the Haight Ashbury district of San Francisco, the
"Drog Store," which patterned its interior after a traditional pharmacy.[163]
Their visual pun was not an analogy but a metonymy, a purposeful association of mainstream prescription use with hippie drug culture.

And, from the mid-1960s on, heavy prescription drug use was a pronounced and frequently troubling aspect of American society. Historian
Nicolas Rasmussen argues that amphetamine use was an important
component to the decade's artistic milieu, especially avant-garde New
York, but he is more adamant and expansive on the commonplace use
of amphetamines, including as a diet pill for women, or as a pep pill for
sports, a practice that extended far into the reaches of professional ath-
letics.[164] While amphetamines began to acquire shades of its menacing
"speed freak" reputation when flamboyant members of the Hell's Angels
motorcycle gang would, in the words of Hunter S. Thompson, "do cart-
wheels" while on "bennies," these colorful stories did not discourage
other users, like the lawyer who admitted to the *New York Times* that
he used amphetamines in order to speed his recovery from his sleeping
pill habit, or the magazine editor who took amphetamine "shots" to help
negotiate his busy bi-coastal lifestyle.[165]

[162] Quotes from "Asleep on Drugs," *Christian Science Monitor*, July 8, 1970, p. 9.
[163] "The Drug Scene: Dependence Grows," *New York Times*, January 8, 1968, p. 1.
[164] Nicolas Rasmussen, *On Speed: The Many Lives of Amphetamine* (New York: New York University Press, 2008), chap. 7.
[165] Hunter S. Thompson, *Hell's Angels: The Strange and Terrible Saga of the Outlaw Motorcycle Gang* (New York: Ballantine Books, 1966), p. 273; Martin Arnold, "The Drug Scene: A Growing Number of America's Elite are Quietly 'Turning On'," *New York Times*, January 10, 1968, p. 26.

The traditional drug companion of amphetamines, barbiturates, did not see the same increase in use – licit or otherwise – as its partner, but that was only because pharmaceutical companies produced new sedatives, including tranquilizers like Valium. While not confined to female consumers, tranquilizers became most associated with housewives because of both heavy use by that group and the anxiety that this use provoked. Feminists who gained a voice in the early 1970s often denounced pills like Valium – which was, at that time, the single most prescribed brand of medicine in the country – as a medical mask disguising the personal pain women encountered when their lives did not measure up to their own ambition or talent.[166] Stories of dependence upon Valium and the dangers it posed also appeared with some regularity in venues like the *Ladies Home Journal* and *McCall's*, and when one of the nation's archetypal housewives, former First Lady Betty Ford, admitted in 1978 that she had "overmedicated" herself with painkillers, American women everywhere were jolted into a critical assessment of their own growing reliance upon prescription medicine.[167]

In a surfeit of drugs and drug use, the American public was periodically warned that doctors were in thrall to a sophisticated pharmaceutical advertising campaign and that the country was, in fact, "overmedicated." Six dollars out of every $10 spent for prescription drugs were unnecessary, one medical professor told a Senate subcommittee in 1967; they were unneeded doses meted out in response to either a clamoring patient or a seductive message proffered by a drug company.[168] In 1969, the federal government launched a public awareness campaign on the dangers of drug use and included some messages specifically targeting middle-class housewives who, the government now believed, were susceptible to over-use of amphetamines and sedatives.[169] While historian Susan Lynn Speaker finds the "overmedication" crisis to be a construct that helped to express "disillusionment with medical care,"[170] no mere intellectual conceit can account for the vast retrenchment in prescription medication that

---

[166] See especially David Herzberg, "'The Pill You Love Can Turn On You': Feminism, Tranquilizers, and the Valium Panic of the 1970s," *American Quarterly* (March 2006): 79–103.
[167] See also Andrea Tone, *The Age of Anxiety: A History of America's Turbulent Affair with Tranquilizers* (New York: Basic Books, 2009).
[168] "Half of the Drugs Prescribed Are Unneeded, Senators Told," *Washington Post Times Herald*, September 14, 1967, p. A3.
[169] "Messages Against Drug Use," *Washington Post Times Herald*, April 24, 1969, p. H10.
[170] Susan Lynn Speaker, "Too Many Pills: Patients, Physicians, and the Myth of Overmedication in America, 1955–1980," PhD diss., University of Pennsylvania. 1992.

occurred once doctors were forced to justify their dispensation of certain "controlled substances" after 1970. Moreover, any time a drug like Valium was re-classed as potentially addictive and subject to controls, its production and consumption figures plummeted. Without a doubt, a lot of prescription pills were floating around prior to the institution of controls, and the puckish humor of countercultural hippies in the Haight who purchased their marijuana from the tidy shelves of the "Drog Store" resonated as much for its insight as it did for its audacity.

Laboratory-engineered drugs and 1960s counterculture collided even more visibly with the use and celebration of LSD (Lysergic Acid Diethylamide). First concocted before World War II, LSD, a potent hallucinogen, had an established (and later controversial) place in military experiments and interrogations throughout the 1950s. During the same time, the drug also gained a notable following in Hollywood, as a small cadre of actors and film professionals, including Cary Grant, experimented with the drug for recreational purposes, to be sure, but also to delve deeper and unlock creative energies that they believed would remain untapped were it not for "acid trips." The exploratory purposes of this group, and in particular the idea that LSD could be used as a path to self-discovery, were echoed years later in the pronouncements of Timothy Leary, a Harvard psychologist who advocated the therapeutic use of psychedelic drugs like LSD. Since the substance was not banned at that point, Leary and his mainly young followers extolled the virtues of LSD without any legal censure, although Harvard did fire Leary when he failed to deliver his scheduled lectures. After his termination, Leary became a free-floating and increasingly more bizarre voice of the counterculture. Appearing before a Senate subcommittee in 1966, he detailed the results of his LSD experiments.[171] "The so-called peril of LSD," Leary told the committee, "resides precisely in its eerie power to release ancient, wise, and I would even say at times holy sources of energy which reside in the human brain."[172] As far as despairing of the country's youth, Leary suggested that it was not drugs but the modern university that had inflicted the most damage by forcing students to think "in linear ways."[173]

At that very same hearing, FDA director Goddard declared his intention "to move vigorously against those who manufacture or distribute

[171] *Hearings before Special Subcommittee of the Committee on Judiciary, US Senate, 89th Congress, January, May, June, July 1966* (Washington, DC: U.S. Government Printing Office, 1966).
[172] Ibid., p. 239.
[173] Ibid., p. 258.

LSD or possess significant quantities," a sign that he and others did not share Leary's reverence for the drug.[174] Still, LSD did not lack colorful defenders before Senate. Goddard's testimony was followed by that of Beatnik poet Allen Ginsburg, who by that time had earned a kind of doyenne status within counterculture. "I want to speak about my own inside feelings," Ginsburg informed the committee.[175] He went on to describe to lawmakers a clash between pacifist student protestors and a belligerent faction of the Hell's Angels; Ken Kesey, author and a friend to Ginsburg, attempted to broker a truce between the groups by passing around LSD. Shortly after that, Ginsburg described, "we settled down to discussing the situation and listening to Joan Baez on the phonograph and chanting Buddhist prayers."[176]

Such eccentric displays confirmed senators and others in their belief that the counterculture and its hedonistic embrace of mind-altering drugs presented a genuine threat to American society. Two years after receiving this testimony, Congress moved to prohibit the legal production and possession of LSD. Unfortunately for those who denounced the counterculture, its most popular drug, marijuana, had spread far beyond the circles of self-identified hippies. By 1969, marijuana offenses accounted for the majority of drug arrests in the country.[177] A year later, the U.S. Treasury was forced to admit that marijuana seizures were "more conveniently measured in tons," nine of which were seized by Customs in June of 1970 alone.[178] More disturbing to defenders of marijuana prohibition, the exaggerated and sometimes outlandish claims advanced by the U.S. government for decades regarding the harms associated with marijuana use were called into question by a broad swath of the drug's recreational users. Judges grew tired of sentencing marijuana smokers, especially when, as one judge admitted, it was clear that the drug was "no more of a public danger or a danger to the user than alcohol."[179] Even a small number of federal government officials voiced skepticism over the harsh sentencing meted out for marijuana offenses; at the same hearing in which FDA director

---

[174] *Hearings before Special Subcommittee of the Committee on Judiciary, US Senate, 89th Congress, January, May, June, July 1966* (Washington, DC: U.S. Government Printing Office, 1966), p. 334.
[175] Ibid., p. 488.
[176] Ibid., p. 492.
[177] Senate Committee on Judiciary, *Report on S.3246, Controlled Dangerous Substances Act of 1969* (Washington, DC: U.S. Government Printing Office, 1969), p. 2.
[178] *Committee on Ways and Means, U.S. House of Representatives, Controlled Dangerous Substances* (Washington, DC: U.S. Government Printing Office, 1970), p. 259.
[179] Ibid.

Goddard shared his alarm over the growing use of LSD, he suggested that the penalties for use of marijuana be dramatically reduced.

Addiction researcher and longtime Bureau of Narcotics gadfly Alfred Lindesmith was quick to seize upon this admission and shrewd in assessing what prompted Goddard's reservations. "Nobody worried very much when police sent thousands of ghetto dwellers to languish in prison for years for puffing on one joint," Lindesmith told the *Wall Street Journal*, but now that "the doctor, the lawyer, the teacher and the business executive and their children are facing the same fate, marijuana has become a cause célèbre."[180] News of certain arrests underscored the shift in the demographics of marijuana use. Alongside noteworthy but unsurprising marijuana busts – like Ken Kesey's two arrests for possession in 1966, or the various arrests of band members of the Rolling Stones in 1967 – the public learned of other marijuana charges, like those against Robert F. Kennedy, Jr., and his cousin, Robert Sargent Shriver III, for possession. Senator Alan Cranston, Democrat of California, could only watch as his son was arrested for smuggling marijuana; Senator Ernest Hollings of South Carolina was in the same position when his son was arrested for possession. Though these incidents were trivial in a statistical sense, they registered an effect on public (and congressional) perceptions of marijuana use as extending well beyond a "fringe" or countercultural group.

Still the most distressing aspect of the country's marijuana laws was that mere possession could result in prison time. Unsuspecting middle-class kids placed in prison found it difficult to negotiate a setting for which they were totally unprepared. When four teenagers were sentenced to the state penitentiary in Idaho for four to five years on account of marijuana possession with intent to sell, they earned the dubious distinction of becoming the youngest prisoners in the institution's history. Sentences such as these rattled local communities; many alarmed readers pointed out that some states had a twenty-five-year sentence for possession, five years more than the typical sentence for murder. Understandably, state and federal prosecutors were disinclined to take marijuana possession cases, for personal as well as practical reasons. "If every marijuana offender was given the maximum sentence or anything approaching it," California's attorney general told the Senate, "there would not be space in the prisons or jails."[181]

---

[180] Quoted in "Marijuana at Issue," *Wall Street Journal*, November 20, 1967, p. 1.
[181] Quoted in Nathan Miller, "Why Pot Penalties are Shrinking," *The Sun*, June 21, 1970, p. PK3.

In no small way, then, marijuana arrests and enforcement prompted a reconsideration of the country's entire illicit drug regime. The dissonance between the penalties meted out for marijuana possession and the growing tolerance for the infraction itself certainly weighed heavily on lawmakers, but one instance in particular – the arrest of Timothy Leary and his two children in 1965 – played a specific and quite considerable role in changing the federal government's tack. Leary appealed his arrest and, in a case that went all the way to the Supreme Court, the resulting 1968 ruling in *Leary v. United States* upended the premise behind the Marihuana Tax Act of 1937 and, in the minds of members of Congress, the case undermined the constitutionality of the Harrison Narcotic Act as well.

These dramatic effects could not be predicted from the rather unspectacular facts of the Leary case. Around the Christmas holidays in 1965, Leary decided to drive his son and his daughter, as well as two friends of theirs, down to Mexico. They left New York on December 20, and two days later they arrived at the International Bridge in Laredo, Texas. They crossed the bridge, attempted to gain entry into Mexico, and were refused. Re-entering the United States, they were stopped and selected for a search. A U.S. Customs official found some scattered marijuana seeds on the floor of the car and three partially smoked joints stowed on Leary's daughter. Leary took responsibility for the drug, which he claimed to have purchased in New York, and was taken into custody along with his daughter. After release on bond and filing his appeal, Leary was re-arrested in the state of California two years later for violation of state marijuana laws; he was subsequently found guilty. For this reason, Leary was actually in prison when the Supreme Court took up his 1965 case. While awaiting the Court's review, Timothy Leary submitted one last document for the Court to consider, the so-called Eagle Brief, a rambling bit of prose arranged in couplet form and published by San Francisco's City Lights Bookstore. "We are in prison because we are American Eagles," Leary began, and his choice of the plural pronoun denoted not just his family's arrest but the persecution of an entire legion of countercultural warriors who rallied around him as well. While not a particularly effective legal intervention, the document did demonstrate just how much more radicalized and obscure Leary had become in the years separating his two arrests, as he proceeded to denounce different forms of authority as various kinds of poultry – turkeys, chickens, and so on – who could only aspire to eagle status. Incoherent though it was, the Eagle Brief attained minor notoriety nonetheless, not least because City

Lights chose to date its publication on the day that Leary escaped from prison in California in 1970.

Fortunately for Leary, the Supreme Court reviewed his case without reference to his "brief"; neither, for that matter, did they consider his repeat offenses, erratic behavior, or his desire to speak as ambassador for the recreational use of illicit drugs. Instead, they considered the terms of the appeal itself. In it Leary argued that in order to obtain the appropriate tax forms to authorize the legal transfer of marijuana, he would be exposing his name and address to authorities, who would then check these against those officially registered to obtain and transfer marijuana. Although, as the Court stated in its majority opinion, Congress had clearly intended for people in the same situation as Leary – that is, those not registered with the IRS as authorized dealers – to be able to obtain a transfer form (provided they were willing to pay the non-registrant fee of $100 to transfer as opposed to the $1 fee charged to registrants), a set of subsequent regulations provided that any attempt to obtain a transfer form by a non-registrant would be reported to the law enforcement authorities. Thus, the Court concluded, Leary was confronted with "a statute which on its face permitted him to acquire the drug legally ... and simultaneously with a system of regulations which, according to the Government, prohibited him from acquiring marihuana under any conditions."[182] As Leary pointed out, any attempt to follow the statute would violate his right against self-incrimination. The court agreed and overturned the conviction.

The decision was interpreted at the time as sounding the death knell for the federal government's use of taxing power to govern illicit drug enforcement efforts. But in fact it did not. First and foremost, the ruling affected only the possession components of the law; illicit trafficking components were unaffected. Yet, in coming before the Congress to propose a new drug regime in 1969, Nixon's attorney general, John Mitchell, was only too happy to cite *Leary*. "We no longer have an effective possession law for the narcotic drugs," Mitchell told the Congress and, while "possession offenses are not the major thrust of Federal law enforcement, they are a necessary concomitant to drug conspiracy cases against large-scale traffickers."[183] This admission was an important one, and it was fundamentally the same insight that judges relied upon to reject the

[182] *Leary v. United States*, 395 US 26 (1968), p. 26.
[183] *Committee on Ways and Means, U.S. House of Representatives, Controlled Dangerous Substances* (Washington, DC: U.S. Government Printing Office, 1970), p. 201.

arguments to decriminalize heroin addiction. Without meaningful criminal possession laws, there was no way to enforce drug prohibition; there was simply no incentive to turn a dealer over to the police, and no ability for law enforcement to infiltrate the world of illicit drug deals.

Perhaps more important, although *Leary* did nothing to undermine the federal government's constitutional claim on taxing power, it did suggest, almost as a matter of common sense, that the taxing power was not a logical choice to effect a regime of total criminal prohibition. One could regulate goods and services through taxes, and one could distinguish licit from illicit transactions and punish the latter, but it was an odd and contradictory posture to levy a tax on something that *no one* was allowed to have. In this way, the government construed *Leary* in a fashion that suggested a determination to effect a regime of total criminal prohibition, at least for marijuana and heroin. Heretofore, complete prohibition had never been attempted, although the circle of permissible possession and sale was drawn so small that, as Timothy Leary might have argued, it had become a metaphorical noose to hang oneself in the American courts.

At the same time, however, the Nixon administration as well as the Congress remained mindful that illicit use of prescription drugs was a growing problem, one that the 1965 Drug Control Amendments did not adequately address. While the 1965 act mandated that drug companies register and perform a one-time inventory of drugs, this inventory was now three years out-of-date and useless; moreover, illicit consumption of amphetamines and other drugs did not come from illicit production but rather from diversion of licit production, and hence registration efforts accomplished little. In 1969, the same year the Nixon administration approached Congress in an effort to rewrite the nation's drug laws, the National Institute of Mental Health estimated that 50 percent of 8 billion amphetamines produced annually were diverted each year.[184] Indeed, as Attorney General Mitchell testified before Congress, there had been a "tremendous upsurge in illicit diversion in the last five years."[185]

The resolution of these multiple policy dilemmas came in the sweeping 1970 Controlled Substances Act. The law classified all drugs in five schedules: Schedule 1 applied to drugs completely prohibited, without any medical value whatsoever, and Schedule 5 applied to drugs determined

---

[184] *Committee on Judiciary, U.S. Senate, Report on S.3246, Controlled Dangerous Substances Act of 1969* (Washington, DC: U.S. Government Printing Office, 1969), p. 4.
[185] *Committee on Ways and Means, U.S. House of Representatives, Controlled Dangerous Substances* (Washington, DC: U.S. Government Printing Office, 1970), p. 202.

to have little to no harmful effects and appropriate for over-the-counter sale without prescription. The gradations between the two extremes – Schedules 2, 3, and 4 – were used to capture drugs that had some recognized medical value, but also posed some risk. Accordingly, various levels of controls were assigned to each category, with Schedule 2 being the most stringent of those applied to licit drugs. In that category, a doctor would have to be able to justify a prescription as medically necessary and, in addition, a pharmacist could offer no refills and no orders by phone. Schedule 2 drug dispensation records also would have to be available for inspection upon request from the government.

While presented as a scientific evaluation, and offered as a lucid and legible categorization of drugs, in reality Schedule 1 was used to accommodate and continue the posture toward drugs regulated under the Harrison Narcotic Act; Schedule 2 drugs, in turn, inherited the practices and norms associated with the Drug Control Abuse Amendments of 1965. In this way, the Controlled Substances Act enshrined in the law the arbitrary distinction drawn between two different groups of drugs when Congress decided, back in 1952, that it could no longer burden the Department of Treasury with new drugs to regulate. The legislation was not a scientifically arbitrated scheme of drugs, but a political framework that consolidated a host of decisions, as well as some failures to decide, how to manage the drug portfolio of the United States.

Significantly, the legislation that created this new drug regime tied the government's power to do so to the grant of federal power under the commerce clause of the constitution, a striking departure from the past drug regulation efforts attached to the power to tax. Though this shift was not unremarked upon, the ambition to consolidate the country's drug laws was most often couched in practical – and not legal – terms. In his final year in office, Lyndon Johnson referenced the "crazy quilt of inconsistent approaches and widely disparate criminal sanctions" that characterized federal statutes on drugs.[186] In that same speech, he requested that the National Commission on Reform of the Federal Criminal Laws review narcotics and other drug laws to recommend reforms "as soon as possible." His successor, Richard Nixon, elevated the efforts to consolidate drug laws to a federal mission, akin to the efforts of Democrats in prior administrations to task the national government with welfare obligations previously reserved for the states. "Within the last decade," Nixon told the Congress in a formal message accompanying his proposals

---

[186] "Johnson Widens Narcotics Fight," *New York Times*, February 8, 1968, p. 1.

to unify drug laws, "the abuse of drugs has grown from essentially a local police problem into a serious national threat to the personal health and safety of millions of Americans." One congressman was even more succinct on the floor of the House: "New laws are needed," he told the chamber, "that are equal to the task of cleaning up the drug problem."[187] Thus the Controlled Substances Act and the drug war that it launched orchestrated two shifts: from taxing power to the commerce clause, and from state prerogative to national power.

Of the two, the proposed legislation's shift in legal authority attracted far less notice. Yet some congressmen did comment on it. Among the most perceptive to do so was Nebraska Republican Senator Roman Hruska, who pointed out that in fact "the first systematized departure from the Harrison Narcotic Act" happened in 1968, when Congress prohibited LSD sale and possession.[188] Building upon the precedent set in 1965 for regulation of amphetamines and barbiturates, Congress chose to prohibit LSD production, sale, and possession under the Food, Drug, and Cosmetic Act using the power afforded to them under the commerce clause. Because LSD was a synthetically manufactured product, and because some still argued for the religious or therapeutic use of hallucinogens, it made sense to lawmakers that these drugs should be grouped with other so-called dangerous drugs, which, since 1965, had been regulated under the authority of the commerce clause.

But narcotics were not. This group, which the government designated as heroin and other opiates (correctly), cocaine and marijuana (incorrectly), had never before been completely prohibited, nor had they been regulated using the commerce clause; they had been controlled exclusively using the power to tax. But, as Congressman John Ashbrook pointed out as he introduced the set of reforms that would become the Controlled Substances Act, the legislation would change "the constitutional basis of control" over narcotics and other drugs "from the taxing power to the commerce power."[189] Congressman MacGregor, a Republican from Minnesota and a staunch conservative, depicted this shift in power in more pointed terms. The proposed legislation would make, MacGregor told his colleagues on the floor, all enforcement "cohesive through the use of the power to regulate interstate

---

[187] Remarks of Monagan in *Congressional Record – House*, 116th Congress, September 23, 1970, p. 3317.

[188] Bayh Hearings, p. 6.

[189] Remarks of Ashbrook in *Congressional Record – House*, 116th Congress, July 1, 1970, p. 22567.

commerce." "The power to tax," he continued, always "a questionable device," he offered, was "no longer relied upon."[190] In testimony before Congress, representatives from the Treasury Department noted this shift as well. In a carefully worded observation, Secretary David M. Kennedy pointed out that the proposed reform would repeal previous legislation "on the ground that the Federal role in control of dangerous substances can be satisfactorily founded on powers other than the taxing power." Needless to say, he told Congress, "[t]he Treasury Department supports this view."[191]

Such was probably an understatement. Some within Treasury more likely rejoiced at the thought of jettisoning drug regulation. For many months before he spoke those words, the marijuana tax in particular had become extremely burdensome. When someone was arrested and charged with an improper "transfer" of marijuana, the law enforcement officials involved notified the nearest district office of the IRS. What followed was a routine but rather tedious political charade: the IRS agent asked the amount of marijuana seized and, using the figure provided by law enforcement, assessed the delinquent tax. The person arrested, already charged with an illegal transfer, was at that point also slapped with quite a large tax fee, one that the IRS had little hope of actually collecting. "Because of recent increased activity in the illegal use of marijuana," Kennedy told the Congress, the "IRS has been obliged to make assessments in numbers and amounts where chances of collection are practically nil."[192]

From various quarters within the government, then, when the shift from taxing to commerce power was discussed, it was with approval. This change dictated an unusual legislative path for the proposed drug overhaul, however. Since the 1950s, the Senate had referred all drug legislation to the judiciary committee, and so when the Nixon administration sent its recommendations to Congress in July 1969, that is precisely where the Senate sent the legislation for consideration. The bill passed the Senate with a unanimous vote in January 1970; at that point, it went to the House. There the chamber split consideration of the bill between Wilbur Mills's taxation committee, House Ways and Means, and Congressman Byrnes's committee, the Committee on Interstate and

---

[190] Remarks of MacGregor in *Congressional Record – House*, 116th Congress, September 23, 1970, p. 3315.

[191] *Committee on Ways and Means, U.S. House of Representatives, Controlled Dangerous Substances* (Washington, DC: U.S. Government Printing Office, 1970), p. 260.

[192] Ibid.

Foreign Commerce. This awkward division meant that the Ways and Means Committee deliberated on a proposal designed to diminish its own power. As Mills conceded, the legislation, if approved, would give the Committee on Interstate and Foreign Commerce "more jurisdiction in the field than it has today," and his own committee "less."[193] Mills was unperturbed by this prospect because he joined others in believing that, more than anything else, the proposal to unify all drug laws was a natural consequence of the move to consolidate the Bureau of Narcotics and Dangerous Drugs, established through executive reorganization in 1968. In justifying the plan before Congress, Attorney General John Mitchell dwelt on the difficulties that different drug laws created for the Bureau. "Today we have one Federal agency responsible for the enforcement of [various drug] laws," he observed, yet "it must approach its enforcement ... with divergent schemes of authority."[194] Bureau agents had arrest powers for some drugs, but not others. They could subpoena information for some types of cases, but not others. These varying and at times conflicting standards introduced practical difficulties in the conduct of Bureau business. As Congressman Boland put it, the proposed reform recognized and in some ways was the logical result of "the new structure of Federal administration of drug statutes created by the Reorganization Plan No. 1 of 1968."[195]

The creation of a unified statute followed the institutional consolidation achieved two years prior and was supported, in no small part, in order to maximize the efficiency and leverage of the new Bureau of Narcotics and Dangerous Drugs. The legislative overhaul was not intended, interestingly enough, to "get tough" on drug use, even though denunciations of especially recreational drug consumption were not hard to find in the debate. Nevertheless, and in contrast to previous drug legislation, sponsors actually questioned the utility of a punishment tack. During Senate consideration, Senator Dodd, the bill's primary sponsor, admitted that the "increasingly longer sentences that had been legislated in the past had not shown the expected overall reduction in drug law violations"; adding that his bill's change to the penalty provisions was "to eliminate all mandatory minimum sentences for drug law violations except for a

---

[193] Remarks of Mills, *Congressional Record – House*, September 23, 1970, 116th Congress, September 23, 1970, p. 3316.

[194] *Committee on Ways and Means, U.S. House of Representatives, Controlled Dangerous Substances* (Washington, DC: U.S. Government Printing Office, 1970), p. 201.

[195] Remarks of Boland in *Congressional Record – House*, 116th Congress, September 23, 1970, p. 33316.

special class of professional criminals."[196] While politicians sounded the alarm on spiraling marijuana use among young people, the House actually scaled back federal sentencing for using the drug. Although Congress invoked the panic aroused by baby boomers' drug use, they had a different goal in mind when they put pen to paper in drafting the 1970 act.

That goal was to create a unified and coherent statutory authority for the BNDD, and to erect a review and regulatory system that could anticipate the arrival of new, medically useful but potentially dangerous drugs. While the classification system devised to accomplish this made sense to most, some questioned it. Congressman Van Deerlin of California expressed his discomfort at the whole proposition, surmising that the schedules provided for medically supported addiction to pharmaceuticals but prohibited and punished addiction to older medicinal drugs like heroin. These addictions were separated most meaningfully by who profited from them, and the congressman remained uneasy that drug companies would continue unchecked. "Until some agency tells us how many Americans really have medical reasons for using these drugs," he confessed during a hearing, "I'm afraid we'll be legislating in the dark."[197] BNDD Director Ingersoll responded by insisting that schedules are just based on a "finding of fact," or scientific results that yielded an obvious classification scheme and decisions within it.[198] The neutrality or scientific nature of the schedules was susceptible to some obvious criticism from the start, however, with the government's decision to group marijuana with heroin and other opiates in Schedule 1 (where it remains today). Widespread recreational use of marijuana gave rise to a public perception, and eventually a scientific consensus, that marijuana did not belong in the same class as addictive opiates, despite Ingersoll's and his successors' claims to the contrary.

Other criticism of the proposed reform came from the country's pharmacists, who were suddenly tasked with the implementation of a new regulatory scheme and charged with the responsibility for maintaining it. As their representatives pointed out in hearings, the entire approach imposed rigorous obligations on pharmacists, but very few on drug manufacturers. "Since pharmacists are not, in fact, responsible for major

[196] *Committee on Judiciary, U.S. Senate, Report on S.3246, Controlled Dangerous Substances Act of 1969* (Washington, DC: U.S. Government Printing Office, 1969), p. 2.
[197] *Subcommittee on Public Health and Welfare, Committee on Interstate and Foreign Commerce, U.S. House of Representatives, Hearings on Drug Abuse Control Amendments* (Washington, DC: Government Printing Office, 1970), p. 63.
[198] Ibid., p. 167.

diversion of drugs in illicit channels," their lobbyists argued, "neither they nor the public should be penalized by costly over-burdensome administrative requirements."[199] Here the pharmacists' groups had an undeniable point: there was no question but that the bill was a drug manufacturers' bill. Senator Dodd, for example, had long been associated with those interests. What was more, lobbyists for the pharmacists complained to sympathetic ears in the House that their efforts to testify before the Senate or get their views in front of the administration while it was formulating its recommendations were all in vain. They were completely shut out of the process; "all of our pleas," a representative complained to the House, "fell on deaf ears."[200]

So, while a quota or a cap on dangerous drugs was by far the simplest and most effective control that could be placed on the surfeit of prescription medicine, the idea was never put before Congress as an option. Limiting production would have appointed drug manufacturers as their own regulators, vigilant stewards directing as much of their product through licit channels as possible. Instead, they produced in copious amounts and let the pharmacists answer for themselves. Given the structure of the bill, it is indeed not too much to say that the Controlled Substances Act was one of the most remarkable feats of trade protectionism in modern U.S. history, though rarely recognized as such. For foreign imports – older painkillers like heroin and morphine, or anesthetics like cocaine – U.S. drug manufacturers successfully lobbied what was a tariff into the ultimate embargo: criminal prohibition. It was, after all, ridiculous to argue that heroin had no medical use; it was originally synthesized and produced as a medicine by the drug companies themselves. Nevertheless, after 1970, agricultural opiates would be labeled criminal, completely severed from their medical origin and use. Yet for domestic drugs, like amphetamines and barbiturates, drug companies went unregulated as producers.

This historical amnesia preserved drug manufacturers' profit margins, but, at the same time, it produced an impossible task for the U.S. government: effect a criminal prohibition of an existing and largely underground market. One of the things that spoke to the extraordinary difficulties the government faced, albeit indirectly, was the tendency for enforcement efforts to "cheat" the established boundaries of government power. No-knock authority, successfully passed months earlier in

---

[199] Ibid., p. 362.
[200] Ibid., p. 373.

the District, was also included in the broader legislative package that included the Controlled Substances Act, though several lawmakers expressed serious misgivings about sanctioning this aggressive instrument. Congressman Carter justified no-knock power by admitting that, "[i]t is a great problem, catching people with the narcotics at hand."[201] Such appeals held little in them to persuade Senator Ervin from North Carolina, a great critic of any sort of government encroachment upon civil liberties. Carter and others might deem no-knock authority as necessary, but Ervin responded by quoting William Pitt the Younger's assertion that necessity was the "argument of tyrants, and the creed of slaves." In addition, asset forfeiture, another dubious tool of drug enforcement, was preserved and expanded upon for Schedule 1 substances, even though, as Congressman Kyras allowed, the provision to confiscate cash, cars, or other assets of someone only charged with a crime was in fact "a pretty harsh section."[202]

In addition to these aggressive tools, another sign that the government faced dismal prospects in effecting a criminal prohibition of an existing trade was the fact that representatives of the Treasury Department could barely disguise the futility of its own – or any – interdiction efforts. Treasury Secretary Kennedy shrugged off interdiction as a solution in any final or meaningful sense: "More than 225 million travelers clear Customs entry procedures annually," he told Congress, "and any individual might be concealing drugs on his person."[203] In the end, rid of any narcotic agent to tell them otherwise, Treasury officials readily conceded that drugs were a trade, and a vibrant one. Prohibition might not produce any results at all since, as Assistant Secretary Rossides allowed in testimony, despite impressive seizures, "[t]here is no solid figure as to how much is missed."[204] Even BNDD Director Ingersoll told a House subcommittee that law enforcement can "at best ... only push back."[205] Still, no one was more forthright than James Goddard, former FDA commissioner who returned to testify on the Controlled Substances Act as a lobbyist for the American Public Health Association. When Congressman

[201] Ibid., p. 292.
[202] Ibid., p. 121.
[203] *Committee on Ways and Means, U.S. House of Representatives, Controlled Dangerous Substances* (Washington, DC: U.S. Government Printing Office, 1970), p. 260.
[204] Ibid., p. 265.
[205] *Subcommittee on Public Health and Welfare, Committee on Interstate and Foreign Commerce, U.S. House of Representatives, Hearings on Drug Abuse Control Amendments* (Washington, DC: U.S. Government Printing Office, 1970), p. 83.

Carter asked him, "How does heroin enter this country at the present time?" Goddard responded that "most of it comes in through the channels of commerce, such as shipping and the airlines." The congressman asked a follow-up question: "Haven't we had a transportation explosion in the past few years?" "Yes," the commissioner acknowledged. The congressman may have paused as he reflected on these logical and rather obvious points that were too often absent from the drug debates. Then he remarked, without much apparent investment and more as an aside, "I wonder sometimes if we were wise to have transferred the Bureau of Narcotics from the Treasury Department?"[206]

Those with reservations regarding the 1970 act likely dismissed any doubts by noting the legislation's dramatic effect on sentencing. To distinguish their efforts from previous moral crusades, supporters of the Controlled Substances Act took pains to stress the reduced penalties for possession in the bill, as well as the abolishment of nearly all federal mandatory minimum sentences for drug violations (when reinstated to federal statutes in the 1980s, Americans of all kinds heralded the change as a "drug war," seemingly unaware of the history of mandatory minimums since World War II). Congressmen also mentioned their support for substantial revision of the model state narcotic act, encouraging state legislators to follow suit and reject incarceration for drug possession. Congressman Boland was explicit about this goal when he offered his hope that the Controlled Substances Act "may serve as an example to the States as they reform their own drug abuse laws."[207] In reaching out to the states, federal lawmakers were soliciting a partner that had only become more important over time. After all, in the 1930s, the last time the states considered their drug laws in any kind of systematic fashion, most local or state police had no interest in drug violations and no meaningful ability to detect them. Now, by the early 1970s, policing drug violations was one very significant way in which law enforcement asserted discretionary power in inner cities across the country.

Certain indications might have encouraged congressional leaders in thinking that states would adopt a treatment approach for simple possession charges. By the time the Controlled Substances Act was signed into law, the federal government supported methadone clinics on an unprecedented scale, and several states followed suit. In New York, for example,

---

[206] Ibid., p. 261.
[207] Remarks of Boland in *Congressional Record – House*, 116th Congress, September 23, 1970, p. 33316.

liberal Republican Governor Nelson Rockefeller proposed a budget for 1971–72 that included a $24 million request for methadone programs.[208] Yet, like the federal government, these experiments in the states lacked the same political conviction that punishment could, and would, elicit. In fact it was Governor Rockefeller who led an aggressive effort in the direction of enforcement: in his State of the State address in January 1973, Rockefeller decried the violence stemming from illicit drug consumption and traffic and vowed to set New York on a different path. The governor proposed, and the legislature subsequently passed, severe mandatory minimums for possession and trafficking. These minimum sentences were so draconian and dramatic in their cumulative effects that they forged, in the words of journalist Eric Schlosser, a "prison industrial complex" – an aggregate of interests deeply vested in promoting incarceration, from statehouse politicians, to prison guard unions, and encompassing even the small town economies that depended upon a local prison for employment opportunities.[209]

Other states followed Rockefeller's lead, mostly because, as the governor himself discovered, imprisonment was an emphatic answer to drug markets revived after the temporary interruption of the "French Connection" and, more subtly, an attractive gesture of certainty in a tumultuous time. And, while it was mainly Republicans who advocated "get tough" drug incarceration throughout statehouses in the early 1970s, the strategy was eventually embraced by Democrats as well. In fact, when federal mandatory minimums for drug violations returned in 1986, it was, as Schlosser points out, Democratic Speaker Tip O'Neil who led the charge to reenact them.

Clearly the prohibition and punishment approach of the federal government was discernable well before lawmakers reversed course on sentencing in the 1980s. Responding to the growing outcry over marijuana

---

[208] Albertean Selmore, "A Study of Locus of Control and Self Concept of Methadone Maintenance and Abstinence Clients," MA thesis, Howard University, 1975, available in Moreland Spingarn Research Center, Howard University, Washington, DC. Eric Schneider argues that New York's retreat from treatment began long before: see Eric C. Schneider, *Smack: Heroin and the American City* (Philadelphia: University of Pennsylvania Press, 2008), pp. 131–2.

[209] See Eric Schlosser, "The Prison Industrial Complex," *The Atlantic*, December 1998, http://www.theatlantic.com/magazine/archive/1998/12/the-prison-industrial-complex/4669/ [accessed May 11, 2011]. Ruth Wilson Gilmore, *Golden Gulag: Prisons, Surplus, Crisis, and Opposition in Globalizing California* (Berkeley: University of California Press, 2007); Robert Perkinson, *Texas Tough: The Rise of America's Prison Empire* (New York: Picador, 2010).

use among young people, Nixon resolved to take a tougher approach on illicit drugs as he opened his bid for reelection. In May 1972, President Nixon declared "war" on heroin, promising to use his new Office for Drug Abuse Law Enforcement (ODALE) to disrupt street-level traffic, initiate supply shortages, and drive addicts into treatment. The simultaneous expansion in federally financed methadone clinics underscored the administration's commitment to treatment – as well as its ambivalence regarding such alternative approaches, insofar as this expansion was less touted than militant enforcement strategies during the 1972 campaign season. By the time Nixon declared his "war," his administration had expanded the Bureau of Narcotics and Dangerous drugs from 600 agents to 1,500.[210] Moreover, throughout the reelection campaign, the administration emphasized enforcement over treatment, featuring Myles Ambrose more prominently than Dr. Jaffe. As Ambrose recalled, during one campaign stop the president appeared pensive as he flew over Brooklyn in a helicopter and the discussion turned to treatment. Finally, the president pointed out the window and remarked, "You and I care about treatment. But those people down there, they want those criminals off the street."[211]

Nixon's overwhelming success at the polls in 1972 was construed by him and by others as a mandate to strengthen illicit drug enforcement still further. Accordingly, in July 1973, Nixon collapsed all drug-related offices into the BNDD and rechristened it the Drug Enforcement Administration (DEA), a consolidation that Nixon hoped to use to disrupt both international and street-level traffic. Patricia Rachal argues that the reorganization plan that created the DEA and established the principle of its organizational preeminence was designed to squelch the interagency feuding between the Bureau of Narcotics and Dangerous Drugs and the U.S. Customs Agency, but she joins Mark H. Moore in noting that the bureaucratic incentives following the plan only added to the tensions and made efficient drug control policy even more difficult to achieve.[212] And, while Edward Jay Epstein overstates the case when he argues that the true intent behind the DEA was to create a police and

[210] See Arnold Isaacs, "White House Makes War on Drugs," *Baltimore Sun*, May 14, 1972, p. A1.

[211] Ambrose recollection as quoted in Frontline, http://www.pbs.org/wgbh/pages/frontline/shows/drugs/etc/script.html [accessed May 11, 2011].

[212] Patricia Rachal, *Federal Narcotics Enforcement: Reorganization and Reform* (Boston: Auburn House, 1982), especially chap. 8; Mark H. Moore, "Problems with Reorganization Plan #2"; for more on bureaucratic incentives driving narcotics enforcement, see James Q. Wilson, *The Investigators: Managing FBI and Narcotic Agents* (New York: Basic Books, 1978).

counterintelligence unit under the personal control of Richard Nixon, the politics driving the reorganization were certainly more than just an earnest effort on the part of the presidency to resolve the Customs and Bureau dispute.[213] John Ingersoll rather quickly sensed the base political ambitions motivating the reorganization, as he resigned that same summer when he was passed over as leader of the newly formed agency, a decision he attributed to his unwillingness to "bow to White House pressures."[214] This remark implied that Ingersoll had steadfastly refused to appoint officials favored by the White House, but it may have also meant that Ingersoll refused to use the powers of the DEA as aggressively or in the precise fashion as the president wanted. During this same period of transition, Dr. Jaffe also resigned and his agency was dissolved, transferred to the NIMH and located far outside the beltway, a physical displacement that symbolized the White House's rejection of a treatment approach.

Between 1968 and 1974, the federal budget for enforcement rose from $3 million to $224 million.[215] At the same time, the nation's investment in treatment experienced equally phenomenal growth: from $18 million in 1966, funding reached $350 million by 1975. Yet, by the end of the 1970s, methadone clinics had lost their federal support, supplanted by punitive enforcement at the national level and sustained – as they are to this day – only by miniscule federal funds and private or local support (or both). What is more, Nixon had proposed his reorganization plan and subsequent creation of the DEA in order to forestall a separate plan, put forward by the National Commission on Marijuana (Schafer Commission), which compiled all drug enforcement functions in a "superagency" that would include treatment and rehabilitation programs as well. Clearly, within the administration, a choice in favor of enforcement, and exclusively enforcement, had been made. Reformers had hoped that consolidating all drug enforcement in the Department of Justice and creating a uniform statute would breathe new life into treatment approaches, undermine mandatory sentencing, and sustain an altogether more judicious approach to illicit drug use. Instead, militant enforcement persisted, mostly because of its usefulness as a coercive instrument in negotiating power in new settings, like policing in urban

[213] See Edward Jay Epstein, *Agency of Fear: Opiates and Political Power in America* (New York: GP Putnam, 1977).

[214] "US Cutting Narcotics Treatment Programs," *New York Times*, July 5, 1973, p. 25.

[215] Epstein, *Agency of Fear*, p. 189.

America, and its success in consolidating Nixon's electoral majorities by recruiting so-called white ethnics to the Republican base.[216] Rather than implement a reasoned response, the DEA launched a war. Yet, as the dust settled and the Nixon administration moved decidedly in favor of prohibition and punishment, not even the most disappointed or chagrined drug reformer could guess just how ambitiously the DEA's agents viewed their writ to wage "war" when they looked abroad.

[216] See Flamm, *Law and Order*; and, for more on that strategy more generally, see Skretny and Sugrue, "White Ethnic Strategy," in *Rightward Bound*, Schulman and Zelizer, eds. (Cambridge: Harvard University Press, 2008), pp. 171–92.

6

The Cost of Denial

Vietnam and the Global Diversity of the Drug Trade

Throughout the 1960s and early '70s, the U.S. government adopted a punishment and prohibitive approach to deal with illicit drug consumption. In so doing, lawmakers demonstrated considerable faith in the formal mechanics of governing, as they cobbled together dramatic legislative overhauls, reorganized and added new layers to the federal government, and issued impressive public vows to stem the tide of illicit drug traffic and use. At the same time and in other areas of American life, public confidence in the instruments and institutions of state power declined precipitously, so much so that observers dubbed the country's frustration a "crisis of liberalism," a widespread disillusionment with key tenets supporting the governing coalition that held power for decades by espousing government manipulation of the economy through interest rates and taxes, social policy benefits for special communities, and Cold War containment policies abroad.

By far the most painful reckoning for the country in this unfolding "crisis" was the U.S. government's intervention in South Vietnam, originally undertaken to forestall communist assumption of power that would likely follow reunification with the North. This decade-long military deployment, launched at the height of Camelot idealism and initially presented as a noble cause, soon became a dispiriting stalemate and, finally, an ignominious and costly defeat. No other saga captured the predicament of state power so completely as the agonizing revelations prompted by U.S. intervention in Vietnam: the government had lied to its people, embraced quixotic and convenient beliefs, sent soldiers to die in a war waged with conflicting tactics and without strategic purpose, and caused the suffering and death of tens of thousands of Vietnamese. Unmasked in its brutality and humiliated by withdrawal and defeat, American power stood revealed as fragile and suspect.

A generation of scholars, dubbed the "New Left," accepted this unflattering view of American intervention abroad, using defeat in Vietnam as leverage for a broader critique of American foreign policy since the Civil War.[1] What had been presented and perceived as benevolent and isolated interventions now appeared to these academics to be a pattern of colonial interference marked by racialized dogmas, ignorance, and government-managed propaganda. While still influential among academics, this interpretation has been considerably revised by newer scholarship, much of which follows the lead of Odd Arne Westad, who argues that, while the Americans and Soviets might have construed their confrontations throughout the developing world as a clash between competing worldviews, these preconceived and self-authorizing beliefs obscured the realities on the ground, and it was those prevailing circumstances, not grand Cold War strategy, that played the biggest role in determining the course of events.[2]

Neither this recent shift in the register of analysis nor the post–Vietnam New Left view of American power exercised abroad have had much to say about the difficulty of initiating and sustaining consistent foreign policy commitment from the U.S. government. Intervention and global influence are the starting points of most scholarship on foreign policy; it is, after all, the subject of study. Yet analysis of drug policy tempers this view. A capacious and occasionally troublesome vehicle, foreign drug policy interventions like eradication programs and military aid were tools of engagement that sustained but often complicated the U.S. government's Cold War agenda for the developing world. These programs impinged upon the host country's sovereignty, installed or bolstered unsavory regimes, and in general offered a unilateral and aggressive face of

---

[1] Important works in this body of scholarship include: William Appleman Williams, *The Tragedy of American Diplomacy* (New York: Norton, 2009); Walter Lafeber, *The New Empire: An Interpretation of American Expansion* (Ithaca: Cornell University Press, 1963); Walter L. Hixson, *The Myth of American Diplomacy: National Identity and US Foreign Policy* (New Haven: Yale University Press, 2009). For work that pays specific attention to race as an instrument and code of empire, see Paul A. Kramer, *The Blood of Government: Race, Empire, the United States and Philippines* (Chapel Hill: University of North Carolina Press, 2006); Eric T. L. Love, *Race Over Empire: Racism and US Imperialism, 1865–1900* (Chapel Hill: University of North Carolina Press, 2004).

[2] Odd Arne Westad, *Global Cold War: Third World Interventions and the Making of Our Times* (New York: Cambridge University Press, 2007). An example of a monograph in this vein is Jana K. Lipman, *Guantanamo: A Working-Class History Between Empire Revolution* (Berkeley: University of California Press, 2009).

American power to prospective allies who by and large would have welcomed a more collaborative relationship. Despite these demerits, drug interventions abroad offered one advantage: they provided a pretext for engagement with the developing world that would otherwise be more politically problematic at home.[3] Especially in the late Cold War as well as in our own time, American reluctance to engage the world shaped the manner and the mechanisms by which it would do so.

Initially, drug policy ventures outside the United States offered the hope of remedying the inadequacies of punitive drug policy at home. Over time, illicit drug interventions abroad ratified elements of different presidential agendas. From the modernization theory in vogue during the Kennedy years to the supply-side economics of Ronald Reagan, drug policy was, to various administrations, a "multiplier" in the foreign policy portfolio, a channel through which other agendas were enacted or reinforced, and a bridge to parts of the world outside of obvious implication in the foreign policy purview – albeit, at the same time, an anachronistic expression of confidence in government power that had been otherwise disowned or discredited. The persistent faith in drug policy interventions suggests that their value lay in part in their enduring legitimacy, their ability to survive financial retrenchment and ideological revision, as well as their versatility and adaptability to different ideas and goals.

At home, a drug policy constructed in a cascading fashion and only around certain drugs meant that a supple "drug war" would survive the country's shift from political divisions based on region to those based on residency. City dwellers who purchased heroin in street deals remained the targets of punishment, while other drug users did not always experience even adequate regulation. Abroad, the malleability of the drug war is best discerned in the shift in the basic purpose and tenor of U.S. foreign drug policy: whereas in the 1950s, the U.S. government used drug policy to indict enemies, by the 1960s, drug interventions were designed primarily to shape and to alter alliances. This change reflected upon the broader shift in U.S. foreign policy from the bipolar rivalry that structured foreign

---

[3] Jonathan Marshall tailors this insight more narrowly, arguing that drug policy "served to overcome congressional reluctance to aid foreign security forces ... in their war against left wing guerrilla movements." See Marshall, "Hidden Agendas in the War on Drugs," *OAH Magazine of History* 6, no. 2 (Fall 1991): 30. Daniel Weimer argues that U.S. intervention in the developing world was a consequence, not a cause, of Nixon-era drug policy: see Weimer, *Seeing Drugs: Modernization, Counterinsurgency, and US Narcotics Control in the Third World, 1969–1976* (Kent, OH: Kent State University Press, 2011). Such a view is possible only if one narrows the analysis chronologically, eliminating prior engagement with the developing world (see Chapter 2), and accepts official reasoning at face value.

engagement of the 1950s to a complex portfolio of global engagement executed in a context of dissipating American economic power and military defeats. This complexity underscored rather than undermined the utility of a "foreign drug war," transforming it from a discrete foreign policy objective into a valued collection of tools to manage relations with the developing world.

Significantly, in creating or reconfiguring connections abroad, U.S. drug policy and the larger foreign policy portfolio of which it was a part ultimately facilitated much more illicit drug traffic than it impeded or intercepted. U.S. soldiers' consumption of amphetamines, marijuana, and heroin in South Vietnam exposed this fact in stark terms, and the revelation of in-country drug use and addiction rendered it poignantly tragic.[4] In the end, this was the sense in which U.S. intervention in Vietnam unveiled the truth of American power abroad: not, as New Left scholarship would have it, as an exposition of a mendacious treachery, but a reckoning both with the realities of global influence as well as the damage inflicted by hasty or misguided alliances forged for expedient purposes. American character, presented as good or evil, was much beside the point: it was the practice of power, including the difficulty in justifying such ambitious international engagement to the American people, that mattered most.

INTERNATIONAL TRADE IN ILLICIT DRUGS

Throughout the postwar era, the international drug policy agenda that attracted the most attention, and warranted the greatest investment in the eyes of U.S. government officials, was the effort to enact a single convention governing the production and import of opium (and its derivatives). Success in this endeavor, long the ambition of U.S. Narcotics Commissioner Harry Anslinger, effectively reinstated the original goal of the 1912 International Opium Convention, that of authorizing an international body to regulate international trade in drugs. Ratification of the original convention took place only after Germany signed the treaty in 1919, a task the country performed as a condition of its surrender following World War I. The League of Nations was subsequently charged with implementing the convention, and its actions, in concert with the

---

[4] For a careful and close examination of drug use among soldiers in Vietnam, as well as an examination of the political purposes to which exaggerated claims regarding the extent to which drugs hampered the combat mission were put, see Jeremy Kuzmarov, *The Myth of the Addicted Army: Vietnam and the Modern War on Drugs* (Amherst: University of Massachusetts Press, 2009).

Americans, produced the first and highly imperfect system of controls that eventually drove much of heroin production underground and into the illicit and informal economy.

The obvious failures of the 1912 convention did not detract from American efforts to duplicate it immediately following World War II, using the United Nations as its new vehicle. In large part this was because, despite the convention's inability to reduce or even effectively regulate heroin production and trade, it did create an international regime premised on prohibition – that is, signatories pledged themselves to consumption and regulation of opium as determined only by medical needs. Moreover, countries pledged to amend or create domestic laws that conformed to this overarching goal. Thus, while not successful as trade regulation, the 1912 convention and its latter day efforts of implementation were effective tools to shape the political behavior of participating states, all the more so because they were imposed by a putatively neutral international body and couched in equally neutral terms. The United States, and U.S. Commissioner Harry Anslinger in particular, embraced this secondary and somewhat hidden objective with an uncommon zealotry throughout the 1950s, styling themselves after the 1912 American delegation, which they viewed as willing to chasten traditional European powers for their colonial vices – yet all the while reproducing patterns of domination in a new context, and applied toward a different purpose. Instead of prioritizing the extraction of raw materials, as traditional imperialists did, Americans sought to "nation-build," or influence the political, institutional, and legal settings of a country in a direction they viewed as desirable.

Left to his own devices, Anslinger probably would have preferred that his entire job as narcotics commissioner consist solely of international duties, which he construed as negotiating treaties, hectoring foreign enemies, and conspiring with sympathetic delegations through backchannels and telegrams, a set of tasks that harkened back to Anslinger's first job in government as a foreign service officer. He relished this role so much that when President Kennedy came into office, Anslinger made an impression on the new president – and not a good one – principally as a member of the U.S. delegation to the 1961 UN effort to craft a new "Single Convention," a unified treaty that would replace and abrogate all previous multilateral treaties (there were nine in force at that time). It was not long before tension surfaced between Anslinger's crusading impulses and the more internationalist inclinations of the Kennedy camp. At the heart of the dispute lay the 1953 Opium Protocol, an interim agreement reached by the UN Commission on Narcotics to designate seven opium-producing countries and control the production and trade of the drug via an indirect method of stock allotment, or assigning shares to a country that determined how much opium it could produce or receive. Like all other agreements before it, the protocol was susceptible to any number of schemes of evasion. Yet the Americans embraced it simply because, unlike other agreements, the 1953 protocol actually named the opium-producing countries and restricted licit opium production to only those enumerated countries. For Anslinger and others, it was a promising starting point.

As the 1953 protocol continued to slowly wend its way through the ratification process, planning for a Single Convention began. Anslinger hoped that the convention would adopt the gains he perceived as notable in the 1953 protocol; to the Kennedy administration, especially its reinvigorated State Department, it seemed clear that it would not. Administration officials like Lee White and narcotics advisor Dean Markham preferred a successful UN treaty, one that received endorsement from as many countries as possible, even if it meant a retreat from the 1953 protocol's designation of opium producers and logic of rationing opium based on medical need. Eager to lead a consensus and broadcast the stature of the United States after a series of embarrassments on the international stage, Kennedy officials clashed with Anslinger and his ally, Assistant Treasury Secretary A. Gilmore Flues. "Surely the controls under the Single Convention," State Department officials reasoned during an interdepartmental meeting on the treaty, "no matter how weak they might be, would be preferable to free trade," meaning, preferable to no treaty at all.[5] It would be better to wait for ratification of the 1953 protocol, Anslinger countered, because if the treaty that emerged as the result of UN deliberations were ratified, "it would no longer be possible for the US to dissuade many countries … from authorizing [opium] production" within their borders.[6] Flues could not refrain from a still more pointed critique, speculating that "the Devil himself must have attended the voting on the Single Convention," for only "his influence could have led the delegates" to forge a treaty that made no attempt to limit opium production at the source. The Kennedy administration responded by asking Flues to vacate his post; on a farewell international tour, Flues urged all the countries he visited not to ratify the 1961 convention.[7]

[5] July 19, 1961 Meeting of Interdepartmental Committee, Minutes. Lee C. White File, General File, *John F. Kennedy Library*, Box 11.
[6] Ibid.
[7] Anslinger to RFK, October 5, 1961, Robert F. Kennedy Papers, Attorney General's Files, General Correspondence, *John F. Kennedy Library*, Box 2.

The unceremonious dismissal of Flues and Anslinger suggested that the Kennedy administration looked to silence more traditional voices of foreign policy – men like John Foster Dulles, the acrimonious and occasionally blustering secretary of state who denounced communism as evil but let many competitive advantages, including missile technology, slip to the Soviets. In their stead the Kennedy administration looked to supply a more youthful, robust, and confident engagement with the world. This commitment took many forms, whether it was assistance to the developing world through the Peace Corps or intervention in it by deploying the Green Berets. These projects, both favorites of the Kennedy White House, cultivated an image of elite achievement and virtuosity: recruitment to these programs was highly competitive, and their demands strained even the most talented members. Yet Kennedy and his advisors openly embraced this change. Rather than the brash "ugly American," uneducated and uninterested in the world, Kennedy would send forth idealistic Peace Corps volunteers or Green Berets who could rappel from helicopters, scale mountains, and embark on foreign adventures already conversant in the native tongue.

In the Kennedy swagger many sensed a more sophisticated Cold War agenda, one detached from crusading impulses and better able to make a rational case to the developing world about the superiority of the American system over the Soviets or Chinese. In reality, the president preached a message that was messianic in a different form. Kennedy's UN delegation assented to the 1961 convention, even absent any significant trade controls, because the treaty still retained the potential for nation-building: signatories were obliged to prohibit opium smoking and eating, coca leaf chewing, and cannabis resin smoking. Even more important, parties to the treaty were required to enact punitive domestic legislation for handling illicit drug use; this stricture is often cited today as the reason why certain European countries that tolerate drug use in practice do not enshrine their beliefs in law.

Viable nation-building tools remained in the 1961 convention, and for the Kennedy administration, wielding these tools remained of paramount concern. Their message to the world, while less ideologically colored than Eisenhower's foreign policy, was nevertheless a kind of amoral proselytizing usually presented as a "modernization theory," a delineation of nation-state evolution that would culminate in something akin to the United States, a democratic republic committed in some degree to capitalist principles. For modernization theory's proponents, the tools of statecraft, including whatever pressure could be asserted under international agreements, should be placed in service of guiding development, enticing countries to "advance" to the next stage while rejecting the false promises that the Soviet or Chinese model issued under the banner of collective ownership and proletarian rule.

Kennedy also replaced investment in global treaties with regional agendas and aggressive bilateral engagement. This preference was manifest in drug policy throughout the sixties – albeit only belatedly, as drug trafficking concerns did not assume importance until much later. Be that as it may, Kennedy initiated what would become a pronounced shift in U.S. foreign drug policy throughout the sixties: bilateral action geared toward supply eradication, crop replacement, and interdiction. Significantly, these actions coexisted with an equally pronounced tendency to ignore or downplay illicit drug trafficking by allies or regimes the United States intended to support for other reasons. Hence, while Kennedy and his followers disowned the melodramatic (and false) accusations delivered by Anslinger on the world stage during the 1950s, they inherited the ambivalence already prevalent in the drug policy portfolio. Political expediency, not policy efficacy, would determine the targets and the tone of drug-related foreign policy.

Then as now, one of the most important bilateral relationships the United States maintained, and certainly the single most important when it came to drug policy, was with Mexico. Throughout the postwar era, the American government estimated that Mexico supplied the overwhelming majority of illicit marijuana and much of the heroin in the United States. Disrupting this supply chain seemed to be a simple solution to the increased traffic in illicit drugs, but doing so unilaterally or too forcefully impinged upon Mexican prerogatives. This bothered Anslinger and his allies but little, and during the commissioner's day "suitcase" agents from the United States operated in Mexico with a kind of marauding cowboy spirit.[8] One agent wrote to a Bureau supervisor in 1960 that he located a corporate group called "Paraventures," an organization that was "actually of two men" who parachute into "difficult areas ... for the purpose of getting adventure films." With a check for $25,000 promised, the two were ready to drop into the Sonora mountain areas for a "complete and comprehensive film of the opium field and heroin laboratories of

---

[8] See Ethan A. Nadelmann, *Cops Across Borders: The Internationalization of US Criminal Law Enforcement* (University Park: Pennsylvania State University Press, 1993); William O. Walker, *Drug Control in the Americas* (Albuquerque: University of New Mexico Press, 1981).

Mexico."⁹ This and other flamboyant schemes found a ready home under Anslinger's stewardship and an American foreign policy establishment that was content to approach Mexico with a mixture of disdain and indifference.

Kennedy and his advisors were determined to rid Mexican relations of such obvious transgressions. Unfortunately for the president, his intention to make Mexico a prominent showpiece in his Alliance for Progress, a massive economic and military aid package intended to advance the "modernization" of Latin America, hit a political roadblock: California. Politicians from across the state remained convinced that ineptitude on both sides of the transnational border between California and Mexico resulted in the enormous influx of illicit drugs into their state. Before Kennedy's seminal 1962 conference on narcotics, Lee White confessed that the "Mexican Situation," by which he meant the conversation regarding Mexico's role in drug trafficking, "may be a fairly delicate one." In light of that fact, he instructed Dean Markham to "establish a pretty clear understanding with the California group as to how far they ought to go in raising the issue." White was so apprehensive about it that he added, "[w]e can always threaten to disinvite the Californians if they don't behave themselves."¹⁰ A joint U.S.-Mexican commission emerged as a result of the conference, one comprised of five Americans and two Mexican officials. Not surprisingly, its first move was to request legislation of the Mexican federal government and individual states to control poppy production.

By the time the commission offered this recommendation, U.S. assistance in destroying poppy fields – both the sort that was covert and that which was acknowledged – was well under way. Flamethrowers, helicopters, and other kinds of material assistance were commonplace, as Anslinger's successor, Henry Giordano, acknowledged before the Senate in 1966.¹¹ Nevertheless, the elevation of Anslinger's occasional scheme to burn a poppy field to a multifaceted aid package from the United States designed to do the same more systematically rankled Mexican politicians,

⁹ Howard W. Chappell to George White, DS, February 3, 1960, Record Group 170, Records of the Drug Enforcement Administration, Office of Enforcement Policy Classified Subject Files, 1932–1967, *NARA*, Box 5.
¹⁰ Lee White to Dean F. Markham, August 27, 1962, Dean F. Markham File, *John F. Kennedy Library*, Box 3.
¹¹ *Hearings before Special Subcommittee of the Committee on the Judiciary, US Senate, 89th Congress, January, May, June, July 1966* (Washington, DC: U.S. Government Printing Office, 1966), p. 453.

whose credibility diminished with each transgression of sovereignty. And it was also the case that powerful *traficantes* or Mexican drug lords did not lack for influence and connections to the Mexican political regime, the military, or to law enforcement on both sides of the border.

As the Americans pressed for indictments, Mexico resisted. In the context of increasingly tense relations, Mexican officials eventually insisted on codifying rules of conduct for American narcotic agents operating within their borders. As Maria Celia Toro argues, the government reached this conclusion not in order to invite Drug Enforcement Administration personnel into Mexico, but to control their already disruptive presence.[12] This insistence on deference to Mexican sovereignty squared with other developments regarding its powerful neighbor to the north. Long an acquiescent victim to stolen archeological treasures, in 1969 the Mexican government signed a bilateral treaty with the United States intended to halt the furtive or unscrupulous transfer of ancient national treasures. As political scientist Lyle C. Brown summarized, by the late 1960s and seventies, Mexico had embarked on a concerted campaign to become more forceful in its dealings with the U.S. government.[13]

For Mexico, these departures from traditional power roles, notable though they were, must be measured against a backdrop of greater suspicion between the two countries and a much greater role for the United States in managing the Mexican response to illicit drug production in Mexico. In the case of drugs, Mexican deference to the United States ran distinctly contrary to the direction of the rest of bilateral relations, and it came about as a result of the aggressive maneuvers of the first California politician to be president: Richard M. Nixon. When Nixon and his National Security Advisor (and future Secretary of State) Henry Kissinger authorized negotiations with Mexico in the spring and summer of 1969, their efforts were immediately complicated over the question of indictments of powerful drug lords. Not only was Mexico reluctant to indict – and especially so using U.S. garnered evidence – the criminal justice system of Mexico was so riddled with corruption and inefficiency, no satisfying result could be predicted from any indictment even if it should occur. In response, the Americans began to advocate systematic poppy and marijuana field destruction, formally dubbed "supply eradication."

---

[12] Maria Celia Toro, "The Internationalization of Police: The DEA in Mexico," *Journal of American History* 86, no. 2 (September 1999): 635.

[13] Lyle C. Brown, "Politics of US Mexico Relations: Problems of the 1970s in Historical Perspective," *Contemporary Mexico*, Wilkie et al., eds. (Berkeley: University of California Press, 1976), p. 472.

In this way, the Americans attempted to "leapfrog" over the inadequacies perceived in the Mexican criminal justice system – as well as the deficiencies of their own. Supply eradication offered the hope of producing results despite corrupt foreign governments, and despite the obvious failure of the punishment approach to stem the tide of illicit drug use within the United States. In the late 1960s, liberals often seized upon supply eradication on precisely these grounds: throwing addicts in jails obviously had not worked, so why not burn a poppy field in Mexico (or elsewhere) and see if that did? As one congressman advocating supply eradication noted on the floor of the House, once drugs enter the American market, "it is very difficult to police their distribution"; another colleague agreed, adding his view that policing drugs at home produced "rather poor results."[14] A seemingly easy answer, supply eradication in fact afforded a foreign government a number of opportunities to dodge American intentions if they chose to do so – and Mexico certainly did. As one unidentified source admitted, the Mexican military would select "fields of marijuana and poppies that are no good," either because of drought or water damage or some other reason, "and they burn[ed] that."[15] Once the U.S. government became aware of this scheme, the DEA began to insist upon "American-observed" burns. This in turn led to more elaborate evasions and, more distressing, even greater marijuana production as *traficantes* began to factor in a sacrificial loss of their cash crop in the name of appeasing the Americans.

The event that inaugurated this bilateral political theater came in 1969, when officials in the Nixon administration realized that Mexico would not, and could not, pursue indictments yet, at the same time, they resisted supply eradication on a more significant scale. As summer negotiations between the two countries stalled, a simultaneous drought in Mexico effected a more drastic shortage in marijuana production than could ever be hoped for or imagined by American drug officials. As supply plummeted, street-level prices for Mexican marijuana skyrocketed across the United States. The Americans seized upon the dynamic in play: if supply could be significantly reduced, the price of marijuana would go up, and American consumers – teenagers especially – might be "priced out" of recreational use of marijuana.

This rationale, offered in earnest and, at times, disingenuously, provided a pretext for Nixon's bold move in late September, a massive search

---

[14] Remarks of Conte, *Congressional Record – House*, 116th Congress, June 4, 1970, p. 18381; Remarks of Biaggi, ibid., p. 18413.
[15] Unidentified source in Brown, "Politics of US Mexico Relations," p. 483.

for stowed marijuana known as "Operation Intercept," conducted by U.S. Customs officials on U.S.-bound travelers at thirty-one different U.S.-Mexico border stations spanning more than 2,000 miles. As newspapers declared at the time, Intercept, which commenced on September 21, 1969, was the largest peacetime search and seizure operation performed by civil authorities in American history. This dramatic effort confirms Vernie Oliveiro's observation that the Nixon administration's actions in support of global enterprise cannot be construed as an abdication of national sovereignty – nor, for that matter, did such actions represent an endorsement of globalization as such.[16] Indeed, it is simplistic and historically insupportable to place globalization as diametrically opposed to national power; moreover, it is equally so to suppose that the U.S. government in general, and the Nixon administration in particular, were merely "reactive" to the rising power of international economic forces. To the contrary, the United States occasionally made a concerted effort to alter the nature and the extent of trade reaching its shores. As the most spectacular of these efforts, "Intercept" demonstrated that Nixon officials had seized upon the great structuring truth of drug traffic: illicit drugs were a trade, and hence anything that impeded the movement of goods or people – and Nixon hoped to do both – would, in turn, diminish the flow of drugs into the United States. Nevertheless it was also true that the bulk of the marijuana supply reached the United States by plane and, in order to successfully interdict those kinds of drug runs, the Americans needed a tip-off in advance. As a result, most "intercepts" of marijuana as the result of Nixon's campaign came at the expense of American tourists and day-trippers, not drug couriers, leading one Mexican businessman to liken the searches to "trying to cure cancer with aspirin."[17]

Yet Intercept constituted a critical intervention nonetheless. First, it underscored the difficulty of staffing the border in a fashion periodically suggested, and sometimes flippantly so, by dozens of congressional members as they chastised the Customs Bureau for letting so many people and cars go by without a thorough search. The very day the Nixon administration launched Intercept, traffic along the border snarled and eventually ground to a halt. Bewildered tourists and travelers negotiated six-hour

[16] Oliveiro makes this point in "The United States, Multinational Enterprises, and the Politics of Globalization," in *The Shock of the Global: The 1970s in Perspective*, Ferguson et al., eds. (Cambridge: Harvard University Press, 2010), pp. 143–55.

[17] As quoted in Dial Torgeson, "Border Narcotics Check Backs Autos 3 ½ Miles Into Tijuana," *Los Angeles Times*, September 19, 1969, p. 1; this article described a full-scale dress rehearsal for Operation Intercept, which was inaugurated days later.

waits at the border – and this was only because Intercept demanded that Customs agents search every car for three minutes, instead of just giving each a perfunctory glance and occasional inspection. San Diego's crossing, funneled through sixteen gates, produced sixteen different lines that stretched for miles back into Mexico. Every so often a motorist would lean on his horn in frustration, and other exasperated travelers joined him, breaking the tedium with a blaring chorus of honking. Over long stretches, fumes from the idling cars made some travelers sick, and nauseous drivers who peeled out of the line for a respite raised the suspicions of border guards who pursued them in search of drugs. When use of the car radio or air conditioning exhausted a car battery, its occupants were forced to push the car over the border, a misfortune that happened with enough frequency to entice a line of tow trucks to wait on the U.S. side.[18] All in all, Operation Intercept amounted to a border-crossing nightmare.

The second and more important realization of Intercept's operational legacy was the fact that border life was intertwined and, even more to the point, the two countries were economically interdependent to some appreciable extent. Indeed, enterprising car mechanics were the only ones to find Operation Intercept a boon to their business. Other companies on both sides of the border suffered, especially businesses dependent upon border traffic, like tourist escapes south of the border, or industry and agriculture dependent upon Mexican day-labor on the U.S. side. Because only the U.S. side introduced the delays, it was not long before Mexican citizens expressed resentment over the frivolous searches, and some grew particularly indignant over body searches of females. That the Operation confiscated very little marijuana – something Americans believed attested to Intercept's success, as smugglers "took a vacation" – only added insult to injury for the Mexicans. Critics were quick to compare the increased security to Cold War boundaries, proclaiming a "grass curtain" had descended across the border. Days into the operation, U.S. Customs officials offended Mexican elites when they held (and searched) Mexican Consul General Robert Urrea in El Paso, Texas. By the end of September, Mexican President Gustavo Diaz Ordaz could no longer contain himself and denounced Intercept as a "bureaucratic mistake" that has "raised a wall of suspicion between our two peoples."[19] Still the Americans would not yield.

[18] "William J. Drummond, "Autos and Tempers Boil Over at Check," *Los Angeles Times*, September 22, 1969.
[19] Dave Smith, "Mexican President Calls Searches at Border a 'Mistake,'" *Los Angeles Times*, October 1, 1969, p. 1.

In early October, London columnist Alistair Cooke took a mischievous delight in filing a report on Intercept for readers of *The Guardian*. No significant marijuana had been seized as a result of the operation, he revealed, but plenty of boozy "junketeers" had been caught red-handed upon their return to the United States with a "bracelet of beads and a belch." His satire of American aspirations squared with Mexican perceptions of border traffic. Accordingly, on October 9, Mexican officials announced a plan to "keep sick or doped-up Americans out of Mexico" – their own Operation Intercept, as it were, a retaliatory plan that Mexicans insisted was instead a "public service instituted by the Mexican government for the comfort of the traveler" aimed at keeping "undesirable persons out of Mexico."[20] Mimicking the impersonal bureaucratic jargon of the United States did not disguise Mexican intentions, and it quickly dawned on U.S. officials that many of these drunken fun-seekers would be U.S. military personnel on their way to Tijuana. In the face of such potential embarrassment, the Americans retreated. One day after Mexico outlined its plans to conduct searches, Operation Intercept was called off.

U.S. officials proclaimed Intercept a success: street-level availability of Mexican marijuana had dropped precipitously and, consequently, prices for it went up. After the conclusion of Operation Intercept, sociologist Lawrence Gooberman examined those claims through a series of interviews with drug users in New York City, most of whom reported difficulty in obtaining Mexican marijuana in the summer and early fall of 1969. As Gooberman pointed out, it was unclear how much of this shortage could be attributed to the drought in Mexico versus Operation Intercept, but this ambiguity did not stop Bureau of Narcotics and Dangerous Drugs (BNDD) director John Ingersoll from celebrating the success of Intercept by noting that the price of Mexican marijuana in New York City was $50 to $60 per pound and, by early October, the price had leaped to $350. Ingersoll would have been more circumspect had he placed his measure for success in context: as Gooberman's interviews revealed, most committed marijuana users simply shifted to hashish, the price of which plummeted over the same time period. Sales were brisk, and one young woman who agreed to share her experience with Gooberman expressed her disappointment that he had not had the opportunity to interview her brother, because "he made a fortune last summer selling hash."[21] Others

[20] "Mexicans Plan Own Intercept," *Hartford Courant*, October 10, 1969, p. 8.
[21] As quoted in Lawrence A. Gooberman, *Operation Intercept: The Multiple Consequences of Public Policy* (New York: Pergamon Press, 1974), p. 52.

adopted or increased their use of amphetamines and barbiturates, also plentiful and cheap, and still others tried heroin – a move that led some to depict the agenda of Intercept in conspiratorial terms. "It's in Nixon's interest to have heroin addicts around," one twenty-three-year-old argued, since "someone who uses smack is a slave, not a revolutionary."[22]

To the extent that Intercept was successful at driving the price of marijuana up, then to that same extent the policy was rife with unintended consequences. Nevertheless, Ingersoll was not alone in his praise for the program, nor was he the only drug policy official to consider an interdiction strategy and changes to a single statistical stream in illicit drug price in one city to be evidence of a causal link.[23] But this tenuous connection was also a temporary one, and subsequent events suggested that affecting the price of marijuana was not the principal goal of Operation Intercept after all. The day after the United States announced the end to the program, a new program, "Operation Cooperation," took its place. This bilateral effort instituted more rigorous searches on traffic venturing across the border in both directions, although searches were now confined to those deemed to be "suspicious."[24] The two governments also began a series of high-level negotiations aimed at "securitizing" the border, a process Gooberman referred to as "permanent upgrading of enforcement."[25] On March 11, 1970, talks concluded with a new agreement between the United States and Mexico on the border, and, in exchange for Mexican promises to pursue drug traffickers, the Americans gave $1 million to Mexico for "technical assistance" in supply eradication and promised to abide by certain rules of conduct for DEA agents in Mexico. By no means was this aid for supply eradication a singular event: for many years afterward, foreign aid destined for Mexico, often channeled through the U.S. Agency for International Development (USAID), was designated specifically for illicit drug crop destruction. In many ways, then, the real target of Operation Intercept was the Mexican government, and its success could best be measured in exacting concessions from that government at a time when Mexico sought to disentangle itself from American power and influence.

[22] Ibid., p. 88.
[23] For a critique of this viewpoint, common among drug interdiction proponents, see Charles F. Manksi, et al., *Informing America's Policy on Illegal Drugs: What We Don't Know Keeps Hurting Us* (Washington, DC: National Academies Press, 2001).
[24] Quote used but not attributed in "Crackdown at Border Still Hurts," *Hartford Courant*, November 2, 1969, p. 37A.
[25] Gooberman, *Operation Intercept*, p. 183.

Contentious and contested relations with Mexico damaged diplomatic ties, but surprised no one. Because of the shared border, Mexico's importance in the U.S. foreign policy portfolio was beyond dispute, and occasionally heated exchanges were a normal part of close relations. Yet the drug policy dynamic in play with Mexico repeated itself in other parts of the world, and with more dramatic effect: the Americans would use supply eradication as a cudgel to execute or enforce a particular agenda, especially with an ally that had in some way displeased the United States. This tendency was well under way as early as 1966, when Assistant Secretary of the Treasury David C. Acheson addressed the Central European Nation Treaty Organization (CENTO), an organization whose membership included Turkey, by far the largest producer and conduit of heroin to the European market. The United States acknowledged the difficulty of altering farming practices in the region, Acheson told the group, and realized that "water cannot be made to flow uphill, that people are not perfect and will make a dollar where they can." Yet, Acheson predicted, synthetic drugs would soon displace legal opium and, as a result, the day of a worldwide ban on poppy cultivation did not seem far away. Thus, the secretary argued, it would seem wise to induce farmers to grow another crop, and develop a new income stream, in anticipation of these events. "In the long run," he told the group, "those around this table must solve the farmer's problem" in order to gain any sort of effective control over opium production.[26]

Though he did not single out Turkey by name, Acheson's unusually frank remarks might have been expected to elicit at least some response. Yet a member of the American delegation to the CENTO conference sounded resigned when he observed that the Turkish delegation sat unperturbed, "no different than it has been in similar meetings."[27] The government of Turkey's apparent indifference to American appeals was soon followed by congressional insistence that Turkey's foreign aid be diminished in light of its refusal to prohibit poppy growth. The American Embassy in Ankara, more sensitive to local concerns as well as to the totality of America's relations with this important Central European Cold War ally, placed its objections to an aggressive drug policy agenda on

---

[26] Acheson, May 18, 1966, Record Group 170, Records of the Drug Enforcement Administration, Office of Enforcement Policy Classified Subject Files, 1932–1967, *NARA*, Box 5.

[27] Meyer, Summary of CENTO Conference, May 24, 1966, Record Group 170, Records of the Drug Enforcement Administration, Office of Enforcement Policy Classified Subject Files, 1932–1967, *NARA*, Box 5.

record. Growing anti-American sentiment in the region meant that "any public action by GOT [government of Turkey] on the poppy cultivation program must have every appearance of a 'sovereign' decision." To wit, the ambassador felt it was "counter-productive" to rest American diplomacy on poppy eradication since, by all appearances, the current Turkish government was prepared to do no more than "renew the assurance" of its "willingness to tackle the problem."[28]

Drug policy officials disagreed. John T. Cusack, a Bureau supervisor sent to Turkey in 1967, argued that increased poppy growth in the provinces of Turkey initiated three years prior accounted for the availability of heroin worldwide. What was more, while poppy growth was licensed and regulated by the Turkish government, Cusack estimated that as much as three quarters of the annual crop was diverted into illicit channels. Production and diversion on such a scale, he told the Bureau of Narcotics commissioner, "creates an oversupply even for the illicit market."[29] Formidable though it was, Turkish poppy production resulted from crop yields in only four of its sixty-seven provinces, down from the growth licensed in forty-two provinces as late as 1958. Prime Minister Süleyman Demirel, only the second democratically elected leader of modern Turkey, hoped that the impressive curtailment of authorized provinces would satisfy American demands, but Turkish officials were forced to concede that the remaining authorized provinces were historically the most productive poppy-growing areas – as well as key to the electoral success of Demirel's governing coalition.[30]

As the Americans increased the pressure, they harped on the Single Convention of 1961, which Turkey had signed and ratified in 1966. But, as they discovered throughout the subsequent year, Demirel was content to placate the Americans while stopping short of prohibition. Upon assuming office, Richard Nixon elevated the importance of drug policy in bilateral relations with Turkey, just as he had done with Mexico. In 1969, Nixon sent his special envoy, Daniel Patrick Moynihan, to Turkey to make an offer to buy the entire opium crop for the year. Turkey rejected the offer outright, insisting on the historic role of poppy production in the

[28] January 21, 1967 cable, AmEmbassy, Ankara, to SecState, Washington, found in ibid., Box 10.
[29] Cusack to Giordano, April 11, 1967, Record Group 170, Records of the Drug Enforcement Administration, Office of Enforcement Policy Classified Subject Files, 1932–1967, *NARA*, Box 10.
[30] For a detailed summary, see Nasuh Uslu, *The Turkish American Relationship Between 1947 and 2003: The History of a Distinctive Alliance* (New York: Nova Science, 2003).

region; Demirel reportedly told Moynihan that, even if he accepted the money, he would not be able to find a Turk willing to plow a poppy field under, such was the pride in and national identification with poppy farming.[31] Shortly thereafter, the *New York Times* reported that Congress was considering withholding a $40 million aid package destined for Turkey unless the country banned opium production.[32] When news of this contemplated move reached Turkey, it produced a firestorm of criticism of the United States, already a bitter subject for many Turks who resented U.S. military bases and political interference in their country.

At this delicate stage in Turkish-American relations, Congress initiated its hearings on the Controlled Substances Act of 1970. Legislators could not resist speculating on the potential effectiveness of supply reduction, either through eradication or by paying Turkish farmers to simply grow another crop. Senator Vanik, frustrated with the imperfections of the criminal approach to drug use in the United States, asked former FDA commissioner what, if anything, would "be wrong with taking some more drastic action?"[33] Goddard, equally disillusioned with penalties at home, offered his view that "subsidizing the Turkish farmers not to grow the poppy is probably more effective a solution than trying to keep blockades at each point of entry,"[34] a reference to the brief experiment of "Operation Intercept," concluded only months prior. Weeks later, Attorney General John Mitchell appeared to testify on the Controlled Substances Act before the House Ways and Means Committee, and while there, he gave a somewhat casual approval of economic sanctions targeting nations that did not support a ban on opium production. Turkish Prime Minister Demirel responded with an immediate rebuke: "statements which are not compatible with the sovereignty of states can not be tolerated."[35]

Demirel's refusal to relent to American demands was not confined to the poppy ban. The prime minister also resisted U.S. requests for unfettered

---

[31] Ibid., p. 225.

[32] This explicit and ultimately more systematic form of pressure on allies by threatening foreign aid was also an elevation of an ad hoc tactic deployed by Bureau agents to the level of official policy; for agents' threats to foreign aid, see Nadelmann, *Cops Across Borders*, p. 134.

[33] *Committee on Ways and Means, U.S. House of Representatives, Controlled Dangerous Substances* (Washington, DC: U.S. Government Printing Office, 1970), p. 242.

[34] *Subcommittee on Public Health and Welfare, Committee on Interstate and Foreign Commerce, U.S. House of Representatives, Hearings on Drug Abuse Control Amendments* (Washington, DC: U.S. Government Priniting Office, 1970), p. 261.

[35] In Uslu, *The Turkish American Relationship*, p. 227.

military access to the Dardanelles for U2 spy planes and bases. Because of U.S. displeasure with his regime, most assume that the Americans either tacitly endorsed or actively helped to engineer the bloodless coup against Demirel on March 12, 1971. As the Turkish military moved to assume power from Demirel, the powerful generals installed Nihat Erim to the post of prime minister; five days later, Erim issued his first decree on licensing opium, further restricting its growth. By the end of June, Erim announced a complete opium prohibition to go into effect in the autumn of 1972.

In the interim, Congress had passed the Foreign Assistance Act of 1971. Section 506 of the new law granted the president the power to suspend foreign aid to any country that, according to the president's determination, had failed to take the appropriate steps to counter the illicit narcotic trade. The introduction of this new threshold was designed, as one of its supporters admitted on the floor of the House, to place the "illegal growing of opium poppies in Turkey" under diplomatic pressure.[36]

Yet it also accomplished much more. Congressional debate on the Foreign Assistance Act was lively and diverse: some legislators hoped foreign aid would be abolished altogether, especially in light of inflation in the American economy, while others decried the proposed cut in the amount of aid in the Foreign Assistance Act as short-sighted and indefensible. Detractors on the right generally agreed with the congressman who insisted that "Uncle Sam" had become "Uncle Sugar" to the developing world, and they pointed to the vote recorded the previous day to raise the debt ceiling as evidence that the country could ill afford programs of such largesse.[37] Foreign aid in fact cost the taxpayer very little, supporters of it countered, and since it developed new markets for American exports, it represented a smart investment rather than blind charity. For these legislators, the Foreign Assistance Act did too little: by sanctioning ill-conceived cuts to vital programs of technical assistance, the act discarded a valuable tenet of U.S. power abroad and ceded ground to the Soviet Union in the battle for hearts and minds in the developing world.

---

[36] Remarks of Rodino, *Congressional Record – House*, 116th Congress, June 4, 1970, p. 18379. Robert David Johnson sees the intense debates over the nature and extent of foreign aid in the 1960s as evidence of congressional assertion of legislation powers vis-à-vis the executive; if so, then a drug threshhold may well be read as a reassertion of executive will. See Johnson, *Congress and the Cold War* (New York: Cambridge University Press, 2006), chap. 4.

[37] Quote from Congressman Carter, *Congressional Record – House*, 116th Congress, June 4, 1970, p. 18399.

FIGURE 6.1. The Bureau of Narcotics took this photo of two women harvesting an abundant crop of poppies in Turkey in 1971 in order to persuade lawmakers to endorse policy interventions designed to eradicate the supply of illicit heroin.

"That support for and interest in our foreign aid programs has declined should be clear," one congressman observed, to anyone who inspected the Foreign Assistance Act.[38]

While the act proposed cuts to foreign subsidies, it soon became clear that the question was not one of economizing in difficult times, but rather one of reinforcing U.S. sovereign power and policy preferences in an interdependent and complex world. As critics of the Foreign Assistance Act made clear, cuts to multilateral banks and agencies that were proposed in the bill meant that the United States would lose value for every dollar spent on foreign aid; the whole logic behind international agencies, they argued, was to maximize the value of the money spent by sharing the burden of institutional and operating costs. Yet such efficiencies came at a cost to American control. "Giving aid to friends is one thing," Congressman Rogers of Florida allowed, as he criticized the concept of

[38] Remarks of Conte, ibid., p. 18381.

foreign aid given to the developing world without any regard to U.S. policy objectives.[39] The "drug rider" introduced in the foreign aid bill – and later repeated with other forms of U.S. assistance – allowed at least the perception of a "quid pro quo," as one congressman put it.[40] Defenders of the new language played upon the resentment of unfettered foreign aid in an era of economic retrenchment at home: recipients, Congressman Biaggi claimed, should "not be allowed to accept millions of hard earned American tax dollars" if they "ignore our pleas for assistance" when it comes to illicit drug traffic.[41]

Yet the discretion or "quid pro quo" enabled by such language materialized only inconsistently, and was most often fueled by a desire to criticize or applaud a particular regime irrespective of drug policy. As an independent standard, the drug threshold meant little: it was never applied uniformly, rarely utilized against allies or friendly regimes, and seldom jeopardized aid or assistance that the United States was otherwise eager to give. Hence, capitalizing on growing American reluctance to engage the developing world, policymakers embraced an ostensibly neutral standard that was in fact a tool to augment and execute more forcefully the administration's agenda for the developing world, while, at the same time, placating Americans who were increasingly reluctant to endorse foreign aid packages.

Satisfied with these changes to foreign aid and placated by the Turkish opium ban, Congress, over the next three years, authorized $35 million in loans to Turkey to fund crop substitution. Even if much of this money had made it into the hands of farmers – and it did not – the funds would not have been comparable to the price illicit poppies could fetch for growers on the black market. It was no real surprise, then, that poppy growth continued despite the ban. Yet American officials seemed appeased despite the failures to fully implement the ban, raising questions as to how much the policy was intended to affect opium production and how much it was used to apply pressure to the Turkish government. That government soon came under tremendous pressure from its own people, who were galled by capitulation to American demands, and with elections restoring civilian rule in 1973, the new Turkish government rescinded the ban and resumed poppy growth in seven provinces in 1974. In response, Congress introduced a slew of bills to cut off aid to Turkey

---

[39] Remarks of Rogers, ibid., p. 18391.
[40] Remarks of Long, ibid., p. 18381.
[41] Remarks of Biaggi, ibid., p. 18391.

but, before any could pass, the United States imposed an arms embargo on the country following the Turkish intervention in Cyprus. By the time the Americans resumed normal relations with Turkey, poppy production had been brought under much tighter regulatory control – so much so, in fact, that the United States would rely on it as a source of licit narcotics whenever its own stockpile was low.

The U.S. government emerged from its struggle with Turkish opium production with new tools to pressure for its agenda, as well as a more militant and emphatic view of drug policy as a component to U.S. power in the world. "We are at war," Assistant Secretary of Treasury Eugene Rossides concluded in 1971, shortly after the military coup in Turkey. "If the Turks refuse to go along with us in this crusade against heroin," he elaborated, "we have to consider them enemies rather than allies."[42] This more assertive stance was buttressed by the BNDD's international expansion. From 1969 to 1971, the Bureau increased its foreign offices from thirteen to twenty-eight. As the Bureau's director, John Ingersoll, extracted his agents from street-level policing in the United States, and he deployed more resources abroad, refocusing the agency's mission by shifting its capabilities.

These priorities matched those of the White House. First and foremost, the president embraced his newfound discretion in dispensing foreign aid. In a statement before the International Narcotics Control Conference in September 1972, President Nixon informed the assembled diplomats that he was now "required by statute to suspend all American economic and military assistance" to any country that contributed, in his judgment, to illicit drug traffic in the United States and, he assured the group, he would "not hesitate to comply fully and promptly with this statute."[43] What was more, shortly after the Turkish opium ban, Nixon decided that opium production and the growing of poppies should be prohibited anywhere and everywhere. The president reached this startling conclusion in part because the medical need for opiates would soon be satisfied by synthetic replacements, the market dominance of which, he was assured, was imminent and inevitable. When one State Department official informed Nixon that the elimination of poppies could have "dire" and "unforeseen" consequences, his views were summarily dismissed. "If we cannot foresee the

[42] As quoted in Edward Jay Epstein, "The Incredible War Against Poppies," *Washington Post*, December 22, 1974, p. B1.

[43] Adam Raphael, "Nixon Warns Drug Producers that Aid May be Stopped," *The Guardian*, September 19, 1972, p. 2.

consequences," one White House official responded, then "why presume they will be 'dire'?"[44]

With no successful synthetic engineered to replace it, the narcotic stockpile of the United States dwindled. By 1974, the United States was forced to solicit allies, including the prodigal Turkish government, for more opium production. The rediscovered utility of licit opium production was underscored, in the minds of American officials, by the revelation that illicit production could shift location, and sometimes dramatically so. When American diplomats approached Turkish officials for opium in the mid-1970s, they no longer considered Asia Minor to be the world's reprobate source of illicit opium. That dubious distinction had passed to Southeast Asia, where the United States had waged a war beginning in 1964.

Surely no postwar foreign policy goal had been more belabored or conspicuous than U.S. support of anti-communism efforts abroad; under this preeminent doctrine, the United States deployed forces in support of South Vietnam. By the same token, no aspect or consequence of American power in the postwar world had been more disguised or disavowed than the enormous influx of illicit drugs into the United States; trade and contact with the world proliferated, and illicit drug traffic rose accordingly. The collision of the announced and deeply espoused worldview of the United States with the realities of American power, especially illicit drug use among U.S. soldiers, meant that when the United States deployed troops to South Vietnam, it would face off against more than just enemies while there.

VIETNAM

Until the late 1960s, any observer of U.S. drug policy in Southeast Asia would have concluded that, in terms of illicit traffic, Thailand posed the biggest problem to the United States. Certainly it claimed the lion's share of attention from the Bureau of Narcotics – as well as its successor agency, the Bureau of Narcotics and Dangerous Drugs. As in other parts of the world, agents stationed in Bangkok suggested that Thai police receive training in the United States at the hands of the Bureau; they were discouraged by Thailand's refusal to prohibit opium smoking; and, throughout the 1950s and early 1960s, narcotic agents sought to implicate the People's Republic of China in the illicit drug trade of Thailand.

---

[44] As quoted in Epstein, "The Incredible War Against Poppies."

In 1962, for example, Bureau agents expressed their frustration with a U.S. Custom's agent working undercover in Thailand by noting his inexperience, best reflected in his omission of "the position of Red China in relation to Thailand traffic" in his official cables.[45]

And any observer of American influence in Southeast Asia more generally would have concluded during the same time that Laos, not South Vietnam, concerned Washington the most. Since parts of Laos included the Golden Triangle, a flourishing bed of poppy growing and refinement run by expelled Kuomintang (KMT) Chinese military command, U.S. diplomats kept a close eye on opium in the country. As early as 1959, the State Department inquired whether Bureau of Narcotic officials would be willing to classify Laos as an opium-producing country under international protocols – that is, as a country authorized to legally grow and export opium or derivatives. Bureau officials refused, offering their sympathy for any proposal "for aiding Laos," but citing the need to reduce – not expand – the number of countries officially permitted to produce opium legally.[46] The request itself and the reluctance to refuse it signaled that the Americans were aware that non-Communists – namely, the scattered forces of Chiang-Kai Shek's Republican military – were behind much of the opium production in the Golden Triangle, and that the Americans were prepared to support it, insofar as money from opium helped establish the power of those same leaders in Laos.

But in fact it was neither Thailand nor Laos that would come to preoccupy American officials throughout the 1960s and seventies; it was South Vietnam, a small country created by the 1954 Geneva Accord that encompassed Cochinchina, the southernmost province of ancient Vietnam and home to the country's largest city, Saigon, as well as the southern portion of Annam – dividing these from northern Annam and Tonkin, the northernmost province, which together became the country of North Vietnam. Whereas North Vietnam immediately rallied behind the Communist leadership of nationalist Ho Chi Minh, South Vietnam suffered through a ruling crisis, as the emperor struggled to maintain power and various factions vied to claim succession or carve out their fiefdom. From the chaos, Ngo Dinh Diệm emerged as a figure akin to

---

[45] Unsigned Memorandum regarding work of Vizzini, November 19, 1962, Record Group 170, Records of the Drug Enforcement Administration, Office of Enforcement Policy Classified Subject Files, 1932–1967, *NARA*, Box 12.

[46] A. L. Tennyson, Chief Counsel, September 4, 1959, Memorandum for the File, Record Group 170, Records of the Drug Enforcement Administration, Office of Enforcement Policy Classified Subject Files, 1932–1967, *NARA*, Box 10.

Chiang Kai-shek in China during the 1920s: a leader with viable patriotic credentials who demonstrated a deft skill at either disposing of warlords or striking efficient bargains with them. While the Geneva agreement dictated that an election be held to unite both North and South Vietnam under one governing regime in 1956, the Americans were content to encourage Diệm to shirk this obligation and establish the idea of an independent South Vietnam instead. They were even more impressed by his subsequent campaign against political rivals outside the bastion of his support in Saigon; doubtless some of the strongmen he defeated had close ties to opium production in the Golden Triangle, and doubtless Diệm's ruling base of bureaucrats in Saigon did as well. Like Chiang Kai-shek more than a decade before, the fact that Diệm was, to the Americans, the most palatable among the political options available did not mean that he was without corruption, or without ties to drug traffic.[47]

Totally unwilling to accept a divided Vietnam, Ho Chi Minh responded by activating the "sleeper cells" of fighters that he had positioned throughout South Vietnam before the partition, a move that was also in violation of the Geneva Accords. This band of largely rural fighters referred to themselves as the National Liberation Front (NLF), but became known, disparagingly, as Viet Cong or VC. Diệm's difficult battle against this guerilla army or "enemy within," begun in earnest in 1960, elicited greater and greater amounts of anxiety and support from the United States. As American dollars and military advisors flowed into South Vietnam, journalists followed, and they soon began filing stories detailing corruption in the Diệm regime, notably its harsh tactics in dealing with Buddhist monks and religious iconography. As criticism of the Diệm regime mounted, a distressed President Kennedy endorsed a coup against Diệm, even though the regime was not noticeably different than strongmen the United States had supported in the past (like Chiang Kai-shek) and would again in the future. Regardless, the successful coup resulted in the assassination of Diệm and his brother, and the horrifying image of their bloodied corpses relayed all over the world preoccupied American officials, until the shocking assassination of President Kennedy only weeks later pushed South Vietnam and its troubles off of the front page and, for the moment, out of the American mind.

Kennedy's successor, Lyndon Johnson, chose to view the fighting in South Vietnam with a kind of determined optimism, believing that the

[47] For a reassessment of Ngo Dinh Diệm, see Ed Miller, "War Stories: The Taylor-Buzzanco Debate and How We Think About the Vietnam War," *Journal of Vietnamese Studies*, 2006.

commitment of more U.S. military strength and economic support to the various regimes that followed Diệm would, at the very least, stave off a communist takeover of South Vietnam, if not vanquish the NLF. American confidence was fueled in part by their contempt for the fighting forces of South Vietnam, which they viewed as corrupt and incompetent. Any U.S.-directed fighting force would perform better, or so they presumed. As the U.S. military arrived in significant numbers, its leaders naturally assumed more and more autonomy for its operations and, implicitly, greater responsibility for the conduct and direction of the war. As the conflict in South Vietnam "Americanized," U.S. officials took a greater interest in illicit drug traffic in that country.

Since Diệm's drive against his opponents in 1957, it had been apparent to American officials that some of the defeated forces "evacuated" their men and their opium-refining equipment to Laos to set up new operations.[48] As major opium traffickers fled in the wake of Diệm's success, the remaining opium circulating in Vietnam was, in the words of one State Department official, "destined for local consumption," either for medicinal reasons, or because there were a considerable number of people who, according to this same diplomat, "still enjoy a good smoke."[49] Importantly, although this knowledge passed through the Bureau of Narcotic's channels, none of it was authored or embraced by narcotic officials. Instead, narcotic agents crafted a narrative according to a familiar script, recasting only some of the characters: illicit drug traffic in Vietnam was the result of Communist agents, whether it be the government of North Vietnam, "Viet Cong" in the south, or even the People's Republic of China. Eager to establish the authority of this interpretation, Gilmore Flues wrote to Commissioner Anslinger in 1961 that, when South Vietnam captured NLF operators with opium in hand, it proved that narcotics were being used "by the communists of North Vietnam as the capital needed for their subversive work," and, moreover, this was another "piece of evidence to fit into our proposition that the communist governments of the Far East are using narcotics as a means of supporting their agents."[50]

[48] William H. McKeldin, ICA, Philippines, to Walter E. O'Brien, Treasury Representative, AmEmbassy, Hong Kong, September 16, 1957, Record Group 170, Records of the Drug Enforcement Administration, Office of Enforcement Policy Classified Subject Files, 1932–1967, *NARA*, Box 10.

[49] Robert E. Barbour, American Consul, Hue, Vietnam, to Department of State, October 17, 1957, Record Group 170, ibid.

[50] Flues to Angslinger, December 1, 1961, ibid.

Despite the Bureau's enthusiasm for this particular version of opium traffic in South Vietnam, information to the contrary continued to come to the agency. Even one of its own agents wrote to the Bureau in 1965 that, while agents stationed in Southeast Asia had "some reports to the effect of Viet Cong infiltrators carr[ying] small quantities of opium for bartering purposes to sustain themselves" – much in the same way as Korean migrants had done more than ten years before – they had "no information" that the "Viet Cong had any program" of trafficking in opium in any systematic sense.[51] This more qualified view was reinforced by the Bureau's old bureaucratic nemesis, the U.S. Customs Agency, agents of which reported in no uncertain terms that the majority of opium traffic from the area originated in Laos, that it had the support of the Laotian government and the U.S. Army, and that it was very often flown in to South Vietnam – including, embarrassingly enough, on American-financed airlines, like Air MeKong.[52]

Still, the Bureau clung to the morality play it had established during the Korean War, and for similar reasons. According to the official remarks of the Bureau, American soldiers were not taking drugs as an act of free will, or an expression of boredom or despair. They were instead the victims of a conniving enemy.[53] As U.S. troop deployment approached the half million mark, Bureau agents worried that the "prospects of our military servicemen providing an increasing market for Viet Cong opium is good." In asserting that the opium trade was in the hands of the NLF, the Bureau district supervisor, along with other Bureau officials, turned a largely unacknowledged but vital fact of the war into evidence: that is, since the NLF controlled the countryside in South Vietnam, it was impossible to imagine opium traffic reaching Saigon without their assistance. In an attempt to account for the fact that the opium trade clearly benefited from the support of South Vietnamese officials throughout Saigon, the Bureau's man put forward an awkward construction: "I cannot concede that the Viet Cong are not involved in the opium traffic," he demurred, and concluded that "corrupt South Vietnamese military officials are in collusion with the Viet Cong" in order to deliver and profit from opium

---

[51] John R. Enright to District Supervisor Taylor, Thailand, November 30, 1965, ibid.

[52] Walter J. Pardian, U.S. Customs Agent, to Commissioner of Customs, June 11, 1963, ibid., Box 7.

[53] This narrative is an unacknowledged but important predecessor to the political purposes that U.S. soldiers' drug use would later be put: see Kuzmarov, *The Myth of the Addicted Army.*

in Saigon.[54] When pressed to follow up these charges days later, the supervisor grew more adamant. "Unquestionably the Viet Cong are engaged in the opium traffic," he contended, "since they control 90 percent of the countryside in South Vietnam." If U.S. military command did not agree with this view, then, the supervisor explained, it is only because they were "in a position to withhold information concerning the narcotic traffic if it conflicts with their objectives and best interest."[55] In other words, there was no way to sketch NLF drug dealing without also implicating the South Vietnamese government in the cities or without conceding that the countryside was firmly in the hands of the enemy. If it occurred to the supervisor, or to Commissioner Giordano, who received these reports, that the traffic was almost entirely in the hands of the South Vietnamese government, then that thought went unaddressed in the Bureau's formal assessments.

The military, on the other hand, could not afford to engage in distorted views regarding the sources of illicit drug use among American soldiers in South Vietnam. Initially, the Military Assistance Command, Vietnam (MACV) learned of drug use among soldiers as an issue of recreational use, and sometimes addiction to, synthetic drugs – a problem that the military, like the country, was slow to apprehend. Prescription-only dispensation of addictive synthetics came late to the military, and the chief pharmacist for the Pentagon complained as early as 1949 that the pharmacies of the Armed Forces did not operate on a "professional basis." In some posts, he told sympathetic officials in the Food and Drug Administration (FDA), doctors directed patients to "the post exchange and buy this, that, or other drugs which in civilian channels would be dispensed on prescription only."[56] Loose and even unauthorized circulation of synthetic drugs on military bases continued despite efforts to the contrary, and in 1955 the president of the California State Board of Pharmacy wrote to the secretary of defense to inform him that "some preparations and devices restricted to sale on prescription only, by rulings of the Federal Drug Administration, are being sold in some military

---

[54] Taylor to Giordano, January 28, 1966, Record Group 170, Records of the Drug Enforcement Administration, Office of Enforcement Policy Classified Subject Files, 1932–1967, *NARA*, Box 10.

[55] Taylor to Giordano, February 1, 1966, ibid.

[56] Memorandum of Telephone Conversation, February 16, 1949, C. E. Hilts, Chief Pharmacist, Pentagon, A. G. Murray, RG 88 Records of the Food and Drug Administration, Division of General Services, General Subject Files, 1938–1974, *NARA*, Box 1184.

installations without restriction. It is my understanding," he added, perhaps to console the secretary, "that some sales are being made other than by authorized military personnel."[57]

Thus, when Senator Burdick acknowledged in 1966 that his subcommittee of the judiciary had been "aware of the drug problem in the armed forces for several years," he referred primarily to abuse of synthetic drugs.[58] The problem was put before Burdick's subcommittee as pertaining to South Vietnam by an ex-Marine and self-professed recovering addict who testified under the pseudonym of "Frank." The one thing he wanted to stress, "Frank" told the legislators, was "how easy it is for a serviceman to cop," meaning to buy drugs. A soldier stationed in South Vietnam could get "the drugs out of the infirmaries," as well as off the base; "Frank" underscored especially the ease of obtaining amphetamines in Da Nang.[59] Historian Nicolas Rasmussen confirms that the military doled out impressive amounts of amphetamines to its soldiers. According to official records, the army and navy together averaged 30–40 5mg Dexedrine pills per soldier per year in Vietnam, enough, Rasmussen writes, "for an inexperienced soldier to stay moderately high for a couple of weeks."[60] In addition to licit use, French-made amphetamines were easy to come by in the black market. One medical survey concluded that, although 3.2 percent of U.S. soldiers arriving in South Vietnam could already be considered heavy amphetamine users, 5.2 percent could be classified as such after one year in action.[61] As the armed forces dosed soldiers with amphetamines intended to boost morale, combat fatigue, and sharpen their senses on patrol, bouts of paranoia sometimes ended in tragic incidents of friendly fire. But these episodes were so infrequent, and so indistinguishable from other chaotic encounters, that no responsible speculation can attempt to account for them.

Army medics who failed to take note of amphetamine use on any consistent basis did sometimes gauge soldiers' use of barbiturates, which the military did not dispense to soldiers as indiscriminately as it did

---

[57] Floyd N. Heffron, Executive Secretary, California State Board of Pharmacy, to Charles E. Wilson, Secretary of Defense, January 11, 1955, RG 88 Records of the Food and Drug Administration, Division of General Services, General Subject Files, 1938–1974, *NARA*, Box 1994.

[58] *Hearings before Special Subcommittee of the Committee on the Judiciary, US Senate, 89th Congress, January, May, June, July 1966* (Washington, DC: U.S. Government Printing Office, 1966), p. 472.

[59] Ibid., p. 481.

[60] Rasmussen, *On Speed*, p. 190.

[61] Summary from ibid., pp. 190–91.

amphetamines. One doctor stationed with the First Cavalry Division observed in his monthly medical report that drugs had been a particular problem in the previous month; whereas before, the division averaged two "serious drug abuse cases per month," suddenly he confronted twenty-two cases of barbiturate abuse.[62] This discovery aroused concern from him and other medical staff stationed in Vietnam, given the potential for lethal overdose when barbiturates were combined with alcohol.

This report may have also caused concern in the medical command of the U.S. Army in Vietnam (USARV), because, although monthly reports were meticulous in detail, discussing anything from rodent infestation to the worrying skin and foot diseases common in monsoon season, they rarely mentioned drug use or abuse at all. This was true even after drug use had become an acknowledged fact of deployment in South Vietnam. In all likelihood, medical staff serving in South Vietnam felt the same way as doctors in the United States did: that it was not their obligation to expose patients to disciplinary proceedings by revealing illicit drug consumption to authorities. Hence even secondary indications were well concealed by medical staff.[63] Although a military history of medical service in Vietnam conceded that the "marked increase in illicit drug abuse" in the late stages of the Vietnam War resulted in "an apparent increased incidence of serum hepatitis," monthly medical reports filed with command attributed hepatitis infections to the drinking of local Vietnamese soda or "eating off the local economy" more generally.[64] One doctor alluded to the possibility of another potential source of infection when he observed that four of the eight cases of hepatitis recorded that month "occurred two to four weeks after R and R trips to Hong Kong, Taipei and Tokyo."[65] This suggestive chronology seemed to be the extent to which medical staff were willing to go to assess, in any official capacity, the problem of drug abuse among U.S. soldiers in South Vietnam.

[62] July 28, 1969, Command Health Report for June 1969, RG 112, Records of the Office of the Surgeon General (Army), Command Health Reports for US Army Units in Vietnam, *NARA*, Box 2.

[63] Kuzmarov argues that military psychiatrists, on the other hand, offered an accurate view of drug use by soldiers, though their involvement dates mainly from 1970 onward: see Kuzmarov, *The Myth of the Addicted Army*, chap. 1.

[64] RG 112, Records of the Office of the Surgeon General (Army), Manuscript and Background Materials on the History of Medical Support of the US Army in Vietnam, 1965–1970, Box 1, "Overview," p. 16, *NARA*.

[65] "Command Health Report for December 1969," p. 13, RG 112, Records of the Office of the Surgeon General (Army), Command Health Reports for US Army Units in Vietnam, *NARA*, Box 2.

Thus the revelation that U.S. soldiers in South Vietnam abused drugs in appreciable numbers came from outside the medical personnel stationed there to treat them. In fact, the "discovery" of illicit drug use among soldiers came from outside the military entirely, and its notoriety seemed to hinge entirely upon the use of one drug: heroin. Early in the fall of 1970, news outlets began to report a dramatic increase in heroin use among U.S. soldiers. By the end of October, a "secret" investigation under way in Congress began to leak information to the press. GIs wrote to Senator Dodd of Connecticut, in charge of the inquiry, to confess their fears that the spiraling use of heroin would jeopardize missions and their own safety. Someday a wounded soldier will yell for a medic, one soldier wrote, only to find that the "medic will be too 'stoned' to help."[66] Historian Jeremy Kuzmarov has given much critical attention to precisely this kind of anecdote, arguing that, to the extent heroin and other drugs were used by soldiers in South Vietnam, this use was largely recreational and did not hamper combat effectiveness in any noticeable way.[67] Yet glimpses of addiction stoked the fears of Americans at home: two months after the Dodd hearings, many Americans read the widely reported story of the Vietnam War veteran who returned home to West Virginia shortly before Christmas and confessed his heroin habit to his mother in the middle of the night as he suffered through withdrawal. "Lots of guys [in Vietnam] are on it," he told his mother; "Officers, enlisted men, lots of them." A few hours later, after his mother returned to sleep, the young man killed himself.[68]

Stories of heroin use continued to circulate as journalists who went abroad to cover the war could not help but notice the drug culture that had sprung up in or immediately adjacent to American base camps. These "scag alleys," wrote one reporter, sold heroin to soldiers for as little as $5, an attractive deal, he mused, for those looking to "keep at bay for a day or so the irritations of military discipline, the boredom of routine jobs, or the anxieties of combat patrols."[69] Another reporter denounced the South Vietnamese government for maintaining a building on a U.S. base, dubbed the "White House," that sold heroin to soldiers directly.

[66] Jack Anderson, "Heroin Endangers GIs Out of Combat," *Washington Post and Times Herald*, October 28, 1970, p. D35.
[67] Kuzmarov, *The Myth of the Addicted Army* passim.
[68] "Viet Veteran Admits Addiction, Kills Self," *Los Angeles Times*, December 20, 1970, p. 4.
[69] Tom Huckley, "It's Always a Dead End On Scag Alley," *New York Times*, June 6, 1971, p. E1.

Military police or other authorities were barred entry because the facility belonged to the Republic of Vietnam (RVN). That same year, NBC news ran a series of reports detailing the ease with which soldiers could obtain heroin, and charged the military with total indifference to the heroin epidemic that was fast taking hold of U.S. soldiers in South Vietnam. A tone of anger and indignation was detectable in all of these stories, whether aroused by the callous profiteering of the South Vietnamese government at the expense of the American soldiers sent to defend it, or the U.S. military's own willingness to ignore or minimize the problem. As Jeremy Kuzmarov points out, media stories, especially of heroin use by U.S. soldiers in Vietnam, became a narrative by which critics of the war could implicitly question its conduct and success, castigating military command for its failures in a way that raised more fundamental questions about the war itself.

While Congress had been aware of – and fairly subdued about – the abuse of synthetics among soldiers in Vietnam, and nearly everyone was aware of and often sympathetic to soldiers' widespread use of marijuana, accusations of heroin use incited an immediate reaction. Congressmen Morgan Murphy and Robert Steele investigated the issue, and reported back to their colleagues that a soldier stationed in South Vietnam was more likely to become a heroin addict than a combat casualty. Senator Dodd excoriated the government of South Vietnam for permitting soldiers in "opium dens," which, as the U.S. military quickly pointed out, were strictly off limits to U.S. personnel. Actually soldiers usually purchased drugs, including heroin, on the black market around a base camp or in urban settings; they went to bars or massage parlors, not opium dens. Just as often, as the military soon discovered, Vietnamese personnel who helped to staff U.S. military bases – especially the cleaning staff, or "hootch maids" – would act as couriers. In this confused transaction across cultures, a drug deal was often made in which, as military investigators found, a dealer did not always know what he or she was selling, and a soldier almost never knew what he or she was buying.[70] When Vietnamese locals noticed that soldiers seemed willing to buy cocaine, they sold heroin to them and simply called it cocaine. Since the staggering purity of heroin available to soldiers – upwards of 95 percent pure, as opposed to the 6 percent purity averaged in a street deal in the United

---

[70] November 8, 1970, RG 472, Records of the US Forces in Southeast Asia, HQ, Military Assistance Command Vietnam (MACV), Provost Marshal, Drug Suppression Division, General Records, *NARA*, Box 1.

States – allowed heroin to be smoked or sniffed instead of injected, there was no reliable and obvious indicator to identify a drug to a buyer. Many soldiers were surprised to discover they had consumed heroin at all, and many experienced no pangs of physical addiction because, among other things, smoking or snorting heroin does not expose a soldier to the same "high" as injecting or mainlining it. So, when soldiers were under the impression they were buying marijuana, they sometimes bought joints laced with an opiate; when purchasing "cocaine" and snorting it, they were actually using heroin. Without any physical craving after the fact, they were none the wiser.

Be that as it may, revelations of heroin use on or around American bases fueled a sense of public outrage and indignation. While support for the war wavered and periodically crested, even staunch supporters of the war condemned the military for its poor care of American soldiers. At times the military's indifference seemed to approach callousness: since the military never performed toxicology tests on corpses of American soldiers prior to August 1970, the command in Vietnam could not even furnish any statistics on how many soldiers had died from illicit drug use before that time. And certainly there were some casualties. "In '68," one veteran recalled, "the Army would swear that there was no one in Vietnam using heroin, but there were all kinds of guys using it," he insisted, including himself. Like others, he traded military-issued food for heroin from Vietnamese families, many of which had a household stash for medicinal use.[71] For these soldiers who were deployed early in the Vietnam War, there are only stories of heroin use, but no statistics.

When heroin use came to light in 1970, appalled members of Congress demanded action. But MACV's response was improvised according to standard military practice and, as a result, it was slower to come than Congress would have liked. Rather than commit to one strategy, the military tested different versions of a treatment approach at the unit level and encouraged the services to devise their own preferred strategy. The army instructed ten of its units to establish "halfway" houses, and gave soldiers who voluntarily submitted to treatment there an amnesty from the disciplinary action that normally would accompany an admission of illicit drug use.[72] Fourth Infantry unit, for example, assured its members that any soldier addicted to illicit drugs could "turn himself in to the

---

[71] Peter Osnos, "Two Veterans Give Details of Drug Use, Attempts to Quit," *Washington Post Times Herald,* April 24, 1973, p. A16.
[72] Huckley, "It's Always a Dead End On Scag Alley," p. E1.

authorities without risk of prosecution." Following counsel from the medical, religious, and legal staff, he would then be awarded a "guardian" who would be "willing to provide emotional support and guidance and whom the individual trusts."[73] Here Fourth Infantry sought to replicate the model of Alcoholics Anonymous and its offspring groups, relying on the stewardship of an assigned mentor – though, presumably, not one struggling with addiction himself.

By the time the military sanctioned treatment outreach on a broader scale, it had already resolved to focus its message on prevention and, as command stated it, put the emphases on reaching the "young soldier."[74] Service members with a movie night in store soon found drug education movies like "Hang Up" and "Trip to Where?" in the film rotation.[75] Every member of the military stationed in South Vietnam received some version of an educational pamphlet, like the one that described "Operation Janus," a brigade-level treatment and amnesty program that was pitched to soldiers in a colloquial fashion. "We want everyone to realize that you just can't compare scag," a slang word for heroin, "to grass" (marijuana), Brigade leaders noted, a distinction that seemed to all but sanction recreational use of the latter. Anyone addicted to heroin would be given one opportunity for treatment, but, should that soldier fail to stay clean, then, as Operation Janus outreach put it, "we just can't afford to have a dude like that in the Brigade." "To sum it up," the pamphlet concluded, the plan had four steps: "(1) going to lay down a true rap about drugs in Nam, (2) find out who is using the hard stuff, (3) help men who are strung out to get down and stay down, and (4) get rid of the ones that won't come down and stay down."[76]

Though rare, some members of the army were willing to go on the record regarding its casual approach to marijuana use among soldiers. "We are after heroin," one lieutenant colonel acknowledged; "our only

---

[73] September 30, 1969 Command Health Report for August 1969, RG 112, Records of the Office of the Surgeon General (Army), Command Health Reports for US Army Units in Vietnam, *NARA*, Box 2.

[74] May 20, 1971, "Drug Abuse Briefing," p. 13, RG 472, Records of the US Forces in Southeast Asia, HQ, Military Assistance Command Vietnam (MACV), Provost Marshal, Drug Suppression Division, General Records, *NARA*, Box 2.

[75] January 3, 1970. Command Health Report for October 1969, RG 112, Records of the Office of the Surgeon General (Army), Command Health Reports for US Army Units in Vietnam, *NARA*, Box 2.

[76] RG 472, Records of the US Forces in Southeast Asia, HQ, Military Assistance Command Vietnam (MACV), Provost Marshal, Drug Suppression Division, General Records, *NARA*, Box 2.

mention of marihuana is that it is illegal."[77] Yet the military services varied in their respective responses to drug use, and not just in terms of how they assessed the dangers posed by different drugs. The Marine Corps, for instance, did not indicate tolerance for any drug; moreover, the service offered no amnesty to its soldiers whatsoever. Instead, they assigned a corporal to talk to all of their men stationed in South Vietnam: "We let him grow his hair a little longer," one Marine commander explained, adding that the corporal also had "a muscular appearance, which we think helps make this approach fairly effective."[78] This informal gambit was acceptable only because of the comparatively small deployment of Marines to South Vietnam; others would require a more sustained and serious effort. In total, MACV assigned 1,800 personnel to drug education, a formidable investment, even though, in all likelihood, only a small percentage of that figure was comprised of personnel assigned exclusively to drug education.[79]

It is difficult to assess the success of the military's prevention outreach efforts. Preliminary surveys of soldiers stationed in South Vietnam revealed that 5–10 percent had used heroin at least once; these figures remained fairly constant for the rest of the deployment, and were revised upward only after the truce in 1973. On the other hand, the amnesty program was, in the eyes of military command, a resounding success. MACV reported that by the summer of 1971, more than 14,000 servicemen had availed themselves of the treatment option under the amnesty program.[80] This was especially welcome to command in light of the clear indications that the military was using the amnesty program to cultivate intelligence on the sources of illicit drug supply in South Vietnam. In a sense, the entire amnesty invitation was designed to produce a robust network of confidential informants, using essentially the same promise made to confidential informants in the United States: leniency. In exchange for treatment,

[77] Minutes of Drug Suppression Council meeting, p. 6, February 25, 1971, RG 472, Records of the US Forces in Southeast Asia, HQ, Military Assistance Command Vietnam (MACV), Provost Marshal, Drug Suppression Division, General Records, *NARA*, Box 2.

[78] Minutes of Drug Suppression Council meeting, p. 7, February 25, 1971, RG 472, Records of the US Forces in Southeast Asia, HQ, Military Assistance Command Vietnam (MACV), Provost Marshal, Drug Suppression Division, General Records, *NARA*, Box 2.

[79] Found in Hearing Before Subcommittee on Drug Abuse in the Military, Committee on Armed Services, US Senate, 92nd Congress (Washington, DC: U.S. Government Printing Office, 1971), p. 269.

[80] AmEmbassy in Saigon to Dept of State, September 7, 1971, RG 472, Records of the US Forces in Southeast Asia, HQ, Military Assistance Command Vietnam (MACV), Provost Marshal, Drug Suppression Division, General Records, *NARA*, Box 2.

soldiers revealed how they obtained drugs. Using such information as it gathered, MACV was prepared to move aggressively. General Abrams, successor to General Westmoreland as head of MACV, increased inspections of vehicles and pedestrian traffic coming in and out of U.S. military bases. He installed a military-run customs unit to inspect Army Post Office (APO) mail, a frequent conduit of drugs at the retail or individual-use level. Abrams also extended the ambit of "off limits" designation to include Vietnamese pharmacies along with opium dens; in one instance, he declared an entire village (Tan Sa Chau Hamlet) off-limits because of its notorious reputation for supplying U.S. troops with drugs.[81]

One of the most aggressive responses to drug use among soldiers in Vietnam was also the most puzzling: despite the strong suggestion that the military condoned marijuana use among soldiers, MACV authorized a series of low-flying helicopter sorties to identify and eradicate marijuana fields across the Delta, the main marijuana-growing region in South Vietnam. As was true for similar combat missions, the U.S. military's forays into the jungle or the hinterland incurred many unintended costs, as one drug official in MACV reminded command. Although the helicopter program had identified and destroyed nearly a half million marijuana plants in just three months, the officer wrote in a report, the missions frightened cattle and upset farmers; what was worse, the marijuana offense rate among American soldiers continued to climb in spite of eradication.[82] MACV responded with a telegram that dismissed the problems encountered on missions: "Unforeseen exigencies," the message read, would be "understood."[83] What was perhaps unforeseen to command was that, in response to helicopter missions, marijuana growers would begin to "hide" their crop by growing it in small batches surrounded by other crops. By September 1970, MACV called for an end to the program. "When the program was first started in 1969," the command observed, "the fields were easy to locate. However, this year the fields are well hidden." What was more, the military was suddenly much

[81] AmEmbassy in Saigon to Dept of State, September 7, 1971, RG 472, Records of the US Forces in Southeast Asia, HQ, Military Assistance Command Vietnam (MACV), Provost Marshal, Drug Suppression Division, General Records, *NARA*, Box 2.

[82] Warren Metzner, RG 472, Records of the US Forces in Southeast Asia, HQ, Military Assistance Command Vietnam (MACV), Provost Marshal, Drug Suppression Division, General Records, *NARA*, Box 1. Original document says "clumb" instead of climb.

[83] Frank Bartimo to BG Smith. RG 472, Records of the US Forces in Southeast Asia, HQ, Military Assistance Command Vietnam (MACV), Provost Marshal, Drug Suppression Division, General Records, *NARA*, Box 1.

more sensitive to the damage such missions inflicted on farmers. Flying at low levels resulted in damage to homes and crops, as well as "stampeded water buffalo, and drowned ducklings."[84] In the end, these "undesirable effects" outweighed the now minimal gains of the program.

Deterred from pursuing eradication, MACV concentrated on the more immediate and engrossing task at hand: collaboration with the government of South Vietnam. It did not take long for military command to surmise that both the government (or RVN in military correspondence, short for Republic of Vietnam) and the military (or ARVN, Army of the Republic of Vietnam) conducted much of the trade in illicit drugs. Already by 1965, the USAID directed its public safety division to invest in South Vietnamese policing, successfully forming a narcotics bureau within the National Police Headquarters in Saigon, one that, Americans hoped, was isolated from corruption.[85] In the following years, the Bureau posted impressive arrest numbers for violations of drug laws. In 1967, police arrested 1,159; in 1968, 1,500; by 1969, they arrested almost 3,000 and, in the first nine months of 1970, police arrested 3,265.[86] But, as the Americans knew, these numbers meant little. Arrests were capricious, for minor infractions or for nothing at all, and meant only a short stay in jail. The prosecuting magistrate of the judiciary branch had no real capability to follow up on arrests, even after it formed its own Narcotics Bureau in 1968.

Unlike other countries with weak or non-existent laws on drug violations, South Vietnam did not lack for statutory authority. But, as MACV commanders noted, while the government had "adequate drug laws," they were "not enforced well."[87] The U.S. military could not conceal its frustration at the RVN's refusal to investigate and imprison wholesale traffickers. "No investigative unit currently exists in RVN to concentrate

---

[84] Confidential telegram from CINCPAC, September 22, 1970, RG 472, Records of the US Forces in Southeast Asia, HQ, Military Assistance Command Vietnam (MACV), Provost Marshal, Drug Suppression Division, General Records, *NARA*, Box 1.

[85] Office of Assistant Chief of Staff, CORDS, PSD Support of Narcotics Control, May 6, 1972, RG 472, Records of the US Forces in Southeast Asia, HQ, Military Assistance Command Vietnam (MACV), Provost Marshal, Drug Suppression Division, General Records, *NARA*, Box 3.

[86] Peter Slusar, Acting Provost Marshal, December 24, 1970, RG 472, Records of the US Forces in Southeast Asia, HQ, Military Assistance Command Vietnam (MACV), Provost Marshal, Drug Suppression Division, General Records, *NARA*, Box 1.

[87] Minutes of the Irregular Practices Committee Hearing, p. 2, March 3, 1971, RG 472, Records of the US Forces in Southeast Asia, HQ, Military Assistance Command Vietnam (MACV), Provost Marshal, Drug Suppression Division, General Records, *NARA*, Box 2.

solely on locating and eradicating large-scale illicit drug operations," one American military official complained.[88] At another U.S. military briefing, MACV's own investigators concluded that high-level police work would be the only strategy to meaningfully curtail the flow of drugs into South Vietnam and the hands of American soldiers. Such work would require "the dedicated support of a well trained local police agency," the briefers acknowledged. "Unfortunately," they added, "Vietnam does not have such a police agency."[89] Naturally the Americans despaired of help from the government or military in South Vietnam: "To date," one report filed in September 1970 read, investigations had shown that drug traffic was "controlled by RVN civilians," and that they were "aided and abetted by transportation facilities from ARVN."[90]

Thus, the myriad efforts undertaken by MACV in response to U.S. soldiers' use of drugs in South Vietnam stalled for want of political will. The Americans could not get very far without South Vietnam, yet in all other respects the Americans remained deeply invested in propping up the succession of Saigon regimes that followed Diệm's ouster. It did not take much prodding for President Richard Nixon to wade into the breach: in fact, reports of U.S. soldiers' addiction to heroin in South Vietnam spurred his commitment to reinvigorate treatment options at home under the leadership of Dr. Jerome Jaffe and DC's Narcotic Treatment Administration leader, Dr. Bob DuPont, and became the public focal point of his "war on drugs." Jeremy Kuzmarov argues that Nixon accepted the dire forecasts of U.S. soldiers' heroin use precisely because he hoped to execute a more forceful "war on drugs." If so, then it is also true that Nixon initially focused his efforts regarding U.S. soldiers on treatment, an obvious duty of the federal government, given the longstanding commitment to care for soldiers coming home from war, especially those who returned wounded.[91] As had been the case in other wars, this obligation was sometimes articulated as a fear of the havoc veterans might wreak on civilian life. The story of one Vietnam War veteran who returned to Utah, became

---

[88] November 8, 1970. RG 472, Records of the US Forces in Southeast Asia, HQ, Military Assistance Command Vietnam (MACV), Provost Marshal, Drug Suppression Division, General Records, *NARA*, Box 1.

[89] May 20, 1971, "Drug Abuse Briefing," p. 8. RG 472, Records of the US Forces in Southeast Asia, HQ, Military Assistance Command Vietnam (MACV), Provost Marshal, Drug Suppression Division, General Records, *NARA*, Box 2.

[90] Colonel John Borders, to CINCPAC, September 1970, RG 472, Records of the US Forces in Southeast Asia, HQ, Military Assistance Command Vietnam (MACV), Provost Marshal, Drug Suppression Division, General Records, *NARA*, Box 1.

[91] See Kathleen J. Frydl, *The GI Bill* (New York: Cambridge University Press, 2009).

a heroin dealer, and successfully peddled narcotics to teenagers stoked these fears. "If President Nixon releases 75,000 such addicted trained killers on our ill-equipped cities," Dr. Julianne Densen-Gerber, executive director of Odyssey House, said when citing the example, "he will be destroying our youth and our whole way of life."[92]

Jerome Jaffe embraced the call to assist the military with his characteristic vigor. Like others before and after him, he hoped that programs and policies crafted for the military might yield benefits beyond the confines of the armed services; namely, in this case, that his work with MACV might lead to, as he put it to the Senate, "developing better ways of dealing with drug abuse in our civilian life."[93] His primary contribution to the crisis in South Vietnam was to help formulate and implement a massive mandatory urine-testing program for soldiers as they completed their tour and prepared to muster-out and return home. In order to "come home clean," as the military urged its soldiers to do, all soldiers scheduled to depart South Vietnam had to submit to urine testing beginning June 22, 1971. If a person was drug-free for five days, the test would register a negative result and require no follow-up, allowing the soldier to return home. If positive, then the soldier was detained for a week of detox.

Months later, Nixon demanded that the military do more than just "dry out" a soldier. Accordingly, the military began the practice of directing soldiers who tested positive to a military base or VA hospital located near his hometown of record for an extended treatment program. Because of the thousands upon thousands of soldiers required to take the urine test, the program produced the biggest boon in the history of urinalysis – and, in that sense, Jaffe's program did indeed affect drug policy at home. In the wake of Jaffe's success, large employers in the United States adopted urine-testing as a method to screen prospective employees for drug use.[94]

Once the system of urinalysis testing was perfected – and this was no easy task – the military rallied behind the program. It shrewdly offered soldiers a powerful inducement to stay drug-free for at least a small window of time, if they had not been so already: a return trip home.

[92] As quoted in James M. Markham, "Odyssey House Director Favors Compulsory Curing of Addicts," *New York Times*, January 11, 1972, p. 28.
[93] Jaffe, *Hearing Before Subcommittee on Drug Abuse in the Military, Committee on Armed Services, US Senate, 92nd Congress* (Washington, DC: U.S. Government Printing Office, 1971), p. 169.
[94] Michael Getler, "GIs Urine Tests Produce Lab Boom," *Washington Post*, September 13, 1971, p. A2.

FIGURE 6.2. Drug reformers hoped that the comprehensive rehabilitation programs they designed for U.S. soldiers addicted to heroin while on active duty in South Vietnam would one day be replicated at home; instead, the most enduring legacy tied to their efforts was the refinement of large-scale urinalysis testing. Here, a technician works on military samples in a Drug Abuse Detection Lab in Germany (1973).

Jaffe's plan also placed the responsibility of treatment on the military's shoulders and the military's dime, but not without a cost. Soldiers certainly received care under the plan, but they were given discharge papers marked with a special "spin number" (384) after they tested positive for drugs.[95] Senator Hughes of Iowa, a recovering alcoholic whose struggles were well known and who was placed in charge of the subcommittee with oversight over the program, belabored the potential damage this could do to a veteran's employment prospects. In hearings with the Department of Defense, he noted that "many employers insist on seeing a veteran's discharge papers." Assistant Secretary of Defense for Health Dr. Wilbur was nonchalant in response: "Apparently this bothers you more than it

---

[95] Falco and Pekkanen, "The Abuse of Drug Abuse," *Washington Post*, p. B1.

bothers me."[96] Wilbur claimed that the ability to glean prior drug use from discharge papers was not significantly different from an employer being informed about a job applicant's medical status in other ways, and he denied that such information would deter employers from hiring discharged veterans. But the military command knew differently, and openly advertised the fact that drug offenses in the military would "close many doors to desirable jobs" in the drug prevention literature distributed to soldiers in South Vietnam.[97]

Just as troubling to the senator was the surge in administrative discharges that came on the heels of the testing and treatment program. All of the armed services discharged more soldiers administratively and with drug "spin numbers" in 1971 than they had done in 1970.[98] Hughes took military leaders to task, wondering out loud if these 5,800 discharges, ostensibly performed in the name of infractions other than drug use – which, owing to Title V of the Draft Extension Act of 1971, the military was compelled to treat – were simply drug discharges by another name. Did military command scrutinize the records of difficult rehabilitation cases for other infractions that could warrant a discharge? "This is a good way to dump the guy without any treatment," the senator reasoned.[99] No racial profile was kept on this subset of discharges, but civil rights advocates at home claimed to discern a racial bias in administrative or dishonorable discharges. The military responded that these discharges ought to be seen in the context of some 40,000 drug infractions that same year; if anything, this validated the senator's concern that the military identified hardcore addicts and discharged them under any possible pretext. Evidence from military records suggests that the senator's suspicions were not without cause. One colonel in Vietnam complained early in 1971 that it simply was not "fair to the straight man to allow junkies to get 'honorables,'" a sentiment that suggested "junkies" would receive something other than honorable discharges.[100] Another lieutenant

---

[96] Hughes and Wilbur, *Hearing before Subcommittee on Drug Abuse in the Military, Committee on Armed Services, US Senate, 92nd Congress* (Washington, DC: U.S. Government Printing Office, 1971), pp. 50–51.

[97] RG 112, Records of the Office of the Surgeon General (Army), General Subject Files, 1960–1969, *NARA*, Box 53.

[98] See *Hearing before Subcommittee on Drug Abuse in the Military, Committee on Armed Services, US Senate, 92nd Congress* (Washington, DC: U.S. Government Printing Office, 1971).

[99] Ibid., p. 177.

[100] Colonel Oltmeyer, Minutes of Drug Suppression Council meeting, February 25, 1971, p. 8. RG 472, Records of the US Forces in Southeast Asia, HQ, Military Assistance

colonel in charge of a recovery center admitted that his facility was powerless when it came to the "'hard core' addicts."[101]

Instead of confronting the complexity of opiate addiction, the military, by all appearances, chose to marginalize and perhaps jettison the most intractable instances of it. MACV's directive to conduct urine tests and rehabilitate soldiers was, one general insisted, "preventive," with the treatment component as secondary to the expected deterrent effects that delaying discharge would have on soldiers who had to undergo urine-testing.[102] In fact, the military seemed vested in distinguishing the drug use in its midst from the "riff-raff" of addicts that the Bureau of Narcotics had depicted and derided for decades back in the United States. Assistant Secretary of Defense Wilbur told the Senate that there could be "no question but that much of the usage in Vietnam is a much more casual type than what we are accustomed to seeing here in this country."[103] At the same time, and in a contradictory fashion, the military also suggested that most soldiers who admitted to or were found using drugs in Vietnam brought the habit with them. It was not the military's fault, military leaders insisted; the draft, including the vast student deferment built into it, meant that the "riff-raff" were issued serial tags. Accordingly, the army predicted a decline in drug use with Nixon's drawdown of U.S. forces because the remaining soldiers "will be more careerist personnel in advisory positions," with fewer young soldiers, and more serious in their devotion to the military.[104]

Instead, the opposite happened. A year after the military acknowledged illicit drug use among soldiers and launched its multipronged approach

Command Vietnam (MACV), Provost Marshal, Drug Suppression Division, General Records, *NARA*, Box 2. This remark also foreshadowed the military's blaming the "drug-addled drafted soldier" for defeat in Vietnam: see Kuzmarov, *The Myth of the Addicted Army.*

[101] Minutes of Drug Suppression Council meeting, February 25, 1971, p. 3, RG 472, Records of the US Forces in Southeast Asia, HQ, Military Assistance Command Vietnam (MACV), Provost Marshal, Drug Suppression Division, General Records, *NARA*, Box 2.

[102] General Greene, Minutes of Drug Suppression Council meeting, February 25, 1971, p. 5. RG 472, Records of the US Forces in Southeast Asia, HQ, Military Assistance Command Vietnam (MACV), Provost Marshal, Drug Suppression Division, General Records, *NARA*, Box 2.

[103] Wilbur in *Hearing before Subcommittee on Drug Abuse in the Military, Committee on Armed Services, US Senate, 92nd Congress* (Washington, DC: U.S. Government Printing Office, 1971), p. 36.

[104] Brigadier General Gard, *Hearing before Subcommittee on Drug Abuse in the Military, Committee on Armed Services, US Senate, 92nd Congress* (Washington, DC: U.S.Government Printing Office, 1971), p. 212.

to suppress it, commanders admitted that the problem appeared to be getting worse.[105] Following the Nixon administration's intervention of treatment and testing, the military still felt that the combined efforts had "not done the job." A frustrated command began to take a more disciplinary and in some ways self-critical view: "It is difficult to imagine that drug abuse could be as widespread as it apparently is if our officers and NCOs were doing their jobs and looking after their men."[106] Still more frustrating to the military was the toll that troop withdrawal took on drug suppression efforts. Reduction in forces had resulted in the disbanding of investigative and inspection units; consequently, the rate of drug offenses rose as troop strength declined. The military attributed this to, among other things, "a phenomenon of statistics," wherein every drug infraction was measured against a smaller denominator, thus yielding a more impressive rate. Yet, as the author of the same memorandum was careful to note, another reason drug offenses may have continued was because, as U.S. troop withdrawal proceeded, the remaining soldiers became "more concentrated in heavily populated areas, where drugs are more readily available."[107]

And this is precisely what happened, as the military knew from its investigations. As one colonel reported in 1971, an estimated "40–50 percent of the troops are using or have experimented with illicit drugs" in South Vietnam, and moreover, "an estimated 5–10 percent of US troops are using [heroin], though its use before 1969," he insisted, "was rare."[108] Heroin began to reach South Vietnam via ARVN networks or air courier from the "Golden Triangle" in formidable quantities beginning in 1970, and U.S. soldiers' use of heroin rose accordingly. Once the network was established, it flourished in the chaos of war and eroding government authority in South Vietnam. A military doctor running a treatment

[105] "In fact, the problem appears to be increasing instead of lessening," p. 2. Minutes of Drug Suppression Council meeting, February 25, 1971, RG 472, Records of the US Forces in Southeast Asia, HQ, Military Assistance Command Vietnam (MACV), Provost Marshal, Drug Suppression Division, General Records, *NARA*, Box 2.

[106] Talking paper, contextually dated as late 1971, RG 472, Records of the US Forces in Southeast Asia, HQ, Military Assistance Command Vietnam (MACV), Provost Marshal, Drug Suppression Division, General Records, *NARA*, Box 2.

[107] September 26, 1972, Memorandum, RG 472, Records of the US Forces in Southeast Asia, HQ, Military Assistance Command Vietnam (MACV), Provost Marshal, Drug Suppression Division, General Records, *NARA*, Box 3.

[108] Minutes of the Irregular Practices Committee Hearing, March 3, 1971, p. 1. RG 472, Records of the US Forces in Southeast Asia, HQ, Military Assistance Command Vietnam (MACV), Provost Marshal, Drug Suppression Division, General Records, *NARA*, Box 2.

facility estimated that "about 60%" of the military's heroin users "have started in country," and "approximately 20–30% were using in the States of which 7–8% are seriously strung out."[109] Subsequent surveys and incident reports revealed that the military's public contention that it had drafted its drug problem was viable for marijuana, but not heroin. Of the 15 percent of military drug users who claimed to start their habit in South Vietnam, anywhere from 9.8 percent of this percentage, up to 11.6 percent (depending upon the reporting period), made this claim as users of heroin.[110] By an overwhelming figure, the illicit drugs most soldiers used was marijuana; to the extent heroin was used, well over half of those users began consuming heroin in South Vietnam.

The military found that most of those arrested for drug infractions or who admitted to drug use in surveys were white, young (18–21 years of age), and in the army.[111] While the rate of whites who used drugs peaked at 88 percent of all users, once heroin was widely available in South Vietnam, that number dipped to 72–77 percent, suggesting that African American soldiers were increasingly likely to experiment with or use heroin. "The average user is a 20 year old high school graduate," a military officer in charge of a treatment facility observed. "We don't find a racial background difference," he added, "but it is more difficult to get a black man to participate in the program."[112] Starting in 1969, the military processed 8,446 illegal drug possession charges for soldiers stationed in Vietnam (up from 4,352 in 1968); by 1970, that figure rose to 11,058, and in 1971, it totaled 11,134 – an unusually high number of drug infractions given the reduction in forces that had taken place in the interim.[113]

[109] Minutes of Drug Suppression Council meeting, February 25, 1971, p. 4. RG 472, Records of the US Forces in Southeast Asia, HQ, Military Assistance Command Vietnam (MACV), Provost Marshal, Drug Suppression Division, General Records, *NARA*, Box 2.

[110] May 20, 1971, "Drug Abuse Briefing," RG 472, Records of the US Forces in Southeast Asia, HQ, Military Assistance Command Vietnam (MACV), Provost Marshal, Drug Suppression Division, General Records, *NARA*, Box 2.

[111] Ibid.

[112] Minutes of Drug Suppression Council meeting, February 25, 1971, RG 472, Records of the US Forces in Southeast Asia, HQ, Military Assistance Command Vietnam (MACV), Provost Marshal, Drug Suppression Division, General Records, *NARA*, Box 2.

[113] First three figures from June 15, 1971, Magnitude of Drug Problem, RG 472, Records of the US Forces in Southeast Asia, HQ, Military Assistance Command Vietnam (MACV), Provost Marshal, Drug Suppression Division, General Records, *NARA*, Box 2; final figure from Briefing, RG 472, Records of the US Forces in Southeast Asia, HQ, Military Assistance Command Vietnam (MACV), Provost Marshal, Drug Suppression Division, General Records, *NARA*, Box 3.

There was no denying that heroin was plentiful and cheap on the streets of Saigon and throughout South Vietnam. The military disregarded the now-dated suggestions from the Bureau of Narcotics that the drug came from the NLF. "There are currently no confirmed indications," military commanders acknowledged in an internal briefing, "that the enemy (VC) are or have been involved in a strategic basis with drug trafficking."[114] In fact, MACV had its own sense of trafficking networks. Much of the production from the Golden Triangle, they learned, was "destined for Saigon." It arrived, commanders described at the same briefing, "aboard military or commercial air flights (including Royal Air Laos and Air Vietnam) often by or in collusion with the crew."[115] Few were aware that the Central Intelligence Agency (CIA) took an active role in supporting this drug traffic, but probably many informed observers supposed that traffic on this scale and with this degree of official complicity must have had some sort of tacit (if not active) American approval.[116]

What the military was slower to apprehend was the extent to which the Triangle had become a major source of illicit heroin in the United States, supplying an estimated one-fourth to one-third of the market by 1972.[117] In June of that year, a young doctoral student at Yale named Alfred McCoy shared some of the findings of his project, "The Politics of Heroin in Southeast Asia," with a Senate subcommittee. Southeast Asia was a major source of heroin to the United States, McCoy asserted, and the government of South Vietnam was complicit in the drug traffic. Although the State Department rebutted some of McCoy's specific assertions, by that time, the Bureau of Narcotics and Dangerous Drugs had given up the ghost. BNDD Director John Ingersoll, busy investing more of his organization's resources in international intelligence and interdiction, informed Congress that between 700 to 1,000 tons of opium were produced in Southeast Asia, roughly half of all opium in the world. What was more, Americans served as middlemen in the traffic networks. Ex-servicemen returned to Saigon to broker new agreements with drug

---

[114] May 20, 1971, "Drug Abuse Briefing,"p. 9. RG 472, Records of the US Forces in Southeast Asia, HQ, Military Assistance Command Vietnam (MACV), Provost Marshal, Drug Suppression Division, General Records, NARA, Box 2.

[115] May 20, 1971, "Drug Abuse Briefing," RG 472, Records of the US Forces in Southeast Asia, HQ, Military Assistance Command Vietnam (MACV), Provost Marshal, Drug Suppression Division, General Records, NARA, Box 2.

[116] Alfred McCoy, *The Politics of Heroin: CIA Complicity in the Gobal Drug Trade* (New York: Lawrence Hill Books, 1991).

[117] Estimate in Senator McGovern, Letter to the Editor, *Washington Post Times Herald*, September 30, 1972, p. A18.

producers, Ingersoll revealed to the Senate, sometimes negotiating deals directly with wholesalers.[118] In response to this new network, the director placed pressure on Thailand and Laos to create drug enforcement agencies and punish trafficking, just as he and the Bureau had done elsewhere. The "potential significance" of their agreement to do so, Ingersoll told Congress, "may be said to be on a par with the recent breakthrough in negotiations with the Turkish Government."[119] This remark was truer than Ingersoll could know: the two nation-building efforts resembled each other most in their negligible long-term effects. Where the Americans pressed for agencies and laws, heroin production and distribution networks adapted and proved resilient against, if not impervious to, the challenges posed by enforcement.

In reciting the BNDD's reformulated views on drug trafficking in Asia, Director Ingersoll distanced himself from the distortions and fabrications of his predecessors. If his agency was to be tasked with curtailing international illicit drug traffic, then, Ingersoll reasoned, his information certainly needed to be much more credible. On the other hand, as a somewhat nonplussed Senator Hughes listened to Ingersoll's testimony, he could not help but seek clarification. Just as Ingersoll was set to leave the hearing, Hughes addressed him in a disarmingly personal fashion. "John," he said at the end of the briefing, "you did not mention China, and maybe I should not at this point." What of all the stories of communist conspiracies? "Previously," the Senator from Iowa reminded Ingersoll, "China was mentioned in testimony before my subcommittee." The director seemed unwilling to disown more than two decades of Bureau accusations any more than he had already done. Maybe Communist China was trafficking in drugs, Ingersoll shrugged, but admitted that he had no indication that it was, nor did he consider it a major priority for the agency.[120]

Enemies, it seemed, could not be blamed for everything. In this and other ways, the perspective on illicit drug traffic and consumption, as well as the purposes of enforcement, had changed during the war. Soldiers who served early tours of duty in Vietnam left behind an America where drugs

---

[118] The most famous dealer who did was Frank Lucas, subject of the film *American Gangster*, and Marc Jacobson, *The Return of Superfly*, New York Magazine, http://nymag.com/nymetro/news/people/features/3649/ [accessed April 27, 2012].

[119] Ingersoll, *Hearing before Subcommittee on Drug Abuse in the Military, Committee on Armed Services, US Senate, 92nd Congress* (Washington, DC: U.S. Government Printing Office, 1971), p. 249.

[120] Ingersoll and Hughes, *Hearing before Subcommittee on Drug Abuse in the Military, Committee on Armed Services, US Senate, 92nd Congress* (Washington, DC: U.S. Government Printing Office, 1971), p. 263.

were regulated by the Treasury Department under the taxing power, and police made few drug arrests. While American soldiers fended off the climactic Tet Offensive in the winter of 1968, Lyndon Johnson prepared to accept a commission's report on criminal justice that noted, among other things, that half of all arrests in the United States were executed for public drunkenness, disorderly conduct, vagrancy, gambling, and "minor sexual deviations."[121] By the time the final platoons returned to the United States from South Vietnam, the discretionary power of law enforcement had shifted from disorder arrests to drug offenses, which police were now far better equipped and motivated to enforce. When the plane delivering the last living American prisoner of war held in North Vietnam landed in March 1973, New York Governor Nelson Rockefeller's decision to bolster the drug enforcement regime by mandating sentencing for drug possession was only weeks old, and Nixon's decision to combine the street-level enforcement performed by the White House Office of Drug Abuse Law Enforcement with the BNDD to form the new Drug Enforcement Administration was only weeks away. The federal government, now fully divested of a taxing scheme to regulate illicit drugs, possessed both the statutes and the institutions to effect a punitive and prohibitive drug regime. For all these dramatic changes, it was not too much to say that soldiers who fought in one war came home to another.

Like U.S. intervention in South Vietnam, the drug war derived its legitimacy in part from the fact that its costs were selectively imposed; not everyone served. A small number of veterans, however, would get caught in them both. Stories of arrests of Vietnam War veterans for drugs, or for crimes committed in order to obtain drugs, made news – a media preoccupation that annoyed the thousands of returning soldiers who struggled to find meaningful work, as employers turned them away based on the misguided notion that "everyone who was in Vietnam ate heroin for breakfast," a stereotype two veteran activists derided in the pages of the *New York Times*.[122] Long lines at Veteran Assistance Centers tested the patience of these men, as did the punctilious paperwork requirements that had to be satisfied in order to obtain special veterans' welfare benefits. In part to buoy the prospects of these veterans, Assistant Secretary of Defense Wilbur was eager to announce the results of one study that

---

[121] See President's Commission on Law Enforcement and the Administration of Justice, *Crime in a Free Society* (Belmont: Dickinson Publishing, 1968).

[122] John P. Rowan and William J. Simon, "The Vietnam-Veteran Blues," *New York Times*, March 29, 1974, p. 35.

found that, although the military grossly underestimated the extent of heroin experimentation among soldiers who served in South Vietnam from 1970 to 1972, once this same cohort of men returned home, they did not exhibit a rate of opiate addiction any higher than a comparable group of civilians.[123] Soldiers may have tried heroin, and a smaller number of them may have developed a dependence on it, but few returned to the states still addicted to it.

While the Pentagon seized on the independent study as a way to exonerate itself from blame for heroin addiction, Dr. Wilbur was most emphatic on the study's potential to dispel the myths surrounding the "addicted army." The "drug abusers" in Vietnam, Wilbur argued, were not "highly deviant men," they were "our sons who have succumbed to the heavy pressures of family separation ... and they deserve much better from society than they are receiving at the present time."[124] Although welcomed by many soldiers who believed the myths surrounding drug use dwarfed any realistic assessment of actual use, Wilbur's message was a hasty one in at least some respects. His assertions rested on extrapolating from a small sample and, as the study's lead author pointed out, there was no reason to think the sample was "atypical of the much larger group of men" in question, but also no "evidence they were typical either."[125] In fact, Wilbur spoke prematurely – only a month after the March truce of 1973 – and his deductions were challenged immediately after he announced them. When looking at a sample of veterans, it was difficult to find heroin addicts; heroin addicts were (and are) a small group, and any given sample size might be too small to capture them. When looking at a sample of heroin addicts, however, it was easy to find veterans. John Helmer, a sociologist at Harvard, responded to Wilbur's calculations by sharing his finding that in Massachusetts, a quarter of heroin addicts were veterans, and most of these were Vietnam War veterans. In New York City, health officials claimed to have in excess of the total number of Vietnam War heroin addicts claimed by Wilbur (2,000) under their care alone (8,000–10,000 were veterans, half of these of the Vietnam War).[126] Even the Veterans Administration admitted to treating

[123] John W. Finney, "Army Reports Few in War in 1970–72 Are Addicts Today," *New York Times*, April 24, 1973, p. 1.

[124] As quoted in William Claiborne, "GI Drug Use Figure Raised, But Few Are Still Addicted," *Washington Post Times Herald*, April 24, 1973, p. A1.

[125] Robins as quoted in M. A. Farber, "Veterans Still Fight Vietnam Drug Habits," *New York Times*, June 2, 1974, p. 1.

[126] "Addicts Uncounted," *New York Times*, April 29, 1973, p. 215.

"at least several times the number of Vietnam addicts" than the Pentagon calculated based on the April 1973 study.[127]

But the strongest criticism of the Pentagon's approach was that the military seemed interested only in heroin use; researchers who had varying interpretations on the incidence of heroin addiction nevertheless agreed that the veterans who used heroin in Vietnam often abused other drugs when they returned home. These included amphetamines and barbiturates, as well as hallucinogens, marijuana, and heavy drinking. A small network of specialized treatment centers sprang up to cater specifically to veterans and their struggles with addiction. "DMZ," for example, played upon a familiar military acronym, but in this case the letters stood for "Drug Mending Zone," a private rehabilitation clinic for veterans. Rather than "normalize" Vietnam War veterans by disavowing addiction, these and other treatment outfits struggled to normalize addiction, just as nearly a generation of treatment advocates had done before them. And, of course, some Vietnam veterans found their way to methadone clinics that had their heyday during the early 1970s – like Reginald Price, who found access to methadone from the District of Columbia's Narcotic Treatment Administration in February 1971. When clinics forced addicts to pick up doses daily, Price says the hassle "got the better of him" and he went back to heroin.[128]

As had been the case in the past, those benefits designated specifically for veterans did not reach all of them, and, in the end, general welfare institutions served as a last resort for veterans. This was true for unemployment benefits as well: a discharge other than honorable meant that a veteran would have to find his way to the local welfare office, because the Veterans Assistance Program could only dispense benefits to veterans who were honorably discharged. Because these administrative or dishonorable discharges were often for drug offenses, veterans found that, in multiple ways, past drug use barred them from the "special citizenship" to which service in combat would have otherwise entitled them. This infuriated veterans and their advocates, including NAACP leader Roy Wilkins, who wrote to the Department of Defense when he learned that the military was considering a blanket amnesty for those who dodged the Vietnam-era draft and fled to other countries. "There would be unfairness in such a proposal," he argued, "because there are thousands of black soldiers

[127] Farber, "Veterans Still Fight Vietnam Drug Habits."
[128] Peter Osnos, "Two Veterans Give Details of Drug Use, Attempts to Quit," *Washington Post, Times Herald*, April 24, 1973, p. A16.

who did not desert from the Armed Forces and yet who did receive less than honorable discharges."[129] The amnesty went forward nonetheless, setting a precedent for the babyboomer generation's interpretation of the obligations of citizenship that would repeat in subsequent years: those privileged enough to evade traditional duties, be these military service or taxes, would be heralded as ideological heroes, while those who were not would bear the burden of those obligations, and find themselves heavily penalized should any misstep occur while laboring under their weight.

While the drug war and the war in South Vietnam took a toll on some veterans' lives, an even smaller group actually took up arms in them both. The DEA continued to support foreign interdiction and supply eradication long after the withdrawal of U.S. troops from South Vietnam, affording returning soldiers the opportunity to put some of their military skills to use after the war. Most active were the efforts in Mexico. In the remote hills of that country's interior, helicopters outfitted with the herbicide paraquat sprayed crops as gunships flew above to counter the gunfire that farmhands would direct at the missions. Since Vietnam War veterans were now the best low-flying helicopter pilots in the world, they were sought after for their expertise. Two Vietnam veterans, Larry Steilen and George F. White, lost their lives while training for or conducting DEA supply eradication missions.[130] Indeed, the reliance upon Vietnam veterans for eradication programs continues to the present day. Ignacio Gómez finds that DynCorp, a private U.S. company that provides military and logistical support to the Colombian anti-narcotics effort, is staffed primarily with U.S. military veterans, especially veterans of the Vietnam War.[131]

Unfortunately for the Americans who held high hopes for eradication, the Mexican government, like their latter-day Colombian colleagues, steered these programs toward their own political purposes. Whereas poppy growers generally maintained close ties to the Mexican ruling regime, marijuana crops flourished in the Sierra Madre, a region the government considered hostile and prone to peasant revolts. To undermine the region's best cash crop, the government ordered that the marijuana fields be sprayed. When traces of paraquat surfaced in marijuana that was sold in the United States, it triggered a panic among users of the

[129] Wilkins to Hoffman, September 6, 1974, Records of the NAACP, Library of Congress Manuscript Division, Part V: 2703.
[130] http://www.justice.gov/dea/agency/10bios.htm
[131] See Ignacio Gómez, "US Mercenaries in Colombia," at http://colombiajournal.org/colombia19.htm [accessed August 1, 2011].

drug. To quell the outrage, the American government denied complicity but quietly jettisoned use of the herbicide.

Paraquat poisoning was only one sense in which the United States was at war, however unwittingly, with its own people. Since World War II, the federal government had amassed an arsenal of tools to punish and prohibit illicit drugs: mandatory sentencing and criminal punishment; no-knock searches, wiretaps, and local law enforcement trained and willing to enforce illicit drug laws; and international supply eradication and aid programs designed to undermine drug production. By the time Mexican poppy growers had adapted to aggressive enforcement in the late 1970s, their reinvigorated supply of heroin to the United States joined the stream of cocaine coming from Bolivia, Peru, and Colombia. Together these two drug waves crested into a new epidemic, one that resulted in a recommitment to the punitive regime crafted over the previous two decades. President Ronald Reagan promised to assert these powers with new vigor. In 1986, he signed National Security Directive 221, proclaiming the war on drugs to be a national-security priority; by the end of the decade, spending on drug control efforts had more than trebled from the 1980 figure of $1.5 billion. Yet none of the instruments deployed in the punitive approach had proven to be effective in curbing addiction, intercepting supply, or interfering with the price or purity of drugs in anything other than a temporary fashion; there was no reason to think that their assembly and collective assertion would bode any differently in the 1980s.

In fact, nothing from the governing conceit to the institutional and operational realities of the United States' punitive drug regime suggested a reasoned or earnest effort to curtail illicit drug use. Instead, the preference for a militant approach to illicit narcotics was a successful state-building strategy to overcome institutional divisions and marshal political support, not just for a prohibitive and punitive anti-narcotic regime, but also for a state engaged in much more activity at home and abroad. In important ways, a "war on drugs" mediated many of the consequences perceived as unwelcome in the reordering of American society and the growth of a powerful central state. First and foremost, the United States abandoned the project of taxing drugs in order to regulate them because taxing power itself became too important, and too controversial, to retain excise taxes as part of the federal portfolio. Second, police in the United States embraced drug enforcement as a way to regain discretionary power lost as part of the professionalization movement within law enforcement and the civil rights movement outside of it. Finally, the U.S.

government found foreign drug policy to be a useful tool in executing its international agenda, and, for that matter, in justifying and explaining it to the American people.

To suggest that the American state adopted a prohibitive and punitive approach to drugs in order to resolve dilemmas embedded within the growth of its own power is to list but one more poignant aspect to the project's futility. Yet this failure might also be the most useful aspect to dwell upon for those who hope to change the course of the nation's drug policy. After all, before there was a "war," there was regulation. While this "usable past" inspires more than it instructs, it should not be discarded for its lack of specificity, for, as former New York Police Department Detective Ralph Salerno reflected in his survey of drug efforts in the late 1980s, "across the country there are twenty-seven thousand people, on all levels of government, in drug enforcement," yet there were not even "twenty-seven people who are being paid by the United States government to sit in a room and *think* about a better approach to the problem."[132] And the government will never designate such a "room" – a space to rethink the state's approach to the handling of illicit drugs – because, as I argue, it is too heavily invested in and reliant upon the modern drug war. Hence it is incumbent upon those who seek such a space to claim it for themselves, and to insist on the validity of regulation and taxes as tools of government power that are ultimately more accountable and less costly than prohibition and punishment.

[132] Salerno, *Oral Histories*, p. 205.

Conclusion

War on Trade – The Drug War as Past and Future

Modern drugs and the war against them have produced a number of alternate states. Countless people, be they broken or bored, frail or fearless, sought refuge in the altered reality produced by drugs. Those who denounced such behavior often endorsed a set of interventions that contradicted other cherished beliefs. Conservatives who normally embraced a minimal state presence nonetheless supported aggressive state actions of interdiction and punishment; isolationists critical of U.S. international engagement came to believe that only extraterritorial action abroad would diminish the supply of drugs at home. Similarly, urban liberals and left-wing intelligentsia who worked to install confidence in the operations of the state began, in the 1980s, to express a skeptical view of the state-sponsored efforts of the "drug war." Like the drug users they claimed to steward, crusaders of either stripe experienced a temporary disconnect when it came to drugs. Significantly, the drug war has produced an "alternate state" in the most literal sense: a statutory structure, law enforcement regime, and international project that stood astride the normal functioning of the state, ostensibly to help strengthen and legitimize its function, but ultimately demonstrating that state's manifest weakness and vulnerability. Whether the drug war was notional, deployed mainly as a rhetorical device, or fully realized, featuring military assaults and, in the case of Manuel Noriega in Panama, toppling a regime, it is a war that has been lost.

Its futility does nothing to undermine its significance as a project of the state. Indeed, there are a number of ways in which the federal government's prosecution of the modern drug war provides a lens through which to view the recent past. First, the state's prosecution of the modern drug war joins with some aspects of African American history, and especially so given the newly restored focus on race discrimination and segregation above the Mason-Dixon line.[1] What is more, while older work on the black freedom movement typically adopted a chronology that culminated in the historic legislation of the Great Society, newer scholarship maps the fight for equality onto urban history – either directly, or by sketching the white backlash that animated suburban development – and brings the story well into the 1970s.[2] Certainly the drug war belongs within the scope of both these narratives: disproportionate police focus on inner cities and differing punishment regimes for drugs resulted in a severe yet highly selective criminal justice apparatus, one that was more motivated and better equipped to apprehend and imprison heroin users in the city than other patterns of illicit drug use. The racial bias inherent in such selectivity has had a profound effect on African Americans and on the urban landscape in almost every respect – politically, culturally, economically, as well as in terms of the built environment and physical space of city life.[3]

Elements of this urban minority experience harken back to the Catholic and Jewish encounter with alcohol prohibition. Indeed, the comparison is provocative, both for its resonances and its departures. There was little question but that the violence committed by those who defied alcohol prohibition as well as the brunt of state power invested in enforcing it fell disproportionately upon urban non-Protestant ethnics who were either recent immigrants or direct descendants from them. This was true even though there was no indication that these same ethnic profiles flouted prohibition to an extent greater than others. Yet, when violent crime made headlines throughout the country in the 1920s, calls for the repeal of prohibition grew stronger, not weaker. As the repeal movement gained in support, it benefited from a diverse coalition: joining the veterans who raucously chanted for beer at their annual conventions, and the Catholics who felt unfairly singled out by the temperance movement, were wealthy

---

[1] For a synthetic overview of this history, see Thomas Sugrue, *Sweet Land of Liberty: The Forgotten Struggle for Civil Rights in the North* (New York: Random House, 2009); see also Robert O. Self, *American Babylon: Race and the Struggle for Postwar Oakland* (Princeton: Princeton University Press, 2005).

[2] See above and also Kevin M. Kruse, *White Flight: Atlanta and the Making of the Modern Conservative Movement* (Princeton: Princeton University Press, 2007); Matthew D. Lassiter, *The Silent Majority: Suburban Politics in the Sunbelt South* (Princeton: Princeton University Press, 2007).

[3] See Eric C. Schneider, *Smack: Heroin and the American City* (Philadelphia: University of Pennsylvania Press, 2008).

Americans who feared that the disappearance of federal excise tax on the legal sale of alcohol would lead the government to rely more upon personal income tax – at this point, paid only by the richest citizens – in order to generate revenue. Moreover, since alcohol prohibition came to most states via constitutional amendment, and was foisted on "wet" states and cities in an abrupt and dramatic fashion, a causal connection between prohibition and the violence that followed seemed plausible, if not obvious, to observers. This connection remained persuasive despite the fact that much of Protestant America harbored deep-seated suspicions regarding the moral character of Catholic ethnics.[4]

Drug prohibition, in contrast, evolved over time, staggering its effects. What was more, the drug-related violence of the sixties and beyond seemed to many to be related to drug use itself, and not the decision to prohibit it. Even today, the association between drug use and crime remains powerful despite the fact that the substance responsible for the most crime – that which is committed in order to obtain it, and that committed under its influence – is alcohol.[5] The refusal to impute any blame for violence in the inner cities to drug prohibition, as opposed to drug use, testifies to, among other things, the enduring power of race to construct an "other," a veil of difference that enables disassociation. Patterns of residential development also abetted the willingness to let inner city, urban America languish in favor of attention to a thriving suburban life. And, although criminalization ultimately had a substantial effect on state and local governments burdened with the cost of the "carceral" state, the decision to prohibit drugs did not represent a substantial loss of revenue, so no outcry denouncing the redistribution of the tax burden followed drug prohibition. Race and racism – including residential segregation, and the construction of "black criminality" – drove a number of the most pointed differences between alcohol and drug prohibition; without these forces, we cannot explain either the drug war or the lack of urgency in repealing it. As Doris Provine argues in her survey of the criminal justice approach to crack cocaine, the country's history of racism "helps to explain the public's otherwise surprising tolerance for failed policies [of

---

[4] Daniel Okrent details these antagonisms in *Last Call: The Rise and Fall of Prohibition* (New York: Scribner, 2011).

[5] See, for example, Bureau of Justice Statistics, "Alcohol and Crime: An Analysis of National Data," available at: http://bjs.ojp.usdoj.gov/content/pub/pdf/ac.pdf [accessed August 1, 2011].

the drug war], even in the face of the tremendous human suffering associated with incarceration."[6]

Still, a focus on race does not adequately account for the rise of the punishment regime, even as incarceration and arrest rates for African Americans make clear some of the purposes to which it was put. A perspective informed by historical materialism, giving primary attention to economic interests, has more to offer in clarifying causality. Indeed, in some ways the criminalization of Schedule I drugs – heroin, marijuana, and cocaine – is the result of the fact that, historically, none was produced domestically on a large scale (something that is still true of poppies and cocoa leaves). Yet synthetic drugs produced under U.S. patents, with similar uses and effects as prohibited drugs, not to mention similar addictive properties, have been classified differently and have no automatic criminal possession charges associated with them. In *The Drug Hang Up: America's Fifty Year Folly*, Rufus King harps on this contradiction, though he does so in a conversational and sometimes mocking tone that distracts from his more serious objectives. As the lawyer most influential in forming the joint American Bar Association and American Medical Association Joint Committee on Narcotic Drugs in the 1950s, King stayed active in the policy world for many years afterward and published his recollections and observations in 1973. In his account, King berates Commissioner Anslinger and his bureaucratic empire and questions the degree of drug dependence for any sort of drug, presenting the anxiety over addiction as a moral panic intentionally aroused by politicians hoping to attract notice for themselves. But King has more than just taunts of Anslinger to offer: as one of the few authors to narrate both narcotic prohibition and the subsequent Drug Abuse Control Act of 1965, he was well positioned to weigh the influence of corporate power. In reciting the many favors bestowed on pharmaceutical companies, King's experience in Washington circles also gives him a knack for seizing the uncanny detail that enhances the argument. He writes that after pharmaceutical companies who provided the Kennedy administration with the drugs requested by Fidel Castro in exchange for releasing prisoners captured during the Bay of Pigs invasion, they were only too happy to call in their chits with the administration, insisting in 1965 negotiations that the Drug Abuse

---

[6] Doris Marie Provine, *Unequal Under Law: Race in the War on Drugs* (Chicago: University of Chicago Press, 2007), p. 12.

Control Amendments include criminal charges for patent infringement and generic copies.

The cumulative result of criminalization of imported narcotics and protection of manufactured synthetics is a confused and highly potent licit and illicit drug market in the United States. OxyContin, a brand name for a synthetic narcotic formulated from oxycodone and similar in potency and medical uses to heroin, and fentanyl (Fentora, Onsolis), another synthetic most similar to morphine, are both Schedule II drugs: that is, controlled substances subject to heavy regulation but sold licitly throughout the United States (though the Beta-Hydroxy formulation of fentanyl is Schedule I). Sad ironies punctuate the dangers inherent in this plentiful array of addictive drugs. Any diligent newspaper reader will know that both OxyContin and fentanyl have been diverted into illicit markets – yet, because both are still used for medical purposes, neither one is prohibited, nor is anyone arrested simply for having them. Perhaps the most surprising turn in the saga of addiction has been the examples of those who initially receive OxyContin to treat pain from serious medical injury and, because of meager or lack of insurance coverage, cannot afford the refills that their pain or their habit demands. As a result they turn to an older, cheaper, and (relatively) easier to obtain painkiller: heroin.[7] Embedded in these anecdotes is the biting truth of failed protectionism that haunts the country: criminal punishment for patents and the prohibition of agricultural opiates has protected the licit market for addictive synthetics, but it has also driven illicit suppliers to become so adept in production and distribution that they can now routinely beat out licit suppliers in price, and often purity as well (the manufacturer of OxyContin is now forbidden to market its most powerful formulation in the United States). Heroin producers and distributors are simply more competitive.

Yet, as Rufus King confesses at several points in his narrative, he cannot account for all the twists and turns in the story of criminal prohibition of illicit narcotics. Why was the Bureau of Narcotics transferred to the Department of Justice, he wonders to his readers. Another aspect of the drug war that fits poorly with materialist interpretations of it is the nature of foreign drug policy as exercised by the U.S. federal government.

---

[7] See Randal C. Archibold, "In Heartland Death, Traces of Heroin Spread," *New York Times*, May 31, 2009, available at http://www.nytimes.com/2009/05/31/us/31border. html?pagewanted=print [accessed September 26, 2012]; for more on the intertwined heroin and OxyContin epidemic afflicting Massachusetts, see the film *Narcotic Misconceptions*, by Nick Martel (2012).

Economic interests certainly speak to those moments when the United States invested the full force of its diplomacy in international production quotas, but this was never all there was to the foreign drug portfolio. Rather, with some striking regularity, the drug war also served as a frame to view the world and the U.S. role within it. Under Anslinger's guidance, the illicit drug traffic became a way to vilify enemies and simultaneously insist on American "innocence." As he explained in 1961, because illicit traffic was "by nature international," the world could be divided into "growing nations and manufacturing nations and 'target' or victim nations"; the United States, he continued, "has always been in the latter category."[8] This provocative rhetorical construction helped to depict U.S. international power, and particularly its early Cold War agenda, as a reaction to sinister antagonists – a move that advanced domestic support for engagement with the world, but only at the expense of a more realistic appraisal of global dynamics and the United States' role in shaping them.

Over time, the U.S. international drug policy agenda became more functional, though no less moralistic, in its purposes. Instead of employing drug policy as a device or a platform to condemn enemies, Kennedy administration officials and their successors embraced it as an indispensable tool of statecraft, one that could be used to pressure allies, bolster particular regimes, and funnel resources. These tendencies became only more pronounced after U.S. defeat in Vietnam, when a fully realized drug war became one in a dwindling set of ways for U.S. officials to justify engagement with and intervention in the developing world. Indeed, outside the scope of this narrative, but within the living memory of most Americans, the United States' efforts in Central and South America throughout the 1980s depended upon both the logic and legitimacy of anti-drug interventions. Jonathan Marshall argues that such interventions could be more accurately viewed as Cold War politics masquerading as drug policy; right-wing anti-communist regimes, no matter what their commitment to anti-drug efforts, consistently benefited from U.S. support.[9] As Marshall points out, governments favored by the United States often had close ties to drug trafficking, a largely unacknowledged relationship that still shapes Central and South American politics to this day. For example, Colombian president Alvaro Uribe, celebrated by the

---

[8] Harry Anslinger, *The Murderers: The Story of Narcotic Gangs* (New York: Farrar, Straus, and Cudahy, 1961), p. 167.

[9] Marshall, *Cocaine Politics: Drugs, Armies, and the CIA in Central America* (Berkeley: University of California Press, 1998).

United States as an implacable foe to the internal guerilla force of FARC throughout the administration of George W. Bush, engaged in all manner of drug trafficking. As he accepted U.S. anti-drug assistance, his domestic program centered not on curtailing illicit drug traffic, but rather on marginalizing labor and reform within Colombia and aligning his administration with right-wing paramilitary organizations.[10]

These and other unsettling components of U.S. policy in Central and South America, while extremely significant, represent only one part of the dependence upon drug policy internationally. The State Department relies upon personnel dedicated to anti-drug efforts to staff its embassy and consulate personnel and, in some areas of the world, to define its diplomatic program. The Bureau of International Narcotics and Law Enforcement Affairs, the State Department office charged with overseeing the unconcealed aspects of U.S. international drug policy, submits plans to Congress as part of the State Department budget proposal. Its African plans for fiscal year 2011 list a robust and rather detailed agenda affecting countries from Benin to Zambia, the most comprehensive program for African engagement to be found anywhere on the State Department's website.[11] This dependence upon drug policy was only underscored when WikiLeaks, an Internet clearinghouse for leaked classified material, released a passel of U.S. government documents that disclosed, among other things, the extent to which the Drug Enforcement Administration (DEA) has been "transformed," in the words of the *New York Times*, into a "global intelligence organization with a reach that extends far beyond narcotics."[12] The *Times* analysis of the leaked diplomatic cables and memoranda concluded that, as Central and South American policy had already demonstrated for more than twenty years, the DEA balanced "diplomacy and law enforcement in places where it can be hard to tell the politicians from the traffickers"; and, moreover, that the DEA had revealed itself to be an "entrepreneurial agency" that has become

[10] For an overview of Uribe's politics of terror, see Daniel Wilkinson, "The Killers of Colombia," *New York Review of Books* 58, no. 11 (June 23, 2011): 38–41.
[11] http://www.state.gov/p/inl/rls/rpt/pbg/fy2011/149369.htm [accessed August 15, 2011].
[12] Ginger Thompson and Scott Shane, "Cables Portray Expanded Reach of Drug Agency," *New York Times*, December 25, 2010 [accessed December 26, 2010]. See also *Frontline*, "A Perfect Terrorist," Season 30, for the story of one DEA informant, David Coleman Headley, who did not receive scrutiny from U.S. law enforcement, presumably because of his relationship to the DEA and despite several Americans urging the FBI to take a look, as he conducted intelligence missions in service to the Pakistani terrorist attacks on the Indian city of Mumbai, which killed 166 people.

"something more than a drug agency," recruited into intelligence collection and covert dealings with goals ranging from anti-terrorism to spying on leftist politicians and groups.[13] From the prosaic chores of everyday embassy work to the subterfuge of covert operations, the U.S. government has come to rely upon drug policy in order to structure and execute its global influence and power.

These various dimensions of the drug war enrich our understanding of modern U.S. history up to and including the present day – but, absent any discussion of political economy, they stand incomplete and unconnected. What is more, without that focus, they lack a critical depth as leverage for critique of the state. What can the drug war tell us about the American experience of modernity, and the state's efforts to define and manage that experience? Historian Charles S. Maier has nominated territoriality, or "control of bordered political space," as the premise for understanding the twentieth century, and he suggests that the crisis or unraveling of the "territorial imperative" serves as the fundamental axis for understanding the recent past and present day.[14] Such a view extends the observations of an array of other scholars who draw from critical theory to argue that, despite its seeming and self-styled inevitability, state sovereignty (including the feelings of nationalism premised upon it) is a social construction, an historical project that often disrupts preexisting ethnic, religious, or even geographic ties, and one that hinders longstanding regional patterns of exchange of goods and people.[15]

If so, then the drug war as waged by the U.S. federal government illustrates a territorial imperative weakened by the state's own hand. It is a dubious undertaking to "manage" modernity by making war on it. It is also a gratuitous one: although economic prosperity ushered in new

[13] Ibid.
[14] Charles S. Maier, "Consigning the Twentieth Century to History: Alternative Narratives for the Modern Era," *American Historical Review* 105, no. 3 (June 2000): 807–31.
[15] Classic articulations of this idea can be found in Benedict Anderson, *Imagined Communities: Reflections on the Origin and Spread of Nationalism* (London: Verso, 1991); and Michael Mann, *The Sources of Social Power, Volume II* (Cambridge: Cambridge University Press, 1993). For an exemplary monograph, see David Blackbourn, *The Long Nineteenth Century: A History of Germany, 1780–1918* (Oxford: Oxford University Press, 1998). Border and frontier studies have been a particularly fruitful area to explore this history. For examples focused on the United States, see Anthony P. Mora, *Border Dilemmas: Racial and National Uncertainties in New Mexico, 1848–1912* (Durham: Duke University Press, 2011); Patricia Nelson Limerick, *The Legacy of Conquest: The Unbroken Past of the American West* (New York: Norton, 1987); and Rachel St. John, *Line in the Sand: A History of the Western US-Mexico Border* (Princeton: Princeton University Press, 2011).

smuggling networks and new possibilities to skirt the law, such incidents paled in significance compared with the ways in which economic success reinforced the legitimacy of the state. Yet, as wealth and state power both accumulated, new problems arose, and these dilemmas altered the context within which drug regulation was considered. Hence the set of choices from which the drug war emerged has its roots in something more than a symbolic crusade, or a stage to enact state sovereignty. Rather, the "war" has its beginnings in the fact that the U.S. federal government was simply not equipped to organize and manage the nation-state that emerged from World War II as a superpower. While the decision to make a concentrated investment in bolstering the federal income tax kept the national government abreast of a modernizing country, it also imperiled the regulatory tools and mission of the federal government in unintended ways. Thus, a strategic move made in the hopes of capitalizing on limited national resources in order to outfit the government for a new era also launched a prolonged, albeit largely unheralded, renegotiation of the instruments and institutions of state power.

Race, class, and various economic concerns all played a role in that process of renegotiation, but it is not a full account of state power simply to acknowledge that other interests successfully insinuated themselves into its exercise. That power merits scrutiny in its own right, both for what it is, and what it is not. The punitive and prohibitive illicit drug regime represents an opportunity to do just that, for, while the obvious success of illicit drug smuggling and widespread illicit drug use are often invoked as implied critiques of state power, it is the drug war itself that points up that power's limits. Indeed, such a state-centered analysis has relevance to the present day. The federal government's withdrawal from the excise tax field restricted the instruments available to it for regulation; subsequent attacks on federal payroll taxes have, in turn, curtailed the federal social policy portfolio. In 2010, President Obama's administration contemplated placing its new mandate to require adults to carry health insurance by 2014 under the federal government's power to tax.[16] While reasonable and in some respects efficient, the move was rejected for fear of provoking the anger of anti-tax crusaders. Instead, the

---

[16] Robert Pear, "Changing Stance, Obama Administration Now Defends Insurance Mandate as a Tax," *New York Times*, July 16, 2010 [accessed online July 17, 2010]. Instead, the administration opted for a hybrid approach, placing the power to compel an insurance mandate under the commerce clause, but the penalty for defying it under taxing authority. See Jacobs and Skocpol, *Health Care Reform and American Politics: What Everyone Needs to Know* (New York: Oxford University Press, 2010).

administration chose to place the mandate under the commerce clause and, as political scientist Gordon Silverstein is not alone in pointing out, this heavily burdened facet of federal power may soon buckle under the weight of strained reasoning and concerted legal challenges.[17]

In our own time, then, federal power, in terms of both capability and legitimacy, has suffered serious blows. Less so the individual states: inheriting the taxes cast off by the federal government, state revenue generation explored new channels, including a uniform sales tax, that resulted in newfound power. And, while the anti-tax movement of our modern era has its roots in a revolt against state collection of property taxes, because states must balance their budget every year, the very success of anti-property tax movements hinges upon the availability of other revenue sources to the states. Indeed, the states have had more than the sales tax to fall back on. Virtually unnoted amidst the reshuffling of excise tax authority was the decision, adopted on a state-by-state basis, to tie income reporting in the states to federal tax returns.[18] The move was by no means obvious: since state income tax preceded the advent of the federal income tax, the two initially had nothing to do with each other in an administrative sense. Whatever ability the state had to assess an individual's income, that was the extent to which income was assessed and then taxed. Throughout the 1950s and '60s, when individual states decided to accept the federal adjusted gross income as the figure upon which to base its tax, it aligned the audit power of the federal government behind its state income tax collection, and a tremendous boon in revenue recovery followed on the heels of this decision.[19]

With reinvigorated revenue collection, the policy programs of the states – including special bonds issued to finance prison construction – flourished.[20] This observation confirms the arguments advanced by Stephen Gardbaum, who challenges the conventional wisdom that

[17] Gordon Silverstein, *Law's Allure: How Law Shapes, Constrains, Saves and Kills Politics* (New York: Cambridge University Press, 2009).

[18] See L. L. Ecker-Racz, "Tax Simplification in This Federal System," *Law and Contemporary Problems* 34 (1969): 781.

[19] James R. Turner, "Federal-State Cooperation in Tax Administration," *William and Mary Law Review*, Issue 4 (1968): 958–71.

[20] For more on the relationship between state politics and prisons, see Ruth Wilson Gilmore, *Golden Gulag: Prisons, Surplus, Crisis, and Opposition in Globalizing California* (Berkeley: University of California Press, 2007); Robert Perkinson, *Texas Tough: The Rise of America's Prison Empire* (New York: Picador, 2010); Ernest Drucker, *A Plague of Prisons: The Epidemiology of Mass Incarceration in America* (New York: New Press, 2011).

individual states lost power to expanded judicial readings of the commerce clause starting with the New Deal. Legal authority, Gardbaum contends, is not necessarily a finite "zero-sum game" wherein a gain in one area (the federal government) entails a loss in another (the states). This observation holds even more truth when it comes to state institutional capacity: individual states expanded both the scope and the efficiency of their operations in tandem with and in response to augmentations in federal power. And, as Gardbaum also notes, the states relied upon new readings of the constitution in order to do so, as the case of levying a uniform sales tax illustrates.[21] If, in its modern form, the federal government has anchored some of its operations in expansive and creative readings of the Constitution, so too have the states.

This perspective shifts the historical grounding of the modern conservative movement. At the very least, it complicates the revival of deference to states' rights espoused as fundamental to conservatives. It also suggests the possibility that the various assaults on federal power do not, in fact, advocate a return to tradition, but instead champion a different departure from it. Such a view is premised upon a more general appreciation of the growth of state power at all levels, and is less preoccupied with the allocation of plenary authority within the federalist system. Stepping away from the trees, legal scholar Bill Stuntz's view of the forest is a blunt and arresting one. The Bill of Rights in the U.S. Constitution, celebrated for articulating restraints upon the state, may have endured, he suggests, not because of its "success at the enterprise of constraining government power." "More likely," he surmises, "its long legal life stems from its failure."[22] Seen from this crude but revealing perspective of aggregate state power, the modern-day movement to allocate more authority to the individual states endows Maier's exhortation to examine the territorial imperative with a deep irony: control over bounded political space could not be achieved in America without enlisting the support of the individual states, and forces unleashed as a part of this political bargain have worked to engineer its demise.

Finally, it is intellectually valid – but even more, politically exigent – to note that the modern drug war, when scrutinized as a state project, raises troubling questions of government accountability. As the history presented here makes clear, the drug war has been seized upon to advance

---

[21] See Gardbaum, "New Deal Constitutionalism and the Unshackling of the States," *University of Chicago Law Review* 64 (1997): 483–566.

[22] Stuntz, *Fighting Crime*, p. 87.

other agendas of state. This fact cheats American citizens out of an honest tally of the deeds and the dilemmas of modern U.S. state power. If law enforcement in urban America did not enforce a drug war, what would it look like? If the State Department could not rely upon drug policy and staff in Africa, just as an example, what would the U.S. commitment to the continent depend upon, and how would it change? These and other questions like them have not been asked, in part because the self-authorizing logic of drug prohibition renders them implausible. In this way, the District of Columbia served not only as a proving ground for much of the federal government's drug war; it foreshadowed its governing equation. Citizens of the nation's capital watched as congressional gambits to advance punishment were foisted upon them without recourse to the ballot box; similarly, as a country, the United States now supports the workings of a national and international drug war project, the dimensions and activities of which cannot be fully recovered or known (despite Wikileaks' best efforts). In some sense, when it comes to the drug war, all Americans live in DC.

Of course, it is not as if eliminating the many components of the drug war would present a *deus ex machina*, a sudden resolution of previously intractable problems by a simple device. But it is certainly true that the drug war's covert operations and dismissal of so many common law and procedural precedents – and the absence of accountability such practices enable – amounts to more than just a list of "shortcuts" that confirm the difficulties encountered when trying to punish a market out of existence. Taken together, they represent a dereliction of democratic oversight that has produced considerable collateral damage. Indeed, this narrative of the drug war raises the prospect that the political and institutional constraints that hemmed in the regulatory project of the federal government have given way, if not given rise, to a state too powerful and too coercive, and one that incurs too many costs, financial and otherwise. For it may well be that, if a state cannot govern using other tools, it will punish its way to power.

THE FUTURE OF DRUG POLICY

The analysis and arguments offered in this book are presented in the hope of informing the political history of the recent past, yet I have made no attempt to disguise my opposition to and criticism of the United States' punitive drug regime. I would therefore be remiss if I failed to offer suggestions for a path forward. Below I enumerate a number of recommendations. Like others, I support abandoning the concept and many of the tools of the "drug war." Unlike others, I rely explicitly upon U.S. political history for precedents and inspiration. Too often we suffer from the misapprehension that our current punitive regime is an ineluctable result of illicit drug use; this book makes clear that there have been other approaches in place in earlier times, and that specific choices well outside of the incidence of drug use and drug traffic influenced the departure from those models. Indeed, it is my hope that recovering the story of illicit drug regulation through taxation and tracing its abandonment captures what J.G.A. Pocock calls the "radical" nature of history: denaturalizing the present way of doing things and laying bare the threads of choice, contingency, and change that had a hand in making it. Such work goes beyond making a case for reform – in historical scholarship, usually presented as a "road not taken" – it makes an implicit and more fundamental claim for potential itself, "making it possible to imagine," in the felicitous wording of Emile Durkheim, other ways and other futures beyond just the ones authorized or suggested by the present.

Recommendation 1: Legalize Marijuana. In 2010, the state of California voted on and rejected Proposition 19, a proposal to decriminalize small-scale production and small-scale consumption of marijuana, as well as a broader provision to allow state municipalities to decide whether it will accept and tax the licit sale of marijuana on any more significant scale. The proposal, formally known as the "Regulate, Control, and Tax Cannabis Act of 2010," would have fared better, perhaps, had it been known by its official name: no one can seriously contend that marijuana production and use is effectively controlled and regulated now, so any plan that promised to do so might have earned more support from voters.

When I traveled to southern California to speak in support of Proposition 19 at an academic conference in the fall of 2010, I was surprised to hear some of the arguments mounted against it. One researcher from RAND predicted chaos should the proposition pass; individual counties in California, she noted in horror to the audience, would be allowed to determine their own specific possession and sale preferences. The variety of conditions for sale and consumption would be bewildering, or so she assumed, and many in the audience seemed willing to agree. What was worse, legal marijuana would be more expensive than illegal marijuana, she argued, and although the two might have similar potencies, she therefore deduced that there would still be brisk sales on the black market.

Listening to these imagined scenarios – and observing the reaction to them – I concluded that collectively, we are not very well acquainted with the history of the repeal of alcohol prohibition.[23] The Twenty-First Amendment that engineered the repeal allowed the individual states to choose their own alcohol control model by licensing, creating a state monopoly, or giving all decisions to the local counties. Following repeal, a bootleg market for alcohol still existed – it thrived up until the 1950s – and states struggled with how to quash it, as well as how to attune alcohol sales to varying local mores and preferences. The industry, led by distilleries and their professional associations, determined that, in the long run, legal sales would be more profitable than illegal ones, essentially a determination that increasing the market share for alcohol would be more profitable than maximizing the value of their current production, and that most customers would prefer to pay more for alcohol that was taxed and legal than bootlegged and furtively purchased and consumed. These decisions meant that the industry was well disposed toward meaningful self-regulation: as one lobbyist put it in 1949, alcohol products faced "the biggest public relations problem of any industry in the nation." After all, he explained, the industry had been successfully demonized and outlawed only years before, and temperance advocates had by no means given up the cause.[24]

Taken together these challenges and incentives disciplined the industry. Unevenly and not without controversy, a system to regulate alcohol production and consumption developed whereby the federal government taxed manufacturers directly (and still does), and states levied a tax at the point of purchase, whether that purchase took place at a licensed retailer or, less frequently, a government-owned store (as is the case in Virginia for hard liquor). Municipalities set the conditions of the purchase, meaning they decided where to locate alcohol retailers, what kinds of alcohol they could carry, and when sales would cease and commence operation. Hence, the variation feared by the RAND researcher and others who contemplated Proposition 19 resembles nothing so much as our current system of alcohol regulation. The reason the system works well is that alcohol manufacturers make more money selling legally, and if diversion of their product is discovered, the threat of losing their legitimate

<hr>

[23] See Garrett Peck, *The Prohibition Hangover: Alcohol in America from Demon Rum to Cult Cabernet* (New Brunswick, NJ: Rutgers University Press, 2009).

[24] As quoted in Patricia A. Morgan, "Power, Politics, and Public Health: The Political Power of the Alcohol Beverage Industry," *Journal of Public Health Policy* 9, no. 2 (Summer 1988): 187.

market appoints them as the most effective watchdog of their distribution chain.

Marijuana is the only illicit drug in the United States where the market is diverse, dispersed, and large enough to interest producers and retailers in investing in licit retail and self-regulation. That this should be the case is no doubt the result of the relative harmlessness of the drug – comparable to alcohol, and in some respects advantageously so – but in a purely technical sense, the drug's risk profile is incidental to why repealing prohibition would work. It is the scale and diversity of marijuana's market that makes legalization possible, and, because of this, doing so would result in much tighter control over marijuana production and consumption than we have today. After all, if you ask teenagers today if it is harder to obtain alcohol or marijuana, they will tell you alcohol. Any criminal will sell to a minor; a business proprietor, concerned with maintaining a license, will not.

Another reason to legalize marijuana on a broad scale is to mandate and control its ever-increasing potency. Whereas medical professionals have long been skeptical of the possibility of physical addiction to marijuana – i.e., a habit that would induce withdrawal symptoms if suddenly stopped – street-level sales of Mexican or U.S. marijuana as well as medical marijuana have put out product that is the highest potency seen in the last thirty years. This point raises yet another parallel to alcohol prohibition, which saw bootleg liquor of truly dangerous alcohol content, to say nothing of the dangerous additives that may be added to bootleg liquor or to marijuana, posing an unknown and potentially dangerous risk to the user.

I believe that the federal government should levy a tax on marijuana producers, thereby monitoring production levels. I believe states should tax marijuana at the point of purchase, and they should regulate the nature and extent of the market, including its potency, either through licensing or state-owned stores. I believe that the move toward medical marijuana is a superfluous one in at least one sense: it does nothing to promote licit consumption on a significant scale, which is by itself the greatest incentive for producers and retailers to stay on the legitimate side of business. On the other hand, it does identify producers and retailers willing to abide by strict regulations; as an intermediate step, then, it can help negotiate the transition between illicit and licit production. I also believe that the more halting and uneven the transition to licit production and consumption, the more difficult it will be to negotiate it. To ask licit producers to police their distribution networks when an incentive to sell on the black market still exists makes them less effective watchdogs of their own product.

Recommendation #2: Decriminalize Possession for Schedule I Drugs and Increase the Size of Local Police Forces. Criminologist Daniel Nagin argues that when punishment is relied upon too heavily, it loses its value as a deterrent.[25] If too many people are arrested and incarcerated, he argues, then the stigma normally associated with these penalties is vastly diminished, if not lost. Pscyhologist Tom Tyler has viewed essentially the same problem from a different angle: if the criminal justice system operates with too much force or caprice in a community, or it is simply perceived to do so, then it loses legitimacy in the eyes of that community.[26] Robbed of its customary authority, the system will not be able to elicit the cooperation essential to its success; what is worse, the self-regulated obedience – the decision to submit to the law even when not immediately compelled to do so – that any well-functioning society relies upon is eroded when the justice system is perceived as fundamentally unfair.[27]

Obviously the drug war has exacerbated both perversions of the criminal justice process when it comes to law enforcement in modern America. I join Steve Levitt and Bill Stuntz in suggesting that police presence, and not criminal punishment, has had more of a role in crime reduction in recent years, and I also endorse the efforts normally associated with community policing as the preeminent strategy to elevate the stature and increase the effectiveness of police in communities across America.[28] I call for an end to criminal punishment for possession of *any* illicit drug, recognizing that, in so doing, I am effectively calling for an end to street-level policing of

---

[25] Daniel S. Nagin, "Criminal Deterrence Research at the Outset of the Twenty First Century," *Crime and Justice* 23 (1998): 1–42.

[26] T. R. Tyler, *Why People Obey The Law: Procedural Justice, Legitimacy, and Compliance* (New Haven: Yale University Press, 1990). See also "Police Fairness," in *Fairness and Effectiveness in Policing: The Evidence*, Skogan and Frydl, eds. (Washington, DC: National Academies Press, 2004), chap. 8, and Jeff Fagan and Tracy Meares, "Punishment, Deterrence and Social Control: The Paradox of Punishment in Minority Communities," *Ohio State Journal of Criminal Law* 6 (2008): 173–229.

[27] Classic texts on self-regulated obedience include: Emile Durkheim on anomie in *Suicide: A Study in Sociology*, Spaulding and Simpson translation (London: Routledge: 1952); on authority and obedience, see Max Weber, *Wirtschaft and Gesellschaft*, Talcott Parsons introduction (London: W. Hodge, 1947).

[28] See Skogan and Frydl, *Fairness and Effectiveness.* Unfortunately, community policing is losing ground to a federal security state: see Sudhir Venkatesh, "How the Federal Government is Killing Community Policing," *New Republic*, September 25, 2012, http://www.tnr.com/article/politics/107675/how-big-brother-killing-community-policing [accessed September 26, 2012].

drug dealing. At the same time, I support a reinvigorated police presence in communities across the United States, and I support any legitimate initiative to involve communities in the process of criminal justice, including especially local police recruitment, regular beat patrols and community meetings, fewer plea bargains and more jury trials.

Some of these recommendations follow the path charted by Portugal in 2000, when it decriminalized possession of illicit drugs and sent users to treatment instead of prison. Following decriminalization, more adults tried drugs, but fewer were addicted and, more important, drug use fell in special communities of concern: teenagers, prisoners, and known addicts.[29] Police in Portugal are required to send an addict discovered with drugs to therapy; here in the United States, local communities should weigh whether they want to pass legislation instituting a similar requirement.

I believe that the illicit production and sale of any drug by someone not licensed to do so should be illegal, and that enforcement of the law should hinge upon the degree to which that activity produces concern and ancillary problems within any given community. In one community, it may be that a local liquor store is causing more problems than anything else; in another, it may be that car rides undertaken to produce and consume methamphetamine pose a danger to everyone else on the road. Local communities should be free to determine the approach to resolve the issue most distressing to them, including the appropriate enforcement strategy and penalties. Finally, I believe anyone under the influence of *any* substance while driving and involved in a car accident should have his or her driving license revoked for a period of ten years, and that any vehicle-involved party who flees the scene of a car accident, or anyone driving without a valid license, should face criminal punishment.

Recommendation #3: Increase Medical Treatment Options and Screening for Addiction. In 2010, the U.S. government spent $74 billion on processing drug offenders through the criminal justice system, while spending $3.6 billion on treatment. Nationwide, local drug courts help

---

[29] See Hatton and Mendoza, "Portugal's Drug Policy Pays Off; US Eyes Lessons," *Washington Post*, December 27, 2010. In his more critical appraisal of Portugal, Michael Specter does allow that "serious drug use is down significantly…; the burden on the criminal justice system has eased; the number of people seeking treatment has grown; and the rates of drug-related deaths and cases of infectious diseases have fallen"; he then expresses reservations similar to those who criticize methadone clinics – i.e., is it ethical to supply an addict with drugs. See Specter, "Getting a Fix," *New Yorker*, October 17, 2011: 36–45.

to channel addicts into treatment and recovery programs and should be retained as arbiters if and when addicts commit crimes – but, apart from that valuable component of criminal justice, the ratio of these spending figures should be reversed.

I believe in expanding all treatment options: clinics and primary care physicians, HMOs and public health programs. I also believe that certain communities should be more attentive to the possibility of addiction and perform more outreach and screening in that regard. First among these is the U.S. military: as *USA Today* reported in December 2009, one in four American soldiers has abused prescription drugs within the previous year, especially the painkiller OxyContin.[30] Physicians across America are already accustomed to prescribing medication to treat addiction – sometimes unscrupulously so, as has been the case throughout modern history – but they usually do so in the context of an existing patient-doctor relationship. Moreover, the typical treatment protocol seems to end there. Private health insurers generally do not cover the cost of substance abuse treatment programs, placing a greater burden on states to fund the cost of programs directly and indirectly (through Medicaid), and limiting the reach and relevance of residential therapy and treatment.

Hence, even in the best-case scenario of an individual who desires treatment, very few opportunities exist to present that individual with realistic options to end substance abuse and dependence. Similar to screening for and awareness of mental health problems more than a decade ago, the medical community must promote its own professional renaissance regarding addiction in order to assess care options and guide patients to them. There is no reason why such an endeavor should not play a crucial part in the Patient Protection and Affordable Care Act of 2010 mandate to produce savings in the health care system: one out of every fourteen hospital stays is related to substance dependency, and medical costs were reduced by more than 25 percent for a group of patients who suffered from addiction and received treatment for it.[31] In fact, authors of the healthcare reform act seem to have understood the paucity of treatment options for addiction and the costs that the failure to treat it impose on the rest of the system; accordingly, the legislation stipulates that substance abuse be considered a chronic disease and that, starting in 2014,

[30] http://www.usatoday.com/news/military/2009–12–16-milhealth_N.htm.
[31] Soros Foundation, "Unforeseen Benefits: Addiction Treatment Reduces Health Care Costs," Open Society Foundation, July 2009.

a healthcare recipient may no longer be denied coverage based on substance abuse disclosed by herself or by a physician.

Recommendation #4: Abolish the DEA and Return International Drug Regulation to the Department of Treasury. When Nixon joined the White House Office of Drug Abuse Law Enforcement, devoted to street-level illicit drug sales, with John Ingersoll's internationally focused Bureau of Narcotics and Dangerous Drugs, two bad ideas were reunited. Nothing about their combination enhanced their prospects for success. I believe the DEA should be abolished.[32]

Recent history tells us that the only effective way to shape trade is to threaten trade. I believe that the Department of Treasury should form an office of international drug sales, and that this office should license international sales of American drugs and imports of the same. It should revive an old practice of U.S. Narcotics Commissioner Harry Anslinger: threaten the export and sale of American drugs if and when a country does not comport itself according to U.S. demands.

I also believe that this same office should adopt a practice from U.S. agriculture, one instituted to ensure price stability: buy crops and then burn them. I believe that any country that is not now currently growing poppy or coca leaves should know that doing so would threaten their supply of U.S.-manufactured drugs. Any country currently growing those crops should be forced, using the same threat, to accept the U.S. Treasury as a buyer of a certain share of production. I believe the Treasury should manipulate its purchase price of a set share of production to reward or punish behavior as they see fit. Of course, it may be that any given country will impose the harshest penalties of this trade-based approach upon the least powerful among them. If so, then sadly that is no different than the power dynamic in place and actively supported by U.S. foreign drug policy in its present form. The only difference would be that a trade-based approach would actually affect the price, purity, and amount of production of poppy and coca, all goals that supposedly support the current approach of the U.S. government.

Finally, many readers of this book will find the drug war to resemble the United States' current "war on terror" in some crucial respects.

[32] For more on the early years of the DEA, see James Q. Wilson, *The Investigators: Managing FBI and Narcotics Agents* (New York: Basic Books, 1978); Patricia Rachal, *Federal Narcotics Enforcement: Reorganization and Reform* (Boston: Auburn House, 1982); and on international activities, see Ethan A. Nadelmann, *Cops Across Borders: The Internationalization of US Law Enforcement* (University Park: Pennsylvania State University Press, 1993): chaps. 3–5.

Though an apt and provocative comparison, it is important to realize that the drug war serves not merely as an analogy, but as a prologue to the current war on terror. Aggressive tactics most commonly associated with the U.S. government actions following September 11 were in fact originally featured in the fully realized drug war of the 1980s: the failure to abide by the Posse Commitatus Act, a post-Reconstruction injunction against the U.S. military performing policing functions at home; aggressive extradition; and the secret deployment of a fighting force against nonstate actors. Given this continuity, it seems natural to assume that various explanations of the drug war would shed some light on the war on terror.

And indeed they do. This latest "war" strikes some as a way to name and to grapple with forces of disorder in the modern world, and as a strategy to reinforce U.S. sovereignty in the face of global dynamics that dissipate state power still further. Some have gone so far as to proclaim the performative aspect of the war on terror – especially airport screening – to be a kind of "security theater," an elaborate staging of government authority that functions at almost a purely symbolic level, doing little to deter or intercept terrorists but making a deep impression upon (and many times irritating) lawful citizens. Also in evidence in the war on terror is a racial and, in this case, a religious subtext underwriting the project and determining its priorities. Islam is a world religion, Al Qaeda has enjoyed popular support throughout Asia and successfully recruited native and Caucasian Americans, yet the composition of the targets of the war on terror is overwhelmingly Arab, and, more disturbing, terrorism has become the lens through which many Americans perceive the Arab world.[33]

In addition, arguments about the drug war specific to this book also apply to the war on terror: clearly, state-building, political strategies, and unspoken agendas are at work as well. As the summer 2010 series "Top Secret America" chronicled in the *Washington Post*, the unprecedented growth of national security intelligence apparatus and the extent of "dataveillance" in the wake of the September 11th attacks is so extensive that reporters dubbed it an "alternative geography of the United States," a set of institutions and programs that are "hidden from public view, lacking in thorough oversight and so unwieldy that [their] effectiveness

[33] True also for Arab Americans: see Howell and Shyrock, "Cracking Down on Diaspora: Arab Detroit and America's War on Terror," *Anthropological Quarterly* 76, no. 3 (2003): 443–62.

is impossible to determine."[34] Just as in the drug war, the war on terror is not fully or even meaningfully captured through the lens of partisan rivalry. While Republicans were most prominent as architects of this latest state project, there has been no shortage of Democrats to help erect and fortify their plans. As before, Democratic eagerness results from some appraisal that political vulnerability would follow a more reluctant or critical approach. Also as before, bipartisan agreement is both a sign of and opportunity for a political agenda that runs deeper than partisan divides – that is, an extension of both state power and discretion. Surely one component of that story is the government reorganization that resulted in the Department of Homeland Security, an institutional expression of resolve in the face of domestic attacks, but one that has been criticized for promoting a siege mentality, fielding inadequate operations, and wasting taxpayers' money through poor accounting and oversight.[35] Yet, despite its demerits and failings – indeed, despite doubts regarding its ultimate utility – "terror" and the war against it have provided an idiom and a set of institutional arrangements to advance other agendas, resulting in the enrichment of private contractors; further entrenchment of security agencies of the U.S. government and individual states, including the "latent function" of providing jobs and public works projects for those associated with it; and the war on terror has also served as a tool to advance certain foreign policy agendas, including, but not limited to, the invasion of Iraq.

Thus the United States is embarked on another metaphorical yet militarized "war." It is obvious that such wars can never be won. In waging these battles, the United States is not at war, it is war, dependent upon this potent stance to forge consensus, organize aspects of its institutional life, understand disorder, and, oddly, make a peace with itself. Victories in such "wars" are pyrrhic indeed, and surrendering governance to these

---

[34] See project website at: http://projects.washingtonpost.com/top-secret-america/ [accessed August 1, 2011].

[35] Much of the best source-reporting on the Department of Homeland Security, and the Transportation Security Agency in particular, can be found in *USA Today*: see, for example, Gary Stoller, "Critics Slam Homeland Security Contracts; Cite Waste, Lack of Oversight," September 10, 2006; and Mimi Hall, "Ex Official Tells of Homeland Security Failures," December 27, 2004. A more recent account of waste as well as the questionable utility of the department can be found in Robert O'Harrow, Jr., "DHS Fusion Centers Portrayed as 'Pools of Ineptitude,' Civil Liberties Intrusions," *Washington Post*, October 2, 2012, found at: http://www.washingtonpost.com/investigations/dhs-fusion-centers-portrayed-as-pools-of-ineptitude-and-civil-liberties-intrusions/2012/10/02/10014440-ocb1-11e2-bd1a-b868e65d57eb_story.html?hpid=z1 [accessed October 3, 2012].

aggressive postures may ultimately exact a price even more difficult to bear than simply the dishonor of forfeiting cherished practices and beliefs belonging to the American political tradition. Poor stewards of freedom bequeath diminished liberty, and they spend the inheritance of the future in blood and treasure as well, leaving a national destiny compromised on several levels, by many hands, and scarred by suffering that was presented, in the indignant words of William Pitt, as a "necessity."

Acknowledgments

I would like to thank the colleagues who provided useful feedback and support throughout the course of this project: Anna Armentrout, Alan Brinkley, Brandi Wilkins Catanese, Charlotte Cowden, Jo Guldi, Kimberly Johnson, Kerwin Klein, Emily Mackil, Joyce Mao, Maureen Miller, Sarah Milov, Adrienne Petty, Jacqui Shine, Gordon Silverstein, and Tyler Stovall. A portion of Chapter 5 was presented at the City College of New York; I am grateful to participants for their comments, especially to Adrienne Petty. Members of the American Political History Seminar at Princeton University, run by Kevin Kruse and Julian Zelizer, provided both helpful comments and stimulation to execute my final push on this manuscript; special thanks go to Paul Frymer for his thoughtful remarks as commentator and to Meg Jacobs for her remarks during the question period.

Second, it is a happy privilege for me to acknowledge the Woodrow Wilson Center in Washington, DC. Without support from the center, this project would not exist. My thanks go especially to Sonya Michel, leader of the U.S. field, as well as to Drew Sample, Philippa Strumm, Joe Brinley, and Don Wolfensberger. Wilson Center staff members Lucy Jilka and Kim Conner lightened my load and gave help when needed. Fellow colleagues in residence inspired and encouraged me in pursuing what was at the time an overwhelming project. I am grateful to Christopher Candland, Katie Benton-Cohen, Devin Fergus, Sara Friedman, Young-sun Hong, Jerome Karabel, Asher Kaufman, Karsten Paerregaard, and David Shirk. My time at the center was also enriched by Maurice Jackson, who provided special help when it came to the history of the District.

Most of all, I want to thank those colleagues who read all or a portion of this manuscript: A. J. Aiséirithe, Sheldon Garon, Gary Gerstle, Melissa Hampton, Pardis Mahdavi, Joe McCartin, Adam McKeown, Bruce Schulman, and the anonymous readers assigned by Cambridge to read this work. Their careful review changed my book from many musings into one story. Errors that remain are my own doing.

While working on this project, friends on Capitol Hill and in DC kept my spirits high and lured me from unproductive seclusion. I am grateful to Amy, Deb and Peter Hernandez, Jane Ruyle, and Shelly Ver Ploeg; thanks also to erstwhile DC residents Shel Garon and Melissa Hampton. This book became a DC story in ways that I did not anticipate. My personal connection to the District turned that into a happy coincidence and, at times, a passionate cause. While research for this project was conducted in many places, I was especially pleased to work at the Martin Luther King Jr. Library's Washingtonia room. My thanks to the staff there for their assistance and for their dedication to maintaining records that preserve voices and struggles that would otherwise be forgotten.

Cambridge University Press dealt efficiently with my manuscript; my thanks especially to my editor, Eric Crahan, for his support and guidance. I'm grateful to Abby Zorbaugh and Robert Dreesen, also at Cambridge, and to Karen Verde, who carefully edited this manuscript. Only weeks before I was ready to send a draft of the book to Eric, my hard drive crashed. Risto Keravuori, "Genius" at the Pentagon City Apple store, fulfilled his job title and earned my thanks when he rescued not just my book, but my hard drive and software as well.

My parents Josef and Ivana Frydl remained steadfast and strong in their support. It was never more needed or appreciated. Finally, I dedicate this book to someone who, as a child of the sixties, will be familiar with some of its subject matter (though such is hardly his distinction). This book is for my first reader and close friend, Larry Janezich, who reminds me that integrity and unreciprocated kindness are our only meaningful successes in this life, and that these daily triumphs vindicate, guide, and discipline us in a difficult world.

Index

Campbell, Nancy, 154
Capote, Truman, 62
Carper, H. H., 144, 145–6, 152
Castro, Fidel, 115, 421
Center for Alcohol Studies, 220
Chiang Kai-shek, 64–6, 83, 87, 114, 389, 390
  and the China Lobby, 64–5
  role in drug trade, 72–4
China
  civil war, 65–6, 72–3
  drug production in, 66, 67–9, 73–4
  opium dealing, 25
  People's Republic of, 73–4, 85, 411
Civil Rights Act (1964), 274
Clark, Ramsey, 287
cocaine, 19, 22, 49–50, 115, 202, 204, 234, 243, 340, 355, 359, 397, 416, 420, 421
Colombia, 415, 423
commerce clause, 180, 274–6, 354–5, 427
Congress on Racial Equality (CORE), 301
Controlled Substances Act (1970), 324, 345, 353–61
Coolidge, Calvin, 20
Costello, Frank, 95, 100
Courtwright, David, 6
Cronkite, Walter, 229–31
Cuba, 264
  under Batista, 94–6, 114–15
  under Castro, 115–17
Cusack, John T., 105, 108, 115, 382

Daniel, Price, 107, 203, 208, 214
Daniel Committee, 107–8, 203–14, 233
Davis, James, 126–8
DEA. *See* Drug Enforcement Agency (DEA)
Demirel. *See* Süleyman Demirel
Department of Defense (DoD), 413–14
Department of Justice, 170, 266
Department of Treasury
  enforcement portfolio of, 20–1, 227, 285
Dewey, Thomas, 90–4
District of Columbia, 123–7, 289, 302–3, 429
  congressional preoccupation with, 13, 129, 210, 308, 324
  drug enforcement and policing in, 127–53, 211, 303–14, 326
Dodd, Thomas, 270
Dole, Vincent, 329–32

Drug Abuse Control Amendments of 1965, 272
Drug Enforcement Agency (DEA), 363–5, 376, 380, 412, 415, 424, 436. *See also* Bureau of Narcotics and Dangerous Drugs (BNDD)
drug use by minors, 201–3, 344–51
drug war
  in Africa, 424
  language of, 28, 290, 423
Dulles, John Foster, 372
Dunbar, Paul, 166, 190
DuPont, Robert, 334–8, 342, 403
Durham-Humphrey, 184–5
Durkheim, Emile, 430

Easter v. *District of Columbia*, 223, 313, 327
Egeberg, Roger, 253, 255
Eisenhower, Dwight, 121, 239, 372
Epstein, Edward, 315, 363
Ervin, Sam, 324, 360
Ewing, Oscar, 24–5

Finlator, John, 271, 286
Fleming, Ian, 118
Flues, A. Gilmore, 371
Flynn, Errol, 115
Food and Drug Administration (FDA), 122, 158, 162–4, 166–7, 180–200, 256, 264, 271, 273, 343, 360, 393
Foreign Assistance Act (1971), 384–6
forfeiture, 155, 271
France
  role in illicit narcotic trade, 24, 102–6
Frydl, Kathleen J., 4, 6, 40, 97, 179, 239, 403

Garland, David, 5, 204
Gaulle, Charles de, 103
General Federation of Women's Clubs (GFWC), 40
Ginsburg, Allen, 181, 349
Giordano, Henry, 269, 281–2, 314, 374, 393
Goddard, James, 350, 360
Goldwater, Barry, 305
Gooberman, Lawrence, 379
Goodell, Charles, 324

Hamilton, Alexander, 20
Hannerz, Ulf, 302